THE DECLINE AND FALL OF THE

ROMAN EMPIRE

VOL. II.

THE DECLINE AND FALL OF THE

ROMAN EMPIRE

VOL. II.

THE HISTORY

OF THE

DECLINE AND FALL OF THE ROMAN EMPIRE

BY

EDWARD GIBBON

EDITED IN SEVEN VOLUMES

WITH INTRODUCTION, NOTES, APPENDICES, AND INDEX

BY

J. B. BURY, M.A.

HON. LITT.D. OF DURHAM; HON. LL.D. OF EDINBURGH
CORRESPONDING MEMBER OF THE IMPERIAL ACADEMY OF SCIENCES, ST. PETERSBURG
FELLOW OF TRINITY COLLEGE, AND REGIUS PROFESSOR OF GREEK
IN THE UNIVERSITY OF DUBLIN

VOL. II.

METHUEN & CO.

36 ESSEX STREET, W.C.

LONDON

1901

Third Edition

CONTENTS OF THE SECOND VOLUME

CHAPTER XV

The Progress of the Christian Religion, and the Sentiments, Manners, Numbers and Condition of the Primitive Christians

	PAGE
Importance of the Inquiry ...	1
Its Difficulties	1
Five Causes of the Growth of Christianity	2
I. THE FIRST CAUSE. Zeal of the Jews	2
Its gradual increase	4
Their Religion better suited to Defence than to Conquest	5
More Liberal Zeal of Christianity ...	6
Obstinacy and Reasons of the Believing Jews	7
The Nazarene Church of Jerusalem	8
The Ebionites	10
The Gnostics ...	11
Their Sects, Progress, and Influence	13
The Dæmons considered as the Gods of Antiquity	15
Abhorrence of the Christians for Idolatry	16
Ceremonies	16
Arts	17
Festivals	18
Zeal for Christianity	19
II. THE SECOND CAUSE. The Doctrine of the Immortality of the Soul among the Philosophers ...	19
Among the Pagans of Greece and Rome ...	20
Among the Barbarians and the Jews	21
Among the Christians	22
Approaching End of the World	23
Doctrine of the Millennium ...	23
Conflagration of Rome and of the World	25
The Pagans devoted to Eternal Punishment	26
Were often converted by their Fears	27
III. THE THIRD CAUSE. Miraculous powers of the Primitive Church	28
Their Truth contested	29
Our perplexity in defining the miraculous Period	30
Use of the Primitive Miracles	31
IV. THE FOURTH CAUSE. Virtues of the first Christians	32
Effects of their Repentance ...	32

CONTENTS

	PAGE
Care of their Reputation	33
Morality of the Fathers	34
Principles of Human Nature	34
The Primitive Christians condemn Pleasure and Luxury ...	35
Their Sentiments concerning Marriage and Chastity	36
Their Aversion to the Business of War and Government ...	38
V. The Fifth Cause. The Christians active in the Government of the Church	39
Its Primitive Freedom and Equality	40
Institution of Bishops as Presidents of the College of Presbyters	41
Provincial Councils	43
Union of the Church	43
Progress of Episcopal Authority	44
Pre-eminence of the Metropolitan Churches	45
Ambition of the Roman Pontiff	45
Laity and Clergy	46
Oblations and Revenue of the Church	47
Distribution of the Revenue	50
Excommunication	51
Public Penance	52
The Dignity of Episcopal Government	53
Recapitulation of the five Causes	54
Weakness of Polytheism	54
The Scepticism of the Pagan World proved favourable to the new Religion	55
And the Peace and Union of the Roman Empire	56
Historical View of the Progress of Christianity	57
In the East	57
The Church of Antioch	59
In Egypt	59
In Rome	60
In Africa and the Western Provinces	62
Beyond the Limits of the Roman Empire	63
General Proportion of Christians and Pagans	65
Whether the first Christians were mean and ignorant	65
Some Exceptions with regard to Learning	66
Some Exceptions with regard to Rank and Fortune	67
Christianity most favourably received by the Poor and Simple	67
Rejected by some eminent Men of the first and second Centuries	68
Their Neglect of Prophecy	68
Their Neglect of Miracles	69
General Silence concerning the Darkness of the Passion ...	69

CHAPTER XVI

The Conduct of the Roman Government towards the Christians, from the Reign of Nero to that of Constantine

Christianity persecuted by the Roman Emperors	71
Inquiry into their Motives	72
Rebellious Spirit of the Jews	72

CONTENTS

A.D.		PAGE
	Toleration of the Jewish Religion	73
	The Jews were a People which followed, the Christians a Sect which deserted, the Religion of their Fathers	74
	Christianity accused of Atheism, and mistaken by the People and Philosophers	75
	The Union and Assemblies of the Christians considered as a dangerous Conspiracy	77
	Their Manners calumniated	79
	Their Imprudent Defence	79
	Idea of the Conduct of the Emperors towards the Christians ...	81
	They neglected the Christians as a Sect of Jews ...	82
	The Fire of Rome under the Reign of Nero	83
	Cruel Punishment of the Christians as the Incendiaries of the City	84
	Remarks on the Passage of Tacitus relative to the Persecution of the Christians by Nero	86
	Oppression of the Jews and Christians by Domitian	89
	Execution of Clemens the Consul	91
	Ignorance of Pliny concerning the Christians	92
	Trajan and his Successors establish a legal Mode of proceeding against them	93
	Popular Clamours	94
	Trials of the Christians	95
	Humanity of the Roman Magistrates	96
	Inconsiderable Number of Martyrs	97
	Example of Cyprian, Bishop of Carthage	99
	His Danger and Flight	99
257	His Banishment	100
	His Condemnation	101
	His Martyrdom	102
	Various Incitements to Martyrdom	103
	Ardour of the first Christians	104
	Gradual Relaxation	106
	Three Methods of escaping Martyrdom	106
	Alternatives of Severity and Toleration	107
	The Ten Persecutions	108
	Supposed Edicts of Tiberius and Marcus Antoninus	108
180	State of the Christians in the Reigns of Commodus and Severus	109
211-249.	Of the Successors of Severus	111
	Of Maximin, Philip, and Decius	112
253-260.	Of Valerian, Gallienus, and his Successors	114
260	Paul of Samosata, his Manners	114
270	He is degraded from the See of Antioch	115
274	The Sentence is executed by Aurelian	116
284-303.	Peace and Prosperity of the Church under Diocletian ...	116
	Progress of Zeal and Superstition among the Pagans	118
	Maximian and Galerius punish a few Christian Soldiers ...	120
	Galerius prevails on Diocletian to begin a general Persecution	121
303	Demolition of the Church of Nicomedia	122
	The first Edict against the Christians	122
	Zeal and Punishment of a Christian	124
	Fire of the Palace of Nicomedia imputed to the Christians ...	124
	Execution of the first Edict	125

A.D.		PAGE
	Demolition of the Churches	126
[303-304.]	Subsequent Edicts	127
303-311.	General Idea of the Persecution	128
	In the Western Provinces, under Constantius and Constantine	128
	In Italy and Africa, under Maximian and Severus	129
	And under Maxentius	130
	In Illyricum and the East, under Galerius and Maximin ...	131
311	Galerius publishes an Edict of Toleration	132
	Peace of the Church	133
	Maximin prepares to renew the Persecution	134
313	End of the Persecutions	135
	Probable Account of the Sufferings of the Martyrs and Confessors	135
	Number of Martyrs	137
	Conclusion	138

CHAPTER XVII

Foundation of Constantinople—Political System of Constantine, and his Successors—Military Discipline—The Palace—The Finances

324	Design of a new Capital	140
	Situation of Byzantium	141
	Description of Constantinople	141
	The Bosphorus	142
	The Port of Constantinople	143
	The Propontis	144
	The Hellespont	144
	Advantages of Constantinople	146
	Foundation of the City	147
	Its Extent	148
	Progress of the Work	150
	Edifices	151
	Population	154
	Privileges	155
330 [May 11] or 334.	Dedication	157
300-500.	Form of Government in the Roman Empire	158
	Hierarchy of the State	159
	Three Ranks of Honour	160
	Four Divisions of Office	160
	I. The Consuls	161
	The Patricians	163
	II. The Prætorian Præfects	165
	The Præfects of Rome and Constantinople	167
	The Proconsuls, Vice-præfects, &c.	169
	The Governors of the Provinces	170
	The Profession of the Law	172
	III. The Military Officers	174
	Distinction of the Troops	176
	Reduction of the Legions	178
	Difficulty of Levies	179
	Increase of Barbarian Auxiliaries	181

CONTENTS

A.D.		PAGE
	IV. Seven Ministers of the Palace	182
	1. The Chamberlain	182
	2. The Master of the Offices	183
	3. The Quæstor	183
	4. The Public Treasurer	185
	Rationales	186
	5. The Private Treasurer	186
	6. The Counts of the Domestics	187
	7. Protectores	187
	Agents, or Official Spies	188
	Use of Torture	189
	Finances	190
	The General Tribute, or Indiction	191
	Assessed in the Form of a Capitation	194
	Capitation on Trade and Industry	198
	Free Gifts	199
	Conclusion	200

CHAPTER XVIII

Character of Constantine—Gothic War—Death of Constantine—Division of the Empire among his three Sons—Persian War—Tragic Death of Constantine the Younger, and Constans—Usurpation of Magnentius— Civil War—Victory of Constantius

A.D.		PAGE
	Character of Constantine	208
	His Virtues	202
	His Vices	202
	His Family	204
	Virtues of Crispus	205
324	Jealousy of Constantine	206
325	Edict of Constantine	207
326	Disgrace and Death of Crispus	208
	The Empress Fausta	210
	The Sons and Nephews of Constantine	212
	Their Education	213
	Manners of the Sarmatians	214
	Their Settlement near the Danube	216
331	The Gothic War	217
334	Expulsion of the Sarmatians	219
337	Death and Funeral of Constantine	220
	Factions of the Court	221
	Massacre of the Princes	222
337	Division of the Empire	224
310	Sapor, King of Persia	224
	State of Mesopotamia and Armenia	225
342	Death of Tiridates	226
337-360.	The Persian War	227
348 [344].	Battle of Singara	227
338, 346, 350.	Siege of Nisibis	229
340	Civil War, and Death of Constantine	231
350	Murder of Constans	232

CONTENTS

A.D.   PAGE

Magnentius and Vetranio assume the Purple 234
Constantius refuses to treat 235
Deposes Vetranio 236
351 Makes War against Magnentius 238
Battle of Mursa 239
352 Conquest of Italy 241
353 Last Defeat and Death of Magnentius 242

CHAPTER XIX

*Constantius sole Emperor—Elevation and Death of Gallus—Danger and
Elevation of Julian—Sarmatian and Persian Wars—Victories of
Julian in Gaul*

Power of the Eunuchs 245
Education of Gallus and Julian 247
351 Gallus declared Cæsar 248
Cruelty and Imprudence of Gallus 248
354 Massacre of the Imperial Ministers 249
Dangerous Situation of Gallus 251
His Disgrace and Death 252
The Danger and Escape of Julian 253
355 He is sent to Athens 255
Recalled to Milan 255
Declared Cæsar 258
Fatal End of Sylvanus 259
357 Constantius visits Rome 260
A new Obelisk 261
357, 358, 359. The Quadian and Sarmatian War 262
358 The Persian Negotiation 265
359 Invasion of Mesopotamia by Sapor 267
Siege of Amida 268
360 Siege of Singara 270
Conduct of the Romans 271
Invasion of Gaul by the Germans 273
Conduct of Julian 274
356 His first Campaign in Gaul 275
357 His second Campaign 277
Battle of Strasburg 278
358 Julian subdues the Franks 280
357, 358, 359. Makes three Expeditions beyond the Rhine 282
Restores the Cities of Gaul 283
Civil administration of Julian 284
Description of Paris 286

CHAPTER XX

*The Motives, Progress, and Effects of the Conversion of Constantine—Legal
Establishment of the Christian, or Catholic Church*

306-337. Date of the Conversion of Constantine 288
His Pagan Superstition 290

CONTENTS

A.D.		PAGE
306-312.	He protects the Christians of Gaul ...	291
313	Edict of Milan	292
	Use and Beauty of the Christian Morality	293
	Theory and Practice of Passive Obedience	294
	Divine Right of Constantine	295
324	General Edict of Toleration	297
	Loyalty and Zeal of the Christian Party	298
	Expectation and Belief of a Miracle	299
	I. The *Labarum*, or Standard of the Cross	301
	II. The Dream of Constantine	301
	III. Appearance of a Cross in the Sky	303
	The Conversion of Constantine might be sincere ...	305
	The fourth Eclogue of Virgil	307
	Devotion and Privileges of Constantine	308
	Delay of his Baptism till the approach of Death ...	309
	Propagation of Christianity	311
312-438.	Change of the National Religion	313
	Distinction of the Spiritual and Temporal Powers ...	314
	State of the Bishops under the Christian Emperors ...	315
	I. Election of Bishops	316
	II. Ordination of the Clergy	318
	III. Property	320
	IV. Civil Jurisdiction	322
	V. Spiritual Censures	324
	VI. Freedom of Public Preaching	326
	VII. Privilege of Legislative Assemblies	327

CHAPTER XXI

Persecution of Heresy—The Schism of the Donatists—The Arian Contro-
versy—Athanasius—Distracted State of the Church and Empire under
Constantine and his Sons—Toleration of Paganism

A.D.		PAGE
312	African Controversy	332
	Councils of Rome and of Arles	333
315	Schism of the Donatists	333
	The Trinitarian Controversy	335
A.C.		
360	The System of Plato	335
	The Logos	336
300	Taught in the School of Alexandria	336
A.D.		
97	Revealed by the Apostle St. John	337
	The Ebionites and Docetes	338
	Mysterious Nature of the Trinity	339
	Zeal of the Christians	340
	Authority of the Church	342
	Factions	343
318	Heterodox Opinions of Arius	344
	Three Systems of the Trinity	344
	I. Arianism	345
	II. Tritheism	345

CONTENTS

A.D.		PAGE
	III. Sabellianism	346
325	Council of Nice	347
	The Homoousion	347
	Arian Creeds	349
	Arian Sects	351
	Faith of the Western, or Latin Church	353
360	Council of Rimini	353
	Conduct of the Emperors in the Arian Controversy	354
324	Indifference of Constantine	354
325	His Zeal	355
328-337.	He persecutes the Arian and the Orthodox Party ...	356
337-361.	Constantius favours the Arians	357
	Arian Councils	359
	Character and Adventures of Athanasius	361
330	Persecution against Athanasius	364
336	His first Exile	366
341 [340].	His Second Exile	367
349 [346].	His Restoration	369
351	Resentment of Constantius	370
353-355.	Councils of Arles and Milan	371
355	Condemnation of Athanasius	373
	Exiles	374
356	Third Expulsion of Athanasius from Alexandria	375
	His Behaviour	377
356-362.	His Retreat	378
	Arian Bishops	381
	Divisions	381
	I. Rome	382
	II. Constantinople	384
	Cruelty of the Arians	386
354, &c.	The Revolt and Fury of the Donatist Circumcellions ...	387
	Their Religious Suicides	389
312-361.	General Character of the Christian Sects	390
	Toleration of Paganism by Constantine	391
	By his Sons	392

CHAPTER XXII

Julian is declared Emperor by the Legions of Gaul—His March and Success—The Death of Constantius—Civil Administration of Julian

	The Jealousy of Constantius against Julian	396
	Fears and Envy of Constantius	397
360	The Legions of Gaul are ordered to march into the East ...	397
	Their Discontents	400
	They proclaim Julian Emperor	400
	His protestations of Innocence	402
	His Embassy to Constantius	404
360, 361.	His fourth and fifth Expeditions beyond the Rhine ...	405
361	Fruitless Treaty and Declaration of War	406
	Julian prepares to attack Constantius	408
	His march from the Rhine into Illyricum	410

CONTENTS   xiii

A.D.   PAGE
    He justifies his Cause 412
    Hostile Preparations 414
361 Death of Constantius 415
361 Julian enters Constantinople 416
361 Is acknowledged by the whole Empire 417
    His civil Government and private Life 417
    Reformation of the Palace 420
    Chamber of Justice 422
    Punishment of the Innocent and the Guilty 423
    Clemency of Julian 425
    His love of Freedom and the Republic 426
    His care of the Grecian Cities 427
    Julian, an Orator and a Judge 428
    His Character 430

CHAPTER XXIII

The Religion of Julian—Universal Toleration—He attempts to restore and reform the Pagan Worship ; to rebuild the Temple of Jerusalem—His artful Persecution of the Christians—Mutual Zeal and Injustice

    Religion of Julian 432
351 His Education and Apostacy 433
    He embraces the Mythology of Paganism 435
    The Allegories 436
    Theological System of Julian 438
    Fanaticism of the Philosophers 439
    Initiation and Fanaticism of Julian 440
    His religious Dissimulation 441
    He writes against Christianity 443
361 Universal Toleration 444
361-363. Zeal and Devotion of Julian in the Restoration of
    Paganism 445
    Reformation of Paganism 447
    The Philosophers 449
    Conversions 451
    The Jews 453
    Description of Jerusalem 454
    Pilgrimages 455
363 Julian attempts to rebuild the Temple 456
    The Enterprise is defeated 458
    Perhaps by a preternatural Event 459
    Partiality of Julian 460
    He prohibits the Christians from teaching Schools ... 461
    Disgrace and Oppression of the Christians 463
    They are condemned to restore the Pagan Temples ... 463
    The Temple and sacred Grove of Daphne 465
    Neglect and Profanation of Daphne 467
362 Removal of the dead Bodies, and Conflagration of the Temple 468
    Julian shuts the Cathedral of Antioch 469
    George of Cappadocia oppresses Alexandria and Egypt ... 470
361 He is massacred by the People 471

A.D.   PAGE
        He is worshipped as a Saint and Martyr   472
362   Restoration of Athanasius   473
        He is persecuted and expelled by Julian   474
361-363. Zeal and Imprudence of the Christians   476

CHAPTER XXIV

Residence of Julian at Antioch—His successful Expedition against the Persians—Passage of the Tigris—The Retreat and Death of Julian— Election of Jovian—He saves the Roman Army by a disgraceful Treaty

        The Cæsars of Julian   479
362   He resolves to march against the Persians   480
        Julian proceeds from Constantinople to Antioch   481
        Licentious Manners of the People of Antioch   482
        Their Aversion to Julian   483
        Scarcity of Corn, and public Discontent   483
        Julian composes a Satire against Antioch   485
314-390. The Sophist Libanius   486
363   March of Julian to the Euphrates   487
        His Design of invading Persia   489
        Disaffection of the King of Armenia   490
        Military Preparations   490
        Julian enters the Persian Territories   492
        His March over the Desert of Mesopotamia   492
        His Success   494
        Description of Assyria   495
363   Invasion of Assyria   497
        Siege of Perisabor   497
        Siege of Maogamalcha   498
        Personal Behaviour of Julian   500
        He transports his Fleet from the Euphrates to the Tigris   ...   502
        Passage of the Tigris and Victory of the Romans   503
        Situation and Obstinacy of Julian   506
        He burns his Fleet   508
        Marches against Sapor   509
        Retreat and Distress of the Roman Army   511
        Julian is mortally wounded   513
363   Death of Julian   515
        Election of the Emperor Jovian   517
        Danger and Difficulty of the Retreat   519
        Negotiation and Treaty of Peace   520
        The Weakness and Disgrace of Jovian   522
        He continues his Retreat to Nisibis   523
        Universal Clamour against the Treaty of Peace   525
        Jovian evacuates Nisibis, and restores the five Provinces to the
                Persians   526
        Reflections on the Death of Julian   527
        On his Funeral   529

MAPS AND PLANS

	PAGE
PLAN OF CONSTANTINOPLE	149
THE ROMAN EMPIRE UNDER DIOCLETIAN	170
MESOPOTAMIA	491

THE HISTORY

OF THE

DECLINE AND FALL OF THE ROMAN EMPIRE

CHAPTER XV

The Progress of the Christian Religion, and the Sentiments, Manners, Numbers, and Condition, of the primitive Christians

A CANDID but rational inquiry into the progress and establishment of Christianity may be considered as a very essential part of the history of the Roman empire. While that great body was invaded by open violence, or undermined by slow decay, a pure and humble religion gently insinuated itself into the minds of men, grew up in silence and obscurity, derived new vigour from opposition, and finally erected the triumphant banner of the cross on the ruins of the Capitol. Nor was the influence of Christianity confined to the period or to the limits of the Roman empire. After a revolution of thirteen or fourteen centuries, that religion is still professed by the nations of Europe, the most distinguished portion of human kind in arts and learning as well as in arms. By the industry and zeal of the Europeans it has been widely diffused to the most distant shores of Asia and Africa; and by the means of their colonies has been firmly established from Canada to Chili, in a world unknown to the ancients.

But this inquiry, however useful or entertaining, is attended with two peculiar difficulties. The scanty and suspicious materials of ecclesiastical history seldom enable us to dispel the dark cloud that hangs over the first age of the church. The great law of impartiality too often obliges us to reveal the imperfections of the uninspired teachers and believers of the gospel; and, to a careless observer, *their* faults may seem to cast a shade on the faith which they professed. But the scandal of the pious Christian, and the fallacious triumph of

Importance of the inquiry

Its difficulties

the Infidel, should cease as soon as they recollect not only *by whom*, but likewise *to whom*, the Divine Revelation was given. The theologian may indulge the pleasing task of describing Religion as she descended from Heaven, arrayed in her native purity. A more melancholy duty is imposed on the historian. He must discover the inevitable mixture of error and corruption which she contracted in a long residence upon earth, among a weak and degenerate race of beings.

Five causes of the growth of Christianity Our curiosity is naturally prompted to inquire by what means the Christian faith obtained so remarkable a victory over the established religions of the earth. To this inquiry, an obvious but satisfactory answer may be returned; that it was owing to the convincing evidence of the doctrine itself, and to the ruling providence of its great Author. But, as truth and reason seldom find so favourable a reception in the world, and as the wisdom of Providence frequently condescends to use the passions of the human heart, and the general circumstances of mankind, as instruments to execute its purpose; we may still be permitted, though with becoming submission, to ask not indeed what were the first, but what were the secondary causes of the rapid growth of the Christian church. It will, perhaps, appear that it was most effectually favoured and assisted by the five following causes: I. The inflexible, and, if we may use the expression, the intolerant zeal of the Christians, derived, it is true, from the Jewish religion, but purified from the narrow and unsocial spirit which, instead of inviting, had deterred the Gentiles from embracing the law of Moses. II. The doctrine of a future life, improved by every additional circumstance which could give weight and efficacy to that important truth. III. The miraculous powers ascribed to the primitive church. IV. The pure and austere morals of the Christians. V. The union and discipline of the Christian republic, which gradually formed an independent and increasing state in the heart of the Roman empire.

THE FIRST CAUSE. Zeal of the Jews I. We have already described the religious harmony of the ancient world, and the facility with which the most different and even hostile nations embraced, or at least respected, each other's superstitions. A single people refused to join in the common intercourse of mankind. The Jews, who, under the Assyrian and Persian monarchies, had languished for many ages the most despised portion of their slaves,[1] emerged from

[1] Dum Assyrios penes, Medosque, et Persas Oriens fuit, despectissima pars servientium. Tacit. Hist. v. 8. Herodotus, who visited Asia whilst it obeyed the

obscurity under the successors of Alexander; and, as they multiplied to a surprising degree in the East, and afterwards in the West, they soon excited the curiosity and wonder of other nations.[2] The sullen obstinacy with which they maintained their peculiar rites and unsocial manners seemed to mark them out a distinct species of men, who boldly professed, or who faintly disguised, their implacable hatred to the rest of human kind.[3] Neither the violence of Antiochus, nor the arts of Herod, nor the example of the circumjacent nations, could ever persuade the Jews to associate with the institutions of Moses the elegant mythology of the Greeks.[4] According to the maxims of universal toleration, the Romans protected a superstition which they despised.[5] The polite Augustus condescended to give orders that sacrifices should be offered for his prosperity in the temple of Jerusalem;[6] while the meanest of the posterity of Abraham, who should have paid the same homage to the Jupiter of the Capitol, would have been an object of abhorrence to himself and to his brethren. But the moderation of the conquerors was insufficient to appease the jealous prejudices of their subjects, who were alarmed and scandalized at the ensigns of paganism, which necessarily introduced themselves into a Roman province.[7] The mad attempt of Caligula to place his own statue in the temple of Jerusalem was defeated by the unanimous resolution of a people

last of those empires, slightly mentions the Syrians of Palestine, who, according to their own confession, had received from Egypt the rite of circumcision. See l. ii. c. 104.

[2] Diodorus Siculus, l. xl. [2 *sqq.*]. Dion Cassius, l. xxxvii. p. 121 [c. 17]. Tacit. Hist. v. 1—9. Justin, xxxvi. 2, 3.

[3] Tradidit arcano quæcunque volumine Moses.
 Non monstrare vias eadem nisi sacra colenti,
 Quæsitum ad fontem solos deducere verpos. [Juvenal, xiv. 102.]
The letter of this law is not to be found in the present volume of Moses. But the wise, the humane Maimonides openly teaches that, if an idolater fall into the water, a Jew ought not to save him from instant death. See Basnage, Histoire des Juifs, l. vi. c. 28.

[4] A Jewish sect, which indulged themselves in a sort of occasional conformity, derived from Herod, by whose example and authority they had been seduced, the name of Herodians. But their numbers were so inconsiderable, and their duration so short, that Josephus has not thought them worthy of his notice. See Prideaux's Connection, vol. ii. p. 285.

[5] Cicero pro Flacco, c. 28.

[6] Philo de Legatione. Augustus left a foundation for a perpetual sacrifice. Yet he approved of the neglect which his grandson Caius expressed towards the temple of Jerusalem. See Sueton. in August. c. 93, and Casaubon's notes on that passage.

[7] See, in particular, Joseph. Antiquitat. xvii. 6 [§ 2], xviii. 3, and de Bel. Judaic. i. 33 [§ 2 *sqq.*], and ii. 9 [§ 2, 3]. Edit. Havercamp.

who dreaded death much less than such an idolatrous profanation.[8] Their attachment to the law of Moses was equal to their detestation of foreign religions. The current of zeal and devotion, as it was contracted into a narrow channel, ran with the strength, and sometimes with the fury, of a torrent.

Its gradual increase

This inflexible perseverance, which appeared so odious, or so ridiculous, to the ancient world, assumes a more awful character, since Providence has deigned to reveal to us the mysterious history of the chosen people. But the devout, and even scrupulous, attachment to the Mosaic religion, so conspicuous among the Jews who lived under the second temple, becomes still more surprising, if it is compared with the stubborn incredulity of their forefathers. When the law was given in thunder from Mount Sinai; when the tides of the ocean and the course of the planets were suspended for the convenience of the Israelites; and when temporal rewards and punishments were the immediate consequences of their piety or disobedience; they perpetually relapsed into rebellion against the visible majesty of their Divine King, placed the idols of the nations in the sanctuary of Jehovah, and imitated every fantastic ceremony that was practised in the tents of the Arabs or in the cities of Phœnicia.[9] As the protection of Heaven was deservedly withdrawn from the ungrateful race, their faith acquired a proportionable degree of vigour and purity. The contemporaries of Moses and Joshua had beheld, with careless indifference, the most amazing miracles. Under the pressure of every calamity, the belief of those miracles has preserved the Jews of a later period from the universal contagion of idolatry; and, in contradiction to every known principle of the human mind, that singular people seems to have yielded a stronger and more ready assent to the traditions of their remote ancestors than to the evidence of their own senses.[10]

[8] Jussi a Caio Cæsare, effigiem ejus in templo locare arma potius sumpsere. Tacit. Hist. v. 9. Philo and Josephus gave a very circumstantial, but a very rhetorical, account of this transaction, which exceedingly perplexed the governor of Syria. At the first mention of this idolatrous proposal, King Agrippa fainted away; and did not recover his senses till the third day.

[9] For the enumeration of the Syrian and Arabian deities, it may be observed that Milton has comprised, in one hundred and thirty very beautiful lines, the two large and learned syntagmas which Selden had composed on that abstruse subject.

[10] "How long will this people provoke me? and how long will it be ere they *believe* me, for all the *signs* which I have shewn among them?" (Numbers, xiv. 11). It would be easy, but it would be unbecoming, to justify the complaint of the Deity, from the whole tenor of the Mosaic history.

The Jewish religion was admirably fitted for defence, but it was never designed for conquest; and it seems probable that the number of proselytes was never much superior to that of apostates. The divine promises were originally made, and the distinguishing rite of circumcision was enjoined, to a single family. When the posterity of Abraham had multiplied like the sands of the sea, the Deity, from whose mouth they received a system of laws and ceremonies, declared himself the proper and, as it were, the national God of Israel; and, with the most jealous care, separated his favourite people from the rest of mankind. The conquest of the land of Canaan was accompanied with so many wonderful and with so many bloody circumstances that the victorious Jews were left in a state of irreconcilable hostility with all their neighbours. They had been commanded to extirpate some of the most idolatrous tribes; and the execution of the Divine will had seldom been retarded by the weakness of humanity. With the other nations they were forbidden to contract any marriages or alliances; and the prohibition of receiving them into the congregation, which, in some cases, was perpetual, almost always extended to the third, to the seventh, or even to the tenth generation. The obligation of preaching to the Gentiles the faith of Moses had never been inculcated as a precept of the law, nor were the Jews inclined to impose it on themselves as a voluntary duty. In the admission of new citizens, that unsocial people was actuated by the selfish vanity of the Greeks, rather than by the generous policy of Rome. The descendants of Abraham were flattered by the opinion that they alone were the heirs of the covenant; and they were apprehensive of diminishing the value of their inheritance, by sharing it too easily with the strangers of the earth. A larger acquaintance with mankind extended their knowledge without correcting their prejudices; and, whenever the God of Israel acquired any new votaries, he was much more indebted to the inconstant humour of polytheism than to the active zeal of his own missionaries.[11] The religion of Moses seems to be instituted for a particular country, as well as for a single nation; and, if a strict obedience had been paid to the order that every male, three times in the year, should present himself before the Lord Jehovah, it would have been impossible that the Jews could ever have spread themselves beyond the narrow limits of the promised

[11] All that relates to the Jewish proselytes has been very ably treated by Basnage, Hist. des Juifs, l. vi. c. 6, 7.

land.[12]   That obstacle was indeed removed by the destruction of the temple of Jerusalem ; but the most considerable part of the Jewish religion was involved in its destruction; and the Pagans, who had long wondered at the strange report of an empty sanctuary,[13] were at a loss to discover what could be the object, or what could be the instruments, of a worship which was destitute of temples and of altars, of priests and of sacrifices. Yet even in their fallen state, the Jews, still asserting their lofty and exclusive privileges, shunned, instead of courting, the society of strangers.   They still insisted with inflexible rigour on those parts of the law which it was in their power to practise. Their peculiar distinctions of days, of meats, and a variety of trivial though burdensome observances, were so many objects of disgust and aversion for the other nations, to whose habits and prejudices they were diametrically opposite.   The painful and even dangerous rite of circumcision was alone capable of repelling a willing proselyte from the door of the synagogue.[14]

More liberal zeal of Christianity

Under these circumstances, Christianity offered itself to the world, armed with the strength of the Mosaic law, and delivered from the weight of its fetters.   An exclusive zeal for the truth of religion and the unity of God was as carefully inculcated in the new as in the ancient system ; and whatever was now revealed to mankind, concerning the nature and designs of the Supreme Being, was fitted to increase their reverence for that mysterious doctrine.   The divine authority of Moses and the prophets was admitted, and even established, as the firmest basis of Christianity.   From the beginning of the world, an uninterrupted series of predictions had announced and prepared the long expected coming of the Messiah, who, in compliance with the gross apprehensions of the Jews, had been more frequently represented under the character of a King and Conqueror, than under that of a Prophet, a Martyr, and the Son of God.   By his expiatory sacrifice, the imperfect sacrifices of the temple were at once consummated and abolished.   The

[12] See Exod. xxiv. 23, Deut. xvi. 16, the commentators, and a very sensible note in the Universal History, vol. i. p. 603, edit. fol.

[13] When Pompey, using or abusing the right of conquest, entered into the Holy of Holies, it was observed with amazement, " Nullâ intus Deûm effigie, vacuam sedem et inania arcana ".   Tacit. Hist. v. 9.   It was a popular saying, with regard to the Jews,

Nil præter nubes et cæli numen adorant.

[14] A second kind of circumcision was inflicted on a Samaritan or Egyptian proselyte.   The sullen indifference of the Talmudists, with respect to the conversion of strangers, may be seen in Basnage, Histoire des Juifs, l. vi. c. 6.

ceremonial law, which consisted only of types and figures, was succeeded by a pure and spiritual worship, equally adapted to all climates, as well as to every condition of mankind; and to the initiation of blood was substituted a more harmless initiation of water. The promise of divine favour, instead of being partially confined to the posterity of Abraham, was universally proposed to the freeman and the slave, to the Greek and to the barbarian, to the Jew and to the Gentile. Every privilege that could raise the proselyte from earth to Heaven, that could exalt his devotion, secure his happiness, or even gratify that secret pride which, under the semblance of devotion, insinuates itself into the human heart, was still reserved for the members of the Christian church; but at the same time all mankind was permitted, and even solicited, to accept the glorious distinction, which was not only proffered as a favour, but imposed as an obligation. It became the most sacred duty of a new convert to diffuse among his friends and relations the inestimable blessing which he had received, and to warn them against a refusal that would be severely punished as a criminal disobedience to the will of a benevolent but all-powerful deity.

The enfranchisement of the church from the bonds of the synagogue was a work however of some time and of some difficulty. The Jewish converts, who acknowledged Jesus in the character of the Messiah foretold by their ancient oracles, respected him as a prophetic teacher of virtue and religion; but they obstinately adhered to the ceremonies of their ancestors, and were desirous of imposing them on the Gentiles, who continually augmented the number of believers. These Judaizing Christians seem to have argued with some degree of plausibility from the divine origin of the Mosaic law, and from the immutable perfections of its great Author. They affirmed *that*, if the Being, who is the same through all eternity, had designed to abolish those sacred rites which had served to distinguish his chosen people, the repeal of them would have been no less clear and solemn than their first promulgation: *that*, instead of those frequent declarations, which either suppose or assert the perpetuity of the Mosaic religion, it would have been represented as a provisionary scheme intended to last only till the coming of the Messiah, who should instruct mankind in a more perfect mode of faith and of worship:[15] *that* the Messiah

Margin note: Obstinacy and reasons of the believing Jews

---

[15] These arguments were urged with great ingenuity by the Jew Orobio, and refuted with equal ingenuity and candour by the Christian Limborch. See the Amica Collatio (it well deserves that name) or account of the dispute between them.

himself, and his disciples who conversed with him on earth, instead of authorizing by their example the most minute observances of the Mosaic law,[16] would have published to the world the abolition of those useless and obsolete ceremonies, without suffering Christianity to remain during so many years obscurely confounded among the sects of the Jewish church. Arguments like these appear to have been used in the defence of the expiring cause of the Mosaic law ; but the industry of our learned divines has abundantly explained the ambiguous language of the Old Testament, and the ambiguous conduct of the apostolic teachers. It was proper gradually to unfold the system of the Gospel, and to pronounce, with the utmost caution and tenderness, a sentence of condemnation so repugnant to the inclination and prejudices of the believing Jews.

The Nazarene church of Jerusalem

The history of the church of Jerusalem affords a lively proof of the necessity of those precautions, and of the deep impression which the Jewish religion had made on the minds of its sectaries. The first fifteen bishops of Jerusalem were all circumcised Jews ; and the congregation over which they presided, united the law of Moses with the doctrine of Christ.[17] It was natural that the primitive tradition of a church which was founded only forty years after the death of Christ, and was governed almost as many years under the immediate inspection of his apostle, should be received as the standard of orthodoxy.[18] The distant churches very frequently appealed to the authority of their venerable Parent, and relieved her distresses by a liberal contribution of alms. But, when numerous and opulent societies were established in the great cities of the empire, in Antioch, Alexandria, Ephesus, Corinth, and Rome, the reverence which Jerusalem had inspired to all the Christian colonies insensibly diminished. The Jewish converts, or, as they were afterwards called, the Nazarenes, who had laid the

---

[16] Jesus . . . circumcisus erat ; cibis utebatur Judaicis ; vestitû simili ; purgatos scabie mittebat ad sacerdotes ; Paschata et alios dies festos religiose observabat : si quos sanavit sabbato, ostendit non tantum ex lege, sed et ex receptis sententiis talia opera sabbato non interdicta. Grotius de veritate Religionis Christianæ, l. v. c. 7. A little afterwards (c. 12) he expatiates on the condescension of the apostles.

[17] Pæne omnes Christum Deum sub legis observatione credebant. Sulpicius Severus, ii. 31. See Eusebius, Hist. Ecclesiast. l. iv. c. 5.

[18] Mosheim de Rebus Christianis ante Constantinum Magnum, p. 153. In this masterly performance, which I shall often have occasion to quote, he enters much more fully into the state of the primitive church than he has an opportunity of doing in his General History.

foundations of the church, soon found themselves overwhelmed by the increasing multitudes that from all the various religions of polytheism inlisted under the banner of Christ; and the Gentiles, who with the approbation of their peculiar apostle had rejected the intolerable weight of Mosaic ceremonies, at length refused to their more scrupulous brethren the same toleration which at first they had humbly solicited for their own practice. The ruin of the temple, of the city, and of the public religion of the Jews, was severely felt by the Nazarenes; as in their manners, though not in their faith, they maintained so intimate a connexion with their impious countrymen, whose misfortunes were attributed by the Pagans to the contempt, and more justly ascribed by the Christians to the wrath, of the Supreme Deity. The Nazarenes retired from the ruins of Jerusalem to the little town of Pella beyond the Jordan, where that ancient church languished above sixty years in solitude and obscurity.[19] They still enjoyed the comfort of making frequent and devout visits to the *Holy City*, and the hope of being one day restored to those seats which both nature and religion taught them to love as well as to revere. But at length, under the reign of Hadrian, the desperate fanaticism of the Jews filled up the measure of their calamities; and the Romans, exasperated by their repeated rebellions, exercised the rights of victory with unusual rigour. The emperor founded, under the name of Ælia Capitolina, a new city on Mount Sion,[20] to which he gave the privileges of a colony; and, denouncing the severest penalties against any of the Jewish people who should dare to approach its precincts, he fixed a vigilant garrison of a Roman cohort to enforce the execution of his orders. The Nazarenes had only one way left to escape the common proscription, and the force of truth was, on this occasion, assisted by the influence of temporal advantages. They elected Marcus for their bishop, a prelate of the race of

[19] Eusebius, l. iii. c. 5. Le Clerc, Hist. Ecclesiast. p. 605. [They retired before the capture.] During this occasional absence, the bishop and church of Pella still retained the title of Jerusalem. In the same manner, the Roman pontiffs resided seventy years at Avignon; and the patriarchs of Alexandria have long since transferred their episcopal seat to Cairo. [The Nazarenes still exist in the vicinity of Bussorah in Southern Babylonia. They are generally known as Mandæans. See W. Brandt, Die mandäische Religion, 1889; and Kessler's articles on Mandæans in Encycl. Britann., and in Herzog and Plitt's Encyclopädie.]

[20] Dion Cassius, l. lxix. [12]. The exile of the Jewish nation from Jerusalem is attested by Aristo of Pella (apud Euseb. l. iv. c. 6), and is mentioned by several ecclesiastical writers; though some of them too hastily extend this interdiction to the whole country of Palestine.

the Gentiles, and most probably a native either of Italy or of some of the Latin provinces. At his persuasion, the most considerable part of the congregation renounced the Mosaic law, in the practice of which they had persevered above a century. By this sacrifice of their habits and prejudices they purchased a free admission into the colony of Hadrian, and more firmly cemented their union with the Catholic church.[21]

The Ebionites   When the name and honours of the church of Jerusalem had been restored to Mount Sion, the crimes of heresy and schism were imputed to the obscure remnant of the Nazarenes which refused to accompany their Latin bishop. They still preserved their former habitation of Pella, spread themselves into the villages adjacent to Damascus, and formed an inconsiderable church in the city of Berœa, or, as it is now called, of Aleppo, in Syria.[22] The name of Nazarenes was deemed too honourable for those Christian Jews, and they soon received from the supposed poverty of their understanding, as well as of their condition, the contemptuous epithet of Ebionites.[23] In a few years after the return of the church of Jerusalem, it became a matter of doubt and controversy whether a man who sincerely acknowledged Jesus as the Messiah, but who still continued to observe the law of Moses, could possibly hope for salvation. The humane temper of Justin Martyr inclined him to answer this question in the affirmative ; and, though he expressed himself with the most guarded diffidence, he ventured to determine in favour of such an imperfect Christian, if he were content to practise the Mosaic ceremonies, without pretending to assert their general use or necessity.

[21] Eusebius, l. iv. c. 6.   Sulpicius Severus, ii. 31.   By comparing their unsatisfactory accounts, Mosheim (p. 327, &c.) has drawn out a very distinct representation of the circumstances and motives of this revolution.

[22] Le Clerc (Hist. Ecclesiast. p. 477, 535) seems to have collected from Eusebius, Jerome, Epiphanius, and other writers, all the principal circumstances that relate to the Nazarenes, or Ebionites.   The nature of their opinions soon divided them into a stricter and a milder sect ; and there is some reason to conjecture that the family of Jesus Christ remained members, at least, of the latter and more moderate party.   [The earliest mention of the Ebionites is in Irenæus, Adv. Hær. i. 22. The earlier Ebionites (= Nazarenes) must be distinguished from the later, Gnostic Ebionites.   For the former see the anti-heretical treatises of Tertullian and Hippolytus, for the latter that of Epiphanius.]

[23] Some writers have been pleased to create an Ebion, the imaginary author of their sect and name.   But we can more safely rely on the learned Eusebius than on the vehement Tertullian or the credulous Epiphanius.   According to Le Clerc, the Hebrew word *Ebjonim* may be translated into Latin by that of *Pauperes*. See Hist. Ecclesiast. p. 477.   [The name was assumed by themselves in reference to the poverty of their condition ; the Fathers contemptuously referred it to their understanding.]

But, when Justin was pressed to declare the sentiment of the church, he confessed that there were very many among the orthodox Christians, who not only excluded their Judaizing brethren from the hope of salvation, but who declined any intercourse with them in the common offices of friendship, hospitality, and social life.[24] The more rigorous opinion prevailed, as it was natural to expect, over the milder; and an external bar of separation was fixed between the disciples of Moses and those of Christ. The unfortunate Ebionites, rejected from one religion as apostates, and from the other as heretics, found themselves compelled to assume a more decided character; and, although some traces of that obsolete sect may be discovered as late as the fourth century, they insensibly melted away either into the church or the synagogue.[25]

While the orthodox church preserved a just medium between _{The Gnostics} excessive veneration and improper contempt for the law of Moses, the various heretics deviated into equal but opposite extremes of error and extravagance. From the acknowledged truth of the Jewish religion the Ebionites had concluded that it could never be abolished. From its supposed imperfections the Gnostics as hastily inferred that it never was instituted by the wisdom of the Deity. There are some objections against the authority of Moses and the prophets, which too readily present themselves to the sceptical mind; though they can only be derived from our ignorance of remote antiquity, and from our incapacity to form an adequate judgment of the divine œconomy. These objections were eagerly embraced, and as petulantly urged, by the vain science of the Gnostics.[26]

[24] See the very curious Dialogue of Justin Martyr with the Jew Tryphon. The conference between them was held at Ephesus, in the reign of Antoninus Pius, and about twenty years after the return of the church of Pella to Jerusalem. For this date consult the accurate note of Tillemont, Mémoires Ecclésiastiques, tom. ii. p. 511.

[25] Of all the systems of Christianity, that of Abyssinia is the only one which still adheres to the Mosaic rites (Geddes's Church History of Æthiopia, and Dissertations de La Grand sur la Relation du P. Lobo). The eunuch of the queen Candace might suggest some suspicions; but, as we are assured (Socrates, i. 19, Sozomen, ii. 24, Ludolphus [Hist. Eth.], p. 281) that the Æthiopians were not converted till the fourth century, it is more reasonable to believe that they respected the Sabbath, and distinguished the forbidden meats, in imitation of the Jews, who, in a very early period, were seated on both sides of the Red Sea. Circumcision had been practised by the most ancient Æthiopians, from motives of health and cleanliness, which seem to be explained in the Recherches Philosophiques sur les Américains, tom. ii. p. 117. [Cp. Art. "Ethiopic Church" in Dict. Chr. Biography.]

[26] Beausobre, Histoire du Manichéisme, l. i. c. 3, has stated their objections, particularly those of Faustus, the adversary of Augustin, with the most learned impartiality. [Perhaps the best introduction to the study of Gnosticism (and of

As those heretics were, for the most part, averse to the pleasures of sense, they morosely arraigned the polygamy of the
patriarchs, the gallantries of David, and the seraglio of Solomon.
The conquest of the land of Canaan, and the extirpation of the
unsuspecting natives, they were at a loss how to reconcile with
the common notions of humanity and justice. But, when they
recollected the sanguinary list of murders, of executions, and
of massacres, which stain almost every page of the Jewish
annals, they acknowledged that the barbarians of Palestine
had exercised as much compassion towards their idolatrous
enemies as they had ever shewn to their friends or countrymen.[27] Passing from the sectaries of the law to the law itself,
they asserted that it was impossible that a religion which consisted only of bloody sacrifices and trifling ceremonies, and
whose rewards as well as punishments were all of a carnal
and temporal nature, could inspire the love of virtue, or restrain
the impetuosity of passion. The Mosaic account of the creation
and fall of man was treated with profane derision by the
Gnostics, who would not listen with patience to the repose
of the Deity after six days' labour, to the rib of Adam, the
garden of Eden, the trees of life and of knowledge, the speaking
serpent, the forbidden fruit, and the condemnation pronounced
against human kind for the venial offence of their first pro-
genitors.[28] The God of Israel was impiously represented by
the Gnostics as a being liable to passion and to error, capricious
in his favour, implacable in his resentment, meanly jealous of
his superstitious worship, and confining his partial providence
to a single people and to this transitory life. In such a char-

Ebionism) is the work of R. A. Lipsius, Quellenkritik des Epiphanios, and his
article on Gnosticismus in Ersch and Gruber's Encyclopædia. The theories of
Harnack and Hilgenfeld as to the origin of Gnosticism are briefly stated in App. 2.
The chief sources for early Gnosticism are : Irenæus, Adv. Hær. (esp. for the
Valentinian heresy), Tertullian, Adv. Hær. (esp. for Marcionism), and two works
of Hippolytus, of which (a) "Against all Heresies " is formally lost, but has been
practically restored, by the ingenuity of Lipsius, from citations of later writers ;
and (b) the "Refutation of all Heresies," of which the greater part was recovered
in this century, in a Ms. found on Mount Athos (the authorship of Hippolytus
was finally proved by Döllinger) ; which discovery led to the identification of the
Philosophumena (of "Pseudo-Origen ") as the first book of the same treatise. It is
to be observed that both Irenæus and Hippolytus apply the word Gnostic in a
wide sense to a whole class of cognate views, not (like Epiphanius) to a special sect ;
Hippolytus, however, chiefly uses it of the Ophites and Syrian Gnostics.]
[27] Apud ipsos fides obstinata, misericordia in promptû : adversus omnes alios
hostile odium. Tacit. Hist. v. 4. Surely Tacitus had seen the Jews with too
favourable an eye. The perusal of Josephus must have destroyed the antithesis.
[28] Dr. Burnet (Archæologia, l. ii. c. 7) has discussed the first chapters of
Genesis with too much wit and freedom.

acter they could discover none of the features of the wise and omnipotent father of the universe.[29] They allowed that the religion of the Jews was somewhat less criminal than the idolatry of the Gentiles; but it was their fundamental doctrine that the Christ whom they adored as the first and brightest emanation of the Deity appeared upon earth to rescue mankind from their various errors, and to reveal a *new* system of truth and perfection. The most learned of the fathers, by a very singular condescension, have imprudently admitted the sophistry of the Gnostics. Acknowledging that the literal sense is repugnant to every principle of faith as well as reason, they deem themselves secure and invulnerable behind the ample veil of allegory, which they carefully spread over every tender part of the Mosaic dispensation.[30]

It has been remarked, with more ingenuity than truth, that the virgin purity of the church was never violated by schism or heresy before the reign of Trajan or Hadrian, about one hundred years after the death of Christ.[31] We may observe, with much more propriety, that, during that period, the disciples of the Messiah were indulged in a freer latitude both of faith and practice than has ever been allowed in succeeding ages. As the terms of communion were insensibly narrowed, and the spiritual authority of the prevailing party was exercised with increasing severity, many of its most respectable adherents, who were called upon to renounce, were provoked to assert, their private opinions, to pursue the consequences of their mistaken principles, and openly to erect the standard of rebellion against the unity of the church. The Gnostics were distinguished as the most polite, the most learned, and the most wealthy of the Christian name, and that general appellation which expressed a superiority of knowledge was either assumed by their own pride or ironically bestowed by the envy of their adversaries.[32] They were almost without exception of the race of the Gentiles, and their principal founders seem to have been

Their sects, progress, and influence

---

[29] The milder Gnostics considered Jehovah, the Creator, as a Being of a mixed nature between God and the Dæmon. Others confounded him with the evil principle. Consult the second century of the general history of Mosheim, which gives a very distinct, though concise, account of their strange opinions on this subject.

[30] See Beausobre, Hist. du Manichéisme, l. i. c. 4. Origen and St. Augustin were among the Allegorists.

[31] Hegesippus, ap. Euseb. l. iii. 32, iv. 22. Clemens, Alexandrin. Stromat. vii. 17.

[32] [It is not necessary to suppose that Gnosticism is referred to in the first Epistle to Timothy, *ad fin.*]

natives of Syria or Egypt, where the warmth of the climate disposes both the mind and the body to indolent and contemplative devotion.   The Gnostics blended with the faith of Christ many sublime but obscure tenets which they derived from oriental philosophy, and even from the religion of Zoroaster, concerning the eternity of matter, the existence of two principles, and the mysterious hierarchy of the invisible world.[33] As soon as they launched out into that vast abyss, they delivered themselves to the guidance of a disordered imagination ; and, as the paths of error are various and infinite, the Gnostics were imperceptibly divided into more than fifty particular sects,[34] of whom the most celebrated appear to have been the Basilidians, the Valentinians, the Marcionites, and, in a still later period, the Manichæans.   Each of these sects could boast of its bishops and congregations, of its doctors and martyrs,[35] and, instead of the four gospels adopted by the church, the heretics produced a multitude of histories, in which the actions and discourses of Christ and of his apostles were adapted to their respective tenets.[36]   The success of the Gnostics was rapid and extensive.[37] They covered Asia and Egypt, established themselves in Rome, and sometimes penetrated into the provinces of the West.   For

[33] In the account of the Gnostics of the second and third centuries, Mosheim is ingenious and candid ; Le Clerc dull, but exact ; Beausobre almost always an apologist ; and it is much to be feared that the primitive fathers are very frequently calumniators.   [Gnosticism originated in Syria, and entered upon a second stage when it passed to Egypt, and came under the influence of Greek philosophy (Basilides, for instance, was affected by the doctrines of the Stoics, Valentinus by Platonism).   A later development is presented in the treatise *Pistis Sophia*, a precious relic of Gnostic literature, preserved in Coptic, edited by Schwartze and Petermann, with Latin translation, in 1851.   See Appendix 2.]

[34] See the catalogues of Irenæus and Epiphanius.   It must indeed be allowed that those writers were inclined to multiply the number of sects which opposed the *unity* of the church.

[35] Eusebius, l. iv. c. 15.   Sozomen, l. ii. c. 32.   See in Bayle, in the article of *Marcion*, a curious detail of a dispute on that subject.   It should seem that some of the Gnostics (the Basilidians) declined, and even refused, the honour of martyrdom.   Their reasons were singular and abstruse.   See Mosheim, p. 359.

[36] See a very remarkable passage of Origen (Proem. ad Lucam).   That indefatigable writer, who had consumed his life in the study of the scriptures, relies for their authenticity on the inspired authority of the church.   It was impossible that the Gnostics could receive our present gospels, many parts of which (particularly in the resurrection of Christ) are directly, and as it might seem designedly, pointed against their favourite tenets.   It is therefore somewhat singular that Ignatius (Epist. ad Smyrn. Patr. Apostol. tom. ii. p. 34, [§ iii. 2]) should choose to employ a vague and doubtful tradition, instead of quoting the certain testimony of the evangelists.

[37] Faciunt favos et vespæ ; faciunt ecclesias et Marcionitæ, is the strong expression of Tertullian, which I am obliged to quote from memory.   [Adv. Marc. iv. 5.]   In the time of Epiphanius (advers. Hæreses, p. 302), the Marcionites were very numerous in Italy, Syria, Egypt, Arabia, and Persia.

the most part they arose in the second century, flourished during the third, and were suppressed in the fourth or fifth, by the prevalence of more fashionable controversies, and by the superior ascendant of the reigning power.   Though they constantly disturbed the peace, and frequently disgraced the name, of religion, they contributed to assist rather than to retard the progress of Christianity.   The Gentile converts, whose strongest objections and prejudices were directed against the law of Moses, could find admission into many Christian societies, which required not from their untutored mind any belief of an antecedent revelation.   Their faith was insensibly fortified and enlarged, and the church was ultimately benefited by the conquests of its most inveterate enemies.[38]

But, whatever difference of opinion might subsist between the Orthodox, the Ebionites, and the Gnostics, concerning the divinity or the obligation of the Mosaic law, they were all equally animated by the same exclusive zeal and by the same abhorrence for idolatry which had distinguished the Jews from the other nations of the ancient world.   The philosopher, who considered the system of polytheism as a composition of human fraud and error, could disguise a smile of contempt under the mask of devotion, without apprehending that either the mockery or the compliance would expose him to the resentment of any invisible, or, as he conceived them, imaginary powers.   But the established religions of Paganism were seen by the primitive Christians in a much more odious and formidable light.   It was the universal sentiment both of the church and of heretics that the dæmons were the authors, the patrons, and the objects of idolatry.[39]   Those rebellious spirits who had been degraded from the rank of angels, and cast down into the infernal pit, were still permitted to roam upon earth, to torment the bodies, and to seduce the minds, of sinful men.   The dæmons soon discovered and abused the natural propensity of the human heart towards devotion, and, artfully withdrawing the adoration of mankind from their Creator, they usurped the place and honours of the Supreme Deity.   By the success of their malicious contrivances, they at once gratified their own vanity

The dæmons considered as the gods of antiquity

[38] Augustin is a memorable instance of this gradual progress from reason to faith.   He was, during several years, engaged in the Manichæan sect.

[39] The unanimous sentiment of the primitive church is very clearly explained by Justin Martyr, Apolog. Major [c. 25], by Athenagoras Legat. c. 22 [25.   πρεσβεία περὶ Χριστιανῶν is the title: best ed. by E. Schwartz, 1891], &c., and by Lactantius, Institut. Divin. ii. 14—19.   [See also Athanasius de incarn. v. 47.]

and revenge, and obtained the only comfort of which they were yet susceptible, the hope of involving the human species in the participation of their guilt and misery. It was confessed, or at least it was imagined, that they had distributed among themselves the most important characters of polytheism, one dæmon assuming the name and attributes of Jupiter, another of Æsculapius, a third of Venus, and a fourth perhaps of Apollo; [40] and that, by the advantage of their long experience and aerial nature, they were enabled to execute, with sufficient skill and dignity, the parts which they had undertaken. They lurked in the temples, instituted festivals and sacrifices, invented fables, pronounced oracles, and were frequently allowed to perform miracles. The Christians, who, by the interposition of evil spirits, could so readily explain every præternatural appearance, were disposed and even desirous to admit the most extravagant fictions of the Pagan mythology. But the belief of the Christian was accompanied with horror. The most trifling mark of respect to the national worship he considered as a direct homage yielded to the dæmon, and as an act of rebellion against the majesty of God.

Abhorrence of the Christians for idolatry

In consequence of this opinion, it was the first but arduous duty of a Christian to preserve himself pure and undefiled by the practice of idolatry. The religion of the nations was not merely a speculative doctrine professed in the schools or preached in the temples. The innumerable deities and rites of polytheism were closely interwoven with every circumstance of business or pleasure, of public or of private life; and it seemed impossible to escape the observance of them, without, at the same time, renouncing the commerce of mankind and all the offices and amusements of society. [41] The important transactions of peace and war were prepared or concluded by solemn sacrifices, in which the magistrate, the senator, and the soldier were obliged to preside or to participate. [42] The public spectacles were an essential part of the cheerful devotion of the Pagans, and the gods were supposed to accept, as the most grateful offering, the games that the prince and people celebrated in honour of their

Ceremonies

[40] Tertullian (Apolog. c. 23 [22]) alleges the confession of the Dæmons themselves as often as they were tormented by the Christian exorcists.

[41] Tertullian has written a most severe treatise against idolatry, to caution his brethren against the hourly danger of incurring that guilt. Recogita silvam, et quantæ latitant spinæ. De Coronâ Militis, c. 10.

[42] The Roman senate was always held in a temple or consecrated place (Aulus Gellius, xiv. 7). Before they entered on business, every senator dropped some wine and frankincense on the altar. Sueton. in August. c. 35.

peculiar festivals.[43] The Christian, who with pious horror avoided the abomination of the circus or the theatre, found himself encompassed with infernal snares in every convivial entertainment, as often as his friends, invoking the hospitable deities, poured out libations to each other's happiness.[44] When the bride, struggling with well-affected reluctance, was forced in hymenæal pomp over the threshold of her new habitation,[45] or when the sad procession of the dead slowly moved towards the funeral pile ;[46] the Christian, on these interesting occasions, was compelled to desert the persons who were the dearest to him, rather than contract the guilt inherent to those impious ceremonies. Every art and every trade that was in the least Arts concerned in the framing or adorning of idols was polluted by the stain of idolatry ;[47] a severe sentence, since it devoted to eternal misery the far greater part of the community, which is employed in the exercise of liberal or mechanic professions. If we cast our eyes over the numerous remains of antiquity, we shall perceive that, besides the immediate representations of the Gods and the holy instruments of their worship, the elegant forms and agreeable fictions, consecrated by the imagination of the Greeks, were introduced as the richest ornaments of the houses, the dress, and the furniture, of the Pagans.[48] Even the arts of music and painting, of eloquence and poetry, flowed from the same impure origin. In the style of the fathers, Apollo and the Muses were the organs of the infernal spirit, Homer and Virgil were the most eminent of his servants, and the beautiful mythology which pervades and animates the compositions of their genius is destined to celebrate the glory of

[43] See Tertullian, De Spectaculis. This severe reformer shews no more indulgence to a tragedy of Euripides than to a combat of gladiators. The dress of the actors particularly offends him. By the use of the lofty buskin, they impiously strive to add a cubit to their stature, c. 23. [Cp. Nöldechen, Z.f. Kirchengesch. xv. 1895, 161 *sqq.*]

[44] The ancient practice of concluding the entertainment with libations may be found in every classic. Socrates and Seneca, in their last moments, made a noble application of this custom. Postquam [*leg.* postremo] stagnum calidæ aquæ introiit, respergens proximos servorum, additâ voce, libare se liquorem illum Jovi Liberatori, Tacit. Annal. xv. 64.

[45] See the elegant but idolatrous hymn of Catullus, on the nuptials of Manlius and Julia. O Hymen, Hymenæe iö ! Quis huic Deo comparare ausit?

[46] The ancient funerals (in those of Misenus and Pallas) are no less accurately described by Virgil than they are illustrated by his commentator Servius. The pile itself was an altar, the flames were fed with the blood of victims, and all the assistants were sprinkled with lustral water.

[47] Tertullian de Idololatria, c. 11.

[48] See every part of Montfaucon's Antiquities. Even the reverses of the Greek and Roman coins were frequently of an idolatrous nature. Here indeed the scruples of the Christian were suspended by a stronger passion.

the dæmons. Even the common language of Greece and Rome
abounded with familiar but impious expressions, which the imprudent Christian might too carelessly utter, or too patiently
hear.[49]

Festivals   The dangerous temptations which on every side lurked in
ambush to surprise the unguarded believer assailed him with
redoubled violence on the days of solemn festivals. So artfully
were they framed and disposed throughout the year that superstition always wore the appearance of pleasure, and often of
virtue.[50] Some of the most sacred festivals in the Roman ritual
were destined to salute the new calends of January with vows
of public and private felicity, to indulge the pious remembrance
of the dead and living, to ascertain the inviolable bounds of
property, to hail, on the return of spring, the genial powers of
fecundity, to perpetuate the two memorable æras of Rome, the
foundation of the city and that of the republic, and to restore,
during the humane license of the Saturnalia, the primitive equality
of mankind. Some idea may be conceived of the abhorrence of
the Christians for such impious ceremonies, by the scrupulous
delicacy which they displayed on a much less alarming occasion.
On days of general festivity, it was the custom of the ancients
to adorn their doors with lamps and with branches of laurel,
and to crown their heads with a garland of flowers. This innocent and elegant practice might, perhaps, have been tolerated
as a mere civil institution. But it most unluckily happened
that the doors were under the protection of the household gods,
that the laurel was sacred to the lover of Daphne, and that
garlands of flowers, though frequently worn as a symbol either
of joy or mourning, had been dedicated in their first origin to
the service of superstition. The trembling Christians, who
were persuaded in this instance to comply with the fashion of
their country and the commands of the magistrate, laboured
under the most gloomy apprehensions, from the reproaches of
their own conscience, the censures of the church, and the de-
nunciations of divine vengeance.[51]

[49] Tertullian de Idololatria, c. 20, 21, 22. If a Pagan friend (on the occasion
perhaps of sneezing) used the familiar expression of "Jupiter bless you," the
Christian was obliged to protest against the divinity of Jupiter.

[50] Consult the most laboured work of Ovid, his imperfect *Fasti*. He finished
no more than the first six months of the year. The compilation of Macrobius is
called the *Saturnalia*, but it is only a small part of the first book that bears any
relation to the title.

[51] Tertullian has composed a defence, or rather panegyric, of the rash action
of a Christian soldier who, by throwing away his crown of laurel, had exposed

Such was the anxious diligence which was required to guard the chastity of the gospel from the infectious breath of idolatry. The superstitious observances of public or private rites were carelessly practised, from education and habit, by the followers of the established religion. But, as often as they occurred, they afforded the Christians an opportunity of declaring and confirming their zealous opposition. By these frequent protestations, their attachment to the faith was continually fortified, and, in proportion to the increase of zeal, they combated with the more ardour and success in the holy war which they had undertaken against the empire of the dæmons.

II. The writings of Cicero [52] represent, in the most lively colours, the ignorance, the errors, and the uncertainty of the ancient philosophers, with regard to the immortality of the soul. When they are desirous of arming their disciples against the fear of death, they inculcate, as an obvious though melancholy position, that the fatal stroke of our dissolution releases us from the calamities of life, and that those can no longer suffer who no longer exist. Yet there were a few sages of Greece and Rome who had conceived a more exalted, and, in some respects, a juster idea of human nature ; though it must be confessed that, in the sublime inquiry, their reason had been often guided by their imagination, and that their imagination had been prompted by their vanity. When they viewed with complacency the extent of their own mental powers when they exercised the various faculties of memory, of fancy, and of judgment, in the most profound speculations, or the most important labours, and when they reflected on the desire of fame, which transported them into future ages far beyond the bounds of death and of the grave ; they were unwilling to confound themselves with the beasts of the field, or to suppose that a being, for whose dignity they entertained the most sincere admiration, could be limited to a spot of earth and to a few years of duration. With this favourable prepossession, they summoned to their aid the science, or rather the language, of

himself and his brethren to the most imminent danger. By the mention of the *emperors* (Severus and Caracalla) it is evident, notwithstanding the wishes of M. de Tillemont, that Tertullian composed his treatise De Coronâ long before he was engaged in the errors of the Montanists. See Mémoires Ecclésiastiques, tom. iii. p. 384. [Date rather 211 ; he joined Montanists, 207. Cp. Nöldechen, Brieger's Ztschr. f. Kirchengeschichte, xi. 1890, p. 352 *sqq.*]

[52] In particular, the first book of the Tusculan Questions, and the treatise De Senectute, and the Somnium Scipionis contain, in the most beautiful language, everything that Grecian philosophy, or Roman good sense, could possibly suggest on this dark but important object.

Metaphysics.   They soon discovered that, as none of the properties of matter will apply to the operations of the mind, the human soul must consequently be a substance distinct from the body, pure, simple, and spiritual, incapable of dissolution, and susceptible of a much higher degree of virtue and happiness after the release from its corporeal prison.   From these spacious and noble principles, the philosophers who trod in the footsteps of Plato deduced a very unjustifiable conclusion, since they asserted, not only the future immortality, but the past eternity of the human soul, which they were too apt to consider as a portion of the infinite and self-existing spirit which pervades and sustains the universe.[53]   A doctrine thus removed beyond the senses and the experience of mankind might serve to amuse the leisure of a philosophic mind ; or, in the silence of solitude, it might sometimes impart a ray of comfort to desponding virtue ; but the faint impression which had been received in the schools was soon obliterated by the commerce and business of active life.   We are sufficiently acquainted with the eminent persons who flourished in the age of Cicero, and of the first Cæsars, with their actions, their characters, and their motives, to be assured that their conduct in this life was never regulated by any serious conviction of the rewards or punishments of a future state.   At the bar and in the senate of Rome the ablest orators were not apprehensive of giving offence to their hearers by exposing that doctrine as an idle and extravagant opinion, which was rejected with contempt by every man of a liberal education and understanding.[54]

among the
Pagans of
Greece and
Rome

Since, therefore, the most sublime efforts of philosophy can extend no farther than feebly to point out the desire, the hope, or at most the probability, of a future state, there is nothing, except a divine revelation, that can ascertain the existence, and describe the condition, of the invisible country which is destined to receive the souls of men after their separation from the body. But we may perceive several defects inherent to the popular religions of Greece and Rome, which rendered them very unequal to so arduous a task.   1. The general system of their

[53] The pre-existence of human souls, so far at least as that doctrine is compatible with religion, was adopted by many of the Greek and Latin fathers.   See Beausobre, Hist. du Manichéisme, l. vi. c. 4.

[54] See Cicero pro Cluent. c. 61. Cæsar ap. Sallust. de Bell. Catilin. c. 50. Juvenal. Satir. ii. 149.

Esse aliquos manes, et subterranea regna,
.   .   .   .
Nec pueri crecount, nisi qui nondum ære lavantur.

mythology was unsupported by any solid proofs; and the wisest among the Pagans had already disclaimed its usurped authority. 2. The description of the infernal regions had been abandoned to the fancy of painters and of poets, who peopled them with so many phantoms and monsters, who dispensed their rewards and punishments with so little equity, that a solemn truth, the most congenial to the human heart, was oppressed and disgraced by the absurd mixture of the wildest fictions.[55] 3. The doctrine of a future state was scarcely considered among the devout poly-theists of Greece and Rome as a fundamental article of faith. The providence of the gods, as it related to public communities rather than to private individuals, was principally displayed on the visible theatre of the present world. The petitions which were offered on the altars of Jupiter or Apollo expressed the anxiety of their worshippers for temporal happiness, and their ignorance or indifference concerning a future life.[56] The im-portant truth of the immortality of the soul was inculcated with more diligence as well as success in India, in Assyria, in Egypt, and in Gaul; and, since we cannot attribute such a difference among the Barbarians to the superior knowledge of the barbarians, we must ascribe it to the influence of an established priesthood, which employed the motives of virtue as the instrument of ambition.[57]

We might naturally expect that a principle, so essential to among the Jews religion, would have been revealed in the clearest terms to the chosen people of Palestine, and that it might safely have been intrusted to the hereditary priesthood of Aaron. It is incum-bent on us to adore the mysterious dispensations of Providence,[58] when we discover that the doctrine of the immortality of the soul is omitted in the law of Moses; it is darkly insinuated by

[55] The xith book of the Odyssey gives a very dreary and incoherent account of the infernal shades. Pindar and Virgil have embellished the picture; but even those poets, though more correct than their great model, are guilty of very strange inconsistencies. See Bayle, Responses aux Questions d'un Provincial, part iii. c. 22.

[56] See the xvith epistle of the first book of Horace, the xiiith Satire of Juvenal, and the iid Satire of Persius: these popular discourses express the sentiment and language of the multitude.

[57] If we confine ourselves to the Gauls, we may observe that they intrusted, not only their lives, but even their money, to the security of another world. Vetus ille mos Gallorum occurrit (says Valerius Maximus, l. ii. c. 6, p. 10), quos, me-moria proditum est, pecunias mutuas, quæ his apud inferos redderentur, dare solitos. The same custom is more darkly insinuated by Mela, l. iii. c. 2. It is almost needless to add that the profits of trade hold a just proportion to the credit of the merchant, and that the Druids derived from their holy profession a character of responsibility which could scarcely be claimed by any other order of men.

[58] The right reverend author of the Divine Legation of Moses assigns a very curious reason for the omission, and most ingeniously retorts it on the unbelievers,

the prophets, and during the long period which elapsed between the Egyptian and the Babylonian servitudes, the hopes as well as fears of the Jews appear to have been confined within the narrow compass of the present life.[59]   After Cyrus had permitted the exiled nation to return into the promised land, and after Ezra had restored the ancient records of their religion, two celebrated sects, the Sadducees and the Pharisees, insensibly arose at Jerusalem.[60]   The former, selected from the more opulent and distinguished ranks of society, were strictly attached to the literal sense of the Mosaic law, and they piously rejected the immortality of the soul, as an opinion that received no countenance from the Divine book, which they revered as the only rule of their faith.   To the authority of scripture the Pharisees added that of tradition, and they accepted, under the name of traditions, several speculative tenets from the philosophy or religion of the eastern nations.   The doctrines of fate or predestination, of angels and spirits, and of a future state of rewards and punishments, were in the number of these new articles of belief; and, as the Pharisees, by the austerity of their manners, had drawn into their party the body of the Jewish people, the immortality of the soul became the prevailing sentiment of the synagogue, under the reign of the Asmonæan princes and pontiffs.   The temper of the Jews was incapable of contenting itself with such a cold and languid assent as might satisfy the mind of a Polytheist; and, as soon as they admitted the idea of a future state, they embraced it with the zeal which has always formed the characteristic of the nation.   Their zeal, however, added nothing to its evidence, or even probability: and it was still necessary that the doctrine of life and immortality, which had been dictated by nature, approved by reason, and received by superstition, should obtain the sanction of Divine truth from the authority and example of Christ.

among the
Christians

When the promise of eternal happiness was proposed to mankind, on condition of adopting the faith and of observing the precepts of the gospel, it is no wonder that so advantageous

---

[59] See Le Clerc (Prolegomena ad Hist. Ecclesiast. sect. 1, c. 8).   His authority seems to carry the greater weight, as he has written a learned and judicious commentary on the books of the Old Testament.

[60] Joseph. Antiquitat. l. xiii. c. 10.   De Bell. Jud. ii. 8.   According to the most natural interpretation of his words, the Sadducees admitted only the Pentateuch; but it has pleased some modern critics to add the prophets to their creed, and to suppose that they contented themselves with rejecting the traditions of the Pharisees.   Dr. Jortin has argued that point in his Remarks on Ecclesiastical History, vol. ii. p. 103.

an offer should have been accepted by great numbers of every religion, of every rank, and of every province in the Roman empire. The ancient Christians were animated by a contempt for their present existence, and by a just confidence of immortality, of which the doubtful and imperfect faith of modern ages cannot give us any adequate notion. In the primitive church, the influence of truth was very powerfully strengthened by an opinion which, however it may deserve respect for its usefulness and antiquity, has not been found agreeable to experience. It was universally believed that the end of the world and the kingdom of Heaven were at hand. The near approach of this wonderful event had been predicted by the apostles; the tradition of it was preserved by their earliest disciples, and those who understood in their literal sense the discourses of Christ himself were obliged to expect the second and glorious coming of the Son of Man in the clouds, before that generation was totally extinguished, which had beheld his humble condition upon earth, and which might still be witness of the calamities of the Jews under Vespasian or Hadrian. The revolution of seventeen centuries has instructed us not to press too closely the mysterious language of prophecy and revelation; but, as long as, for wise purposes, this error was permitted to subsist in the church, it was productive of the most salutary effects on the faith and practice of Christians, who lived in the awful expectation of that moment when the globe itself, and all the various race of mankind, should tremble at the appearance of their divine judge.[61]

The ancient and popular doctrine of the Millennium was intimately connected with the second coming of Christ. As the works of the creation had been finished in six days, their duration in their present state, according to a tradition which was attributed to the prophet Elijah, was fixed to six thousand years.[62] By the same analogy it was inferred that this long period of labour and contention, which was now almost elapsed,[63]

Margin notes: Approaching end of the world — Doctrine of the Millennium

[61] This expectation was countenanced by the twenty-fourth chapter of St. Matthew, and by the first epistle of St. Paul to the Thessalonians. Erasmus removes the difficulty by the help of allegory and metaphor; and the learned Grotius ventures to insinuate that, for wise purposes, the pious deception was permitted to take place.

[62] See Burnet's Sacred Theory, part iii. c. 5. This tradition may be traced as high as the author of the Epistle of Barnabas, who wrote in the first century, and who seems to have been half a Jew.

[63] The primitive church of Antioch computed almost 6000 years from the creation of the world to the birth of Christ. Africanus, Lactantius, and the Greek church, have reduced that number to 5500, and Eusebius has contented

would be succeeded by a joyful Sabbath of a thousand years; and that Christ, with the triumphant band of the saints and the elect who had escaped death, or who had been miraculously revived, would reign upon earth till the time appointed for the last and general resurrection. So pleasing was this hope to the mind of believers that the *New Jerusalem*, the seat of this blissful kingdom, was quickly adorned with all the gayest colours of the imagination. A felicity consisting only of pure and spiritual pleasure would have appeared too refined for its inhabitants, who were still supposed to possess their human nature and senses. A garden of Eden, with the amusements of the pastoral life, was no longer suited to the advanced state of society which prevailed under the Roman empire. A city was therefore erected of gold and precious stones, and a supernatural plenty of corn and wine was bestowed on the adjacent territory; in the free enjoyment of whose spontaneous productions the happy and benevolent people was never to be restrained by any jealous laws of exclusive property.[64] The assurance of such a Millennium was carefully inculcated by a succession of fathers from Justin Martyr[65] and Irenæus, who conversed with the immediate disciples of the apostles, down to Lactantius, who was preceptor to the son of Constantine.[66] Though it might not be universally received, it appears to have been the reigning sentiment of the orthodox believers; and it seems so well adapted to the desires and apprehensions of mankind that it must have contributed, in a very considerable degree, to the progress of the Christian faith. But, when the edifice of the church was almost completed, the temporary support was laid aside. The doctrine of Christ's reign upon earth was at first treated as a profound allegory, was considered

himself with 5200 years. These calculations were formed on the Septuagint, which was universally received during the six first centuries. The authority of the Vulgate and of the Hebrew text has determined the moderns, Protestants as well as Catholics, to prefer a period of about 4000 years; though, in the study of profane antiquity, they often find themselves straitened by those narrow limits. [Cp. App. 3.]

[64] Most of these pictures were borrowed from a misinterpretation of Isaiah, Daniel, and the Apocalypse. One of the grossest images may be found in Irenæus (l. 5, p. 455 [c. 33]), the disciple of Papias, who had seen the apostle St. John.

[65] See the second dialogue of Justin with Tryphon and the seventh book of Lactantius. It is unnecessary to allege all the intermediate fathers, as the fact is not disputed. Yet the curious reader may consult Daillé de Usu Patrum, l. iii. c. 4.

[66] The testimony of Justin, of his own faith and that of his orthodox brethren, in the doctrine of a Millennium, is delivered in the clearest and most solemn manner (Dialog. cum. Tryphonte Jud. p. 177, 178, edit. Benedictin). If in the beginning of this important passage there is anything like an inconsistency, we may impute it, as we think proper, either to the author or to his transcribers.

by degrees as a doubtful and useless opinion, and was at length rejected as the absurd invention of heresy and fanaticism.[67] A mysterious prophecy, which still forms a part of the sacred canon, but which was thought to favour the exploded sentiment, has very narrowly escaped the proscription of the church.[68]

Whilst the happiness and glory of a temporal reign were promised to the disciples of Christ, the most dreadful calamities were denounced against an unbelieving world. The edification of the new Jerusalem was to advance by equal steps with the destruction of the mystic Babylon; and, as long as the emperors who reigned before Constantine persisted in the profession of idolatry, the epithet of Babylon was applied to the city and to the empire of Rome. A regular series was prepared of all the moral and physical evils which can afflict a flourishing nation; intestine discord, and the invasion of the fiercest barbarians from the unknown regions of the North; pestilence and famine, comets and eclipses, earthquakes and inundations.[69] All these were only so many preparatory and alarming signs of the great catastrophe of Rome, when the country of the Scipios and Cæsars should be consumed by a flame from Heaven, and the city of the seven hills, with her palaces, her temples, and her triumphal arches, should be buried in a vast lake of fire and brimstone. It might, however, afford some consolation to Roman vanity, that the period of their empire would be that

Conflagration of Rome and of the world

[67] Dupin, Bibliothèque Ecclésiastique, tom. i. p. 223, tom. ii. p. 366, and Mosheim, p. 720; though the latter of these learned divines is not altogether candid on this occasion.

[68] In the Council of Laodicea (about the year 360) the Apocalypse was tacitly excluded from the sacred canon, by the same churches of Asia to which it is addressed; and we may learn from the complaint of Sulpicius Severus that their sentence had been ratified by the greater number of Christians of his time. From what causes, then, is the Apocalypse at present so generally received by the Greek, the Roman, and the Protestant churches? The following ones may be assigned. 1. The Greeks were subdued by the authority of an impostor who, in the sixth century, assumed the character of Dionysius the Areopagite. 2. A just apprehension, that the grammarians might become more important than the theologians, engaged the Council of Trent to fix the seal of their infallibility on all the books of Scripture, contained in the Latin Vulgate, in the number of which the Apocalypse was fortunately included (Fra Paolo, Istoria del Concilio Tridentino, l. ii). 3. The advantage of turning those mysterious prophecies against the See of Rome inspired the Protestants with uncommon veneration for so useful an ally. See the ingenious and elegant discourses of the present bishop of Lichfield on that unpromising subject. [It may be considered certain that the Apocalypse of "John" was composed under Domitian (as Mommsen holds), to whose persecution of Christians there are allusions. But there is nothing in the work to show that it was written by the author of the Gospel.]

[69] Lactantius (Institut. Divin. vii. 15, &c.) relates the dismal tale of futurity with great spirit and eloquence.

of the world itself; which, as it had once perished by the element of water, was destined to experience a second and a speedy destruction from the element of fire. In the opinion of a general conflagration, the faith of the Christian very happily coincided with the tradition of the East, the philosophy of the Stoics, and the analogy of Nature; and even the country which, from religious motives, had been chosen for the origin and principal scene of the conflagration, was the best adapted for that purpose by natural and physical causes; by its deep caverns, beds of sulphur, and numerous volcanoes, of which those of Ætna, of Vesuvius, and of Lipari, exhibit a very imperfect representation. The calmest and most intrepid sceptic could not refuse to acknowledge that the destruction of the present system of the world by fire was in itself extremely probable. The Christian, who founded his belief much less on the fallacious arguments of reason than on the authority of tradition and the interpretation of scripture, expected it with terror and confidence, as a certain and approaching event; and, as his mind was perpetually filled with the solemn idea, he considered every disaster that happened to the empire as an infallible symptom of an expiring world.[70]

The Pagans devoted to eternal punishment

The condemnation of the wisest and most virtuous of the Pagans, on account of their ignorance or disbelief of the divine truth, seems to offend the reason and the humanity of the present age.[71] But the primitive church, whose faith was of a much firmer consistence, delivered over, without hesitation, to eternal torture the far greater part of the human species. A charitable hope might perhaps be indulged in favour of Socrates, or some other sages of antiquity, who had consulted the light of reason before that of the gospel had arisen.[72] But it was

[70] On this subject every reader of taste will be entertained with the third part of Burnet's Sacred Theory. He blends philosophy, scripture, and tradition, into one magnificent system; in the description of which he displays a strength of fancy not inferior to that of Milton himself.

[71] And yet, whatever may be the language of individuals, it is still the public doctrine of all the Christian churches; nor can even our own refuse to admit the conclusions which must be drawn from the viiith and the xviiith of her Articles. The Jansenists, who have so diligently studied the works of the fathers, maintain this sentiment with distinguished zeal; and the learned M. de Tillemont never dismisses a virtuous emperor without pronouncing his damnation. Zuinglius is perhaps the only leader of a party who has ever adopted the milder sentiment, and he gave no less offence to the Lutherans than to the Catholics. See Bossuet, Histoire des Variations des Eglises Protestantes, l. ii. c. 19—22.

[72] Justin and Clemens of Alexandria allow that some of the philosophers were instructed by the Logos; confounding its double signification of the human reason and of the Divine Word.

unanimously affirmed that those who, since the birth or the death of Christ, had obstinately persisted in the worship of the dæmons, neither deserved, nor could expect, a pardon from the irritated justice of the Deity. These rigid sentiments, which had been unknown to the ancient world, appear to have infused a spirit of bitterness into a system of love and harmony. The ties of blood and friendship were frequently torn asunder by the difference of religious faith; and the Christians, who, in this world, found themselves oppressed by the power of the Pagans, were sometimes seduced by resentment and spiritual pride to delight in the prospect of their future triumph. "You are fond of spectacles," exclaims the stern Tertullian; "expect the greatest of all spectacles, the last and eternal judgment of the universe. How shall I admire, how laugh, how rejoice, how exult, when I behold so many proud monarchs, and fancied gods, groaning in the lowest abyss of darkness; so many magistrates, who persecuted the name of the Lord, liquefying in fiercer fires than they ever kindled against the Christians; so many sage philosophers blushing in red hot flames, with their deluded scholars; so many celebrated poets trembling before the tribunal, not of Minos, but of Christ; so many tragedians, more tuneful in the expression of their own sufferings; so many dancers——!" But the humanity of the reader will permit me to draw a veil over the rest of this infernal description, which the zealous African pursues in a long variety of affected and unfeeling witticisms.[73]

Doubtless there were many among the primitive Christians of a temper more suitable to the meekness and charity of their profession. There were many who felt a sincere compassion for the danger of their friends and countrymen, and who exerted the most benevolent zeal to save them from the impending destruction. The careless Polytheist, assailed by new and unexpected terrors, against which neither his priests nor his philosophers could afford him any certain protection, was very frequently terrified and subdued by the menace of eternal tortures. His fears might assist the progress of his faith and reason; and, if he could once persuade himself to suspect that

Were often converted by their fears

---

[73] Tertullian, De Spectaculis, c. 30. In order to ascertain the degree of authority which the zealous African had acquired, it may be sufficient to allege the testimony of Cyprian, the doctor and guide of all the western churches. (See Prudent. Hymn. xiii. 100.) As often as he applied himself to his daily study of the writings of Tertullian, he was accustomed to say, "*Da mihi magistrum;* Give me my master". (Hieronym. de Viris Illustribus, tom. i. p. 284 [c. 53; leg. *da magistrum*].)

the Christian religion might possibly be true, it became an easy task to convince him that it was the safest and most prudent party that he could possibly embrace.

THE THIRD
CAUSE.
Miraculous
powers of the
primitive
church
III. The supernatural gifts, which even in this life were ascribed to the Christians above the rest of mankind, must have conduced to their own comfort, and very frequently to the conviction of infidels. Besides the occasional prodigies, which might sometimes be affected by the immediate interposition of the Deity when he suspended the laws of Nature for the service of religion, the Christian church, from the time of the apostles and their first disciples,[74] has claimed an uninterrupted succession of miraculous powers, the gift of tongues, of vision and of prophecy, the power of expelling dæmons, of healing the sick, and of raising the dead. The knowledge of foreign languages was frequently communicated to the contemporaries of Irenæus, though Irenæus himself was left to struggle with the difficulties of a barbarous dialect whilst he preached the gospel to the natives of Gaul.[75] The divine inspiration, whether it was conveyed in the form of a waking or of a sleeping vision, is described as a favour very liberally bestowed on all ranks of the faithful, on women as on elders, on boys as well as upon bishops. When their devout minds were sufficiently prepared by a course of prayer, of fasting, and of vigils, to receive the extraordinary impulse, they were transported out of their senses, and delivered in extasy what was inspired, being mere organs of the Holy Spirit, just as a pipe or flute is of him who blows into it.[76] We may add that the design of these visions was, for the most part, either to disclose the future history, or to guide the present administration, of the church. The expulsion of the dæmons from the bodies of those unhappy persons whom they had been permitted to torment was considered as a signal, though ordinary, triumph of religion, and is repeatedly alleged by the ancient apologists as the most convincing evidence of the truth of Christianity. The awful ceremony was usually performed in a public manner, and in the presence of a great number of

[74] Notwithstanding the evasions of Dr. Middleton, it is impossible to overlook the clear traces of visions and inspiration, which may be found in the apostolic fathers.

[75] Irenæus adv. Hæres. Proem. p. 3. Dr. Middleton (Free Inquiry, p. 96, &c.) observes that, as this pretension of all others was the most difficult to support by art, it was the soonest given up. The observation suits his hypothesis.

[76] Athenagoras in Legatione. Justin Martyr, Cohort. ad Gentes. Tertullian advers. Marcionit. l. iv. These descriptions are not very unlike the prophetic fury for which Cicero (de Divinat. ii. 54) expresses so little reverence.

spectators; the patient was relieved by the power or skill of the exorcist, and the vanquished dæmon was heard to confess that he was one of the fabled gods of antiquity, who had impiously usurped the adoration of mankind.[77]   But the miraculous cure of diseases, of the most inveterate or even præternatural kind, can no longer occasion any surprise, when we recollect that in the days of Irenæus, about the end of the second century, the resurrection of the dead was very far from being esteemed an uncommon event; that the miracle was frequently performed on necessary occasions, by great fasting and the joint supplication of the church of the place, and that the persons thus restored to their prayers had lived afterwards among them many years.[78]   At such a period, when faith could boast of so many wonderful victories over death, it seems difficult to account for the scepticism of those philosophers who still rejected and derided the doctrine of the resurrection.   A noble Grecian had rested on this important ground the whole controversy, and promised Theophilus, bishop of Antioch, that, if he could be gratified with the sight of a single person who had been actually raised from the dead, he would immediately embrace the Christian religion.   It is somewhat remarkable that the prelate of the first eastern church, however anxious for the conversion of his friend, thought proper to decline this fair and reasonable challenge.[79]

The miracles of the primitive church, after obtaining the *Their truth* sanction of ages, have been lately attacked in a very free *contested* and ingenious inquiry;[80] which, though it has met with the most favourable reception from the Public, appears to have excited a general scandal among the divines of our own as well as of the other Protestant churches of Europe.[81]   Our different sentiments on this subject will be much less influenced by any

[77] Tertullian (Apolog. c. 23) throws out a bold defiance to the Pagan magistrates.   Of the primitive miracles, the power of exorcising is the only one which has been assumed by Protestants.

[78] Irenæus adv. Hæreses, l. ii. 56, 57; l. v. c. 6.   Mr. Dodwell (Dissertat. ad Irenæum, ii. 42) concludes that the second century was still more fertile in miracles than the first.

[79] Theophilus ad Autolycum, l. i. p. 345.   Edit. Benedictin.   Paris, 1742 [c. 13 ed Migne, vol. 7, p. 1041].

[80] Dr. Middleton sent out his Introduction in the year 1747, published his Free Inquiry in 1749, and before his death, which happened in 1750, he had prepared a vindication of it against his numerous adversaries.

[81] The university of Oxford conferred degrees on his opponents.   From the indignation of Mosheim (p. 221), we may discover the sentiments of Lutheran divines.

particular arguments than by our habits of study and reflection; and, above all, by the degree of the evidence which we have accustomed ourselves to require for the proof of a miraculous event. The duty of an historian does not call upon him to interpose his private judgment in this nice and important controversy; but he ought not to dissemble the difficulty of adopting such a theory as may reconcile the interest of religion with that of reason, of making a proper application of that theory, and of defining with precision the limits of that happy period, exempt from error and from deceit, to which we might be disposed to extend the gift of supernatural powers. From the first of the fathers to the last of the popes, a succession of bishops, of saints, of martyrs, and of miracles is continued without interruption, and the progress of superstition was so gradual and almost imperceptible that we know not in what particular link we should break the chain of tradition. Every age bears testimony to the wonderful events by which it was distinguished, and its testimony appears no less weighty and respectable than that of the preceding generation, till we are insensibly led on to accuse our own inconsistency, if in the eighth or in the twelfth century we deny to the venerable Bede, or to the holy Bernard, the same degree of confidence which, in the second century, we had so liberally granted to Justin or to Irenæus.[82] If the truth of any of those miracles is appreciated by their apparent use and propriety, every age had unbelievers to convince, heretics to confute, and idolatrous nations to convert; and sufficient motives might always be produced to justify the interposition of Heaven. And yet, since every friend to revelation is persuaded of the reality, and every reasonable man is convinced of the cessation, of miraculous powers, it is evident that there must have been *some period* in which they were either suddenly or gradually withdrawn from the Christian church. Whatever æra is chosen for that purpose, the death of the apostles, the conversion of the Roman empire, or the extinction of the Arian heresy,[83] the insensibility of the Christians who

Our perplexity in defining the miraculous period

[82] It may seem somewhat remarkable that Bernard of Clairvaux, who records so many miracles of his friend St. Malachi, never takes any notice of his own, which, in their turn, however, are carefully related by his companions and disciples. In the long series of ecclesiastical history, does there exist a single instance of a saint asserting that he himself possessed the gift of miracles?

[83] The conversion of Constantine is the æra which is most usually fixed by Protestants. The more rational divines are unwilling to admit the miracles of the fourth, whilst the more credulous are unwilling to reject those of the fifth century.

lived at that time will equally afford a just matter of surprise. They still supported their pretensions after they had lost their power. Credulity performed the office of faith; fanaticism was permitted to assume the language of inspiration, and the effects of accident or contrivance were ascribed to supernatural causes. The recent experience of genuine miracles should have instructed the Christian world in the ways of Providence, and habituated their eye (if we may use a very inadequate expression) to the style of the divine artist. Should the most skilful painter of modern Italy presume to decorate his feeble imitations with the name of Raphael or of Correggio, the insolent fraud would be soon discovered and indignantly rejected.

Whatever opinion may be entertained of the miracles of the primitive church since the time of the apostles, this unresisting softness of temper, so conspicuous among the believers of the second and third centuries, proved of some accidental benefit to the cause of truth and religion. In modern times, a latent, and even involuntary, scepticism adheres to the most pious dispositions. Their admission of supernatural truths is much less an active consent than a cold and passive acquiescence. Accustomed long since to observe and to respect the invariable order of Nature, our reason, or at least our imagination, is not sufficiently prepared to sustain the visible action of the Deity. But, in the first ages of Christianity, the situation of mankind was extremely different. The most curious, or the most credulous, among the Pagans were often persuaded to enter into a society which asserted an actual claim of miraculous powers. The primitive Christians perpetually trod on mystic ground, and their minds were exercised by the habits of believing the most extraordinary events. They felt, or they fancied, that on every side they were incessantly assaulted by dæmons, comforted by visions, instructed by prophecy, and surprisingly delivered from danger, sickness, and from death itself, by the supplications of the church. The real or imaginary prodigies, of which they so frequently conceived themselves to be the objects, the instruments, or the spectators, very happily disposed them to adopt, with the same ease, but with far greater justice, the authentic wonders of the evangelic history; and thus miracles that exceeded not the measure of their own experience inspired them with the most lively assurance of mysteries which were acknowledged to surpass the limits of their understanding. It is this deep impression of supernatural truths which has been so much celebrated under the name of faith; a state of mind

Use of the primitive miracles

described as the surest pledge of the divine favour and of future felicity, and recommended as the first or perhaps the only merit of a Christian. According to the more rigid doctors, the moral virtues, which may be equally practised by infidels, are destitute of any value or efficacy in the work of our justification.

THE FOURTH CAUSE. Virtues of the first Christians

IV. But the primitive Christian demonstrated his faith by his virtues ; and it was very justly supposed that the divine persuasion, which enlightened or subdued the understanding, must, at the same time, purify the heart, and direct the actions, of the believer. The first apologists of Christianity who justify the innocence of their brethren, and the writers of a later period who celebrate the sanctity of their ancestors, display, in the most lively colours, the reformation of manners which was introduced into the world by the preaching of the gospel. As it is my intention to remark only such human causes as were permitted to second the influence of revelation, I shall slightly mention two motives which might naturally render the lives of the primitive Christians much purer and more austere than those of their Pagan contemporaries, or their degenerate successors ; repentance for their past sins, and the laudable desire of supporting the reputation of the society in which they were engaged.

Effects of their repentance

It is a very ancient reproach, suggested by the ignorance or the malice of infidelity, that the Christians allured into their party the most atrocious criminals, who, as soon as they were touched by a sense of remorse, were easily persuaded to wash away, in the water of baptism, the guilt of their past conduct, for which the temples of the gods refused to grant them any expiation. But this reproach, when it is cleared from misrepresentation, contributes as much to the honour as it did to the increase of the church.[84] The friends of Christianity may acknowledge without a blush that many of the most eminent saints had been before their baptism the most abandoned sinners. Those persons who in the world had followed, though in an imperfect manner, the dictates of benevolence and propriety, derived such a calm satisfaction from the opinion of their own rectitude, as rendered them much less susceptible of the sudden emotions of shame, of grief, and of terror, which have given birth to so many wonderful conversions. After the example of their Divine Master, the missionaries of the gospel disdained not the

---

[84] The imputations of Celsus and Julian, with the defence of the fathers, are very fairly stated by Spanheim, Commentaire sur les Césars de Julian, p. 468.

society of men, and especially of women, oppressed by the consciousness, and very often by the effects, of their vices. As
they emerged from sin and superstition to the glorious hope of
immortality, they resolved to devote themselves to a life, not
only of virtue, but of penitence. The desire of perfection
became the ruling passion of their soul; and it is well known
that, while reason embraces a cold mediocrity, our passions
hurry us, with rapid violence, over the space which lies between
the most opposite extremes.

When the new converts had been enrolled in the number of *Care of their*
the faithful and were admitted to the sacraments of the church, *reputation.*
they found themselves restrained from relapsing into their past
disorders by another consideration of a less spiritual, but of a
very innocent and respectable nature. Any particular society
that has departed from the great body of the nation or the
religion to which it belonged immediately becomes the object
of universal as well as invidious observation. In proportion to
the smallness of its numbers, the character of the society may
be affected by the virtue and vices of the persons who compose
it; and every member is engaged to watch with the most
vigilant attention over his own behaviour and over that of his
brethren, since, as he must expect to incur a part of the common
disgrace, he may hope to enjoy a share of the common reputation. When the Christians of Bithynia were brought before the
tribunal of the younger Pliny, they assured the proconsul that,
far from being engaged in any unlawful conspiracy, they were
bound by a solemn obligation to abstain from the commission
of those crimes which disturb the private or public peace of
society, from theft, robbery, adultery, perjury, and fraud.[85]
Near a century afterwards, Tertullian, with an honest pride,
could boast that very few Christians had suffered by the hand
of the executioner, except on account of their religion.[86] Their
serious and sequestered life, averse to the gay luxury of the age,
insured them to chastity, temperance, economy, and all the
sober and domestic virtues. As the greater number were of
some trade or profession, it was incumbent on them, by the
strictest integrity and the fairest dealing, to remove the
suspicions which the profane are too apt to conceive against
the appearances of sanctity. The contempt of the world
exercised them in the habits of humility, meekness, and

[85] Plin. Epist. x. 97.
[86] Tertullian, Apolog. c. 44. He adds, however, with some degree of hesitation,
" Aut si [et] aliud, jam non Christianus".

patience. The more they were persecuted, the more closely they adhered to each other. Their mutual charity and unsuspecting confidence has been remarked by infidels, and was too often abused by perfidious friends.[87]

Morality of the fathers

It is a very honourable circumstance for the morals of the primitive Christians, that even their faults, or rather errors, were derived from an excess of virtue. The bishops and doctors of the church, whose evidence attests, and whose authority might influence, the professions, the principles, and even the practice, of their contemporaries, had studied the scriptures with less skill than devotion, and they often received, in the most literal sense, those rigid precepts of Christ and the apostles to which the prudence of succeeding commentators has applied a looser and more figurative mode of interpretation. Ambitious to exalt the perfection of the gospel above the wisdom of philosophy, the zealous fathers have carried the duties of self-mortification, of purity, and of patience, to a height which it is scarcely possible to attain, and much less to preserve, in our present state of weakness and corruption. A doctrine so extraordinary and so sublime must inevitably command the veneration of the people; but it was ill calculated to obtain the suffrage of those worldly philosophers who, in the conduct of this transitory life, consult only the feelings of nature and the interest of society.[88]

Principle of human nature

There are two very natural propensities which we may distinguish in the most virtuous and liberal dispositions, the love of pleasure and the love of action. If the former be refined by art and learning, improved by the charms of social intercourse, and corrected by a just regard to economy, to health, and to reputation, it is productive of the greatest part of the happiness of private life. The love of action is a principle of a much stronger and more doubtful nature. It often leads to anger, to ambition, and to revenge; but, when it is guided by the sense of propriety and benevolence, it becomes the parent of every virtue; and, if those virtues are accompanied with equal abilities, a family, a state, or an empire may be indebted for their safety and prosperity to the undaunted courage of a single man. To the love of pleasure we may therefore ascribe most of the agreeable, to the love of action we may attribute

---

[87] The philosopher Peregrinus (of whose life and death Lucian has left us so entertaining an account) imposed, for a long time, on the credulous simplicity of the Christians of Asia.

[88] See a very judicious treatise of Barbeyrac sur la Morale des Pères.

most of the useful and respectable qualifications. The character in which both the one and the other should be united and harmonized would seem to constitute the most perfect idea of human nature. The insensible and inactive disposition, which should be supposed alike destitute of both, would be rejected, by the common consent of mankind, as utterly incapable of procuring any happiness to the individual, or any public benefit to the world. But it was not in *this* world that the primitive Christians were desirous of making themselves either agreeable or useful.

The acquisition of knowledge, the exercise of our reason or fancy, and the cheerful flow of unguarded conversation, may employ the leisure of a liberal mind. Such amusements, however, were rejected with abhorrence, or admitted with the utmost caution, by the severity of the fathers, who despised all knowledge that was not useful to salvation, and who considered all levity of discourse as a criminal abuse of the gift of speech. In our present state of existence, the body is so inseparably connected with the soul that it seems to be our interest to taste, with innocence and moderation, the enjoyments of which that faithful companion is susceptible. Very different was the reasoning of our devout predecessors ; vainly aspiring to imitate the perfection of angels, they disdained, or they affected to disdain, every earthly and corporeal delight.[89] Some of our senses indeed are necessary for our preservation, others for our subsistence, and others again for our information, and thus far it was impossible to reject the use of them. The first sensation of pleasure was marked as the first moment of their abuse. The unfeeling candidate for Heaven was instructed, not only to resist the grosser allurements of the taste or smell, but even to shut his ears against the profane harmony of sounds, and to view with indifference the most finished productions of human art. Gay apparel, magnificent houses, and elegant furniture were supposed to unite the double guilt of pride and of sensuality: a simple and mortified appearance was more suitable to the Christian who was certain of his sins and doubtful of his salvation. In their censures of luxury, the fathers are extremely minute and circumstantial ;[90] and among the various articles which excite their pious indignation, we may enumerate false hair, garments of any colour except white,

The primitive Christians condemn pleasure and luxury

---

[89] Lactant. Institut. Divin. l. vi. c. 20, 21, 22.
[90] Consult a work of Clemens of Alexandria, intitled the Pædagogue, which contains the rudiments of ethics, as they were taught in the most celebrated of the Christian schools.

instruments of music, vases of gold or silver, downy pillows (as Jacob reposed his head on a stone), white bread, foreign wines, public salutations, the use of warm baths, and the practice of shaving the beard, which, according to the expression of Tertullian, is a lie against our own faces, and an impious attempt to improve the works of the Creator.[91]   When Christianity was introduced among the rich and the polite, the observation of these singular laws was left, as it would be at present, to the few who were ambitious of superior sanctity.   But it is always easy, as well as agreeable, for the inferior ranks of mankind to claim a merit from the contempt of that pomp and pleasure, which fortune has placed beyond their reach.   The virtue of the primitive Christians, like that of the first Romans, was very frequently guarded by poverty and ignorance.

Their senti-
ments con-
cerning mar-
riage and
chastity
    The chaste severity of the fathers, in whatever related to the commerce of the two sexes, flowed from the same principle; their abhorrence of every enjoyment which might gratify the sensual, and degrade the spiritual, nature of man.   It was their favourite opinion that, if Adam had preserved his obedience to the Creator, he would have lived for ever in a state of virgin purity, and that some harmless mode of vegetation might have peopled paradise with a race of innocent and immortal beings.[92]   The use of marriage was permitted only to his fallen posterity, as a necessary expedient to continue the human species, and as a restraint, however imperfect, on the natural licentiousness of desire.   The hesitation of the orthodox casuists on this interesting subject betrays the perplexity of men, unwilling to approve an institution which they were compelled to tolerate.[93]   The enumeration of the very whimsical laws, which they most circumstantially imposed on the marriage-bed, would force a smile from the young, and a blush from the fair.   It was their unanimous sentiment that a first marriage was adequate to all the purposes of nature and of society.   The sensual connexion was refined into a resemblance of the mystic union of Christ with his church, and was pronounced to be indissoluble either by divorce or by death.   The practice of second nuptials was branded with the name of a legal adultery; and the persons who were guilty of so scandalous an offence against Christian

[91] Tertullian, de Spectaculis, c. 23.   Clemens Alexandrin. Pædagog. l. iii. c. 8.
[92] Beausobre, Hist. Critique du Manichéisme, l. vii. c. 3.   Justin, Gregory of Nyssa, Augustin, &c., strongly inclined to this opinion.
[93] Some of the Gnostic heretics were more consistent; they rejected the use of marriage.

purity were soon excluded from the honours, and even from the alms, of the church.[94] Since desire was imputed as a crime, and marriage was tolerated as a defect, it was consistent with the same principles to consider a state of celibacy as the nearest approach to the divine perfection. It was with the utmost difficulty that ancient Rome could support the institution of six vestals;[95] but the primitive church was filled with a great number of persons of either sex who had devoted themselves to the profession of perpetual chastity.[96] A few of these, among whom we may reckon the learned Origen, judged it the most prudent to disarm the tempter.[97] Some were insensible and some were invincible against the assaults of the flesh. Disdaining an ignominious flight, the virgins of the warm climate of Africa encountered the enemy in the closest engagement; they permitted priests and deacons to share their bed, and gloried amidst the flames in their unsullied purity. But insulted Nature sometimes vindicated her rights, and this new species of martyrdom served only to introduce a new scandal into the church.[98] Among the Christian ascetics, however (a name which they soon acquired from their painful exercise), many, as they were less presumptuous, were probably more successful. The loss of sensual pleasure was supplied and compensated by spiritual pride. Even the multitude of Pagans were inclined to estimate the merit of the sacrifice by its apparent difficulty; and it was in the praise of these chaste spouses of Christ that the fathers have poured forth the troubled stream of their eloquence.[99] Such are the early traces of monastic principles and institutions

[94] See a chain of tradition, from Justin Martyr to Jerome, in the Morale des Pères; c. iv. 6—26.

[95] See a very curious Dissertation on the Vestals, in the Mémoires de l'Académie des Inscriptions, tom. iv. p. 161—227. Notwithstanding the honours and rewards which were bestowed on those virgins, it was difficult to procure a sufficient number; nor could the dread of the most horrible death always restrain their incontinence.

[96] Cupiditatem procreandi aut unam scimus aut nullam. Minucius Felix, c. 31. Justin. Apolog. Major [29]. Athenagoras in Legat. c. 28. Tertullian de Cultu Femin. l. ii.

[97] Eusebius, l. vi. 8. Before the fame of Origen had excited envy and persecution, this extraordinary action was rather admired than censured. As it was his general practice to allegorize scripture, it seems unfortunate that, in this instance only, he should have adopted the literal sense.

[98] Cyprian Epist. 4, and Dodwell Dissertat. Cyprianic. iii. Something like this rash attempt was long afterwards imputed to the founder of the order of Fontevrault. Bayle has amused himself and his readers on that very delicate subject.

[99] Dupin (Bibliothèque Ecclésiastique, tom. i. p. 195) gives a particular account of the dialogue of the ten virgins, as it was composed by Methodius, bishop of Tyre. The praises of virginity are excessive.

which, in a subsequent age, have counterbalanced all the temporal advantages of Christianity.[100]

The Christians were not less averse to the business than to the pleasures of this world. The defence of our persons and property they knew not how to reconcile with the patient doctrine which enjoined an unlimited forgiveness of past injuries and commanded them to invite the repetition of fresh insults. Their simplicity was offended by the use of oaths, by the pomp of magistracy, and by the active contention of public life, nor could their humane ignorance be convinced that it was lawful on any occasion to shed the blood of our fellow-creatures, either by the sword of justice or by that of war; even though their criminal or hostile attempts should threaten the peace and safety of the whole community.[101] It was acknowledged that, under a less perfect law, the powers of the Jewish constitution had been exercised, with the approbation of Heaven, by inspired prophets and by anointed kings. The Christians felt and confessed that such institutions might be necessary for the present system of the world, and they cheerfully submitted to the authority of their Pagan governors. But, while they inculcated the maxims of passive obedience, they refused to take any active part in the civil administration or the military defence of the empire. Some indulgence might perhaps be allowed to those persons who, before their conversion, were already engaged in such violent and sanguinary occupations;[102] but it was impossible that the Christians, without renouncing a more sacred duty, could assume the character of soldiers, of magistrates, or of princes.[103] This indolent, or even criminal, disregard to the public welfare exposed them to the contempt and reproaches of the Pagans, who very frequently asked, What must be the fate of the empire, attacked on every side by the barbarians, if all mankind should

---

[100] The Ascetics (as early as the second century) made a public profession of mortifying their bodies, and of abstaining from the use of flesh and wine. Mosheim, p. 310.

[101] See the Morale des Pères. The same patient principles have been revived since the Reformation by the Socinians, the modern Anabaptists, and the Quakers. Barclay, the apologist of the Quakers, has protected his brethren by the authority of the primitive Christians, p. 542—549.

[102] Tertullian, Apolog. c. 21, De Idololatriâ, c. 17, 18. Origen contra Celsum, l. v. p. 253, [p. 1232, Migne, Patr. G. xi.,] l. vii. p. 348, [1457,] l. viii. p. 423—428, [1620, *sqq.*].

[103] Tertullian (De Coronâ Militis, c. 11) suggests to them the expedient of deserting; a counsel which, if it had been generally known, was not very proper to conciliate the favour of the emperors towards the Christian sect.

adopt the pusillanimous sentiments of the new sect?[104] To this insulting question the Christian apologists returned obscure and ambiguous answers, as they were unwilling to reveal the secret cause of their security; the expectation that, before the conversion of mankind was accomplished, war, government, the Roman empire and the world itself would be no more. It may be observed that, in this instance likewise, the situation of the first Christians coincided very happily with their religious scruples, and that their aversion to an active life contributed rather to excuse them from the service, than to exclude them from the honours, of the state and army.

V. But the human character, however it may be exalted or depressed by a temporary enthusiasm, will return, by degrees, to its proper and natural level, and will resume those passions that seem the most adapted to its present condition. The primitive Christians were dead to the business and pleasures of the world; but their love of action, which could never be entirely extinguished, soon revived, and found a new occupation in the government of the church. A separate society, which attacked the established religion of the empire, was obliged to adopt some form of internal policy, and to appoint a sufficient number of ministers, intrusted not only with the spiritual functions, but even with the temporal direction, of the Christian commonwealth. The safety of that society, its honour, its aggrandisement, were productive, even in the most pious minds, of a spirit of patriotism, such as the first of the Romans had felt for the republic, and sometimes, of a similar indifference in the use of whatever means might probably conduce to so desirable an end. The ambition of raising themselves or their friends to the honours and offices of the church was disguised by the laudable intention of devoting to the public benefit the power and consideration which, for that purpose only, it became their duty to solicit. In the exercise of their functions, they were frequently called upon to detect the errors of heresy, or the arts of faction, to oppose the designs of perfidious brethren, to stigmatize their characters with deserved infamy, and to expel them from the bosom of a society whose peace and happiness they had attempted to disturb. The ecclesiastical governors of the Christians were taught to unite the wisdom of the serpent with the innocence of the dove; but, as the former was refined, so

THE FIFTH CAUSE. The Christians active in the government of the church

---

[104] As well as we can judge from the mutilated representation of Origen (l. viii. p. 423 [1620]), his adversary, Celsus, had urged his objection with great force and candour.

the latter was insensibly corrupted, by the habits of government. In the church as well as in the world the persons who were placed in any public station rendered themselves considerable by their eloquence and firmness, by their knowledge of mankind, and by their dexterity in business ; and, while they concealed from others, and, perhaps, from themselves, the secret motives of their conduct, they too frequently relapsed into all the turbulent passions of active life, which were tinctured with an additional degree of bitterness and obstinacy from the infusion of spiritual zeal.

Its primitive freedom and equality The government of the church has often been the subject, as well as the prize, of religious contention. The hostile disputants of Rome, of Paris, of Oxford and of Geneva have alike struggled to reduce the primitive and apostolic model [105] to the respective standards of their own policy. The few who have pursued this inquiry with more candour and impartiality are of opinion [106] that the apostles declined the office of legislation, and rather chose to endure some partial scandals and divisions than to exclude the Christians of a future age from the liberty of varying their forms of ecclesiastical government according to the changes of times and circumstances. The scheme of policy which, under their approbation, was adopted for the use of the first century may be discovered from the practice of Jerusalem, of Ephesus, or of Corinth. The societies which were instituted in the cities of the Roman empire were united only by the ties of faith and charity. Independence and equality formed the basis of their internal constitution. The want of discipline and human learning was supplied by the occasional assistance of the *prophets*,[107] who were called to that function, without distinction of age, of sex, or of natural abilities, and who, as often as they felt the divine impulse, poured forth the effusions of the spirit in the assembly of the faithful. But these extraordinary gifts were frequently abused or misapplied by the prophetic teachers. They displayed them at an improper season, presumptuously disturbed the service of the assembly, and by their pride or mistaken zeal they introduced, particularly into

[105] The aristocratical party in France, as well as in England, has strenuously maintained the divine origin of bishops. But the Calvinistical presbyters were impatient of a superior ; and the Roman Pontiff refused to acknowledge an equal. See Fra Paolo.

[106] In the history of the Christian hierarchy, I have, for the most part, followed the learned and candid Mosheim.

[107] For the prophets of the primitive church, see Mosheim, Dissertationes ad Hist. Eccles. pertinentes, tom. ii. p. 132—208.

the apostolic church of Corinth, a long and melancholy train of disorders.[108] As the institution of prophets became useless, and even pernicious, their powers were withdrawn and their office abolished. The public functions of religion were solely intrusted to the established ministers of the church, the *bishops* and the *presbyters;* two appellations which, in their first origin, appear to have distinguished the same office and the same order of persons. The name of Presbyter was expressive of their age, or rather of their gravity and wisdom. The title of Bishop denoted their inspection over the faith and manners of the Christians who were committed to their pastoral care. In proportion to the respective numbers of the faithful, a larger or smaller number of these *episcopal presbyters* guided each infant congregation with equal authority and with united councils.[109]

But the most perfect equality of freedom requires the directing hand of a superior magistrate; and the order of public deliberations soon introduces the office of a president, invested at least with the authority of collecting the sentiments, and of executing the resolutions, of the assembly. A regard for the public tranquillity, which would so frequently have been interrupted by annual or by occasional elections, induced the primitive Christians to constitute an honourable and perpetual magistracy, and to choose one of the wisest and most holy among their presbyters to execute, during his life, the duties of their ecclesiastical governor. It was under these circumstances that the lofty title of Bishop began to raise itself above the humble appellation of presbyter; and, while the latter remained the most natural distinction for the members of every Christian senate, the former was appropriated to the dignity of its new president.[110] The advantages of this episcopal form of government, which appears to have been introduced before the end of

Institution of bishops as presidents of the college of presbyters

---

[108] See the Epistles of St. Paul, and of Clemens, to the Corinthians.

[109] Hooker's Ecclesiastical Polity, l. vii. [On bishops and presbyters, see Appendix 4.]

[110] See Jerome ad Titum, c. 1, and Epistol. 85 (in the Benedictine edition, 101), and the elaborate apology of Blondel, pro sententiâ Hieronymi. The ancient state, as it is described by Jerome, of the bishop and presbyters of Alexandria receives a remarkable confirmation from the patriarch Eutychius (Annal. tom. i. p. 330, Vers. Pocock), whose testimony I know not how to reject, in spite of all the objections of the learned Pearson in his Vindiciæ Ignatianæ, part i. c. 11. [If Ignatius suffered under Trajan, and the Epistles ascribed to him are genuine, it would follow that episcopal government was fully organized in some churches in the East at the beginning of the second century, for those documents assume the institution. See below, p. 98, and App. 4.]

the first century,[111] were so obvious, and so important for the
future greatness, as well as the present peace, of Christianity,
that it was adopted without delay by all the societies which
were already scattered over the empire, had acquired in a very
early period the sanction of antiquity,[112] and is still revered by
the most powerful churches, both of the East and of the West,
as a primitive and even as a divine establishment.[113] It is needless to observe that the pious and humble presbyters who were
first dignified with the episcopal title could not possess, and
would probably have rejected, the power and pomp which now
encircles the tiara of the Roman pontiff, or the mitre of a
German prelate. But we may define, in a few words, the
narrow limits of their original jurisdiction, which was chiefly of
a spiritual, though in some instances of a temporal, nature.[114]
It consisted in the administration of the sacraments and discipline of the church, the superintendency of religious ceremonies,
which imperceptibly increased in number and variety, the consecration of ecclesiastical ministers, to whom the bishop assigned
their respective functions, the management of the public fund,
and the determination of all such differences as the faithful
were unwilling to expose before the tribunal of an idolatrous
judge. These powers, during a short period, were exercised
according to the advice of the presbyteral college, and with the
consent and approbation of the assembly of Christians. The
primitive bishops were considered only as the first of their
equals, and the honourable servants of a free people. Whenever the episcopal chair became vacant by death, a new president
was chosen among the presbyters by the suffrage of the whole

[111] See the introduction to the Apocalypse. Bishops, under the name of angels,
were already instituted in seven cities of Asia. And yet the epistle of Clemens
(which is probably of as ancient a date) does not lead us to discover any traces of
episcopacy either at Corinth or Rome. [The date of the first letter (the second
is spurious) of Clement is generally admitted to be about 100 A.D.; it is an
admonition addressed by the Roman to the Corinthian church. The author is
supposed by some to be no other than Flavius Clemens, the cousin of Domitian
who was put to death by him for ἀθεότης, by others to be one of his freedmen,
(so Lightfoot, who has edited the letter in his Apostolic Fathers).]

[112] Nulla Ecclesia sine Episcopo, has been a fact as well as a maxim since the
time of Tertullian and Irenæus.

[113] After we have passed the difficulties of the first century, we find the episcopal
government universally established, till it was interrupted by the republican genius
of the Swiss and German reformers.

[114] See Mosheim in the first and second centuries. Ignatius (ad Smyrnæos, c.
3, &c.) is fond of exalting the episcopal dignity. Le Clerc (Hist. Eccles. p. 569)
very bluntly censures his conduct. Mosheim, with a more critical judgment (p.
161), suspects the purity even of the smaller epistles.

congregation, every member of which supposed himself invested with a sacred and sacerdotal character.[115]

Such was the mild and equal constitution by which the Christians were governed more than a hundred years after the death of the apostles. Every society formed within itself a separate and independent republic : and, although the most distant of these little states maintained a mutual as well as friendly intercourse of letters and deputations, the Christian world was not yet connected by any supreme authority or legislative assembly. As the numbers of the faithful were gradually multiplied, they discovered the advantages that might result from a closer union of their interest and designs. Towards the end of the second century, the churches of Greece and Asia adopted the useful institutions of provincial synods, and they may justly be supposed to have borrowed the model of a representative council from the celebrated examples of their own country, the Amphictyons, the Achæan league, or the assemblies of the Ionian cities. It was soon established as a custom and as a law that the bishops of the independent churches should meet in the capital of the province at the stated periods of spring and autumn. Their deliberations were assisted by the advice of a few distinguished presbyters, and moderated by the presence of a listening multitude.[116] Their decrees, which were styled Canons, regulated every important controversy of faith and discipline; and it was natural to believe that a liberal effusion of the Holy Spirit would be poured on the united assembly of the delegates of the Christian people. The institution of synods was so well suited to private ambition and to public interest that in the space of a few years it was received throughout the whole empire. A regular correspondence was established between the provincial councils, which mutually communicated and approved their respective proceedings; and the Catholic church soon assumed the form, and acquired the strength, of a great federative republic.[117]

Provincial councils

Union of the church

[115] Nonne et Laici sacerdotes sumus? Tertullian, Exhort. ad Castitat. c. 7. As the human heart is still the same, several of the observations which Mr. Hume has made on Enthusiasm (Essays, vol. i. p. 76, quarto edit.) may be applied even to real inspiration.

[116] Acta Concil. Carthag. apud Cyprian. Edit. Fell, p. 158. This council was composed of eighty-seven bishops from the provinces of Mauritania, Numidia, and Africa; some presbyters and deacons assisted at the assembly; præsente plebis maximâ parte.

[117] Aguntur præterea per Græcias illas, certis in locis concilia, &c. Tertullian de Jejuniis, c. 13. The African mentions it as a recent and foreign institution. The coalition of the Christian churches is very ably explained by Mosheim, p. 164—170.

Progress of
episcopal
authority

As the legislative authority of the particular churches was
insensibly superseded by the use of councils, the bishops obtained
by their alliance a much larger share of executive and arbitrary
power ; and, as soon as they were connected by a sense of their
common interest, they were enabled to attack, with united
vigour, the original rights of their clergy and people. The prelates of the third century imperceptibly changed the language
of exhortation into that of command, scattered the seeds of future
usurpations, and supplied, by scripture allegories and declama-
tory rhetoric, their deficiency of force and of reason. They
exalted the unity and power of the church, as it was represented
in the EPISCOPAL OFFICE, of which every bishop enjoyed an equal
and undivided portion.[118] Princes and magistrates, it was often
repeated, might boast an earthly claim to a transitory dominion ;
it was the episcopal authority alone which was derived from the
Deity, and extended itself over this and over another world.
The bishops were the vicegerents of Christ, the successors of the
apostles, and the mystic substitutes of the high priest of the
Mosaic law. Their exclusive privilege of conferring the sacerdotal character invaded the freedom both of clerical and of
popular elections ; and if, in the administration of the church,
they still consulted the judgment of the presbyters or the
inclination of the people, they most carefully inculcated the
merit of such a voluntary condescension. The bishops acknowledged the supreme authority which resided in the assembly of
their brethren ; but, in the government of his peculiar diocese,
each of them exacted from his *flock* the same implicit obedience
as if that favourite metaphor had been literally just, and as if
the shepherd had been of a more exalted nature than that of
his sheep.[119] This obedience, however, was not imposed without some efforts on one side, and some resistance on the other.
The democratical part of the constitution was, in many places,
very warmly supported by the zealous or interested opposition
of the inferior clergy. But their patriotism received the ignominious epithets of faction and schism ; and the episcopal cause
was indebted for its rapid progress to the labours of many active
prelates, who, like Cyprian of Carthage, could reconcile the
arts of the most ambitious statesman with the Christian

[118] Cyprian, in his admired treatise De Unitate Ecclesiæ, p. 75—86.

[119] We may appeal to the whole tenor of Cyprian's conduct, of his doctrine,
and of his Epistles. Le Clerc, in a short life of Cyprian (Bibliothèque Universelle,
tom. xii. p. 207—378), has laid him open with great freedom and accuracy.

virtues which seem adapted to the character of a saint and martyr.[120]

The same causes which at first had destroyed the equality of the presbyters introduced among the bishops a pre-eminence of rank, and from thence a superiority of jurisdiction. As often as in the spring and autumn they met in provincial synod, the difference of personal merit and reputation was very sensibly felt among the members of the assembly, and the multitude was governed by the wisdom and eloquence of the few. But the order of public proceedings required a more regular and less invidious distinction; the office of perpetual presidents in the councils of each province was conferred on the bishops of the principal city, and these aspiring prelates, who soon acquired the lofty titles of Metropolitans and Primates, secretly prepared themselves to usurp over their episcopal brethren the same authority which the bishops had so lately assumed above the college of presbyters.[121] Nor was it long before an emulation of pre-eminence and power prevailed among the metropolitans themselves, each of them affecting to display, in the most pompous terms, the temporal honours and advantages of the city over which he presided; the numbers and opulence of the Christians who were subject to their pastoral care; the saints and martyrs who had arisen among them, and the purity with which they preserved the tradition of the faith, as it had been transmitted through a series of orthodox bishops from the apostle or the apostolic disciple, to whom the foundation of their church was ascribed.[122] From every cause, either of a civil or of an ecclesiastical nature, it was easy to foresee that Rome must enjoy the respect, and would soon claim the obedience, of the provinces. The society of the faithful bore a just proportion to the capital of the empire; and the Roman church was the greatest, the most numerous, and, in regard to the West, the most ancient of all the Christian establishments, many of which had received their religion from the pious labours of her missionaries. Instead of *one* apostolic founder, the utmost boast of Antioch, of Ephesus, or of Corinth, the banks of the Tiber were supposed to have been honoured with the preaching and martyrdom of

Pre-eminence of the metropolitan churches

Ambition of the Roman pontiff

---

[120] If Novatus, Felicissimus, &c., whom the bishop of Carthage expelled from his church, and from Africa, were not the most detestable monsters of wickedness, the zeal of Cyprian must occasionally have prevailed over his veracity. For a very just account of these obscure quarrels, see Mosheim, p. 497—512.

[121] Mosheim, p. 269, 574. Dupin, Antiquæ Eccles. Disciplin., p. 19, 20.

[122] Tertullian, in a distinct treatise, has pleaded against the heretics the right of prescription, as it was held by the apostolic churches.

the *two* most eminent among the apostles ;[123] and the bishops of Rome very prudently claimed the inheritance of whatsoever prerogatives were attributed either to the person or to the office of St. Peter.[124]   The bishops of Italy and of the provinces were disposed to allow them a primacy of order and association (such was their very accurate expression) in the Christian aristocracy.[125]   But the power of a monarch was rejected with abhorrence, and the aspiring genius of Rome experienced, from the nations of Asia and Africa, a more vigorous resistance to her spiritual, than she had formerly done to her temporal, dominion. The patriotic Cyprian, who ruled with the most absolute sway the church of Carthage and the provincial synods, opposed with resolution and success the ambition of the Roman pontiff, artfully connected his own cause with that of the eastern bishops, and, like Hannibal, sought out new allies in the heart of Asia.[126] If this Punic war was carried on without any effusion of blood, it was owing much less to the moderation than to the weakness of the contending prelates.   Invectives and excommunications were *their* only weapons ; and these, during the progress of the whole controversy, they hurled against each other with equal fury and devotion.   The hard necessity of censuring either a pope, or a saint and martyr, distresses the modern Catholics, whenever they are obliged to relate the particulars of a dispute in which the champions of religion indulged such passions as seem much more adapted to the senate or to the camp.[127]

Laity and clergy

The progress of the ecclesiastical authority gave birth to the memorable distinction of the laity and of the clergy, which had been unknown to the Greeks and Romans.[128]   The former of

[123] The journey of St. Peter to Rome is mentioned by most of the ancients (see Eusebius, ii. 25), maintained by all the Catholics, allowed by some Protestants (see Pearson and Dodwell de Success. Episcop. Roman.), but has been vigorously attacked by Spanheim (Miscellanea Sacra, iii. 3).   According to father Hardouin, the monks of the thirteenth century, who composed the Æneid, represented St. Peter under the allegorical character of the Trojan hero.

[124] It is in French only that the famous allusion to St. Peter's name is exact. Tu es *Pierre* et sur cette *pierre.*—The same is imperfect in Greek, Latin, Italian, &c., and totally unintelligible in our Teutonic languages.

[125] Irenæus adv. Hæreses, iii. 3.   Tertullian de Præscription., c. 36, and Cyprian Epistol. 27, 55, 71, 75.   Le Clerc (Hist. Eccles. p. 764) and Mosheim (p. 258, 578) labour in the interpretation of these passages.   But the loose and rhetorical style of the fathers often appears favourable to the pretensions of Rome.

[126] See the sharp epistle from Firmilianus, bishop of Cæsarea, to Stephen, bishop of Rome, ap. Cyprian Epistol. 75.

[127] Concerning this dispute of the re-baptism of heretics, see the epistles of Cyprian, and the seventh book of Eusebius.

[128] For the origin of these words, see Mosheim, p. 141.   Spanheim, Hist. Ecclesiast. p. 633.   The distinction of *Clerus* and *Laicus* was established before the time of Tertullian.

these appellations comprehended the body of the Christian people; the latter, according to the signification of the word, was appropriated to the chosen portion that had been set apart for the service of religion; a celebrated order of men which has furnished the most important, though not always the most edifying, subjects for modern history. Their mutual hostilities sometimes disturbed the peace of the infant church, but their zeal and activity were united in the common cause, and the love of power, which (under the most artful disguises) could insinuate itself into the breasts of bishops and martyrs, animated them to increase the number of their subjects, and to enlarge the limits of the Christian empire. They were destitute of any temporal force, and they were for a long time discouraged and oppressed, rather than assisted, by the civil magistrate; but they had acquired, and they employed within their own society, the two most efficacious instruments of government, rewards and punishments; the former derived from the pious liberality, the latter from the devout apprehensions, of the faithful.

I. The community of goods, which had so agreeably amused the imagination of Plato,[129] and which subsisted in some degree among the austere sect of the Essenians,[130] was adopted for a short time in the primitive church. The fervour of the first proselytes prompted them to sell those worldly possessions which they despised, to lay the price of them at the feet of the apostles, and to content themselves with receiving an equal share out of the general distribution.[131] The progress of the Christian religion relaxed, and gradually abolished, this generous institution, which, in hands less pure than those of the apostles, would too soon have been corrupted and abused by the returning selfishness of human nature; and the converts who embraced the new religion were permitted to retain the possession of their patrimony, to receive legacies and inheritances, and to increase their separate property by all the lawful means of trade and industry. Instead of an absolute sacrifice, a moderate proportion was accepted by the ministers of the gospel; and in their weekly or monthly assemblies, every believer, according to the exigency of the occasion, and the measure of his wealth

Oblations and revenue of the church

---

[129] The community instituted by Plato is more perfect than that which Sir Thomas More had imagined for his Utopia. The community of women, and that of temporal goods, may be considered as inseparable parts of the same system.

[130] Joseph. Antiquitat. xviii. 2.   Philo, de Vit. Contemplativ.

[131] See the Acts of the Apostles, c. ii. 4, 5, with Grotius's Commentary. Mosheim, in a particular dissertation, attacks the common opinion with very inconclusive arguments.

and piety, presented his voluntary offering for the use of the common fund.[132] Nothing, however inconsiderable, was refused; but it was diligently inculcated that, in the article of Tythes, the Mosaic law was still of divine obligation; and that, since the Jews, under a less perfect discipline, had been commanded to pay a tenth part of all that they possessed, it would become the disciples of Christ to distinguish themselves by a superior degree of liberality,[133] and to acquire some merit by resigning a superfluous treasure, which must so soon be annihilated with the world itself.[134] It is almost unnecessary to observe that the revenue of each particular church, which was of so uncertain and fluctuating a nature, must have varied with the poverty or the opulence of the faithful, as they were dispersed in obscure villages, or collected in the great cities of the empire. In the time of the emperor Decius, it was the opinion of the magistrates that the Christians of Rome were possessed of very considerable wealth; that vessels of gold and silver were used in their religious worship; and that many among their proselytes had sold their lands and houses to increase the public riches of the sect, at the expense, indeed, of their unfortunate children, who found themselves beggars, because their parents had been saints.[135] We should listen with

---

[132] Justin. Martyr, Apolog. Major, c. 89. Tertullian, Apolog. c. 39.

[133] Irenæus ad Hæres. l. iv. c. 27, 34. Origen in Num. Hom. ii. Cyprian de Unitat. Eccles. Constitut. Apostol. l. ii. c. 34, 35, with the notes of Cotelerius. The Constitutions introduce this divine precept by declaring that priests are as much above kings, as the soul is above the body. Among the tythable articles, they enumerate corn, wine, oil, and wood. On this interesting subject, consult Prideaux's History of Tythes, and Fra Paolo delle Materie Beneficiarie; two writers of a very different character.

[134] The same opinion which prevailed about the year 1000 was productive of the same effects. Most of the donations express their motive, "appropinquante mundi fine". See Mosheim's General History of the Church, vol. i. p. 457.

[135] Tum summa cura est fratribus,
(Ut sermo testatur loquax)
Offerre, fundis venditis
Sestertiorum millia.
Addicta avorum prædia
Fœdis sub auctionibus,
Successor exheres gemit
Sanctis egens parentibus.
Hæc occuluntur abditis
Ecclesiarum in angulis,
Et summa pietas creditur
Nudare dulces liberos.

Prudent, περὶ στεφάνων, Hymn 2.

The subsequent conduct of the deacon Laurence only proves how proper a use was made of the wealth of the Roman church; it was undoubtedly very considerable;

distrust to the suspicions of strangers and enemies : on this occasion, however, they receive a very specious and probable colour from the two following circumstances, the only ones that have reached our knowledge, which define any precise sums, or convey any distinct idea. Almost at the same period, the bishop of Carthage, from a society less opulent than that of Rome, collected a hundred thousand sesterces (above eight hundred and fifty pounds sterling), on a sudden call of charity, to redeem the brethren of Numidia, who had been carried away captives by the barbarians of the desert.[136] About an hundred years before the reign of Decius, the Roman church had received, in a single donation, the sum of two hundred thousand sesterces from a stranger of Pontus, who proposed to fix his residence in the capital.[137] These oblations, for the most part, were made in money ; nor was the society of Christians either desirous or capable of acquiring, to any considerable degree, the incumbrance of landed property. It had been provided by several laws, which were enacted with the same design as our statutes of mortmain, that no real estates should be given or bequeathed to any corporate body, without either a special privilege or a particular dispensation from the emperor or from the senate ;[138] who were seldom disposed to grant them in favour of a sect, at first the object of their contempt, and at last of their fears and jealousy. A transaction, however, is related under the reign of Alexander Severus, which discovers that the restraint was sometimes eluded or suspended, and that the Christians were permitted to claim and to possess lands within the limits of Rome itself.[139] The progress of Christianity and the civil confusion of the empire contributed to relax the severity of the laws ; and, before the close of the third century, many considerable estates were bestowed on the opulent churches of Rome, Milan, Carthage, Antioch, Alexandria, and the other great cities of Italy and the provinces.

but Fra Paolo (c. 3) appears to exaggerate when he supposes that the successors of Commodus were urged to persecute the Christians by their own avarice, or that of their Prætorian præfects.
[136] Cyprian, Epistol. 62.
[137] Tertullian de Præscriptionibus, c. 30. [The stranger was the heretic Marcion.]
[138] Diocletian gave a rescript, which is only a declaration of the old law : " Collegium, si nullo speciali privilegio subnixum sit, hereditatem capere non posse, dubium non est". Fra Paolo (c. 4) thinks that these regulations had been much neglected since the reign of Valerian.
[139] Hist. August. p. 131 [xviii. 49, 6]. The ground had been public ; and was now disputed between the society of Christians and that of butchers.

The bishop was the natural steward of the church; the public stock was intrusted to his care, without account or control; the presbyters were confined to their spiritual functions, and the more dependent order of deacons was solely employed in the management and distribution of the ecclesiastical revenue.[140] If we may give credit to the vehement declamations of Cyprian, there were too many among his African brethren who, in the execution of their charge, violated every precept, not only of evangelic perfection, but even of moral virtue. By some of these unfaithful stewards, the riches of the church were lavished in sensual pleasures, by others they were perverted to the purposes of private gain, of fraudulent purchases, and of rapacious usury.[141] But, as long as the contributions of the Christian people were free and unconstrained, the abuse of their confidence could not be very frequent, and the general uses to which their liberality was applied reflected honour on the religious society. A decent portion was reserved for the maintenance of the bishop and his clergy; a sufficient sum was allotted for the expenses of the public worship, of which the feasts of love, the *agapæ*, as they were called, constituted a very pleasing part. The whole remainder was the sacred patrimony of the poor. According to the discretion of the bishop, it was distributed to support widows and orphans, the lame, the sick, and the aged of the community; to comfort strangers and pilgrims, and to alleviate the misfortunes of prisoners and captives, more especially when their sufferings had been occasioned by their firm attachment to the cause of religion.[142] A generous intercourse of charity united the most distant provinces, and the smaller congregations were cheerfully assisted by the alms of their more opulent brethren.[143] Such an institution, which paid less regard to the merit than to the distress of the object, very materially conduced to the progress of Christianity. The Pagans, who were actuated by a sense of humanity, while they derided the doctrines, acknowledged the benevolence, of the new sect.[144] The prospect of immediate relief and of future protection allured into its hospitable bosom

[140] Constitut. Apostol. ii. 35.

[141] Cyprian. de Lapsis, p. 89, Epistol. 65. The charge is confirmed by the 19th and 20th canon of the council of Illiberis.

[142] See the apologies of Justin, Tertullian, &c.

[143] The wealth and liberality of the Romans to their most distant brethren is gratefully celebrated by Dionysius of Corinth, ap. Euseb. l. iv. c. 23.

[144] See Lucian in Peregrin. Julian (Epist. 49) seems mortified that the Christian charity maintains not only their own, but likewise the heathen poor.

many of those unhappy persons whom the neglect of the world would have abandoned to the miseries of want, of sickness, and of old age. There is some reason likewise to believe that great numbers of infants who, according to the inhuman practice of the times, had been exposed by their parents were frequently rescued from death, baptized, educated, and maintained by the piety of the Christians, and at the expense of the public treasure.[145]

II. It is the undoubted right of every society to exclude from its communion and benefits such among its members as reject or violate those regulations which have been established by general consent. In the exercise of this power, the censures of the Christian church were chiefly directed against scandalous sinners, and particularly those who were guilty of murder, of fraud, or of incontinence ; against the authors, or the followers, of any heretical opinions which had been condemned by the judgment of the episcopal order ; and against those unhappy persons who, whether from choice or from compulsion, had polluted themselves after their baptism by any act of idolatrous worship. The consequences of excommunication were of a temporal as well as a spiritual nature. The Christian against whom it was pronounced was deprived of any part in the oblations of the faithful. The ties both of religious and of private friendship were dissolved ; he found himself a profane object of abhorrence to the persons whom he the most esteemed, or by whom he had been the most tenderly beloved ; and, as far as an expulsion from a respectable society could imprint on his character a mark of disgrace, he was shunned or suspected by the generality of mankind. The situation of these unfortunate exiles was in itself very painful and melancholy ; but, as it usually happens, their apprehensions far exceeded their sufferings. The benefits of the Christian communion were those of eternal life, nor could they erase from their minds the awful opinion, that to those ecclesiastical governors by whom they were condemned the Deity had committed the keys of Hell and of Paradise. The heretics, indeed, who might be supported by the consciousness of their intentions, and by the flattering hope that they alone had discovered the true path of salvation, endeavoured to regain, in their separate assemblies, those comforts, temporal as

margin note: Excommunication

[145] Such, at least, has been the laudable conduct of more modern missionaries, under the same circumstances. Above three thousand new-born infants are annually exposed in the streets of Pekin. See Le Comte, Mémoires sur la Chine, and the Recherches sur les Chinois et les Egyptiens, tom. i. p. 61.

well as spiritual, which they no longer derived from the great
society of Christians. But almost all those who had reluctantly
yielded to the power of vice or idolatry were sensible of their
fallen condition, and anxiously desirous of being restored to the
benefits of the Christian communion.

With regard to the treatment of these penitents, two opposite
opinions, the one of justice, the other of mercy, divided the
primitive church. The more rigid and inflexible casuists refused
them for ever, and without exception, the meanest place in the
holy community, which they had disgraced or deserted, and,
leaving them to the remorse of a guilty conscience, indulged
them only with a faint ray of hope that the contrition of their
life and death might possibly be accepted by the Supreme
Being.[146] A milder sentiment was embraced, in practice as
well as in theory, by the purest and most respectable of the
Christian churches.[147] The gates of reconciliation and of Heaven
were seldom shut against the returning penitent; but a severe
and solemn form of discipline was instituted, which, while it
served to expiate his crime, might powerfully deter the spectators
from the imitation of his example. Humbled by a public
confession, emaciated by fasting, and clothed in sackcloth, the
penitent lay prostrate at the door of the assembly, imploring,
with tears, the pardon of his offences, and soliciting the prayers
of the faithful.[148] If the fault was of a very heinous nature,
whole years of penance were esteemed an inadequate satisfaction
to the Divine Justice; and it was always by slow and painful
gradations that the sinner, the heretic, or the apostate was
re-admitted into the bosom of the church. A sentence of
perpetual excommunication was, however, reserved for some
crimes of an extraordinary magnitude, and particularly for the
inexcusable relapses of those penitents who had already experienced and abused the clemency of their ecclesiastical superiors.
According to the circumstances or the number of the guilty, the
exercise of the Christian discipline was varied by the discretion
of the bishops. The councils of Ancyra and Illiberis were held
about the same time, the one in Galatia, the other in Spain;
but their respective canons, which are still extant, seem to

Public pen-
ance

---

[146] The Montanists and the Novatians, who adhered to this opinion with the
greatest rigour and obstinacy, found *themselves* at last in the number of excommunicated heretics. See the learned and copious Mosheim, Secul. ii. and iii.

[147] Dionysius ap. Euseb. iv. 23. Cyprian, de Lapsis.

[148] Cave's Primitive Christianity, part iii. c. 5. The admirers of antiquity regret
the loss of this public penance.

breathe a very different spirit. The Galatian, who after his baptism had repeatedly sacrificed to idols, might obtain his pardon by a penance of seven years, and, if he had seduced others to imitate his example, only three years more were added to the term of his exile. But the unhappy Spaniard, who had committed the same offence, was deprived of the hope of reconciliation, even in the article of death ; and his idolatry was placed at the head of a list of seventeen other crimes, against which a sentence, no less terrible, was pronounced. Among these we may distinguish the inexpiable guilt of calumniating a bishop, a presbyter, or even a deacon.[149]

The well-tempered mixture of liberality and rigour, the judicious dispensation of rewards and punishments, according to the maxims of policy as well as justice, constituted the *human* strength of the church. The bishops, whose paternal care extended itself to the government of both worlds, were sensible of the importance of these prerogatives, and, covering their ambition with the fair pretence of the love of order, they were jealous of any rival in the exercise of a discipline so necessary to prevent the desertion of those troops which had inlisted themselves under the banner of the cross, and whose numbers every day became more considerable. From the imperious declamations of Cyprian we should naturally conclude that the doctrines of excommunication and penance formed the most essential part of religion ; and that it was much less dangerous for the disciples of Christ to neglect the observance of the moral duties than to despise the censures and authority of their bishops. Sometimes we might imagine that we were listening to the voice of Moses, when he commanded the earth to open, and to swallow up, in consuming flames, the rebellious race which refused obedience to the priesthood of Aaron ; and we should sometimes suppose that we heard a Roman consul asserting the majesty of the republic, and declaring his inflexible resolution to enforce the rigour of the laws. " If such irregularities are suffered with impunity (it is thus that the bishop of Carthage chides the lenity of his colleague), if such irregularities are suffered, there is an end of EPISCOPAL VIGOUR ;[150] an end of the sublime and

The dignity of episcopal government

---

[149] See in Dupin, Bibliothèque Ecclésiastique, tom. ii. p. 304—313, a short but rational exposition of the canons of those councils, which were assembled in the first moments of tranquillity after the persecution of Diocletian. This persecution had been much less severely felt in Spain than in Galatia ; a difference which may, in some measure, account for the contrast of their regulations.

[150] Cyprian. Epist. 69 [59].

divine power of governing the church, an end of Christianity itself." Cyprian had renounced those temporal honours which it is probable he would never have obtained; but the acquisition of such absolute command over the consciences and understanding of a congregation, however obscure or despised by the world, is more truly grateful to the pride of the human heart than the possession of the most despotic power imposed by arms and conquest on a reluctant people.

Recapitulation of the five causes   In the course of this important, though perhaps tedious, inquiry, I have attempted to display the secondary causes which so efficaciously assisted the truth of the Christian religion. If among these causes we have discovered any artificial ornaments, any accidental circumstances, or any mixture of error and passion, it cannot appear surprising that mankind should be the most sensibly affected by such motives as were suited to their imperfect nature. It was by the aid of these causes, exclusive zeal, the immediate expectation of another world, the claim of miracles, the practice of rigid virtue, and the constitution of the primitive church, that Christianity spread itself with so much success in the Roman empire. To the first of these the Christians were indebted for their invincible valour, which disdained to capitulate with the enemy whom they were resolved to vanquish. The three succeeding causes supplied their valour with the most formidable arms. The last of these causes united their courage, directed their arms, and gave their efforts that irresistible weight which even a small band of well-trained and intrepid volunteers has so often possessed over an undisciplined multitude, ignorant of the subject, and careless of the event of Weakness of the war. In the various religions of Polytheism, some wandering Polytheism fanatics of Egypt and Syria, who addressed themselves to the credulous superstition of the populace, were perhaps the only order of priests [151] that derived their whole support and credit from their sacerdotal profession, and were very deeply affected by a personal concern for the safety or prosperity of their tutelar deities. The ministers of Polytheism, both in Rome and in the provinces, were, for the most part, men of a noble birth, and of an affluent fortune, who received, as an honourable distinction, the care of a celebrated temple, or of a public sacrifice, exhibited, very frequently at their own expense, the sacred games,[152] and with cold indifference performed the

[151] The arts, the manners, and the vices of the priests of the Syrian goddess are very humorously described by Apuleius, in the eighth book of his Metamorphoses.
[152] The office of Asiarch was of this nature, and it is frequently mentioned in

ancient rites, according to the laws and fashion of their country. As they were engaged in the ordinary occupations of life, their zeal and devotion were seldom animated by a sense of interest, or by the habits of an ecclesiastical character. Confined to their respective temples and cities, they remained without any connexion of discipline or government; and, whilst they acknowledged the supreme jurisdiction of the senate, of the college of pontiffs, and of the emperor, those civil magistrates contented themselves with the easy task of maintaining, in peace and dignity, the general worship of mankind. We have already seen how various, how loose, and how uncertain were the religious sentiments of Polytheists. They were abandoned, almost without control, to the natural workings of a superstitious fancy. The accidental circumstances of their life and situation determined the object, as well as the degree, of their devotion; and, as long as their adoration was successively prostituted to a thousand deities, it was scarcely possible that their hearts could be susceptible of a very sincere or lively passion for any of them.

When Christianity appeared in the world, even these faint and imperfect impressions had lost much of their original power. Human reason, which, by its unassisted strength, is incapable of perceiving the mysteries of faith, had already obtained an easy triumph over the folly of Paganism; and, when Tertullian or Lactantius employ their labours in exposing its falsehood and extravagance, they are obliged to transcribe the eloquence of Cicero or the wit of Lucian. The contagion of these sceptical writings had been diffused far beyond the number of their readers. The fashion of incredulity was communicated from the philosopher to the man of pleasure or business, from the noble to the plebeian, and from the master to the menial slave who waited at his table, and who eagerly listened to the freedom of his conversation. On public occasions the philosophic part of mankind affected to treat with respect and decency the religious institutions of their country; but their secret contempt penetrated through the thin and awkward disguise; and even the people, when they discovered that their deities were rejected and derided by those whose

The scepticism of the Pagan world proved favourable to the new religion

Aristides, the Inscriptions, &c. It was annual and elective. None but the vainest citizens could desire the honour; none but the most wealthy could support the expense. See in the Patres Apostol. tom. ii. p. 200, with how much indifference Philip the Asiarch conducted himself in the martyrdom of Polycarp. There were likewise Bithyniarchs, Lyciarchs, &c. [Cp. Pauly-Wissowa, Encycl., *sub* Asiarches.]

rank or understanding they were accustomed to reverence, were filled with doubts and apprehensions concerning the truth of those doctrines to which they had yielded the most implicit belief.   The decline of ancient prejudice exposed a very numerous portion of human kind to the danger of a painful and comfortless situation.   A state of scepticism and suspense may amuse a few inquisitive minds.   But the practice of superstition is so congenial to the multitude that, if they are forcibly awakened, they still regret the loss of their pleasing vision. Their love of the marvellous and supernatural, their curiosity with regard to future events, and their strong propensity to extend their hopes and fears beyond the limits of the visible world, were the principal causes which favoured the establishment of Polytheism.   So urgent on the vulgar is the necessity of believing that the fall of any system of mythology will most probably be succeeded by the introduction of some other mode of superstition.   Some deities of a more recent and fashionable cast might soon have occupied the deserted temples of Jupiter and Apollo, if, in the decisive moment, the wisdom of Providence had not interposed a genuine revelation, fitted to inspire the most rational esteem and conviction, whilst, at the same time, it was adorned with all that could attract the curiosity, the wonder, and the veneration of the people.   In their actual disposition, as many were almost disengaged from their artificial prejudices, but equally susceptible and desirous of a devout attachment ; an object much less deserving would have been sufficient to fill the vacant place in their hearts, and to gratify the uncertain eagerness of their passions.   Those who are inclined to pursue this reflection, instead of viewing with astonishment the rapid progress of Christianity, will perhaps be surprised that its success was not still more rapid and still more universal.

as well as the peace and union of the Roman empire

It has been observed, with truth as well as propriety, that the conquests of Rome prepared and facilitated those of Christianity.   In the second chapter of this work we have attempted to explain in what manner the most civilized provinces of Europe, Asia, and Africa were united under the dominion of one sovereign, and gradually connected by the most intimate ties of laws, of manners, and of language.   The Jews of Palestine, who had fondly expected a temporal deliverer, gave so cold a reception to the miracles of the divine prophet that it was found unnecessary to publish, or at least to preserve, any Hebrew gospel.[153]   The authentic histories of the actions of Christ were

[153] The modern critics are not disposed to believe what the fathers almost un-

composed in the Greek language, at a considerable distance from Jerusalem, and after the Gentile converts were grown extremely numerous.[154] As soon as those histories were translated into the Latin tongue, they were perfectly intelligible to all the subjects of Rome, excepting only to the peasants of Syria and Egypt, for whose benefit particular versions were afterwards made. The public highways, which had been constructed for the use of the legions, opened an easy passage for the Christian missionaries from Damascus to Corinth, and from Italy to the extremity of Spain or Britain; nor did those spiritual conquerors encounter any of the obstacles which usually retard or prevent the introduction of a foreign religion into a distant country. There is the strongest reason to believe that before the reigns of Diocletian and Constantine, the faith of Christ had been preached in every province, and in all the great cities of the empire; but the foundation of the several congregations, the numbers of the faithful who composed them, and their proportion to the unbelieving multitude, are now buried in obscurity, or disguised by fiction and declamation. Such imperfect circumstances, however, as have reached our knowledge concerning the increase of the Christian name in Asia and Greece, in Egypt, in Italy, and in the West, we shall now proceed to relate, without neglecting the real or imaginary acquisitions which lay beyond the frontiers of the Roman empire.

Historical view of the progress of Christianity

The rich provinces that extend from the Euphrates to the Ionian sea were the principal theatre on which the apostle of the Gentiles displayed his zeal and piety. The seeds of the gospel, which he had scattered in a fertile soil, were diligently cultivated by his disciples; and it should seem that, during the two first centuries, the most considerable body of Christians was contained within those limits. Among the societies which were instituted in Syria, none were more ancient or more illustrious than those of Damascus, of Berœa or Aleppo, and of Antioch. The prophetic introduction of the Apocalypse has

in the East

animously assert, that St. Matthew composed a Hebrew gospel, of which only the Greek translation is extant. It seems, however, dangerous to reject their testimony. [Ματθαῖος μὲν οὖν Ἑβραΐδι διαλέκτῳ τὰ λόγια συνεγράψατο, Papias ap. Euseb., H. E., iii., 39 and 16. Our Greek Matthew is not a translation of this, but may have been compiled from it and Mark, which is generally believed now to be the earliest of the four gospels.]

154 Under the reigns of Nero and Domitian, and in the cities of Alexandria, Antioch, Rome, and Ephesus. See Mill, Prolegomena ad Nov. Testament, and Dr. Lardner's fair and extensive collection, vol. xv.

described and immortalized the seven churches of Asia :—
Ephesus, Smyrna, Pergamus, Thyatira,[155] Sardes, Laodicea, and
Philadelphia ; and their colonies were soon diffused over that
populous country. In a very early period, the islands of Cyprus
and Crete, the provinces of Thrace and Macedonia, gave a
favourable reception to the new religion ; and Christian republics
were soon founded in the cities of Corinth, of Sparta, and of
Athens.[156]   The antiquity of the Greek and Asiatic churches
allowed a sufficient space of time for their increase and multiplication, and even the swarms of Gnostics and other heretics
serve to display the flourishing condition of the orthodox church,
since the appellation of heretics has always been applied to the
less numerous party. To these domestic testimonies we may
add the confession, the complaints, and the apprehensions of
the Gentiles themselves. From the writings of Lucian, a
philosopher who had studied mankind, and who describes their
manners in the most lively colours, we may learn that, under
the reign of Commodus, his native country of Pontus was filled
with Epicureans and *Christians*.[157] Within fourscore years after
the death of Christ,[158] the humane Pliny laments the magnitude
of the evil which he vainly attempted to eradicate. In his
very curious epistle to the emperor Trajan, he affirms that the
temples were almost deserted, that the sacred victims scarcely
found any purchasers, and that the superstition had not only
infected the cities, but had even spread itself into the villages
and the open country of Pontus and Bithynia.[159]

[155] The Alogians (Epiphanius de Hæres. 51) disputed the genuineness of the
Apocalypse, because the church of Thyatira was not yet founded.   Epiphanius, who
allows the fact, extricates himself from the difficulty by ingeniously supposing that
St. John wrote in the spirit of prophecy. See Abauzit, Discours sur l'Apocalypse.

[156] The epistles of Ignatius and Dionysius (ap. Euseb. iv. 23) point out many
churches in Asia and Greece. That of Athens seems to have been one of the least
flourishing.

[157] Lucian in Alexandro, c. 25.   Christianity, however, must have been very un-
equally diffused over Pontus ; since in the middle of the third century there were no
more than seventeen believers in the extensive diocese of Neo-Cæsarea. See M.
de Tillemont, Mémoires Ecclésiast. tom. iv. p. 675, from Basil and Gregory of
Nyssa, who were themselves natives of Cappadocia.

[158] According to the ancients, Jesus Christ suffered under the consulship of the
two Gemini, in the year 29 of our present æra. Pliny was sent into Bithynia
(according to Pagi) in the year 110. [The evening on which the moon was first
visible began the Jewish month ; and by astronomical calculation of the times of
conjunction we can determine that the 15th of Nisan might have fallen on Friday
in the years 27, 30, 33 and 34 A.D. (29 is excluded). But the question is complicated by the uncertainty at what time the Jewish day began, See Wieseler,
Synopsis, p. 407.]

[159] Plin. Epist. x. 97.

Without descending into a minute scrutiny of the expressions, The church of or of the motives of those writers who either celebrate or lament the progress of Christianity in the East, it may in general be observed that none of them have left us any grounds from whence a just estimate might be formed of the real numbers of the faithful in those provinces. One circumstance, however, has been fortunately preserved, which seems to cast a more distinct light on this obscure but interesting subject. Under the reign of Theodosius, after Christianity had enjoyed, during more than sixty years, the sunshine of Imperial favour, the ancient and illustrious church of Antioch consisted of one hundred thousand persons, three thousand of whom were supported out of the public oblations.[160] The splendour and dignity of the queen of the East, the acknowledged populousness of Cæsarea, Seleucia, and Alexandria, and the destruction of two hundred and fifty thousand souls in the earthquake which afflicted Antioch under the elder Justin,[161] are so many convincing proofs that the whole number of its inhabitants was not less than half a million, and that the Christians, however multiplied by zeal and power, did not exceed a fifth part of that great city. How different a proportion must we adopt when we compare the persecuted with the triumphant church, the West with the East, remote villages with populous towns, and countries recently converted to the faith with the place where the believers first received the appellation of Christians! It must not, however, be dissembled that, in another passage, Chrysostom, to whom we are indebted for this useful information, computes the multitude of the faithful as even superior to that of the Jews and Pagans.[162] But the solution of this apparent difficulty is easy and obvious. The eloquent preacher draws a parallel between the civil and the ecclesiastical constitution of Antioch; between the list of Christians who had acquired Heaven by baptism and the list of citizens who had a right to share the public liberality. Slaves, strangers, and infants were comprised in the former; they were excluded from the latter.

The extensive commerce of Alexandria, and its proximity to In Egypt Palestine, gave an easy entrance to the new religion. It was at

---

[160] Chrysostom. Opera, tom. vii. p. 658, 810.

[161] John Malala, tom. ii. p. 144 [p. 420, ed. Bonn]. He draws the same conclusion with regard to the populousness of Antioch.

[162] Chrysostom. tom. i. p. 592. I am indebted for these passages, though not for my inference, to the learned Dr. Lardner, Credibility of the Gospel History, vol. xii. p. 370.

first embraced by great numbers of the Therapeutæ, or Essenians of the lake Mareotis, a Jewish sect which had abated much of its reverence for the Mosaic ceremonies. The austere life of the Essenians, their fasts and excommunications, the community of goods, the love of celibacy, their zeal for martyrdom, and the warmth though not the purity of their faith, already offered a very lively image of the primitive discipline.[163] It was in the school of Alexandria that the Christian theology appears to have assumed a regular and scientifical form; and, when Hadrian visited Egypt, he found a church, composed of Jews and of Greeks, sufficiently important to attract the notice of that inquisitive prince.[164] But the progress of Christianity was for a long time confined within the limits of a single city, which was itself a foreign colony, and, till the close of the second century, the predecessors of Demetrius were the only prelates [A.D. 189-232] of the Egyptian church. Three bishops were consecrated by the hands of Demetrius, and the number was increased to twenty [233-249] by his successor Heraclas.[165] The body of the natives, a people distinguished by a sullen inflexibility of temper,[166] entertained the new doctrine with coldness and reluctance; and even in the time of Origen it was rare to meet with an Egyptian who had surmounted his early prejudices in favour of the sacred animals of his country.[167] As soon, indeed, as Christianity ascended the throne, the zeal of those barbarians obeyed the prevailing impulsion; the cities of Egypt were filled with bishops, and the deserts of Thebais swarmed with hermits.

In Rome   A perpetual stream of strangers and provincials flowed into the capacious bosom of Rome. Whatever was strange or odious,

---

[163] Basnage, Histoire des Juifs, l. 2, c. 20, 21, 22, 23, has examined, with the most critical accuracy, the curious treatise of Philo which describes the Therapeutæ. By proving that it was composed as early as the time of Augustus, Basnage has demonstrated, in spite of Eusebius (l. ii. c. 17), and a crowd of modern Catholics, that the Therapeutæ were neither Christians nor monks. It still remains probable that they changed their name, preserved their manners, adopted some new articles of faith, and gradually became the fathers of the Egyptian Ascetics. [The Therapeutæ were not Essenes (for whom see Grätz Gesch. der Juden. vol. 3), for they did not secede from the synagogues. P. C. Lucius (Die Therapeuten. 1879) tried to prove that they did not exist, and that Philo's treatise (to which the earliest reference is in Eusebius) is a forgery, c. 300, A.D. The genuineness is defended by Mr. Conybeare in his recent ed. and P. Wendland, die Therapeuten, 1896.]

[164] See a letter of Hadrian, in the Augustan History, p. 245 [xxix. 8, 1].

[165] For the succession of Alexandrian bishops, consult Renaudot's History, p. 24, &c. This curious fact is preserved by the patriarch Eutychius (Annal. tom. i. p. 334, Vers. Pocock [date 10th century]), and its internal evidence would alone be a sufficient answer to all the objections which Bishop Pearnos has urged in the Vindiciæ Ignatianæ.

[166] Ammian. Marcellin. xxii. 16.

[167] Origen contra Celsum, l. i. p. 40 [p. 757, Migne].

whoever was guilty or suspected, might hope, in the obscurity of that immense capital, to elude the vigilance of the law. In such a various conflux of nations, every teacher, either of truth or of falsehood, every founder, whether of a virtuous or a criminal association, might easily multiply his disciples or accomplices. The Christians of Rome, at the time of the accidental persecution of Nero, are represented by Tacitus as already amounting to a very great multitude,[168] and the language of that great historian is almost similar to the style employed by Livy, when he relates the introduction and the suppression of the rites of Bacchus. After the Bacchanals had awakened the severity of the senate, it was likewise apprehended that a very great multitude, as it were *another people*, had been initiated into those abhorred mysteries. A more careful inquiry soon demonstrated that the offenders did not exceed seven thousand; a number, indeed, sufficiently alarming, when considered as the object of public justice.[169] It is with the same candid allowance that we should interpret the vague expressions of Tacitus, and in a former instance of Pliny, when they exaggerate the crowds of deluded fanatics who had forsaken the established worship of the gods. The church of Rome was undoubtedly the first and most populous of the empire; and we are possessed of an authentic record which attests the state of religion in that city, about the middle of the third century, and after a peace of thirty-eight years. The clergy, at that time, consisted of a bishop, forty-six presbyters, seven deacons, as many sub-deacons, forty-two acolytes, and fifty readers, exorcists, and porters. The number of widows, of the infirm, and of the poor, who were maintained by the oblations of the faithful, amounted to fifteen hundred.[170] From reason, as well as from the analogy of Antioch, we may venture to estimate the Christians of Rome at about fifty thousand. The populousness of that great capital cannot, perhaps, be exactly ascertained; but the most modest calculation will not surely reduce it lower than a million of inhabitants, of whom the Christians might constitute at the most a twentieth part.[171]

[168] Ingens multitudo is the expression of Tacitus, xv. 44.

[169] T. Liv. xxxix. 13, 15, 16, 17. Nothing could exceed the horror and consternation of the senate on the discovery of the Bacchanalians, whose depravity is described, and perhaps exaggerated, by Livy.

[170] Eusebius, l. vi. c. 43. The Latin translator (M. de Valois) has thought proper to reduce the number of presbyters to forty-four.

[171] This proportion of the presbyters and of the poor to the rest of the people was originally fixed by Burnet (Travels into Italy, p. 168), and is approved by Moyle

The western provincials appeared to have derived the knowledge of Christianity from the same source which had diffused among them the language, the sentiments, and the manners of Rome. In this more important circumstance, Africa, as well as Gaul, was gradually fashioned to the imitation of the capital. Yet, notwithstanding the many favourable occasions which might invite the Roman missionaries to visit their Latin provinces, it was late before they passed either the sea or the Alps ; [172] nor can we discover in those great countries any assured traces either of faith or of persecution that ascend higher than the reign of the Antonines.[173] The slow progress of the gospel in the cold climate of Gaul was extremely different from the eagerness with which it seems to have been received on the burning sands of Africa. The African Christians soon formed one of the principal members of the primitive church. The practice introduced into that province of appointing bishops to the most inconsiderable towns, and very frequently to the most obscure villages, contributed to multiply the splendour and importance of their religious societies, which during the course of the third century were animated by the zeal of Tertullian, directed by the abilities of Cyprian, and adorned by the eloquence of Lactantius. But if, on the contrary, we turn our eyes towards Gaul, we must content ourselves with discovering, in the time of Marcus Antoninus, the feeble and united congregations of Lyons and Vienna ; and, even as late as the reign of Decius, we are assured that in a few cities only, Arles, Narbonne, Toulouse, Limoges, Clermont, Tours, and Paris, some scattered churches were supported by the devotion of a small number of Christians.[174] Silence is indeed very consistent

(vol. ii. p. 151). They were both unacquainted with the passage of Chrysostom, which converts their conjecture almost into a fact [see above, p. 59. Cp. App. 5].

[172] Serius trans Alpes, religione Dei susceptâ. Sulpicius Severus, l. ii. [32, 1]. These were the celebrated martyrs of Lyons. See Eusebius, v. 1. Tillemont, Mém. Ecclésiast. tom. ii. p. 316. According to the Donatists, whose assertion is confirmed by the tacit acknowledgment of Augustin, Africa was the last of the provinces which received the gospel. Tillemont, Mém. Ecclésiast. tom. i. p. 754.

[173] Tum primum intra Gallias martyria visa. Sulp. Severus, l. ii. [ib.]. With regard to Africa, see Tertullian ad Scapulam, c. 3. It is imagined that the Scyllitan martyrs were the first (Acta Sincera Ruinart. p. 34). One of the adversaries of Apuleius seems to have been a Christian. Apolog. p. 496, 497, edit. Delphin.

[174] Raræ in aliquibus civitatibus ecclesiæ, paucorum Christianorum devotione, resurgerent. Acta Sincera, p. 130. Gregory of Tours, l. i. c. 28. Mosheim, p. 207, 449. There is some reason to believe that, in the beginning of the fourth century, the extensive dioceses of Liège, of Treves, and of Cologne composed a single bishopric, which had been very recently founded. See Mémoires de Tillemont, tom. vi. part i. p. 43, 411. [Duchesne, Mémoires sur l'origine des diocèses episc. dans l'ancienne Gaule, 1890.]

with devotion, but, as it is seldom compatible with zeal, we may perceive and lament the languid state of Christianity in those provinces which had exchanged the Celtic for the Latin tongue; since they did not, during the three first centuries, give birth to a single ecclesiastical writer. From Gaul, which claimed a just pre-eminence of learning and authority over all the countries on this side of the Alps, the light of the gospel was more faintly reflected on the remote provinces of Spain and Britain; and, if we may credit the vehement assertions of Tertullian, they had already received the first rays of the faith when he addressed his apology to the magistrates of the emperor Severus.[175] But the obscure and imperfect origin of the western churches of Europe has been so negligently recorded that, if we would relate the time and manner of their foundation, we must supply the silence of antiquity by those legends which avarice or superstition long afterwards dictated to the monks in the lazy gloom of their convents.[176] Of these holy romances, that of the apostle St. James can alone, by its single extravagance, deserve to be mentioned. From a peaceful fisherman of the lake of Gennesareth, he was transformed into a valorous knight, who charged at the head of the Spanish chivalry in their battles against the Moors. The gravest historians have celebrated his exploits; the miraculous shrine of Compostella displayed his power; and the sword of a military order, assisted by the terrors of the Inquisition, was sufficient to remove every objection of profane criticism.[177]

The progress of Christianity was not confined to the Roman empire; and, according to the primitive fathers, who interpret facts by prophecy, the new religion within a century after the death of its divine author, had already visited every part of the globe. "There exists not," says Justin Martyr, "a people, whether Greek or barbarian, or any other race of men, by whatsoever appellation or manners they may be distinguished, however ignorant of arts or agriculture, whether they dwell under

Beyond the limits of the Roman empire

---

[175] The date of Tertullian's Apology is fixed, in a dissertation of Mosheim, to the year 198. [197-8. His Ad Nationes, written either just before or just after, or partly before and partly after, the Apologeticum, covers the same ground briefly.]

[176] In the fifteenth century, there were few who had either inclination or courage to question, whether Joseph of Arimathea founded the monastery of Glastonbury, and whether Dionysius the Areopagite preferred the residence of Paris to that of Athens.

[177] The stupendous metamorphosis was performed in the ninth century. See Mariana (Hist. Hispan. l. vii. c. 13, tom. i. p. 285, edit. Hag. Com. 1733), who, in every sense, imitates Livy, and the honest detection of the legend of St. James by Dr. Geddes, Miscellanies, vol. ii. p. 221.

tents, or wander about in covered waggons, among whom prayers are not offered up in the name of a crucified Jesus to the Father and Creator of all things." [178]   But this splendid exaggeration, which even at present it would be extremely difficult to reconcile with the real state of mankind, can be considered only as the rash sally of a devout but careless writer, the measure of whose belief was regulated by that of his wishes. But neither the belief nor the wishes of the fathers can alter the truth of history.   It will still remain an undoubted fact, that the barbarians of Scythia and Germany who afterwards subverted the Roman monarchy were involved in the darkness of paganism; and that even the conversion of Iberia, of Armenia, or of Æthiopia, was not attempted with any degree of success till the sceptre was in the hands of an orthodox emperor. [179]   Before that time the various accidents of war and commerce might indeed diffuse an imperfect knowledge of the gospel among the tribes of Caledonia, [180] and among the borderers of the Rhine, the Danube, and the Euphrates. [181] Beyond the last-mentioned river, Edessa was distinguished by a firm and early adherence to the faith. [182]   From Edessa the principles of Christianity were easily introduced into the Greek and Syrian cities which obeyed the successors of Artaxerxes;

[178] Justin Martyr, Dialog. cum Tryphon. p. 341.   Irenæus adv. Hæres. l. i. c. 10.   Tertullian adv. Jud. c. 7.   See Mosheim, p. 203.

[179] See the fourth century of Mosheim's History of the Church.   Many, though very confused circumstances, that relate to the conversion of Iberia and Armenia, may be found in Moses of Chorene, l. ii. c. 78—89.   [Milman notes that Gibbon "had expressed his intention of withdrawing the words 'of Armenia,' from the text of future editions" (Vindication, Works, iv. 577).   Christianity spread at an early time in Armenia, but its beginnings are enveloped in obscurity, and the traditions are largely legendary.   The history of the Armenian church begins with Gregory Lusavoritch (Illuminator), consecrated bishop by Leontius of Cappadocia, to which see the Armenian bishopric was at first subject.   The main source for Gregory is an early Life incorporated in the history of Tiridates by Agathangelus (translated by Langlois, Fr. Hist. Graec. vol. v.).   See further Appendix 18.]

[180] According to Tertullian, the Christian faith had penetrated into parts of Britain inaccessible to the Roman arms.   About a century afterwards, Ossian, the son of Fingal, is *said* to have disputed, in his extreme old age, with one of the foreign missionaries, and the dispute is still extant, in verse, and in the Erse language.   See Mr. Macpherson's Dissertation on the Antiquity of Ossian's Poems, p. 10.

[181] The Goths, who ravaged Asia in the reign of Gallienus, carried away great numbers of captives; some of whom were Christians, and became missionaries. See Tillemont, Mémoires Ecclésiast. tom. iv. p. 44.

[182] The legend of Abgarus, fabulous as it is, affords a decisive proof that, many years before Eusebius wrote his history, the greatest part of the inhabitants of Edessa had embraced Christianity.   Their rivals, the citizens of Carrhæ, adhered, on the contrary, to the cause of Paganism, as late as the sixth century.

but they do not appear to have made any deep impression on the minds of the Persians, whose religious system, by the labours of a well-disciplined order of priests, had been constructed with much more art and solidity than the uncertain mythology of Greece and Rome.[183]

From this impartial, though imperfect, survey of the progress of Christianity, it may, perhaps, seem probable that the number of its proselytes has been excessively magnified by fear on the one side and by devotion on the other. According to the irreproachable testimony of Origen,[184] the proportion of the faithful was very inconsiderable when compared with the multitude of an unbelieving world; but, as we are left without any distinct information, it is impossible to determine, and it is difficult even to conjecture, the real numbers of the primitive Christians. The most favourable calculation, however, that can be deduced from the examples of Antioch and of Rome will not permit us to imagine that more than a twentieth part of the subjects of the empire had enlisted themselves under the banner of the cross before the important conversion of Constantine. But their habits of faith, of zeal, and of union seemed to multiply their numbers; and the same causes which contributed to their future increase served to render their actual strength more apparent and more formidable.

General proportion of Christians and Pagans

Such is the constitution of civil society that, whilst a few persons are distinguished by riches, by honours, and by knowledge, the body of the people is condemned to obscurity, ignorance, and poverty. The Christian religion, which addressed itself to the whole human race, must consequently collect a far greater number of proselytes from the lower than from the superior ranks of life. This innocent and natural circumstance has been improved into a very odious imputation, which seems to be less strenuously denied by the apologists than it is urged by the adversaries of the faith; that the new sect of Christians was almost entirely composed of the dregs of the populace, of peasants and mechanics, of boys and women, of beggars and slaves; the last of whom might sometimes introduce the missionaries into the rich and noble families to which they belonged.

Whether the first Christians were mean and ignorant

---

[183] According to Bardesanes (ap. Euseb. Præpar. Evangel.), there were some Christians in Persia before the end of the second century. In the time of Constantine (see his Epistle to Sapor, Vit. l. iv. c. 13), they composed a flourishing church. Consult Beausobre, Hist. Critique du Manichéisme, tom. i. p. 180, and the Bibliotheca Orientalis of Assemani.

[184] Origen contra Celsum, l. viii. p. 424 [p. 1621, (πάνυ ὀλίγοι). Cp. App. 5.]

These obscure teachers (such was the charge of malice and infidelity) are as mute in public as they are loquacious and dogmatical in private.   Whilst they cautiously avoid the dangerous encounter of philosophers, they mingle with the rude and illiterate crowd, and insinuate themselves into those minds, whom their age, their sex, or their education has the best disposed to receive the impression of superstitious terrors.[185]

Some exceptions with regard to learning

This unfavourable picture, though not devoid of a faint resemblance, betrays, by its dark colouring and distorted features, the pencil of an enemy.   As the humble faith of Christ diffused itself through the world, it was embraced by several persons who derived some consequence from the advantages of nature or fortune.   Aristides, who presented an eloquent apology to the emperor Hadrian, was an Athenian philosopher.[186]   Justin Martyr had sought divine knowledge in the schools of Zeno, of Aristotle, of Pythagoras, and of Plato, before he fortunately was accosted by the old man, or rather the angel, who turned his attention to the study of the Jewish prophets.[187]   Clemens of Alexandria had acquired much various reading in the Greek, and Tertullian in the Latin, language.   Julius Africanus and Origen possessed a very considerable share of the learning of their times; and, although the style of Cyprian is very different from that of Lactantius, we might almost discover that both those writers had been public teachers of rhetoric.   Even the study of philosophy was at length introduced among the Christians, but it was not always productive of the most salutary effects; knowledge was as often the parent of heresy as of devotion, and the description which was designed for the followers of Artemon may, with equal propriety, be applied to the various sects that resisted the successors of the apostles.   "They presume to alter the holy scriptures, to abandon the ancient rule of faith, and to

[185] Minucius Felix, c. 8, with Wowerus's notes.   Celsus ap. Origen., l. iii. p. 138, 142, [p. 984, *sqq.*].   Julian ap. Cyril. l. vi. p. 206.   Edit. Spanheim.

[186] Euseb. Hist. Eccles. iv. 3.   Hieronym. Epist. 83, [*leg.* 84.   But in Migne's arrangement, ep. 70, vol. i. p. 667.   Since Gibbon wrote there have been discovered, not the Apology of Aristides in its original form, but materials for reconstructing it.   These consist of (1) a Syriac version or paraphrase found on Mount Sinai by Mr. J. Rendel Harris (published in Robinson's Texts and Studies, 1891), (2) a fragment of an Armenian translation (published at Venice by the Mechitarists, 1878), (3) a loose Greek reproduction, incorporated in the Tale of Barlaam and Josaphat (see Robinson, *loc. cit.*).   In the second superscription of the Syriac version, the work is addressed to Antoninus Pius, which is inconsistent with the statement of Eusebius, who, however, had not seen the book.]

[187] The story is prettily told in Justin's Dialogues.   Tillemont (Mém. Ecclésiast. tom. ii. p. 334), who relates it after him, is sure that the old man was a disguised angel.

form their opinions according to the subtile precepts of logic. The science of the church is neglected for the study of geometry, and they lose sight of Heaven while they are employed in measuring the earth. Euclid is perpetually in their hands. Aristotle and Theophrastus are the objects of their admiration; and they express an uncommon reverence for the works of Galen. Their errors are derived from the abuse of the arts and sciences of the infidels, and they corrupt the simplicity of the Gospel by the refinements of human reason." [188]

Nor can it be affirmed with truth that the advantages of birth and fortune were always separated from the profession of Christianity. Several Roman citizens were brought before the tribunal of Pliny, and he soon discovered that a great number of persons of *every order* of men in Bithynia had deserted the religion of their ancestors. [189] His unsuspected testimony may, in this instance, obtain more credit than the bold challenge of Tertullian, when he addresses himself to the fears as well as to the humanity of the proconsul of Africa, by assuring him that, if he persists in his cruel intentions, he must decimate Carthage, and that he will find among the guilty many persons of his own rank, senators and matrons of noblest extraction, and the friends or relations of his most intimate friends. [190] It appears, however, that about forty years afterwards the emperor Valerian was persuaded of the truth of this assertion, since in one of his rescripts he evidently supposes that senators, Roman knights, and ladies of quality were engaged in the Christian sect. [191] The church still continued to increase its outward splendour as it lost its internal purity; and in the reign of Diocletian the palace, the courts of justice, and even the army concealed a multitude of Christians who endeavoured to reconcile the interests of the present with those of a future life.

And yet these exceptions are either too few in number, or too recent in time, entirely to remove the imputation of ignorance and obscurity which has been so arrogantly cast on the first proselytes of Christianity. Instead of employing in our defence

with regard to rank and fortune

Christianity most favourably received by the poor and simple

---

[188] Eusebius, v. 28. It may be hoped that none, except the heretics, gave occasion to the complaint of Celsus (ap. Origen., l. ii. p. 77) that the Christians were perpetually correcting and altering their Gospels.

[189] Plin. Epist. x. 97. Fuerunt alii similis amentiæ, cives Romani . . . Multi enim omnis ætatis, *omnis ordinis*, utriusque sexûs, etiam vocantur in periculum et vocabuntur.

[190] Tertullian ad Scapulam. Yet even his rhetoric rises no higher than to claim a *tenth* part of Carthage.

[191] Cyprian. Epist. 79 [80].

the fictions of later ages, it will be more prudent to convert the occasion of scandal into a subject of edification. Our serious thoughts will suggest to us that the apostles themselves were chosen by providence among the fishermen of Galilee, and that, the lower we depress the temporal condition of the first Christians, the more reason we shall find to admire their merit and success. It is incumbent on us diligently to remember that the kingdom of heaven was promised to the poor in spirit, and that minds afflicted by calamity and the contempt of mankind cheerfully listen to the divine promise of future happiness; while, on the contrary, the fortunate are satisfied with the possession of this world; and the wise abuse in doubt and dispute their vain superiority of reason and knowledge.

Rejected by some eminent men of the first and second centuries

We stand in need of such reflections to comfort us for the loss of some illustrious characters, which in our eyes might have seemed the most worthy of the heavenly present. The names of Seneca, of the elder and the younger Pliny, of Tacitus, of Plutarch, of Galen, of the slave Epictetus, and of the emperor Marcus Antoninus, adorn the age in which they flourished, and exalt the dignity of human nature. They filled with glory their respective stations, either in active or contemplative life; their excellent understandings were improved by study; Philosophy had purified their minds from the prejudices of the popular superstition; and their days were spent in the pursuit of truth and the practice of virtue. Yet all these sages (it is no less an object of surprise than of concern) overlooked or rejected the perfection of the Christian system. Their language or their silence equally discover their contempt for the growing sect, which in their time had diffused itself over the Roman empire. Those among them who condescend to mention the Christians consider them only as obstinate and perverse enthusiasts, who exacted an implicit submission to their mysterious doctrines, without being able to produce a single argument that could engage the attention of men of sense and learning.[192]

Their neglect of prophecy

It is at least doubtful whether any of these philosophers perused the apologies which the primitive Christians repeatedly published in behalf of themselves and of their religion; but it is much to be lamented that such a cause was not defended by

[192] Dr. Lardner, in his first and second volume of Jewish and Christian testimonies, collects and illustrates those of Pliny the younger, of Tacitus, of Galen, of Marcus Antoninus, and perhaps of Epictetus (for it is doubtful whether that philosopher means to speak of the Christians). The new sect is totally unnoticed by Seneca, the elder Pliny, and Plutarch [and Dion Chrysostom].

abler advocates. They expose with superfluous wit and eloquence the extravagance of Polytheism. They interest our compassion by displaying the innocence and sufferings of their injured
brethren. But, when they would demonstrate the divine origin
of Christianity, they insist much more strongly on the predictions which announced, than on the miracles which accompanied,
the appearance of the Messiah. Their favourite argument
might serve to edify a Christian or to convert a Jew, since both
the one and the other acknowledge the authority of those
prophecies, and both are obliged, with devout reverence, to
search for their sense and their accomplishment. But this
mode of persuasion loses much of its weight and influence,
when it is addressed to those who neither understand nor
respect the Mosaic dispensation and the prophetic style.[193] In
the unskilful hands of Justin and of the succeeding apologists,
the sublime meaning of the Hebrew oracles evaporates in
distant types, affected conceits, and cold allegories ; and even
their authenticity was rendered suspicious to an unenlightened
Gentile by the mixture of pious forgeries, which, under the
names of Orpheus, Hermes, and the Sibyls,[194] were obtruded on
him as of equal value with the genuine inspirations of Heaven.
The adoption of fraud and sophistry in the defence of revelation
too often reminds us of the injudicious conduct of those poets
who load their *invulnerable* heroes with a useless weight of
cumbersome and brittle armour.

But how shall we excuse the supine inattention of the Pagan and of mir-
and philosophic world to those evidences which were presented acles
by the hand of Omnipotence, not to their reason, but to their
senses ? During the age of Christ, of his apostles, and of their
first disciples, the doctrine which they preached was confirmed
by innumerable prodigies. The lame walked, the blind saw,
the sick were healed, the dead were raised, dæmons were
expelled, and the laws of Nature were frequently suspended General
silence con-
cerning the
darkness of

[193] If the famous prophecy of the Seventy Weeks had been alleged to a Roman the passion
philosopher, would he not have replied in the words of Cicero, "Quæ tandem ista
auguratio est, annorum potius quam aut mensium aut dierum?" De Divinatione,
ii. 30. Observe with what irreverence Lucian (in Alexandro, c. 13), and his
friend Celsus ap. Origen. (l. vii. p. 327, [p. 1440, Migne]), express themselves
concerning the Hebrew prophets.

[194] The Philosophers, who derided tne more ancient predictions of the Sibyls,
would easily have detected the Jewish and Christian forgeries, which have been
so triumphantly quoted by the fathers, from Justin Martyr to Lactantius. When
the Sibylline verses had performed their appointed task, they, like the system of
the millennium, were quietly laid aside. The Christian Sibyl had unluckily fixed
the ruin of Rome for the year 195, A.U.C. 948.

for the benefit of the church. But the sages of Greece and
Rome turned aside from the awful spectacle, and, pursuing the
ordinary occupations of life and study, appeared unconscious of
any alterations in the moral or physical government of the
world. Under the reign of Tiberius, the whole earth,[195] or at
least a celebrated province of the Roman empire,[196] was involved
in a præternatural darkness of three hours. Even this miraculous event, which ought to have excited the wonder, the curiosity,
and the devotion of mankind, passed without notice in an age
of science and history.[197] It happened during the lifetime of
Seneca and the elder Pliny, who must have experienced the
immediate effects, or received the earliest intelligence, of the
prodigy. Each of these philosophers, in a laborious work, has
recorded all the great phenomena of Nature, earthquakes,
meteors, comets, and eclipses, which his indefatigable curiosity
could collect.[198] Both the one and the other have omitted to
mention the greatest phenomenon to which the mortal eye has
been witness since the creation of the globe. A distinct
chapter of Pliny [199] is designed for eclipses of an extraordinary
nature and unusual duration; but he contents himself with
describing the singular defect of light which followed the
murder of Cæsar, when, during the greatest part of the year,
the orb of the sun appeared pale and without splendour. This
season of obscurity, which cannot surely be compared with the
præternatural darkness of the Passion, had been already celebrated by most of the poets [200] and historians of that memorable
age.[201]

---

[195] The fathers, as they are drawn out in battle array by Dom Calmet (Dissertations sur la Bible, tom. iii. p. 295—308), seem to cover the whole earth with
darkness, in which they are followed by most of the moderns.

[196] Origen ad Matth. c. 27, and a few modern critics, Beza, Le Clerc, Lardner,
&c., are desirous of confining it to the land of Judea.

[197] The celebrated passage of Phlegon is now wisely abandoned. When Tertullian assures the Pagans that the mention of the prodigy is found in Arcanis
(not Archivis) vestris (see his Apology, c. 21), he probably appeals to the Sibylline
verses, which relate it exactly in the words of the gospel [*archiuis* is in all the
Mss. except one, which has *arcanis*, and is certainly right. See Bindley's ed. p.
78. The official report of Pilate is said to be meant.]

[198] Seneca Quæst. Natur. i. 1, 15, vi. 1, vii. 17. Plin. Hist. Natur. l. ii.

[199] Plin. Hist. Natur. ii. 30 [a chapter remarkable for its brevity].

[200] Virgil. Georgic. i. 466. Tibullus, l. i. [*leg.* ii.]. Eleg. v. ver. 75. Ovid.
Metamorph. xv. 782. Lucan. Pharsal. i. 540. The last of these poets places this
prodigy before the civil war.

[201] See a public epistle of M. Antony in Joseph. Antiquit. xiv. 12. Plutarch in
Cæsar. p. 471 [c. 69]. Appian. Bell. Civil. l. iv. Dion Cassius, l. xlv. p. 431
[c. 17]. Julius Obsequens, c. 128. His little treatise is an abstract of Livy's
prodigies.

CHAPTER XVI

*The Conduct of the Roman Government towards the Christians, from
the Reign of Nero to that of Constantine*

IF we seriously consider the purity of the Christian religion, the Christianity persecuted by the Roman emperors
sanctity of its moral precepts, and the innocent as well as
austere lives of the greater number of those who, during the
first ages, embraced the faith of the gospel, we should naturally
suppose that so benevolent a doctrine would have been received
with due reverence, even by the unbelieving world ; that the
learned and the polite, however they might deride the miracles,
would have esteemed the virtues of the new sect ; and that the
magistrates, instead of persecuting, would have protected an
order of men who yielded the most passive obedience to the
laws, though they declined the active cares of war and government.   If, on the other hand, we recollect the universal toleration of Polytheism, as it was invariably maintained by the faith
of the people, the incredulity of philosophers, and the policy of
the Roman senate and emperors, we are at a loss to discover
what new offence the Christians had committed, what new
provocation could exasperate the mild indifference of antiquity,
and what new motives could urge the Roman princes, who
beheld, without concern, a thousand forms of religion subsisting
in peace under their gentle sway, to inflict a severe punishment
on any part of their subjects, who had chosen for themselves a
singular, but an inoffensive, mode of faith and worship.

The religious policy of the ancient world seems to have
assumed a more stern and intolerant character, to oppose the
progress of Christianity.   About fourscore years after the death
of Christ, his innocent disciples were punished with death, by
the sentence of a proconsul of the most amiable and philosophic
character, and, according to the laws of an emperor, distinguished
by the wisdom and justice of his general administration.   The
apologies which were repeatedly addressed to the successors of
Trajan, are filled with the most pathetic complaints, that the
Christians, who obeyed the dictates, and solicited the liberty, of
conscience, were alone, among all the subjects of the Roman

empire, excluded from the common benefits of their auspicious government. The deaths of a few eminent martyrs have been recorded with care ; and from the time that Christianity was invested with the supreme power, the governors of the church have been no less diligently employed in displaying the cruelty, than in imitating the conduct, of their Pagan adversaries. To separate (if it be possible) a few authentic, as well as interesting, facts, from an undigested mass of fiction and error, and to relate, in a clear and rational manner, the causes, the extent, the duration, and the most important circumstances of the persecutions to which the first Christians were exposed, is the design of the present Chapter.

Inquiry into their motives

The sectaries of a persecuted religion, depressed by fear, animated with resentment, and perhaps heated by enthusiasm, are seldom in a proper temper of mind calmly to investigate, or candidly to appreciate, the motives of their enemies, which often escape the impartial and discerning view even of those who are placed at a secure distance from the flames of persecution. A reason has been assigned for the conduct of the emperors towards the primitive Christians, which may appear the more specious and probable as it is drawn from the acknowledged genius of Polytheism. It has already been observed that the religious concord of the world was principally supported by the implicit assent and reverence which the nations of antiquity expressed for their respective traditions and ceremonies. It might therefore be expected that they would unite with indignation against any sect of people which should separate itself from the communion of mankind, and, claiming the exclusive possession of divine knowledge, should disdain every form of worship, except its own, as impious and idolatrous. The rights of toleration were held by mutual indulgence ; they were justly forfeited by a refusal of the accustomed tribute. As the payment of this tribute was inflexibly refused by the Jews, and by them alone, the consideration of the treatment which they experienced from the Roman magistrates will serve to explain how far these speculations are justified by facts, and will lead us to discover the true causes of the persecution of Christianity.

Rebellious spirit of the Jews

Without repeating what has been already mentioned of the reverence of the Roman princes and governors for the temple of Jerusalem, we shall only observe that the destruction of the temple and city was accompanied and followed by every circumstance that could exasperate the minds of the conquerors, and authorize religious persecution by the most specious arguments

of political justice and the public safety. From the reign of
Nero to that of Antoninus Pius, the Jews discovered a fierce
impatience of the dominion of Rome, which repeatedly broke
out in the most furious massacres and insurrections. Humanity
is shocked at the recital of the horrid cruelties which they
committed in the cities of Egypt, of Cyprus, and of Cyrene,
where they dwelt in treacherous friendship with the unsuspecting natives;[1] and we are tempted to applaud the severe
retaliation which was exercised by the arms of the legions
against a race of fanatics, whose dire and credulous superstition
seemed to render them the implacable enemies not only of the
Roman government, but of human kind.[2] The enthusiasm of
the Jews was supported by the opinion that it was unlawful for
them to pay taxes to an idolatrous master; and by the flattering
promise which they derived from their ancient oracles, that a
conquering Messiah would soon arise, destined to break their
fetters and to invest the favourites of heaven with the empire of
the earth. It was by announcing himself as their long-expected
deliverer, and by calling on all the descendants of Abraham to
assert the hope of Israel, that the famous Barchochebas collected
a formidable army, with which he resisted, during two years, the
power of the emperor Hadrian.[3]

Notwithstanding these repeated provocations, the resentment
of the Roman princes expired after the victory; nor were their
apprehensions continued beyond the period of war and danger.
By the general indulgence of polytheism, and by the mild
temper of Antoninus Pius, the Jews were restored to their
ancient privileges, and once more obtained the permission of
circumcising their children, with the easy restraint that they
should never confer on any foreign proselyte that distinguishing
mark of the Hebrew race.[4] The numerous remains of that

Toleration of the Jewish religion

[1] In Cyrene they massacred 220,000 Greeks; in Cyprus, 240,000; in Egypt, a
very great multitude. Many of these unhappy victims were sawed asunder,
according to a precedent to which David had given the sanction of his example.
The victorious Jews devoured the flesh, licked up the blood, and twisted the
entrails like a girdle round their bodies. See Dion Cassius, l. lxviii. p. 1145
[c. 32].

[2] Without repeating the well-known narratives of Josephus, we may learn from
Dion (l. lxix. p. 1162 [c. 14]) that in Hadrian's war 580,000 Jews were cut off
by the sword, besides an infinite number which perished by famine, by disease,
and by fire.

[3] For the sect of the Zealots, see Basnage, Histoire des Juifs, l. i. c. 17, for the
characters of the Messiah, according to the Rabbis, l. v. c. 11, 12, 13, for the
actions of Barchochebas, l. vii. c. 12.

[4] It is to Modestinus, a Roman lawyer (l. vi. regular.), that we are indebted
for a distinct knowledge of the Edict of Antoninus. See Casaubon ad Hist.
August. p. 27.

people, though they were still excluded from the precincts
of Jerusalem, were permitted to form and to maintain considerable establishments both in Italy and in the provinces, to
acquire the freedom of Rome, to enjoy municipal honours, and
to obtain, at the same time, an exemption from the burdensome
and expensive offices of society. The moderation or the contempt of the Romans gave a legal sanction to the form of
ecclesiastical police which was instituted by the vanquished sect.
The patriarch, who had fixed his residence at Tiberias, was
empowered to appoint his subordinate ministers and apostles, to
exercise a domestic jurisdiction, and to receive from his dispersed
brethren an annual contribution.[5] New synagogues were frequently erected in the principal cities of the empire; and the
sabbaths, the fasts, and the festivals, which were either commanded by the Mosaic law or enjoined by the traditions of the
Rabbis, were celebrated in the most solemn and public manner.[6]
Such gentle treatment insensibly assuaged the stern temper of
the Jews. Awakened from their dream of prophecy and conquest,
they assumed the behaviour of peaceable and industrious subjects.
Their irreconcileable hatred of mankind, instead of flaming out
in acts of blood and violence, evaporated in less dangerous
gratifications. They embraced every opportunity of over-reach-
ing the idolaters in trade; and they pronounced secret and
ambiguous imprecations against the haughty kingdom of Edom.[7]

The Jews were a people which followed, the Christians a sect which deserted, the religion of their fathers

Since the Jews, who rejected with abhorrence the deities
adored by their sovereign and by their fellow-subjects, enjoyed,
however, the free exercise of their unsocial religion; there
must have existed some other cause, which exposed the disciples
of Christ to those severities from which the posterity of Abraham
was exempt. The difference between them is simple and obvious;
but, according to the sentiments of antiquity, it was of the
highest importance. The Jews were a *nation;* the Christians
were a *sect;* and, if it was natural for every community to respect
the sacred institutions of their neighbours, it was incumbent on
them to persevere in those of their ancestors. The voice of

[5] See Basnage, Histoire des Juifs, l. iii. c. 2, 3. The office of Patriarch was
suppressed by Theodosius the younger.
[6] We need only mention the purim, or deliverance of the Jews from the rage of
Haman, which, till the reign of Theodosius, was celebrated with insolent triumph
and riotous intemperance. Basnage, Hist. des Juifs, l. vi. c. 17, l. viii. c. 6.
[7] According to the false Josephus, Tsepho, the grandson of Esau, conducted
into Italy the army of Æneas, king of Carthage. Another colony of Idumæans,
flying from the sword of David, took refuge in the dominions of Romulus. For
these, or for other reasons of equal weight, the name of Edom was applied by the
Jews to the Roman empire.

oracles, the precepts of philosophers and the authority of the laws unanimously enforced this national obligation. By their lofty claim of superior sanctity, the Jews might provoke the Polytheists to consider them as an odious and impure race. By disdaining the intercourse of other nations they might deserve their contempt. The laws of Moses might be for the most part frivolous or absurd; yet, since they had been received during many ages by a large society, his followers were justified by the example of mankind; and it was universally acknowledged that they had a right to practise what it would have been criminal in them to neglect. But this principle which protected the Jewish synagogue afforded not any favour or security to the primitive church. By embracing the faith of the Gospel, the Christians incurred the supposed guilt of an unnatural and unpardonable offence. They dissolved the sacred ties of custom and education, violated the religious institutions of their country, and presumptuously despised whatever their fathers had believed as true, or had reverenced as sacred. Nor was this apostacy (if we may use the expression) merely of a partial or local kind; since the pious deserter who withdrew himself from the temples of Egypt or Syria would equally disdain to seek an asylum in those of Athens or Carthage. Every Christian rejected with contempt the superstitions of his family, his city, and his province. The whole body of Christians unanimously refused to hold any communion with the gods of Rome, of the empire, and of mankind. It was in vain that the oppressed believer asserted the inalienable rights of conscience and private judgment. Though his situation might excite the pity, his arguments could never reach the understanding, either of the philosophic or of the believing part of the Pagan world. To their apprehensions, it was no less a matter of surprise that any individuals should entertain scruples against complying with the established mode of worship, than if they had conceived a sudden abhorrence to the manners, the dress, or the language of their native country.[8]

The surprise of the Pagans was soon succeeded by resentment; and the most pious of men were exposed to the unjust but dangerous imputation of impiety. Malice and prejudice con-

Christianity accused of atheism, and mistaken by the people and philosophers

---

[8] From the arguments of Celsus, as they are represented and refuted by Origen (l. v. p. 247—259 [p. 1276, *sqq.*]), we may clearly discover the distinction that was made between the Jewish *people* and the Christian *sect*. See in the Dialogue of Minucius Felix (c. 5, 6) a fair and not inelegant description of the popular sentiments, with regard to the desertion of the established worship.

curred in representing the Christians as a society of atheists, who, by the most daring attack on the religious constitution of the empire, had merited the severest animadversion of the civil magistrate. They had separated themselves (they gloried in the confession) from every mode of superstition which was received in any part of the globe by the various temper of polytheism; but it was not altogether so evident what deity or what form of worship they had substituted to the gods and temples of antiquity. The pure and sublime idea which they entertained of the Supreme Being escaped the gross conception of the Pagan multitude, who were at a loss to discover a spiritual and solitary God, that was neither represented under any corporeal figure or visible symbol, nor was adored with the accustomed pomp of libations and festivals, of altars and sacrifices.[9] The sages of Greece and Rome, who had elevated their minds to the contemplation of the existence and attributes of the First Cause, were induced, by reason or by vanity, to reserve for themselves and their chosen disciples the privilege of this philosophical devotion.[10] They were far from admitting the prejudices of mankind as the standard of truth; but they considered them as flowing from the original disposition of human nature; and they supposed that any popular mode of faith and worship which presumed to disclaim the assistance of the senses would, in proportion as it receded from superstition, find itself incapable of restraining the wanderings of the fancy and the visions of fanaticism. The careless glance which men of wit and learning condescended to cast on the Christian revelation served only to confirm their hasty opinion, and to persuade them that the principle, which they might have revered, of the divine unity was defaced by the wild enthusiasm, and annihilated by the airy speculations, of the new sectaries. The author of a celebrated dialogue which has been attributed to Lucian, whilst he affects to treat the mysterious subject of the Trinity in a style of ridicule and contempt, betrays his own ignorance of the weakness of human reason, and of the inscrutable nature of the divine perfections.[11]

[9] Cur nullas aras habent? templa nulla? nulla nota simulacra? . . . Unde autem, vel quis ille, aut ubi, Deus unicus, solitarius, destitutus? Minucius Felix, c. 10. The Pagan interlocutor goes on to make a distinction in favour of the Jews, who had once a temple, altars, victims, &c.

[10] It is difficult (says Plato) to attain, and dangerous to publish, the knowledge of the true God. See the Théologie des Philosophes, in the Abbé d'Olivet's French translation of Tully de Naturâ Deorum, tom. i. p. 275.

[11] The author of the Philopatris [a much later work; cp. App. 1, ad init.] perpetu-

It might appear less surprising that the founder of Christianity should not only be revered by his disciples as a sage and a prophet, but that he should be adored as a God. The Polytheists were disposed to adopt every article of faith which seemed to offer any resemblance, however distant or imperfect, with the popular mythology; and the legends of Bacchus, of Hercules, and of Æsculapius had, in some measure, prepared their imagination for the appearance of the Son of God under a human form.[12] But they were astonished that the Christians should abandon the temples of those ancient heroes who, in the infancy of the world, had invented arts, instituted laws, and vanquished the tyrants or monsters who infested the earth; in order to choose, for the exclusive object of their religious worship, an obscure teacher who, in a recent age, and among a barbarous people, had fallen a sacrifice either to the malice of his own countrymen or to the jealousy of the Roman government. The Pagan multitude, reserving their gratitude for temporal benefits alone, rejected the inestimable present of life and immortality which was offered to mankind by Jesus of Nazareth. His mild constancy in the midst of cruel and voluntary sufferings, his universal benevolence, and the sublime simplicity of his actions and character were insufficient, in the opinion of those carnal men, to compensate for the want of fame, of empire, and of success; and, whilst they refused to acknowledge his stupendous triumph over the powers of darkness and of the grave, they misrepresented, or they insulted, the equivocal birth, wandering life, and ignominious death of the divine Author of Christianity.[13]

The personal guilt which every Christian had contracted, in thus preferring his private sentiment to the national religion, The union and assemblies of the Christians considered as a dangerous conspiracy

ally treats the Christians as a company of dreaming enthusiasts, δαιμόνιοι αἰθέριοι αἰθεροβατοῦντες ἀεροβατοῦντες, &c., and in one place manifestly alludes to the vision, in which St. Paul was transported to the third heaven. In another place, Triephon, who personates a Christian, after deriding the Gods of Paganism, proposes a mysterious oath,

Ὑψιμέδοντα θεὸν, μέγαν, ἄμβροτον, οὐρανίωνα,
Υἱὸν πατρὸς, πνεῦμα ἐκ πατρὸς ἐκπορευόμενον
Ἐν ἐκ τριῶν, καὶ ἐξ ἑνὸς τρία.

Ἀριθμέειν με διδάσκεις (is the profane answer of Critias) καὶ ὅρκος ἢ ἀριθμητική οὐκ οἶδα γὰρ τί λέγεις· ἓν τρία, τρία ἕν!

[12] According to Justin Martyr (Apolog. Major, c. 70—85), the dæmon, who had gained some imperfect knowledge of the prophecies, purposely contrived this resemblance, which might deter, though by different means, both the people and the philosophers from embracing the faith of Christ.

[13] In the first and second books of Origen, Celsus treats the birth and character of our Saviour with the most impious contempt. The orator Libanius praises Porphyry and Julian for confuting the folly of a sect which styled a dead man of Palestine God, and the Son of God. Socrates, Hist. Ecclesiast. iii. 23.

was aggravated, in a very high degree, by the number and
union of the criminals. It is well known, and has been already
observed, that Roman policy viewed with the utmost jealousy
and distrust any association among its subjects ; and that the
privileges of private corporations, though formed for the most
harmless or beneficial purposes, were bestowed with a very
sparing hand.[14]   The religious assemblies of the Christians, who
had separated themselves from the public worship, appeared of
a much less innocent nature : they were illegal in their principle
and in their consequences might become dangerous ; nor were
the emperors conscious that they violated the laws of justice,
when, for the peace of society, they prohibited those secret
and sometimes nocturnal meetings.[15]   The pious disobedience
of the Christians made their conduct, or perhaps their designs,
appear in a much more serious and criminal light ; and the
Roman princes, who might perhaps have suffered themselves to
be disarmed by a ready submission, deeming their honour concerned in the execution of their commands, sometimes attempted
by rigorous punishments to subdue this independent spirit,
which boldly acknowledged an authority superior to that of the
magistrate.   The extent and duration of this spiritual conspiracy
seemed to render it every day more deserving of his animadversion.   We have already seen that the active and successful zeal
of the Christians had insensibly diffused them through every
province and almost every city of the empire.   The new converts
seemed to renounce their family and country, that they might
connect themselves in an indissoluble band of union with a
peculiar society, which everywhere assumed a different character
from the rest of mankind.   Their gloomy and austere aspect,
their abhorrence of the common business and pleasures of life,
and their frequent predictions of impending calamities,[16] inspired
the Pagans with the apprehension of some danger which would
arise from the new sect, the more alarming as it was the more
obscure.   " Whatever," says Pliny, " may be the principle of

[14] The emperor Trajan refused to incorporate a company of 150 firemen, for
the use of the city of Nicomedia.   He disliked all associations.   See Plin. Epist.
x. 42, 43.

[15] The proconsul Pliny had published a general edict against unlawful meetings.
The prudence of the Christians suspended their Agapæ ; but it was impossible
for them to omit the exercise of public worship.

[16] As the prophecies of the Antichrist, approaching conflagration, &c., provoked
those Pagans whom they did not convert, they were mentioned with caution and
reserve ; and the Montanists were censured for disclosing too freely the dangerous
secret.   See Mosheim, p. 413.

their conduct, their inflexible obstinacy appeared deserving of punishment." [17]

The precautions with which the disciples of Christ performed the offices of religion were at first dictated by fear and necessity; but they were continued from choice. By imitating the awful secrecy which reigned in the Eleusinian mysteries, the Christians had flattered themselves that they should render their sacred institutions more respectable in the eyes of the Pagan world. [18] But the event, as it often happens to the operations of subtile policy, deceived their wishes and their expectations. It was concluded that they only concealed what they would have blushed to disclose. Their mistaken prudence afforded an opportunity for malice to invent, and for suspicious credulity to believe, the horrid tales which described the Christians as the most wicked of human kind, who practised in their dark recesses every abomination that a depraved fancy could suggest, and who solicited the favour of their unknown God by the sacrifice of every moral virtue. There were many who pretended to confess or to relate the ceremonies of this abhorred society. It was asserted, "that a new-born infant, entirely covered over with flour, was presented, like some mystic symbol of initiation, to the knife of the proselyte, who unknowingly inflicted many a secret and mortal wound on the innocent victim of his error; that, as soon as the cruel deed was perpetrated, the sectaries drank up the blood, greedily tore asunder the quivering members, and pledged themselves to eternal secrecy, by a mutual consciousness of guilt. It was as confidently affirmed that this inhuman sacrifice was succeeded by a suitable entertainment, in which intemperance served as a provocative to brutal lust; till, at the appointed moment, the lights were suddenly extinguished, shame was banished, nature was forgotten; and, as accident might direct, the darkness of the night was polluted by the incestuous commerce of sisters and brothers, of sons and of mothers." [19]

But the perusal of the ancient apologies was sufficient to remove even the slightest suspicion from the mind of a candid

Their manners calumniated

Their imprudent defence

[17] Neque enim dubitabam, quodcunque esset quod faterentur (such are the words of Pliny), pervicaciam certe et inflexibilem obstinationem debere puniri.

[18] See Mosheim's Ecclesiastical History, vol. i. p. 101, and Spanheim, Remarques sur les Césars de Julien, p. 468, &c.

[19] See Justin Martyr, Apolog. i. 35 [c. 26, *sqq.*], ii. 14 [12]. Athenagoras in Legation, c. 27. Tertullian, Apolog. c. 7, 8, 9. Minucius Felix, c. 9, 10, 30, 31. The last of these writers relates the accusation in the most elegant and circumstantial manner. The answer of Tertullian is the boldest and most vigorous.

adversary. The Christians, with the intrepid security of innocence, appeal from the voice of rumour to the equity of the magistrates. They acknowledge that, if any proof can be produced of the crimes which calumny has imputed to them, they are worthy of the most severe punishment. They provoke the punishment, and they challenge the proof. At the same time they urge, with equal truth and propriety, that the charge is not less devoid of probability than it is destitute of evidence; they ask whether any one can seriously believe that the pure and holy precepts of the Gospel, which so frequently restrain the use of the most lawful enjoyments, should inculcate the practice of the most abominable crimes; that a large society should resolve to dishonour itself in the eyes of its own members; and that a great number of persons of either sex, and every age and character, insensible to the fear of death or infamy, should consent to violate those principles which nature and education had imprinted most deeply in their minds.[20] Nothing, it should seem, could weaken the force or destroy the effect of so unanswerable a justification, unless it were the injudicious conduct of the apologists themselves, who betrayed the common cause of religion, to gratify their devout hatred to the domestic enemies of the church. It was sometimes faintly insinuated, and sometimes boldly asserted, that the same bloody sacrifices, and the same incestuous festivals, which were so falsely ascribed to the orthodox believers, were in reality celebrated by the Marcionites, by the Carpocratians, and by several other sects of the Gnostics, who, notwithstanding they might deviate into the paths of heresy, were still actuated by the sentiments of men, and still governed by the precepts of Christianity.[21] Accusations of a similar kind were retorted upon the church by the schismatics who had departed from its communion;[22] and it was confessed on all sides that the most

[20] In the persecution of Lyons, some Gentile slaves were compelled, by the fear of tortures, to accuse their Christian master. The church of Lyons, writing to their brethren of Asia, treat the horrid charge with proper indignation and contempt. Euseb. Hist. Eccles. v. 1.

[21] See Justin Martyr, Apolog. i. 35 [26]. Irenæus adv. Hæres. i. 24. Clemens Alexandrin., Stromat. l. iii. p. 438 [ed. Paris; ed. Migne, vol. 6, p. 1136]. Euseb. iv. 8. It would be tedious and disgusting to relate all that the succeeding writers have imagined, all that Epiphanius has received, and all that Tillemont has copied. M. de Beausobre (Hist. du Manichéisme, l. ix. c. 8, 9) has exposed, with great spirit, the disingenuous arts of Augustin and Pope Leo I.

[22] When Tertullian became a Montanist, he aspersed the morals of the church which he had so resolutely defended. "Sed majoris est Agape, quia per hanc adolescentes tui cum sororibus dormiunt, appendices scilicet gulæ lascivia et luxuria." De Jejuniis, c. 17. The 35th canon of the council of Illiberis provides

scandalous licentiousness of manners prevailed among great
numbers of those who affected the name of Christians. A
Pagan magistrate, who possessed neither leisure nor abilities to
discern the almost imperceptible line which divides the orthodox
faith from heretical pravity, might easily have imagined that
their mutual animosity had extorted the discovery of their
common guilt. It was fortunate for the repose, or at least for
the reputation, of the first Christians, that the magistrates sometimes proceeded with more temper and moderation than is
usually consistent with religious zeal, and that they reported, as
the impartial result of their judicial inquiry, that the sectaries
who had deserted the established worship appeared to them
sincere in their professions and blameless in their manners;
however they might incur, by their absurd and excessive
superstition, the censure of the laws.[23]

History, which undertakes to record the transactions of the
past, for the instruction of future, ages, would ill deserve that
honourable office, if she condescended to plead the cause of
tyrants, or to justify the maxims of persecution. It must, however, be acknowledged that the conduct of the emperors who
appeared the least favourable to the primitive church is by no
means so criminal as that of modern sovereigns who have
employed the arm of violence and terror against the religious
opinions of any part of their subjects. From their reflections,
or even from their own feelings, a Charles V. or a Louis XIV.
might have acquired a just knowledge of the rights of conscience,
of the obligation of faith, and of the innocence of error. But
the princes and magistrates of ancient Rome were strangers to
those principles which inspired and authorized the inflexible
obstinacy of the Christians in the cause of truth, nor could they
themselves discover in their own breasts any motive which
would have prompted them to refuse a legal, and as it were a
natural, submission to the sacred institutions of their country.
The same reason which contributes to alleviate the guilt, must
have tended to abate the rigour, of their persecutions. As
they were actuated, not by the furious zeal of bigots, but by the
temperate policy of legislators, contempt must often have relaxed,
and humanity must frequently have suspended, the execution of
those laws which they enacted against the humble and obscure

Idea of the conduct of the emperors towards the Christians

against the scandals which too often polluted the vigils of the church, and disgraced
the Christian name in the eyes of unbelievers.

[23] Tertullian (Apolog. c. 2) expatiates on the fair and honourable testimony of
Pliny, with much reason, and some declamation.

followers of Christ. From the general view of their character
and motives we might naturally conclude : I. That a considerable
time elapsed before they considered the new sectaries as an
object deserving of the attention of government. II. That, in
the conviction of any of their subjects who were accused of so
very singular a crime, they proceeded with caution and reluctance. III. That they were moderate in the use of punishments ; and IV. That the afflicted church enjoyed many intervals
of peace and tranquillity. Notwithstanding the careless indifference which the most copious and the most minute of the
Pagan writers have shewn to the affairs of the Christians,[24] it
may still be in our power to confirm each of these probable
suppositions by the evidence of authentic facts.

They neg-
lected the
Christians as
a sect of Jews

I. By the wise dispensation of Providence, a mysterious veil
was cast over the infancy of the church, which, till the faith of
the Christians was matured and their numbers were multiplied,
served to protect them not only from the malice, but even from
the knowledge, of the Pagan world. The slow and gradual
abolition of the Mosaic ceremonies afforded a safe and innocent
disguise to the more early proselytes of the Gospel. As they
were far the greater part of the race of Abraham, they were
distinguished by the peculiar mark of circumcision, offered up
their devotions in the Temple of Jerusalem till its final destruction, and received both the Law and the Prophets as the
genuine inspirations of the Deity. The Gentile converts, who
by a spiritual adoption had been associated to the hope of Israel,
were likewise confounded under the garb and appearance of
Jews,[25] and, as the Polytheists paid less regard to articles of
faith than to the external worship, the new sect, which carefully
concealed, or faintly announced, its future greatness and ambition, was permitted to shelter itself under the general toleration
which was granted to an ancient and celebrated people in the
Roman empire. It was not long, perhaps, before the Jews
themselves, animated with a fiercer zeal and a more jealous
faith, perceived the gradual separation of their Nazarene
brethren from the doctrine of the synagogue ; and they would
gladly have extinguished the dangerous heresy in the blood of
its adherents. But the decrees of heaven had already disarmed

[24] In the various compilation of the Augustan History, (a part of which was
composed under the reign of Constantine), there are not six lines which relate to
the Christians ; nor has the diligence of Xiphilin discovered their name in the large
history of Dion Cassius.

[25] An obscure passage of Suetonius (in Claud. c. 25) may seem to offer a proof
how strangely the Jews and Christians of Rome were confounded with each other.

their malice; and, though they might sometimes exert the licentious privilege of sedition, they no longer possessed the administration of criminal justice; nor did they find it easy to infuse into the calm breast of a Roman magistrate the rancour of their own zeal and prejudice. The provincial governors declared themselves ready to listen to any accusation that might affect the public safety; but, as soon as they were informed that it was a question not of facts but of words, a dispute relating only to the interpretation of the Jewish laws and prophecies, they deemed it unworthy of the majesty of Rome seriously to discuss the obscure differences which might arise among a barbarous and superstitious people. The innocence of the first Christians was protected by ignorance and contempt; and the tribunal of the Pagan magistrate often proved their most assured refuge against the fury of the synagogue.[26] If, indeed, we were disposed to adopt the traditions of a too credulous antiquity, we might relate the distant peregrinations, the wonderful achievements, and the various deaths, of the twelve apostles; but a more accurate inquiry will induce us to doubt whether any of those persons who had been witnesses to the miracles of Christ were permitted, beyond the limits of Palestine, to seal with their blood the truth of their testimony.[27] From the ordinary term of human life, it may very naturally be presumed that most of them were deceased before the discontent of the Jews broke out into that furious war which was terminated only by the ruin of Jerusalem. During a long period, from the death of Christ to that memorable rebellion, we cannot discover any traces of Roman intolerance, unless they are to be found in the sudden, the transient, but the cruel persecution, which was exercised by Nero against the Christians of the capital, thirty-five years after the former, and only two years before the latter of those great events. The character of the philosophic historian, to whom we are principally indebted for the knowledge of this singular transaction, would alone be sufficient to recommend it to our most attentive consideration.

In the tenth year of the reign of Nero, the capital of the The fire of Rome under the reign of Nero

[26] See in the xviiith and xxvth chapters of the Acts of the Apostles, the behaviour of Gallio, proconsul of Achaia, and of Festus, procurator of Judæa.

[27] In the time of Tertullian and Clemens of Alexandria, the glory of martyrdom was confined to St. Peter, St. Paul, and St. James. It was gradually bestowed on the rest of the apostles, by the more recent Greeks, who prudently selected for the theatre of their preaching and sufferings, some remote country beyond the limits of the Roman empire. See Mosheim p. 81, and Tillemont, Mémoires Ecclésiastiques, tom. i. part iii.

[A.D. 65] empire was afflicted by a fire which raged beyond the memory or example of former ages. [28] The monuments of Grecian art and of Roman virtue, the trophies of the Punic and Gallic wars, the most holy temples, and the most splendid palaces were involved in one common destruction. Of the fourteen regions or quarters into which Rome was divided, four only subsisted entire, three were levelled with the ground, and the remaining seven, which had experienced the fury of the flames, displayed a melancholy prospect of ruin and desolation. The vigilance of government appears not to have neglected any of the precautions which might alleviate the sense of so dreadful a calamity. The Imperial gardens were thrown open to the distressed multitude, temporary buildings were erected for their accommodation, and a plentiful supply of corn and provisions was distributed at a very moderate price. [29] The most generous policy seemed to have dictated the edicts which regulated the disposition of the streets and the construction of private houses ; and, as it usually happens in an age of prosperity, the conflagration of Rome, in the course of a few years, produced a new city, more regular and more beautiful than the former. But all the prudence and humanity affected by Nero on this occasion were insufficient to preserve him from the popular suspicion. Every crime might be imputed to the assassin of his wife and mother ; nor could the prince who prostituted his person and dignity on the theatre be deemed incapable of the most extravagant folly. The voice of rumour accused the emperor as the incendiary of his own capital ; and, as the most incredible stories are the best adapted to the genius of an enraged people, it was gravely reported, and firmly believed, that Nero, enjoying the calamity which he had occasioned, amused himself with singing to his lyre the destruction of ancient Troy. [30] To divert a suspicion which the power of despotism was unable to suppress the emperor resolved to substitute in his own place some fictitious criminals. " With this view (continues Tacitus) he inflicted the most exquisite tortures on those men, who, under the vulgar appellation of Christians, were already branded with deserved infamy. They derived their name and origin from

Cruel punish-
ment of the
Christians as
the incen-
diaries of the
city

[28] Tacit. Annal. xv. 38—44. Sueton. in Neron. c. 38. Dion Cassius, l. lxii. p. 1014 [c. 16]. Orosius, vii. 7.

[29] The price of wheat (probably of the *modius*) was reduced as low as *terni nummi;* which would be equivalent to about fifteen shillings the English quarter.

[30] We may observe, that the rumour is mentioned by Tacitus with a very becoming distrust and hesitation, whilst it is greedily transcribed by Suetonius, and solemnly confirmed by Dion.

Christ, who, in the reign of Tiberius, had suffered death, by the sentence of the procurator Pontius Pilate.[31] For a while this dire superstition was checked ; but it again burst forth, and not only spread itself over Judæa, the first seat of this mischievous sect, but was even introduced into Rome, the common asylum which receives and protects whatever is impure, whatever is atrocious. The confessions of those who were seized, discovered a great multitude of their accomplices, and they were all convicted, not so much for the crime of setting fire to the city, as for their hatred of human kind.[32] They died in torments, and their torments were embittered by insult and derision. Some were nailed on crosses ; others sewn up in the skins of wild beasts, and exposed to the fury of dogs ; others again, smeared over with combustible materials, were used as torches to illuminate the darkness of the night. The gardens of Nero were destined for the melancholy spectacle, which was accompanied with a horse race, and honoured with the presence of the emperor, who mingled with the populace in the dress and attitude of a charioteer. The guilt of the Christians deserved, indeed, the most exemplary punishment, but the public abhorrence was changed into commiseration, from the opinion that those unhappy wretches were sacrificed, not so much to the public welfare, as to the cruelty of a jealous tyrant."[33] Those who survey, with a curious eye, the revolutions of mankind may observe that the gardens and circus of Nero on the Vatican, which were polluted with the blood of the first Christians, have

[31] This testimony is alone sufficient to expose the anachronism of the Jews, who place the birth of Christ near a century sooner (Basnage, Histoire des Juifs, l. v. c. 14, 15). We may learn from Josephus (Antiquitat. xviii. 3), that the procuratorship of Pilate corresponded with the last ten years of Tiberius, A.D. 27—37. As to the particular time of the death of Christ, a very early tradition fixed it to the 25th of March, A.D. 29, under the consulship of the two Gemini (Tertullian adv. Judæos, c. 8). This date, which is adopted by Pagi, cardinal Noris, and Le Clerc, seems at least as probable as the vulgar æra, which is placed (I know not from what conjectures) four years later. [See above, p. 58, n. 158.]

[32] *Odio humani generis convicti.* These words may either signify the hatred of mankind towards the Christians, or the hatred of the Christians towards mankind. I have preferred the latter sense, as the most agreeable to the style of Tacitus, and to the popular error, of which a precept of the Gospel (see Luke xiv. 26) had been, perhaps, the innocent occasion. My interpretation is justified by the authority of Lipsius ; of the Italian, the French, and the English translators of Tacitus ; of Mosheim (p. 102), of Le Clerc (Historia Ecclesiast. p. 427), of Dr. Lardner (Testimonies, vol. i. p. 345), and of the bishop of Gloucester (Divine Legation, vol. iii. p. 38). But as the word *convicti* does not unite very happily with the rest of the sentence, James Gronovius has preferred the reading of *conjuncti*, which is authorized by the valuable Ms. of Florence. [The interpretation adopted by Gibbon is certainly correct, but there is no reason to question the reading *convicti*.]

[33] Tacit. Annal. xv. 44.

been rendered still more famous by the triumph and by the abuse of the persecuted religion. On the same spot,[34] a temple, which far surpasses the ancient glories of the Capitol, has been since erected by the Christian Pontiffs, who, deriving their claim of universal dominion from an humble fisherman of Galilee, have succeeded to the throne of the Cæsars, given laws to the barbarian conquerors of Rome, and extended their spiritual jurisdiction from the coast of the Baltic to the shores of the Pacific Ocean.

But it would be improper to dismiss this account of Nero's persecution, till we have made some observations, that may serve to remove the difficulties with which it is perplexed and to throw some light on the subsequent history of the church.

Remarks on the passage of Tacitus, relative to the persecution of the Christians by Nero

1. The most sceptical criticism is obliged to respect the truth of this extraordinary fact, and the integrity of this celebrated passage of Tacitus. The former is confirmed by the diligent and accurate Suetonius, who mentions the punishment which Nero inflicted on the Christians, a sect of men who had embraced a new and criminal superstition.[35] The latter may be proved by the consent of the most ancient manuscripts; by the inimitable character of the style of Tacitus; by his reputation, which guarded his text from the interpolations of pious fraud; and by the purport of his narration, which accused the first Christians of the most atrocious crimes, without insinuating that they possessed any miraculous or even magical powers above the rest of mankind.[36]   2. Notwithstanding it is probable that

[34] Nardini Roma Antica, p. 487. Donatus de Româ Antiquâ, l. iii. p. 449.

[35] Sueton. in Nerone, c. 16. The epithet of *malefica*, which some sagacious commentators have translated *magical*, is considered by the more rational Mosheim as only synonymous to the *exitiabilis* of Tacitus.

[36] The passage concerning Jesus Christ, which was inserted into the text of Josephus between the time of Origen and that of Eusebius, may furnish an example of no vulgar forgery. The accomplishment of the prophecies, the virtues, miracles and resurrection of Jesus are distinctly related. Josephus acknowledges that he was the Messiah, and hesitates whether he should call him a man. If any doubt can still remain concerning this celebrated passage, the reader may examine the pointed objections of Le Fevre (Havercamp. Joseph. tom. ii. p. 267—273), the laboured answers of Daubuz (p. 187—232), and the masterly reply (Bibliothèque Ancienne et Moderne, tom. vii. p. 237—288) of an anonymous critic, whom I believe to have been the learned Abbé de Longuerue. [Most unluckily book xviii. of the Antiquities, in which the passage occurs (c. 3, 3), is not contained in the Palatinus, the best Ms. of the work. It has found defenders in recent times, and Ewald has given reasons for regarding it as not entirely spurious but tainted with interpolations. There is another noteworthy passage in xx. 9, 1, about the death of St. James, "brother of Jesus, called the Christ".]

Tacitus was born some years before the fire of Rome,[37] he could derive only from reading and conversation the knowledge of an event which happened during his infancy. Before he gave himself to the Public, he calmly waited till his genius had attained its full maturity, and he was more than forty years of age, when a grateful regard for the memory of the virtuous Agricola extorted from him the most early of those historical compositions which will delight and instruct the most distant posterity. After making a trial of his strength in the life of Agricola and the description of Germany, he conceived, and at length executed, a more arduous work ; the history of Rome, in thirty books, from the fall of Nero to the accession of Nerva. The administration of Nerva introduced an age of justice and prosperity, which Tacitus had destined for the occupation of his old age ;[38] but, when he took a nearer view of his subject, judging, perhaps, that it was a more honourable or a less invidious office to record the vices of past tyrants than to celebrate the virtues of a reigning monarch, he chose rather to relate, under the form of annals, the actions of the four immediate successors of Augustus. To collect, to dispose, and to adorn a series of fourscore years in an immortal work, every sentence of which is pregnant with the deepest observations and the most lively images, was an undertaking sufficient to exercise the genius of Tacitus himself during the greatest part of his life. In the last years of the reign of Trajan, whilst the victorious monarch extended the power of Rome beyond its ancient limits, the historian was describing, in the second and fourth books of his annals, the tyranny of Tiberius ;[39] and the emperor Hadrian must have succeeded to the throne, before Tacitus, in the regular prosecution of his work, could relate the fire of the capital and the cruelty of Nero towards the unfortunate Christians. At the distance of sixty years, it was the duty of the annalist to adopt the narratives of contemporaries ; but it was natural for the philosopher to indulge himself in the description of the origin, the progress, and the character of the new sect, not so much according to the knowledge or prejudices of the age of Nero, as according to those of the time of Hadrian.

3. Tacitus very frequently trusts to the curiosity or reflection

[37] See the lives of Tacitus, by Lipsius and the Abbé de la Bléterie, Dictionnaire de Bayle à l'article TACITE, and Fabricius, Biblioth. Latin. tom. ii. p. 386, edit. Ernest.

[38] Principatum Divi Nervæ et imperium Trajani, uberiorem securioremque materiam senectuti seposui. Tacit. Hist. i. [1].

[39] See Tacit. Annal. ii. 61, iv. 4.

of his readers to supply those intermediate circumstances and ideas which, in his extreme conciseness, he has thought proper to suppress. We may, therefore, presume to imagine some probable cause which could direct the cruelty of Nero against the Christians of Rome, whose obscurity, as well as innocence, should have shielded them from his indignation, and even from his notice. The Jews, who were numerous in the capital, and oppressed in their own country, were a much fitter object for the suspicions of the emperor and of the people ; nor did it seem unlikely that a vanquished nation, who already discovered their abhorrence of the Roman yoke, might have recourse to the most atrocious means of gratifying their implacable revenge. But the Jews possessed very powerful advocates in the palace, and even in the heart of the tyrant ; his wife and mistress, the beautiful Poppæa, and a favourite player of the race of Abraham, who had already employed their intercession in behalf of the obnoxious people.[40] In their room it was necessary to offer some other victims, and it might easily be suggested, that, although the genuine followers of Moses were innocent of the fire of Rome, there had arisen among them a new and pernicious sect of GALILÆANS, which was capable of the most horrid crimes. Under the appellation of GALILÆANS, two distinctions of men were confounded, the most opposite to each other in their manners and principles ; the disciples who had embraced the faith of Jesus of Nazareth,[41] and the zealots who had followed the standard of Judas the Gaulonite.[42] The former were the friends, and the latter were the enemies, of human kind ; and the only resemblance between them consisted in the same inflexible constancy which, in the defence of their cause, rendered them insensible of death and tortures. The followers of Judas, who impelled their countrymen into rebellion, were soon buried under the ruins of Jerusalem ; whilst those of Jesus, known by the more celebrated name of Christians, diffused

---

[40] The player's name was Aliturus. Through the same channel, Josephus (De Vitâ suâ, c. 3) about two years before, had obtained the pardon and release of some Jewish priests, who were prisoners at Rome.

[41] The learned Dr. Lardner (Jewish and Heathen Testimonies, vol. ii. p. 102, 103), has proved that the name of Galilæans was a very ancient and, perhaps, the primitive appellation of the Christians.

[42] Joseph. Antiquitat. xviii. 1, 2. Tillemont, Ruine des Juifs, p. 742. The sons of Judas were crucified in the time of Claudius. His grandson Eleazar, after Jerusalem was taken, defended a strong fortress with 960 of his most desperate followers. When the battering ram had made a breach, they turned their swords against their wives, their children, and at length against their own breasts. They died to the last man.

themselves over the Roman empire. How natural was it for Tacitus, in the time of Hadrian, to appropriate to the Christians the guilt and the sufferings which he might, with far greater truth and justice, have attributed to a sect whose odious memory was almost extinguished! 4. Whatever opinion may be entertained of this conjecture (for it is no more than a conjecture), it is evident that the effect, as well as the cause, of Nero's persecution were confined to the walls of Rome;[43] that the religious tenets of the Galilæans, or Christians, were never made a subject of punishment or even of inquiry; and that, as the idea of their sufferings was, for a long time, connected with the idea of cruelty and injustice, the moderation of succeeding princes inclined them to spare a sect, oppressed by a tyrant whose rage had been usually directed against virtue and innocence.

It is somewhat remarkable that the flames of war consumed almost at the same time the temple of Jerusalem and the Capitol of Rome;[44] and it appears no less singular that the tribute which devotion had destined to the former should have been converted by the power of an assaulting victor to restore and adorn the splendour of the latter.[45] The emperors levied a general capitation tax on the Jewish people; and, although the sum assessed on the head of each individual was inconsiderable, the use for which it was designed, and the severity with which it was exacted, were considered as an intolerable grievance.[46] Since the officers of the revenue extended their unjust claim to many persons who were strangers to the blood or religion of the Jews, it was impossible that the Christians, who had so often

Oppression of the Jews and Christians by Domitian

[43] See Dodwell. Paucitat. Mart. l. xiii. The Spanish Inscription in Gruter, p. 238, No. 9, is a manifest and acknowledged forgery, contrived by that noted impostor Cyriacus of Ancona, to flatter the pride and prejudices of the Spaniards. See Ferreras, Histoire d Espagne, tom. i. p. 192. [Gibbon's conjecture is not happy, and need not be considered seriously.]

[44] The Capitol was burnt during the civil war between Vitellius and Vespasian, the 19th of December, A.D. 69. On the 10th of August, A.D. 70, the Temple of Jerusalem was destroyed by the hands of the Jews themselves, rather than by those of the Romans.

[45] The new Capitol was dedicated by Domitian. Sueton. in Domitian. c. 5. Plutarch in Poplicola, tom. i. p. 230, edit. Bryan. The gilding alone cost 12,000 talents (above two millions and a half). It was the opinion of Martial (l. ix. Epigram 3) that, if the emperor had called in his debts, Jupiter himself, even though he had made a general auction of Olympus, would have been unable to pay two shillings in the pound.

[46] With regard to the tribute, see Dion Cassius, l. lxvi. p. 1082 [c. 7] with Reimarus's notes. Spanheim, de Usû Numismatum, tom. ii. p. 571, and Basnage, Histoire des Juifs, l. vii. c. 2,

sheltered themselves under the shade of the synagogue, should now escape this rapacious persecution. Anxious as they were to avoid the slightest infection of idolatry, their conscience forbade them to contribute to the honour of that dæmon who had assumed the character of the Capitoline Jupiter. As a very numerous, though declining, party among the Christians still adhered to the law of Moses, their efforts to dissemble their Jewish origin were detected by the decisive test of circumcision,[47] nor were the Roman magistrates at leisure to inquire into the difference of their religious tenets. Among the Christians who were brought before the tribunal of the emperor, or, as it seems more probable, before that of the procurator of Judæa, two persons are said to have appeared, distinguished by their extraction, which was more truly noble than that of the greatest monarchs. These were the grandsons of St. Jude the apostle, who himself was the brother of Jesus Christ.[48] Their natural pretensions to the throne of David might perhaps attract the respect of the people, and excite the jealousy of the governor; but the meanness of their garb and the simplicity of their answers soon convinced him that they were neither desirous nor capable of disturbing the peace of the Roman empire. They frankly confessed their royal origin and their near relation to the Messiah; but they disclaimed any temporal views, and professed that his kingdom, which they devoutly expected, was purely of a spiritual and angelic nature. When they were examined concerning their fortune and occupation, they shewed their hands hardened with daily labour, and declared that they derived their whole subsistence from the cultivation of a farm near the village of Cocaba, of the extent of about twenty-four English acres,[49] and of the value of

47 Suetonius (in Domitian. c. 12) had seen an old man of ninety publicly examined before the procurator's tribunal. This is what Martial calls, Mentula tributis damnata.

48 This appellation was at first understood in the most obvious sense, and it was supposed that the brothers of Jesus were the lawful issue of Joseph and of Mary. A devout respect for the virginity of the Mother of God suggested to the Gnostics, and afterwards to the orthodox Greeks, the expedient of bestowing a second wife on Joseph. The Latins (from the time of Jerome) improved on that hint, asserted the perpetual celibacy of Joseph, and justified, by many similar examples, the new interpretation that Jude, as well as Simon and James, who are styled the brothers of Jesus Christ, were only his first cousins. See Tillemont, Mém. Ecclésiast. tom. i. part iii. and Beausobre, Hist. Critique du Manichéisme, l. ii. c. 2.

49 Thirty-nine πλέθρα, squares of an hundred feet each, which, if strictly computed, would scarcely amount to nine acres. But the probability of circumstances, the practice of other Greek writers, and the authority of M. de Valois, inclined me to believe that the πλέθρον is used to express the Roman jugerum,

nine thousand drachms, or three hundred pounds sterling. The grandsons of St. Jude were dismissed with compassion and contempt.[50]

But, although the obscurity of the house of David might pro- Execution of tect them from the suspicions of a tyrant, the present greatness consul the of his own family alarmed the pusillanimous temper of Domitian, [A.D. 95] which could only be appeased by the blood of those Romans whom he either feared, or hated, or esteemed. Of the two sons of his uncle Flavius Sabinus,[51] the elder was soon convicted of treasonable intentions, and the younger, who bore the name of Flavius Clemens, was indebted for his safety to his want of courage and ability.[52] The emperor, for a long time, distinguished so harmless a kinsman by his favour and protection, bestowed on him his own niece Domitilla, adopted the children of that marriage to the hope of the succession, and invested their father with the honours of the consulship. But he had scarcely finished the term of his annual magistracy, when, on a slight pretence, he was condemned and executed ; Domitilla was banished to a desolate island on the coast of Campania ;[53] and sentences either of death or of confiscation were pronounced against a great number of persons who were involved in the same accusation. The guilt imputed to their charge was that of *Atheism* and *Jewish manners ;*[54] a singular association of ideas, which cannot with any propriety be applied except to the Christians, as they were obscurely and imperfectly viewed by the magistrates and by the writers of that period. On the strength of so probable an interpretation, and too eagerly admitting the suspicions of a tyrant as an evidence of their honourable crime, the church has placed both Clemens and Domitilla among its first martyrs, and has branded the cruelty of Domitian with the name of the second persecution. But

[50] Eusebius, iii. 20. The story is taken from Hegesippus.

[51] See the death and character of Sabinus in Tacitus (Hist. iii. 74, 75). Sabinus was the elder brother, and, till the accession of Vespasian, had been considered as the principal support of the Flavian family.

[52] Flavium Clementem patruelem suum *contemptissimæ inertiæ* . . . ex tenuissimâ suspicione interemit. Sueton. in Domitian. c. 15.

[53] The isle of Pandataria, according to Dion. Bruttius Præsens (apud Euseb. iii. 18) banishes her to that of Pontia, which was not far distant from the other. That difference, and a mistake, either of Eusebius or of his transcribers, have given occasion to suppose two Domitillas, the wife and the niece of Clemens. See Tillemont, Mémoires Ecclésiastiques, tom. ii. p. 224.

[54] Dion, l. lxvii. p. 1112 [c. 14]. If the Bruttius Præsens, from whom it is probable that he collected this account, was the correspondent of Pliny (Epistol. vii. 3), we may consider him as a contemporary writer,

this persecution (if it deserves that epithet) was of no long duration. A few months after the death of Clemens and the banishment of Domitilla, Stephen, a freedman belonging to the latter, who had enjoyed the favour, but who had not surely embraced the faith, of his mistress, assassinated the emperor in his palace.[55] The memory of Domitian was condemned by the senate ; his acts were rescinded ; his exiles recalled ; and under the gentle administration of Nerva, while the innocent were restored to their rank and fortunes, even the most guilty either obtained pardon or escaped punishment.[56]

[A.D. 96, Sept. 18]

II. About ten years afterwards, under the reign of Trajan, the younger Pliny was intrusted by his friend and master with the government of Bithynia and Pontus. He soon found himself at a loss to determine by what rule of justice or of law he should direct his conduct in the execution of an office the most repugnant to his humanity. Pliny had never assisted at any judicial proceedings against the Christians, with whose name alone he seems to be acquainted ; and he was totally uninformed with regard to the nature of their guilt, the method of their conviction, and the degree of their punishment. In this perplexity he had recourse to his usual expedient, of submitting to the wisdom of Trajan an impartial and, in some respects, a favourable account of the new superstition, requesting the emperor that he would condescend to resolve his doubts and to instruct his ignorance.[57] The life of Pliny had been employed in the acquisition of learning, and in the business of the world. Since the age of nineteen he had pleaded with distinction in the tribunals of Rome,[58] filled a place in the senate, had been invested with the honours of the consulship, and had formed very numerous connexions with every order of men, both in Italy and in the provinces. From *his* ignorance, therefore, we may derive some useful information. We may assure ourselves that when he accepted the government of Bithynia there were no general laws or decrees of the senate in force against the Christians ; that neither Trajan nor any of his virtuous predecessors, whose edicts were received into the civil

Ignorance of Pliny concerning the Christians
[Appointed legatus A.D. 111]

[A.D. 112]

---

[55] Suet. in Domit. c. 17.   Philostratus in Vit. Apollon. l. viii.

[56] Dion, l. lxviii. p. 1118 [c. 1].   Plin. Epistol. iv. 22.

[57] Plin. Epistol. x. 97.   The learned Mosheim expresses himself (p. 147, 232) with the highest approbation of Pliny's moderate and candid temper.   Notwithstanding Dr. Lardner's suspicions (see Jewish and Heathen Testimonies, vol. ii. p. 46), I am unable to discover any bigotry in his language or proceedings.

[58] Plin. Epist. v. 8.   He pleaded his first cause A.D. 81 ; the year after the famous eruptions of Mount Vesuvius, in which his uncle lost his life.

and criminal jurisprudence, had publicly declared their intentions concerning the new sect; and that, whatever proceedings had been carried on against the Christians, there were none of sufficient weight and authority to establish a precedent for the conduct of a Roman magistrate.

The answer of Trajan, to which the Christians of the succeeding age have frequently appealed, discovers as much regard for justice and humanity as could be reconciled with his mistaken notions of religious policy.[59] Instead of displaying the implacable zeal of an inquisitor, anxious to discover the most minute particles of heresy and exulting in the number of his victims, the emperor expresses much more solicitude to protect the security of the innocent than to prevent the escape of the guilty. He acknowledges the difficulty of fixing any general plan; but he lays down two salutary rules, which often afforded relief and support to the distressed Christians. Though he directs the magistrates to punish such persons as are legally convicted, he prohibits them, with a very humane inconsistency, from making any inquiries concerning the supposed criminals. Nor was the magistrate allowed to proceed on every kind of information. Anonymous charges the emperor rejects, as too repugnant to the equity of his government; and he strictly requires, for the conviction of those to whom the guilt of Christianity is imputed, the positive evidence of a fair and open accuser. It is likewise probable that the persons who assumed so invidious an office were obliged to declare the grounds of their suspicions, to specify (both in respect to time and place) the secret assemblies which their Christian adversary had frequented, and to disclose a great number of circumstances which were concealed with the most vigilant jealousy from the eye of the profane. If they succeeded in their prosecution, they were exposed to the resentment of a considerable and active party, to the censure of the more liberal portion of mankind, and to the ignominy which, in every age and country, has attended the character of an informer. If, on the contrary, they failed in their proofs, they incurred the severe, and perhaps capital, penalty which, according to a law published by the emperor Hadrian, was inflicted on those who falsely attributed to their fellow-citizens the crime of Christianity. The violence of

Trajan and his successors establish a legal mode of proceeding against them [A.D. 112]

---

[59] Plin. Epist. x. 98. [Tillemont's date, 104; Mommsen's, 112.] Tertullian (Apolog. c. 5) considers this rescript as a relaxation of the ancient penal laws, " quas Trajanus ex parte frustratus est"; and yet Tertullian, in another part of his Apology, exposes the inconsistency of prohibiting inquiries and enjoining punishments.

personal or superstitious animosity might sometimes prevail over the most natural apprehensions of disgrace and danger; but it cannot surely be imagined that accusations of so unpromising an appearance were either lightly or frequently undertaken by the Pagan subjects of the Roman empire.[60]

Popular
clamours

The expedient which was employed to elude the prudence of the laws affords a sufficient proof how effectually they disappointed the mischievous designs of private malice or superstitious zeal.   In a large and tumultuous assembly, the restraints of fear and shame, so forcible on the minds of individuals, are deprived of the greatest part of their influence.   The pious Christian, as he was desirous to obtain or to escape the glory of martyrdom, expected, either with impatience or with terror, the stated returns of the public games and festivals.   On those occasions, the inhabitants of the great cities of the empire were collected in the circus of the theatre, where every circumstance of the place, as well as of the ceremony, contributed to kindle their devotion and to extinguish their humanity.   Whilst the numerous spectators, crowned with garlands, perfumed with incense, purified with the blood of victims, and surrounded with the altars and statues of their tutelar deities, resigned themselves to the enjoyment of pleasures which they considered as an essential part of their religious worship; they recollected that the Christians alone abhorred the gods of mankind, and by their absence and melancholy on these solemn festivals seemed to insult or to lament the public felicity.   If the empire had been afflicted by any recent calamity, by a plague, a famine, or an unsuccessful war; if the Tiber had, or if the Nile had not, risen beyond its banks; if the earth had shaken, or if the temperate order of the seasons had been interrupted, the superstitious Pagans were convinced that the crimes and the impiety of the Christians, who were spared by the excessive lenity of the government, had at length provoked the Divine Justice. It was not among a licentious and exasperated populace that the forms of legal proceedings could be observed; it was not in an amphitheatre, stained with the blood of wild beasts and gladiators, that the voice of compassion could be heard.   The impatient clamours of the multitude denounced the Christians

---

[60] Eusebius (Hist. Ecclesiast. l. iv. c. 9) has preserved the edict of Hadrian. He has likewise (c. 13) given us one still more favourable under the name of Antoninus; the authenticity of which is not so universally allowed.   [See Appendix 6.]   The second Apology of Justin contains some curious particulars relative to the accusations of Christians.

as the enemies of gods and men, doomed them to the severest tortures, and, venturing to accuse by name some of the most distinguished of the new sectaries, required, with irresistible vehemence, that they should be instantly apprehended and cast to the lions.[61] The provincial governors and magistrates who presided in the public spectacles were usually inclined to gratify the inclinations, and to appease the rage, of the people by the sacrifice of a few obnoxious victims. But the wisdom of the emperors protected the church from the danger of these tumultuous clamours and irregular accusations, which they justly censured as repugnant both to the firmness and to the equity of their administration. The edicts of Hadrian and of Antoninus Pius expressly declared that the voice of the multitude should never be admitted as legal evidence to convict or to punish those unfortunate persons who had embraced the enthusiasm of the Christians.[62]

III. Punishment was not the inevitable consequence of con- Trials of the viction, and the Christians, whose guilt was the most clearly Christians proved by the testimony of witnesses, or even by their voluntary confession, still retained in their own power the alternative of life or death. It was not so much the past offence, as the actual resistance, which excited the indignation of the magistrate. He was persuaded that he offered them an easy pardon, since, if they consented to cast a few grains of incense upon the altar, they were dismissed from the tribunal in safety and with applause. It was esteemed the duty of a humane judge to endeavour to reclaim, rather than to punish, those deluded enthusiasts. Varying his tone according to the age, the sex, or the situation of the prisoners, he frequently condescended to set before their eyes every circumstance which could render life more pleasing, or death more terrible ; and to solicit, nay, to intreat them, that they would show some compassion to themselves, to their families, and to their friends.[63] If threats and persuasions proved ineffectual, he had often recourse to violence ; the scourge and the rack were called in to supply the deficiency of argument, and every art of cruelty was employed to subdue such inflexible and, as it appeared to the Pagans,

[61] See Tertullian (Apolog. c. 40). The acts of the martyrdom of Polycarp exhibit a lively picture of these tumults, which were usually fomented by the malice of the Jews.

[62] These regulations are inserted in the above-mentioned edicts of Hadrian and Pius. See the apology of Melito (apud Euseb. l. iv. c. 26).

[63] See the rescript of Trajan, and the conduct of Pliny. The most authentic acts of the martyrs abound in these exhortations.

such criminal obstinacy. The ancient apologists of Christianity
have censured, with equal truth and severity, the irregular
conduct of their persecutors, who, contrary to every principle
of judicial proceeding, admitted the use of torture, in order to
obtain not a confession but a denial of the crime which was the
object of their inquiry.[64] The monks of succeeding ages, who,
in their peaceful solitudes, entertained themselves with diversi-
fying the death and sufferings of the primitive martyrs, have
frequently invented torments of a much more refined and ingenious nature. In particular, it has pleased them to suppose
that the zeal of the Roman magistrates, disdaining every consideration of moral virtue or public decency, endeavoured to
seduce those whom they were unable to vanquish, and that,
by their orders, the most brutal violence was offered to those
whom they found it impossible to seduce. It is related that
pious females, who were prepared to despise death, were sometimes condemned to a more severe trial, and called upon to
determine whether they set a higher value on their religion or
on their chastity. The youths to whose licentious embraces
they were abandoned received a solemn exhortation from the
judge to exert their most strenuous efforts to maintain the
honour of Venus against the impious virgin who refused to burn
incense on her altars. Their violence, however, was commonly
disappointed ; and the seasonable interposition of some miraculous power preserved the chaste spouses of Christ from the
dishonour even of an involuntary defeat. We should not, indeed, neglect to remark that the more ancient, as well as
authentic, memorials of the church are seldom polluted with
these extravagant and indecent fictions.[65]

Humanity of
the Roman
magistrates
    The total disregard of truth and probability in the representa-
tion of these primitive martyrdoms was occasioned by a very
natural mistake. The ecclesiastical writers of the fourth or
fifth centuries ascribed to the magistrates of Rome the same
degree of implacable and unrelenting zeal which filled their
own breasts against the heretics or the idolaters of their own
times. It is not improbable that some of those persons who

[64] In particular, see Tertullian (Apolog. c. 2, 3), and Lactantius (Institut. Divin.
v. 9). Their reasonings are almost the same ; but we may discover that one of
these apologists had been a lawyer and the other a rhetorician.
[65] See two instances of this kind of torture in the Acta Sincera Martyrum
published by Ruinart, p. 160, 399. Jerome, in his Legend of Paul the Hermit,
tells a strange story of a young man, who was chained naked on a bed of flowers,
and assaulted by a beautiful and wanton courtezan. He quelled the rising temptation by biting off his tongue.

were raised to the dignities of the empire might have imbibed the prejudices of the populace, and that the cruel disposition of others might occasionally be stimulated by motives of avarice or of personal resentment.[66] But it is certain, and we may appeal to the grateful confessions of the first Christians, that the greatest part of those magistrates who exercised in the provinces the authority of the emperor, or of the senate, and to whose hands alone the jurisdiction of life and death was intrusted, behaved like men of polished manners and liberal educations, who respected the rules of justice, and who were conversant with the precepts of philosophy. They frequently declined the odious task of persecution, dismissed the charge with contempt, or suggested to the accused Christian some legal evasion by which he might elude the severity of the laws.[67] Whenever they were invested with a discretionary power,[68] they used it much less for the oppression than for the relief and benefit of the afflicted church. They were far from condemning all the Christians who were accused before their tribunal, and very far from punishing with death all those who were convicted of an obstinate adherence to the new superstition. Contenting themselves, for the most part, with the milder chastisements of imprisonment, exile, or slavery in the mines,[69] they left the unhappy victims of their justice some reason to hope that a prosperous event, the accession, the marriage, or the triumph of an emperor might speedily restore them, by a general pardon, to their former state. The martyrs, devoted to immediate execution by the Roman magistrates, appear to have been selected from the most opposite extremes. They were either bishops and presbyters, the persons the most distinguished among the Christians by their rank and influence, and whose example might strike terror into the whole sect;[70] or else they were

Inconsiderable number of martyrs

[66] The conversion of his wife provoked Claudius Herminianus, governor of Cappadocia, to treat the Christians with uncommon severity. Tertullian ad Scapulam, c. 3.

[67] Tertullian, in his epistle to the governor of Africa, mentions several remarkable instances of lenity and forbearance which had happened within his knowledge.

[68] Neque enim in universum aliquid quod quasi certam formam habeat constitui potest : an expression of Trajan which gave a very great latitude to the governors of provinces.

[69] In metalla damnamur, in insulas relegamur. Tertullian, Apolog. c. 12. The mines of Numidia contained nine bishops, with a proportionable number of their clergy and people, to whom Cyprian addressed a pious epistle of praise and comfort. See Cyprian, Epistol. 76, 77.

[70] Though we cannot receive with entire confidence either the epistles or the acts of Ignatius (they may be found in the 2d volume of the Apostolic Fathers), yet we may quote that bishop of Antioch as one of those *exemplary* martyrs. He was sent in chains to Rome as a public spectacle ; and, when he arrived at Troas, he

the meanest and most abject among them, particularly those of the servile condition, whose lives were esteemed of little value, and whose sufferings were viewed by the ancients with too careless an indifference.[71] The learned Origen, who, from his experience as well as reading, was intimately acquainted with the history of the Christians, declares, in the most express terms, that the number of martyrs was very inconsiderable.[72] His authority would alone be sufficient to annihilate that formidable army of martyrs whose relics, drawn for the most part from the catacombs of Rome, have replenished so many churches,[73] and whose marvellous achievements have been the subject of so many volumes of holy romance.[74] But the general assertion of Origen may be explained and confirmed by the particular testimony of his friend Dionysius, who, in the immense city of Alexandria, and under the rigorous persecution of Decius, reckons only ten men and seven women who suffered for the profession of the Christian name.[75]

---

received the pleasing intelligence that the persecution of Antioch was already at an end. [The Acts are certainly spurious; the Epistles are doubtless genuine, though some German critics still question Lightfoot's conclusions. The question is closely connected with the origin of episcopacy which is assumed in the Letters. They are edited by Lightfoot in his " Apostolic Fathers ". Cp. App. 4.]

[71] Among the martyrs of Lyons (Euseb. l. v. c. 1), the slave Blandina was distinguished by more exquisite tortures. Of the five martyrs so much celebrated in the acts of Felicitas and Perpetua, two were of a servile, and two others of a very mean, condition. [Acts of the Martyrdom of Perp. and Felic., Harris and Gifford, 1890.]

[72] Origen. advers. Celsum. l. iii. p. 116 [p. 929]. His words deserve to be transcribed. " 'Ολίγοι κατὰ καιροὺς, καὶ σφόδρα εὐαρίθμητοι περὶ [leg. ὑπὲρ] τῶν Χριστιανῶν θεοσεβείας τεθνήκασι."

[73] If we recollect that all the Plebeians of Rome were not Christians, and that all the Christians were not saints and martyrs, we may judge with how much safety religious honours can be ascribed to bones or urns indiscriminately taken from the public burial-place. After ten centuries of a very free and open trade, some suspicions have arisen among the more learned Catholics. They now require, as a proof of sanctity and martyrdom, the letters B. M., a vial full of red liquor, supposed to be blood, or the figure of a palm tree. But the two former signs are of little weight, and with regard to the last it is observed by the critics, 1. That the figure, as it is called, of a palm is perhaps a cypress, and perhaps only a stop, the flourish of a comma, used in the monumental inscriptions. 2. That the palm was the symbol of victory among the Pagans. 3. That among the Christians it served as the emblem, not only of martyrdom, but in general of a joyful resurrection. See the epistle of P. Mabillon, on the worship of unknown saints, and Muratori sopra le Antichità Italiane, Dissertat. lviii.

[74] As a specimen of these legends, we may be satisfied with 10'000 Christian soldiers crucified in one day, either by Trajan or Hadrian, on Mount Ararat. See Baronius ad Martyrologium Romanum; Tillemont, Mém. Ecclésiast. tom. ii. part ii. p. 438; and Geddes's Miscellanies, vol. ii. p. 203. The abbreviation of MIL. which may signify either soldiers or thousands is said to have occasioned some extraordinary mistakes.

[75] Dionysius ap. Euseb. l. vi. c. 41. One of the seventeen was likewise accused of robbery [falsely].

During the same period of persecution, the zealous, the eloquent, the ambitious Cyprian, governed the church, not only of Carthage, but even of Africa. He possessed every quality which could engage the reverence of the faithful or provoke the suspicions and resentment of the Pagan magistrates. His character as well as his station seemed to mark out that holy prelate as the most distinguished object of envy and of danger.[76] The experience, however, of the life of Cyprian is sufficient to prove that our fancy has exaggerated the perilous situation of a Christian bishop ; and that the dangers to which he was exposed were less imminent than those which temporal ambition is always prepared to encounter in the pursuit of honours. Four Roman emperors, with their families, their favourites, and their adherents, perished by the sword in the space of ten years, during which the bishop of Carthage guided, by his authority and eloquence, the counsels of the African church. It was only in the third year of his administration that he had reason, during a few months, to apprehend the severe edicts of Decius, the vigilance of the magistrate, and the clamours of the multitude, who loudly demanded that Cyprian, the leader of the Christians, should be thrown to the lions. Prudence suggested the necessity of a temporary retreat, and the voice of prudence was obeyed. He withdrew himself into an obscure solitude, from whence he could maintain a constant correspondence with the clergy and people of Carthage ; and, concealing himself till the tempest was past, he preserved his life, without relinquishing either his power or his reputation. His extreme caution did not, however, escape the censure of the more rigid Christians who lamented, or the reproaches of his personal enemies who insulted, a conduct which they considered as a pusillanimous and criminal desertion of the most sacred duty.[77] The propriety of reserving himself for the future exigencies of the church, the example of several holy bishops,[78] and the

---

[76] The letters of Cyprian exhibit a very curious and original picture both of the *man* and of the *times*. See likewise the two lives of Cyprian, composed with equal accuracy, though with very different views ; the one by Le Clerc (Bibliothèque Universelle, tom. xii. p. 208—378), the other by Tillemont, Mémoires Ecclésiastiques, tom. iv. part i. p. 76—459. [His name was Thascius Cæcilius Cyprianus. The best ed. of his works is that of Hartel in the Vienna Corpus Script. eccl. Lat.]

[77] See the polite but severe epistle of the clergy of Rome to the bishop of Carthage (Cyprian, Epist. 8, 9). Pontius labours with the greatest care and diligence to justify his master against the general censure.

[78] In particular those of Dionysius of Alexandria and Gregory Thaumaturgus of Neo-Cæsarea. See Euseb. Hist. Ecclesiast. l. vi. c. 40, and Mémoires de Tillemont, tom. iv. part. ii. p. 685.

divine admonitions which, as he declares himself, he frequently
received in visions and ecstacies, were the reasons alleged in his
justification.[79] But his best apology may be found in the
cheerful resolution with which, about eight years afterwards, he
suffered death in the cause of religion. The authentic history
of his martyrdom has been recorded with unusual candour and
impartiality. A short abstract, therefore, of its most important
circumstances will convey the clearest information of the spirit,
and of the forms, of the Roman persecutions.[80]

A.D. 257.
His banish-
ment
When Valerian was consul for the third, and Gallienus for
the fourth, time, Paternus, proconsul of Africa, summoned
Cyprian to appear in his private council-chamber. He there
acquainted him with the Imperial mandate which he had just
received,[81] that those who had abandoned the Roman religion
should immediately return to the practice of the ceremonies of
their ancestors. Cyprian replied without hesitation that he
was a Christian and a bishop, devoted to the worship of the
true and only Deity, to whom he offered up his daily supplications for the safety and prosperity of the two emperors, his
lawful sovereigns. With modest confidence he pleaded the
privilege of a citizen, in refusing to give any answer to some
invidious and, indeed, illegal questions which the proconsul
had proposed. A sentence of banishment was pronounced as
the penalty of Cyprian's disobedience; and he was conducted,
[Col. Iulia;
now Kurba]
without delay, to Curubis, a free and maritime city of Zeugitana,
in a pleasant situation, a fertile territory, and at the distance of
about forty miles from Carthage.[82] The exiled bishop enjoyed
the conveniencies of life and the consciousness of virtue. His

[79] See Cyprian, Epist. 16, and his life by Pontius. [Cp. Epp. 7, 12, 14, 43.]

[80] We have an original life of Cyprian by the deacon Pontius, the companion of
his exile, and the spectator of his death; and we likewise possess the ancient proconsular acts of his martyrdom. These two relations are consistent with each other
and with probability; and, what is somewhat remarkable, they are both unsullied
by any miraculous circumstances.

[81] It should seem that these were circular orders, sent at the same time to all the
governors. Dionysius (ap. Euseb. l. vii. c. 11) relates the history of his own banishment from Alexandria almost in the same manner. But, as he escaped and
survived the persecution, we must account him either more or less fortunate than
Cyprian.

[82] See Plin. Hist. Natur. v. 3. Cellarius, Geograph, Antiq. part iii. p. 96.
Shaw's Travels, p. 90; and for the adjacent country (which is terminated by Cape
Bona, or the promontory of Mercury), l'Afrique de Marmol. tom. ii. p. 494. There
are the remains of an aqueduct near Curubis, or Curbis, at present altered into
Gurbes [Kurba; Korbes is Col. Iulia Karpis]; and Dr. Shaw read an inscription
[C.I.L. 8, 980], which styles that city *Colonia Fulvia* [not Fulvia, but Iulia]. The
deacon Pontius (in Vit. Cyprian. c. 12) calls it "Apricum et competentem locum,
hospitium pro voluntate secretum, et quicquid apponi eis ante promissum est, qui
regnum et justitiam Dei quærunt".

reputation was diffused over Africa and Italy; an account of his behaviour was published for the edification of the Christian world;[83] and his solitude was frequently interrupted by the letters, the visits, and the congratulations of the faithful. On the arrival of a new proconsul in the province, the fortune of Cyprian appeared for some time to wear a still more favourable aspect. He was recalled from banishment; and, though not yet permitted to return to Carthage, his own gardens in the neighbourhood of the capital were assigned for the place of his residence.[84]

At length, exactly one year [85] after Cyprian was first appre- His condem-hended, Galerius Maximus, proconsul of Africa, received the [258 A.D.] Imperial warrant for the execution of the Christian teachers. The bishop of Carthage was sensible that he should be singled out for one of the first victims; and the frailty of nature tempted him to withdraw himself, by a secret flight, from the danger and the honour of martyrdom; but, soon recovering that fortitude which his character required,[86] he returned to his gardens, and patiently expected the ministers of death. Two officers of rank, who were intrusted with that commission, placed Cyprian between them in a chariot; and, as the proconsul was not then at leisure, they conducted him, not to a prison, but to a private house in Carthage, which belonged to one of them. An elegant supper was provided for the entertainment of the bishop, and his Christian friends were permitted for the last time to enjoy his society, whilst the streets were filled with a multitude of the faithful, anxious and alarmed at the approaching fate of their spiritual father.[87] In the morning he appeared before the tribunal of the proconsul, who, after informing himself of the name and situation of Cyprian, commanded him to offer sacrifice, and pressed him to reflect on the consequences of his disobedience. The refusal of Cyprian was firm and decisive; and the magistrate,

[83] See Cyprian, Epistol. 77. Edit. Fell.

[84] Upon his conversion, he had sold those gardens for the benefit of the poor. The indulgence of God (most probably the liberality of some Christian friend) restored them to Cyprian. See Pontius, c. 15.

[85] When Cyprian, a twelvemonth before, was sent into exile, he dreamt that he should be put to death the next day. The event made it necessary to explain that word as signifying a year. Pontius, c. 12.

[86] [But cp. Ep. 83.]

[87] Pontius (c. 15) acknowledges that Cyprian, with whom he supped, passed the night custodiâ delicatâ. The bishop exercised a last and very proper act of jurisdiction, by directing that the younger females who watched in the street should be removed from the dangers and temptations of a nocturnal crowd. Act. Proconsularia, c. 2.

when he had taken the opinion of his council, pronounced with some reluctance the sentence of death. It was conceived in the following terms: "That Thascius Cyprianus should be immediately beheaded, as the enemy of the gods of Rome, and as the chief and ringleader of a criminal association, which he had seduced into an impious resistance against the laws of the most holy emperors, Valerian and Gallienus".[88] The manner of his execution was the mildest and least painful that could be inflicted on a person convicted of any capital offence : nor was the use of torture admitted to obtain from the bishop of Carthage either the recantation of his principles or the discovery of his accomplices.

His martyr-
dom.
[Sept. 14]

As soon as the sentence was proclaimed, a general cry of "We will die with him" arose at once among the listening multitude of Christians who waited before the palace gates. The generous effusions of their zeal and affection were neither serviceable to Cyprian nor dangerous to themselves. He was led away under a guard of tribunes and centurions, without resistance and without insult, to the place of his execution, a spacious and level plain near the city, which was already filled with great numbers of spectators. His faithful presbyters and deacons were permitted to accompany their holy bishop. They assisted him in laying aside his upper garment, spread linen on the ground to catch the precious relics of his blood, and received his orders to bestow five-and-twenty pieces of gold on the executioner. The martyr then covered his face with his hands, and at one blow his head was separated from his body. His corpse remained during some hours exposed to the curiosity of the Gentiles ; but in the night it was removed, and transported in a triumphal procession and with a splendid illumination to the burial-place of the Christians. The funeral of Cyprian was publicly celebrated without receiving any interruption from the Roman magistrates ; and those among the faithful who had performed the last offices to his person and his memory were secure from the danger of inquiry or of punishment. It is remarkable that of so great a multitude of bishops in the province of Africa Cyprian was the first who was esteemed worthy to obtain the crown of martyrdom.[89]

---

[88] See the original sentence in the Acts, c. 4, and in Pontius, c. 17.   The latter expresses it in a more rhetorical manner.

[89] Pontius, c. 19.   M. de Tillemont (Mémoires, tom. iv. part i. p. 450, note 50) is not pleased with so positive an exclusion of any former martyrs of the episcopal rank.

It was in the choice of Cyprian either to die a martyr or to live Various in- an apostate, but on that choice depended the alternative of citements to martyrdom honour or infamy. Could we suppose that the bishop of Carthage had employed the profession of the Christian faith only as the instrument of his avarice or ambition, it was still incumbent on him to support the character which he had assumed ; [90] and, if he possessed the smallest degree of manly fortitude, rather to expose himself to the most cruel tortures than by a single act to exchange the reputation of a whole life for the abhorrence of his Christian brethren and the contempt of the Gentile world. But, if the zeal of Cyprian was supported by the sincere conviction of the truth of those doctrines which he preached, the crown of martyrdom must have appeared to him as an object of desire rather than of terror. It is not easy to extract any distinct ideas from the vague though eloquent declamations of the Fathers or to ascertain the degree of immortal glory and happiness which they confidently promised to those who were so fortunate as to shed their blood in the cause of religion.[91] They inculcated with becoming diligence that the fire of martyrdom supplied every defect and expiated every sin ; that, while the souls of ordinary Christians were obliged to pass through a slow and painful purification, the triumphant sufferers entered into the immediate fruition of eternal bliss, where, in the society of the patriarchs, the apostles, and the prophets, they reigned with Christ, and acted as his assessors in the universal judgment of mankind. The assurance of a lasting reputation upon earth, a motive so congenial to the vanity of human nature, often served to animate the courage of the martyrs. The honours

[90] Whatever opinion we may entertain of the character or principles of Thomas Becket, we must acknowledge that he suffered death with a constancy not unworthy of the primitive martyrs. See Lord Lyttelton's History of Henry II. vol. ii. p. 592, &c.

[91] See, in particular, the treatise of Cyprian de Lapsis, p. 87—98, edit. Fell. The learning of Dodwell (Dissertat. Cyprianic. xii. xiii.) and the ingenuity of Middleton (Free Inquiry, p. 162, &c.) have left scarcely anything to add concerning the merit, the honours, and the motives of the martyrs. [In the Decian persecution, many Christians had *lapsed* or denied their faith ; cp. Cyprian Epp. 11, 34, 59, &c. Afterwards the question arose as to their being received back into the church. Some were ready to receive them by indulgences from confessors and martyrs ; but there was another party (strong at Rome) which strenuously opposed this policy. Cyprian took a moderate view, and the First Council of Carthage decided that the church could remit all such offences, but that the indulgences of martyrs were ineffectual. The leading representative of the rigorous view was Novatian. The controversy was a precursor of the great Donatist schism, which turned on the same question of church discipline, see c. xxi. Cp. below, n. 101 and n. 104.]

which Rome or Athens bestowed on those citizens who had fallen in the cause of their country were cold and unmeaning demonstrations of respect, when compared with the ardent gratitude and devotion which the primitive church expressed towards the victorious champions of the faith. The annual commemoration of their virtues and sufferings was observed as a sacred ceremony, and at length terminated in religious worship. Among the Christians who had publicly confessed their religious principles, those who (as it very frequently happened) had been dismissed from the tribunal or the prisons of the Pagan magistrates obtained such honours as were justly due to their imperfect martyrdom and their generous resolution. The most pious females courted the permission of imprinting kisses on the fetters which they had worn and on the wounds which they had received. Their persons were esteemed holy, their decisions were admitted with deference, and they too often abused, by their spiritual pride and licentious manners, the pre-eminence which their zeal and intrepidity had acquired.[92] Distinctions like these, whilst they display the exalted merit, betray the inconsiderable number, of those who suffered and of those who died for the profession of Christianity.

Ardour of the first Christians   The sober discretion of the present age will more readily censure than admire, but can more easily admire than imitate, the fervour of the first Christians; who, according to the lively expression of Sulpicius Severus, desired martyrdom with more eagerness than his own contemporaries solicited a bishopric.[93] The epistles which Ignatius composed as he was carried in chains through the cities of Asia breathe sentiments the most repugnant to the ordinary feelings of human nature. He earnestly beseeches the Romans that, when he should be exposed in the amphitheatre, they would not, by their kind but unseasonable intercession, deprive him of the crown of glory; and he declares his resolution to provoke and irritate the wild beasts which might be employed as the instruments of his death.[94] Some stories are related of the courage of martyrs

---

[92] Cyprian. Epistol. 5, 6, 7, 22, 24, and de Unitat. Ecclesiæ. The number of pretended martyrs has been very much multiplied by the custom which was introduced of bestowing that honourable name on confessors.

[93] Certatim gloriosa in certamina ruebatur; multoque avidius tum martyria gloriosis mortibus quærebantur, quam nunc Episcopatus pravis ambitionibus appetuntur. Sulpicius Severus, l. ii. He might have omitted the word *nunc*.

[94] See Epist. ad Roman. c. 4, 5, ap. Patres Apostol. tom. ii. p. 27. It suited the purpose of Bishop Pearson (see Vindiciæ Ignatianæ, part ii. c. 9) to justify, by a profusion of examples and authorities, the sentiments of Ignatius.

who actually performed what Ignatius had intended; who exasperated the fury of the lions, pressed the executioner to hasten his office, cheerfully leaped into the fires which were kindled to consume them, and discovered a sensation of joy and pleasure in the midst of the most exquisite tortures. Several examples have been preserved of a zeal impatient of those restraints which the emperors had provided for the security of the church. The Christians sometimes supplied by their voluntary declaration the want of an accuser, rudely disturbed the public service of Paganism,[95] and, rushing in crowds round the tribunal of the magistrates, called upon them to pronounce and to inflict the sentence of the law. The behaviour of the Christians was too remarkable to escape the notice of the ancient philosophers; but they seem to have considered it with much less admiration than astonishment. Incapable of conceiving the motives which sometimes transported the fortitude of believers beyond the bounds of prudence or reason, they treated such an eagerness to die as the strange result of obstinate despair, of stupid insensibility, or of superstitious frenzy.[96] "Unhappy men!" exclaimed the proconsul Antoninus to the Christians of Asia; "unhappy men! if you are thus weary of your lives, is it so difficult for you to find ropes and precipices?"[97] He was extremely cautious (as it is observed by a learned and pious historian) of punishing men who had found no accusers but themselves, the Imperial laws not having made any provision for so unexpected a case; condemning, therefore, a few as a warning to their brethren, he dismissed the multitude with indignation and contempt.[98] Notwithstanding this real or affected disdain, the intrepid constancy of the faithful was productive of more salutary effects on those minds which nature or grace had disposed for the easy reception of religious truth.

[95] The story of Polyeuctes, on which Corneille has founded a very beautiful tragedy, is one of the most celebrated, though not perhaps the most authentic, instances of this excessive zeal. We should observe that the 60th canon of the council of Illiberis refuses the title of martyrs to those who exposed themselves to death by publicly destroying the idols. [Polyeuctes is first mentioned in Gregory of Tours, Hist. Fr. vii, 6. His *Acta* are published by Aubé in Polyeucte dans l'histoire, 1882.]

[96] See Epictetus, l. iv. c. 7 (though there is some doubt whether he alludes to the Christians), Marcus Antoninus de Rebus suis, l. xi. c. 3, Lucian. in Peregrin.

[97] Tertullian ad Scapul. c. 5. The learned are divided between three persons of the same name, who were all proconsuls of Asia. I am inclined to ascribe this story to Antoninus Pius, who was afterwards emperor; and who may have governed Asia under the reign of Trajan.

[98] Mosheim, de Rebus Christ. ante Constantin. p. 235.

On these melancholy occasions, there were many among the Gentiles who pitied, who admired, and who were converted. The generous enthusiasm was communicated from the sufferer to the spectators ; and the blood of martyrs, according to a well-known observation, became the seed of the church.

Gradual relaxation

But, although devotion had raised, and eloquence continued to inflame, this fever of the mind, it insensibly gave way to the more natural hopes and fears of the human heart, to the love of life, the apprehension of pain, and the horror of dissolution. The more prudent rulers of the church found themselves obliged to restrain the indiscreet ardour of their followers, and to distrust a constancy which too often abandoned them in the hour of trial.[99] As the lives of the faithful became less mortified and austere, they were every day less ambitious of the honours of martyrdom ; and the soldiers of Christ, instead of distinguishing themselves by voluntary deeds of heroism, frequently deserted their post, and fled in confusion before the enemy whom it was their duty to resist.   There were three methods, however, of escaping the flames of persecution, which were not attended with an equal degree of guilt : the first, indeed, was generally allowed to be innocent ; the second was of a doubtful, or at least of a venial, nature ; but the third implied a direct and criminal apostacy from the Christian faith.

Three methods of escaping martyrdom

I. A modern inquisitor would hear with surprise that, whenever an information was given to a Roman magistrate of any person within his jurisdiction who had embraced the sect of the Christians, the charge was communicated to the party accused, and that a convenient time was allowed him to settle his domestic concerns and to prepare an answer to the crime which was imputed to him.[100]   If he entertained any doubt of his own constancy, such a delay afforded him the opportunity of preserving his life and honour by flight, of withdrawing himself into some obscure retirement or some distant province, and of patiently expecting the return of peace and security.   A measure so consonant to reason was soon authorized by the advice and example of the most holy prelates, and seems to have been censured by few, except by the Montanists, who deviated into heresy by their strict and obstinate adherence to the rigour of

[99] See the Epistle of the Church at Smyrna, ap. Euseb. Hist. Eccles. l. iv. c. 15.

[100] In the second apology of Justin, there is a particular and very curious instance of this legal delay.   The same indulgence was granted to accused Christians in the persecution of Decius ; and Cyprian (de Lapsis) expressly mentions the " Dies negantibus præstitutus ".

ancient discipline.[101] II. The provincial governors, whose zeal was less prevalent than their avarice, had countenanced the practice of selling certificates, (or libels as they were called), which attested that the persons therein mentioned had complied with the laws and sacrificed to the Roman deities. By producing these false declarations, the opulent and timid Christians were enabled to silence the malice of an informer and to reconcile, in some measure, their safety with their religion. A slight penance atoned for this profane dissimulation.[102] III. In every persecution there were great numbers of unworthy Christians who publicly disowned or renounced the faith which they had professed ; and who confirmed the sincerity of their abjuration by the legal acts of burning incense or of offering sacrifices. Some of these apostates had yielded on the first menace or exhortation of the magistrate ; whilst the patience of others had been subdued by the length and repetition of tortures. The affrighted countenances of some betrayed their inward remorse, while others advanced, with confidence and alacrity, to the altars of the gods.[103] But the disguise which fear had imposed subsisted no longer than the present danger. As soon as the severity of the persecution was abated, the doors of the churches were assailed by the returning multitude of penitents, who detested their idolatrous submission, and who solicited, with equal ardour, but with various success, their readmission into the society of Christians.[104]

IV. Notwithstanding the general rules established for the conviction and punishment of the Christians, the fate of those sectaries, in an extensive and arbitrary government, must still, in a great measure, have depended on their own behaviour, the

Alternatives of severity and toleration

---

[101] Tertullian considers flight from persecution as an imperfect, but very criminal apostacy, as an impious attempt to elude the will of God, &c. &c. He has written a treatise on this subject (see p. 536—544, edit. Rigalt.), which is filled with the wildest fanaticism and the most incoherent declamation. It is, however, somewhat remarkable that Tertullian did not suffer martyrdom himself.

[102] The *Libellatici*, who are chiefly known by the writings of Cyprian, are described, with the utmost precision, in the copious commentary of Mosheim, p. 483 —489.

[103] Plin. Epistol. x. 97, Dionysius Alexandrin. ap. Euseb. l. vi. c. 41. Ad prima statim verba minantis inimici maximus fratrum numerus fidem suam prodidit ; nec prostratus est persecutionis impetu, sed voluntario lapsu seipsum prostravit. Cyprian. Opera, p. 89. Among these deserters were many priests, and even bishops.

[104] It was on this occasion that Cyprian wrote his treatise De Lapsis and many of his epistles. The controversy concerning the treatment of penitent apostates does not occur among the Christians of the preceding century. Shall we ascribe this to the superiority of their faith and courage or to our less intimate knowledge of their history ?

circumstances of the times, and the temper of their supreme as well as subordinate rulers. Zeal might sometimes provoke, and prudence might sometimes avert or assuage, the superstitious fury of the Pagans. A variety of motives might dispose the provincial governors either to enforce or to relax the execution of the laws ; and of these motives the most forcible was their regard not only for the public edicts, but for the secret intentions of the emperor, a glance from whose eye was sufficient to kindle or to extinguish the flames of persecution. As often as any occasional severities were exercised in the different parts of the empire, the primitive Christians lamented and perhaps magnified their own sufferings ; but the celebrated number of *ten* persecutions has been determined by the ecclesiastical writers of the fifth century, who possessed a more distinct view of the prosperous or adverse fortunes of the church, from the age of Nero to that of Diocletian. The ingenious parallels of the *ten* plagues of Egypt and of the *ten* horns of the Apocalypse first suggested this calculation to their minds ; and in their application of the faith of prophecy to the truth of history they were careful to select those reigns which were indeed the most hostile to the Christian cause.[105] But these transient persecutions served only to revive the zeal, and to restore the discipline, of the faithful : and the moments of extraordinary rigour were compensated by much longer intervals of peace and security. The indifference of some princes and the indulgence of others permitted the Christians to enjoy, though not perhaps a legal, yet an actual and public, toleration of their religion.

The apology of Tertullian contains two very ancient, very singular, but at the same time very suspicious, instances of Imperial clemency ; the edicts published by Tiberius and by Marcus Antoninus, and designed not only to protect the innocence of the Christians, but even to proclaim those stupendous miracles which had attested the truth of their doctrine. The first of these examples is attended with some difficulties which might perplex the sceptical mind.[106] We are required to believe *that* Pontius Pilate informed the emperor of the unjust sentence

The ten persecutions

Supposed edicts of Tiberius and Marcus Antoninus

---

[105] See Mosheim, p. 97. Sulpicius Severus was the first author of this computation ; though he seemed desirous of reserving the tenth and greatest persecution for the coming of the Antichrist.

[106] The testimony given by Pontius Pilate is first mentioned by Justin. The successive improvements which the story has acquired (as it passed through the hands of Tertullian, Eusebius, Epiphanius, Chrysostom, Orosius, Gregory of Tours, and the authors of the several editions of the acts of Pilate) are very fairly stated by Dom. Calmet, Dissertat. sur l'Ecriture, tom. iii. p. 651, &c.

of death which he had pronounced against an innocent, and, as it appeared, a divine, person ; and that, without acquiring the merit, he exposed himself to the danger, of martyrdom ; *that* Tiberius, who avowed his contempt for all religion, immediately conceived the design of placing the Jewish Messiah among the gods of Rome ; *that* his servile senate ventured to disobey the commands of their master ; *that* Tiberius, instead of resenting their refusal, contented himself with protecting the Christians from the severity of the laws, many years before such laws were enacted, or before the church had assumed any distinct name or existence ; and lastly, *that* the memory of this extraordinary transaction was preserved in the most public and authentic records, which escaped the knowledge of the historians of Greece and Rome, and were only visible to the eyes of an African Christian, who composed his apology one hundred and sixty years after the death of Tiberius. The edict of Marcus Antoninus is supposed to have been the effect of his devotion and gratitude for the miraculous deliverance which he had obtained in the Marcomannic war. The distress of the legions, the seasonable tempest of rain and hail, of thunder and lightning, and the dismay and defeat of the barbarians, have been celebrated by the eloquence of several Pagan writers. If there were any Christians in that army, it was natural that they should ascribe some merit to the fervent prayers which, in the moment of danger, they had offered up for their own and the public safety. But we are still assured by monuments of brass and marble, by the Imperial medals, and by the Antonine column, that neither the prince nor the people entertained any sense of this signal obligation, since they unanimously attribute their deliverance to the providence of Jupiter and to the interposition of Mercury. During the whole course of his reign, Marcus despised the Christians as a philosopher, and punished them as a sovereign.[107]

By a singular fatality, the hardships which they had endured under the government of a virtuous prince immediately ceased on the accession of a tyrant, and, as none except themselves had experienced the injustice of Marcus, so they alone were protected by the lenity of Commodus. The celebrated Marcia, the most favoured of his concubines, and who at length contrived the murder of her Imperial lover, entertained a singular affection for the oppressed church ; and, though it was impos- *State of the Christians in the reigns of Commodus and Severus. A.D. 180*

---

[107] On this miracle, as it is commonly called, of the Thundering Legion, see the admirable criticism of Mr. Moyle, in his Works, vol. ii. p. 81—390.

sible that she could reconcile the practice of vice with the precepts of the Gospel, she might hope to atone for the frailties of her sex and profession, by declaring herself the patroness of the Christians.[108]   Under the gracious protection of Marcia, they passed in safety the thirteen years of a cruel tyranny; and, when the empire was established in the house of Severus, they formed a domestic but more honourable connexion with the new court.   The emperor was persuaded that, in a dangerous sickness, he had derived some benefit, either spiritual or physical, from the holy oil with which one of his slaves had anointed him.   He always treated with peculiar distinction several persons of both sexes who had embraced the new religion.   The nurse as well as the preceptor of Caracalla were Christians; and, if that young prince ever betrayed a sentiment of humanity, it was occasioned by an incident which, however trifling, bore some relation to the cause of Christianity.[109]   Under the reign of Severus, the fury of the populace was checked ; the rigour of ancient laws was for some time suspended ; and the provincial governors were satisfied with receiving an annual present from the churches within their jurisdiction, as the price, or as the reward, of their moderation.[110]   The controversy concerning the precise time of the celebration of Easter armed the bishops of Asia and Italy against each other, and was considered as the most important business of this period of leisure and A.D. 198   tranquillity.[111]   Nor was the peace of the church interrupted till the increasing numbers of proselytes seem at length to have attracted the attention, and to have alienated the mind, of Severus.   With the design of restraining the progress of Chris-[c. A.D. 202]   tianity, he published an edict which, though it was designed to affect only the new converts, could not be carried into strict execution without exposing to danger and punishment the most zealous of their teachers and missionaries.   In this mitigated persecution, we may still discover the indulgent spirit of

---

[108] Dion Cassius, or rather his abbreviator Xiphilin, l. lxxii. p. 1206 [4].   Mr. Moyle (p. 266) has explained the condition of the church under the reign of Commodus.   [Cp. Görres, Jahrb. für protestantische Theologie X. 401 *sqq.*]

[109] Compare the life of Caracalla in the Augustan History with the epistle of Tertullian to Scapula.   Dr. Jortin (Remarks on Ecclesiastical History, vol. ii. p. 5, &c.) considers the cure of Severus by the means of holy oil, with a strong desire to convert it into a miracle.   [Wirth dates Tertullian's letter 21½ A.D.]

[110] Tertullian de Fugâ, c, 13.   The present was made during the feast of the Saturnalia ; and it is a matter of serious concern to Tertullian that the faithful should be confounded with the most infamous professions which purchased the connivance of the government.

[111] Euseb. l. v. c. 23, 24.   Mosheim, p. 435—447.

Rome and of Polytheism, which so readily admitted every excuse in favour of those who practised the religious ceremonies of their fathers.[112]

But the laws which Severus had enacted soon expired with the authority of that emperor; and the Christians, after this accidental tempest, enjoyed a calm of thirty-eight years.[113] Till this period they had usually held their assemblies in private houses and sequestered places. They were now permitted to erect and consecrate convenient edifices for the purpose of religious worship;[114] to purchase lands, even at Rome itself, for the use of the community; and to conduct the elections of their ecclesiastical ministers in so public, but at the same time in so exemplary, a manner as to deserve the respectful attention of the Gentiles.[115] This long repose of the church was accompanied with dignity. The reigns of those princes who derived their extraction from the Asiatic provinces proved the most favourable to the Christians; the eminent persons of the sect, instead of being reduced to implore the protection of a slave or concubine, were admitted into the palace in the honourable characters of priests and philosophers; and their mysterious doctrines, which were already diffused among the people, insensibly attracted the curiosity of their sovereign. When the empress Mammæa passed through Antioch, she expressed a desire of conversing with the celebrated Origen, the fame of whose piety and learning was spread over the East. Origen obeyed so flattering an invitation, and, though he could not expect to succeed in the conversion of an artful and ambitious woman, she listened with pleasure to his eloquent exhortations, and honourably dismissed him to his retirement in Palestine.[116] The sentiments of Mammæa were adopted by her son Alexander,

Of the successors of Severus. A.D. 211-249

112 Judæos fieri sub gravi pœna vetuit. Idem etiam de Christianis sanxit. Hist. August. p. 70 [x. 17, 1]. [See A. Wirth, Quaestiones Severianae, 1888.]

113 Sulpicius Severus, l. ii. p. 384. This computation (allowing for a single exception) is confirmed by the history of Eusebius, and by the writings of Cyprian.

114 The antiquity of Christian churches is discussed by Tillemont (Mémoires Ecclésiastiques, tom. iii. part ii. p. 68—72), and by Mr. Moyle (vol. i. p. 378—398). The former refers the first construction of them to the peace of Alexander Severus; the latter to the peace of Gallienus.

115 See the Augustan History, p. 130 [xviii. 45, 7]. The emperor Alexander adopted their method of publicly proposing the names of those persons who were candidates for ordination. It is true that the honour of this practice is likewise attributed to the Jews.

116 Euseb. Hist. Ecclesiast. l. vi. c. 21. Hieronym. de Script. Eccles. c. 54. Mammæa was styled a holy and pious woman, both by the Christians and the Pagans. From the former, therefore, it was impossible that she should deserve that honourable epithet.

and the philosophic devotion of that emperor was marked by a
singular but injudicious regard for the Christian religion. In
his domestic chapel he placed the statues of Abraham, of
Orpheus, of Apollonius, and of Christ, as an honour justly due
to those respectable sages who had instructed mankind in the
various modes of addressing their homage to the supreme and
universal deity.[117]   A purer faith, as well as worship, was openly
professed and practised among his household.   Bishops, perhaps

A.D. 235   for the first time, were seen at court ; and after the death of
Alexander, when the inhuman Maximin discharged his fury on
the favourites and servants of his unfortunate benefactor, a
great number of Christians, of every rank, and of both sexes,
were involved in the promiscuous massacre, which, on their
account, has improperly received the name of Persecution.[118]

Of Maximin,   Notwithstanding the cruel disposition of Maximin, the effects
Philip and   of his resentment against the Christians were of a very local
Decius   and temporary nature, and the pious Origen, who had been
proscribed as a devoted victim, was still reserved to convey the

A.D. 244   truths of the Gospel to the ear of monarchs.[119]   He addressed
several edifying letters to the emperor Philip, to his wife, and
to his mother ; and, as soon as that prince, who was born in
the neighbourhood of Palestine, had usurped the Imperial
sceptre, the Christians acquired a friend and a protector.   The
public and even partial favour of Philip towards the sectaries
of the new religion, and his constant reverence for the ministers
of the church, gave some colour to the suspicion, which prevailed in his own times, that the emperor himself was become
a convert to the faith ;[120]   and afforded some grounds for a

[117] See the Augustan History, p. 123 [xviii. 29, 2]. Mosheim (p. 465) seems to
refine too much on the domestic religion of Alexander.   His design of building a
public temple to Christ (Hist. August. p. 129, [ib. 43, 6]) and the objection which
was suggested either to him or in similar circumstances to Hadrian appear to have
no other foundation than an improbable report, invented by the Christians and
credulously adopted by an historian of the age of Constantine.

[118] Euseb. l. vi. c. 28.   It may be presumed that the success of the Christians
had exasperated the increasing bigotry of the Pagans.   Dion Cassius, who composed his history under the former reign, had most probably intended for the use
of his master those counsels of persecution which he ascribes to a better age and to
the favourite of Augustus.   Concerning this oration of Mæcenas, or rather of Dion,
I may refer to my own unbiassed opinion (vol. i. p. 55, Not. 25) and to the Abbé
de la Blèterie (Mémoires de l'Académie, tom. xxiv. p. 303, tom. xxv. p. 432).

[119] Orosius, l. vii. c. 19, mentions Origen as the object of Maximin's resentment ;
and Firmilianus, a Cappadocian bishop of that age, gives a just and confined idea
of this persecution (apud Cyprian. Epist. 75).

[120] The mention of those princes who were publicly supposed to be Christians,
as we find it in an epistle of Dionysius of Alexandria (ap. Euseb. l. vii. c. 10), evidently alludes to Philip and his family, and forms a contemporary evidence that

fable which was afterwards invented, that he had been purified by confession and penance from the guilt contracted by the murder of his innocent predecessor.[121] The fall of Philip in- A.D. 249 troduced, with the change of masters, a new system of government, so oppressive to the Christians that their former condition, ever since the time of Domitian, was represented as a state of perfect freedom and security, if compared with the rigorous treatment which they experienced under the short reign of Decius.[122] The virtues of that prince will scarcely allow us to suspect that he was actuated by a mean resentment against the favourites of his predecessor, and it is more reasonable to believe that, in the prosecution of his general design to restore the purity of Roman manners, he was desirous of delivering the empire from what he condemned as a recent and criminal [Edict 250 superstition. The bishops of the most considerable cities were A.D.] removed by exile or death; the vigilance of the magistrates prevented the clergy of Rome during sixteen months from proceeding to a new election; and it was the opinion of the Christians that the emperor would more patiently endure a competitor for the purple than a bishop in the capital.[123] Were it possible to suppose that the penetration of Decius had discovered pride under the disguise of humility, or that he could foresee the temporal dominion which might insensibly arise from the claims of spiritual authority, we might be less surprised

such a report had prevailed; but the Egyptian bishop, who lived at an humble distance from the court of Rome, expresses himself with a becoming diffidence concerning the truth of the fact. The epistles of Origen (which were extant in the time of Eusebius, see l. vi. c. 36) would most probably decide this curious, rather than important, question.

[121] Euseb. l. vi. c. 34. The story, as is usual, has been embellished by succeeding writers, and is confuted, with much superfluous learning, by Frederick Spanheim (Opera Varia, tom. ii. p. 400, &c.).

[122] Lactantius, de Mortibus Persecutorum, c. 3, 4. After celebrating the felicity and increase of the church, under a long succession of good princes, he adds, "Extitit post annos plurimos, execrabile animal, Decius, qui vexaret Ecclesiam". [The object of Decius was to enforce universal observance of the national religion, and he was successful in inducing many Christians to concede external compliance to the pagan ceremonials, by sacrifice and sprinkling incense on the altars of the gods. Many Christians purchased *libelli* from the magistrates certifying that they were free from the imputation of Christianity, and were hence called *libellatici*. The chief sources are Cyprian's Letters and his De Lapsis; fragments of Dionysius, Bishop of Alexandria, who hid himself during the persecution, in Eusebius, H. E., vi. 40—42; and the Vita of Gregory Thaumaturgus by Gregory of Nyssa.]

[123] Euseb. l. vi. c. 39. Cyprian. Epistol. 55. The see of Rome remained vacant from the martyrdom of Fabianus, the 20th of January, A.D. 250, till the election of Cornelius, the 4th of June, A.D. 251. Decius had probably left Rome, since he was killed before the end of that year.

that he should consider the successors of St. Peter as the most formidable rivals to those of Augustus.

Of Valerian,
Gallienus and
his successors.
A.D. 253-260

The administration of Valerian was distinguished by a levity and inconstancy, ill-suited to the gravity of the *Roman Censor*. In the first part of his reign, he surpassed in clemency those princes who had been suspected of an attachment to the Christian faith. In the last three years and a half, listening to the insinuations of a minister addicted to the superstitions of Egypt, he adopted the maxims, and imitated the severity, of his predecessor Decius.[124] The accession of Gallienus, which increased the calamities of the empire, restored peace to the church; and the Christians obtained the free exercise of their religion, by an edict addressed to the bishops and conceived in such terms as seemed to acknowledge their office and public character.[125] The ancient laws, without being formally repealed, were suffered to sink into oblivion; and (excepting only some hostile intentions which are attributed to the emperor Aurelian [126]) the disciples of Christ passed above forty years in a state of prosperity, far more dangerous to their virtue than the severest trials of persecution.

[261 A.D.]

Paul of Sam-
osata, his
manners.
A.D. 260

The story of Paul of Samosata, who filled the metropolitan see of Antioch, while the East was in the hands of Odenathus and Zenobia, may serve to illustrate the condition and character of the times. The wealth of that prelate was a sufficient evidence of his guilt, since it was neither derived from the inheritance of his fathers nor acquired by the arts of honest industry. But Paul considered the service of the church as a very lucrative profession.[127] His ecclesiastical jurisdiction was venal and rapacious; he extorted frequent contributions from the most

---

[124] Euseb. l. vii. c. 10. Mosheim (p. 548) has very clearly shown that the Præfect Macrianus and the Egyptian *Magus* are one and the same person.

[125] Eusebius (l. vii. c. 13) gives us a Greek version of this Latin edict, which seems to have been very concise. By another edict he directed that the *Cœmeteria* should be restored to the Christians.

[126] Euseb. l. vii. c. 30. Lactantius de M. P. c. 6. Hieronym. in Chron. p. 177 [ad ann. 2290]. Orosius, l. vii. c. 23. Their language is in general so ambiguous and incorrect that we are at a loss to determine how far Aurelian had carried his intentions before he was assassinated. [He intended to rescind the edict of Gallienus.] Most of the moderns (except Dodwell, Dissertat. Cyprian. xi. 64) have seized the occasion of gaining a few extraordinary martyrs.

[127] Paul was better pleased with the title of *Ducenarius*, than with that of bishop. The *Ducenarius* was an Imperial procurator, so called from his salary of two hundred *Sestertia*, or 1600*l.* a year. (See Salmasius ad Hist. August. p. 124.) Some critics suppose that the bishop of Antioch had actually obtained such an office from Zenobia, while others consider it only as a figurative expression of his pomp and insolence.

opulent of the faithful, and converted to his own use a considerable part of the public revenue. By his pride and luxury the Christian religion was rendered odious in the eyes of the Gentiles. His council chamber and his throne, the splendour with which he appeared in public, the suppliant crowd who solicited his attention, the multitude of letters and petitions to which he dictated his answers, and the perpetual hurry of business in which he was involved, were circumstances much better suited to the state of a civil magistrate [128] than to the humility of a primitive bishop. When he harangued his people from the pulpit, Paul affected the figurative style and the theatrical gestures of an Asiatic sophist, while the cathedral resounded with the loudest and most extravagant acclamations in the praise of his divine eloquence. Against those who resisted his power, or refused to flatter his vanity, the prelate of Antioch was arrogant, rigid, and inexorable; but he relaxed the discipline, and lavished the treasures, of the church on his dependent clergy, who were permitted to imitate their master in the gratification of every sensual appetite. For Paul indulged himself very freely in the pleasures of the table, and he had received into the episcopal palace two young and beautiful women, as the constant companions of his leisure moments. [129]

Notwithstanding these scandalous vices, if Paul of Samosata had preserved the purity of the orthodox faith, his reign over the capital of Syria would have ended only with his life; and, had a seasonable persecution intervened, an effort of courage might perhaps have placed him in the rank of saints and martyrs. Some nice and subtle errors, which he imprudently adopted and obstinately maintained, concerning the doctrine of the Trinity, excited the zeal and indignation of the eastern churches. [130] From Egypt to the Euxine sea, the bishops were

He is degraded from the see of Antioch. A.D. 270

---

[128] Simony was not unknown in those times; and the clergy sometimes bought what they intended to sell. It appears that the bishopric of Carthage was purchased by a wealthy matron, named Lucilla, for her servant Majorinus. The price was 400 *Folles.* (Monument. Antiq. ad calcem Optati, p. 263.) Every *Follis* contained 125 pieces of silver, and the whole sum may be computed at about 2400*l.*

[129] If we are desirous of extenuating the vices of Paul, we must suspect the assembled bishops of the East of publishing the most malicious calumnies in circular epistles addressed to all the churches of the empire (ap. Euseb. l. vii. c. 30).

[130] His heresy (like those of Noetus and Sabellius, in the same century) tended to confound the mysterious distinction of the divine persons. See Mosheim, p. 702, &c.

in arms and in motion. Several councils were held, confutations were published, excommunications were pronounced, ambiguous explanations were by turns accepted and refused, treaties were concluded and violated, and, at length, Paul of Samosata was degraded from his episcopal character, by the sentence of seventy or eighty bishops, who assembled for that purpose at Antioch, and who, without consulting the rights of the clergy or people, appointed a successor by their own authority. The manifest irregularity of this proceeding increased the numbers of the discontented faction ; and as Paul, who was no stranger to the arts of courts, had insinuated himself into the favour of Zenobia, he maintained above four years the possession of the episcopal house and office. The victory of Aurelian changed the face of the East, and the two contending parties, who applied to each other the epithets of schism and heresy, were either commanded or permitted to plead their cause before the tribunal of the conqueror. This public and very singular trial affords a convincing proof that the existence, the property, the privileges, and the internal policy of the Christians were acknowledged, if not by the laws, at least by the magistrates, of the empire. As a Pagan and as a soldier, it could scarcely be expected that Aurelian should enter into the discussion, whether the sentiments of Paul or those of his adversaries were most agreeable to the true standard of the orthodox faith. His determination, however, was founded on the general principles of equity and reason. He considered the bishops of Italy as the most impartial and respectable judges among the Christians, and, as soon as he was informed that they had unanimously approved the sentence of the council, he acquiesced in their opinion, and immediately gave orders that Paul should be compelled to relinquish the temporal possessions belonging to an office of which, in the judgment of his brethren, he had been regularly deprived. But, while we applaud the justice, we should not overlook the policy, of Aurelian ; who was desirous of restoring and cementing the dependence of the provinces on the capital by every means which could bind the interest or prejudices of any part of his subjects.[131]

The sentence is executed by Aurelian. A.D. 274

Peace and prosperity of the church under Diocletian. A.D. 284—303

Amidst the frequent revolutions of the empire, the Christians still flourished in peace and prosperity ; and, notwithstanding a celebrated æra of martyrs has been deduced from the accession

---

[131] Euseb. Hist. Ecclesiast. l. vii. c. 30. We are entirely indebted to him for the curious story of Paul of Samosata.

of Diocletian,[132] the new system of policy, introduced and maintained by the wisdom of that prince, continued, during more than eighteen years, to breathe the mildest and most liberal spirit of religious toleration. The mind of Diocletian himself was less adapted indeed to speculative inquiries than to the active labours of war and government. His prudence rendered him averse to any great innovation, and, though his temper was not very susceptible of zeal or enthusiasm, he always maintained an habitual regard for the ancient deities of the empire. But the leisure of the two empresses, of his wife Prisca and of Valeria his daughter, permitted them to listen with more attention and respect to the truths of Christianity, which in every age has acknowledged its important obligations to female devotion.[133] The principal eunuchs, Lucian[134] and Dorotheus, Gorgonius and Andrew, who attended the person, possessed the favour, and governed the household of Diocletian, protected by their powerful influence the faith which they had embraced. Their example was imitated by many of the most considerable officers of the palace, who, in their respective stations, had the care of the Imperial ornaments, of the robes, of the furniture, of the jewels, and even of the private treasury; and, though it might sometimes be incumbent on them to accompany the emperor when he sacrificed in the temple,[135] they enjoyed, with their wives, their children, and their slaves, the free exercise of the Christian religion. Diocletian and his colleagues frequently conferred the most important offices on those persons who avowed their abhorrence for the worship of the gods, but who had displayed abilities proper for the service of the state. The bishops held an honourable rank in their respective provinces, and were treated with distinction and respect, not only by the people, but by the magistrates themselves. Almost in every city, the ancient churches were found insufficient to contain the increasing multitude of proselytes; and in their place more stately and capacious edifices were erected for the public worship

---

[132] The æra of Martyrs, which is still in use among the Copts and the Abyssinians, must be reckoned from the 29th of August, A.D. 284; as the beginning of the Egyptian year was nineteen days earlier than the real accession of Diocletian. See Dissertation Préliminaire à l'Art de vérifier les Dates.

[133] The expression of Lactantius (de M. P. c. 15), "sacrificio pollui coegit," implies their antecedent conversion to the faith; but does not seem to justify the assertion of Mosheim (p. 912) that they had been privately baptized

[134] M. de Tillemont (Memoires Ecclésiastiques, tom. v. part i. p. 11, 12) has quoted, from the Spicilegium of Dom. Luc d'Acheri [iii. 297], a very curious instruction which bishop Theonas composed for the use of Lucian

[135] Lactantius de M. P. c. 10.

of the faithful. The corruption of manners and principles, so forcibly lamented by Eusebius,[136] may be considered, not only as a consequence, but as a proof, of the liberty which the Christians enjoyed and abused under the reign of Diocletian. Prosperity had relaxed the nerves of discipline. Fraud, envy, and malice prevailed in every congregation. The presbyters aspired to the episcopal office, which every day became an object more worthy of their ambition. The bishops, who contended with each other for ecclesiastical pre-eminence, appeared by their conduct to claim a secular and tyrannical power in the church ; and the lively faith which still distinguished the Christians from the Gentiles was shewn much less in their lives than in their controversial writings.

Progress of zeal and superstition among the Pagans

Notwithstanding this seeming security, an attentive observer might discern some symptoms that threatened the church with a more violent persecution than any which she had yet endured. The zeal and rapid progress of the Christians awakened the Polytheists from their supine indifference in the cause of those deities whom custom and education had taught them to revere. The mutual provocations of a religious war, which had already continued above two hundred years, exasperated the animosity of the contending parties. The Pagans were incensed at the rashness of a recent and obscure sect which presumed to accuse their countrymen of error and to devote their ancestors to eternal misery. The habits of justifying the popular mythology against the invectives of an implacable enemy produced in their minds some sentiments of faith and reverence for a system which they had been accustomed to consider with the most careless levity. The supernatural powers assumed by the church inspired at the same time terror and emulation. The followers of the established religion intrenched themselves behind a similar fortification of prodigies ; invented new modes of sacrifice, of expiation, and of initiation ;[137] attempted to revive the credit of their expiring oracles ;[138] and listened with eager credulity

[136] Eusebius, Hist. Ecclesiast. l. viii. c. i. The reader who consults the original will not accuse me of heightening the picture. Eusebius was about sixteen years of age at the accession of the emperor Diocletian.

[137] We might quote, among a great number of instances, the mysterious worship of Mithras, and the Taurobolia ; the latter of which became fashionable in the time of the Antonines (see a Dissertation of M. de Boze, in the Mémoires de l'Académie des Inscriptions, tom. ii. p. 443). The romance of Apuleius is as full of devotion as of satire.

[138] The impostor Alexander very strongly recommended the oracle of Trophonius at Mallos, and those of Apollo at Claros and Miletus (Lucian, tom. ii. p. 236, edit. Reitz). The last of these, whose singular history would furnish a very

to every impostor who flattered their prejudices by a tale of wonders.[139] Both parties seemed to acknowledge the truth of those miracles which were claimed by their adversaries; and, while they were contented with ascribing them to the arts of magic and to the power of dæmons, they mutually concurred in restoring and establishing the reign of superstition.[140] Philosophy, her most dangerous enemy, was now converted into her most useful ally. The groves of the academy, the gardens of Epicurus, and even the portico of the Stoics, were almost deserted, as so many different schools of scepticism or impiety;[141] and many among the Romans were desirous that the writings of Cicero should be condemned and suppressed by the authority of the senate.[142] The prevailing sect of the new Platonicians judged it prudent to connect themselves with the priests, whom perhaps they despised, against the Christians, whom they had reason to fear. These fashionable philosophers prosecuted the design of extracting allegorical wisdom from the fictions of the Greek poets; instituted mysterious rites of devotion for the use of their chosen disciples; recommended the worship of the ancient gods as the emblems or ministers of the Supreme Deity, and composed against the faith of the Gospel many elaborate treatises,[143] which have since been committed to the flames by the prudence of orthodox emperors.[144]

curious episode, was consulted by Diocletian before he published his edicts of persecution (Lactantius, de M. P. c. 11).

[139] Besides the ancient stories of Pythagoras and Aristeas, the cures performed at the shrine of Æsculapius and the fables related of Apollonius of Tyana were frequently opposed to the miracles of Christ; though I agree with Dr. Lardner (see Testimonies, vol. iii. p. 253, 352) that, when Philostratus composed the life of Apollonius, he had no such intention.

[140] It is seriously to be lamented that the Christian fathers, by acknowledging the supernatural or, as they deem it, the infernal part of Paganism, destroy with their own hands the great advantage which we might otherwise derive from the liberal concessions of our adversaries.

[141] Julian (p. 301, edit. Spanheim) expresses a pious joy that the providence of the gods had extinguished the impious sects, and for the most part destroyed the books of the Pyrrhonians and Epicureans, which had been very numerous, since Epicurus himself composed no less than 300 volumes. See Diogenes Laertius, l. x. c. 26.

[142] Cumque alios audiam mussitare indignanter, et dicere oportere statui per Senatum, aboleantur ut hæc scripta, quibus Christiana Religio comprobetur et vetustatis opprimatur auctoritas. Arnobius adversus Gentes, l. iii. p. 103, 104. He adds very properly, Erroris convincite Ciceronem . . . nam intercipere scripta, et publicatam velle submergere lectionem, non est Deum [Deos] defendere sed veritatis testificationem timere.

[143] Lactantius (Divin. Institut. l. v. c. 2, 3) gives a very clear and spirited account of two of these philosophic adversaries of the faith. The large treatise of Porphyry against the Christians consisted of thirty books, and was composed in Sicily about the year 270.

[144] See Socrates, Hist. Ecclesiast. l. i. c. 9, and Codex Justinian. l. i. tit. l. i. 3.

Maximian
and Galerius
punish a
few Christian
soldiers

Although the policy of Diocletian and the humanity of Constantius inclined them to preserve inviolate the maxims of toleration, it was soon discovered that their two associates Maximian and Galerius entertained the most implacable aversion for the name and religion of the Christians. The minds of those princes had never been enlightened by science; education had never softened their temper. They owed their greatness to their swords, and in their most elevated fortune they still retained their superstitious prejudices of soldiers and peasants. In the general administration of the provinces they obeyed the laws which their benefactor had established; but they frequently found occasions of exercising within their camp and palaces a secret persecution,[145] for which the imprudent zeal of the Christians sometimes offered the most specious pretences. A sentence of death was executed upon Maximilianus, an African youth, who had been produced by his own father before the magistrate as a sufficient and legal recruit, but who obstinately persisted in declaring that his conscience would not permit him to embrace the profession of a soldier.[146] It could scarcely be expected that any government should suffer the action of Marcellus the centurion to pass with impunity. On the day of a public festival, that officer threw away his belt, his arms, and the ensigns of his office, and exclaimed with a loud voice that he would obey none but Jesus Christ the eternal King, and that he renounced for ever the use of carnal weapons and the service of an idolatrous master. The soldiers, as soon as they recovered from their astonishment, secured the person of Marcellus. He was examined in the city of Tingi by the president of that part of Mauritania; and, as he was convicted by his own confession, he was condemned and beheaded for the crime of desertion.[147] Examples of such a nature savour much

[Tangier]

---

[145] Eusebius, l. viii. c. 4. c. 17. He limits the number of military martyrs, by a remarkable expression (σπανίως τούτων εἶς που καὶ δεύτερος), of which neither his Latin nor French translations have rendered the energy. Notwithstanding the authority of Eusebius, and the silence of Lactantius, Ambrose, Sulpicius, Orosius, &c. it has been long believed that the Thebæan legion, consisting of 6000 Christians, suffered martyrdom, by the order of Maximian, in the valley of the Pennine Alps. The story was first published about the middle of the fifth century by Eucherius, bishop of Lyons, who received it from certain persons, who received it from Isaac, bishop of Geneva, who is said to have received it from Theodore bishop of Octodurum. The abbey of St. Maurice still subsists, a rich monument of the credulity of Sigismund, king of Burgundy. See an excellent Dissertation in the xxxvith volume of the Bibliothèque Raisonnée, p. 427—454.

[146] See the Acta Sincera, p. 299. The accounts of his martyrdom and of that of Marcellus bear every mark of truth and authenticity.

[147] Acta Sincera, p. 302.

less of religious persecution than of martial or even civil law : but they served to alienate the mind of the emperors, to justify the severity of Galerius, who dismissed a great number of Christian officers from their employments, and to authorize the opinion that a sect of enthusiasts which avowed principles so repugnant to the public safety must either remain useless, or would soon become dangerous, subjects of the empire.

After the success of the Persian war had raised the hopes and the reputation of Galerius, he passed a winter with Diocletian in the palace of Nicomedia ; and the fate of Christianity became the object of their secret consultations.[148] The experienced emperor was still inclined to pursue measures of lenity ; and, though he readily consented to exclude the Christians from holding any employments in the household or the army, he urged in the strongest terms the danger as well as cruelty of shedding the blood of those deluded fanatics. Galerius at length extorted from him the permission of summoning a council, composed of a few persons the most distinguished in the civil and military departments of the state. The important question was agitated in their presence, and those ambitious courtiers easily discerned that it was incumbent on them to second, by their eloquence, the importunate violence of the Cæsar. It may be presumed that they insisted on every topic which might interest the pride, the piety, or the fears, of their sovereign in the destruction of Christianity. Perhaps they represented that the glorious work of the deliverance of the empire was left imperfect, as long as an independent people was permitted to subsist and multiply in the heart of the provinces. The Christians (it might speciously be alleged), re-nouncing the gods and the institutions of Rome, had constituted a distinct republic, which might yet be suppressed before it had acquired any military force ; but which was already governed by its own laws and magistrates, was possessed of a public treasure, and was intimately connected in all its parts by the frequent assemblies of the bishops, to whose decrees their numerous and opulent congregations yielded an implicit obe-dience. Arguments like these may seem to have determined the reluctant mind of Diocletian to embrace a new system of persecution : but, though we may suspect, it is not in our power

Galerius prevails on Diocletian to begin a general persecution

---

[148] De M. P. c. 11. Lactantius (or whoever was the author of this little treatise) was, at that time, an inhabitant of Nicomedia ; but it seems difficult to conceive how he could acquire so accurate a knowledge of what passed in the Imperial cabinet. [Cp. Append. 1 ad init.]

to relate, the secret intrigues of the palace, the private views and resentments, the jealousy of women or eunuchs, and all those trifling but decisive causes which so often influence the fate of empires and the councils of the wisest monarchs.[149]

Demolition of the church of Nicomedia. A. D. 303, 23rd Feb.

The pleasure of the emperors was at length signified to the Christians, who, during the course of this melancholy winter, had expected, with anxiety, the result of so many secret consultations. The twenty-third of February, which coincided with the Roman festival of the Terminalia,[150] was appointed (whether from accident or design) to set bounds to the progress of Christianity. At the earliest dawn of day, the Prætorian præfect,[151] accompanied by several generals, tribunes, and officers of the revenue, repaired to the principal church of Nicomedia, which was situated on an eminence in the most populous and beautiful part of the city. The doors were instantly broken open; they rushed into the sanctuary; and, as they searched in vain for some visible object of worship, they were obliged to content themselves with committing to the flames the volumes of holy scripture. The ministers of Diocletian were followed by a numerous body of guards and pioneers, who marched in order of battle, and were provided with all the instruments used in the destruction of fortified cities. By their incessant labour, a sacred edifice, which towered above the Imperial palace, and had long excited the indignation and envy of the Gentiles, was in a few hours levelled with the ground.[152]

The first edict against the Christians 24th of February

The next day the general edict of persecution was published;[153] and, though Diocletian, still averse to the effusion of blood, had moderated the fury of Galerius, who proposed that every one refusing to offer sacrifice should immediately be burnt alive, the penalties inflicted on the obstinacy of the Christians might be deemed sufficiently rigorous and effectual. It was enacted that their churches, in all the provinces of the empire, should be

[149] The only circumstance which we can discover is the devotion and jealousy of the mother of Galerius. She is described by Lactantius as Deorum montium cultrix; mulier admodum superstitiosa. She had a great influence over her son, and was offended by the disregard of some of her Christian servants.

[150] The worship and festival of the God Terminus are elegantly illustrated by M. de Boze, Mém. de l'Académie des Inscriptions, tom. i. p. 50.

[151] In our only Ms. of Lactantius, we read profectus; but reason and the authority of all the critics allow us, instead of that word, which destroys the sense of the passage, to substitute præfectus.

[152] Lactantius de M. P. c. 12, gives a very lively picture of the destruction of the church.

[153] Mosheim (p. 922—926), from many scattered passages of Lactantius and Eusebius, has collected a very just and accurate notion of this edict; though he sometimes deviates into conjecture and refinement.

demolished to their foundations; and the punishment of death was denounced against all who should presume to hold any secret assemblies for the purpose of religious worship. The philosophers, who now assumed the unworthy office of directing the blind zeal of persecution, had diligently studied the nature and genius of the Christian religion; and, as they were not ignorant that the speculative doctrines of the faith were supposed to be contained in the writings of the prophets, of the evangelists, and of the apostles, they most probably suggested the order that the bishops and presbyters should deliver all their sacred books into the hands of the magistrates; who were commanded, under the severest penalties, to burn them in a public and solemn manner. By the same edict, the property of the church was at once confiscated; and the several parts of which it might consist were either sold to the highest bidder, united to the Imperial domain, bestowed on the cities and corporations, or granted to the solicitations of rapacious courtiers. After taking such effectual measures to abolish the worship, and to dissolve the government of the Christians, it was thought necessary to subject to the most intolerable hardships the condition of those perverse individuals who should still reject the religion of Nature, of Rome, and of their ancestors. Persons of a liberal birth were declared incapable of holding any honours or employments; slaves were for ever deprived of the hopes of freedom, and the whole body of the people were put out of the protection of the law. The judges were authorized to hear and to determine every action that was brought against a Christian. But the Christians were not permitted to complain of any injury which they themselves had suffered; and thus those unfortunate sectaries were exposed to the severity, while they were excluded from the benefits, of public justice. This new species of martyrdom, so painful and lingering, so obscure and ignominious, was, perhaps, the most proper to weary the constancy of the faithful; nor can it be doubted that the passions and interest of mankind were disposed on this occasion to second the designs of the emperors. But the policy of a well-ordered government must sometimes have interposed in behalf of the oppressed Christians; nor was it possible for the Roman princes entirely to remove the apprehension of punishment, or to connive at every act of fraud and violence, without exposing their own authority and the rest of their subjects to the most alarming dangers.[154]

---

[154] Many ages afterwards, Edward I. practised with great success the same mode of persecution against the clergy of England. See Hume's History of England, vol. ii. p. 300, last 4to edition.

Zeal and
punishment
of a Christian

This edict was scarcely exhibited to the public view, in the most conspicuous place of Nicomedia, before it was torn down by the hands of a Christian, who expressed, at the same time, by the bitterest invectives, his contempt as well as abhorrence for such impious and tyrannical governors. His offence, according to the mildest laws, amounted to treason, and deserved death. And, if it be true that he was a person of rank and education, those circumstances could serve only to aggravate his guilt. He was burnt, or rather roasted, by a slow fire; and his executioners, zealous to revenge the personal insult which had been offered to the emperors, exhausted every refinement of cruelty, without being able to subdue his patience, or to alter the steady and insulting smile which in his dying agonies he still preserved in his countenance. The Christians, though they confessed that his conduct had not been strictly conformable to the laws of prudence, admired the divine fervour of his zeal; and the excessive commendations which they lavished on the memory of their hero and martyr contributed to fix a deep impression of terror and hatred in the mind of Diocletian.[155]

Fire of the
palace of
Nicomedia
imputed to
the Chris-
tians

His fears were soon alarmed by the view of a danger from which he very narrowly escaped. Within fifteen days the palace of Nicomedia, and even the bed-chamber of Diocletian, were twice in flames; and, though both times they were extinguished without any material damage, the singular repetition of the fire was justly considered as an evident proof that it had not been the effect of chance or negligence. The suspicion naturally fell on the Christians; and it was suggested, with some degree of probability, that those desperate fanatics, provoked by their present sufferings and apprehensive of impending calamities, had entered into a conspiracy with their faithful brethren, the eunuchs of the palace, against the lives of two emperors, whom they detested as the irreconcileable enemies of the church of God. Jealousy and resentment prevailed in every breast, but especially in that of Diocletian. A great number of persons, distinguished either by the offices which they had filled or by the favour which they had enjoyed, were thrown into prison. Every mode of torture was put in practice, and the court, as well as city, was polluted with many bloody

[155] Lactantius only calls him quidam, etsi non recte, magno tamen animo, &c. c. 12. Eusebius (l. viii. c. 5) adorns him with secular honours. Neither have condescended to mention his name; but the Greeks celebrate his memory under that of John. See Tillemont, Mémoires Ecclésiastiques, tom. v. part ii. p. 320.

executions.[156]   But, as it was found impossible to extort any discovery of this mysterious transaction, it seems incumbent on us either to presume the innocence, or to admire the resolution, of the sufferers.   A few days afterwards Galerius hastily withdrew himself from Nicomedia, declaring that, if he delayed his departure from that devoted palace, he should fall a sacrifice to the rage of the Christians.   The ecclesiastical historians, from whom alone we derive a partial and imperfect knowledge of this persecution, are at a loss how to account for the fears and dangers of the emperors.   Two of these writers, a Prince and a Rhetorician, were eye-witnesses of the fire of Nicomedia.   The one ascribes it to lightning and the divine wrath; the other affirms that it was kindled by the malice of Galerius himself.[157]

As the edict against the Christians was designed for a general law of the whole empire, and as Diocletian and Galerius, though they might not wait for the consent, were assured of the concurrence, of the western princes, it would appear more consonant to our ideas of policy that the governors of all the provinces should have received secret instructions to publish, on one and the same day, this declaration of war within their respective departments.   It was at least to be expected that the convenience of the public highways and established posts would have enabled the emperors to transmit their orders with the utmost dispatch from the palace of Nicomedia to the extremities of the Roman world; and that they would not have suffered fifty days to elapse before the edict was published in Syria, and near four months before it was signified to the cities of Africa.[158]   This delay may perhaps be imputed to the cautious temper of Diocletian, who had yielded a reluctant consent to the measures of persecution, and who was desirous of trying the experiment under his more immediate eye, before he gave way to the disorders and discontent which it must inevitably occasion in the distant provinces.   At first, indeed, the magistrates were restrained from the effusion of blood; but the use of every other severity was permitted and even recommended to their zeal; nor could the Christians, though they cheerfully

Execution of the first edict

---

[156] Lactantius de M. P. c. 13, 14.   Potentissimi quondam Eunuchi necati, per quos Palatium et ipse constabat.   Eusebius (l. viii. c. 6.) mentions the cruel extortions of the eunuchs, Gorgonius and Dorotheus, and of Anthemius, bishop of Nicomedia; and both those writers describe, in a vague but tragical manner, the horrid scenes which were acted even in the Imperial presence.

[157] See Lactantius, Eusebius, and Constantine, ad Cœtum Sanctorum, c. 25. Eusebius confesses his ignorance of the cause of the fire.

[158] Tillemont, Mémoires Ecclésiast. tom. v. part i. p. 43.

resigned the ornaments of their churches, resolve to interrupt their religious assemblies or to deliver their sacred books to the flames. The pious obstinacy of Felix, an African bishop, appears to have embarrassed the subordinate ministers of the government. The curator of his city sent him in chains to the proconsul. The proconsul transmitted him to the Prætorian præfect of Italy; and Felix, who disdained even to give an evasive answer, was at length beheaded at Venusia, in Lucania, a place on which the birth of Horace has conferred fame.[159] This precedent, and perhaps some Imperial rescript, which was issued in consequence of it, appeared to authorize the governors of provinces in punishing with death the refusal of the Christians to deliver up their sacred books. There were undoubtedly many persons who embraced this opportunity of obtaining the crown of martyrdom; but there were likewise too many who purchased an ignominious life by discovering and betraying the holy scripture into the hands of infidels. A great number even of bishops and presbyters acquired, by this criminal compliance, the opprobrious epithet of *Traditors;* and their offence was productive of much present scandal, and of much future discord, in the African church.[160]

Demolition of the churches

The copies, as well as the versions, of scripture were already so multiplied in the empire that the most severe inquisition could no longer be attended with any fatal consequences; and even the sacrifice of those volumes which, in every congregation, were preserved for public use required the consent of some treacherous and unworthy Christians. But the ruin of the churches was easily effected by the authority of the government and by the labour of the Pagans. In some provinces, however, the magistrates contented themselves with shutting up the places of religious worship. In others, they more literally complied with the terms of the edict; and, after taking away the doors, the benches, and the pulpit, which they burnt, as it were in a funeral pile, they completely demolished the remainder of the edifice.[161] It is perhaps to this melancholy

---

[159] See the Acta Sincera of Ruinart, p. 353; those of Felix of Thibara, or Tibiur, appear much less corrupted than in the other editions, which afford a lively specimen of legendary licence.

[160] See the first book of Optatus of Milevis against the Donatists at Paris, 1700 [*leg.* 1702], edit. Dupin. He lived under the reign of Valens.

[161] The ancient monuments, published at the end of Optatus, p. 261, &c. describe, in a very circumstantial manner, the proceedings of the governors in the destruction of churches. They made a minute inventory of the plate, &c. which they found in them. That of the Church of Cirta, in Numidia, is still extant. It

occasion that we should apply a very remarkable story, which is related with so many circumstances of variety and improbability that it serves rather to excite than to satisfy our curiosity.   In a small town in Phrygia, of whose name as well as situation we are left ignorant, it should seem that the magistrates and the body of the people had embraced the Christian faith ; and, as some resistance might be apprehended to the execution of the edict, the governor of the province was supported by a numerous detachment of legionaries.   On their approach the citizens threw themselves into the church, with the resolution either of defending by arms that sacred edifice or of perishing in its ruins.   They indignantly rejected the notice and permission which was given them to retire, till the soldiers, provoked by their obstinate refusal, set fire to the building on all sides, and consumed, by this extraordinary kind of martyrdom, a great number of Phrygians, with their wives and children.[162]

Some slight disturbances, though they were suppressed almost as soon as excited, in Syria and the frontiers of Armenia, afforded the enemies of the church a very plausible occasion to insinuate that those troubles had been secretly fomented by the intrigues of the bishops, who had already forgotten their ostentatious professions of passive and unlimited obedience.[163] The resentment, or the fears, of Diocletian at length transported him beyond the bounds of moderation which he had hitherto preserved, and he declared, in a series of cruel edicts, his intention of abolishing the Christian name.   By the first of these edicts, the governors of the provinces were directed to apprehend all persons of the ecclesiastical order ; and the prisons, destined for the vilest criminals, were soon filled with a

Subsequent edicts

[Second edict. A.D. 303]

consisted of two chalices of gold, and six of silver; six urns, one kettle, seven lamps, all likewise of silver ; besides a large quantity of brass utensils, and wearing apparel.

[162] Lactantius (Institut. Divin. v. 11) confines the calamity to the *conventiculum*, with its congregation.   Eusebius (viii. 11) extends it to a whole city, and introduces something very like a regular siege.   His ancient Latin translator, Rufinus, adds the important circumstance of the permission given to the inhabitants of retiring from thence.   As Phrygia reached to the confines of Isauria, it is possible that the restless temper of those independent Barbarians may have contributed to this misfortune.

[163] Eusebius, l. viii. c. 6.   M. de Valois (with some probability) thinks that he has discovered the Syrian rebellion in an oration of Libanius; and that it was a rash attempt of the tribune Eugenius, who with only five hundred men seized Antioch, and might perhaps allure the Christians by the promise of religious toleration.   From Eusebius (l. ix. c. 8), as well as from Moses of Chorene (Hist. Armen. l. ii. c. 77, &c.), it may be inferred that Christianity was already introduced into Armenia.   [See Appendix 18.]

multitude of bishops, presbyters, deacons, readers, and exorcists. By a second edict, the magistrates were commanded to employ *[Third edict. A.D 303]* every method of severity which might reclaim them from their odious superstition and oblige them to return to the established worship of the gods. This rigorous order was ex- *[Fourth edict. A.D. 304, before end of March]* tended by a subsequent edict to the whole body of Christians, who were exposed to a violent and general persecution.[164] Instead of those salutary restraints, which had required the direct and solemn testimony of an accuser, it became the duty as well as the interest of the imperial officers to discover, to pursue, and to torment the most obnoxious among the faithful. Heavy penalties were denounced against all who should presume to save a proscribed sectary from the just indignation of the gods, and of the emperors. Yet, notwithstanding the severity of this law, the virtuous courage of many of the Pagans, in concealing their friends or relations, affords an honourable proof that the rage of superstition had not extinguished in their minds the sentiments of nature and humanity.[165]

General idea of the perse-cution

Diocletian had no sooner published his edicts against the Christians than, as if he had been desirous of committing to other hands the work of persecution, he divested himself of the Imperial purple. The character and situation of his colleagues and successors sometimes urged them to enforce, and sometimes inclined them to suspend the execution of these rigorous laws; nor can we acquire a just and distinct idea of this important period of ecclesiastical history, unless we separately consider the state of Christianity, in the different parts of the empire, during the space of ten years, which elapsed between the first edicts of Diocletian and the final peace of the church.

In the western provinces under Con-stantius and Constantine

The mild and humane temper of Constantius was averse to the oppression of any part of his subjects. The principal offices of his palace were exercised by Christians. He loved their persons, esteemed their fidelity, and entertained not any dislike to their religious principles. But, as long as Constantius remained in the subordinate station of Cæsar, it was not in his power openly to reject the edicts of Diocletian or to disobey the commands of Maximian. His authority contributed, however, to alleviate the sufferings which he pitied and abhorred.

[164] See Mosheim, p. 938; the text of Eusebius very plainly shews that the governors, whose powers were enlarged, not restrained, by the new laws, could punish with death the most obstinate Christians, as an example to their brethren. [For 4th edict, see Euseb Mart. Pal. c. 3.]

[165] Athanasius, p. 833, ap. Tillemont, Mém. Ecclésiast. tom. v. part i. p. 90.

He consented, with reluctance, to the ruin of the churches; but he ventured to protect the Christians themselves from the fury of the populace and from the rigour of the laws. The provinces of Gaul (under which we may probably include those of Britain) were indebted for the singular tranquillity which they enjoyed to the gentle interposition of their sovereign.[166] But Datianus, the president or governor of Spain, actuated either by zeal or policy, chose rather to execute the public edicts of the emperors than to understand the secret intentions of Constantius; and it can scarcely be doubted that his provincial administration was stained with the blood of a few martyrs.[167] The elevation of Constantius to the supreme and independent dignity of Augustus gave a free scope to the exercise of his virtues, and the shortness of his reign did not prevent him from establishing a system of toleration, of which he left the precept and the example to his son Constantine. His fortunate son, from the first moment of his accession declaring himself the protector of the church, at length deserved the appellation of the first emperor who publicly professed and established the Christian religion. The motives of his conversion, as they may variously be deduced from benevolence, from policy, from conviction, or from remorse; and the progress of the revolution which, under his powerful influence, and that of his sons, rendered Christianity the reigning religion of the Roman empire, will form a very interesting and important chapter in the second volume of this history. At present it may [Chap. xx.] be sufficient to observe that every victory of Constantine was productive of some relief or benefit to the church.

The provinces of Italy and Africa experienced a short but In Italy and violent persecution. The rigorous edicts of Diocletian were Africa, under Maximian strictly and cheerfully executed by his associate Maximian, and Severus who had long hated the Christians, and who delighted in acts

[166] Eusebius, l. viii. c. 13. Lactantius de M. P. c. 15. Dodwell (Dissertat. Cyprian. xi. 75) represents them as inconsistent with each other. But the former evidently speaks of Constantius in the station of Cæsar, and the latter of the same prince in the rank of Augustus. [On the religious policy of Constantius, see papers of Görres in Zeitschrift für wiss. Theologie, vol 31 1888, p. 72 *sqq.*, and 33, 1890 p 469 *sqq.*]

[167] Datianus is mentioned in Gruter's Inscriptions, as having determined the limits between the territories of Pax Julia, and those of Ebora, both cities in the southern part of Lusita..ia. [This inscription is not genuine. See No. 17 of the False Inscriptions at end of C. I. L., vol. 2.] If we recollect the neighbourhood of those places to Cape St. Vincent, we may suspect that the celebrated deacon and martyr of that name has been inaccurately assigned by Prudentius, &c. to Saragossa, or Valentia. See the pompous history of his sufferings, in the Mémoires de Tillemont, tom. v. part ii. p. 58-85. Some critics are of opinion that the department of Constantius, as Cæsar, did not include Spain, which still continued under the immediate jurisdiction of Maximian. [See vol. i. p. 354.]

of blood and violence. In the autumn of the first year of the persecution, the two emperors met at Rome to celebrate their triumph; several oppressive laws appear to have issued from their secret consultations, and the diligence of the magistrates was animated by the presence of their sovereigns. After Diocletian had divested himself of the purple, Italy and Africa were administered under the name of Severus, and were exposed, without defence, to the implacable resentment of his master Galerius. Among the martyrs of Rome, Adauctus deserves the notice of posterity. He was of a noble family in Italy, and had raised himself, through the successive honours of the palace, to the important office of treasurer of the private demesnes. Adauctus is the more remarkable for being the only person of rank and distinction who appears to have suffered death during the whole course of this general persecution.[168]

under Maxentius
The revolt of Maxentius immediately restored peace to the churches of Italy and Africa; and the same tyrant who oppressed every other class of his subjects showed himself just, humane, and even partial, towards the afflicted Christians. He depended on their gratitude and affection, and very naturally presumed that the injuries which they had suffered, and the dangers which they still apprehended from his most inveterate enemy, would secure the fidelity of a party already considerable by their numbers and opulence.[169] Even the conduct of Maxentius towards the bishops of Rome and Carthage may be considered as the proof of his toleration, since it is probable that the most orthodox princes would adopt the same measures with regard to their established clergy. Marcellus, the former of those prelates, had thrown the capital into confusion by the severe penance which he imposed on a great number of Christians, who, during the late persecution, had renounced or dissembled their religion. The rage of faction broke out in frequent and violent seditions; the blood of the faithful was shed by each other's hands; and the exile of Marcellus, whose prudence seems to have been less eminent than his zeal, was found to be the only measure capable of restoring peace to the distracted church of Rome.[170] The behaviour of Mensurius,

---

[168] Eusebius, l. viii. c. 11. Gruter, Inscript. p. 1171. No. 18. Rufinus has mistaken the office of Adauctus, as well as the place of his martyrdom.

[169] Eusebius, l. viii. c. 14. But, as Maxentius was vanquished by Constantine, it suited the purpose of Lactantius to place his death among those of the persecutors. [On toleration of Maxentius see Görres, Z. f. wiss. Theol. 33, p. 206.]

[170] The epitaph of Marcellus is to be found in Gruter, Inscrip. p. 1172, No. 3, and it contains all that we know of his history. Marcellinus and Marcellus, whose

bishop of Carthage, appears to have been still more reprehensible. A deacon of that city had published a libel against the emperor. The offender took refuge in the episcopal palace; and, though it was somewhat early to advance any claims of ecclesiastical immunities, the bishop refused to deliver him up to the officers of justice. For this treasonable resistance, Mensurius was summoned to court, and, instead of receiving a legal sentence of death or banishment, he was permitted, after a short examination, to return to his diocese.[171] Such was the happy condition of the Christian subjects of Maxentius that, whenever they were desirous of procuring for their own use any bodies of martyrs, they were obliged to purchase them from the most distant provinces of the East. A story is related of Aglae, a Roman lady, descended from a consular family, and possessed of so ample an estate that it required the management of seventy-three stewards. Among these, Boniface was the favourite of his mistress; and, as Aglae mixed love with devotion, it is reported that he was admitted to share her bed. Her fortune enabled her to gratify the pious desire of obtaining some sacred relics from the East. She intrusted Boniface with a considerable sum of gold and a large quantity of aromatics; and her lover, attended by twelve horsemen and three covered chariots, undertook a remote pilgrimage, as far as Tarsus in Cilicia.[172]

The sanguinary temper of Galerius, the first and principal author of the persecution, was formidable to those Christians whom their misfortunes had placed within the limits of his dominions; and it may fairly be presumed that many persons of a middle rank, who were not confined by the chains either of wealth or of poverty, very frequently deserted their native

in Illyricum and the East, under Galerius and Maximin

---

names follow in the list of popes, are supposed by many critics to be different persons; but the learned Abbé de Longuerue was convinced that they were one and the same.

> Veridicus rector, lapsis [*leg.* lapsos] quia crimina flere
> Prædixit, miseris fuit omnibus hostis amarus.
> Hinc furor, hinc odium; sequitur discordia, lites,
> Seditio, cædes; solvuntur fœdera pacis.
> Crimen ob alterius, Christum qui in pace negavit,
> Finibus expulsus patriæ est feritate Tyranni.
> Hæc breviter Damasus voluit comperta referre:
> Marcelli [ut] populus meritum cognoscere posset.

We may observe, that Damasus was made bishop of Rome, A.D. 366. [Cp. App. 7.]

[171] Optatus contr. Donatist. l. i. c. 17, 18.

[172] The Acts of the Passion of St. Boniface, which abound in miracles and declamation, are published by Ruinart (p. 283-291) both in Greek and Latin, from the authority of very ancient manuscripts.

country, and sought a refuge in the milder climate of the West. As long as he commanded only the armies and provinces of Illyricum, he could with difficulty either find or make a considerable number of martyrs, in a warlike country, which had entertained the missionaries of the Gospel with more coldness and reluctance than any other part of the empire.[173] But, when Galerius had obtained the supreme power and the government of the East, he indulged in their fullest extent his zeal and cruelty, not only in the provinces of Thrace and Asia, which acknowledged his immediate jurisdiction, but in those of Syria, Palestine, and Egypt, where Maximin gratified his own inclination by yielding a rigorous obedience to the stern commands of his benefactor.[174] The frequent disappointments of his ambitious views, the experience of six years of persecution, and the salutary reflections which a lingering and painful distemper suggested to the mind of Galerius, at length convinced him that the most violent efforts of despotism are insufficient to extirpate a whole people or to subdue their religious prejudices. Desirous of repairing the mischief that he had occasioned, he published in his own name, and in those of Licinius and Constantine, a general edict, which, after a pompous recital of the Imperial titles, proceeded in the following manner :

Galerius publishes an edict of toleration. [A.D. 311, April 30]

" Among the important cares which have occupied our mind for the utility and preservation of the empire, it was our intention to correct and re-establish all things according to the ancient laws and public discipline of the Romans. We were particularly desirous of reclaiming, into the way of reason and nature, the deluded Christians, who had renounced the religion and ceremonies instituted by their fathers, and, presumptuously despising the practice of antiquity, had invented extravagant laws and opinions, according to the dictates of their fancy, and had collected a various society from the different provinces of our empire. The edicts which we have published to enforce the worship of the gods, having exposed many of the Christians to danger and distress, many having suffered death, and many

[173] During the four first centuries there exist few traces of either bishops or bishoprics in the western Illyricum. It has been thought probable that the primate of Milan extended his jurisdiction over Sirmium, the capital of that great province. See the Geographia Sacra of Charles de St. Paul, p. 68-76, with the observations of Lucas Holstenius.

[174] The eighth book of Eusebius, as well as the supplement concerning the martyrs of Palestine, principally relate to the persecution of Galerius and Maximin. The general lamentations with which Lactantius opens the fifth book of his Divine Institutions allude to their cruelty.

more, who still persist in their impious folly, being left destitute of *any* public exercise of religion, we are disposed to extend to those unhappy men the effects of our wonted clemency. We permit them, therefore, freely to profess their private opinions, and to assemble in their conventicles without fear or molestation, provided always that they preserve a due respect to the established laws and government. By another rescript we shall signify our intentions to the judges and magistrates; and we hope that our indulgence will engage the Christians to offer up their prayers to the Deity whom they adore, for our safety and prosperity, for their own, and for that of the republic." [175] It is not usually in the language of edicts and manifestoes that we should search for the real character or the secret motives of princes; but, as these were the words of a dying emperor, his situation, perhaps, may be admitted as a pledge of his sincerity.

When Galerius subscribed this edict of toleration, he was well assured that Licinius would readily comply with the inclinations of his friend and benefactor, and that any measures in favour of the Christians would obtain the approbation of Constantine. But the emperor would not venture to insert in the preamble the name of Maximin, whose consent was of the greatest importance, and who succeeded a few days afterwards to the provinces of Asia. In the first six months, however, of his new reign, Maximin affected to adopt the prudent counsels of his predecessor; and, though he never condescended to secure the tranquillity of the church by a public edict, Sabinus, [A.D. 311] his Prætor ianpræfect, addressed a circular letter to all the governors and magistrates of the provinces, expatiating on the Imperial clemency, acknowledging the invincible obstinacy of the Christians, and directing the officers of justice to cease their ineffectual prosecutions and to connive at the secret assemblies of those enthusiasts. In consequence of these orders, great numbers of Christians were released from prison or delivered from the mines. The confessors, singing hymns of triumph, returned into their own countries; and those who had yielded to the violence of the tempest solicited with tears of repentance their re-admission into the bosom of the church. [176]

Peace of the church

---

[175] Eusebius (l. viii. c. 17) has given us a Greek version, and Lactantius (de M. P. c. 34) the Latin original, of this memorable edict. Neither of these writers seems to recollect how directly it contradicts whatever they have just affirmed of the remorse and repentance of Galerius.

[176] Eusebius, l. ix. c. 1. He inserts the epistle of the præfect.

134 THE DECLINE AND FALL

Maximin
prepares to
renew the
persecution

[End of 312
A.D.]

But this treacherous calm was of short duration; nor could the Christians of the East place any confidence in the character of their sovereign. Cruelty and superstition were the ruling passions of the soul of Maximin. The former suggested the means, the latter pointed out the objects, of persecution. The emperor was devoted to the worship of the gods, to the study of magic, and to the belief of oracles. The prophets or philosophers, whom he revered as the favourites of heaven, were frequently raised to the government of provinces and admitted into his most secret counsels. They easily convinced him that the Christians had been indebted for their victories to their regular discipline, and that the weakness of Polytheism had principally flowed from a want of union and subordination among the ministers of religion. A system of government was therefore instituted, which was evidently copied from the policy of the church. In all the great cities of the empire, the temples were repaired and beautified by the order of Maximin; and the officiating priests of the various deities were subjected to the authority of a superior pontiff, destined to oppose the bishop and to promote the cause of Paganism. These pontiffs acknowledged, in their turn, the supreme jurisdiction of the metropolitans or high priests of the province, who acted as the immediate vicegerents of the emperor himself. A white robe was the ensign of their dignity; and these new prelates were carefully selected from the most noble and opulent families. By the influence of the magistrates and of the sacerdotal order, a great number of dutiful addresses were obtained, particularly from the cities of Nicomedia, Antioch, and Tyre, which artfully represented the well-known intentions of the court as the general sense of the people; solicited the emperor to consult the laws of justice rather than the dictates of his clemency; expressed their abhorrence of the Christians; and humbly prayed that those impious sectaries might at least be excluded from the limits of their respective territories. The answer of Maximin to the address which he obtained from the citizens of Tyre is still extant. He praises their zeal and devotion in terms of the highest satisfaction, descants on the obstinate impiety of the Christians, and betrays, by the readiness with which he consents to their banishment, that he considered himself as receiving, rather than as conferring, an obligation. The priests, as well as the magistrates, were empowered to enforce the execution of his edicts, which were engraved on tables of brass; and, though it was recommended to them to avoid the effusion of blood, the most cruel and ignominious punishments were inflicted on the refractory Christians.[177]

The Asiatic Christians had everything to dread from the severity of a bigoted monarch, who prepared his measures of violence with such deliberate policy. But a few months had scarcely elapsed before the edicts published by the two western emperors obliged Maximin to suspend the prosecution of his designs : the civil war, which he so rashly undertook against Licinius, employed all his attention ; and the defeat and death of Maximin soon delivered the church from the last and most implacable of her enemies.[178]

In this general view of the persecution, which was first authorized by the edicts of Diocletian, I have purposely refrained from describing the particular sufferings and deaths of the Christian martyrs. It would have been an easy task, from the history of Eusebius, from the declamations of Lactantius, and from the most ancient acts, to collect a long series of horrid and disgustful pictures, and to fill many pages with racks and scourges, with iron hooks, and red-hot beds, and with all the variety of tortures which fire and steel, savage beasts and more savage executioners, could inflict on the human body. These melancholy scenes might be enlivened by a crowd of visions and miracles destined either to delay the death, to celebrate the triumph, or to discover the relics, of those canonized saints who suffered for the name of Christ. But I cannot determine what I ought to transcribe, till I am satisfied how much I ought to believe. The gravest of the ecclesiastical historians, Eusebius himself, indirectly confesses that he has related whatever might redound to the glory, and that he has suppressed all that could tend to the disgrace, of religion.[179] Such an acknowledgment

End of the persecutions

Probable account of the sufferings of the martyrs and confessors

[177] See Eusebius, l. viii. c. 14, l. ix. c. 2-8. Lactantius de M. P. c. 36. These writers agree in representing the arts of Maximin ; but the former relates the execution of several martyrs, while the latter expressly affirms, occidi servos Dei vetuit. [For Maximin's persecutions, cp. Görres, Brieger's Z. f. Kirchengesch. xi. 333 *sqq.*]

[178] A few days before his death, he published a very ample edict of toleration, in which he imputes all the severities which the Christians suffered to the judges and governors, who had misunderstood his intentions. See the Edict. in Eusebius, l. ix. c. 10. [Summer, 313 A.D.]

[179] Such is the *fair* deduction from two remarkable passages in Eusebius, [H. E.] l. viii. c. 2, and de Martyr. Palestin. c. 12. The prudence of the historian has exposed his own character to censure and suspicion. It is well known that he himself had been thrown into prison ; and it was suggested that he had purchased his deliverance by some dishonourable compliance. The reproach was urged in his lifetime, and even in his presence, at the council of Tyre. See Tillemont, Mémoires Ecclésiastiques, tom. viii. part i. p. 67. [Milman admits that the authority of Eusebius is "loose" and "by no means scrupulous".]

will naturally excite a suspicion that a writer who has so openly violated one of the fundamental laws of history has not paid a very strict regard to the observance of the other ; and the suspicion will derive additional credit from the character of Eusebius, which was less tinctured with credulity, and more practised in the arts of courts, than that of almost any of his contemporaries. On some particular occasions, when the magistrates were exasperated by some personal motives of interest or resentment, when the zeal of the martyrs urged them to forget the rules of prudence, and perhaps of decency, to overturn the altars, to pour out imprecations against the emperors, or to strike the judge as he sat on his tribunal, it may be presumed that every mode of torture, which cruelty could invent or constancy could endure, was exhausted on those devoted victims.[180] Two circumstances, however, have been unwarily mentioned, which insinuate that the general treatment of the Christians who had been apprehended by the officers of justice was less intolerable than it is usually imagined to have been. 1. The confessors who were condemned to work in the mines were permitted, by the humanity or the negligence of their keepers, to build chapels and freely to profess their religion in the midst of those dreary habitations.[181] 2. The bishops were obliged to check and to censure the forward zeal of the Christians, who voluntarily threw themselves into the hands of the magistrates. Some of these were persons oppressed by poverty and debts, who blindly sought to terminate a miserable existence by a glorious death. Others were allured by the hope that a short confinement would expiate the sins of a whole life ; and others, again, were actuated by the less honourable motive of deriving a plentiful subsistence, and perhaps a considerable profit, from the alms which the charity of the faithful bestowed on the prisoners.[182] After the church had triumphed over all her enemies, the interest as well as vanity of the captives prompted them to magnify the merit of their respective

---

[180] The ancient, and perhaps authentic, account of the sufferings of Tarachus and his companions (Acta Sincera, Ruinart, p. 419-448) is filled with strong expressions of resentment and contempt, which could not fail of irritating the magistrate. The behaviour of Ædesius to Hierocles, præfect of Egypt, was still more extraordinary, λόγοις τε καὶ ἔργοις τὸν δικαστὴν . . . περιβαλών. Euseb. de Martyr. Palestin. c. 5.

[181] Euseb. de Martyr. Palestin. c. 13.

[182] Augustin. Collat. Carthagin. Dei, iii. c. 13, ap. Tillemont, Mémoires Ecclésiastiques, tom v. part i. p. 46. The controversy with the Donatists has reflected some, though perhaps a partial, light on the history of the African church.

suffering. A convenient distance of time or place gave an ample scope to the progress of fiction; and the frequent instances which might be alleged of holy martyrs, whose wounds had been instantly healed, whose strength had been renewed, and whose lost members had miraculously been restored, were extremely convenient for the purpose of removing every difficulty and of silencing every objection. The most extravagant legends, as they conduced to the honour of the church, were applauded by the credulous multitude, countenanced by the power of the clergy, and attested by the suspicious evidence of ecclesiastical history.

The vague descriptions of exile and imprisonment, of pain and torture, are so easily exaggerated or softened by the pencil of an artful orator that we are naturally induced to inquire into a fact of a more distinct and stubborn kind; the number of persons who suffered death, in consequence of the edicts published by Diocletian, his associates, and his successors. The recent legendaries record whole armies and cities, which were at once swept away by the undistinguishing rage of persecution. The more ancient writers content themselves with pouring out a liberal effusion of loose and tragical invectives, without condescending to ascertain the precise number of those persons who were permitted to seal with their blood their belief of the gospel. From the history of Eusebius, it may however be collected that only nine bishops were punished with death; and we are assured, by his particular enumeration of the martyrs of Palestine, that no more than ninety-two Christians were entitled to that honourable appellation.[183] As we are unacquainted with the degree of episcopal zeal and courage which

---

[183] Eusebius de Martyr. Palestin. c. 13. He closes his narration by assuring us that these were the martyrdoms inflicted in Palestine during the *whole* course of the persecution. The fifth chapter of his eighth book, which relates to the province of Thebais in Egypt, may seem to contradict our moderate computation; but it will only lead us to admire the artful management of the historian. Choosing for the scene of the most exquisite cruelty the most remote and sequestered country of the Roman empire, he relates that in Thebais from ten to one hundred persons had frequently suffered martyrdom in the same day. But when he proceeds to mention his own journey into Egypt, his language insensibly becomes more cautious and moderate. Instead of a large, but definite number, he speaks of many Christians (πλείους), and most artfully selects two ambiguous words (ἱστορήσαμεν, and ὑπομείναντας), which may signify either what he had seen or what he had heard; either the expectation or the execution of the punishment. Having thus provided a secure evasion, he commits the equivocal passage to his readers and translators; justly conceiving that their piety would induce them to prefer the most favourable sense. There was perhaps some malice in the remark of Theodorus Metochita, that all who, like Eusebius, had been conversant with the Egyptians delighted in an obscure and intricate style. (See Valesius ad loc.)

prevailed at that time, it is not in our power to draw any useful inferences from the former of these facts; but the latter may serve to justify a very important and probable conclusion. According to the distribution of Roman provinces, Palestine may be considered as the sixteenth part of the Eastern empire;[184] and since there were some governors who, from a real or affected clemency, had preserved their hands unstained with the blood of the faithful,[185] it is reasonable to believe that the country which had given birth to Christianity produced at least the sixteenth part of the martyrs who suffered death within the dominions of Galerius and Maximin; the whole might consequently amount to about fifteen hundred; a number which, if it is equally divided between the ten years of the persecution, will allow an annual consumption of one hundred and fifty martyrs. Allotting the same proportion to the provinces of Italy, Africa, and perhaps Spain, where, at the end of two or three years, the rigour of the penal laws was either suspended or abolished, the multitude of Christians in the Roman empire on whom a capital punishment was inflicted by a judicial sentence will be reduced to somewhat less than two thousand persons. Since it cannot be doubted that the Christians were more numerous, and their enemies more exasperated, in the time of Diocletian, than they had ever been in any former persecution, this probable and moderate computation may teach us to estimate the number of primitive saints and martyrs who sacrificed their lives for the important purpose of introducing Christianity into the world.

Conclusion   We shall conclude this chapter by a melancholy truth which obtrudes itself on the reluctant mind; that even admitting, without hesitation or inquiry, all that history has recorded, or devotion has feigned, on the subject of martyrdoms, it must still be acknowledged that the Christians, in the course of their intestine dissensions, have inflicted far greater severities on each other than they had experienced from the zeal of infidels. During the ages of ignorance which followed the subversion of the Roman empire in the West, the bishops of the Imperial city extended their dominion over the laity as well as clergy

[184] When Palestine was divided into three, the præfecture of the East contained forty-eight provinces. As the ancient distinctions of nations were long since abolished, the Romans distributed the provinces according to a general proportion of their extent and opulence. [Cp. Appendix 11.]
[185] Ut gloriari possint nullum se innocentium peremisse, nam et ipse audivi aliquos gloriantes, quia administratio sua in hâc parte fuerit incruenta. Lactant. Institut. Divin. v. 11.

of the Latin church. The fabric of superstition which they had erected, and which might long have defied the feeble efforts of reason, was at length assaulted by a crowd of daring fanatics, who, from the twelfth to the sixteenth century, assumed the popular character of reformers. The church of Rome defended by violence the empire which she had acquired by fraud ; a system of peace and benevolence was soon disgraced by proscriptions, wars, massacres, and the institution of the holy office. And, as the reformers were animated by the love of civil, as well as of religious, freedom, the Catholic princes connected their own interest with that of the clergy, and enforced by fire and the sword the terrors of spiritual censures. In the Netherlands alone, more than one hundred thousand of the subjects of Charles the Fifth are said to have suffered by the hand of the executioner ; and this extraordinary number is attested by Grotius,[186] a man of genius and learning, who preserved his moderation amidst the fury of contending sects, and who composed the annals of his own age and country, at a time when the invention of printing had facilitated the means of intelligence and increased the danger of detection. If we are obliged to submit our belief to the authority of Grotius, it must be allowed that the number of Protestants who were executed in a single province and a single reign far exceeded that of the primitive martyrs in the space of three centuries and of the Roman empire. But, if the improbability of the fact itself should prevail over the weight of evidence ; if Grotius should he convicted of exaggerating the merit and sufferings of the Reformers ; [187] we shall be naturally led to inquire what confidence can be placed in the doubtful and imperfect monuments of ancient credulity ; what degree of credit can be assigned to a courtly bishop, and a passionate declaimer, who, under the protection of Constantine, enjoyed the exclusive privilege of recording the persecutions inflicted on the Christians by the vanquished rivals, or disregarded predecessors of their gracious sovereign.

---

[186] Grot. Annal. de Rebus Belgicis, l. i. p. 12, edit. fol.

[187] Fra Paolo (Istoria del Concilio Tridentino, l. iii.) reduces the number of Belgic martyrs to 50,000. In learning and moderation, Fra Paolo was not inferior to Grotius. The priority of time gives some advantage to the evidence of the former, which he loses on the other hand by the distance of Venice from the Netherlands.

CHAPTER XVII

Foundation of Constantinople—Political System of Constantine, and his Successors—Military Discipline—The Palace—The Finances

THE unfortunate Licinius was the last rival who opposed the greatness, and the last captive who adorned the triumph, of Constantine. After a tranquil and prosperous reign, the conqueror bequeathed to his family the inheritance of the Roman empire: a new capital, a new policy, and a new religion; and the innovations which he established have been embraced and consecrated by succeeding generations. The age of the great Constantine and his sons is filled with important events; but the historian must be oppressed by their number and variety, unless he diligently separates from each other the scenes which are connected only by the order of time. He will describe the political institutions that gave strength and stability to the empire, before he proceeds to relate the wars and revolutions which hastened its decline. He will adopt the division, unknown to the ancients, of civil and ecclesiastical affairs: the victory of the Christians and their intestine discord will supply copious and distinct materials both for edification and for scandal.

Design of a new capital. A.D. 324 [326 ?] After the defeat and abdication of Licinius, his victorious rival proceeded to lay the foundations of a city destined to reign in future times the mistress of the East, and to survive the empire and religion of Constantine. The motives, whether of pride or of policy, which first induced Diocletian to withdraw himself from the ancient seat of government, had acquired additional weight by the example of his successors and the habits of forty years. Rome was insensibly confounded with the dependent kingdoms which had once acknowledged her supremacy; and the country of the Cæsars was viewed with cold indifference by a martial prince, born in the neighbourhood of the Danube, educated in the courts and armies of Asia, and invested with the purple by the legions of Britain. The Italians, who had received Constantine as their deliverer, submissively obeyed the edicts which he sometimes condescended to address to the senate and people of Rome; but they were seldom honoured with the presence of their new sovereign. During the vigour of his age, Constantine, according to the various exigencies of peace and war, moved with slow dignity, or with active diligence, along the frontiers of his extensive dominions; and was always prepared to take the field either against a foreign or a domestic enemy. But, as he gradually reached the summit of prosperity and the decline of life, he began to meditate the design of fixing in a more permanent station the strength as well as majesty of the throne. In the choice of an advantageous situation, he preferred the confines of Europe and Asia; to curb, with a powerful arm, the barbarians who dwelt between the Danube and the Tanais; to watch with an eye of jealousy the conduct of the Persian monarch, who indignantly supported the yoke of an ignominious treaty. With these views Diocletian had selected and embellished the residence of Nicomedia: but the memory of Diocletian was justly abhorred by the protector of the church; and Constantine was not insensible to the ambition of founding a city which might perpetuate the glory of his own name. During the late operations of the war against Licinius, he had sufficient opportunity to contemplate, both as a soldier and as a statesman, the incomparable position of Byzantium; and to observe how strongly it was guarded by nature against an hostile attack, whilst it was accessible on every side to the benefits of commercial intercourse. Many ages before Constantine, one of the most judicious historians of antiquity[1] had described the advantages of a situation, from whence a feeble colony of Greeks derived the command of the sea and the honours of a flourishing and independent republic.[2]

Situation of Byzantium

If we survey Byzantium in the extent which it acquired with the august name of Constantinople, the figure of the Imperial city may be represented under that of an unequal triangle.

Description of Constantinople

---

[1] Polybius, l. iv. p. 423, edit. Casaubon [c. 45]. He observes that the peace of the Byzantines was frequently disturbed, and the extent of their territory contracted, by the inroads of the wild Thracians.

[2] The navigator Byzas, who was styled the son of Neptune, founded the city 656 [*leg.* 657] years before the Christian æra. His followers were drawn from Argos and Megara. Byzantium was afterwards rebuilt and fortified by the Spartan general Pausanias. See Scaliger Animadvers. ad Euseb. p. 81. Ducange, Constantinopolis, l. i. part i. cap. 15, 16. With regard to the wars of the Byzantines against Philip, the Gauls, and the kings of Bithynia, we should trust none but the ancient writers who lived before the greatness of the Imperial city had excited a spirit of flattery and fiction.

The obtuse point, which advances towards the east and the shores of Asia, meets and repels the waves of the Thracian Bosphorus. The northern side of the city is bounded by the harbour; and the southern is washed by the Propontis, or sea of Marmara. The basis of the triangle is opposed to the west, and terminates the continent of Europe. But the admirable form and division of the circumjacent land and water cannot, without a more ample explanation, be clearly or sufficiently understood.

The Bosphorus

The winding channel through which the waters of the Euxine flow with a rapid and incessant course towards the Mediterranean received the appellation of Bosphorus, a name not less celebrated in the history than in the fables of antiquity.[3] A crowd of temples and of votive altars, profusely scattered along its steep and woody banks, attested the unskilfulness, the terrors, and the devotion of the Grecian navigators, who, after the example of the Argonauts, explored the dangers of the inhospitable Euxine. On these banks tradition long preserved the memory of the palace of Phineus, infested by the obscene harpies;[4] and of the sylvan reign of Amycus, who defied the son of Leda to the combat of the Cestus.[5] The straits of the Bosphorus are terminated by the Cyanean rocks, which, according to the description of the poets, had once floated on the face of the waters, and were destined by the gods to protect the entrance of the Euxine against the eye of profane curiosity.[6] From the Cyanean rocks to the point and harbour of Byzantium, the winding length of the Bosphorus extends about sixteen miles,[7] and its most ordinary breadth may

[3] The Bosphorus has been very minutely described by Dionysius of Byzantium, who lived in the time of Domitian (Hudson, Geograph. Minor. tom. iii.), and by Gilles or Gyllius, a French traveller of the XVIth century. Tournefort (Lettre XV.) seems to have used his own eyes and the learning of Gyllius.

[4] There are very few conjectures so happy as that of Le Clerc (Bibliothèque Universelle, tom. i. p. 148), who supposes that the harpies were only locusts. The Syriac or Phœnician name of those insects, their noisy flight, the stench and devastation which they occasion, and the north wind which drives them into the sea, all contribute to form this striking resemblance.

[5] The residence of Amycus was in Asia, between the old and the new castles, at a place called Laurus Insana. That of Phineus was in Europe, near the village of Mauromole and the Black Sea. See Gyllius de Bosph. l. ii. c. 23. Tournefort, Lettre XV.

[6] The deception was occasioned by several pointed rocks, alternately covered and abandoned by the waves. At present there are two small islands, one towards either shore: that of Europe is distinguished by the column of Pompey.

[7] The ancients computed one hundred and twenty stadia, or fifteen Roman miles. They measured only from the new castles, but they carried the straits as far as the town of Chalcedon.

be computed at about one mile and a half. The *new* castles of Europe and Asia are constructed, on either continent, upon the foundations of two celebrated temples, of Serapis and of Jupiter Urius. The *old* castles, a work of the Greek emperors, command the narrowest part of the channel, in a place where the opposite banks advance within five hundred paces of each other. These fortresses were restored and strengthened by Mahomet the Second, when he meditated the siege of Constantinople:[8] but the Turkish conqueror was most probably ignorant that, near two thousand years before his reign, Darius had chosen the same situation to connect the two continents by a bridge of boats.[9] At a small distance from the old castles we discover the little town of Chrysopolis, or Scutari, which may almost be considered as the Asiatic suburb of Constantinople. The Bosphorus, as it begins to open into the Propontis, passes between Byzantium and Chalcedon. The latter of those cities was built by the Greeks, a few years before the former; and the blindness of its founders, who overlooked the superior advantages of the opposite coast, has been stigmatized by a proverbial expression of contempt.[10]

The harbour of Constantinople, which may be considered as The port an arm of the Bosphorus, obtained, in a very remote period, the denomination of the *Golden Horn*. The curve which it describes might be compared to the horn of a stag, or, as it should seem, with more propriety, to that of an ox.[11] The epithet of *golden* was expressive of the riches which every wind wafted from the most distant countries into the secure and capacious port of Constantinople. The river Lycus, formed by the conflux of two little streams, pours into the harbour[12] a perpetual supply of fresh water, which serves to cleanse the

---

[8] Ducas, Hist. c. 34. Leunclavius, Hist. Turcica Mussulmanica, l. xv. p. 577. Under the Greek empire these castles were used as state prisons, under the tremendous name of Lethe, or towers of oblivion.

[9] Darius engraved in Greek and Assyrian letters on two marble columns the names of his subject nations, and the amazing numbers of his land and sea forces. The Byzantines afterwards transported these columns into the city, and used them for the altars of their tutelar deities. Herodotus, l. iv. c. 87.

[10] Namque artissimo inter Europam Asiamque divortio Byzantium in extremâ Europâ posuere Græci, quibus, Pythium Apollinem consulentibus ubi conderent urbem, redditum oraculum est, quærerent sedem *cæcorum* terris adversam. Eâ ambage Chalcedonii monstrabantur, quod priores illuc advecti prævisâ locorum utilitate pejora legissent. Tacit. Annal. xii. 62.

[11] Strabo, l. x. p. 492. Most of the antlers are now broke off; or, to speak less figuratively, most of the recesses of the harbour are filled up. See Gyllius de Bosphoro Thracio, l. i. c. 5.

[12] [It flowed into the Propontis. See Plan.]

bottom and to invite the periodical shoals of fish to seek their retreat in that convenient recess. As the vicissitudes of tides are scarcely felt in those seas, the constant depth of the harbour allows goods to be landed on the quays without the assistance of boats; and it has been observed that in many places the largest vessels may rest their prows against the houses, while their sterns are floating in the water.[13] From the mouth of the Lycus to that of the harbour this arm of the Bosphorus is more than seven miles in length. The entrance is about five hundred yards broad, and a strong chain could be occasionally drawn across it, to guard the port and city from the attack of an hostile navy.[14]

The Propontis   Between the Bosphorus and the Hellespont, the shores of Europe and Asia receding on either side inclose the sea of Marmara, which was known to the ancients by the denomination of Propontis. The navigation from the issue of the Bosphorus to the entrance of the Hellespont is about one hundred and twenty miles. Those who steer their westward course through the middle of the Propontis may at once descry the high lands of Thrace and Bithynia, and never lose sight of the lofty summit of Mount Olympus, covered with eternal snows.[15] They leave on the left a deep gulf, at the bottom of which Nicomedia was seated, the imperial residence of Diocletian; and they pass the small islands of Cyzicus and Proconnesus before they cast anchor at Gallipoli; where the sea, which separates Asia from Europe, is again contracted into a narrow channel.

The Helles-pont   The geographers who, with the most skilful accuracy, have surveyed the form and extent of the Hellespont, assign about sixty miles for the winding course, and about three miles for the ordinary breadth of those celebrated straits.[16] But the

---

[13] Procopius de Ædificiis, l. i. c. 5. His description is confirmed by modern travellers. See Thévenot, part i. l. i. c. 15. Tournefort, Lettre XII. Niebuhr, Voyage d'Arabie, p. 22. [The description of Himerius is rhetorical, or. 16.]

[14] See Ducange, C. P. l. i. part i. c. 16, and his Observations sur Villehardouin, p. 289. The chain was drawn from the Acropolis near the modern Kiosk to the tower of Galata, and was supported at convenient distances by large wooden piles.

[15] Thévenot (Voyages au Levant, part i. l. i. c. 14) contracts the measure to 125 small Greek miles. Belon (Observations, l. ii. c. 1) gives a good description of the Propontis, but contents himself with the vague expression of one day and one night's sail. When Sandys (Travels, p. 21) talks of 150 furlongs in length as well as breadth, we can only suppose some mistake of the press in the text of that judicious traveller.

[16] See an admirable dissertation of M. d'Anville upon the Hellespont or Dardanelles, in the Mémoires de l'Académie des Inscriptions, tom. xxviii. p. 318-

narrowest part of the channel is found to the northward of the old Turkish castles between the cities of Sestus and Abydus. It was here that the adventurous Leander braved the passage of the flood for the possession of his mistress.[17] It was here likewise, in a place where the distance between the opposite banks cannot exceed five hundred paces, that Xerxes imposed a stupendous bridge of boats, for the purpose of transporting into Europe an hundred and seventy myriads of barbarians.[18] A sea contracted within such narrow limits may seem but ill to deserve the singular epithet of *broad,* which Homer, as well as Orpheus, has frequently bestowed on the Hellespont. But our ideas of greatness are of a relative nature : the traveller, and especially the poet, who sailed along the Hellespont, who pursued the windings of the stream, and contemplated the rural scenery, which appeared on every side to terminate the prospect, insensibly lost the remembrance of the sea ; and his fancy painted those celebrated straits with all the attributes of a mighty river flowing with a swift current, in the midst of a woody and inland country, and at length, through a wide mouth, discharging itself into the Ægean or Archipelago.[19] Ancient Troy,[20] seated on an eminence at the foot of Mount Ida, overlooked the mouth of the Hellespont, which scarcely received an accession of waters from the tribute of those immortal rivulets Simois and Scamander. The Grecian camp had stretched twelve

346. Yet even that ingenious geographer is too fond of supposing new and perhaps imaginary *measures,* for the purpose of rendering ancient writers as accurate as himself. The stadia employed by Herodotus in the description of the Euxine, the Bosphorus, &c. (l. iv. c. 85). must undoubtedly be all of the same species ; but it seems impossible to reconcile them either with truth or with each other. [Length of Propontis about 40 miles, breadth 1 mile.]

[17] The oblique distance between Sestus and Abydus was thirty stadia. The improbable tale of Hero and Leander is exposed by M. Mahudel, but is defended on the authority of poets and medals by M. de la Nauze. See the Académie des Inscriptions, tom. vii. Hist. p. 74. Mém. p. 240.

[18] See the seventh book of Herodotus, who has erected an elegant trophy to his own fame and to that of his country. The review appears to have been made with tolerable accuracy ; but the vanity, first of the Persians and afterwards of the Greeks, was interested to magnify the armament and the victory. I should much doubt whether the *invaders* have ever outnumbered the *men* of any country which they attacked.

[19] See Wood's observations on Homer, p. 320. I have, with pleasure, selected this remark from an author who in general seems to have disappointed the expectation of the public as a critic, and still more as a traveller. He had visited the banks of the Hellespont; he had read Strabo; he ought to have consulted the Roman itineraries; how was it possible for him to confound Ilium and Alexandria Troas (Observations, p. 340, 341), two cities which were sixteen miles distant from each other .

[20] Demetrius of Scepsis wrote sixty books on thirty lines of Homer's Catalogue. The XIIIth Book of Strabo is sufficient for *our* curiosity.

miles along the shore from the Sigæan to the Rhœtean promontory; and the flanks of the army were guarded by the bravest chiefs who fought under the banners of Agamemnon. The first of those promontories was occupied by Achilles with his invincible Myrmidons, and the dauntless Ajax pitched his tents on the other. After Ajax had fallen a sacrifice to his disappointed pride and to the ingratitude of the Greeks, his sepulchre was erected on the ground where he had defended the navy against the rage of Jove and of Hector; and the citizens of the rising town of Rhœteum celebrated his memory with divine honours.[21] Before Constantine gave a just preference to the situation of Byzantium, he had conceived the design of erecting the seat of empire on this celebrated spot, from whence the Romans derived their fabulous origin. The extensive plain which lies below ancient Troy, towards the Rhœtean promontory and the tomb of Ajax, was first chosen for his new capital; and, though the undertaking was soon relinquished, the stately remains of unfinished walls and towers attracted the notice of all who sailed through the straits of the Hellespont.[22]

Advantages of Constantinople

We are at present qualified to view the advantageous position of Constantinople; which appears to have been formed by Nature for the centre and capital of a great monarchy. Situated in the forty-first degree of latitude, the imperial city commanded, from her seven hills,[23] the opposite shores of Europe and Asia; the climate was healthy and temperate, the soil fertile, the harbour secure and capacious; and the approach on the side of the continent was of small extent and easy defence. The Bosphorus and Hellespont may be considered as the two gates of Constantinople; and the prince who possessed those important passages could always shut them against a naval enemy and open them to the fleets of commerce. The preserva-

[21] Strabo, l. xiii. p. 595. The disposition of the ships which were drawn upon dry land, and the posts of Ajax and Achilles, are very clearly described by Homer. See Iliad ix. [leg. viii.] 220.

[22] Zosim. l. ii. p. 105 [c. 30]. Sozomen, l. ii. c. 3. Theophanes, p. 18. Nicephorus Callistus, l. vii. p. 48. Zonaras, tom. ii. l. xiii. p. 6 [3]. Zosimus places the new city between Ilium and Alexandria, but this apparent difference may be reconciled by the large extent of its circumference. [There is some doubt about the text of Zosimus, see Mendelssohn ad. loc.] Before the foundation of Constantinople, Thessalonica is mentioned by Cedrenus (p. 283) [i. 496. Bonn]. and Sardica by Zonaras, as the intended capital. [Cp. also Anon. Continuator of Dion (prob. Peter the Patrician), Müller, F. H. G. 4, 199.] They both suppose, with very little probability, that the emperor, if he had not been prevented by a prodigy, would have repeated the mistake of the *blind* Chalcedonians.

[23] Pocock's Description of the East, vol. ii. part ii. p. 127. His plan of the seven hills is clear and accurate. That traveller is seldom so satisfactory.

tion of the eastern provinces may, in some degree, be ascribed to the policy of Constantine, as the barbarians of the Euxine, who in the preceding age had poured their armaments into the heart of the Mediterranean, soon desisted from the exercise of piracy, and despaired of forcing this insurmountable barrier. When the gates of the Hellespont and Bosphorus were shut, the capital still enjoyed, within their spacious inclosure, every production which could supply the wants, or gratify the luxury, of its numerous inhabitants. The sea-coast of Thrace and Bithynia, which languish under the weight of Turkish oppression, still exhibits a rich prospect of vineyards, of gardens, and of plentiful harvests ; and the Propontis has ever been renowned for an inexhaustible store of the most exquisite fish, that are taken in their stated seasons without skill and almost without labour.[24] But, when the passages of the Straits were thrown open for trade, they alternately admitted the natural and artificial riches of the north and south, of the Euxine, and of the Mediterranean. Whatever rude commodities were collected in the forests of Germany and Scythia, as far as the sources of the Tanais and the Borysthenes ; whatsoever was manufactured by the skill of Europe or Asia ; the corn of Egypt, and the gems and spices of the farthest India, were brought by the varying winds into the port of Constantinople, which, for many ages, attracted the commerce of the ancient world.[25]

The prospect of beauty, of safety, and of wealth, united in a single spot, was sufficient to justify the choice of Constantine. But, as some decent mixture of prodigy and fable has, in every age, been supposed to reflect a becoming majesty on the origin of great cities,[26] the emperor was desirous of ascribing his resolution, not so much to the uncertain counsels of human policy, as to the infallible and eternal decrees of divine wisdom. In one of his laws he has been careful to instruct posterity that, in obedience to the commands of God, he laid the everlasting foundations of Constantinople :[27] and, though he has not con-

Foundation of the city

---

[24] See Belon, Observations, c. 72-76. Among a variety of different species, the Pelamides, a sort of Thunnies, were the most celebrated. We may learn from Polybius, Strabo, and Tacitus that the profits of the fishery constituted the principal revenue of Byzantium.

[25] See the eloquent description of Busbequius, epistol. i. p. 64, Est in Europa ; habet in conspectu Asiam, Ægyptum, Africamque a dextrâ : quæ tametsi contiguæ non sunt, maris tamen navigandique commoditate veluti junguntur. A sinistra vero Pontus est Euxinus, &c.

[26] Datur hæc venia antiquitati, ut, miscendo humana divinis, primordia urbium augustiora faciat, T. Liv. in proem.

[27] He says in one of his laws, pro commoditate Urbis quam æterno nomine, jubente Deo, donavimus. Cod. Theodos. l. xiii. tit. v. leg. 7.

descended to relate in what manner the celestial inspiration was communicated to his mind, the defect of his modest silence has been liberally supplied by the ingenuity of succeeding writers, who describe the nocturnal vision which appeared to the fancy of Constantine, as he slept within the walls of Byzantium. The tutelar genius of the city, a venerable matron sinking under the weight of years and infirmities, was suddenly transformed into a blooming maid, whom his own hands adorned with all the symbols of imperial greatness.[28] The monarch awoke, interpreted the auspicious omen, and obeyed, without hesitation, the will of heaven. The day which gave birth to a city or colony was celebrated by the Romans with such ceremonies as had been ordained by a generous superstition ;[29] and, though Constantine might omit some rites which savoured too strongly of their Pagan origin, yet he was anxious to leave a deep impression of hope and respect on the minds of the spectators. On foot, with a lance in his hand, the emperor himself led the solemn procession ; and directed the line which was traced as the boundary of the destined capital ; till the growing circumference was observed with astonishment by the assistants, who, at length, ventured to observe that he had already exceeded the most ample measure of a great city. " I shall still advance," replied Constantine, " till HE, the invisible guide who marches before me, thinks proper to stop." [30] Without presuming to investigate the nature or motives of this extraordinary conductor, we shall content ourselves with the more humble task of describing the extent and limits of Constantinople.[31]

Extent   In the actual state of the city, the palace and gardens of the Seraglio occupy the eastern promontory, the first of the seven hills, and cover about one hundred and fifty acres of our own

[28] The Greeks, Theophanes, Cedrenus, and the author of the Alexandrian Chronicle, confine themselves to vague and general expressions. For a more particular account of the vision, we are obliged to have recourse to such Latin writers as William of Malmesbury. See Ducange, C. P. l. i. p. 24, 25.

[29] See Plutarch in Romul. tom. i. p. 49, edit. Bryan. Among other ceremonies, a large hole, which had been dug for that purpose, was filled up with handfuls of earth, which each of the settlers brought from the place of his birth, and thus adopted his new country.

[30] Philostorgius, l. ii. c. 9. This incident, though borrowed from a suspected writer, is characteristic and probable.

[31] See in the Mémoires de l'Académie, tom. xxxv. p. 747-758, a dissertation of M. d'Anville on the extent of Constantinople. He takes the plan inserted in the Imperium Orientale of Banduri as the most complete ; but, by a series of very nice observations, he reduces the extravagant proportion of the scale, and instead of 9500, determines the circumference of the city as consisting of about 7800 French *toises.*

measure. The seat of Turkish jealousy and despotism is erected
on the foundations of a Grecian republic; but it may be supposed that the Byzantines were tempted by the conveniency
of the harbour to extend their habitations on that side beyond
the modern limits of the Seraglio. The new walls of Constantine
stretched from the port to the Propontis across the enlarged
breadth of the triangle, at the distance of fifteen stadia from
the ancient fortification; and with the city of Byzantium they
inclosed five of the seven hills, which, to the eyes of those
who approach Constantinople, appear to rise above each other
in beautiful order.[32] About a century after the death of the
founder, the new building, extending on one side up the harbour,
and on the other along the Propontis, already covered the
narrow ridge of the sixth, and the broad summit of the seventh,
hill. The necessity of protecting those suburbs from the
incessant inroads of the barbarians engaged the younger
Theodosius to surround his capital with an adequate and
permanent inclosure of walls.[33] From the eastern promontory
to the golden gate, the extreme length of Constantinople
was about three Roman miles;[34] the circumference measured
between ten and eleven; and the surface might be computed
as equal to about two thousand English acres. It is impossible
to justify the vain and credulous exaggerations of modern
travellers, who have sometimes stretched the limits of Constantinople over the adjacent villages of the European, and
even of the Asiatic, coast.[35] But the suburbs of Pera and

[32] Codinus Antiquitat. Const. p. 12. He assigns the church of St. Antony as
the boundary on the side of the harbour. It is mentioned in Ducange, l. iv. c.
6.; but I have tried, without success, to discover the exact place where it was
situated. [The Monastery of St. Antony, Kauleas, near the Neôrion (see Plan).
The two hills outside Constantine's wall are v. and vi.; and the space between the
wall and that of Theodosius was never included in the Regions of the city, but
was called exokionion and was divided into seven quarters (*deuteron, triton, &c.*),
except Blachernæ, which formed Region xiv. See plan, and Mordtmann, Esquisse
top. de Constantinople, p. 2.]

[33] The new wall of Theodosius was constructed in the year 413. In 447 it was
thrown down by an earthquake, and rebuilt in three months by the diligence of the
præfect Cyrus. The suburb of the Blachernæ was first taken into the city in the
reign of Heraclius. Ducange Const. l. i. c. 10, 11. [The triple defence of Theodosius ii. can be clearly traced: (1) inner wall of Anthemius; (2) the outer wall
of Cyrus; (3) a ditch and counterscarp, representing a third wall (Mordtmann,
ib. p. 11).]

[34] The measurement is expressed in the Notitia by 14,075 feet. It is reasonable
to suppose hat hese were Greek feet; the proportion of which has been ingeniously determined by M. d'Anville. He compares the 180 feet with the 78
Hashemite cubits which in different writers are assigned for the height of St.
Sophia. Each of these cubits was equal to 27 French inches.

[35] The accurate Thévenot (l. i. c. 15) walked in one hour and three quarters

Galata, though situate beyond the harbour, may deserve to be considered as a part of the city;[36] and this addition may perhaps authorize the measure of a Byzantine historian, who assigns sixteen Greek (about fourteen Roman) miles for the circumference of his native city.[37] Such an extent may seem not worthy of an imperial residence. Yet Constantinople must yield to Babylon and Thebes,[38] to ancient Rome, to London, and even to Paris.[39]

Progress of the work

The master of the Roman world, who aspired to erect an eternal monument of the glories of his reign, could employ in the prosecution of that great work the wealth, the labour, and all that yet remained of the genius, of obedient millions. Some estimate may be formed of the expense bestowed with imperial liberality on the foundation of Constantinople, by the allowance of about two millions five hundred thousand pounds for the construction of the walls, the porticoes, and the aqueducts.[40] The forests that overshadowed the shores of the Euxine, and the celebrated quarries of white marble in the little island of Proconnesus, supplied an inexhaustible stock of materials, ready to be conveyed, by the convenience of a short water-carriage, to the harbour of Byzantium.[41] A multitude

round two of the sides of the triangle, from the Kiosk of the Seraglio to the seven towers. D'Anville examines with care, and receives with confidence, this decisive testimony, which gives a circumference of ten or twelve miles. The extravagant computation of Tournefort (Lettre XI.) of thirty-four or thirty miles, without including Scutari, is a strange departure from his usual character.

[36] The sycæ, or fig-trees, formed the thirteenth region, and were very much embellished by Justinian. It has since borne the names of Pera and Galata. The etymology of the former is obvious; that of the latter is unknown. See Ducange Const. l. i. c. 22, and Gyllius de Byzant. l. iv. c. 10. [It seems probable that Galata was the quarter of Celtic mercenaries in 3rd century B.C., and hence, like the country of Galatia, derived its name.]

[37] One hundred and eleven stadia, which may be translated into modern Greek miles each of seven stadia, or 660 sometimes only 600, French toises. See d'Anville, Mesures tinéraires, p. 53.

[38] When the ancient texts which describe the size of Babylon and Thebes are settled, the exaggerations reduced, and the measures ascertained, we find that those famous cities filled the great but not incredible circumference of about twenty-five or thirty miles. Compare d'Anville, Mém. de l'Acad. tom. xxxviii. p. 235, with his Description de l'Egypte, p. 201, 202.

[39] If we divide Constantinople and Paris into equal squares of 50 French toises, the former contains 850, and the latter 1160 of those divisions.

[40] Six hundred centenaries, or sixty thousand pounds weight of gold. This sum is taken from Codinus Antiquit. Const. p. 11; but, unless that contemptible author had derived his information from some purer sources, he would probably have been unacquainted with so obsolete a mode of reckoning.

[41] For the forests of the Black Sea, consult Tournefort, Lettre XVI.; for the marble quarries of Proconnesus, see Strabo, l. xiii. p. 588. The latter had already furnished the materials of the stately buildings of Cyzicus.

of labourers and artificers urged the conclusion of the work with incessant toil : but the impatience of Constantine soon discovered that, in the decline of the arts, the skill as well as numbers of his architects bore a very unequal proportion to the greatness of his designs. The magistrates of the most distant provinces were therefore directed to institute schools, to appoint professors, and by the hopes of rewards and privileges, to engage in the study and practice of architecture a sufficient number of ingenious youths, who had received a liberal educa-tion.[42] The buildings of the new city were executed by such artificers as the reign of Constantine could afford ; but they were decorated by the hands of the most celebrated masters of the age of Pericles and Alexander. To revive the genius of Phidias and Lysippus surpassed indeed the power of a Roman emperor ; but the immortal productions which they had be-queathed to posterity were exposed without defence to the rapacious vanity of a despot. By his commands the cities of Greece and Asia were despoiled of their most valuable orna-ments.[43] The trophies of memorable wars, the objects of religious veneration, the most finished statues of the gods and heroes, of the sages and poets, of ancient times, contributed to the splendid triumph of Constantinople ; and gave occasion to the remark of the historian Cedrenus,[44] who observes, with some enthusiasm, that nothing seemed wanting except the souls of the illustrious men whom those admirable monuments were intended to represent. But it is not in the city of Con-stantine, nor in the declining period of an empire when the human mind was depressed by civil and religious slavery, that we should seek for the souls of Homer and of Demos-thenes.

During the siege of Byzantium, the conqueror had pitched Edifices his tent on the commanding eminence of the second hill. To perpetuate the memory of his success, he chose the same

[42] See the Codex Theodos. l. xiii. tit. iv. leg. 1.   This law is dated in the year 334, and was addressed to the præfect of Italy, whose jurisdiction extended over Africa.   The commentary of Godefroy on the whole title well deserves to be consulted.

[43] Constantinoplis dedicatur pœne omnium urbium nuditate. Hieronym. Chron. p. 181. See Codinus, p. 8, 9.   The author of the Antiquitat. Const. l. iii. (apud Banduri Imp. Orient. tom. i. p. 41), enumerates Rome, Sicily, Antioch, Athens, and a long list of other cities.   The provinces of Greece and Asia Minormay be supposed to have yielded the richest booty.

[44] Hist. Compend. p. 369 [i. 648, Bonn].   He describes the statue, or rather bust, of Homer with a degree of taste which plainly indicates that Cedrenus copied the style of a more fortunate age.

advantageous position for the principal Forum ; [45] which appears
to have been of a circular, or rather elliptical form. The two
opposite entrances formed triumphal arches; the porticoes, which
inclosed it on every side, were filled with statues ; and the
centre of the Forum was occupied by a lofty column, of which
a mutilated fragment is now degraded by the appellation of the
burnt pillar. This column was erected on a pedestal of white
marble twenty feet high ; and was composed of ten pieces of
porphyry, each of which measured above ten feet in height
and about thirty-three in circumference.[46]   On the summit of
the pillar, above one hundred and twenty feet from the ground,
stood the colossal statue of Apollo.   It was of bronze, had been
transported either from Athens or from a town of Phrygia, and
was supposed to be the work of Phidias.   The artist had represented the god of day, or, as it was afterwards interpreted,
the emperor Constantine himself, with a sceptre in his right
hand, the globe of the world in his left, and a crown of rays
glittering on his head.[47]   The Circus, or Hippodrome, was a
stately building about four hundred paces in length and one
hundred in breadth.[48]   The space between the two *metœ* or
goals was filled with statues and obelisks ; and we may still
remark a very singular fragment of antiquity ; the bodies of
three serpents, twisted into one pillar of brass.   Their triple
heads had once supported the golden tripod which, after the
defeat of Xerxes, was consecrated in the temple of Delphi by
the victorious Greeks.[49]   The beauty of the Hippodrome has

[45] Zosim. l. ii. p. 106 [c. 30].   Chron. Alexandrin. vel Paschal. p. 284 [528,
Bonn].   Ducange Const. l. i. c. 24.   Even the last of those writers seems to
confound the Forum of Constantine with the Augusteum, or court of the palace.
I am not satisfied whether I have properly distinguished what belongs to the one
and the other.   [See App. 9.]

[46] The most tolerable account of this column is given by Pocock.   Description
of the East, vol. ii. part ii. p. 131.   But it is still in many instances perplexed and
unsatisfactory.

[47] Ducange Const. l. i. c. 24, p. 76, and his notes ad Alexiad. p. 382.   The
statue of Constantine or Apollo was thrown down under the reign of Alexis
Comnenus.

[48] Tournefort (Lettre XII) computes the Atmeidan at four hundred paces.
If he means geometrical paces of five feet each, it was three hundred *toises*
in length, about forty more than the great Circus of Rome.   See d'Anville,
Mesures Itinéraires, p. 73.   [According to the measurements of M. Paspatês the
length was 320 yards long, 79 yards broad.]

[49] The guardians of the most holy relics would rejoice if they were able to
produce such a chain of evidence as may be alleged on this occasion.   See
Banduri ad Antiquitat. Const. p. 668.   Gyllius de Byzant. l. ii. c. 13.   1. The
original consecration of the tripod and pillar in the temple of Delphi may be
proved from Herodotus and Pausanias.   2. The Pagan Zosimus agrees with the
three ecclesiastical historians, Eusebius, Socrates, and Sozomen, that the sacred

been long since defaced by the rude hands of the Turkish conquerors ; but, under the similar appellation of Atmeidan, it still serves as a place of exercise for their horses.   From the throne, whence the emperor viewed the Circensian games, a winding staircase [50] descended to the palace ; a magnificent edifice, which scarcely yielded to the residence of Rome itself, and which, together with the dependent courts, gardens, and porticoes, covered a considerable extent of ground upon the banks of the Propontis between the Hippodrome and the church of St. Sophia.[51]   We might likewise celebrate the baths, which still retained the name of Zeuxippus, after they had been enriched, by the munificence of Constantine, with lofty columns, various marbles, and above threescore statues of bronze.[52]   But we should deviate from the design of this history, if we attempted minutely to describe the different buildings or quarters of the city.   It may be sufficient to observe that whatever could adorn the dignity of a great capital, or contribute to the benefit or pleasure of its numerous inhabitants, was contained within the walls of Constantinople. A particular description, composed about a century after its foundation, enumerates a capitol or school of learning, a circus,

ornaments of the temple of Delphi were removed to Constantinople by the order of Constantine ; and among these the serpentine pillar of the Hippodrome is particularly mentioned.   3. All the European travellers who have visited Constantinople, from Buondelmonte to Pocock, describe it in the same place, and almost in the same manner ; the differences between them are occasioned only by the injuries which it has sustained from the Turks.   Mahomet the Second broke the underjaw of one of the serpents with a stroke of his battle-axe.   Thévenot, l. i. c. 17. [Zosimus mentions only a tripod of Apollo with a statue of the god on it (ii. 31), but not the serpent coils, and therefore (so Mendelssohn) not the Platæan dedication.]

[50] The Latin name *Cochlea* was adopted by the Greeks, and very frequently occurs in the Byzantine history.   Ducange Const. l. ii. c. i. p. 104.

[51] There are three topographical points which indicate the situation of the palace.   1. The staircase, which connected it with the Hippodrome or Atmeidan. 2. A small artificial port on the Propontis, from whence there was an easy ascent, by a flight of marble steps, to the gardens of the palace.   3. The Augusteum was a spacious court, one side of which was occupied by the front of the palace, and another by the church of St. Sophia.   [See App. 9]

[52] Zeuxippus was an epithet of Jupiter, and the baths were a part of old Byzantium.   The difficulty of assigning their true situation has not been felt by Ducange.   History seems to connect them with St. Sophia and the palace ; but the original plan, inserted in Banduri, places them on the other side of the city, near the harbour.   [They were close to the Palace and Hippodrome, on south side of the Augusteum, see App. 9.]   For their beauties, see Chron. Paschal., p. 285, and Gyllius de Byzant. l. ii. c. 7.   Christodorus (see Antiquitat. Const. l. vii.) composed inscriptions in verse for each of the statues.   He was a Theban poet in genius as well as in birth :

Bœotum in crasso jurares aëre natum.

two theatres, eight public, and one hundred and fifty-three private, baths, fifty-two porticoes, five granaries, eight aqueducts or reservoirs of water, four spacious halls for the meetings of the senate or courts of justice, fourteen churches, fourteen palaces, and four thousand three hundred and eighty-eight houses, which, for their size or beauty, deserved to be distinguished from the multitude of plebeian habitations.[53]

Population   The populousness of his favoured city was the next and most serious object of the attention of its founder. In the dark ages which succeeded the translation of the empire, the remote and the immediate consequences of that memorable event were strangely confounded by the vanity of the Greeks and the credulity of the Latins.[54] It was asserted and believed that all the noble families of Rome, the senate, and the equestrian order, with their innumerable attendants, had followed their emperor to the banks of the Propontis ; that a spurious race of strangers and plebeians was left to possess the solitude of the ancient capital ; and that the lands of Italy, long since converted into gardens, were at once deprived of cultivation and inhabitants.[55] In the course of this history, such exaggerations will be reduced to their just value : yet, since the growth of Constantinople cannot be ascribed to the general increase of mankind and of industry, it must be admitted that this artificial colony was raised at the expense of the ancient cities of the empire. Many opulent senators of Rome, and of the Eastern provinces, were probably invited by Constantine to adopt for their country the fortunate spot which he had chosen for his own residence. The invitations of a master are scarcely to be distinguished from commands ; and the liberality of the emperor obtained a ready and cheerful obedience. He bestowed on his favourites the palaces which he had built in the several quarters of the city, assigned them lands and pensions

[53] See the Notitia. Rome only reckoned 1780 large houses, *domus ;* but the word must have had a more dignified signification. No *insulæ* are mentioned at Constantinople. The old capital consisted of 424 streets, the new of 322.

[54] Liutprand, Legatio ad Imp. Nicephorum, p. 153 [c. 62]. The modern Greeks have strangely disfigured the antiquities of Constantinople. We might excuse the errors of the Turkish or Arabian writers ; but it is somewhat astonishing that the Greeks, who had access to the authentic materials preserved in their own language, should prefer fiction to truth and loose tradition to genuine history. In a single page of Codinus we may detect twelve unpardonable mistakes ; the reconciliation of Severus and Niger, the marriage of their son and daughter, the siege of Byzantium by the Macedonians, the invasion of the Gauls, which recalled Severus to Rome, the *sixty* years which elapsed from his death to the foundation of Constantinople, &c.

[55] Montesquieu, Grandeur et Décadence des Romains, c. 17.

for the support of their dignity,[56] and alienated the demesnes of Pontus and Asia, to grant hereditary estates by the easy tenure of maintaining a house in the capital.[57]   But these encouragements and obligations soon became superfluous, and were gradually abolished.   Wherever the seat of government is fixed, a considerable part of the public revenue will be expended by the prince himself, by his ministers, by the officers of justice, and by the domestics of the palace.   The most wealthy of the provincials will be attracted by the powerful motives of interest and duty, of amusement and curiosity.   A third and more numerous class of inhabitants will insensibly be formed, of servants, of artificers, and of merchants, who derive their subsistence from their own labour and from the wants or luxury of the superior ranks.   In less than a century, Constantinople disputed with Rome itself the pre-eminence of riches and numbers.   New piles of buildings, crowded together with too little regard to health or convenience, scarcely allowed the intervals of narrow streets for the perpetual throng of men, of horses, and of carriages.   The allotted space of ground was insufficient to contain the increasing people; and the additional foundations, which, on either side, were advanced into the sea, might alone have composed a very considerable city.[58]

The frequent and regular distributions of wine and oil, of corn or bread, of money or provisions, had almost exempted the poorer citizens of Rome from the necessity of labour.   The magnificence of the first Cæsars was in some measure imitated by the founder of Constantinople : [59] but his liberality, however

Privileges

---

[56] Themist. Orat. iii. p. 48. edit Hardouin. Sozomen, l. ii. c. 3.   Zosim. l. ii. p. 107 [32]. Anonym. Valesian. p. 715 [§ 30]. If we could credit Codinus (p. 10), Constantine built houses for the senators on the exact model of their Roman palaces, and gratified them, as well as himself, with the pleasure of an agreeable surprise; but the whole story is full of fictions and inconsistencies.

[57] The law by which the younger Theodosius, in the year 438, abolished this tenure may be found among the Novellæ of that emperor at the end of the Theodosian Code, tom. vi. nov. 12. M. de Tillemont (Hist. des Empereurs, tom. iv. p. 371), has evidently mistaken the nature of these estates. With a grant from the Imperial demesnes, the same condition was accepted as a favour which would justly have been deemed a hardship, if it had been imposed upon private property.

[58] The passages of Zosimus, of Eunapius, of Sozomen, and of Agathias, which relate to the increase of buildings and inhabitants at Constantinople, are collected and connected by Gyllius de Byzant. l. i. c. 3. Sidonius Apollinaris (in Panegyr. Anthem. 56, p. 290, edit. Sirmond) describes the moles that were pushed forwards into the sea; they consisted of the famous Puzzolan sand, which hardens in the water.

[59] Sozomen, l. ii. c. 3, Philostorg. l. ii. c. 9, Codin. Antiq. Const. p. 8.   It appears by Socrates, l. ii. c. 13, that the daily allowances of the city consisted of eight myriads of σίτου, which we may either translate with Valesius by the words modii

it might excite the applause of the people, has incurred the censure of posterity. A nation of legislators and conquerors might assert their claim to the harvests of Africa, which had been purchased with their blood ; and it was artfully contrived by Augustus that, in the enjoyment of plenty, the Romans should lose the memory of freedom. But the prodigality of Constantine could not be excused by any consideration either of public or private interest ; and the annual tribute of corn imposed upon Egypt for the benefit of his new capital was applied to feed a lazy and indolent populace, at the expense of the husbandmen of an industrious province.[60] Some other regulations of this emperor are less liable to blame, but they are less deserving of notice. He divided Constantinople into fourteen regions or quarters,[61] dignified the public council with the appellation of Senate,[62] communicated to the citizens the privileges of Italy,[63] and bestowed on the rising city the title of

of corn or consider as expressive of the number of loaves of bread. [Cp. also Zosimus, ii. 32 ; Photius, p. 475, a. 39, ed. Bekker ; Codinus, de or cp. p. 16, 4, ed. Bekk. (ἄρτους ἡμερησίους). We must understand loaves, not modii (nor medimni, as Finlay thought ; 1 med. = 6 mod.). See E. Gebhardt, das Verpflegungswesen von Rom und Constantinopel, 1881.]

[60] See Cod. Theodos. l. xiii. and xiv. [16] and Cod. Justinian. Edict. xii. tom. ii. p. 648, edit. Genev. See the beautiful complaint of Rome in the poem of Claudian de Bell. Gildonico, ver. 46—64.

> Cum subiit par Roma mihi divisaque sumsit
> Æquales aurora togas : Ægyptia rura
> In partem cessere novam.

[Cp. also Libanius περὶ τῶν ἱερ. 184, ed. Reiske ; Themistius, Or. 4, p. 52   C. I. L., i. p. 394.]

[61] The regions of Constantinople are mentioned in the code of Justinian, and particularly described in the Notitia of the younger Theodosius ; but, as the four last of them are not included within the wall of Constantine, it may be doubted whether this division of the city should be referred to the founder.

[62] Senatum constituit secundi ordinis ; *Claros* vocavit. Anon. Valesian. p. 715 [§ 30]. The senators of old Rome were styled *Clarissimi*. See a curious note of Valesius ad Ammian. Marcellin. xxii. 9. From the 11th epistle of Julian, it should seem that the place of senator was considered as a burthen rather than as an honour ; but the Abbé de la Bléterie (Vie de Jovien, t. ii. p. 371) has shewn that this epistle could not relate to Constantinople. Might we not read, instead of the celebrated name of Βυζαντίοις, the obscure but more probable word Βισανθηνοις ? Bisanthe or Rhœdestus, now Rhodosto, was a small maritime city of Thrace. See Stephan. Byz. de Urbibus, p. 225, and Cellar Geograph. tom. i. p. 849. [Certain gold medallions with Emperor standing and the legend Senatus, on the reverse, have been shown to refer to the foundation of the new senate (Kenner, *Wiener numism. Zeit.*, 3, 117). Hertlein, p. 491, keeps Βυζαντίοις but notices Gibbon's conjecture.]

[63] Cod. Theodos. l. xiv. 13. The Commentary of Godefroy (t. v. p. 220) is long, but perplexed ; nor indeed is it easy to ascertain in what the Jus Italicum could consist, after the freedom of the city had been communicated to the whole empire. [Jus Italicum gave exemption from tributum or land-tax,—an exemption which Italy herself had recently lost.]

Colony, the first and most favoured daughter of ancient Rome. The venerable parent still maintained the legal and acknowledged supremacy which was due to her age, to her dignity, and to the remembrance of her former greatness.[64]

As Constantine urged the progress of the work with the impatience of a lover, the walls, the porticoes, and the principal edifices, were completed in a few years, or, according to another account, in a few months;[65] but this extraordinary diligence should excite the less admiration, since many of the buildings were finished in so hasty and imperfect a manner that, under the succeeding reign, they were preserved with difficulty from impending ruin.[66] But, while they displayed the vigour and freshness of youth, the founder prepared to celebrate the dedication of his city.[67] The games and largesses which crowned the pomp of this memorable festival may easily be supposed; but there is one circumstance of a more singular and permanent nature, which ought not entirely to be overlooked. As often as the birthday of the city returned, the statue of Constantine, framed, by his order, of gilt wood, and bearing in its right hand a small image of the genius of the place, was erected on a triumphal car. The guards, carrying white tapers, and clothed in their richest apparel, accompanied the solemn procession as it moved through the Hippodrome. When it was opposite to the throne of the reigning emperor, he rose from

Dedication. A.D. 330 or 334

[A.D. 30, May 11]

[64] Julian (Orat. i. p. 8) celebrates Constantinople as not less superior to all other cities than she was inferior to Rome itself. His learned commentator (Spanheim, p. 75, 76), justifies this language by several parallel and contemporary instances. Zosimus, as well as Socrates and Sozomen, flourished after the division of the empire between the two sons of Theodosius, which established a perfect *equality* between the old and the new capital.

[65] Codinus (Antiquitat. p. 8), affirms that the foundations of Constantinople were laid in the year of the world 5837 (A.D. 329), on the 26th of September, and that the city was dedicated the 11th of May 5838 (A.D. 330). He connects these dates with several characteristic epochs, but they contradict each other; the authority of Codinus is of little weight, and the space which he assigns must appear insufficient. The term of ten years is given us by Julian (Orat. i. p. 8), and Spanheim labours to establish the truth of it (p. 69-75), by the help of two passages from Themistius (Orat. iv. p. 58), and of Philostorgius (l. ii. c. 9), which form a period from the year 324 to the year 334. Modern critics are divided concerning this point of chronology, and their different sentiments are very accurately discussed by Tillemont, Hist. des Empereurs, tom. iv. p. 619-625. [The date of dedication, 11th May 330, is certain, see Idatius, *Descr. Consul.*, Chron. Pasch. p. 285, Hesychius, F. H. G. 4, p. 154, cp. Malalas, p. 322, Cedren. i. p. 497. The foundation of Western Wall was laid Nov. 4, 326, acc. to Anon. Band. i. 3.]

[66] Themistius, Orat. iii. p. 47. Zosim. l. ii. p. 108. Constantine himself, in one of his laws (Cod. Theod. l. xv. tit. 1), betrays his impatience.

[67] Cedrenus and Zonaras, faithful to the mode of superstition which prevailed in their own times, assure us that Constantinople was consecrated to the Virgin Mother of God.

his seat, and with grateful reverence adored the memory of his predecessor.[68]   At the festival of the dedication, an edict, engraved on a column of marble, bestowed the title of SECOND or NEW ROME on the city of Constantine.[69]   But the name of Constantinople[70] has prevailed over that honourable epithet; and, after the revolution of fourteen centuries, still perpetuates the fame of its author.[71]

Form of government

The foundation of a new capital is naturally connected with the establishment of a new form of civil and military administration.   The distinct view of the complicated system of policy, introduced by Diocletian, improved by Constantine, and completed by his immediate successors, may not only amuse the fancy by the singular picture of a great empire, but will tend to illustrate the secret and internal causes of its rapid decay. In the pursuit of any remarkable institution, we may be frequently led into the more early or the more recent times of the Roman history; but the proper limits of this inquiry will be included within a period of about one hundred and thirty years, from the accession of Constantine to the publication of the Theodosian code;[72] from which, as well as from the *Notitia* of the east and west,[73] we derive the most copious and authentic information of the state of the empire.   This variety of objects will suspend, for some time, the course of the narrative; but

[68] The earliest and most complete account of this extraordinary ceremony may be found in the Alexandrian Chronicle, p. 285 [Chr. Pasch. p. 529-30].   Tillemont, and the other friends of Constantine, who are offended with the air of Paganism which seems unworthy of a Christian Prince, had a right to consider it as doubtful, but they were not authorized to omit the mention of it.

[69] Sozomen, l. ii. c. 2. Ducange, C. P. l. i. c. 6.   Velut ipsius Romæ filiam, is the expression of Augustin. de Civitat. Dei, l. v. c. 25.

[70] Eutropius, l. x. c. 8.   Julian. Orat. i. p. 8.   Ducange C. P. l. i. c. 5.   The name of Constantinople is extant on the medals of Constantine.

[71] The lively Fontenelle (Dialogues des Morts, xii.) affects to deride the vanity of human ambition, and seems to triumph in the disappointment of Constantine, whose immortal name is now lost in the vulgar appellation of Istambol, a Turkish corruption of εἰς τὴν πόλιν.   Yet the original name is still preserved, 1. By the nations of Europe.   2. By the modern Greeks.   3. By the Arabs, whose writings are diffused over the wide extent of their conquests in Asia and Africa.   See d'Herbelot Bibliothèque Orientale, p. 275.   4. By the more learned Turks, and by the emperor himself in his public mandates.   Cantemir's History of [Growth and Decay of] the Othman [Ottoman] Empire, p. 51 [Eng. Tr., 1734].

[72] The Theodosian code was promulgated A.D. 438.   See the Prolegomena of Godefroy, c. i. p. 185.

[73] Pancirolus, in his elaborate Commentary, assigns to the Notitia a date almost similar to that of the Theodosian code: but his proofs, or rather conjectures, are extremely feeble.   I should be rather inclined to place this useful work between the final division of the empire (A.D. 395), and the successful invaion of Gaul by the Barbarians (A.D. 407).   See Histoire des anciens Peuples des l'Europe, tom. vii. p. 40.   [Cp. App. 11.]

OF THE ROMAN EMPIRE 159

the interruption will be censured only by those readers who are insensible to the importance of laws and manners, while they peruse, with eager curiosity, the transient intrigues of a court, or the accidental event of a battle.

The manly pride of the Romans, content with substantial power, had left to the vanity of the east the forms and cere- monies of ostentatious greatness.[74] But when they lost even the semblance of those virtues which were derived from their ancient freedom, the simplicity of Roman manners was in- sensibly corrupted by the stately affectation of the courts of Asia. The distinctions of personal merit and influence, so conspicuous in a republic, so feeble and obscure under a monarchy, were abolished by the despotism of the emperors; who substituted in their room a severe subordination of rank and office, from the titled slaves, who were seated on the steps of the throne, to the meanest instruments of arbitrary power. This multitude of abject dependents was interested in the support of the actual government, from the dread of a revolu- tion, which might at once confound their hopes and intercept the reward of their services. In this divine hierarchy (for such it is frequently styled) every rank was marked with the most scrupulous exactness, and its dignity was displayed in a variety of trifling and solemn ceremonies, which it was a study to learn and a sacrilege to neglect.[75] The purity of the Latin language was debased by adopting, in the intercourse of pride and flattery, a profusion of epithets, which Tully would scarcely have understood, and which Augustus would have rejected with indignation. The principal officers of the empire were saluted, even by the sovereign himself, with the deceitful titles of your *Sincerity,* your *Gravity,* your *Excellency,* your *Eminence,* your *sublime and wonderful Magnitude,* your *illustrious and mag- nificent Highness.*[76] The codicils or patents of their office were curiously emblazoned with such emblems as were best adapted to explain its nature and high dignity; the image or portrait of the reigning emperors; a triumphal car; the book of man-

Hierarchy of the state

[74] Scilicet externæ superbiæ sueto, non inerat notitia nostri (perhaps *nostrae*); apud quos vis Imperii valet, inania transmittuntur. Tacit. Annal. xv. 31. The gradation from the style of freedom and simplicity to that of form and servitude may be traced in the Epistles of Cicero, of Pliny, and of Symmachus.

[75] The emperor Gratian, after confirming a law of precedency published by Valentinian, the father of his *Divinity,* thus continues: Siquis igitur indebitum sibi locum usurpaverit, nulla se ignoratione defendat ; sitque plane *sacrilegii* reus, qui *divina* præcepta neglexerit. Cod. Theod. l. vi. tit. v. leg. 2.

[76] Consult the *Notitia Dignitatum,* at the end of the Theodosian Code, tom. vi. p. 316.

dates placed on a table, covered with a rich carpet, and illuminated by four tapers; the allegorical figures of the provinces which they governed; or the appellations and standards of the troops whom they commanded. Some of these official ensigns were really exhibited in their hall of audience; others preceded their pompous march whenever they appeared in public; and every circumstance of their demeanour, their dress, their ornaments, and their train, was calculated to inspire a deep reverence for the representatives of supreme majesty. By a philosophic observer, the system of the Roman government might have been mistaken for a splendid theatre, filled with players of every character and degree, who repeated the language, and imitated the passions, of their original model.[77]

Three ranks of honour

All the magistrates of sufficient importance to find a place in the general state of the empire were accurately divided into three classes. 1. The *Illustrious.* 2. The *Spectabiles,* or *Respectable:* And, 3. The *Clarissimi;* whom we may translate by the word *Honourable.* In the times of Roman simplicity, the last-mentioned epithet was used only as a vague expression of deference, till it became at length the peculiar and appropriated title of all who were members of the senate,[78] and consequently of all who, from that venerable body, were selected to govern the provinces. The vanity of those who, from their rank and office, might claim a superior distinction above the rest of the senatorial order was long afterwards indulged with the new appellation of *Respectable;* but the title of *Illustrious* was always reserved to some eminent personages who were obeyed or reverenced by the two subordinate classes. It was communicated only, I. To the consuls and patricians; II. To the prætorian præfects, with the præfects of Rome and Constantinople; III. To the masters general of the cavalry and the infantry; and, IV. To the seven ministers of the palace, who exercised their *sacred* functions about the person of the emperor.[79] Among those

[Four divisions of Illustres]

[77] Pancirolus ad Notitiam utriusque Imperii, p. 39. But his explanations are obscure, and he does not sufficiently distinguish the painted emblems from the effective ensigns of office.

[78] In the Pandects, which may be referred to the reigns of the Antonines, *Clarissimus* is the ordinary and legal title of a senator. [Another important title is that of *vir consularis* (origin uncertain). All *clarissimi* who were admitted into the senate had this rank, which must be carefully distinguished from *consularis* in the old sense of ex-consul. Some provincial governorships could only be held by *consulares;* hence the *Consularis* of — &c.]

[79] Pancirol. p. 12-17. I have not taken any notice of the two inferior ranks, *Perfectissimus* and *Egregius,* which were given to many persons who were not raised to the senatorial dignity. [For example, the urban prefect was perfectissimus; likewise the governors of dioceses under Diocletian and Constantine. But, as these

illustrious magistrates who were esteemed co-ordinate with each other, the seniority of appointment gave place to the union of dignities.[80] By the expedient of honorary codicils, the emperors, who were fond of multiplying their favours, might sometimes gratify the vanity, though not the ambition, of impatient courtiers.[81]

I. As long as the Roman consuls were the first magistrates The consuls of a free state, they derived their right to power from the choice of the people. As long as the emperors condescended to disguise the servitude which they imposed, the consuls were still elected by the real or apparent suffrage of the senate. From the reign of Diocletian, even these vestiges of liberty were abolished, and the successful candidates who were invested with the annual honours of the consulship affected to deplore the humiliating condition of their predecessors. The Scipios and the Catos had been reduced to solicit the votes of plebeians, to pass through the tedious and expensive forms of a popular election, and to expose their dignity to the shame of a public refusal; while their own happier fate had reserved them for an age and government in which the rewards of virtue were assigned by the unerring wisdom of a gracious sovereign.[82] In the epistles which the emperor addressed to the two consuls elect, it was declared that they were created by his sole authority.[83] Their names and portraits, engraved on gilt tablets of ivory, were dispersed over the empire as presents to the provinces, the cities, the magistrates, the senate, and the people.[84] Their solemn inauguration was performed at the place of the

and lesser officials were promoted to senatorial rank, they became *clarissimi* or *spectabiles.* The rank of *egregius* is not found after Constantine; that of *perfectissimus* lingered longer and was still borne by the governor of Dalmatia in the early years of the fifth century.]

[80] Cod. Theodos. l. vi. tit. vi. The rules of precedency are ascertained with the most minute accuracy by the emperors and illustrated with equal prolixity by their learned interpreter.

[81] Cod. Theodos. l. vi. tit. xxii.

[82] Ausonius (in Gratiarum Actione) basely expatiates on this unworthy topic, which is managed by Mamertinus (Panegyr. Vet. xi. 16, 19) with somewhat more freedom and ingenuity.

[83] Cum de Consulibus in annum creandis solus mecum volutarem . . . te Consulem et designavi, et declaravi, et priorem nuncupavi; are some of the expressions employed by the emperor Gratian to his preceptor the poet Ausonius.

[84] Immanesque . . . dentes,
Qui secti ferro in tabulas auroque micantes
Inscripti rutilum cælato consule nomen
Per proceres et vulgus eant.
Claud. in ii. Cons. Stilichon. 346.
Montfaucon has represented some of these tablets or diptychs; see Supplément à 'Antiquité expliquée, tom. iii. p. 220.

imperial residence; and, during a period of one hundred and twenty years, Rome was constantly deprived of the presence of her ancient magistrates.[85] On the morning of the first of January, the consuls assumed the ensigns of their dignity. Their dress was a robe of purple, embroidered in silk and gold, and sometimes ornamented with costly gems.[86] On this solemn occasion they were attended by the most eminent officers of the state and army, in the habit of senators; and the useless fasces, armed with the once formidable axes, were borne before them by the lictors.[87] The procession moved from the palace [88] to the Forum, or principal square of the city; where the consuls ascended their tribunal, and seated themselves in the curule chairs, which were framed after the fashion of ancient times. They immediately exercised an act of jurisdiction, by the manumission of a slave, who was brought before them for that purpose; and the ceremony was intended to represent the celebrated action of the elder Brutus, the author of liberty and of the consulship, when he admitted among his fellow-citizens the faithful Vindex, who had revealed the conspiracy of the Tarquins.[89] The public festival was continued during several days in all the

[85] Consule lætatur post plurima sæcula viso
Pallanteus apex : agnoscunt rostra curules
Auditas quondam proavis : desuetaque cingit
Regius auratis Fora fascibus Ulpia lictor.
i. in vi. Cons. Honorii, 643.
From the reign of Carus to the sixth consulship of Honorius, there was an interval of one hundred and twenty years, during which the emperors were always absent from Rome on the first day of January. See the Chronologie de Tillemont, tom. iii. iv. and v.

[86] See Claudian in Cons. Prob. et Olybrii, 178, &c., and in iv. Cons. Honorii, 585, &c.; though in the latter it is not easy to separate the ornaments of the emperor from those of the consul. Ausonius received, from the liberality of Gratian, a *vestis palmata*, or robe of state, in which the figure of the emperor Constantius was embroidered.

[87] Cernis ut armorum proceres legumque potentes
Patricios sumunt habitus, et more Gabino
Discolor incedit legio, positisque parumper
Bellorum signis sequitur vexilla Quirini?
Lictori cedunt aquilæ, ridetque togatus
Miles, et in mediis effulget curia castris.
Claud. in iv. Cons. Honorii, 5.
—— *strictasque* procul radiare *secures*.
In Cons. Prob. 229 [232].

[88] See Valesius ad Ammian. Marcellin. l. xxii. c. 7.

[89] Auspice mox læto [laetum] sonuit clamore tribunal
Te fastos ineunte quater ; sollemnia ludit
Omnia [omina] libertas : deductum Vindice morem
Lex servat [celebrat], famulusque jugo laxatus erili
Ducitur, et grato remeat securior ictu.
Claud. in iv. Cons. Honorii, 611.

principal cities ; in Rome, from custom ; in Constantinople, from imitation ; in Carthage, Antioch, and Alexandria, from the love of pleasure and the superfluity of wealth.[90] In the two capitals of the empire the annual games of the theatre, the circus, and the amphitheatre,[91] cost four thousand pounds of gold, (about) one hundred and sixty thousand pounds sterling : and if so heavy an expense surpassed the faculties or the inclination of the magistrates themselves, the sum was supplied from the imperial treasury.[92] As soon as the consuls had discharged these customary duties, they were at liberty to retire into the shade of private life, and to enjoy, during the remainder of the year, the undisturbed contemplation of their own greatness. They no longer presided in the national councils ; they no longer executed the resolutions of peace or war. Their abilities (unless they were employed in more effective offices) were of little moment ; and their names served only as the legal date of the year in which they had filled the chair of Marius and of Cicero. Yet it was still felt and acknowledged, in the last period of Roman servitude, that this empty name might be compared, and even preferred, to the possession of substantial power. The title of consul was still the most splendid object of ambition, the noblest reward of virtue and loyalty. The emperors themselves, who disdained the faint shadow of the republic, were conscious that they acquired an additional splendour and majesty as often as they assumed the annual honours of the consular dignity.[93]

The proudest and most perfect separation which can be found in any age or country between the nobles and the people is perhaps that of the Patricians and the Plebeians, as it was established in the first age of the Roman republic. Wealth and

The Patricians

---

[90] Celebrant quidem solemnes istos dies, omnes ubique urbes quæ sub legibus agunt ; et Roma de more, et Constantinopolis de imitatione, et Antochia pro luxu, et discincta Carthago, et domus fluminis Alexandria sed Treviri Principis beneficio. Ausonius in Grat. Actione.

[91] Claudian (in Cons. Mall. Theodori, 279-331) describes, in a lively and fanciful manner, the various games of the circus, the theatre, and the amphitheatre, exhibited by the new consul. The sanguinary combats of gladiators had already been prohibited.

[92] Procopius in Hist. Arcana, c. 26. [20 centenaria = 2000 (not 4000) lbs. of gold.]

[93] In Consulatu honos sine labore suscipitur (Mamertin. in Panegyr. Vet. xi. 2). This exalted idea of the consulship is borrowed from an Oration (iii. p. 107) pronounced by Julian in the servile court of Constantius. See the Abbé de la Bléterie (Mémoires de l'Académie, tom. xxiv. p. 289), who delights to pursue the vestiges of the old constitution, and who sometimes finds them in his copious fancy. [Before the end of the fourth century, the arrangement was made that one consul was appointed by the western, the other by the eastern, emperor.]

honours, the offices of the state, and the ceremonies of religion, were almost exclusively possessed by the former; who, preserving the purity of their blood with the most insulting jealousy,[94] held their clients in a condition of specious vassalage.   But these distinctions, so incompatible with the spirit of a free people, were removed, after a long struggle, by the persevering efforts of the Tribunes.   The most active and successful of the Plebeians accumulated wealth, aspired to honours, deserved triumphs, contracted alliances, and, after some generations, assumed the pride of ancient nobility.[95]   The Patrician families, on the other hand, whose original number was never recruited till the end of the commonwealth, either failed in the ordinary course of nature, or were extinguished in so many foreign and domestic wars, or, through a want of merit or fortune, insensibly mingled with the mass of the people.[96]   Very few remained who could derive their pure and genuine origin from the infancy of the city, or even from that of the republic, when Cæsar and Augustus, Claudius and Vespasian, created from the body of the senate a competent number of new Patrician families, in the hope of perpetuating an order which was still considered as honourable and sacred.[97]   But these artificial supplies (in which the reigning house was always included) were rapidly swept away by the rage of tyrants, by frequent revolutions, by the change of manners, and by the intermixture of nations.[98]   Little more

[94] Intermarriages between the Patricians and Plebeians were prohibited by the laws of the XII. Tables; and the uniform operations of human nature may attest that the custom survived the law.   See in Livy (iv. 1-6), the pride of family urged by the consul, and the rights of mankind asserted by the tribune Canuleius.

[95] See the animated pictures drawn by Sallust, in the Jugurthine war, of the pride of the nobles, and even of the virtuous Metellus, who was unable to brook the idea that the honour of the consulship should be bestowed on the obscure merit of his lieutenant Marius (c. 64).   Two hundred years before, the race of the Metelli themselves were confounded among the Plebeians of Rome; and from the etymology of their name of *Cæcilius*, there is reason to believe that those haughty nobles derived their origin from a sutler.

[96] In the year of Rome 800, very few remained, not only of the old Patrician families, but even of those which had been created by Cæsar and Augustus (Tacit. Annal. xi. 25).   The family of Scaurus (a branch of the Patrician Æmilii) was degraded so low that his father, who exercised the trade of a charcoal merchant, left him only ten slaves, and somewhat less than three hundred pounds sterling (Valerius Maximus, l. iv. c. 4, n. 11, Aurel. Victor in Scauro).   The family was saved from oblivion by the merit of the son.

[97] Tacit. Annal. xi. 25, Dion Cassius, l. lii. p. 693 [c. 42].   The virtues of Agricola, who was created a Patrician by the emperor Vespasian, reflected honour on that ancient order; but his ancestors had not any claim beyond an equestrian nobility.

[98] This failure would have been almost impossible, if it were true, as Casaubon compels Aurelius Victor to affirm (ad. Sueton. in Cæsar. c. 42.   See Hist. August. p. 203 [—c. 3], and Casaubon, Comment. p. 220), that Vespasian created at once

was left when Constantine ascended the throne than a vague
and imperfect tradition that the Patricians had once been the
first of the Romans.   To form a body of nobles, whose influence
may restrain, while it secures, the authority of the monarch,
would have been very inconsistent with the character and policy
of Constantine ; but, had he seriously entertained such a design,
it might have exceeded the measure of his power to ratify, by
an arbitrary edict, an institution which must expect the sanction
of time and of opinion.   He revived, indeed, the title of PA-
TRICIANS, but he revived it as a personal, not as an hereditary, distinction.   They yielded only to the transient superiority of the
annual consuls ; but they enjoyed the pre-eminence over all the
great officers of state, with the most familiar access to the
person of the prince.   This honourable rank was bestowed on
them for life ; and, as they were usually favourites and ministers
who had grown old in the Imperial court, the true etymology of
the word was perverted by ignorance and flattery ; and the
Patricians of Constantine were reverenced as the adopted
Fathers of the emperor and the republic.[99]

II. The fortunes of the Prætorian præfects were essentially *The Prætorian præ-
fects*
different from those of the consuls and patricians.   The latter
saw their ancient greatness evaporate in a vain title.   The
former, rising by degrees from the most humble condition, were
invested with the civil and military administration of the Roman
world.   From the reign of Severus to that of Diocletian, the
guards and the palace, the laws and the finances, the armies and
the provinces, were intrusted to their superintending care ; and,
like the Vizirs of the East, they held with one hand the seal,
and with the other the standard, of the empire.   The ambition
of the præfects, always formidable and sometimes fatal to the
masters whom they served, was supported by the strength of the
prætorian bands ; but after those haughty troops had been
weakened by Diocletian, and finally suppressed by Constantine,
the præfects, who survived their fall, were reduced without
difficulty to the station of useful and obedient ministers.   When
they were no longer responsible for the safety of the emperor's
person, they resigned the jurisdiction which they had hitherto
claimed and exercised over all the departments of the palace.

a thousand Patrician families.   But this extravagant number is too much even for
the whole senatorial order, unless we should include all the Roman knights who
were distinguished by the permission of wearing the laticlave.
   [99] Zosimus, l. ii. p. 118 [c. 40] ; and Godefroy ad Cod. Theodos. l. vi. tit. vi.
[These Patricians had precedence of all dignitaries except the consuls in office.
But they were hardly regarded as adoptive fathers of the emperor.]

They were deprived by Constantine of all military command, as soon as they had ceased to lead into the field, under their immediate orders, the flower of the Roman troops; and at length, by a singular revolution, the captains of the guard were transformed into the civil magistrates of the provinces. According to the plan of government instituted by Diocletian, the four princes had each their prætorian præfect;[100] and, after the monarchy was once more united in the person of Constantine, he still continued to create the same number of FOUR PRÆFECTS, and intrusted to their care the same provinces which they already administered. 1. The præfect of the East stretched his ample jurisdiction into the three parts of the globe which were subject to the Romans, from the cataracts of the Nile to the banks of the Phasis, and from the mountains of Thrace to the frontiers of Persia. 2. The important provinces of Pannonia, Dacia, Macedonia, and Greece, once acknowledged the authority of the præfect of Illyricum. 3. The power of the præfect of Italy was not confined to the country from whence he derived his title; it extended over the additional territory of Rhætia as far as the banks of the Danube, over the dependent islands of the Mediterranean, and over that part of the continent of Africa which lies between the confines of Cyrene and those of Tingitania. 4. The præfect of the Gauls comprehended under that plural denomination the kindred provinces of Britain and Spain, and his authority was obeyed from the wall of Antoninus to the foot of Mount Atlas.[101]

After the Prætorian præfects had been dismissed from all military command,[102] the civil functions which they were ordained to exercise over so many subject nations were adequate to the ambition and abilities of the most consummate ministers. To their wisdom was committed the supreme administration of justice and of the finances, the two objects which, in a state of peace, comprehend almost all the respective duties of the sovereign and of the people; of the former, to protect the citizens who are obedient to the laws; of the latter, to contribute the share of their property which is required for the

[100] [It is probable that the Cæsars had præt. prefects as well as the Augusti; but there is not evidence that there were 4 prefects regularly under Constantine. See App. 6 and 15.]

[101] Zosimus, l. ii. p. 109, 110 [c. 33]. If we had not fortunately possessed this satisfactory account of the division of the power and provinces of the Prætorian præfects, we should frequently have been perplexed amidst the copious details of the Code, and the circumstantial minuteness of the Notitia.

[102] [By Constantine; not entirely by Diocletian. The only duty which still connected them with the army was that of providing the supplies for the soldiers; and this was a consequence of their financial functions.]

expenses of the state.[103] The coin, the highways, the posts, the granaries, the manufactures, whatever could interest the public prosperity was moderated by the authority of the Prætorian præfects. As the immediate representatives of the Imperial majesty, they were empowered to explain, to enforce, and on some occasions to modify, the general edicts by their discretionary proclamations. They watched over the conduct of the provincial governors,[104] removed the negligent, and inflicted punishments on the guilty. From all the inferior jurisdictions, an appeal in every matter of importance, either civil or criminal, might be brought before the tribunal of the præfect: but *his* sentence was final and absolute ; and the emperors themselves refused to admit any complaints against the judgment or the integrity of a magistrate whom they honoured with such unbounded confidence.[105] His appointments were suitable to his dignity ; [106] and, if avarice was his ruling passion, he enjoyed frequent opportunities of collecting a rich harvest of fees, of presents, and of perquisites. Though the emperors no longer dreaded the ambition of their præfects, they were attentive to counterbalance the power of this great office by the uncertainty and shortness of its duration.[107]

From their superior importance and dignity, Rome and Constantinople were alone excepted from the jurisdiction of the prætorian præfects. The immense size of the city and the experience of the tardy, ineffectual operation of the laws had furnished the policy of Augustus with a specious pretence for introducing a new magistrate, who alone could restrain a servile and turbulent populace by the strong arm of arbitrary power.[108]

The præfects of Rome and Constantinople

[103] [The prefect was head of the office for the collection of inland revenue. The emperor only intervened when the ordinary taxes were insufficient or a remission of arrears was expedient.]

[104] [Whom they practically appointed.]

[105] See a law of Constantine himself. A præfectis autem prætorio provocare non sinimus. Cod. Justinian. l. vii. tit. lxii. leg. 19. Charisius, a lawyer of the time of Constantine (Heinec. Hist. Juris Romani, p. 349), who admits this law as a fundamental principle of jurisprudence, compares the prætorian præfects to the masters of the horse of the ancient dictators. Pandect. l. i. tit. xi.

[106] When Justinian, in the exhausted condition of the empire, instituted a prætorian præfect for Africa, he allowed him a salary of one hundred pounds of gold. Cod. Justinian. l. i. tit. xxvii. leg. 1.

[107] For this, and the other dignities of the empire, it may be sufficient to refer to the ample commentaries of Pancirolus and Godefroy, who have diligently collected and accurately digested in their proper order all the legal and historical materials. From those authors Dr. Howell (History of the World, vol. ii. p. 24-77) had deduced a very distinct abridgment of the state of the Roman empire.

[108] Tacit. Annal. vi. 11. Euseb. in Chron. p. 155. Dion Cassius, in the oration of Mæcenas (l. lii. p. 675 [21]), describes the prerogatives of the præfect of the city as they were established in his own time.

Valerius Messalla was appointed the first præfect of Rome, that
his reputation might countenance so invidious a measure : but,
at the end of a few days, that accomplished citizen [109] resigned
his office, declaring with a spirit worthy of the friend of Brutus,
that he found himself incapable of exercising a power incompatible with public freedom.[110] As the sense of liberty became less
exquisite, the advantages of order were more clearly understood;
and the præfect, who seemed to have been designed as a terror
only to slaves and vagrants, was permitted to extend his civil
and criminal jurisdiction over the equestrian and noble families
of Rome. The prætors, annually created as the judges of law
and equity, could not long dispute the possession of the Forum
with a vigorous and permanent magistrate, who was usually
admitted into the confidence of the prince. Their courts were
deserted, their number, which had once fluctuated between
twelve and eighteen,[111] was gradually reduced to two or three,
and their important functions were confined to the expensive
obligation [112] of exhibiting games for the amusement of the
people. After the office of the Roman consuls had been changed
into a vain pageant, which was rarely displayed in the capital,
the præfects assumed their vacant place in the senate, and were
soon acknowledged as the ordinary presidents of that venerable
assembly. They received appeals from the distance of one
hundred miles ; and it was allowed as a principle of jurisprudence, that all municipal authority was derived from them
alone.[113] In the discharge of his laborious employment, the

---

[109] The fame of Messalla has been scarcely equal to his merit. In the earliest
youth he was recommended by Cicero to the friendship of Brutus. He followed
the standard of the republic till it was broken in the fields of Philippi : he then
accepted and deserved the favour of the most moderate of the conquerors ; and
uniformly asserted his freedom and dignity in the court of Augustus. The triumph
of Messalla was justified by the conquest of Aquitain. As an orator he disputed
the palm of eloquence with Cicero himself. Messalla cultivated every muse, and
was the patron of every man of genius. He spent his evenings in philosophic
conversation with Horace ; assumed his place at table between Delia and Tibullus ;
and amused his leisure by encouraging the poetical talents of young Ovid.

[110] Incivilem esse potestatem contestans, says the translator of Eusebius. Tacitus
expresses the same idea in other words : quasi nescius exercendi.

[111] See Lipsius, Excursus D. ad 1 lib. Tacit. Annal.

[112] Heineccii Element. Juris Civilis secund. ordinem Pandect. tom. i. p. 70. See
likewise Sparheim de Usu Numismatum, tom. ii. dissertat. x. p. 219. In the year
450, Marcian published a law that *three* citizens should be annually created Prætors
of Constantinople by the choice of the senate, but with their own consent. Cod.
Justinian. l. i. tit. xxxix. leg. 2.

[113] Quidquid igitur intra urbem admittitur, ad P. U. videtur pertinere ; sed et
siquid intra centesimum milliarium. Ulpian in Pandect. l. i. tit. xiii. n. 1. He
proceeds to enumerate the various offices of the præfect, who, in the code of
Justinian (l. i. tit. xxxix. leg. 3), is declared to precede and command all city
magistrates, sine injuriâ ac detrimento honoris alieni.

governor of Rome was assisted by fifteen officers, some of whom had been originally his equals, or even his superiors. The principal departments were relative to the command of a numerous watch, established as a safeguard against fires, robberies, and nocturnal disorders; the custody and distribution of the public allowance of corn and provisions; the care of the port, of the aqueducts, of the common sewers, and of the navigation and bed of the Tiber; the inspection of the markets, the theatres, and of the private as well as public works. Their vigilance ensured the three principal objects of a regular police, safety, plenty, and cleanliness; and, as a proof of the attention of government to preserve the splendour and ornaments of the capital, a particular inspector was appointed for the statues; the guardian, as it were, of that inanimate people, which, according to the extravagant computation of an old writer, was scarcely inferior in number to the living inhabitants of Rome. About thirty years after the foundation of Constantinople, a [359 A.D similar magistrate was created in that rising metropolis, for the same uses, and with the same powers. A perfect equality was established between the dignity of the *two* municipal, and that of the *four* prætorian, præfects.[114]

Those who, in the Imperial hierarchy, were distinguished by the title of *Respectable*, formed an intermediate class between the *illustrious* præfects and the *honourable* magistrates of the provinces. In this class the proconsuls of Asia, Achaia, and Africa claimed a pre-eminence, which was yielded to the remembrance of their ancient dignity; and the appeal from their tribunal to that of the præfects was almost the only mark of their dependence.[115] But the civil government of the empire was distributed into thirteen great DIOCESES, each of which equalled the just measure of a powerful kingdom. The first of these dioceses was subject to the jurisdiction of the *count* of

The proconsuls, vice-præfects, &c.

---

[114] Besides our usual guides, we may observe that Felix Cantelorius has written a separate treatise, De Præfecto Urbis; and that many curious details concerning the police of Rome and Constantinople are contained in the fourteenth book of the Theodosian Code. [E. Léotard, De præf. urbana quarto p. C. sæculo. 1873.]

[115] Eunapius affirms that the proconsul of Asia was independent of the præfect; which must, however, be understood with some allowance: the jurisdiction of the vice-præfect he most assuredly disclaimed. Pancirolus, p. 161. [The proconsuls of Asia and Africa had precedence of all the other provincial governors, and were subordinate neither to the vicars of Asia and Africa, nor to the prætorian prefects. (Theodosius I. gave the proconsul of Asia the position of vicar over the Islands and the Hellespont.) The proconsul of Achaia was subordinate to the prefect of Illyricum, but not to the vicar of Macedonia, All three were appointed by the emperor without the intervention of the Prætorian Prefect.]

the east ; and we may convey some idea of the importance and variety of his functions, by observing that six hundred apparitors, who would be styled at present either secretaries, or clerks, or ushers, or messengers, were employed in his immediate office.[116] The place of *Augustal prœfect* of Egypt was no longer filled by a Roman knight ; but the name was retained ; and the extra- ordinary powers which the situation of the country and the temper of the inhabitants had once made indispensable were still continued to the governor. The eleven remaining dioceses, of Asiana, Pontica, and Thrace ; of Macedonia, Dacia,[117] and Pannonia or Western Illyricum ; of Italy and Africa ; of Gaul, Spain, and Britain ; were governed by twelve *vicars* or *vice- prœfects*,[118] whose name sufficiently explains the nature and dependence of their office. It may be added that the lieuten- ant-generals of the Roman armies, the military counts and dukes, who will be hereafter mentioned, were allowed the rank and title of *Respectable*.

The governors of the pro- vinces

As the spirit of jealousy and ostentation prevailed in the councils of the emperors, they proceeded with anxious diligence to divide the substance, and to multiply the titles of power. The vast countries which the Roman conquerors had united under the same simple form of administration were imper- ceptibly crumbled into minute fragments ; till at length the whole empire was distributed into one hundred and sixteen provinces, each of which supported an expensive and splendid establishment. Of these, three were governed by *proconsuls*, thirty-seven by *consulars*, five by *correctors*, and seventy-one by *presidents*. The appellations of these magistrates were different ; they ranked in successive order, the ensigns of their dignity

---

116 The proconsul of Africa had four hundred apparitors ; and they all received large salaries, either from the treasury or the province. See Pancirol. p. 26, and Cod. Justinian. l. xii. tit. lvi. lvii. [The *comes orientis* seems to be a survival of the diocesan counts who were instituted by Constantine (c. A.D. 327) to control and check the vicarii, of whom they had precedence. The institution seems not to have survived its author, except in the case of *Oriens Aegyptus et Mesopotamia*, where the vicar appears in 331 A.D. (Cod. Theod. i. 16, 6) with the title of count ; perhaps the distinction was due (as Schiller has suggested) to the fact that Egypt was part of his province. Some time between 365 and 386 the administration of Egypt was taken from him, and that country became a separate diocese.]

117 [Dacia, from Constantine forward, had no vicar but was directly under the prætorian prefect of Italia et Illyricum, or Illyricum. See App. 15.]

118 In Italy there was likewise the *Vicar* of *Rome*. It has been much disputed, whether his jurisdiction measured one hundred miles from the city, or whether it stretched over the ten southern provinces of Italy, [He was vicar of the *prætorian prefect* of Italy, not of the *præfectus urbis*, and he administered the ten provinces, of which the revenue went to Rome. The rest of Italy, under the vicarius Italiæ, was distinguished as *annonaria*.]

were curiously varied, and their situation, from accidental circumstances, might be more or less agreeable or advantageous.
But they were all (excepting only the proconsuls) alike included
in the class of *honourable* persons; and they were alike intrusted,
during the pleasure of the prince, and under the authority of
the præfects or their deputies, with the administration of justice
and the finances in their respective districts. The ponderous
volumes of the Codes and Pandects [119] would furnish ample
materials for a minute inquiry into the system of provincial
government, as in the space of six centuries it was improved by
the wisdom of the Roman statesmen and lawyers. It may be
sufficient for the historian to select two singular and salutary
provisions intended to restrain the abuse of authority. 1. For
the preservation of peace and order, the governors of the provinces were armed with the sword of justice. They inflicted
corporal punishments, and they exercised, in capital offences,
the power of life and death. But they were not authorized
to indulge the condemned criminal with the choice of his own
execution, or to pronounce a sentence of the mildest and most
honourable kind of exile. These prerogatives were reserved to
the præfects, who alone could impose the heavy fine of fifty
pounds of gold : their vicegerents were confined to the trifling
weight of a few ounces.[120] This distinction, which seems to
grant the larger, while it denies the smaller, degree of authority,
was founded on a very rational motive. The smaller degree
was infinitely more liable to abuse. The passions of a provincial
magistrate might frequently provoke him into acts of oppression which affected only the freedom or the fortunes of the
subject ; though, from a principle of prudence, perhaps of
humanity, he might still be terrified by the guilt of innocent
blood. It may likewise be considered that exile, considerable
fines, or the choice of an easy death relate more particularly
to the rich and the noble ; and the persons the most exposed
to the avarice or resentment of a provincial magistrate were
thus removed from his obscure persecution to the more august

[119] Among the works of the celebrated Ulpian, there was one in ten books
concerning the office of a proconsul, whose duties in the most essential articles were
the same as those of an ordinary governor of a province.

[120] The presidents, or consulars, could impose only two ounces; the vice-præfects,
three ; the proconsuls, count of the east, and præfect of Egypt, six. See Heineccii
Jur. Civil. tom. i. p. 75. Pandect. l. xlviii. tit. xix. n. 8. Cod. Justinian. l. i. tit.
liv. leg. 4, 6. [The name *praesides* came in when Gallienus excluded senators
from governorships of imperial provinces and appointed knights. The title
correctores was first used in Italy. Cp. above, vol. i., App. 20.]

and impartial tribunal of the Prætorian præfect. 2. As it was reasonably apprehended that the integrity of the judge might be biassed, if his interest was concerned or his affections were engaged ; the strictest regulations were established to exclude any person, without the special dispensation of the emperor, from the government of the province where he was born;[121] and to prohibit the governor or his son from contracting marriage with a native or an inhabitant ;[122] or from purchasing slaves, lands, or houses, within the extent of his jurisdiction.[123]   Notwithstanding these rigorous precautions, the emperor Constantine, after a reign of twenty-five years, still deplores the venal and oppressive administration of justice, and expresses the warmest indignation that the audience of the judge, his dispatch of business, his seasonable delays, and his final sentence were publicly sold, either by himself or by the officers of his court.   The continuance, and perhaps the impunity, of these crimes is attested by the repetition of important laws and ineffectual menaces.[124]

The profession of the law

All the civil magistrates were drawn from the profession of the law.   The celebrated Institutes of Justinian are addressed to the youth of his dominions, who had devoted themselves to the study of Roman jurisprudence ; and the sovereign condescends to animate their diligence by the assurance that their skill and ability would in time be rewarded by an adequate share in the government of the republic.[125]   The rudiments of this lucrative science were taught in all the considerable cities of the east and west ; but the most famous school was that of Berytus,[126] on the coast of Phœnicia ; which flourished above

---

[121] Ut nulli patriæ suæ administratio sine speciali principis permissu permittatur. Cod. Justinian. i. i. tit. xli.   This law was first enacted by the emperor Marcus, after the rebellion of Cassius (Dion. l. lxxi.).   The same regulation is observed in China, with equal strictness and with equal effect.

[122] Pandect. l. xxiii. tit. ii. n. 38, 57, 63.

[123] In jure continetur, ne quis in administratione constitutus aliquid comparet. Cod. Theod. l. viii. tit. xv. leg. 1.   This maxim of common law was enforced by a series of edicts (see the remainder of the title) from Constantine to Justin.   From this prohibition, which is extended to the meanest offices of the governor, they except only clothes and provisions.   The purchase within five years may be recovered ; after which, on information, it devolves to the treasury.

[124] Cessent rapaces jam nunc officialium manus ; cessent, inquam ; nam si moniti non cessaverint, gladiis præcidentur, &c.   Cod. Theod. l. i. tit. vii. leg. 1.   Zeno enacted that all governors should remain in the province, to answer any accusations, fifty days after the expiration of their power.   Cod. Justinian. l. ii. tit. xlix. leg. 1.

[125] Summâ igitur ope, et alacri studio has leges nostras accipite ; et vosmetipsos sic eruditos ostendite, ut spes vos pulcherrima foveat ; toto legitimo opere perfecto, posse etiam nostram rempublicam in partibus ejus vobis credendis gubernari. Justinian. in proem. Institutionum.

[126] The splendour of the school of Berytus, which preserved in the east the

three centuries from the time of Alexander Severus, the author
perhaps of an institution so advantageous to his native country.
After a regular course of education, which lasted five years, the
students dispersed themselves through the provinces, in search
of fortune and honours; nor could they want an inexhaustible
supply of business in a great empire, already corrupted by the
multiplicity of laws, of arts, and of vices. The court of the
Prætorian præfect of the east could alone furnish employment
for one hundred and fifty advocates, sixty-four of whom were
distinguished by peculiar privileges, and two were annually
chosen with a salary of sixty pounds of gold, to defend the
causes of the treasury. The first experiment was made of their
judicial talents, by appointing them to act occasionally as assessors to the magistrates; from thence they were often raised
to preside in the tribunals before which they had pleaded.
They obtained the government of a province; and, by the aid
of merit, of reputation, or of favour, they ascended, by successive steps, to the *illustrious* dignities of the state.[127] In the

language and jurisprudence of the Romans, may be computed to have lasted from
the third to the middle of the sixth century. Heinecc. Jur. Rom. Hist. p. 351-356.
  [127] As in a former period I have traced the civil and military promotion of
Pertinax, I shall here insert the civil honours of Mallius Theodorus. 1. He was
distinguished by his eloquence, while he pleaded as an advocate in the court of the
Prætorian præfect. 2. He governed one of the provinces of Africa, either as
president or consular, and deserved, by his administration, the honour of a brass
statue. 3. He was appointed vicar, or vice-præfect, of Macedonia. 4. Quæstor.
5. Count of the sacred largesses. 6. Prætorian præfect of the Gauls; whilst he
might yet be represented as a young man. 7. After a retreat, perhaps a disgrace,
of many years, which Mallius (confounded by some critics with the poet Manilius,
see Fabricius Bibliothec. Latin. Edit. Ernest. tom. i. c. 18, p. 501), employed in
the study of the Grecian philosophy, he was named Prætorian præfect of Italy, in
the year 397. 8. While he still exercised that great office, he was created, in the
year 399, consul for the West; and his name, on account of the infamy of his
colleague, the eunuch Eutropius, often stands alone in the Fasti. 9. In the year
408, Mallius was appointed a second time prætorian præfect of Italy. Even in
the venal panegyric of Claudian, we may discover the merit of Mallius Theodorus,
who, by a rare felicity, was the intimate friend both of Symmachus and of St.
Augustin. See Tillemont, Hist. des Emp. tom. v. p. 1110-1114. [Inscriptions
supply us with more illustrations of official careers under the Constantinian
monarchy. The career of Caelius Saturninus (C. I. L. 6, 1704) occasioned an
important study by Mommsen in the *Memorie d. Institut. d. corr. arch.* ii. 299;
and that of L. Aradius Valerius Proculus is recorded fully in C. I. L. 6. 1690 and
1691. Proculus began his career apparently as one of the *legati* subordinate to
the proconsul of Africa (this is Mommsen's explanation of *legato pro præt. prov.
Numidiae*). He was then sent to Gallicia to revise the taxation (as *peraequator
census*); after which he became governor successively of Byzacena; Europe and
Thrace (temporarily combined); and Sicily; then proconsul of Africa. He finally
attained to the prætorian prefecture and the prefecture of the City of Rome. We
know from other sources that he was præf. urbi in 337, and ordinary consul in 340
A.D. The career constantly began with the post of advocatus fisci (Caelius
Saturninus is an instance) or of advocate in the ordinary law-courts.]

practice of the bar, these men had considered reason as the instrument of dispute; they interpreted the laws according to the dictates of private interest; and the same pernicious habits might still adhere to their characters in the public administration of the state. The honour of a liberal profession has indeed been vindicated by ancient and modern advocates, who have filled the most important stations with pure integrity and consummate wisdom: but in the decline of Roman jurisprudence, the ordinary promotion of lawyers was pregnant with mischief and disgrace. The noble art, which had once been preserved as the sacred inheritance of the patricians, was fallen into the hands of freedmen and plebeians,[128] who, with cunning rather than with skill, exercised a sordid and pernicious trade. Some of them procured admittance into families for the purpose of fomenting differences, of encouraging suits, and of preparing a harvest of gain for themselves or their brethren. Others, recluse in their chambers, maintained the dignity of legal professors by furnishing a rich client with subtleties to confound the plainest truth and with arguments to colour the most unjustifiable pretensions. The splendid and popular class was composed of the advocates, who filled the Forum with the sound of their turgid and loquacious rhetoric. Careless of fame and of justice, they are described, for the most part, as ignorant and rapacious guides, who conducted their clients through a maze of expense, of delay, and of disappointment; from whence, after a tedious series of years, they were at length dismissed, when their patience and fortune were almost exhausted.[129]

The military officers

III. In the system of policy introduced by Augustus, the governors, those at least of the Imperial provinces, were invested with the full powers of the sovereign himself. Ministers of peace and war, the distribution of rewards and punishments depended on them alone, and they successively appeared on their tribunal in the robes of civil magistracy, and in complete armour at the head of the Roman legions.[130] The influence of

[128] Mamertinus in Panegyr. Vet. xi. 20. Asterius apud Photium, p. 1500.

[129] The curious passage of Ammianus (l. xxx. c. 4), in which he paints the manners of contemporary lawyers, affords a strange mixture of sound sense, false rhetoric, and extravagant satire. Godefroy (Prolegom. ad Cod. Theod. c. i. p. 185) supports the historian by similar complaints and authentic facts. In the fourth century, many camels might have been laden with law-books. Eunapius in Vet. Edesii, p. 72. [The advocate (also called *iuris peritus* and *scholasticus*) in the new Monarchy takes the place which under the Principate was filled by the *iuris consultus*, from whom the old *advocatus* was carefully distinguished.]

[130] See a very splendid example in the Life of Agricola, particularly c. 20, 21. The lieutenant of Britain was intrusted with the same powers which Cicero, proconsul of Cilicia, had exercised in the name of the senate and people.

the revenue, the authority of law, and the command of a military force concurred to render their power supreme and absolute; and whenever they were tempted to violate their allegiance, the loyal province which they involved in their rebellion was scarcely sensible of any change in its political state. From the time of Commodus to the reign of Constantine, near one hundred governors might be enumerated, who, with various success, erected the standard of revolt; and though the innocent were too often sacrificed, the guilty might be sometimes prevented, by the suspicious cruelty of their master.[131] To secure his throne and the public tranquillity from these formidable servants, Constantine resolved to divide the military from the civil administration; and to establish, as a permanent and professional distinction, a practice which had been adopted only as an occasional expedient. The supreme jurisdiction exercised by the Prætorian præfects over the armies of the empire was transferred to the two *masters general* whom he instituted, the one for the *cavalry*, the other for the *infantry*; and, though each of these *illustrious* officers was more peculiarly responsible for the discipline of those troops which were under his immediate inspection, they both indifferently commanded in the field the several bodies, whether of horse or foot, which were united in the same army.[132] Their number was soon doubled by the division of the east and west; and, as separate generals of the same rank and title were appointed on the four important frontiers of the Rhine, of the Upper and the Lower Danube, and of the Euphrates, the defence of the Roman empire was at length committed to eight masters general of the cavalry and infantry. Under their orders, thirty-five military commanders were stationed in the provinces: three in Britain, six in Gaul, one in Spain, one in Italy, five on the Upper, and four on the Lower Danube; in Asia eight, three in Egypt, and four in

---

[131] The Abbé Dubos, who has examined with accuracy (see Hist. de la Monarchie Françoise, tom. i. p. 41-100, edit. 1742) the institutions of Augustus and of Constantine, observes that, if Otho had been put to death the day before he executed his conspiracy, Otho would now appear in history as innocent as Corbulo.

[132] Zosimus, l. ii. p. 110 [33]. Before the end of the reign of Constantius, the *magistri militum* were already increased to four. See Valesius ad Ammian. l. xvi. c. 7. [We first meet *magistri militum* about 315 (Cod. Theod. ii. i. 1). The titles *mag. ped.* and *mag. eq.* survived in the west, but were superseded in the east by the titles *mag. utriusque militiae* or *mag. eq. et ped.* The masters who were in attendance at the imperial court were distinguished from those stationed on the frontiers by the addition *in praesenti*. For the increase of the number of magistri between Constantius and the time of the Notitia cf. Ammianus, xxvi. 5, and Zosimus, iv. 27.]

Africa.   The titles of *counts*, and *dukes*,[133] by which they were properly distinguished, have obtained in modern languages so very different a sense that the use of them may occasion some surprise.   But it should be recollected that the second of those appellations is only a corruption of the Latin word which was indiscriminately applied to any military chief.   All these provincial generals were therefore *dukes ;* but no more than ten among them were dignified with the rank of *counts* or companions, a title of honour, or rather of favour, which had been recently invented in the court of Constantine.[134]   A gold belt was the ensign which distinguished the office of the counts and dukes ; and besides their pay, they received a liberal allowance, sufficient to maintain one hundred and ninety servants, and one hundred and fifty-eight horses.   They were strictly prohibited from interfering in any matter which related to the administration of justice or the revenue ; but the command which they exercised over the troops of their department was independent of the authority of the magistrates.   About the same time that Constantine gave a legal sanction to the ecclesiastical order, he instituted in the Roman empire the nice balance of the civil and the military powers.   The emulation, and sometimes the discord, which reigned between two professions of opposite interests and incompatible manners, was productive of beneficial and of pernicious consequences.   It was seldom to be expected that the general and the civil governor of a province should either conspire for the disturbance, or should unite for the service, of their country.   While the one delayed to offer the assistance which the other disdained to solicit, the troops very frequently remained without orders or without supplies ; the public safety was betrayed, and the defenceless subjects were left exposed to the fury of the Barbarians.   The divided administration which had been formed by Constantine relaxed the vigour of the state, while it secured the tranquillity of the monarch.

Distinction of the troops   The memory of Constantine has been deservedly censured for another innovation, which corrupted military discipline and pre-

[133] Though the military counts and dukes are frequently mentioned, both in history and the codes, we must have recourse to the Notitia for the exact knowledge of their number and stations.   For the institution, rank, privileges, &c., of the counts in general, see Cod. Theod. l. vi. tit. xii.-xx., with the Commentary of Godefroy.   [As a rule the sphere of the dux or comes corresponded to that of the praeses or civil governor of a province, but in some cases was larger, as in that of the *dux Libyarum*.]

[134] [Derived from the *comites* who attended the Princeps when he visited the provinces.]

pared the ruin of the empire. The nineteen years which preceded his final victory over Licinius had been a period of licence
and intestine war. The rivals who contended for the possession
of the Roman world had withdrawn the greatest part of their
forces from the guard of the general frontier; and the principal
cities which formed the boundary of their respective dominions
were filled with soldiers, who considered their countrymen as
their most implacable enemies. After the use of these internal
garrisons had ceased with the civil war, the conqueror wanted
either wisdom or firmness to revive the severe discipline of
Diocletian, and to suppress a fatal indulgence which habit had
endeared and almost confirmed to the military order. From the
reign of Constantine, a popular and even legal distinction was
admitted between the *Palatines* [135] and the *Borderers ;* the troops of
the court as they were improperly styled, and the troops of the
frontier. The former, elevated by the superiority of their pay
and privileges, were permitted, except in the extraordinary
emergencies of war, to occupy their tranquil stations in the
heart of the provinces. The most flourishing cities were
oppressed by the intolerable weight of quarters. The soldiers
insensibly forgot the virtues of their profession, and contracted
only the vices of civil life. They were either degraded by the
industry of mechanic trades, or enervated by the luxury of baths
and theatres. They soon became careless of their martial
exercises, curious in their diet and apparel; and, while they inspired terror to the subjects of the empire, they trembled at the
hostile approach of the Barbarians. [136] The chain of fortifications
which Diocletian and his colleagues had extended along the
banks of the great rivers was no longer maintained with the
same care or defended with the same vigilance. The numbers
which still remained under the name of the troops of the
frontier might be sufficient for the ordinary defence. But their
spirit was degraded by the humiliating reflection that *they* who
were exposed to the hardships and dangers of a perpetual warfare were rewarded only with about two-thirds of the pay and

[135] Zosimus, l. ii. p. 111. The distinction between the two classes of Roman
troops is very darkly expressed in the historians, the laws, and the *Notitia*. Consult,
however, the copious *paratitlon*, or abstract, which Godefroy has drawn up of the
seventh book, de Re Militari, of the Theodosian Code, l. vii. tit. i. leg. 18, l. viii.
tit. i. leg. 10. [Gibbon uses "Palatines" as equivalent to Palatines and Comitatenses—an erroneous use. See Appendix 12.]

[136] Ferox erat in suos miles et rapax, ignavus vero in hostes et fractus. Ammian.
l. xxii. c. 4. He observes that they loved downy beds and houses of marble ; and
that their cups were heavier than their swords.

emoluments which were lavished on the troops of the court. Even the bands or legions that were raised the nearest to the level of those unworthy favourites were in some measure disgraced by the title of honour which they were allowed to assume. It was in vain that Constantine repeated the most dreadful menaces of fire and sword against the Borderers who should dare to desert their colours, to connive at the inroads of the Barbarians, or to participate in the spoil.[137]   The mischiefs which flow from injudicious counsels are seldom removed by the application of partial severities ; and, though succeeding princes laboured to restore the strength and numbers of the frontier garrisons, the empire, till the last moment of its dissolution, continued to languish under the mortal wound which had been so rashly or so weakly inflicted by the hand of Constantine.

Reduction of the legion

The same timid policy, of dividing whatever is united, of reducing whatever is eminent, of dreading every active power, and of expecting that the most feeble will prove the most obedient, seems to pervade the institutions of several princes, and particularly those of Constantine. The martial pride of the legions, whose victorious camps had so often been the scene of rebellion, was nourished by the memory of their past exploits and the consciousness of their actual strength. As long as they maintained their ancient establishment of six thousand men, they subsisted, under the reign of Diocletian, each of them singly, a visible and important object in the military history of the Roman empire. A few years afterwards these gigantic bodies were shrunk to a very diminutive size ; and, when *seven* legions, with some auxiliaries, defended the city of Amida against the Persians, the total garrison, with the inhabitants of both sexes, and the peasants of the deserted country, did not exceed the number of twenty thousand persons.[138]   From this fact, and from similar examples, there is reason to believe that the constitution of the legionary troops, to which they partly owed their valour and discipline, was dissolved by Constantine ; and that the bands of Roman infantry, which still assumed the same names and the same honours, consisted only of one thousand or fifteen hundred men.[139]   The conspiracy of so many separate

---

[137] Cod. Theod. l. vii. tit. i. leg. 1, tit. xii. leg. 1.   See Howell's Hist. of the World, vol. ii. p. 19.   That learned historian, who is not sufficiently known, labours to justify the characters and policy of Constantine.

[138] Ammian. l. xix. c. 2.   He observes (c. 5), that the desperate sallies of two Gallic legions were like an handful of water thrown on a great conflagration.

[139] Pancirolus ad Notitiam, p. 96.   Mémoires de l'Académie des Inscriptions, tom. xxv. p. 491.   [This is partly true, but not altogether.   See Appendix 12. The *Notitia* gives 62 legions in the West, 70 in the East—Gibbon's 132.]

detachments, each of which was awed by the sense of its own weakness, could easily be checked ; and the successors of Constantine might indulge their love of ostentation, by issuing their orders to one hundred and thirty-two legions, inscribed on the muster-roll of their numerous armies. The remainder of their troops was distributed into several hundred cohorts of infantry, and squadrons of cavalry. Their arms, and titles, and ensigns were calculated to inspire terror, and to display the variety of nations who marched under the imperial standard. And not a vestige was left of that severe simplicity which, in the ages of freedom and victory, had distinguished the line of battle of a Roman army from the confused host of an Asiatic monarch.[140] A more particular enumeration, drawn from the *Notitia*, might exercise the diligence of an antiquary ; but the historian will content himself with observing that the number of permanent stations or garrisons established on the frontiers of the empire amounted to five hundred and eighty-three ; and that, under the successors of Constantine, the complete force of the military establishment was computed at six hundred and forty-five thousand soldiers.[141] An effort so prodigious surpassed the wants of a more ancient, and the faculties of a later, period.

In the various states of society, armies are recruited from very different motives. Barbarians are urged by the love of war ; the citizens of a free republic may be prompted by a principle of duty ; the subjects, or at least the nobles, of a monarchy are animated by a sentiment of honour ; but the timid and luxurious inhabitants of a declining empire must be allured into the service by the hopes of profit, or compelled by the dread of punishment. The resources of the Roman treasury were exhausted by the increase of pay, by the repetition of donatives, and by the invention of new emoluments and indulgences, which, in the opinion of the provincial youth, might compensate the hardships and dangers of a military life. Yet, although the stature was lowered,[142] although slaves, at least by a tacit con-

Difficulty of levies

---

[140] Romana acies unius prope formæ erat et hominum et armorum genere.— Regia acies varia magis multis gentibus dissimilitudine armorum auxiliorumque erat. T. Liv. l. xxxvii. c. 39, 40. Flaminius, even before the event, had compared the army of Antiochus to a supper, in which the flesh of one vile animal was diversified by the skill of the cooks. See the life of Flaminius in Plutarch.

[141] Agathias, l. v. p. 157, edit. Louvre [P. 305, ed. Bonn. A.D. 558. This was the estimate on paper ; the actual strength 150,000. For an estimate by Mommsen, see App. 12. The number of frontier garrisons, in the *Notitia*, is 305, not 583.]

[142] Valentinian (Cod. Theodos. l. vii. tit. xiii. leg. 3) fixes the standard at five feet seven inches, about five feet four inches and a half English measure. It had formerly been five feet ten inches, and in the best corps six Roman feet. Sed tunc erat amplior multitudo, et plures sequebantur militiam armatam. Vegetius de Re Militari, l. i. c. 5.

nivance, were indiscriminately received into the ranks, the insurmountable difficulty of procuring a regular and adequate supply of volunteers obliged the emperors to adopt more effectual and coercive methods. The lands bestowed on the veterans, as the free reward of their valour, were henceforward granted under a condition, which contains the first rudiments of the feudal tenures; that their sons, who succeeded to the inheritance, should devote themselves to the profession of arms, as soon as they attained the age of manhood ; and their cowardly refusal was punished by the loss of honour, of fortune, or even of life.[143] But, as the annual growth of the sons of the veterans bore a very small proportion to the demands of the service, levies of men were frequently required from the provinces, and every proprietor was obliged either to take up arms, or to procure a substitute, or to purchase his exemption by the payment of a heavy fine. The sum of forty-two pieces of gold, to which it was *reduced*, ascertains the exorbitant price of volunteers and the reluctance with which the government admitted of this alternative.[144] Such was the horror for the profession of a soldier which had affected the minds of the degenerate Romans that many of the youth of Italy and the provinces chose to cut off the fingers of their right hand to escape from being pressed into the service ; and this strange expedient was so commonly practised as to deserve the severe animadversion of the laws [145] and a peculiar name in the Latin language.[146]

[143] See the two titles, De Veteranis, and De Filiis Veteranorum, in the seventh book of the Theodosian Code. The age at which their military service was required varied from twenty-five to sixteen. If the sons of the veterans appeared with a horse, they had a right to serve in the cavalry ; two horses gave them some valuable privileges.

[144] Cod. Theod. l. vii. tit. xiii. leg. 7. According to the historian Socrates (see Godefroy ad. loc.), the same emperor Valens sometimes required eighty pieces of gold for a recruit. In the following law it is faintly expressed that slaves shall not be admitted inter optimas lectissimorum militum turmas.

[145] The person and property of a Roman knight, who had mutilated his two sons, were sold by public auction by the order of Augustus (Sueton. in August. c. 27). The moderation of that artful usurper proves that this example of severity was justified by the spirit of the times. Ammianus makes a distinction between the effeminate Italians and the hardy Gauls (l. xv. c. 12). Yet only fifteen years afterwards, Valentinian, in a law addressed to the præfect of Gaul, is obliged to enact that these cowardly deserters shall be burnt alive (Cod. Theod. l. vii. tit. xiii. leg. 5). Their numbers in Illyricum were so considerable that the province complained of a scarcity of recruits (id. leg. 10).

[146] They were called *Murci*. *Murcidus* is found in Plautus and Festus, to denote a lazy and cowardly person, who, according to Arnobius and Augustin, was under the immediate protection of the goddess *Murcia*. From this particular instance of cowardice, *murcare* is used as synonymous to *mutilare*, by the writers of the middle Latinity. See Lindenbrogius, and Valesius ad Ammian. Marcellin. l. xv. c. 12.

The introduction of Barbarians into the Roman armies be- Increase of came every day more universal, more necessary, and more fatal. ^{Barbarian} ^{auxiliaries} The most daring of the Scythians, of the Goths, and of the Germans, who delighted in war, and who found it more profitable to defend than to ravage the provinces, were enrolled, not only in the auxiliaries of their respective nations, but in the legions themselves, and among the most distinguished of the Palatine troops. As they freely mingled with the subjects of the empire, they gradually learned to despise their manners and to imitate their arts. They abjured the implicit reverence which the pride of Rome had exacted from their ignorance, while they acquired the knowledge and possession of those advantages by which alone she supported her declining greatness. The Barbarian soldiers who displayed any military talents were advanced, without exception, to the most important commands ; and the names of the tribunes, of the counts and dukes, and of the generals themselves, betray a foreign origin, which they no longer condescended to disguise. They were often entrusted with the conduct of a war against their countrymen ; and, though most of them preferred the ties of allegiance to those of blood, they did not always avoid the guilt, or at least the suspicion, of holding a treasonable correspondence with the enemy, of inviting his invasion, or of sparing his retreat. The camps and the palace of the son of Constantine were governed by the powerful faction of the Franks, who preserved the strictest connexion with each other and with their country, and who resented every personal affront as a national indignity.[147] When the tyrant Caligula was suspected of an intention to invest a very extraordinary candidate with the consular robes, the sacrilegious profanation would have scarcely excited less astonishment, if, instead of a horse, the noblest chieftain of Germany or Britain had been the object of his choice. The revolution of three centuries had produced so remarkable a change in the prejudices of the people that, with the public approbation, Constantine shewed his successors the example of bestowing the honours of the consulship on the Barbarians who, by their merit and services, had deserved to be ranked among the first of the Romans.[148] But as these hardy veterans, who had been edu-

[147] Malarichus—adhibitis Francis quorum eâ tempestate in palatio multitudo florebat, erectius jam loquebatur tumultuabaturque. Ammian. l. xv. c. 5.
[148] Barbaros omnium primus, ad usque fasces auxerat et trabeas consulares. Ammian. l. xx. c. 10. Eusebius (in Vit. Constantin. l. iv. c. 7) and Aurelius Victor seem to confirm the truth of this assertion ; yet in the thirty-two consular Fasti of the reign of Constantine I cannot discover the name of a single Barbarian,   I

cated in the ignorance or contempt of the laws, were incapable of exercising any civil offices, the powers of the human mind were contracted by the irreconcileable separation of talents as well as of professions. The accomplished citizens of the Greek and Roman republics, whose characters could adapt themselves to the bar, the senate, the camp, or the schools, had learned to write, to speak, and to act, with the same spirit, and with equal abilities.

Seven minis-
ters of the
palace IV. Besides the magistrates and generals, who at a distance from the court diffused their delegated authority over the provinces and armies, the emperor conferred the rank of *Illustrious* on seven of his more immediate servants, to whose fidelity he entrusted his safety, or his counsels, or his treasures. 1. The private apartments of the palace were governed by a favourite eunuch, who, in the language of that age, was styled The chamber-
lain the *præpositus* or præfect of the sacred bed-chamber. His duty was to attend the emperor in his hours of state, or in those of amusement, and to perform about his person all those menial services which can only derive their splendour from the influence of royalty. Under a prince who deserved to reign, the great chamberlain (for such we may call him) was an useful and humble domestic; but an artful domestic, who improves every occasion of unguarded confidence, will insensibly acquire over a feeble mind that ascendant which harsh wisdom and uncomplying virtue can seldom obtain. The degenerate grand-sons of Theodosius, who were invisible to their subjects and contemptible to their enemies, exalted the præfects of their bed-chamber above the heads of all the ministers of the palace;[149] and even his deputy, the first of the splendid train of slaves who waited in the presence, was thought worthy to rank before the *respectable* proconsuls of Greece or Asia. The jurisdiction of the chamberlain was acknowledged by the *counts*, or superintendents, who regulated the two important provinces of the magnificence of the wardrobe and of the luxury of the imperial table.[150] 2. The principal administration of public affairs was committed to the diligence and abilities of the *master*

should therefore interpret the liberality of that prince, as relative to the ornaments, rather than to the office, of the consulship.

[149] Cod. Theod. l. vi. tit. 8.

[150] By a very singular metaphor, borrowed from the military character of the first emperors, the steward of their household was styled the count of their camp (comes castrensis). Cassiodorius very seriously represents to him that his own fame, and that of the empire, must depend on the opinion which foreign ambassadors may conceive of the plenty and magnificence of the royal table (Variar. l. vi. epistol. 9).

of the offices.[151] He was the supreme magistrate of the palace, inspected the discipline of the civil and military *schools*, and received appeals from all parts of the empire; in the causes which related to that numerous army of privileged persons who, as the servants of the court, had obtained, for themselves and families, a right to decline the authority of the ordinary judges. The correspondence between the prince and his subjects was managed by the four *scrinia* or offices of this minister of state. The first was appropriated to memorials, the second to epistles, the third to petitions, and the fourth to papers and orders of a miscellaneous kind.[152] Each of these was directed by an inferior *master* of *respectable* dignity, and the whole business was dispatched by an hundred and forty-eight secretaries, chosen for the most part from the profession of the law, on account of the variety of abstracts of reports and references which frequently occurred in the exercise of their several functions. From a condescension, which in former ages would have been esteemed unworthy of the Roman majesty, a particular secretary was allowed for the Greek language; and interpreters were appointed to receive the ambassadors of the Barbarians: but the department of foreign affairs, which constitutes so essential a part of modern policy, seldom diverted the attention of the master of the offices. His mind was more seriously engaged by the general direction of the posts and arsenals of the empire. There were thirty-four cities, fifteen in the east, and nineteen in the west, in which regular companies of workmen were perpetually employed in fabricating defensive armour, offensive weapons of all sorts, and military engines, which were deposited in the arsenals, and occasionally delivered for the service of the troops.[153] 3. In the course of nine centuries, the office of *quæstor* had experienced a very singular revolution. In the infancy of Rome, two inferior magistrates were annually elected by the people, to relieve the consuls from the invidious manage-

The master of the offices

The quæstor

---

[151] Gutherius (de Officiis Domûs Augustæ, l. ii. c. 20, l. iii.) has very accurately explained the functions of the master of the offices and the constitution of his subordinate *scrinia*. But he vainly attempts, on the most doubtful authority, to deduce from the time of the Antonines, or even of Nero, the origin of a magistrate who cannot be found in history before the reign of Constantine. [His importance —if not his origin—probably dated from the reign of Constantine, and gradually developed during the fourth century. The original title was *tribunus et mag. off.* (Cod. Theod. ii. 9. 1), which further obscures the origin.]

[152] [*Scr. dispositionum*, of which one duty was to make dispositions in case of an imperial journey.]

[153] [It should not be overlooked that the mag. off. was head of the school of agentes in rebus; see below, note 170.]

ment of the public treasure ; [154] a similar assistant was granted
to every proconsul, and to every prætor, who exercised a military
or provincial command ; with the extent of conquest, the two
quæstors were gradually multiplied to the number of four, of
eight, of twenty, and, for a short time, perhaps, of forty ; [155]
and the noblest citizens ambitiously solicited an office which
gave them a seat in the senate, and a just hope of obtaining
the honours of the republic.   Whilst Augustus affected to
maintain the freedom of election, he consented to accept the
annual privilege of recommending, or rather indeed of nominat-
ing, a certain proportion of candidates ; and it was his custom
to select one of these distinguished youths, to read his orations
or epistles in the assemblies of the senate.[156]   The practice of
Augustus was imitated by succeeding princes ; the occasional
commission was established as a permanent office ; and the
favoured quæstor, assuming a new and more illustrious character,
alone survived the suppression of his ancient and useless colleagues.[157]   As the orations which he composed in the name of
the emperor [158] acquired the force, and, at length, the form of

[154] Tacitus (Annal. xi. 22) says that the first quæstors were elected by the
people, sixty-four years after the foundation of the republic ; but he is of opinion
that they had, long before that period, been annually appointed by the consuls,
and even by the kings.   But this obscure point of antiquity is contested by other
writers.   [Mommsen (Staatsrecht, 2, p. 525) thinks that the quæstorship originated
simultaneously with the consulsnip.]

[155] Tacitus (Annal. xi. 22) seems to consider twenty [fixed by Sulla] as the
highest number of quæstors ; and Dion. (l. xliii. p. 374 [c. 47 ; cp. 51]) insinuates
that, if the dictator Cæsar once created forty, it was only to facilitate the payment
of an immense debt of gratitude.   Yet the augmentation which he made of prætors
subsisted under the succeeding reigns.

[156] Sueton. in August. c. 65, and Torrent. ad loc. Dion. Cas. p. 755.

[157] The youth and inexperience of the quæstors, who entered on that important
office in their twenty-fifth year (Lips. Excurs. ad Tacit. l. iii. D.), engaged Augustus
to remove them from the management of the treasury ; and, though they were restored by Claudius, they seem to have been finally dismissed by Nero (Tacit. Annal.
xxii. 29.   Sueton. in Aug. c. 36, in Claud. c. 24, Dion. p. 696 [liii. 2], 961 [lx. 24],
&c. ;   Plin. Epistol. x. 20, et alib.).   In the provinces of the Imperial division, the
place of the quæstors was more ably supplied by the *procurators* (Dion. Cass. p. 707
[liii. 15] ; Tacit. in Vit. Agricol. c. 15) ; or, as they were afterwards called, *rationales*
(Hist. August. p. 130 [xviii. 45, 46]).   But in the provinces of the senate we may
still discover a series of quæstors till the reign of Marcus Antoninus (see the
Inscriptions of Gruter, the Epistles of Pliny, and a decisive fact in the Augustan
history, p. 64).   From Ulpian we may learn (Pandect. l. i. tit. 13) that, under the
government of the house of Severus, their provincial administration was abolished ;
and in the subsequent troubles the annual or triennial elections of quæstors must
have naturally ceased.   [The quæstorship continued to exist under the Constantinian monarchy, but it became virtually a municipal office at Rome, and the
quæstors were no longer "commended" by the Emperor, but were entirely
appointed by the Senate.   Their chief function was to defray the cost of games.]

[158] Cum patris nomine et epistolas ipse dictaret, et edicta conscriberet, orationesque
in senatu recitaret, etiam quæstoris vice.   Sueton. in Tit. c. 6.   The office must

absolute edicts, he was considered as the representative of the
legislative power, the oracle of the council, and the original
source of the civil jurisprudence.   He was sometimes invited to
take his seat in the supreme judicature of the Imperial consistory,
with the Prætorian præfects, and the master of the offices ; and he
was frequently requested to resolve the doubts of inferior judges ;
but, as he was not oppressed with a variety of subordinate business, his leisure and talents were employed to cultivate that dignified style of eloquence which, in the corruption of taste and
language, still preserves the majesty of the Roman laws.[159]   In
some respects, the office of the Imperial quæstor may be compared with that of a modern chancellor ; but the use of a great
seal, which seems to have been adopted by the illiterate
Barbarians, was never introduced to attest the public acts of
the emperors.   4. The extraordinary title of *count of the sacred*   The public
largesses was bestowed on the treasurer-general of the revenue,   treasurer
with the intention perhaps of inculcating that every payment
flowed from the voluntary bounty of the monarch.   To conceive
the almost infinite detail of the annual and daily expense of the
civil and military administration in every part of a great empire
would exceed the powers of the most vigorous imagination.
The actual account employed several hundred persons, distributed into eleven different offices, which were artfully contrived
to examine and control their respective operations.   The
multitude of these agents had a natural tendency to increase ;
and it was more than once thought expedient to dismiss to
their native homes the useless supernumeraries, who, deserting
their honest labours, had pressed with too much eagerness into
the lucrative profession of the finances.[160]   Twenty-nine pro-

have acquired new dignity, which was occasionally executed by the heir-apparent
of the empire.   Trajan entrusted the same care to Hadrian his quæstor and
cousin. See Dodwell, Prælection. Cambden. x. xi. p. 362-394. [It is not at all
likely that the *quæstor* of the new Monarchy can be derived from the quæstor who
read the orations of Augustus in the Senate. Mommsen proposes (Ephem. Epig.
5, 625 ff.) to derive him from the *vicarius a consiliis sacris*, the president (as he
believes) of the consistorium. In any case he was probably instituted by Constantine (Zos. v. 32). As a rule, he had precedence of the master of offices. Observe
that to both these officials were diverted functions which formerly belonged to the
præt. prefect. The quæstor took his place in the consistorium (cp. App. 10),
while the master of offices superseded him as commander of the palace guards.]
[159]——————— Terris edicta daturus ;
  Supplicibus responsa.—Oracula regis
  Eloquio crevere tuo ; nec dignius unquam
  Majestas meminit sese Romana locutam.
Claudian in Consulat. Mall. Theodor. 33. See likewise Symmachus (Epistol. i.
17 [= 23, ed. Seeck]), and Cassiodorius (Variar. vi. 5).
[160] Cod. Theod. l. vi. tit. 30. Cod Justinian. l. xii. tit. 24. [The *sacred largesses*

[Rationales] vincial receivers, of whom eighteen were honoured with the title of count, corresponded with the treasurer; and he extended his jurisdiction over the mines, from whence the precious metals were extracted, over the mints, in which they were converted into the current coin, and over the public treasuries of the most important cities, where they were deposited for the service of the state. The foreign trade of the empire was regulated by this minister, who directed likewise all the linen and woollen manufactures, in which the successive operations of spinning, weaving, and dyeing were executed, chiefly by women of a servile condition, for the use of the palace and army. Twenty-six of these institutions are enumerated in the west, where the arts had been more recently introduced, and a still larger proportion may be allowed for the industrious pro-

The private treasurer

vinces of the east.[161] 5. Besides the public revenue, which an absolute monarch might levy and expend according to his pleasure, the emperors, in the capacity of opulent citizens, possessed a very extensive property, which was administered by the *count*, or treasurer, of *the private estate*. Some part had perhaps been the ancient demesnes of kings and republics; some accessions might be derived from the families which were successively invested with the purple; but the most considerable portion flowed from the impure source of confiscations and forfeitures. The Imperial estates were scattered through the provinces, from Mauritania to Britain; but the rich and fertile soil of Cappadocia tempted the monarch to acquire in that country his fairest possessions,[162] and either Constantine or his successors embraced the occasion of justifying avarice by religious zeal. They suppressed the rich temple of the goddess of war supported the dignity of a sovereign prince; and they applied to their private use the consecrated lands, which were inhabited by six thousand

corresponds to the fiscus of the principate. The title *comes sacrarum largitionum* came into use about the middle of the fourth century; under Constantine he was called *rationalis summæ rei* (C. I. L. 6, 1145), and had the rank of a *count of the first order*. At first a *perfectissimus*, he finally became an *illustris*.]

[161] In the departments of the two counts of the treasury, the eastern part of the *Notitia* happens to be very defective. It may be observed that we had a treasury-chest in London, and a gynecæum or manufacture [of wool] at Winchester. But Britain was not thought worthy either of a mint or of an arsenal. Gaul alone possessed three of the former, and eight of the latter.

[162] Cod. Theod. l. vi. tit. xxx. leg. 2, and Godefroy ad loc. [With Diocletian there ceased to be any real distinction between the fiscus and the res privata, but the double treasury was maintained. Under Diocletian the title was *magister;* Constantine changed it to *rationalis rei privatae;* subsequently this minister is called *comes largitionum privatarum.*]

subjects or slaves of the Deity and her ministers.[163] But these were not the valuable inhabitants; the plains that stretch from the foot of Mount Argæus to the banks of the Sarus bred a generous race of horses, renowned above all others in the ancient world for their majestic shape and incomparable swiftness. These *sacred* animals, destined for the service of the palace and the Imperial games, were protected by the laws from the profanation of a vulgar master.[164] The demesnes of Cappadocia were important enough to require the inspection of a *count ;*[165] officers of an inferior rank were stationed in the other parts of the empire ; and the deputies of the private, as well as those of the public, treasurer were maintained in the exercise of their independent functions, and encouraged to control the authority of the provincial magistrates.[166] 6, 7. The chosen bands of cavalry and infantry which guarded the person of the emperor, were under the immediate command of the *two counts of the domestics.* The whole number consisted of three thousand five hundred men, divided into seven *schools,* or troops, of five hundred each ; and in the east, this honourable service was almost entirely appropriated to the Armenians. Whenever, on public ceremonies, they were drawn up in the courts and porticoes of the palace, their lofty stature, silent order, and splendid arms of silver and gold displayed a martial pomp, not unworthy of the Roman majesty.[167] From the seven schools two companies of horse and foot were selected, of the protectors, whose advantageous station was the hope and reward of the most deserving soldiers. They mounted guard in the interior apartments, and were occasionally dispatched into the provinces to execute with celerity and vigour the orders of their master.[168]

The counts of the domestics

Protectores

---

[163] Strabon. Geograph. l. xii. p. 809. The other temple of Comana, in Pontus, was a colony from that of Cappadocia, l. xii. p. 825. The president Des Brosses (see his Saluste, tom. ii. p. 21) conjectures that the deity adored in both Comanas was Beltis, the Venus of the east, the goddess of generation ; a very different being indeed from the goddess of war.

[164] Cod. Theod. l. x. tit. vi. de Grege Dominico. Godefroy has collected every circumstance of antiquity relative to the Cappadocian horses. One of the finest breeds, the Palmatian, was the forfeiture of a rebel, whose estate lay about sixteen miles from Tyana, near the great road between Constantinople and Antioch.

[165] Justinian (Novell. 30 [44, ed Zachariä]) subjected the province of the count of Cappadocia to the immediate authority of the favourite eunuch who presided over the sacred bed-chamber. [The divina domus Cappadociae is placed under the praep. sacri cubiculi in the Notitia orientis, x.]

[166] Cod. Theod. l. vi. tit. leg. 4, &c.

[167] Pancirolus, p. 102, 136. The appearance of these military domestics is described in the Latin poem of Corippus, de Laudibus Justin. l. iii. 157-179, p. 419, 420 of the Appendix Hist. Byzantin. Rom. 1777. [See Appendix 13.]

[168] Ammianus Marcellinus, who served so many years, obtained only the rank of a Protector. The first ten among these honourable soldiers were *Clarissimi,*

The counts of the domestics had succeeded to the office of the Prætorian præfects; like the præfects, they aspired from the service of the palace to the command of armies.

Agents or official spies   The perpetual intercourse between the court and the provinces was facilitated by the construction of roads and the institution of posts. But these beneficial establishments were accidentally connected with a pernicious and intolerable abuse. Two or three hundred *agents* or messengers were employed, under the jurisdiction of the master of the offices, to announce the names of the annual consuls and the edicts or victories of the emperors. They insensibly assumed the licence of reporting whatever they could observe of the conduct either of magistrates or of private citizens; and were soon considered as the eyes of the monarch,[169] and the scourge of the people. Under the warm influence of a feeble reign, they multiplied to the incredible number of ten thousand, disdained the mild though frequent admonitions of the laws, and exercised in the profitable management of the posts a rapacious and insolent oppression. These official spies, who regularly corresponded with the palace, were encouraged, by favour and reward, anxiously to watch the progress of every treasonable design, from the faint and latent symptoms of disaffection to the actual preparation of an open revolt. Their careless or criminal violation of truth and justice was covered by the consecrated mask of zeal; and they might securely aim their poisoned arrows at the breast either of the guilty or the innocent, who had provoked their resentment or refused to purchase their silence. A faithful subject, of Syria perhaps, or of Britain, was exposed to the danger, or at least to the dread, of being dragged in chains to the court of Milan or Constantinople, to defend his life and fortune against the malicious charge of these privileged informers. The ordinary administration was conducted by those methods which extreme necessity can alone palliate; and the defects of evidence were diligently supplied by the use of torture.[170]

[169] Xenophon, Cyropæd. l. viii. Brisson, de Regno Persico, l. i. No. 190, p. 264. The emperors adopted with pleasure this Persian metaphor. [Originally, like the *frumentarii*, superintendents of the supplies of public corn, the *agentes in rebus* acted as secret police and became so much detested that Diocletian abolished them. They were revived as a military *schola*, and employed in the same way as confidential agents.]

[170] For the *Agentes in Rebus*, see Ammian. l. xv. c. 3, l. xvi. c. 5, l. xxii. c. 7, with the curious annotations of Valesius. Cod. Theod. l. vi. t. xxvii., xxviii., xxix. Among the passages collected in the Commentary of Godefroy, the most remarkable one is from Libanius, in his discourse concerning the death of Julian.

The deceitful and dangerous experiment of the criminal *question*, as it is emphatically styled, was admitted, rather than approved, in the jurisprudence of the Romans. They applied this sanguinary mode of examination only to servile bodies, whose sufferings were seldom weighed by those haughty republicans in the scale of justice or humanity: but they would never consent to violate the sacred person of a citizen, till they possessed the clearest evidence of his guilt.[171] The annals of tyranny, from the reign of Tiberius to that of Domitian, circumstantially relate the executions of many innocent victims; but, as long as the faintest remembrance was kept alive of the national freedom and honour, the last hours of a Roman were secure from the danger of ignominious torture.[172] The conduct of the provincial magistrates was not, however, regulated by the practice of the city or the strict maxims of the civilians. They found the use of torture established, not only among the slaves of oriental despotism, but among the Macedonians, who obeyed a limited monarch; among the Rhodians, who flourished by the liberty of commerce; and even among the sage Athenians, who had asserted and adorned the dignity of human kind.[173] The acquiescence of the provincials encouraged their governors to acquire, or perhaps to usurp, a discretionary power of employing the rack, to extort from vagrants or plebeian criminals the confession of their guilt, till they insensibly proceeded to confound the distinction of rank and to disregard the privileges of Roman citizens. The apprehensions of the subjects urged them to solicit, and the interest of the sovereign engaged him to grant, a variety of special exemptions, which tacitly allowed, and even authorized, the general use of torture. They protected all persons of illustrious or honourable rank, bishops and their presbyters, professors of the liberal arts, soldiers and their families, municipal officers, and their posterity to the third generation, and all

[171] The Pandects (l. xlviii. tit. xviii.) contain the sentiments of the most celebrated civilians on the subject of torture. They strictly confine it to slaves; and Ulpian himself is ready to acknowledge that Res est fragilis, et periculosa, et quæ veritatem fallat.

[172] In the conspiracy of Piso against Nero, Epicharis (libertina mulier) was the only person tortured; the rest were *intacti tormentis*. It would be superfluous to add a weaker, and it would be difficult to find a stronger, example. Tacit. Annal. xv. 57.

[173] Dicendum . . . de institutis Atheniensium, Rhodiorum, doctissimorum hominum, apud quos etiam (id quod acerbissimum est) liberi civesque torquentur. Cicero. Partit. Orat. c. 34. We may learn from the trial of Philotas the practice of the Macedonians (Diodor. Sicul. l. xvii. p. 604. Q. Curt. l. vi. c. 11).

children under the age of puberty.[174] But a fatal maxim was introduced into the new jurisprudence of the empire, that in the case of treason, which included every offence that the subtlety of lawyers could derive from an *hostile intention* towards the prince or republic,[175] all privileges were suspended, and all conditions were reduced to the same ignominious level. As the safety of the emperor was avowedly preferred to every consideration of justice or humanity, the dignity of age and the tenderness of youth were alike exposed to the most cruel tortures ; and the terrors of a malicious information, which might select them as the accomplices, or even as the witnesses, perhaps, of an imaginary crime, perpetually hung over the heads of the principal citizens of the Roman world.[176]

Finances   These evils, however terrible they may appear, were confined to the smaller number of Roman subjects, whose dangerous situation was in some degree compensated by the enjoyment of those advantages, either of nature or of fortune, which exposed them to the jealousy of the monarch. The obscure millions of a great empire have much less to dread from the cruelty than from the avarice of their masters ; and *their* humble happiness is principally affected by the grievance of excessive taxes, which, gently pressing on the wealthy, descend with accelerated weight on the meaner and more indigent classes of society. An ingenious philosopher [177] has calculated the universal measure of the public impositions by the degrees of freedom and servitude ; and ventures to assert that, according to an invariable law of nature, it must always increase with the former, and diminish in a just proportion to the latter. But this reflection, which would tend to alleviate the miseries of despotism, is contradicted at least by the history of the Roman empire ; which accuses the same princes of despoiling the senate of its authority and the provinces of their wealth. Without abolishing all the various customs and duties on merchandises, which are imperceptibly discharged by the

[174] Heineccius (Element. Jur. Civil. part vii. p. 81) has collected these exemptions into one view.

[175] This definition of the sage Ulpian (Pandect. l. xlviii. tit. iv.) seems to have been adapted to the court of Caracalla rather than to that of Alexander Severus. See the Codes of Theodosius and Justinian ad leg. Juliam majestatis.

[176] Arcadius Charisius is the oldest lawyer quoted in the Pandects to justify the universal practice of torture in all cases of treason; but this maxim of tyranny, which is admitted by Ammianus (l. xix. c. 12) with the most respectful terror, is enforced by several laws of the successors of Constantine. See Cod. Theod. l. ix. tit. xxxv. In majestatis crimine omnibus æqua est conditio.

[177] Montesquieu, Esprit des Loix, l. xii. c. 13.

apparent choice of the purchaser, the policy of Constantine and his successors preferred a simple and direct mode of taxation, more congenial to the spirit of an arbitrary government.[178]

The name and use of the *indictions*,[179] which serve to ascertain the chronology of the middle ages, was derived from the regular practice of the Roman tributes.[180] The emperor subscribed with his own hand, and in purple ink, the solemn edict, or indiction, which was fixed up in the principal city of each diocese during two months previous to the first day of September. And, by a very easy connexion of ideas, the word *indiction* was transferred to the measure of tribute which it prescribed, and to the annual term which it allowed for the payment. This general estimate of the supplies was proportioned to the real and imaginary wants of the state ; but, as often as the expense exceeded the revenue, or the revenue fell short of the computation, an additional tax, under the name of *superindiction*, was imposed on the people, and the most valuable attribute of sovereignty was communicated to the Prætorian præfects, who,

The general tribute, or indiction

---

[178] Mr. Hume (Essays, vol. i. p. 389) has seen this important truth, with some degree of perplexity.

[179] The cycle of indictions, which may be traced as high as the reign of Constantius, or perhaps of his father Constantine, is still employed by the papal court : but the commencement of the year has been very reasonably altered to the first of January. See l'Art de vérifier les Dates, p. xi. ; and Dictionnaire Raison. de la Diplomatique, tom. ii. p. 25 ; two accurate treatises, which come from the workshop of the Benedictines. [A fifteen-yearly valuation of property, for purposes of taxation, was as old as Hadrian (Mommsen, Staatsrecht, ii. 975). The financial year or "indiction" ran from 1st Sept. to 31st Aug., and thus included unequal parts of two calendar years ; as a mode of chronology, it came into general use in the course of the fifth century. On this system 312-13 A.D. was regarded as the first year of the first fifteen-year cycle. Accordingly, if we wish to determine the indiction corresponding to any year, we subtract 312 and divide the difference by 15 ; the remainder is the indiction to which the first eight months of the given year (and the last four of the preceding year) belong. Take 700 A.D. : (700 − 312) ÷ 15 = 25 with a remainder of 13 ; therefore 1st Sept. 699 A.D. to 31st Aug. 700 A.D. is a 13th indiction. (If there is no remainder, the indiction is 15.) It is clear that the converse process requires a knowledge of the approximate period in terms of Anni Domini. Thus, if we know the date of the reign of Justinian ii., we may determine the indiction, say, of the first year in that reign, and so reckon which year corresponds to Ind. 13.—In the twelfth century this usage changed ; the period of fifteen years was called the indiction ; and the Birth of Christ was adopted as the starting-point. A year was known as the first, second, &c. year of such and such an indiction.—It is also to be observed that in Egypt (under the empire) the indictional year did not begin on 1st Sept. or any fixed date, but varied from year to year. This has been shown by Wilcken (*Hermes*, 19, 293 *sqq.*), whereas it had been formerly thought (by Hartel) that the Egyptian ind. began on some day between 11th and 15th June.]

[180] The first twenty-eight titles of the eleventh book of the Theodosian Code are filled with the circumstantial regulations on the important subject of tributes ; but they suppose a clearer knowledge of fundamental principles than it is at present in our power to attain.

on some occasions, were permitted to provide for the unforeseen
and extraordinary exigencies of the public service. The execution of these laws (which it would be tedious to pursue in their
minute and intricate detail) consisted of two distinct operations ; the resolving the general imposition into its constituent
parts, which were assessed on the provinces, the cities, and
the individuals of the Roman world, and the collecting the
separate contributions of the individuals, the cities, and the
provinces, till the accumulated sums were poured into the
Imperial treasuries. But, as the account between the monarch
and the subject was perpetually open, and as the renewal of the
demand anticipated the perfect discharge of the preceding
obligation, the weighty machine of the finances was moved by
the same hands round the circle of its yearly revolution. Whatever was honourable or important in the administration of the
revenue was committed to the wisdom of the præfects and their
provincial representatives ; the lucrative functions were claimed
by a crowd of subordinate officers, some of whom depended on
the treasurer, others on the governor of the province ; and who,
in the inevitable conflicts of a perplexed jurisdiction, had frequent opportunities of disputing with each other the spoils of
the people. The laborious offices, which could be productive only
of envy and reproach, of expense and danger, were imposed on
the *Decurions*, who formed the corporations of the cities, and
whom the severity of the Imperial laws had condemned to sustain the burthens of civil society.[181] The whole landed property
of the empire (without excepting the patrimonial estates of the
monarch) was the object of ordinary taxation ; and every new
purchaser contracted the obligations of the former proprietor.
An accurate *census*,[182] or survey, was the only equitable mode
of ascertaining the proportion which every citizen should be
obliged to contribute for the public service ; and from the well-
known period of the indictions there is reason to believe that
this difficult and expensive operation was repeated at the
regular distance of fifteen years. The lands were measured by
surveyors, who were sent into the provinces ; their nature,
whether arable or pasture, or vineyards or woods, was dis-

---

[181] The title concerning the Decurions (l. xii. tit. i.) is the most ample in the
whole Theodosian Code ; since it contains not less than one hundred and ninety-
two distinct laws to ascertain the duties and privileges of that useful order of
citizens.

[182] Habemus enim et hominum numerum qui delati sunt, et agrûm modum.
Eumenius in Panegyr. Vet. viii. 6.   See Cod. Theod. l. xiii. tit. x., xi. with Godefroy's Commentary.

tinctly reported; and an estimate was made of their common value from the average produce of five years. The numbers of slaves and of cattle constituted an essential part of the report; an oath was administered to the proprietors, which bound them to disclose the true state of their affairs; and their attempts to prevaricate, or elude the intention of the legislator, were severely watched, and punished as a capital crime which included the double guilt of treason and sacrilege.[183] A large portion of the tribute was paid in money; and of the current coin of the empire, gold alone could be legally accepted.[184] The remainder of the taxes, according to the proportions determined by the annual indiction, was furnished in a manner still more direct, and still more oppressive. According to the different nature of lands, their real produce, in the various articles of wine or oil, corn or barley, wood or iron, was transported by the labour or at the expense of the provincials to the Imperial magazines, from whence they were occasionally distributed, for the use of the court, of the army, and of the two capitals, Rome and Constantinople. The commissioners of the revenue were so frequently obliged to make considerable purchases that they were strictly prohibited from allowing any compensation or from receiving in money the value of those supplies which were exacted in kind. In the primitive simplicity of small communities, this method may be well adapted to collect the almost voluntary offerings of the people; but it is at once susceptible of the utmost latitude and of the utmost strictness, which in a corrupt and absolute monarchy must introduce a perpetual contest between the power of oppression and the arts of fraud.[185] The agriculture of the Roman provinces was insensibly ruined, and, in the progress of despotism, which tends to disappoint its own purpose, the emperors were

---

[183] Siquis sacrilegâ vitem falce succiderit, aut feracium ramorum fœtus hebetaverit, quo declinet fidem censuum, et mentiatur callide paupertatis ingenium, mox detectus capitale subibit exitium, et bona ejus in fisci jura migrabunt. Cod. Theod. l. xiii. tit. xi. leg. 1. Although this law is not without its studied obscurity, it is, however, clear enough to prove the minuteness of the inquisition, and the disproportion of the penalty.

[184] The astonishment of Pliny would have ceased. Equidem miror P. R. victis gentibus argentum semper imperitasse non aurum. Hist. Natur. xxxiii. 15.

[185] Some precautions were taken (see Cod. Theod. l. xi. tit. ii. and Cod. Justinian. l. x. tit. xxvii. leg. 1, 2, 3) to restrain the magistrates from the abuse of their authority, either in the exaction or in the purchase of corn: but those who had learning enough to read the orations of Cicero against Verres (iii. de Frumento) might instruct themselves in all the various arts of oppression, with regard to the weight, the price, the quality, and the carriage. The avarice of an unlettered governor would supply the ignorance of precept or precedent.

obliged to derive some merit from the forgiveness of debts, or the remission of tributes, which their subjects were utterly incapable of paying. According to the new division of Italy, the fertile and happy province of Campania, the scene of the early victories and of the delicious retirements of the citizens of Rome, extended between the sea and the Apennine from the Tiber to the Silarus. Within sixty years after the death of Constantine, and on the evidence of an actual survey, an exemption was granted in favour of three hundred and thirty thousand English acres of desert and uncultivated land; which amounted to one-eighth of the whole surface of the province. As the footsteps of the Barbarians had not yet been seen in Italy, the cause of this amazing desolation, which is recorded in the laws, can be ascribed only to the administration of the Roman emperors.[186]

Assessed in the form of a capitation   Either from design or from accident, the mode of assessment seemed to unite the substance of a land-tax with the forms of a capitation.[187] The returns which were sent of every province or district expressed the number of tributary subjects and the amount of the public impositions. The latter of these sums was divided by the former; and the estimate, that such a province contained so many *capita*, or heads of tribute, and that each *head* was rated at such a price, was universally received, not only in the popular, but even in the legal computation. The value of a tributary head must have varied, according to many accidental, or at least fluctuating, circumstances; but

[186] Cod. Theod. l. xi. tit. xxviii. leg. 2, published the 24th of March, A.D. 395, by the emperor Honorius, only two months after the death of his father Theodosius. He speaks of 528,042 Roman jugera, which I have reduced to the English measure. The jugerum contained 28,800 square Roman feet.

[187] Godefroy (Cod. Theod. tom. vi. p. 116) argues with weight and learning on the subject of the capitation; but, while he explains the *caput* as a share or measure of property, he too absolutely excludes the idea of a personal assessment. [The old land tax or *tributum* (so called in imperial provinces; *stipendium* in senatorial) now became the *capitatio terrena* (or *iugatio*), and the assessment was made on a valuation, not of the produce, but of the capital. In the Eastern part of the empire, property was divided into a number of unities which paid the same tax, and consequently differed in size according to the value of the land. (Seven classes of land were distinguished: 1, wine-producing; 2, 3, oil-producing; 4, 5, 6, arable; 7, pasture.) The unity or *iugum* was valued at 1000 solidi, and might be made up of land of different classes. Under Diocletian this tax was paid in kind, though assessed in money (*annonae*, measures of corn, and *capita*, units of hay, &c., being equated with money-values), but after Constantine's monetary reforms the payment could be made in coin. Landed proprietors had, beside this tax, to supply rations for the support of the government officials and the army. The *cap. terrena* must be distinguished from the *cap. humana* or poll-tax, which is very obscure, but possibly fell on the coloni, as it certainly did on widows and orphans (so Schiller). Compare Mommsen's article in Hermes, 3, 429 *sqq.*; Schiller, *R.G.* ii. 68 *sqq.*]

some knowledge has been preserved of a very curious fact, the more important, since it relates to one of the richest provinces of the Roman empire, and which now flourishes as the most splendid of the European kingdoms. The rapacious ministers of Constantius had exhausted the wealth of Gaul, by exacting twenty-five pieces of gold for the annual tribute of every head. The humane policy of his successor reduced the capitation to seven pieces.[188] A moderate proportion between these opposite extremes of extravagant oppression and of transient indulgence may therefore be fixed at sixteen pieces of gold, or about nine pounds sterling, the common standard perhaps of the impositions of Gaul.[189] But this calculation, or rather indeed the facts from whence it is deduced, cannot fail of suggesting two difficulties to a thinking mind, who will be at once surprised by the *equality* and by the *enormity* of the capitation. An attempt to explain them may perhaps reflect some light on the interesting subject of the finances of the declining empire.

I. It is obvious that, as long as the immutable constitution of human nature produces and maintains so unequal a division of property, the most numerous part of the community would be deprived of their subsistence by the equal assessment of a tax from which the sovereign would derive a very trifling revenue. Such indeed might be the theory of the Roman capitation; but in the practice, this unjust equality was no longer felt, as the tribute was collected on the principle of a *real*, not of a *personal*,

[188] Quid profuerit (*Julianus*) anhelantibus extremâ penuriâ Gallis, hinc maxime claret, quod primitus partes eas ingressus, pro *capitibus* singulis tributi nomine vicenos quinos aureos reperit flagitari; discedens vero septenos tantum munera universa complentes. Ammian. l. xvi. c. 5. [The *caput* is the *iugum*.]

[189] In the calculation of any sum of money under Constantine and his successors, we need only refer to the excellent discourse of Mr. Greaves on the Denarius for the proof of the following principles: 1. That the ancient and modern Roman pound, containing 5256 grains of Troy weight, is about one-twelfth lighter than the English pound, which is composed of 5760 of the same grains. 2. That the pound of gold, which had once been divided into forty-eight *aurei*, was at this time coined into seventy-two smaller pieces of the same denomination. 3. That five of these aurei were the legal tender for a pound of silver, and that consequently the pound of gold was exchanged for fourteen pounds eight ounces of silver according to the Roman, or about thirteen pounds according to the English, weight. 4. That the English pound of silver is coined into sixty-two shillings. From these elements we may compute the Roman pound of gold, the usual method of reckoning large sums, at forty pounds sterling; and we may fix the currency of the *aureus* at somewhat more than eleven shillings. [Before Diocletian 70 aurei were struck from a pound of gold. Diocletian raised the value of the aureus from $\frac{1}{70}$ to $\frac{1}{60}$, and Constantine reduced it again, but to $\frac{1}{72}$. This new Constantinian aureus was also called *Solidus* (whence Ital. *soldo*, French *sou*). Schiller has shown that from 307 to 323 there was a transitional period in which the $\frac{1}{72}$ lb. aureus was struck in the west, but not in the east. Röm. Gesch. ii. p. 222.]

imposition.   Several indigent citizens contributed to compose a single *head*, or share of taxation ; while the wealthy provincial, in proportion to his fortune, alone represented several of those imaginary beings.   In a poetical request, addressed to one of the last and most deserving of the Roman princes who reigned in Gaul, Sidonius Apollinaris personifies his tribute under the figure of a triple monster, the Geryon of the Grecian fables, and entreats the new Hercules that he would most graciously be pleased to save his life by cutting off three of his heads.[190]   The fortune of Sidonius far exceeded the customary wealth of a poet; but, if he had pursued the allusion, he must have painted many of the Gallic nobles with the hundred heads of the deadly Hydra spreading over the face of the country and devouring the substance of an hundred families.   II. The difficulty of allowing an annual sum of about nine pounds sterling, even for the aver- age of the capitation of Gaul, may be rendered more evident by the comparison of the present state of the same country, as it is now governed by the absolute monarch of an industrious, wealthy, and affectionate people.   The taxes of France cannot be magni- fied, either by fear or by flattery, beyond the annual amount of eighteen millions sterling, which ought perhaps to be shared among four and twenty millions of inhabitants.[191]   Seven millions of these, in the capacity of fathers or brothers or husbands, may discharge the obligations of the remaining multitude of women and children ; yet the equal proportion of each tributary subject will scarcely rise above fifty shillings of our money,

---

[190] Geryones nos esse puta, monstrumque tribitum,
       Hic *capita*, ut vivam, tu mihi tolle *tria*.
                              Sidon. Apollinar. Carm. xiii.
The reputation of Father Sirmond led me to expect more satisfaction than I have found in his note (p. 144) on this remarkable passage.   The words, suo vel *suorum* nomine, betray the perplexity of the commentator.

[191] This assertion, however formidable it may seem, is founded on the original registers of births, deaths, and marriages, collected by public authority, and now deposited in the *Contrôle Général* at Paris.   The annual average of births through- out the whole kingdom, taken in five years (from 1770 to 1774, both inclusive), is 479,649 boys and 449,269 girls, in all 928,918 children.   The province of French Hainault alone furnishes 9906 births : and we are assured, by an actual enumeration of the people, annually repeated from the year 1773 to the year 1776, that, upon an average, Hainault contains 257,097 inhabitants.   By the rules of fair analogy, we might infer that the ordinary proportion of annual births to the whole people, is about 1 to 26 ; and that the kingdom of France contains 24,151,868 persons of both sexes and of every age.   If we content ourselves with the more moderate proportion of 1 to 25, the whole population will amount to 23,222,950.   From the diligent researches of the French government (which are not unworthy of our own imitation), we may hope to obtain a still greater degree of certainty on this im portant subject.

instead of a proportion almost four times as considerable, which was regularly imposed on their Gallic ancestors. The reason of this difference may be found, not so much in the relative scar-city or plenty of gold and silver, as in the different state of society in ancient Gaul and in modern France. In a country where personal freedom is the privilege of every subject, the whole mass of taxes, whether they are levied on property or on consumption, may be fairly divided among the whole body of the nation. But the far greater part of the lands of ancient Gaul, as well as of the other provinces of the Roman world, were cultivated by slaves, or by peasants whose dependent condition was a less rigid servitude.[192] In such a state the poor were maintained at the expense of the masters, who enjoyed the fruits of their labour ; and, as the rolls of tribute were filled only with the names of those citizens who possessed the means of an honourable, or at least of a decent, subsistence, the comparative smallness of their numbers explains and justifies the high rate of their capitation. The truth of this assertion may be illustrated by the following example : The Ædui, one of the most powerful and civilized tribes or *cities* of Gaul, occupied an ex-tent of territory which now contains above five hundred thousand inhabitants in the two ecclesiastical dioceses of Autun and Nevers :[193] and with the probable accession of those of Châlons and Macon,[194] the population would amount to eight hundred

[192] Cod. Theod. l. v. tit. ix., x., xi. Cod. Justinian. l. xi. tit. lxiii. Coloni appellantur qui conditionem debent genitali solo, propter agriculturam sub dominio possessorum. Augustin. de Civitate Dei, l. x. c. 1.

[193] The ancient jurisdiction of (*Augustodunum*) Autun in Burgundy, the capital of the Ædui, comprehended the adjacent territory of (*Noviodunum*) Nevers. See d'Anville, Notice de l'ancienne Gaule, p. 491. The two dioceses of Autun and Nevers are now composed, the former of 610, and the latter of 160, parishes. The registers of births, taken during eleven years, in 476 parishes of the same province of Burgundy, and multiplied by the moderate proportion of 25 (see Messance, Re-cherches sur la Population, p. 142), may authorize us to assign an average number of 656 persons for each parish, which being again multiplied by the 770 parishes of the diocese of Nevers and Autun will produce the sum of 505,120 persons for the extent of country which was once possessed by the Ædui.

[194] We might derive an additional supply of 301,750 inhabitants from the dioceses of Châlons (*Cabillonum*) and of Macon (*Matisco*) ; since they contain, the one 200, and the other 260, parishes. This accession of territory might be justified by very specious reasons. 1. Châlons and Macon were undoubtedly with-in the original jurisdiction of the Ædui (see d'Anville, Notice, p. 187, 443). 2. In the *Notitia* of Gaul, they are enumerated not as *Civitates*, but merely as *Castra*. 3. They do not appear to have been episcopal seats before the fifth and sixth centuries. Yet there is a passage in Eumenius (Panegyr. Vet. viii. 7) which very forcibly deters me from extending the territory of the Ædui, in the reign of Constantine, along the beautiful banks of the navigable Saône.

thousand souls. In the time of Constantine, the territory of the Ædui afforded no more than twenty-five thousand *heads* of capitation, of whom seven thousand were discharged by that prince from the intolerable weight of tribute.[195]   A just analogy would seem to countenance the opinion of an ingenious historian,[196] that the free and tributary citizens did not surpass the number of half a million ; and if, in the ordinary administration of government, their annual payments may be computed at about four millions and a half of our money, it would appear that, although the share of each individual was four times as considerable, a fourth part only of the modern taxes of France was levied on the Imperial province of Gaul.[197]   The exactions of Constantius may be calculated at seven millions sterling, which were reduced to two millions by the humanity or the wisdom of Julian.

Capitation on trade and industry

But this tax or capitation on the proprietors of land would have suffered a rich and numerous class of free citizens to escape. With the view of sharing that species of wealth which is derived from art or labour, and which exists in money or in merchandise, the emperors imposed a distinct and personal tribute on the trading part of their subjects.[198]   Some exemptions, very strictly confined both in time and place, were allowed to the proprietors who disposed of the produce of their own estates.   Some indulgence was granted to the profession of the liberal arts : but every other branch of commercial industry was affected by the severity of the law.   The honourable merchant of Alexandria, who imported the gems and spices of India for the use of the western world ; the usurer, who derived from the interest of money a silent and ignominious profit ; the ingenious manufacturer, the diligent mechanic, and even the most obscure retailer of a sequestered village, were obliged to admit the officers of the revenue into the partnership of their gain : and the sovereign of the Roman empire, who tolerated the profession, consented to share the infamous salary, of public prostitutes. As this general tax upon industry was collected every fourth year, it was styled the *Lustral Contribution :* and the his-

---

[195] Eumenius in Panegyr. Vet. viii. 11.   [The land of the Ædui contained 32,000 capita of land, which the discharge of 7000 reduced to 25,000.   The passage of Eumenius was first explained rightly by Savigny.   Smith (ed. of Gibbon, ii. 341) has a good note on the errors of Gibbon's computation.]

[196] L'Abbé du Bos, Hist. Critique de la M. F. tom i. p. 121.

[197] [Gibbon does not take into account the other taxes in the Empire.]

[198] See Cod. Theod. l. xiii. tit. i. and iv.

torian Zosimus[199] laments that the approach of the fatal
period was announced by the tears and terrors of the citizens,
who were often compelled by the impending scourge to embrace the most abhorred and unnatural methods of procuring
the sum at which their property had been assessed. The testimony of Zosimus cannot indeed be justified from the charge of
passion and prejudice; but, from the nature of this tribute, it
seems reasonable to conclude that it was arbitrary in the distribution, and extremely rigorous in the mode of collecting.
The secret wealth of commerce, and the precarious profits of art
or labour, are susceptible only of a discretionary valuation, which
is seldom disadvantageous to the interest of the treasury; and,
as the person of the trader supplies the want of a visible and
permanent security, the payment of the imposition, which, in
the case of a land-tax, may be obtained by the seizure of property, can rarely be extorted by any other means than those of
corporal punishments. The cruel treatment of the insolvent
debtors of the state is attested, and was perhaps mitigated, by a
very humane edict of Constantine, who, disclaiming the use of
racks and of scourges, allots a spacious and airy prison for the
place of their confinement.[200]

These general taxes were imposed and levied by the absolute Free gifts
authority of the monarch; but the occasional offerings of the
coronary gold still retained the name and semblance of popular
consent. It was an ancient custom that the allies of the republic, who ascribed their safety or deliverance to the success of
the Roman arms; and even the cities of Italy, who admired the
virtues of their victorious general; adorned the pomp of his
triumph by their voluntary gifts of crowns of gold, which, after
the ceremony, were consecrated in the temple of Jupiter, to
remain a lasting monument of his glory to future ages. The
progress of zeal and flattery soon multiplied the number, and
increased the size, of these popular donations; and the triumph
of Cæsar was enriched with two thousand eight hundred and
twenty-two massy crowns, whose weight amounted to twenty
thousand four hundred and fourteen pounds of gold. This
treasure was immediately melted down by the prudent dictator,

---

[199] Zosimus, l. ii. p. 115 [c. 38]. There is probably as much passion and prejudice in the attack of Zosimus as in the elaborate defence of the memory of Constantine by the zealous Dr. Howell. Hist. of the World, vol. ii. p. 20. [The
lustralis collatio was also called chrysargyron.]

[200] Cod. Theod. l. xi. tit. vii. leg. 3.

who was satisfied that it would be more serviceable to his soldiers than to the gods: his example was imitated by his successors; and the custom was introduced of exchanging these splendid ornaments for the more acceptable present of the current gold coin of the empire.[201] The spontaneous offering was at length exacted as the debt of duty; and, instead of being confined to the occasion of a triumph, it was supposed to be granted by the several cities and provinces of the monarchy as often as the emperor condescended to announce his accession, his consulship, the birth of a son, the creation of a Cæsar, a victory over the Barbarians, or any other real or imaginary event which graced the annals of his reign. The peculiar free gift of the senate of Rome was fixed by custom at sixteen hundred pounds of gold, or about sixty-four thousand pounds sterling. The oppressed subjects celebrated their own felicity, that their sovereign should graciously consent to accept this feeble but voluntary testimony of their loyalty and gratitude.[202]

Conclusion   A people elated by pride, or soured by discontent, are seldom qualified to form a just estimate of their actual situation. The subjects of Constantine were incapable of discerning the decline of genius and manly virtue, which so far degraded them below the dignity of their ancestors; but they could feel and lament the rage of tyranny, the relaxation of discipline, and the increase of taxes. The impartial historian, who acknowledges the justice of their complaints, will observe some favourable circumstances which tended to alleviate the misery of their condition. The threatening tempest of Barbarians, which so soon subverted the foundations of Roman greatness, was still repelled, or suspended, on the frontiers. The arts of luxury and literature were cultivated, and the elegant pleasures of society were enjoyed, by the inhabitants of a considerable portion of the globe. The forms, the pomp, and the expense of the civil administration contributed to restrain the irregular licence of the soldiers; and, although the laws were violated by power or perverted by

[201] See Lipsius de Magnitud. Romanâ, l. ii. c. 9. The Tarragonese Spain presented the emperor Claudius with a crown of gold of seven, and Gaul with another of nine, *hundred* pounds' weight. I have followed the rational emendation of Lipsius.

[202] Cod. Theod. l. xii. tit. xiii. The senators were supposed to be exempt from the *Aurum Coronarium;* but the *Auri Oblatio*, which was required at their hands, was precisely of the same nature. [The amount mentioned in the text was that paid on the Decennalia of Valentinian ii. (Symmachus, *Relat.* 13, 3). The senators had also to pay a regular tax, the *follis*, paid by the emperor himself as a senator, which did not free him from the land tax, if he were a proprietor. The follis was of three grades: 8, 4, and 2 pounds of gold.]

subtlety, the sage principles of the Roman jurisprudence preserved a sense of order and equity, unknown to the despotic governments of the east. The rights of mankind might derive some protection from religion and philosophy ; and the name of freedom, which could no longer alarm, might sometimes admonish, the successors of Augustus that they did not reign over a nation of slaves or barbarians.[203]

---

[203] The great Theodosius, in his judicious advice to his son (Claudian in iv. Consulat. Honorii, 214, &c.), distinguishes the station of a Roman prince from that of a Partnian monarch. Virtue was necessary for the one ; birth might suffice for the other. [In connexion with Constantine's finance, it should be observed that the oppressiveness of taxation in the latter part of his reign, as noticed by Zosimus, ii. 38, was probably caused in a great measure by the enormous expenses connected with the foundation of his new city (cp. Schiller, ii. 226). We must notice too the immunities from taxation which he allowed to certain favoured classes and communities ; e.g., to physicians and professors, Cod. Theod. 13, 4, 1 ; Athens received supplies of corn, Julian, Or. i. 10.]

CHAPTER XVIII

Character of Constantine—Gothic War—Death of Constantine—
Division of the Empire among his three Sons—Persian War—
Tragic Deaths of Constantine the Younger and Constans—
Usurpation of Magnentius—Civil War—Victory of Constantius

Character of Constantine

THE character of the prince who removed the seat of empire and introduced such important changes into the civil and religious constitution of his country has fixed the attention, and divided the opinions, of mankind. By the grateful zeal of the Christians, the deliverer of the church has been decorated with every attribute of a hero, and even of a saint; while the discontent of the vanquished party has compared Constantine to the most abhorred of those tyrants, who, by their vice and weakness, dishonoured the Imperial purple. The same passions have in some degree been perpetuated to succeeding generations, and the character of Constantine is considered, even in the present age, as an object either of satire or of panegyric. By the impartial union of those defects which are confessed by his warmest admirers and of those virtues which are acknowledged by his most implacable enemies, we might hope to delineate a just portrait of that extraordinary man, which the truth and candour of history should adopt without a blush.[1] But it would soon appear that the vain attempt to blend such discordant colours, and to reconcile such inconsistent qualities, must produce a figure monstrous rather than human, unless it is viewed in its proper and distinct lights by a careful separation of the different periods of the reign of Constantine.

His virtues

The person, as well as the mind, of Constantine had been enriched by nature with her choicest endowments. His stature was lofty, his countenance majestic, his deportment graceful; his strength and activity were displayed in every manly exercise,

[1] On ne se trompera point sur Constantin, en croyant tout le mal qu'en dit Eusèbe, et tout le bien qu'en dit Zosime. Fleury, Hist. Ecclésiastique, t. iii. p. 233. Eusebius and Zosimus form indeed the two extremes of flattery and invective. The intermediate shades are expressed by those writers whose character or situation variously tempered the influence of their religious zeal.

and from his earliest youth to a very advanced season of life, he preserved the vigour of his constitution by a strict adherence to the domestic virtues of chastity and temperance. He delighted in the social intercourse of familiar conversation; and, though he might sometimes indulge his disposition to raillery with less reserve than was required by the severe dignity of his station, the courtesy and liberality of his manners gained the hearts of all who approached him. The sincerity of his friendship has been suspected; yet he shewed, on some occasions, that he was not incapable of a warm and lasting attachment. The disadvantage of an illiterate education had not prevented him from forming a just estimate of the value of learning; and the arts and sciences derived some encouragement from the munificent protection of Constantine. In the dispatch of business, his diligence was indefatigable; and the active powers of his mind were almost continually exercised in reading, writing, or meditating, in giving audience to ambassadors, and in examining the complaints of his subjects. Even those who censured the propriety of his measures were compelled to acknowledge that he possessed magnanimity to conceive, and patience to execute, the most arduous designs, without being checked either by the prejudices of education or by the clamours of the multitude. In the field, he infused his own intrepid spirit into the troops, whom he conducted with the talents of a consummate general; and to his abilities, rather than to his fortune, we may ascribe the signal victories which he obtained over the foreign and domestic foes of the republic. He loved glory, as the reward, perhaps as the motive, of his labours. The boundless ambition, which, from the moment of his accepting the purple at York, appears as the ruling passion of his soul, may be justified by the dangers of his own situation, by the character of his rivals, by the consciousness of superior merit, and by the prospect that his success would enable him to restore peace and order to the distracted empire. In his civil wars against Maxentius and Licinius, he had engaged on his side the inclinations of the people, who compared the undissembled vices of those tyrants with the spirit of wisdom and justice which seemed to direct the general tenor of the administration of Constantine.[2]

---

[2] The virtues of Constantine are collected for the most part from Eutropius and the younger Victor, two sincere pagans, who wrote after the extinction of his family. Even Zosimus and the *Emperor* Julian acknowledge his personal courage and military achievements.

His vices

Had Constantine fallen on the banks of the Tiber, or even in the plains of Hadrianople, such is the character which, with a few exceptions, he might have transmitted to posterity. But the conclusion of his reign (according to the moderate and indeed tender sentence of a writer of the same age) degraded him from the rank which he had acquired among the most deserving of the Roman princes.[3] In the life of Augustus, we behold the tyrant of the republic converted, almost by imperceptible degrees, into the father of his country and of human kind. In that of Constantine, we may contemplate a hero, who had so long inspired his subjects with love and his enemies with terror, degenerating into a cruel and dissolute monarch, corrupted by his fortune, or raised by conquest above the

A.D.
323-337

necessity of dissimulation. The general peace which he maintained during the last fourteen years of his reign was a period of apparent splendour rather than of real prosperity; and the old age of Constantine was disgraced by the opposite yet reconcileable vices of rapaciousness and prodigality. The accumulated treasures found in the palaces of Maxentius and Licinius were lavishly consumed; the various innovations introduced by the conqueror were attended with an increasing expense; the cost of his buildings, his court, and his festivals, required an immediate and plentiful supply; and the oppression of the people was the only fund which could support the magnificence of the sovereign.[4] His unworthy favourites, enriched by the boundless liberality of their master, usurped with impunity the privilege of rapine and corruption.[5] A secret but universal decay was felt in every part of the public administration, and the emperor himself, though he still retained the obedience, gradually lost the esteem, of his subjects. The dress and manners, which, towards the decline of life, he chose

---

[3] See Eutropius, x. 6. In primo Imperii tempore optimis principibus, ultimo mediis comparandus. From the ancient Greek version of Pæanius (edit. Havercamp. p. 697), I am inclined to suspect that Eutropius had originally written *vix* mediis; and that the offensive monosyllable was dropped by the wilful inadvertency of transcribers. Aurelius Victor [Epit. 41] expresses the general opinion by a vulgar and indeed obscure proverb. *Trachala* decem annis præstantissimus; duodecim sequentibus *latro*; decem novissimis *pupillus* ob immodicas profusiones.

[4] Julian. Orat. i. p. 8 [9, ed Hertl.], in a flattering discourse pronounced before the son of Constantine; and Cæsares, p. 335. Zosimus, p. 114, 115 [ii. 38]. The stately buildings of Constantinople, &c., may be quoted as a lasting and unexceptionable proof of the profuseness of their founder.

[5] The impartial Ammianus deserves all our confidence. Proximorum fauces aperuit primus omnium Constantinus. L. xvi. c. 8. Eusebius himself confesses the abuse (Vit. Constantin. l. iv. c. 29, 54); and some of the imperial laws feebly point out the remedy. See above, p. 172 of this volume.

to affect, served only to degrade him in the eyes of mankind. The Asiatic pomp, which had been adopted by the pride of Diocletian, assumed an air of softness and effeminacy in the person of Constantine. He is represented with false hair of various colours, laboriously arranged by the skilful artists of the times; a diadem of a new and more expensive fashion; a profusion of gems and pearls, of collars and bracelets, and a variegated flowing robe of silk, most curiously embroidered with flowers of gold. In such apparel, scarcely to be excused by the youth and folly of Elagabalus, we are at a loss to discover the wisdom of an aged monarch and the simplicity of a Roman veteran.[6] A mind thus relaxed by prosperity and indulgence was incapable of rising to that magnanimity which disdains suspicion and dares to forgive. The deaths of Maximian and Licinius may perhaps be justified by the maxims of policy, as they are taught in the schools of tyrants; but an impartial narrative of the executions, or rather murders, which sullied the declining age of Constantine, will suggest to our most candid thoughts the idea of a prince who could sacrifice without reluctance the laws of justice and the feelings of nature to the dictates either of his passions or of his interest.

The same fortune which so invariably followed the standard of Constantine seemed to secure the hopes and comforts of his domestic life. Those among his predecessors who had enjoyed the longest and most prosperous reigns, Augustus, Trajan, and Diocletian, had been disappointed of posterity; and the frequent revolutions had never allowed sufficient time for any Imperial family to grow up and multiply under the shade of the purple. But the royalty of the Flavian line, which had been first ennobled by the Gothic Claudius, descended through several generations; and Constantine himself derived from his royal father the hereditary honours which he transmitted to his children. The emperor had been twice married. Minervina, the obscure but lawful object of his youthful attachment,[7] had left

His family [marginal note]

---

[6] Julian, in the Cæsars, attempts to ridicule his uncle. His suspicious testimony is confirmed however by the learned Spanheim, with the authority of medals (see Commentaire, p. 156, 299, 397, 459). Eusebius (Orat. c. 5) alleges that Constantine dressed for the public, not for himself. Were this admitted, the vainest coxcomb could never want an excuse.

[7] Zosimus [ii. 20] and Zonaras [13, 2] agree in representing Minervina as the concubine of Constantine: but Ducange has very gallantly rescued her character, by producing a decisive passage from one of the panegyrics: "Ab ipso fine pueritiæ te [ilico] matrimonii legibus dedisti [tradidisti]". Incert. Pan. vi. § 4. [The reference is probably to an early (and childless) marriage of Constantine, not to Minervina, who was doubtless his concubine. Cp. Seeck, Gesch. des Untergangs der ant. Welt, i. p. 442. It has been doubted whether the three younger sons were

[Flavius
Julius
Crispus: Fl.
Claudius Con-
stantinus, Fl.
Jul. Con-
stantius, Fl.
Jul. Constans] him only one son, who was called Crispus. By Fausta, the daughter of Maximian, he had three daughters, and three sons, known by the kindred names of Constantine, Constantius, and Constans. The unambitious brothers of the great Constantine, Julius Constantius, Dalmatius, and Hannibalianus,[8] were permitted to enjoy the most honourable rank, and the most affluent fortune, that could be consistent with a private station. The youngest of the three lived without a name, and died without posterity. His two elder brothers obtained in marriage the daughters of wealthy senators, and propagated new branches of the Imperial race. Gallus and Julian afterwards became the most illustrious of the children of Julius Constantius, the *Patrician*. The two sons of Dalmatius, who had been decorated with the vain title of *censor*, were named Dalmatius and Hannibalianus. The two sisters of the great Constantine, Anastasia and Eutropia, were bestowed on Optatus and Nepotianus, two senators of noble birth and of consular dignity. His third sister, Constantia, was distinguished by her pre-eminence of greatness and of misery. She remained the widow of the vanquished Licinius ; and it was by her entreaties that an innocent boy, the offspring of their marriage, preserved for some time, his life, the title of Cæsar, and a precarious hope of the succession. Besides the females and the allies of the Flavian house, ten or twelve males, to whom the language of modern courts would apply the title of princes of the blood, seemed, according to the order of their birth, to be destined either to inherit or to support the throne of Constantine. But in less than thirty years, this numerous and increasing family was reduced to the persons of Constantius and Julian, who alone had survived a series of crimes and calamities, such as the tragic poets have deplored in the devoted lines of Pelops and of Cadmus.

Virtues of
Crispus

Crispus, the eldest son of Constantine, and the presumptive heir of the empire, is represented by impartial historians as an amiable and accomplished youth. The care of his education, or at least of his studies, was entrusted to Lactantius, the most eloquent of the Christians ; a præceptor admirably qualified to

the children of Fausta; Zosimus denies it (ii. 39). We have to accept the fact that the first eight years of the marriage were fruitless, Constantine being born in 315-16 if Julian's statement is true, Or. i. 10, p. 25. Mommsen thinks they may have been adopted by Fausta : C. I. L. 10, 678.]

[8] Ducange (Familiæ Byzantinæ, p. 44) bestows on him, after Zonaras, the name of Constantine ; a name somewhat unlikely, as it was already occupied by the elder brother. That of Hannibalianus is mentioned in the Paschal Chronicle, and is approved by Tillemont, Hist. des Empereurs, tom. iv. p. 527. [The correct form of the second brother's name is Delmatius.]

form the taste, and to excite the virtues, of his illustrious disciple.[9] At the age of seventeen, Crispus was invested with the title
of Cæsar, and the administration of the Gallic provinces, where [1st March,
the inroads of the Germans gave him an early occasion of $^{\text{A.D. 317}]}$
signalizing his military prowess. In the civil war which broke
out soon afterwards, the father and son divided their powers;
and this history has already celebrated the valour as well as
conduct displayed by the latter in forcing the straits of the Hellespont, so obstinately defended by the superior fleet of Licinius.
This naval victory contributed to determine the event of the
war; and the names of Constantine and of Crispus were united
in the joyful acclamations of their eastern subjects : who loudly
proclaimed that the world had been subdued, and was now
governed, by an emperor endowed with every virtue; and by
his illustrious son, a prince beloved of heaven, and the lively
image of his father's perfections. The public favour, which
seldom accompanies old age, diffused its lustre over the youth
of Crispus. He deserved the esteem, and he engaged the affections, of the court, the army, and the people. The experienced
merit of a reigning monarch is acknowledged by his subjects
with reluctance, and frequently denied with partial and discontented murmurs; while, from the opening virtues of his successor, they fondly conceive the most unbounded hopes of private
as well as public felicity.[10]

This dangerous popularity soon excited the attention of Con- Jealousy of
stantine, who, both as a father and as a king, was impatient of $^{\text{Constantine.}}_{\text{A.D. 324,}}$
an equal. Instead of attempting to secure the allegiance of his $^{\text{October 10}}$
son, by the generous ties of confidence and gratitude, he resolved [A.D. 324,
to prevent the mischiefs which might be apprehended from dis- $^{8\text{th Nov.}]}$
satisfied ambition. Crispus soon had reason to complain that,
while his infant brother Constantius was sent, with the title of
Cæsar, to reign over his peculiar department of the Gallic provinces,[11] *he*, a prince of mature years, who had performed such

<hr/>

[9] Jerom. in Chron. The poverty of Lactantius may be applied either to the
praise of the disinterested philosopher or to the shame of the unfeeling patron.
See Tillemont, Mém. Ecclésiast. tom. vi. part i. p. 345.   Dupin, Bibliothèque
Ecclésiast. tom i. p. 205. Lardner's Credibility of the Gospel History, part ii. vol.
vii. p. 66.

[10] Euseb. Hist. Ecclesiast. l. x. c. 9. Eutropius (x. 6) styles him "egregium
virum"; and Julian (Orat. i.) very plainly alludes to the exploits of Crispus in the
civil war. See Spanheim, Comment. p. 92.

[11] Compare Idatius and the Paschal Chronicle with Ammianus, l. xiv. c. 5.
The *year* in which Constantius was created Cæsar seems to be more accurately
fixed by the two chronologists; but the historian who lived in his court could not
be ignorant of the *day* of the anniversary. [The day is Nov. 8; so Idatius, con-

recent and signal services, instead of being raised to the superior
rank of Augustus, was confined almost a prisoner to his father's
court; and exposed, without power or defence, to every calumny
which the malice of his enemies could suggest.   Under such
painful circumstances, the royal youth might not always be able
to compose his behaviour, or suppress his discontent; and we may
be assured that he was encompassed by a train of indiscreet or
perfidious followers, who assiduously studied to inflame, and who
were perhaps instructed to betray, the unguarded warmth of his
resentment.   An edict of Constantine, published about this time,
manifestly indicates his real or affected suspicions that a secret
conspiracy had been formed against his person and government.
By all the allurements of honours and rewards, he invites informers of every degree to accuse without exception his magistrates or ministers, his friends or his most intimate favourites,
protesting, with a solemn asseveration, that he himself will listen
to the charge, that he himself will revenge his injuries; and
concluding with a prayer, which discovers some apprehension of
danger, that the providence of the Supreme Being may still
continue to protect the safety of the emperor and of the
empire.[12]

A.D. 325,
October 1

The informers, who complied with so liberal an invitation,
were sufficiently versed in the arts of courts to select the friends
and adherents of Crispus as the guilty persons; nor is there
any reason to distrust the veracity of the emperor, who had
promised an ample measure of revenge and punishment.   The
policy of Constantine maintained, however, the same appearances of regard and confidence towards a son whom he began
to consider as his most irreconcileable enemy.   Medals were
struck with the customary vows for the long and auspicious
reign of the young Cæsar;[13] and as the people, who was not
admitted into the secrets of the palace, still loved his virtues
and respected his dignity, a poet who solicits his recall from
exile, adores with equal devotion the majesty of the father and
that of the son.[14]   The time was now arrived for celebrating

Disgrace and
death of Cris-
pus. A.D.
326, July

firmed by the Fasti of Philocalus, C. I. L. i. p. 379.   Ammian's *Oct.* is a slip for
Nov.]   For the appointment of the new Cæsar to the provinces of Gaul, see
Julian, Orat. i. p. 12; Godefroy, Chronol. Legum, p. 26; and Blondel de la
Primauté de l'Eglise, p. 1183.   [Idatius gives 324 A.D., Chron. Pasch. 325 A.D.
The right year is in Jerome, Chron. 323 A.D.   Cp. Stobbe, *Philologus*, 32, p. 85.]
[12] Cod. Theod. l. ix. tit. iv. [leg. 1, 4].   Godefroy suspected the secret motives of
this law.   Comment. tom. iii. p. 9.   [But it is very doubtful whether such secret
motives, and not rather flagrant abuses, led to this edict.]
[13] Ducange, Fam. Byzant. p. 28.   Tillemont, tom. iv. p. 610.
[14] His name was Porphyrius Optatianus.   The date of his panegyric, written

the august ceremony of the twentieth year of the reign of Constantine; and the emperor, for that purpose, removed his court from Nicomedia to Rome, where the most splendid preparations had been made for his reception. Every eye and every tongue affected to express their sense of the general happiness, and the veil of ceremony and dissimulation was drawn for a while over the darkest designs of revenge and murder.[15] In the midst of the festival, the unfortunate Crispus was apprehended by order of the emperor, who laid aside the tenderness of a father, without assuming the equity of a judge. The examination was short and private; [16] and, as it was thought decent to conceal the fate of the young prince from the eyes of the Roman people, he was sent under a strong guard to Pola, in Istria, where, soon afterwards, he was put to death, either by the hand of the executioner or by the more gentle operation of poison.[17] The Cæsar Licinius, a youth of amiable manners, was involved in the ruin of Crispus; [18] and the stern [A.D. 326] jealousy of Constantine was unmoved by the prayers and tears of his favourite sister, pleading for the life of a son, whose rank was his only crime, and whose loss she did not long survive. The story of these unhappy princes, the nature and evidence of their guilt, the forms of their trial, and the circumstances of their death, were buried in mysterious obscurity; and the

according to the taste of the age in vile acrostics, is settled by Scaliger ad Euseb. p. 250. Tillemont, tom. iv. p. 607 [cp. p. 221], and Fabricius, Biblioth. Latin. l. iv. c. 1. [Clinton gives the date as 325 A.D. Jerome, Chron., enters it under 329 A.D.]

[15] Zosim. l. ii. p. 103 [29]. Godefroy, Chronol. Legum, p. 28.

[16] Ἀκρίτως, *without a trial*, is the strong, and most probably the just, expression of Suidas. The elder Victor, who wrote under the next reign, speaks with becoming caution. "Natû grandior incertum quâ causâ patris judicio occidisset." If we consult the succeeding writers, Eutropius, the younger Victor, Orosius, Jerom, Zosimus, Philostorgius, and Gregory of Tours; their knowledge will appear gradually to increase, as their means of information must have diminished; a circumstance which frequently occurs in historical disquisition. [See Appendix 14.]

[17] Ammianus (l. xiv. c. 11) uses the general expression of *peremptum*. Codinus (p. 34 [63, ed. Bonn]) beheads the young prince; but Sidonius Apollinaris (Epistol. v. 8), for the sake perhaps of an antithesis to Fausta's *warm* bath, chooses to administer a draught of *cold* poison. [All critics are agreed as to the date, 326, though Chron. Alex. gives 325. The true causes of the tragedy are enveloped in a tantalizing veil of obscurity. It may be noted that the name of Crispus was often erased on inscriptions; cp. C. I. L. 10, 517, &c.]

[18] Sororis filium, commodæ indolis juvenem. Eutropius, x. 6 [date, see Jerome, Chron.]. May I not be permitted to conjecture that Crispus had married Helena, the daughter of the Emperor Licinius, and that on the happy delivery of the princess, in the year 322, a general pardon was granted by Constantine? [So Seeck.] See Ducange, Fam. Byzant. p. 47, and the law (l. ix. tit. xxxviii. [leg. 1]) of the Theodosian Code, which has so much embarrassed the interpreters. Godefroy, tom. iii. p. 267. [As to the younger Licinius, cp. Appendix 14.]

courtly bishop, who has celebrated in an elaborate work the
virtues and piety of his hero, observes a prudent silence on
the subject of these tragic events.[19] Such haughty contempt
for the opinion of mankind, whilst it imprints an indelible
stain on the memory of Constantine, must remind us of the
very different behaviour of one of the greatest monarchs of
the present age. The Czar Peter, in the full possession of
despotic power, submitted to the judgment of Russia, of
Europe, and of posterity, the reasons which had compelled him
to subscribe to the condemnation of a criminal, or at least of a
degenerate, son.[20]

The empress
Fausta

The innocence of Crispus was so universally acknowledged
that the modern Greeks, who adore the memory of their
founder, are reduced to palliate the guilt of a parricide, which
the common feelings of human nature forbade them to justify.
They pretend that, as soon as the afflicted father discovered
the falsehood of the accusation by which his credulity had been
so fatally misled, he published to the world his repentance
and remorse ; that he mourned forty days, during which he
abstained from the use of the bath and all the ordinary
comforts of life ; and that, for the lasting instruction of posterity,
he erected a golden statue of Crispus, with this memorable
inscription : TO MY SON, WHOM I UNJUSTLY CONDEMNED.[21] A
tale so moral and so interesting would deserve to be supported
by less exceptionable authority ; but, if we consult the more
ancient and authentic writers, they will inform us that the
repentance of Constantine was manifested only in acts of blood
and revenge ; and that he atoned for the murder of an innocent
son, by the execution, perhaps, of a guilty wife. They ascribe
the misfortunes of Crispus to the arts of his stepmother Fausta,
whose implacable hatred, or whose disappointed love, renewed
in the palace of Constantine the ancient tragedy of Hippolytus
and of Phædra.[22] Like the daughter of Minos, the daughter
of Maximian accused her son-in-law of an incestuous attempt

[19] See the Life of Constantine, particularly l. ii. c. 19, 20. Two hundred and
fifty years afterwards, Evagrius (l. iii. c. 41) deduced from the silence of Eusebius
a vain argument against the reality of the fact.
[20] Histoire de Pierre le Grand, par Voltaire, part ii. c. x.
[21] In order to prove that the statue was erected by Constantine, and afterwards
concealed by the malice of the Arians, Codinus very readily creates (p. 34) two
witnesses, Hippolytus and the younger Herodotus, to whose imaginary histories he
appeals with unblushing confidence.
[22] Zosimus (l. ii. p. 103 [29]) may be considered as our original. The ingenuity
of the moderns, assisted by a few hints from the ancients, has illustrated and improved his obscure and imperfect narrative. [For Seeck's view, see App. 14.]

on the chastity of his father s wife ; and easily obtained, from the jealousy of the emperor, a sentence of death against a young prince whom she considered with reason as the most formidable rival of her own children. But Helena, the aged mother of Constantine, lamented and revenged the untimely fate of her grandson Crispus : nor was it long before a real or pretended discovery was made, that Fausta herself entertained a criminal connexion with a slave belonging to the Imperial stables.[23] Her condemnation and punishment were the instant consequences of the charge ; and the adulteress was suffocated by the steam of a bath, which, for that purpose, had been heated to an extraordinary degree.[24] By some it will perhaps be thought, that the remembrance of a conjugal union of twenty years, and the honour of their common offspring, the destined heirs of the throne, might have softened the obdurate heart of Constantine ; and persuaded him to suffer his wife, however guilty she might appear, to expiate her offences in a solitary prison. But it seems a superfluous labour to weigh the propriety, unless we could ascertain the truth, of this singular event ; which is attended with some circumstances of doubt and perplexity. Those who have attacked, and those who have defended, the character of Constantine have alike disregarded two very remarkable passages of two orations pronounced under the succeeding reign. The former celebrates the virtues, the beauty, and the fortune of the empress Fausta, the daughter, wife, sister, and mother of so many princes.[25] The latter asserts, in explicit terms, that the mother of the younger Constantine, who was slain three years after his father's

---

[23] Philostorgius, l. ii. c. 4. Zosimus (l. ii. p. 104, 116 [29 ; 39]) imputes to Constantine the death of two wives : of the innocent Fausta, and of an adulteress who was the mother of his three successors. According to Jerom, three or four years elapsed between the death of Crispus and that of Fausta. The elder Victor is prudently silent. [Thus Jerome's date would be c. 329 A.D. Greg. of Tours, H. F. i. 36, suggests 326 (so Tillemont, iv. p. 224). Clinton decides for 327.]

[24] If Fausta was put to death, it is reasonable to believe that the private apartments of the palace were the scene of her execution. The orator Chrysostom indulges his fancy by exposing the naked empress on a desert mountain, to be devoured by wild beasts.

[25] Julian. Orat. i. [p. 10, ed. Hertl.]. He seems to call her the mother of Crispus. She might assume that title by adoption. At least, she was not considered as his mortal enemy. Julian compares the fortune [not the fate] of Fausta with that of Parysatis, the Persian queen. A Roman would have more naturally recollected the second Agrippina :—

Et moi, qui sur le trône ai suivi mes ancêtres :
Moi, fille, femme, sœur et mère de vos maîtres.

death, survived to weep over the fate of her son.[26] Notwithstanding the positive testimony of several writers of the Pagan as well as of the Christian religion, there may still remain some reason to believe, or at least to suspect, that Fausta escaped the blind and suspicious cruelty of her husband. The deaths of a son, and of a nephew, with the execution of a great number of respectable and perhaps innocent friends,[27] who were involved in their fall, may be sufficient, however, to justify the discontent of the Roman people, and to explain the satirical verses affixed to the palace-gate, comparing the splendid and bloody reigns of Constantine and Nero.[28]

The sons and nephews of Constantine

By the death of Crispus, the inheritance of the empire seemed to devolve on the three sons of Fausta, who have been already mentioned under the names of Constantine, of Constantius, and of Constans. These young princes were successively invested with the title of Cæsar; and the dates of their promotion may be referred to the tenth, the twentieth, and the thirtieth years of the reign of their father.[29] This conduct, though it tended to multiply the future masters of the Roman world, might be excused by the partiality of paternal affection; but it is not easy to understand the motives of the emperor, when he endangered the safety both of his family and of his people, by the unnecessary elevation of his two nephews, Dalmatius and Hannibalianus. The former was raised, by the title of Cæsar, to an equality with his cousins. In favour of the latter, Constantine invented the new and singular appellation of *Nobilissimus*;[30] to which he annexed the flattering distinction of a robe of purple and gold. But of the whole series of Roman princes in any age of the empire, Hannibalianus alone was distinguished by the

---

[26] Monod. in Constantin. Jun. c. 4, ad Calcem. Eutrop. edit. Havercamp. The orator styles her the most divine and pious of queens. [Ranke, *Weltgeschichte*, iii. 521, accepts the evidence of this document and rejects the execution of Fausta. But the *Monodia* has nothing to do with Constantine; see Appendix 1.]

[27] Interfecit numerosos amicos. Eutrop. x. 6.

[28] Saturni aurea sæcula quis requirat?
Sunt hæc gemmea, sed Neroniana.

Sidon. Apollinar. v. 8.

It is somewhat singular, that these satirical lines should be attributed, not to an obscure libeller, or a disappointed patriot, but to Ablavius [Ablabius], prime minister and favourite of the emperor. We may now perceive that the imprecations of the Roman people were dictated by humanity, as well as by superstition. Zosim. l. ii. p. 105 [29 ad fin., 30 ad in.].

[29] Euseb. Orat. in Constantin. c. 3. These dates are sufficiently correct to justify the orator. [The right dates are 317, 323, 333 respectively.]

[30] Zosim. l. ii. p. 117 [c. 39]. Under the predecessors of Constantine, *Nobilissimus* was a vague epithet rather than a legal and determined title. [Delmatius is named on coins: nob. Cæs. and princ. iuventutis, Cohen, 6.]

title of KING; a name which the subjects of Tiberius would have
detested, as the profane and cruel insult of capricious tyranny.
The use of such a title, even as it appears under the reign of
Constantine, is a strange and unconnected fact, which can
scarcely be admitted on the joint authority of imperial medals
and contemporary writers.[31]

The whole empire was deeply interested in the education of *Their educa-*
these five youths, the acknowledged successors of Constantine. *tion*
The exercises of the body prepared them for the fatigues of war
and the duties of active life. Those who occasionally mention
the education or talents of Constantius allow that he excelled
in the gymnastic arts of leaping and running; that he was a
dexterous archer, a skilful horseman, and a master of all the
different weapons used in the service either of the cavalry or of
the infantry.[32] The same assiduous cultivation was bestowed,
though not perhaps with equal success, to improve the minds of
the sons and nephews of Constantine.[33] The most celebrated
professors of the Christian faith, of the Grecian philosophy, and
of the Roman jurisprudence were invited by the liberality of the
emperor, who reserved for himself the important task of instructing the royal youths in the science of government and the
knowledge of mankind. But the genius of Constantine himself
had been formed by adversity and experience. In the free intercourse of private life, and amidst the dangers of the court of
Galerius, he had learned to command his own passions, to encounter those of his equals, and to depend for his present safety
and future greatness on the prudence and firmness of his
personal conduct. His destined successors had the misfortune
of being born and educated in the Imperial purple. Incessantly
surrounded with a train of flatterers, they passed their youth in

[31] Adstruunt nummi veteres ac singulares. Spanheim de Usu Numismat.
Dissertat. xii. vol. ii. p. 357 [cp. Eckhel, 8, p. 174]. Ammianus speaks of this
Roman king (l. xiv. c. 1) and Valesius ad loc. The Valesian fragment styles him
King of kings; and the Paschal Chronicle (p. 286 [p. 532, ed. Bonn]), by employing the word 'Ρῆγα, acquires the weight of Latin evidence. [Pontic and Armenian regions were assigned to him in 335 A.D. with the title of *rex regum.* He
was thus to be a vassal king, subordinate to the Emperors. Observe that 'Ρῆγα
(not βασιλέα) is used of him in the Paschal Chronicle. Mommsen guesses that
Bosporus (in the Chersonesus) was included in this kingdom, from the fact that
the last coin of Bosporus dates from 335 A.D. (Róm. Ges. v. 289).]

[32] His dexterity in martial exercise is celebrated by Julian (Orat. i. p. 11 [12],
Orat. ii. p. 53 [67], and allowed by Ammianus (l. xxi. c. 16).

[33] Euseb. in Vit. Constantin. l. iv. c. 51. Julian. Orat. i. p. 11-16, with Spanheim's elaborate Commentary. Libanius, Orat. iii. p. 109 [ed. Paris, 1627].
Constantius studied with laudable diligence; but the dulness of his fancy prevented
him from succeeding in the art of poetry, or even of rhetoric.

the enjoyment of luxury and the expectation of a throne ; nor would the dignity of their rank permit them to descend from that elevated station from whence the various characters of human nature appear to wear a smooth and uniform aspect. The indulgence of Constantine admitted them at a very tender age to share the administration of the empire ; and they studied the art of reigning at the expense of the people entrusted to their care. The younger Constantine was appointed to hold his court in Gaul ; and his brother Constantius exchanged that department, the ancient patrimony of their father, for the more opulent, but less martial, countries of the East. Italy, the Western Illyricum, and Africa were accustomed to revere Constans, the third of his sons, as the representative of the great Constantine. He fixed Dalmatius on the Gothic frontier, to which he annexed the government of Thrace, Macedonia, and Greece. The city of Cæsarea was chosen for the residence of Hannibalianus ; and the provinces of Pontus, Cappadocia, and the Lesser Armenia were destined to form the extent of his new kingdom. For each of these princes a suitable establishment was provided. A just proportion of guards, of legions, and of auxiliaries was allotted for their respective dignity and defence. The ministers and generals who were placed about their persons were such as Constantine could trust to assist, and even to control, these youthful sovereigns in the exercise of their delegated power. As they advanced in years and experience, the limits of their authority were insensibly enlarged : but the emperor always reserved for himself the title of Augustus ; and, while he shewed the *Cæsars* to the armies and provinces, he maintained every part of the empire in equal obedience to its supreme head.[34] The tranquillity of the last fourteen years of his reign was scarcely interrupted by the contemptible insurrection of a camel-driver in the island of Cyprus,[35] or by the active part which the policy of Constantine engaged him to assume in the wars of the Goths and Sarmatians.

Manners of the Sarmatians

Among the different branches of the human race, the Sar-

[34] Eusebius ([Vita C.] l. iv. c. 51, 52), with a design of exalting the authority and glory of Constantine, affirms that he divided the Roman empire as a private citizen might have divided his patrimony. His distribution of the provinces may be collected from Eutropius, the two Victors, and the Valesian fragment. [On this division see Appendix 15.]

[35] Calocerus, the obscure leader of this rebellion, or rather tumult, was apprehended and burnt alive in the market-place of Tarsus, by the vigilance of Dalmatius. See the elder Victor, the chronicle of Jerom, and the doubtful traditions of Theophanes and Cedrenus.

matians form a very remarkable shade; as they seem to unite the manners of the Asiatic barbarians with the figure and complexion of the ancient inhabitants of Europe. According to the various accidents of peace and war, of alliance or conquest, the Sarmatians were sometimes confined to the banks of the Tanais; and they sometimes spread themselves over the immense plains which lie between the Vistula and the Volga.[36] The care of their numerous flocks and herds, the pursuit of game, and the exercise of war, or rather of rapine, directed the vagrant motions of the Sarmatians. The moveable camps or cities, the ordinary residence of their wives and children, consisted only of large waggons, drawn by oxen and covered in the form of tents. The military strength of the nation was composed of cavalry; and the custom of their warriors, to lead in their hand one or two spare horses, enabled them to advance and to retreat with a rapid diligence which surprised the security, and eluded the pursuit, of a distant enemy.[37] Their poverty of iron prompted their rude industry to invent a sort of cuirass, which was capable of resisting a sword or javelin, though it was formed only of horses' hoofs, cut into thin and polished slices, carefully laid over each other in the manner of scales or feathers, and strongly sewed upon an under-garment of coarse linen.[38] The offensive arms of the Sarmatians were short daggers, long lances, and a weighty bow with a quiver of arrows. They were reduced to the necessity of employing fish bones for the points of their weapons; but the custom of dipping them in a venomous liquor that poisoned the wounds which they inflicted is alone sufficient to prove the most savage manners; since a people impressed with a sense of humanity would have abhorred so cruel a practice, and a nation skilled in the arts of war would have disdained so impotent a resource.[39] Whenever these Barbarians

[36] Cellarius has collected the opinions of the ancients concerning the European and Asiatic Sarmatia; and M. d'Anville has applied them to modern geography with the skill and accuracy which always distinguishes that excellent writer.

[37] Ammian. l. xvii. c. 12. The Sarmatian horses were castrated, to prevent the mischievous accidents which might happen from the noisy and ungovernable passions of the males.

[38] Pausanias, l. i. p. 50, edit. Kuhn [c. 21]. That inquisitive traveller had carefully examined a Sarmatian cuirass, which was preserved in the temple of Æsculapius at Athens.

[39]   Aspicis et mitti sub adunco toxica ferro,
      Et telum causas mortis habere duas.
                Ovid. ex Ponto, l. iv. ep. 7, ver. 7.
See in the Recherches sur les Américains, tom. ii. p. 236-271, a very curious dissertation on poisoned darts. The venom was commonly extracted from the vegetable reign; but that employed by the Scythians appears to have been drawn from

issued from their deserts in quest of prey, their shaggy beards, uncombed locks, the furs with which they were covered from head to foot, and their fierce countenances, which seemed to express the innate cruelty of their minds, inspired the more civilized provincials of Rome with horror and dismay.

Their settlement near the Danube   The tender Ovid, after a youth spent in the enjoyment of fame and luxury, was condemned to an hopeless exile on the frozen banks of the Danube, where he was exposed, almost without defence, to the fury of these monsters of the desert, with whose stern spirits he feared that his gentle shade might hereafter be confounded. In his pathetic, but sometimes unmanly, lamentations,[40] he describes, in the most lively colours, the dress and manners, the arms and inroads of the Getæ and Sarmatians, who were associated for the purposes of destruction; and from the accounts of history there is some reason to believe that these Sarmatians were the Jazygæ, one of the most numerous and warlike tribes of the nation. The allurements of plenty engaged them to seek a permanent establishment on the frontiers of the empire. Soon after the reign of Augustus, they obliged the Dacians, who subsisted by fishing on the banks of the river Theiss or Tibiscus, to retire into the hilly country, and to abandon to the victorious Sarmatians the fertile plains of the Upper Hungary, which are bounded by the course of the Danube and the semi-circular inclosure of the Carpathian mountains.[41] In this advantageous position, they watched or suspended the moment of attack, as they were provoked by injuries or appeased by presents; they gradually acquired the skill of using more dangerous weapons; and, although the Sarmatians did not illustrate their name by any memorable exploits, they occasionally assisted their eastern and western neighbours, the Goths and the Germans, with a formidable

the viper and a mixture of human blood. The use of poisoned arms, which has been spread over both worlds, never preserved a savage tribe from the arms of a disciplined enemy.

[40] The nine books of Poetical Epistles, which Ovid composed during the seven first years of his melancholy exile, possess, besides the merit of elegance, a double value. They exhibit a picture of the human mind under very singular circumstances; and they contain many curious observations, which no Roman, except Ovid, could have an opportunity of making. Every circumstance which tends to illustrate the history of the Barbarians has been drawn together by the very accurate Count de Buat. Hist. Ancienne des Peuples de l'Europe, tom. iv. c. xvi. p. 286-317. [For Sarmatians cp. App. 16.]

[41] The Sarmatians [? *leg.* Sarmatian] Jazygæ were settled on the banks of the Pathissus or Tibiscus, when Pliny, in the year 79, published his Natural History. See l. iv. c. 25. In the time of Strabo and Ovid, sixty or seventy years before, they appear to have inhabited beyond the Getæ, along the coast of the Euxine.

body of cavalry. They lived under the irregular aristocracy of their chieftains;[42] but, after they had received into their bosom the fugitive Vandals, who yielded to the pressure of the Gothic power, they seem to have chosen a king from that nation, and from the illustrious race of the Astingi, who had formerly dwelt on the shores of the Northern ocean.[43]

This motive of enmity must have inflamed the subjects of contention, which perpetually arise on the confines of warlike and independent nations. The Vandal princes were stimulated by fear and revenge; the Gothic kings aspired to extend their dominion from the Euxine to the frontiers of Germany: and the waters of the Maros, a small river which falls into the Theiss, were stained with the blood of the contending Barbarians. After some experience of the superior strength and number of their adversaries, the Sarmatians implored the protection of the Roman monarch, who beheld with pleasure the discord of the nations, but who was justly alarmed by the progress of the Gothic arms. As soon as Constantine had declared himself in favour of the weaker party, the haughty Araric, king of the Goths, instead of expecting the attack of the legions, boldly passed the Danube, and spread terror and devastation through the province of Mæsia. To oppose the inroad of this destroying host, the aged emperor took the field in person; but on this occasion either his conduct or his fortune betrayed the glory which he had acquired in so many foreign and domestic wars. He had the mortification of seeing his troops fly before an inconsiderable detachment of the Barbarians, who pursued them to the edge of their fortified camp and obliged him to consult his safety by a precipitate and ignominious retreat.[44] The event of a second and more successful action retrieved the honour of the Roman name; and the powers of art and discipline prevailed, after an obstinate contest, over the efforts of irregular valour. The broken army of the Goths abandoned the field of battle, the wasted province, and the passage of the Danube: and, although the eldest of

The Gothic war, A.D. 331

[42] Principes Sarmatarum Jazygum penes quos civitatis regimen . . . plebem quoque et vim equitum quâ solâ valent offerebant. Tacit. Hist. iii. 5. This offer was made in the civil war between Vitellius and Vespasian.

[43] This hypothesis of a Vandal king reigning over Sarmatian subjects seems necessary to reconcile the Goth Jornandes with the Greek and Latin historians of Constantine. It may be observed that Isidore, who lived in Spain under the dominion of the Goths, gives them for enemies, not the Vandals, but the Sarmatians. See his Chronicle in Grotius, p. 709.

[44] [There seems to be no evidence for this defeat of Constantine. It is a curious error of Gibbon.]

A.D. 332,
April 20th
the sons of Constantine was permitted to supply the place of his father, the merit of the victory, which diffused universal joy, was ascribed to the auspicious counsels of the emperor himself.

He contributed at least to improve this advantage, by his negotiations with the free and warlike people of Chersonesus,[45] whose capital, situate on the western coast of the Tauric or Crimæan peninsula, still retained some vestiges of a Grecian colony, and was governed by a perpetual magistrate, assisted by a council of senators, emphatically styled the Fathers of the City. The Chersonites were animated against the Goths by the memory of the wars which, in the preceding century, they had maintained with unequal forces against the invaders of their country. They were connected with the Romans by the mutual benefits of commerce; as they were supplied from the provinces of Asia with corn and manufactures, which they purchased with their only productions, salt, wax, and hides. Obedient to the requisition of Constantine, they prepared, under the conduct of their magistrate Diogenes, a considerable army, of which the principal strength consisted in crossbows and military chariots. The speedy march and intrepid attack of the Chersonites, by diverting the attention of the Goths, assisted the operations of the imperial generals. The Goths, vanquished on every side, were driven into the mountains, where, in the course of a severe campaign, above an hundred thousand were computed to have perished by cold and hunger. Peace was at length granted to their humble supplications; the eldest son of Araric was accepted as the most valuable hostage; and Constantine endeavoured to convince their chiefs, by a liberal distribution of honours and rewards, how far the friendship of the Romans was preferable to their enmity. In the expressions of his gratitude towards the faithful Chersonites,

---

[45] I may stand in need of some apology for having used, without scruple, the authority of Constantine Porphyrogenitus, in all that relates to the wars and negotiations of the Chersonites. I am aware that he was a Greek of the tenth century, and that his accounts of ancient history are frequently confused and fabulous. But on this occasion his narrative is, for the most part, consistent and probable; nor is there much difficulty in conceiving that an emperor might have access to some secret archives, which had escaped the diligence of meaner historians. For the situation and history of Chersone, see Peyssonel des Peuples barbares qui ont habité les Bords du Danube, c. xvi. p. 84-90. [Const. Porph., de Adm. Imp. c. 53. See St. Martin (note on Lebeau, i. 326), who points out that Gibbon has confounded the city of Cherson, to which Constantine Porph. refers, with the whole peninsula. He is also mistaken in describing the Stephanephoros (who was annually elected) as a perpetual magistrate. Milman calls attention to St. Martin's note.]

the emperor was still more magnificent. The pride of the nation was gratified by the splendid and almost royal decorations bestowed on their magistrate and his successors. A perpetual exemption from all duties was stipulated for their vessels which traded to the ports of the Black Sea. A regular subsidy was promised, of iron, corn, oil, and of every supply which could be useful either in peace or war. But it was thought that the Sarmatians were sufficiently rewarded by their deliverance from impending ruin ; and the emperor, perhaps with too strict an economy, deducted some part of the expenses of the war from the customary gratifications which were allowed to that turbulent nation.[46]

Exasperated by this apparent neglect, the Sarmatians soon forgot, with the levity of Barbarians, the services which they had so lately received and the dangers which still threatened their safety. Their inroads on the territory of the empire provoked the indignation of Constantine to leave them to their fate, and he no longer opposed the ambition of Geberic, a renowned warrior, who had recently ascended the Gothic throne. Wisumar, the Vandal king, whilst alone and unassisted he defended his dominions with undaunted courage, was vanquished and slain in a decisive battle, which swept away the flower of the Sarmatian youth. The remainder of the nation embraced the desperate expedient of arming their slaves, a hardy race of hunters and herdsmen, by whose tumultuary aid they revenged their defeat and expelled the invader from their confines. But they soon discovered that they had exchanged a foreign for a domestic enemy, more dangerous and more implacable. Enraged by their former servitude, elated by their present glory, the slaves, under the name of Limigantes, claimed and usurped the possession of the country which they had saved. Their masters, unable to withstand the ungoverned fury of the populace, preferred the hardships of exile to the tyranny of their servants. Some of the fugitive Sarmatians solicited a less ignominious dependence, under the hostile standard of the Goths. A more numerous band retired beyond the Carpathian mountains, among the Quadi, their German allies, and were easily admitted to share a superfluous waste of uncultivated land. But the far greater part of the distressed nation turned their eyes towards the fruitful provinces of Rome. Imploring the protection and forgiveness of

Expulsion of the Sarmatians. A.D. 334

---

[46] [This is a misconception. No such "deduction" is mentioned in the sources.]

the emperor, they solemnly promised, as subjects in peace and as soldiers in war, the most inviolable fidelity to the empire which should graciously receive them into its bosom. According to the maxims adopted by Probus and his successors, the offers of this Barbarian colony were eagerly accepted; and a competent portion of lands, in the provinces of Pannonia, Thrace, Macedonia, and Italy, were immediately assigned for the habitation and subsistence of three hundred thousand Sarmatians.[47]

Death and funeral of Constantine. A.D. 335, 25th July

By chastising the pride of the Goths, and by accepting the homage of a suppliant nation, Constantine asserted the majesty of the Roman empire; and the ambassadors of Æthiopia, Persia and the most remote countries of India congratulated the peace and prosperity of his government.[48] If he reckoned, among the favours of fortune, the death of his eldest son, of his nephew, and perhaps of his wife, he enjoyed an uninterrupted flow of private as well as public felicity, till the thirtieth year of his reign; a period which none of his predecessors, since Augustus, had been permitted to celebrate. Constantine survived that solemn festival about ten months; and, at the mature age of sixty-four, after a short illness, he ended his memorable life at

A.D. 337, 22nd May

the palace of Aquyrion, in the suburbs of Nicomedia, whither he had retired for the benefit of the air, and with the hope of recruiting his exhausted strength by the use of the warm baths. The excessive demonstrations of grief, or at least of mourning, surpassed whatever had been practised on any former occasion. Notwithstanding the claims of the senate and people of ancient Rome, the corpse of the deceased emperor, according to his last request, was transported to the city which was destined to pre-

[47] The Gothic and Sarmatian wars are related in so broken and imperfect a manner that I have been obliged to compare the following writers, who mutually supply, correct, and illustrate each other. Those who will take the same trouble, may acquire a right of criticizing my narrative. Ammianus, l. xvii. c. 12. Anonym. Valesian. p. 715. Eutropius, x. 7, Sextus Rufus de Provinciis, c. 26. Julian. Orat. i. p. 9, and Spanheim, Comment. p. 94. Hieronym. in Chron. Euseb. in Vit. Constantin. l. iv. c. 6. Socrates, l. i. c. 18. Sozomen, l. i. c. 8. Zosimus, l. ii. p. 108 [c. 21]. Jornandes de Reb. Geticis, c. 22. Isidorus in Chron. p. 709; in Hist. Gothorum Grotii. Constantin. Porpnyrogenitus de administrat. Imperii. c. 53, p. 208, edit. Meursii. [Add Joan of Antioch, fr. 171 (Müller, F. H. G. 4). It has been conjectured by Böcking that the Sarmatian settlements in Ausonius *Mosella* 819 were made at this time. Sarmatic games were instituted (C. I. L. i. 407) and Constantine is called Sarmaticus in inscriptions. See Henzen, 5576; Eckhel, 8, 87, 101, 107.]

[48] Eusebius (in Vit. Const. l. iv. c. 50) remarks three circumstances relative to these Indians. 1. They came from the shores of the eastern ocean; a description which might be applied to the coast of China or Coromandel. 2. They presented shining gems, and unknown animals. 3. They protested their kings had erected statues to represent the supreme majesty of Constantine.

serve the name and memory of its founder. The body of Constantine, adorned with the vain symbols of greatness, the purple and diadem, was deposited on a golden bed in one of the apartments of the palace, which for that purpose had been splendidly furnished and illuminated. The forms of the court were strictly maintained. Every day, at the appointed hours, the principal officers of the state, the army, and the household, approaching the person of their sovereign with bended knees and a composed countenance, offered their respectful homage as seriously as if he had been still alive. From motives of policy, this theatrical representation was for some time continued ; nor could flattery neglect the opportunity of remarking that Constantine alone, by the peculiar indulgence of heaven, had reigned after his death.[49]

But this reign could subsist only in empty pageantry ; and it was soon discovered that the will of the most absolute monarch is seldom obeyed, when his subjects have no longer anything to hope from his favour, or to dread from his resentment. The same ministers and generals who bowed with such reverential awe before the inanimate corpse of their deceased sovereign were engaged in secret consultations to exclude his two nephews, Dalmatius and Hannibalianus, from the share which he had assigned them in the succession of the empire. We are too imperfectly acquainted with the court of Constantine to form any judgment of the real motives which influenced the leaders of the conspiracy ; unless we should suppose that they were actuated by a spirit of jealousy and revenge against the præfect Ablavius, a proud favourite, who had long directed the counsels and abused the confidence of the late emperor. The arguments by which they solicited the concurrence of the soldiers and people are of a more obvious nature : and they might with decency, as well as truth, insist on the superior rank of the children of Constantine, the danger of multiplying the number of sovereigns, and the impending mischiefs which threatened the republic, from the discord of so many rival princes, who were not connected by the tender sympathy of fraternal affection. The intrigue was conducted with zeal and secrecy till a loud and

Factions of the court

[49] Funus relatum in urbem sui nominis, quod sane P. R. ægerrime tulit. Aurelius Victor (Caes. 41). Constantine had prepared for himself a stately tomb in the church of the Holy Apostles. Euseb. l. iv. c. 60. The best, and indeed almost the only, account of the sickness, death, and funeral of Constantine, is contained in the fourth book of his Life, by Eusebius. [The Cæsars did not become Augusti till 9th September, and the dead emperor nominally reigned in the four intervening months.]

unanimous declaration was procured from the troops that they would suffer none except the sons of their lamented monarch to reign over the Roman empire.[50] The younger Dalmatius, who was united with his collateral relations by the ties of friendship and interest, is allowed to have inherited a considerable share of the abilities of the great Constantine ; but, on this occasion, he does not appear to have concerted any measures for supporting, by arms, the just claims which himself and his royal brother derived from the liberality of their uncle.[51] Astonished and overwhelmed by the tide of popular fury, they seem to have remained, without the power of flight or of resistance, in the hands of their implacable enemies. Their fate was suspended till the arrival of Constantius, the second, and perhaps the most favoured, of the sons of Constantine.

Massacre of the princes The voice of the dying emperor had recommended the care of his funeral to the piety of Constantius ; and that prince, by the vicinity of his eastern station, could easily prevent the diligence of his brothers, who resided in their distant government of Italy and Gaul. As soon as he had taken possession of the palace of Constantinople, his first care was to remove the apprehensions of his kinsmen by a solemn oath, which he pledged for their security. His next employment was to find some specious pretence which might release his conscience from the obligation of an imprudent promise. The arts of fraud were made subservient to the designs of cruelty ; and a manifest forgery was attested by a person of the most sacred character. From the hands of the bishop of Nicomedia, Constantius received a fatal scroll affirmed to be the genuine testament of his father ; in which the emperor expressed his suspicions that he had been poisoned by his brother ; and conjured his sons to revenge his death, and to consult their own safety by the punishment of the guilty.[52] Whatever reasons might have been alleged by these unfortunate

[50] Eusebius (l. iv. c. 6) terminates his narrative by this loyal declaration of the troops, and avoids all the invidious circumstances of the subsequent massacre.

[51] The character of Dalmatius is advantageously, though concisely, drawn by Eutropius (x. 9). Dalmatius Cæsar prosperrimâ indole, neque patruo absimilis, *haud multo* post oppressus est factione militari. As both Jerom and the Alexandrian Chronicle mention the third year of the Cæsar, which did not commence till the 18th or 24th of September, A.D. 337, it is certain that these military factions continued above four months.

[52] I have related this singular anecdote on the authority of Philostorgius, l. ii. c. 16. But, if such a pretext was ever used by Constantine and his adherents, it was laid aside with contempt, as soon as it had served their immediate purpose. Athanasius (tom. i. p. 856) mentions the oath which Constantius had taken for the security of his kinsmen. [The story is very doubtful.]

princes to defend their life and honour against so incredible an accusation, they were silenced by the furious clamours of the soldiers, who declared themselves at once their enemies, their judges, and their executioners. The spirit, and even the forms, of legal proceedings were repeatedly violated in a promiscuous massacre ; which involved the two uncles of Constantius, seven of his cousins, of whom Dalmatius and Hannibalianus were the most illustrious, the patrician Optatus, who had married a sister of the late emperor, and the præfect Ablavius, whose power and riches had inspired him with some hopes of obtaining the purple. If it were necessary to aggravate the horrors of this bloody scene, we might add that Constantius himself had espoused the daughter of his uncle Julius, and that he had bestowed his sister in marriage on his cousin Hannibalianus. These alliances, which the policy of Constantine, regardless of the public [53] prejudice, had formed between the several branches of the Imperial house, served only to convince mankind that these princes were as cold to the endearments of conjugal affection, as they were insensible to the ties of consanguinity and the moving entreaties of youth and innocence. Of so numerous a family Gallus and Julian alone, the two youngest children of Julius Constantius, were saved from the hands of the assassins, till their rage, satiated with slaughter, had in some measure subsided. The emperor Constantius, who, in the absence of his brothers, was the most obnoxious to guilt and reproach, discovered, on some future occasions, a faint and transient remorse for those cruelties, which the perfidious councils of his ministers and the irresistible violence of the troops had extorted from his unexperienced youth.[54]

[53] Conjugia sobrinarum diu ignorata, tempora addito percrebuisse. Tac. Ann. xii. 6, and Lipsius ad loc. The repeal of the ancient law, and the practice of five hundred years, were insufficient to eradicate the prejudices of the Romans ; who still considered the marriages of cousins-german as a species of imperfect incest (Augustin de Civitate Dei, xv. 6) ; and Julian, whose mind was biassed by superstition and resentment, stigmatizes these unnatural alliances between his own cousins with the opprobrious epithet of γάμων τε οὐ γάμων (Orat. vii. p. 228 [296]). The jurisprudence of the canons has since revived and enforced this prohibition, without being able to introduce it either into the civil or the common law of Europe. See on the subject of these marriages, Taylor's Civil Law, p. 331 ; Brouer, de Jure Connub. l. ii. c. 12 ; Hericourt, des Loix Ecclésiastiques, part iii. c. 5 ; Fleury, Institutions du Droit Canonique, tom. i. p. 331. Paris, 1767 ; and Fra Paolo, Istoria del Concilio Trident. l. viii.

[54] Juian (ad S. P. Q. Athen. p. 270 [i. p. 348, ed. Hertl.]) charges his cousin Constantius with the whole guilt of a massacre from which he himself so narrowly escaped. His assertion is confirmed by Athanasius, who, for reasons of a very different nature, was not less an enemy of Constantius (tom. i. p. 856 [ad. mon. 69]). Zosimus joins in the same accusation. But the three abbreviators, Eutropius and the Victors, use very qualifying expressions ; "sinente potius quam jubente ;" "incertum quo suasore ;" "vi militum". [But Julian also says Constantius acted under compulsion ; cp. Or. i. p. 19.]

Division of
the empire.
A.D. 337,
11th Sept. [?]
The massacre of the Flavian race was succeeded by a new division of the provinces; which was ratified in a personal interview of the three brothers. Constantine, the eldest of the Cæsars, obtained, with a certain pre-eminence of rank, the possession of the new capital, which bore his own name and that of his father. Thrace and the countries of the east were allotted for the patrimony of Constantius; and Constans was acknowledged as the lawful sovereign of Italy, Africa, and the western Illyricum. The armies submitted to their hereditary right; and they condescended, after some delay, to accept [9th Sept.,
A.D. 337] from the Roman Senate the title of *Augustus*. When they first assumed the reins of government, the eldest of these princes was twenty-one, the second twenty, and the third only seventeen, years of age.[55]

Sapor, king
of Persia.
A.D 310
[September]
While the martial nations of Europe followed the standards of his brothers, Constantius, at the head of the effeminate troops of Asia, was left to sustain the weight of the Persian war. At the decease of Constantine, the throne of the east was filled by Sapor, son of Hormouz or Hormisdas, and grandson of Narses, who, after the victory of Galerius, had humbly confessed the superiority of the Roman power. Although Sapor was in the thirtieth year of his long reign, he was still in the vigour of youth, as the date of his accession, by a very strange fatality, had preceded that of his birth. The wife of Hormouz remained pregnant at the time of her husband's death; and the uncertainty of the sex, as well as of the event, excited the ambitious hopes of the princes of the house of Sassan. The apprehensions of civil war were at length removed, by the positive assurance of the Magi that the widow of Hormouz had conceived, and would safely produce, a son. Obedient to the voice of superstition, the Persians prepared, without delay, the ceremony of his coronation. A royal bed, on which the queen lay in state, was exhibited in the midst of the palace; the diadem was placed on the spot which might be supposed to conceal the future heir of Artaxerxes, and the prostrate Satraps adored the majesty of their invisible and insensible sovereign.[56]

[55] Euseb. in Vit. Constantin. l. iv. c. 69. Zosimus, l. ii. p. 117 [39]. Idat. in Chron. See two notes of Tillemont, Hist. des Empereurs, tom. iv. p. 1086-1091 [p. 666-668]. The reign of the eldest brother at Constantinople is noticed only in the Alexandrian Chronicle. [But see App. 15.]

[56] Agathias, who lived in the sixth century, is the author of this story (l. iv. p. 135, edit. Louvre [p. 262, ed. Bonn]). He derived his information from some extracts of the Persian Chronicles, obtained and translated by the interpreter Sergius, during his embassy at that court. The coronation of the mother of Sapor is likewise mentioned by Schikard (Tarikh. p. 116) and d'Herbelot (Bibliothèque Orientale, p. 763). [Tabari does not mention the ceremony; Noldeke, 51-2.]

If any credit can be given to this marvellous tale, which seems however to be countenanced by the manners of the people and by the extraordinary duration of his reign, we must admire not only the fortune, but the genius, of Sapor. In the soft sequestered education of a Persian harem, the royal youth could discover the importance of exercising the vigour of his mind and body; and, by his personal merit, deserved a throne, on which he had been seated while he was yet unconscious of the duties and temptations of absolute power. His minority was exposed to the almost inevitable calamities of domestic discord; his capital was surprised and plundered by Thair, a powerful king of Yemen, or Arabia; and the majesty of the royal family was degraded by the captivity of a princess, the sister of the deceased king. But, as soon as Sapor attained the age of manhood, the presumptuous Thair, his nation, and his country fell beneath the first effort of the young warrior; who used his victory with so judicious a mixture of rigour and clemency that he obtained from the fears and gratitude of the Arabs the title of *Dhoulacnaf*, or protector of the nation.[57]   [Dhū-l-Iknāf]

The ambition of the Persian, to whom his enemies ascribe the virtues of a soldier and a statesman, was animated by the desire of revenging the disgrace of his fathers, and of wresting from the hands of the Romans the five provinces beyond the Tigris. The military fame of Constantine, and the real or apparent strength of his government, suspended the attack; and, while the hostile conduct of Sapor provoked the resentment, his artful negotiations amused the patience, of the imperial court. The death of Constantine was the signal of war,[58] and the actual condition of the Syrian and Armenian frontier seemed to encourage the Persians by the prospect of a rich spoil and an easy conquest. The example of the massacres of the palace diffused a spirit of licentiousness and sedition among the troops of the east, who were no longer restrained by their habits of obedience to a veteran commander. By the prudence of Constantius, who, from the interview with his brothers in Pannonia,

State of Mesopotamia and Armenia

---

[57] D'Herbelot, Bibliothèque Orientale, p. 764.

[58] Sextus Rufus (c. 26.), who on this occasion is no contemptible authority, affirms that the Persians sued in vain for peace, and that Constantine was preparing to march against them: yet the superior weight of the testimony of Eusebius obliges us to admit the preliminaries, if not the ratification, of the treaty. See Tillemont, Hist. des Empereurs, tom. iv. p. 420. [An important feature in connexion with these wars is Sapor's persecution of the Christians in his dominion. See Ruinart, Acta sinc. p. 584 *sqq.*, and Görres, Das Christenthum im Sassanidenreiche, in Zeitschr. f. wiss. Theol., vol. 31, 1888, p. 449 *sqq.*]

immediately hastened to the banks of the Euphrates, the legions
were gradually restored to a sense of duty and discipline; but
the season of anarchy had permitted Sapor to form the siege of
Nisibis, and to occupy several of the most important fortresses
[A.D. 338]   of Mesopotamia.[59]   In Armenia, the renowned Tiridates had
long enjoyed the peace and glory which he deserved by his
valour and fidelity to the cause of Rome.   The firm alliance
which he maintained with Constantine was productive of
spiritual as well as of temporal benefits: by the conversion of
Tiridates, the character of a saint was applied to that of a hero,
the Christian faith was preached and established from the
Euphrates to the shores of the Caspian, and Armenia was
attached to the empire by the double ties of policy and of
religion.   But, as many of the Armenian nobles still refused to
abandon the plurality of their gods and of their wives, the
public tranquillity was disturbed by a discontented faction,
which insulted the feeble age of their sovereign, and impatiently
A.D. 342   expected the hour of his death.   He died at length after a
[But see
Appendix 18]   reign of fifty-six years, and the fortune of the Armenian monarchy expired with Tiridates.   His lawful heir was driven
into exile, the Christian priests were either murdered or expelled from their churches, the barbarous tribes of Albania
were solicited to descend from their mountains; and two of
the most powerful governors, usurping the ensigns or the powers
of royalty, implored the assistance of Sapor, and opened the
gates of their cities to the Persian garrisons.   The Christian
party, under the guidance of the Archbishop of Artaxata, the
immediate successor of St. Gregory the Illuminator, had recourse to the piety of Constantius.   After the troubles had
continued about three years, Antiochus, one of the officers of
the household, executed with success the imperial commission
of restoring Chosroes, the son of Tiridates, to the throne of his
fathers, of distributing honours and rewards among the faithful
servants of the house of Arsaces, and of proclaiming a general
amnesty, which was accepted by the greater part of the rebellious
Satraps.   But the Romans derived more honour than advantage
from this revolution.   Chosroes was a prince of a puny stature,
and a pusillanimous spirit.   Unequal to the fatigues of war,
averse to the society of mankind, he withdrew from his capital
to a retired palace, which he built on the banks of the river

---

[59] Julian. Orat. i. p. 20 [p. 24, ed. Hertl.   From some successes gained possibly
in the campaign of this year Constantius won the title of Adiabenicus Maximus.
C. I. L. 3, 3705].

Eleutherus, and in the centre of a shady grove; where he consumed his vacant hours in the rural sports of hunting and hawking. To secure this inglorious ease, he submitted to the conditions of peace which Sapor condescended to impose; the payment of an annual tribute, and the restitution of the fertile province of Atropatene, which the courage of Tiridates and the victorious arms of Galerius had annexed to the Armenian monarchy.[60]

During the long period of the reign of Constantius, the provinces of the east were afflicted by the calamities of the Persian war. The irregular incursions of the light troops alternately spread terror and devastation beyond the Tigris and beyond the Euphrates, from the gates of Ctesiphon to those of Antioch; and this active service was performed by the Arabs of the desert, who were divided in their interest and affections; some of their independent chiefs being enlisted in the party of Sapor, whilst others had engaged their doubtful fidelity to the emperor.[61] The more grave and important operations of the war were conducted with equal vigour; and the armies of Rome and Persia encountered each other in nine bloody fields, in two of which Constantius himself commanded in person.[62] The event of the day was most commonly adverse to the Romans, but in the battle of Singara[63] their imprudent valour

The Persian war.
A.D. 337-360

Battle of Singara.
A.D. 348
[A.D. 344]

---

[60] Julian. Orat. 1. p. 20, 21 [24, 25]. Moses of Chorene, l. ii. c. 89, l. iii. c. 1-9, p. 226-240. The perfect agreement between the vague hints of the contemporary orator and the circumstantial narrative of the national historian gives light to the former and weight to the latter. For the credit of Moses it may be likewise observed that the name of Antiochus is found a few years before in a civil office of inferior dignity. See Godefroy, Cod. Theod. tom. vi. p. 350. [For the Armenian affairs see Append. 18.]

[61] Ammianus (xiv. 4) gives a lively description of the wandering and predatory life of the Saracens, who stretched from the confines of Assyria to the cataracts of the Nile. It appears from the adventures of Malchus, which Jerom has related in so entertai ing a manner, that the high road between Beroea and Edessa was infested by these robbers. See Hieronym. tom. i. p. 256.

[62] We shall take from Eutropius the general idea of the war (x. 10). A Persis enim multa et gravia perpessus, sæpe captis oppidis, obsessis urbibus, cæsis exercitibus, nullumque ei contra Saporem prosperum prælium fuit, nisi quod apud Singaram, &c. This honest account is confirmed by the hints of Ammianus, Rufus, and Jerom. The two first orations of Julian and the third oration of Libanius exhibit a more flattering picture; but the recantation of both those orators, after the death of Constantius, while it restores us to the possession of the truth, degrades their own character, and that of the emperor. The commentary of Spanheim on the first oration of Julian is profusely learned. See likewise the judicious observations of Tillemont, Hist. des Empereurs, tom. iv. p. 656. [Julian puts the campaign about six years before the revolt of Magnentius, that would be 344 (Or. i. p. 32, ἕκτον που μάλιστα μετὰ τὸν πόλεμον ἔτος). See App. 17.]

[63] [Singara, now called Sinjár, is situated due west of Nineveh (Môsil), and about the same distance—a geographical degree, roughly—east of the river

had almost achieved a signal and decisive victory.   The
stationary troops of Singara retired on the approach of Sapor,
who passed the Tigris over three bridges, and occupied near the
village of Hilleh an advantageous camp, which, by the labour of
his numerous pioneers, he surrounded in one day with a deep
ditch and a lofty rampart.   His formidable host, when it was
drawn out in order of battle, covered the banks of the river,
the adjacent heights, and the whole extent of a plain of above
twelve miles, which separated the two armies.   Both were alike
impatient to engage ; but the Barbarians, after a slight resistance, fled in disorder ; unable to resist, or desirous to weary,
the strength of the heavy legions, who, fainting with heat and
thirst, pursued them across the plain, and cut in pieces a line of
cavalry, clothed in complete armour, which had been posted
before the gates of the camp to protect their retreat.   Constantius, who was hurried along in the pursuit, attempted,
without effect, to restrain the ardour of his troops, by representing to them the dangers of the approaching night and the
certainty of completing their success with the return of day.
As they depended much more on their own valour than on the
experience or the abilities of their chief, they silenced by their
clamours his timid remonstrances ; and rushing with fury to
the charge filled up the ditch, broke down the rampart, and
dispersed themselves through the tents, to recruit their exhausted strength and to enjoy the rich harvest of their labours.
But the prudent Sapor had watched the moment of victory.
His army, of which the greater part, securely posted on the
heights, had been spectators of the action, advanced in silence,
and under the shadow of the night ; and his Persian archers,
guided by the illumination of the camp, poured a shower of
arrows on a disarmed and licentious crowd.   The sincerity of
history [64] declares that the Romans were vanquished with a
dreadful slaughter, and that the flying remnant of the legions
was exposed to the most intolerable hardships.   Even the
tenderness of panegyric, confessing that the glory of the
emperor was sullied by the disobedience of his soldiers, chooses
to draw a veil over the circumstances of this melancholy retreat.
Yet one of those venal orators, so jealous of the fame of Con-

Chaboras.   See map in Sachau's Reise in Syrien und Mesopotamien, 1883, and
p. 327 *sqq ;* or Mr. Le Strange's map in Journal of Asiatic Soc., Jan., 1895.]

[64] Acerrimâ nocturnâ concertatione pugnatum est, nostrorum copiis ingenti strage
confossis.   Ammian. xviii. 5.   See likewise Eutropius, x. 10, and S. Rufus
[Festus] c. 27.

stantius, relates with amazing coolness an act of such incredible cruelty, as, in the judgment of posterity, must imprint a far deeper stain on the honour of the imperial name. The son of Sapor, the heir of his crown, had been made a captive in the Persian camp. The unhappy youth, who might have excited the compassion of the most savage enemy, was scourged, tortured, and publicly executed by the inhuman Romans.[65]

Whatever advantages might attend the arms of Sapor in the field, though nine repeated victories diffused among the nations the fame of his valour and conduct, he could not hope to succeed in the execution of his designs, while the fortified towns of Mesopotamia, and, above all, the strong and ancient city of Nisibis, remained in the possession of the Romans. In the space of twelve years, Nisibis, which, since the time of Lucullus, had been deservedly esteemed the bulwark of the east, sustained three memorable sieges against the power of Sapor, and the disappointed monarch, after urging his attacks above sixty, eighty, and an hundred days, was thrice repulsed with loss and ignominy.[66] This large and populous city was situate about two days' journey from the Tigris, in the midst of a pleasant and fertile plain at the foot of Mount Masius. A treble inclosure of brick walls was defended by a deep ditch;[67] and the intrepid assistance of Count Lucilianus and his garrison was seconded by the desperate courage of the people. The citizens of Nisibis were animated by the exhortations of their bishop,[68] enured to arms by the presence of danger, and convinced of the intentions of Sapor to plant a Persian colony in their room and to lead them away into distant and barbarous captivity. The event of the two former sieges elated their confidence, and

Margin notes: Siege of Nisibis; [Nisibin]; A.D. 338, 346 [349-], 350

[65] Libanius, Orat. iii. p. 133, with Julian. Orat. i. p. 24 [29-30], and Spanheim's Commentary, p. 179.

[66] See Julian. Orat. i. p. 27 [29], Orat. ii. p. 62 [79], &c., with the Commentary of Spanheim (p. 188-202), who illustrates the circumstances, and ascertains the time of the three sieges of Nisibis. Their dates are likewise examined by Tillemont (Hist. des Empereurs, tom. iv. p. 668, 671, 674). Something is added from Zosimus, l. iii. p. 151 [8], and the Alexandrine Chronicle, p. 290.

[67] Sallust, Fragment. lxxxiv. edit. Brosses, and Plutarch in Lucull. tom. iii. p. 184. Nisibis is now reduced to one hundred and fifty houses; the marshy lands produce rice, and the fertile meadows as far as Mosul and the Tigris, are covered with the ruins of towns and villages. See Niebuhr, Voyages, tom. ii. p. 300-309. [Compare Sachau's description (op. cit. p. 391): "200 poor huts built chiefly of mud and straw," most of them inhabited by Jews.]

[68] The miracles which Theodoret (l. ii. c. 30) ascribes to St. James, Bishop of Edessa, were at least performed in a worthy cause, the defence of his country. He appeared on the walls under the figure of the Roman emperor, and sent an army of gnats to sting the trunks of the elephants, and to discomfit the host of the new Senacherib.

exasperated the haughty spirit of the Great King, who advanced
[A.D. 49] a third time towards Nisibis, at the head of the united forces of
Persia and India.   The ordinary machines invented to batter or
undermine the walls were rendered ineffectual by the superior
skill of the Romans ; and many days had vainly elapsed, when
Sapor embraced a resolution, worthy of an eastern monarch,
who believed that the elements themselves were subject to his
power.   At the stated season of the melting of the snows in
Armenia, the river Mygdonius, which divides the plain and the
city of Nisibis, forms, like the Nile,[69] an inundation over the
adjacent country.   By the labour of the Persians, the course of
the river was stopped below the town, and the waters were confined on every side by solid mounds of earth.   On this artificial
lake, a fleet of armed vessels, filled with soldiers and with
engines which discharged stones of five hundred pounds' weight,
advanced in order of battle, and engaged, almost upon a level,
the troops which defended the ramparts.   The irresistible force
of the waters was alternately fatal to the contending parties,
till at length a portion of the walls, unable to sustain the accumulated pressure, gave way at once, and exposed an ample
breach of one hundred and fifty feet.   The Persians were instantly driven to the assault, and the fate of Nisibis depended
on the event of the day.   The heavy armed cavalry, who led
the van of a deep column, were embarrassed in the mud, and
great numbers were drowned in the unseen holes which had
been filled by the rushing waters.   The elephants, made
furious by their wounds, increased the disorder, and trampled
down thousands of the Persian archers.   The Great King, who,
from an exalted throne, beheld the misfortunes of his arms,
sounded, with reluctant indignation, the signal of the retreat,
and suspended for some hours the prosecution of the attack.
But the vigilant citizens improved the opportunity of the night ;
and the return of day discovered a new wall of six feet in
height, rising every moment to fill up the interval of the
breach.   Notwithstanding the disappointment of his hopes,
and the loss of more than twenty thousand men, Sapor still

[69] Julian. Orat. i. p. 27.   Though Niebuhr (tom. ii. p. 307) allows a very considerable swell to the Mygdonius, over which he saw a bridge of *twelve* arches ;
it is difficult, however, to understand this parallel of a trifling rivulet with a mighty
river.   There are many circumstances obscure, and almost unintelligible, in the
description of these stupendous water-works.   [The river (now called Jaghjagha)
is split into three arms where the bridge spans it.   Sachau, who describes the bridge
as old but in tolerably good condition, saw the river very full (viel und reissend
fliessendes Wasser, p. 390).]

pressed the reduction of Nisibis, with an obstinate firmness which could have yielded only to the necessity of defending the eastern provinces of Persia against a formidable invasion of the Massagetæ.[70] Alarmed by this intelligence, he hastily [A.D. 350] relinquished the siege, and marched with rapid diligence from the banks of the Tigris to those of the Oxus. The danger and difficulties of the Scythian war engaged him soon afterwards to conclude, or at least to observe, a truce with the Roman emperor, which was equally grateful to both princes; as Constantius himself, after the deaths of his two brothers, was involved, by the revolutions of the west, in a civil contest, which required and seemed to exceed the most vigorous exertion of his undivided strength.

After the partition of the empire three years had scarcely Civil war, elapsed, before the sons of Constantine seemed impatient to con- and death of vince mankind that they were incapable of contenting themselves Constantine. with the dominions which they were unqualified to govern. A.D. 340, The eldest of those princes soon complained that he was de- March frauded of his just proportion of the spoils of their murdered kinsmen; and, though he might yield to the superior guilt and merit of Constantius, he exacted from Constans the cession of the African provinces, as an equivalent for the rich countries of Macedonia and Greece, which his brother had acquired by the death of Dalmatius. The want of sincerity which Constantine experienced in a tedious and fruitless negotiation exasperated the fierceness of his temper; and he eagerly listened to those favourites who suggested to him that his honour, as well as his interest, was concerned in the prosecution of the quarrel. At the head of a tumultuary band, suited for rapine rather than for conquest, he suddenly broke into the dominions of Constans, by the way of the Julian Alps, and the country round Aquileia felt the first effects of his resentment. The measures of Constans, who then resided in Dacia, were directed with more prudence and ability. On the news of his brother's invasion, he dispatched a select and disciplined body of his Illyrian troops, proposing to follow them in person with the remainder of his forces. But the conduct of his lieutenants soon terminated the unnatural contest. By the artful appear-

---

[70] We are obliged to Zonaras (tom. ii. l. xiii. p. 11 [7]) for this invasion of the Massagetæ, which is perfectly consistent with the general series of events, to which we are darkly led by the broken history of Ammianus. [In memory of the brave resistance and the raising of the siege of Nisibis Constantius founded "Persian Games" in May 350. See Corp. Ins. Lat. i. p. 393.]

ances of flight, Constantine was betrayed into an ambuscade, which had been concealed in a wood, where the rash youth, with a few attendants, was surprised, surrounded, and slain. His body, after it had been found in the obscure stream of the Alsa, obtained the honours of an imperial sepulchre; but his provinces transferred their allegiance to the conqueror, who, refusing to admit his elder brother Constantius to any share in these new acquisitions, maintained the undisputed possession of more than two-thirds of the Roman empire.[71]

Murder of
Constans.
A.D. 350.
February

The fate of Constans himself was delayed about ten years longer, and the revenge of his brother's death was reserved for the more ignoble hand of a domestic traitor. The pernicious tendency of the system introduced by Constantine was displayed in the feeble administration of his sons; who, by their vices and weakness, soon lost the esteem and affections of their people. The pride assumed by Constans, from the unmerited success of his arms, was rendered more contemptible by his want of abilities and application. His fond partiality towards some German captives, distinguished only by the charms of youth, was an object of scandal to the people;[72] and Magnentius, an ambitious soldier, who was himself of barbarian extraction, was encouraged by the public discontent to assert the honour of the Roman name.[73] The chosen bands of Jovians and Herculians, who acknowledged Magnentius as their leader, maintained the most respectable and important station in the

[71] The causes and the events of this civil war are related with much perplexity and contradiction. I have chiefly followed Zonaras, and the younger Victor. The monody (ad calcem Eutrop. edit. Havercamp [but cp. App. 1]) pronounced on the death of Constantine, might have been very instructive; but prudence and false taste engaged the orator to involve himself in vague declamation. [Eutropius and others make Constantine invade his brother's land without reason or provocation (Zosimus, ii. 41, states that Constans sent soldiers to murder Constantine). The dissatisfaction of Constantine at the territorial division, given as the cause of the quarrel by Victor, Epit. 41, and Zosimus, and adopted by Gibbon, may be right. Schiller thinks it was a "Kompetenzkonflikt," Constantine claiming a sort of primacy over his brothers, and supports his view by certain coins, which suggest that Constantine held an isolated position among the Augusti (ii. 241).]

[72] Quarum (*gentium*) obsides pretio quæsitos pueros venustiores, quod cultius habuerat, libidine hujusmodi arsisse *pro certo* habetur [Cæs. 41]. Had not the depraved tastes of Constans been publicly avowed, the elder Victor, who held a considerable office in his brother's reign, would not have asserted it in such positive terms.

[73] Julian. Orat. i. and ii. Zosim. l. ii. p. 134 [42]. Victor in Epitome. There is reason to believe that [Fl. Magnus] Magnentius was born in one of those Barbarian Colonies which Constantius Chlorus had established in Gaul (see this History, vol. i. p. 362). His behaviour may remind us of the patriot Earl of Leicester, the famous Simon de Montfort, who could persuade the good people of England that he, a Frenchman by birth, had taken arms to deliver them from foreign favourites.

Imperial camp. The friendship of Marcellinus, count of the sacred largesses, supplied with a liberal hand the means of seduction. The soldiers were convinced, by the most specious arguments, that the republic summoned them to break the bonds of hereditary servitude and, by the choice of an active and vigilant prince, to reward the same virtues which had raised the ancestors of the degenerate Constans from a private condition to the throne of the world. As soon as the conspiracy was ripe for execution, Marcellinus, under the pretence of celebrating his son's birthday, gave a splendid entertainment to the *illustrious* and *honourable* persons of the court of Gaul, which then resided in the city of Autun. The intemperance [Augustodunum] of the feast was artfully protracted till a very late hour of the night; and the unsuspecting guests were tempted to indulge themselves in a dangerous and guilty freedom of conversation. On a sudden the doors were thrown open, and Magnentius, who had retired for a few moments, returned into the apartment, invested with the diadem and purple. The conspirators in- [A.D. 350, 18th Jan.] stantly saluted him with the titles of Augustus and Emperor. The surprise, the terror, the intoxication, the ambitious hopes, and the mutual ignorance of the rest of the assembly, prompted them to join their voices to the general acclamation. The guards hastened to take the oath of fidelity; the gates of the town were shut; and, before the dawn of day, Magnentius became master of the troops and treasure of the palace and city of Autun. By his secrecy and diligence he entertained some hopes of surprising the person of Constans, who was pursuing in the adjacent forest his favourite amusement of hunting, or perhaps some pleasures of a more private and criminal nature. The rapid progress of fame allowed him, however, an instant for flight, though the desertion of his soldiers and subjects deprived him of the power of resistance. Before he could reach a seaport in Spain, where he intended to embark, he was overtaken near Helena,[74] at the foot of the Pyrenees, by a party of light cavalry, whose chief, regardless of the sanctity of a temple, executed his commission by the murder of the son of Constantine.[75]

---

[74] This ancient city had once flourished under the name of Illiberis (Pomponius Mela, ii. 5). The munificence of Constantine gave it new splendour, and his mother's name. Helena (it is still called Elne) became the seat of a bishop, who long afterwards transferred his residence to Perpignan, the capital of modern Rousillon. See d'Anville, Notice de l'Ancienne Gaule, p. 380; Longuerue, Description de la France, p. 223, and the Marca Hispanica, l. i. c. 2.

[75] Zosimus, l. ii. p. 119, 120 [42]; Zonaras, tom. ii. l. xiii. p. 13 [6], and the Abbreviators.

As soon as the death of Constans had decided this easy but important revolution, the example of the court of Autun was imitated by the provinces of the west. The authority of Magnentius was acknowledged through the whole extent of the two great præfectures of Gaul and Italy;[76] and the usurper prepared, by every act of oppression, to collect a treasure, which might discharge the obligation of an immense donative and supply the expenses of a civil war. The martial countries of Illyricum, from the Danube to the extremity of Greece, had long obeyed the government of Vetranio, an aged general, beloved for the simplicity of his manners, and who had acquired some reputation by his experience and services in war.[77] Attached, by habit, by duty, and by gratitude, to the house of Constantine, he immediately gave the strongest assurances to the only surviving son of his late master that he would expose, with unshaken fidelity, his person and his troops, to inflict a just revenge on the traitors of Gaul. But the legions of Vetranio were seduced rather than provoked by the example of rebellion; their leader soon betrayed a want of firmness, or a want of sincerity; and his ambition derived a specious pretence from the approbation of the princess Constantina. That cruel and aspiring woman, who had obtained from the great Constantine her father the rank of *Augusta*, placed the diadem with her own hands on the head of the Illyrian general; and seemed to expect from his victory the accomplishment of those unbounded hopes of which she had been disappointed by the death of her husband Hannibalianus. Perhaps it was without the consent of Constantina that the new emperor formed a necessary, though dishonourable, alliance with the usurper of the west, whose purple was so recently stained with her brother's blood.[78]

[76] [This fact is confirmed in detail by inscriptions: see list in Schiller, ii. 249. In religion, Magnentius was probably a pagan; he permitted pagan sacrifices. But he professed to be a Christian of Nicene views, sought the support of Athanasius, and issued coins with the anti-Arian symbol Α ρ Ω.]

[77] Eutropius (x. 10) describes Vetranio with more temper, and probably with more truth, than either of the two Victors. Vetranio was born of obscure parents in the wildest parts of Mæsia; and so much had his education been neglected that, after his elevation, he studied the alphabet. [For the part played by Constantina see Chron. Pasch. i, 539, 540. The coins seem to support the hypothesis that Vetranio was loyal; see next note. Vetranio coins with Concordia militum, and Virtus Augustorum, are referred by Schiller to an understanding between Vetranio and Constantius.]

[78] The doubtful, fluctuating conduct of Vetranio is described by Julian in his first oration [p. 32 *sqq.*, ed. Hertl.] and accurately explained by Spanheim, who discusses the situation and behaviour of Constantina. [Schiller (ii. 250 *sqq.*) discusses the conduct of Vetranio and concludes that he was loyal throughout to the house of Constantine; that he assumed the purple lest a true rebel should be pro-

The intelligence of these important events, which so deeply affected the honour and safety of the Imperial house, recalled the arms of Constantius from the inglorious prosecution of the Persian war. He recommended the care of the east to his lieutenants, and afterwards to his cousin Gallus, whom he raised from a prison to a throne; and marched towards Europe, with a mind agitated by the conflict of hope and fear, of grief and indignation. On his arrival at Heraclea in Thrace, the emperor gave audience to the ambassadors of Magnentius and Vetranio. The first author of the conspiracy, Marcellinus, who in some measure had bestowed the purple on his new master, boldly accepted this dangerous commission; and his three colleagues were selected from the illustrious personages of the state and army. These deputies were instructed to soothe the resentment, and to alarm the fears, of Constantius. They were empowered to offer him the friendship and alliance of the western princes, to cement their union by a double marriage; of Constantius with the daughter of Magnentius, and of Magnentius himself with the ambitious Constantina; and to acknowledge in the treaty the pre-eminence of rank, which might justly be claimed by the emperor of the east. Should pride and mistaken piety urge him to refuse these equitable conditions, the ambassadors were ordered to expatiate on the inevitable ruin which must attend his rashness, if he ventured to provoke the sovereigns of the west to exert their superior strength and to employ against him that valour, those abilities, and those legions, to which the house of Constantine had been indebted for so many triumphs. Such propositions and such arguments appeared to deserve the most serious attention; the answer of Constantius was deferred till the next day; and, as he had reflected on the importance of justifying a civil war in the opinion of the people, he thus addressed his council, who listened with real or affected credulity: "Last night," said he, "after I retired to rest, the shade of the great Constantine, embracing the corpse of my murdered brother, rose before my eyes; his well-known voice awakened me to revenge, forbade me to despair of the republic, and assured me of the success and immortal glory which would crown the justice of my arms". The authority of such a vision, or rather of the prince who alleged it, silenced every doubt, and excluded all negotiation. The ignominious terms of peace were rejected with disdain. One of the ambassadors of the tyrant

Constantius refuses to treat.
A.D. 350

[November]

claimed; and that the dramatic scene of his repentance and resignation was pre-arranged between himself and Constantius.]

was dismissed with the haughty answer of Constantius; his colleagues, as unworthy of the privileges of the law of nations, were put in irons; and the contending powers prepared to wage an implacable war.[79]

Deposes Ve-
tranio.
A.D. 350,
Dec. 25

Such was the conduct, and such perhaps was the duty, of the brother of Constans towards the perfidious usurper of Gaul. The situation and character of Vetranio admitted of milder measures; and the policy of the eastern emperor was directed to disunite his antagonists, and to separate the forces of Illyricum from the cause of rebellion. It was an easy task to deceive the frankness and simplicity of Vetranio, who, fluctuating some time between the opposite views of honour and interest, displayed to the world the insincerity of his temper, and was insensibly engaged in the snares of an artful negotiation. Constantius acknowledged him as a legitimate and equal colleague in the empire, on condition that he would renounce his disgraceful alliance with Magnentius and appoint a place of interview on the frontiers of their respective provinces, where they might pledge their friendship by mutual vows of fidelity and regulate by common consent the future operations of the civil war. In consequence of this agreement, Vetranio advanced to the city

[Sona]

of Sardica,[80] at the head of twenty thousand horse and of a more numerous body of infantry; a power so far superior to the forces of Constantius that the Illyrian emperor appeared to command the life and fortunes of his rival, who, depending on the success of his private negotiations, had seduced the troops, and undermined the throne, of Vetranio. The chiefs, who had secretly embraced the party of Constantius, prepared in his favour a public spectacle, calculated to discover and inflame the passions of the multitude.[81] The united armies were commanded to assemble in a large plain near the city. In the centre, according to the rules of ancient discipline, a military tribunal, or rather scaffold, was erected, from whence the emperors were accustomed, on solemn and important occasions, to harangue the troops. The well-ordered ranks of Romans and Barbarians, with drawn swords or with erected spears, the squadrons of

---

[79] See Peter the Patrician, in the Excerpta Legationum, p. 27.

[80] Zonaras, t. ii. l. xiii. p. 16 [c. 7]. The position of Sardica, near the modern city of Sophia, appears better suited to this interview than the situation of either Naissus or Sirmium, where it is placed by Jerom, Socrates, and Sozomen.

[81] See the two first orations of Julian, particularly p. 31; and Zosimus, l. ii. p. 122 [c. 44]. The distinct narrative of the historian serves to illustrate the diffuse, but vague, descriptions of the orator. [Cp. also Them. Orat. 3, p. 45 C, and 4, p. 56 B · Libanius, Vita, p. 58, Reiske.—Ammian, 21, 8, 1.]

cavalry and the cohorts of infantry, distinguished by the variety of their arms and ensigns, formed an immense circle round the tribunal ; and the attentive silence which they preserved was sometimes interrupted by loud bursts of clamour or of applause. In the presence of this formidable assembly, the two emperors were called upon to explain the situation of public affairs : the precedency of rank was yielded to the royal birth of Constantius ; and, though he was indifferently skilled in the arts of rhetoric, he acquitted himself, under these difficult circumstances, with firmness, dexterity, and eloquence. The first part of his oration seemed to be pointed only against the tyrant of Gaul ; but, while he tragically lamented the cruel murder of Constans, he insinuated that none, except a brother, could claim a right to the succession of his brother. He displayed, with some complacency, the glories of his Imperial race ; and recalled to the memory of the troops the valour, the triumphs, the liberality of the great Constantine, to whose sons they had engaged their allegiance by an oath of fidelity, which the ingratitude of his most favoured servants had tempted them to violate. The officers, who surrounded the tribunal and were instructed to act their parts in this extraordinary scene, confessed the irresistible power of reason and eloquence by saluting the emperor Constantius as their lawful sovereign. The contagion of loyalty and repentance was communicated from rank to rank ; till the plain of Sardica resounded with the universal acclamation of " Away with these upstart usurpers ! Long life and victory to the son of Constantine ! Under his banners alone we will fight and conquer." The shout of thousands, their menacing gestures, the fierce clashing of their arms, astonished and subdued the courage of Vetranio, who stood, amidst the defection of his followers, in anxious and silent suspense. Instead of embracing the last refuge of generous despair, he tamely submitted to his fate ; and taking the diadem from his head, in view of both armies, fell prostrate at the feet of his conqueror. Constantius used his victory with prudence and moderation ; and raising from the ground the aged suppliant, whom he affected to style by the endearing name of Father, he gave him his hand to descend from the throne. The city of Prusa was assigned for the exile or retirement of the abdicated monarch, who lived six years in the enjoyment of ease and affluence. He often expressed his grateful sense of the goodness of Constantius, and, with a very amiable simplicity, advised his benefactor to resign the sceptre of the world, and to seek for content (where alone

it could be found) in the peaceful obscurity of a private
condition.[82]

The behaviour of Constantius on this memorable occasion
was celebrated with some appearance of justice; and his
courtiers compared the studied orations which a Pericles or a
Demosthenes addressed to the popu¹ ce of Athens with the
victorious eloquence which had persu ed an armed multitude
to desert and depose the object of their partial choice.[83]   The
approaching contest with Magnentius was of a more serious
and bloody kind.   The tyrant advanced by rapid marches to
encounter Constantius, at the head of a numerous army, composed
of Gauls and Spaniards, of Franks and Saxons; of those
provincials who supplied the strength of the legions, and of
those barbarians who were dreaded as the most formidable
enemies of the republic.   The fertile plains [84] of the Lower
Pannonia, between the Drave, the Save, and the Danube,
presented a spacious theatre; and the operations of the civil
war were protracted during the summer months by the skill
or timidity of the combatants.[85]   Constantius had declared his
intention of deciding the quarrel in the fields of Cibalis, a
name that would animate his troops by the remembrance of
the victory which, on the same auspicious ground, had been
obtained by the arms of his father Constantine.   Yet, by the
impregnable fortifications with which the emperor encompassed
his camp, he appeared to decline, rather than to invite, a
general engagement.   It was the object of Magnentius to tempt
or to compel his adversary to relinquish this advantageous
position; and he employed, with that view, the various marches,
evolutions, and stratagems, which the knowledge of the art of

[82] The younger Victor assigns to his exile the emphatical appellation of
"Voluptarium otium".   Socrates (l. ii. c. 28) is the voucher for the correspondence with the emperor, which would seem to prove that Vetranio was, indeed,
prope ad stultitiam simplicissimus.

[83] Eum Constantius . . . facundiæ vi dejectum Imperio in privatum otium
removit.   Quæ gloria post natum Imperium soli processit eloquio clementiâque,
&c.   Aurelius Victor, Julian, and Themistius (Orat. iii and iv) adorn this exploit
with all the artificial and gaudy colouring of their rhetoric.

[84] Busbequius (p. 112) traversed the Lower Hungary and Sclavonia at a time
when they were reduced almost to a desert by the reciprocal hostilities of the
Turks and Christians.   Yet he mentions with admiration the unconquerable fertility
of the soil; and observes that the height of the grass was sufficient to conceal a
loaded waggon from his sight.   See likewise Browne's Travels, in Harris's
Collection, vol. ii. p. 762, &c.

[85] Zosimus gives a very large account of the war and the negotiation (l. ii. p.
123-130 [c. 45-49]).   But, as he neither shews himself a soldier nor a politician, his
narrative must be weighed with attention, and received with caution.

war could suggest to an experienced officer. He carried by assault the important town of Siscia ; made an attack on the city of Sirmium, which lay in the rear of the Imperial camp ; attempted to force a passage over the Save into the eastern provinces of Illyricum ; and cut in pieces a numerous detachment, which he had allured into the narrow passes of Adarne. During the greater part of the summer, the tyrant of Gaul shewed himself master of the field. The troops of Constantius were harassed and dispirited ; his reputation declined in the eye of the world ; and his pride condescended to solicit a treaty of peace, which would have resigned to the assassin of Constans the sovereignty of the provinces beyond the Alps. These offers were enforced by the eloquence of Philip the Imperial ambassador ; and the council as well as the army of Magnentius were disposed to accept them. But the haughty usurper, careless of the remonstrances of his friends, gave orders that Philip should be detained as a captive, or at least as a hostage ; while he dispatched an officer to reproach Constantius with the weakness of his reign, and to insult him by the promise of a pardon, if he would instantly abdicate the purple. "That he should confide in the justice of his cause and the protection of an avenging Deity," was the only answer which honour permitted the emperor to return. But he was so sensible of the difficulties of his situation that he no longer dared to retaliate the indignity which had been offered to his representative. The negotiation of Philip was not, however, ineffectual, since he determined Sylvanus, the Frank, a general of merit and reputation, to desert with a considerable body of cavalry, a few days before the battle of Mursa.

The city of Mursa, or Essek, celebrated in modern times for a bridge of boats five miles in length over the river Drave and the adjacent morasses,[86] has been always considered as a place of importance in the wars of Hungary. Magnentius, directing his march towards Mursa, set fire to the gates, and, by a sudden assault, had almost scaled the walls of the town. The vigilance of the garrison extinguished the flames ; the approach of Constantius left him no time to continue the operations of the siege ; and the emperor soon removed the only obstacle that could embarrass his motions, by forcing a

Battle of Mursa. A.D. 351, Sept. 28

---

[86] This remarkable bridge, which is flanked with towers, and supported on large wooden piles, was constructed, A.D. 1566, by Sultan Soliman, to facilitate the march of his armies into Hungary. See Browne's Travels, and Busching's System of Geography, vol. ii. p. 90.

body of troops which had taken post in an adjoining amphi-theatre. The field of battle round Mursa was a naked and level plain: on this ground the army of Constantius formed, with the Drave on their right; while their left, either from the nature of their disposition or from the superiority of their cavalry, extended far beyond the right flank of Magnentius.[87] The troops on both sides remained under arms in anxious expectation during the greatest part of the morning; and the son of Constantine, after animating his soldiers by an eloquent speech, retired into a church at some distance from the field of battle, and committed to his generals the conduct of this decisive day.[88] They deserved his confidence by the valour and military skill which they exerted. They wisely began the action upon the left; and, advancing their whole wing of cavalry in an oblique line, they suddenly wheeled it on the right flank of the enemy, which was unprepared to resist the impetuosity of their charge. But the Romans of the West soon rallied, by the habits of discipline; and the Barbarians of Germany supported the renown of their national bravery. The engagement soon became general; was maintained with various and singular turns of fortune; and scarcely ended with the darkness of the night. The signal victory which Constantius obtained is attributed to the arms of his cavalry. His cuirassiers are described as so many massy statues of steel, glittering with their scaly armour, and breaking with their ponderous lances the firm array of the Gallic legions. As soon as the legions gave way, the lighter and more active squadrons of the second line rode sword in hand into the intervals, and completed the disorder. In the meanwhile, the huge bodies of the Germans were exposed almost naked to the dexterity of the oriental archers; and whole troops of those Barbarians were urged by anguish and despair to precipitate themselves into the broad and rapid stream of the Drave.[89] The number of the slain

[87] This position, and the subsequent evolutions, are clearly, though concisely, described by Julian, Orat. i. p. 36 [p. 44, ed. Hertl.].

[88] Sulpicius Severus, l. ii. p. 405 [ed. Lugd. Bat. 1647; c. 38]. The emperor passed the day in prayer with Valens, the Arian bishop of Mursa, who gained his confidence by announcing the success of the battle. M. de Tillemont (Hist. des Empereurs, tom. iv. p. 1110) very properly remarks the silence of Julian with regard to the personal prowess of Constantius in the battle of Mursa. The silence of flattery is sometimes equal to the most positive and authentic evidence.

[89] Julian, Orat. i. p. 36, 37 [45, 46, ed. Hertl.] ; and Orat. ii. p. 59, 60. Zonaras, tom. ii. l. xiii. p. 17 [8]. Zosimus, l. ii. p. 130-133 [49-52]. The last of these celebrates the dexterity of the archer Menelaus, who could discharge three arrows at the same time; an advantage which, according to his apprehension of military affairs, materially contributed to the victory of Constantius.

was computed at fifty-four thousand men, and the slaughter
of the conquerors was more considerable than that of the
vanquished ; [90] a circumstance which proves the obstinacy of
the contest, and justifies the observation of an ancient writer
that the forces of the empire were consumed in the fatal battle
of Mursa, by the loss of a veteran army, sufficient to defend
the frontiers or to add new triumphs to the glory of Rome.[91]
Notwithstanding the invectives of a servile orator, there is not
the least reason to believe that the tyrant deserted his own
standard in the beginning of the engagement.   He seems
to have displayed the virtues of a general and of a soldier till
the day was irrecoverably lost, and his camp in the possession
of the enemy.   Magnentius then consulted his safety, and,
throwing away the imperial ornaments, escaped with some
difficulty from the pursuit of the light horse, who incessantly
followed his rapid flight from the banks of the Drave to the
foot of the Julian Alps.[92]

The approach of winter supplied the indolence of Con- Conquest of
stantius with specious reasons for deferring the prosecution of Italy. A.D. 352
the war till the ensuing spring.   Magnentius had fixed his
residence in the city of Aquileia, and shewed a seeming resolution to dispute the passage of the mountains and morasses
which fortified the confines of the Venetian province.   The
surprisal of a castle in the Alps by the secret march of the
Imperialists could scarcely have determined him to relinquish
the possession of Italy, if the inclinations of the people had
supported the cause of their tyrant.[93]   But the memory of

[90] According to Zonaras, Constantius, out of 80,000 men, lost 30,000, and
Magnentius lost 24,000 out of 36,000.   The other articles of this account seem
probable and authentic, but the numbers of the tyrant's army must have been
mistaken, either by the author or his transcribers.   Magnentius had collected the
whole force of the West, Romans and Barbarians, into one formidable body, which
cannot fairly be estimated at less than 100,000 men.   Julian, Orat. i. p. 34, 35 [75,
76].

[91] Ingentes R. I. vires eâ dimicatione consumptæ sunt, ad quælibet bella externa
idoneæ, quæ multum triumphorum possent securitatisque conferre.   Eutropius, x.
13.   The younger Victor expresses himself to the same effect. [Cp. Sulpicius
Severus, Chron. 2, 38.]

[92] On this occasion, we must prefer the unsuspected testimony of Zosimus and
Zonaras to the flattering assertions of Julian.   The younger Victor paints the
character of Magnentius in a singular light : " Sermonis acer, animi tumidi, et
immodice timidus ; artifex tamen ad occultandam audaciæ specie formidinem ".
Is it most likely that in the battle of Mursa his behaviour was governed by nature
or by art ?   I should incline for the latter.

[93] Julian. Orat. i. p. 38, 39 [48, 49].   In that place, however, as well as in
Oration ii. p. 97 [124], he insinuates the general disposition of the senate, the
people, and the soldiers of Italy, towards the party of the emperor.

the cruelties exercised by his ministers, after the unsuccessful revolt of Nepotian, had left a deep impression of horror and resentment on the minds of the Romans. That rash youth, the son of the princess Eutropia, and the nephew of Constantine, had seen with indignation the sceptre of the West usurped by a perfidious barbarian. Arming a desperate troop of slaves and gladiators, he overpowered the feeble guard of the domestic tranquillity of Rome, received the homage of the senate, and, assuming the title of Augustus, precariously reigned during a tumult of twenty-eight days. The march of some regular forces put an end to his ambitious hopes: the rebellion was extinguished in the blood of Nepotian, of his mother Eutropia, and of his adherents; and the proscription was extended to all who had contracted a fatal alliance with the name and family of Constantine.[94] But, as soon as Constantius, after the battle of Mursa, became master of the sea-coast of Dalmatia, a band of noble exiles, who had ventured to equip a fleet in some harbour of the Hadriatic, sought protection and revenge in his victorious camp. By their secret intelligence with their countrymen, Rome and the Italian cities were persuaded to display the banners of Constantius on their walls. The grateful veterans, enriched by the liberality of the father, signalized their gratitude and loyalty to the son. The cavalry, the legions, and the auxiliaries of Italy renewed their oath of allegiance to Constantius; and the usurper, alarmed by the general desertion, was compelled, with the remains of his faithful troops, to retire beyond the Alps into the provinces of Gaul. The detachments, however, which were ordered either to press or to intercept the flight of Magnentius, conducted themselves with the usual imprudence of success; and allowed him, in the plains of Pavia, an opportunity of turning on his pursuers and of gratifying his despair by the carnage of a useless victory.[95]

[A.D. 350, July]

[Before Sept., A.D. 352]

Last defeat and death of Magnentius. A.D. 353, August 10 [11]

The pride of Magnentius was reduced, by repeated misfortunes, to sue, and to sue in vain, for peace. He first dispatched a senator, in whose abilities he confided, and

[94] The elder Victor describes in a pathetic manner the miserable condition of Rome: "Cujus stolidum ingenium adeo P. R. patribusque exitio fuit, uti passim domus, fora, viæ, templaque, cruore, cadaveribusque opplerentur bustorum modo". Athanasius (tom. i. p. 677) deplores the fate of several illustrious victims, and Julian (Orat. ii. p. 58 [74]) execrates the cruelty of Marcellinus, the implacable enemy of the house of Constantine. [June is given as the date in Idatius and Chron. Pasch.; but Rossi argues for July; Rev. Arch. 6, 375.]

[95] Zosim. l. ii. p. 133 [52]. Victor in Epitome. The panegyrists of Constantius, with their usual candour, forget to mention this accidental defeat.

afterwards several bishops, whose holy character might obtain a more favourable audience, with the offer of resigning the purple, and the promise of devoting the remainder of his life to the service of the emperor. But Constantius, though he granted fair terms of pardon and reconciliation to all who abandoned the standard of rebellion,[96] avowed his inflexible resolution to inflict a just punishment on the crimes of an assassin, whom he prepared to overwhelm on every side by the effort of his victorious arms. An Imperial fleet acquired the easy possession of Africa and Spain, confirmed the wavering faith of the Moorish nations, and landed a considerable force, which passed the Pyrenees, and advanced towards Lyons, the last and fatal station of Magnentius.[97] The temper of the tyrant, which was never inclined to clemency, was urged by distress to exercise every act of oppression which could extort an immediate supply from the cities of Gaul.[98] Their patience was at length exhausted ; and Treves, the seat of prætorian government, gave the signal of revolt by shutting her gates against Decentius, who had been raised by his brother to the rank either of Cæsar or of Augustus.[99] From Treves, Decentius was obliged to retire to Sens, where he was soon surrounded by an [Senones] army of Germans, whom the pernicious arts of Constantius had introduced into the civil dissensions of Rome.[100]   In the meantime the Imperial troops forced the passages of the Cottian Alps, and in the bloody combat of Mount Seleucus irrevocably fixed the title of Rebels on the party of Magnentius.[101] He was unable to bring another army into the field ; the fidelity of his

[96] Zonaras, tom. ii. l. xiii. p. 17. Julian, in several places of the two orations, expatiates on the clemency of Constantius to the rebels.

[97] Zosim. l. ii. p. 133 [ib.]. Julian, Orat. i. p. 40 [50]; ii. p. 74 [95].

[98] Ammian. xv. 6. Zosim. l. ii. p. 133. Julian, who (Orat. i. p. 40) inveighs against the cruel effects of the tyrant's despair, mentions (Orat. i. p. 34) the oppressive edicts which were dictated by his necessities, or by his avarice. His subjects were compelled to purchase the Imperial demesnes ; a doubtful and dangerous species of property, which, in case of a revolution, might be imputed to them as a treasonable usurpation.

[99] The medals of Magnentius celebrate the victories of the *two* Augusti, and of the Cæsar. The Cæsar was another brother, named Desiderius. See Tillemont, Hist. des Empereurs, tom. iv. p. 757. [Decentius was only Cæsar. The two Augusti (*Augustorum*) on the coins are Magnentius and Constantius. Magnentius posed as the colleague of Constantius.]

[100] Julian, Orat. i. p. 40, ii. p. 74, with Spanheim, p. 263. His Commentary illustrates the transactions of this civil war. Mons Seleuci was a small place in the Cottian Alps, a few miles distant from Vapincum, or Gap, an episcopal city of Dauphiné. See d'Anville, Notice de la Gaule, p. 464 ; and Longuerue, Description de la France, p. 327.

[101] Zosimus, l. ii. p. 134 [52]. Liban. Orat. x. p. 268, 269. The latter most vehemently arraigns this cruel and selfish policy of Constantius.

guards was corrupted : and, when he appeared in public to animate them by his exhortations, he was saluted with an unanimous shout of "Long live the emperor Constantius!" The tyrant, who perceived that they were preparing to deserve pardon and rewards by the sacrifice of the most obnoxious criminal, prevented their design by falling on his sword ;[102] a death more easy and more honourable than he could hope to obtain from the hands of an enemy, whose revenge would have been coloured with the specious pretence of justice and fraternal piety.   The example of suicide was imitated by Decentius, who strangled [A.D. 353, 12th Aug.] himself on the news of his brother's death.   The author of the conspiracy, Marcellinus, had long since disappeared in the battle of Mursa,[103] and the public tranquillity was confirmed by the execution of the surviving leaders of a guilty and unsuccessful faction.   A severe inquisition was extended over all who, either from choice or from compulsion, had been involved in the cause of rebellion.   Paul, surnamed Catena, from his superior skill in the judicial exercise of tyranny, was sent to explore the latent remains of the conspiracy in the remote province of Britain. The honest indignation expressed by Martin, vice-præfect of the island, was interpreted as an evidence of his own guilt ; and the governor was urged to the necessity of turning against his breast the sword with which he had been provoked to wound the Imperial minister.   The most innocent subjects of the West were exposed to exile and confiscation, to death and torture ; and, as the timid are always cruel, the mind of Constantius was inaccessible to mercy.[104]

---

[102] Julian, Orat. i. p. 40. Zosimus, l. ii. p. 134 [53]. Socrates, l. ii. c. 32. Sozomen, l. iv. c. 7.   The younger Victor describes his death with some horrid circumstances : Transfosso latere, ut erat vasti corporis, vulnere naribusque et ore cruorem effundens, exspiravit. If we can give credit to Zonaras, the tyrant, before he expired, had the pleasure of murdering with his own hands his mother and his brother Desiderius. [The date 11th Aug. must be accepted from Idatiur   Gibbon took 10th Aug. from Chron. Pasch., which gives the wrong year, 354.]

[103] Julian (Orat. i. p. 58, 59) seems at a loss to determine whether he inflicted on himself the punishment of his crimes, whether he was drowned in the Drave, or whether he was carried by the avenging demons from the field of battle to his destined place of eternal tortures.

[104] Ammian. xiv. 5 ; xxi. 16. [Several inscriptions are extant celebrating the victory of Constantius; e.g., C. I. L. 6, 1158 : restitutor urbis Romæ atque orbis et extinctor pestiferæ tyrannidis. Magnentius had been described as liberator orbis terrarum, &c. Cod. Theod. 15, 14, 5, and 9, 38, 2, annul all the acts of the tyrant.]

CHAPTER XIX

Constantius sole Emperor—Elevation and Death of Gallus—Danger and Elevation of Julian—Sarmatian and Persian Wars—Victories of Julian in Gaul

THE divided provinces of the empire were again united by the victory of Constantius; but, as that feeble prince was destitute of personal merit, either in peace or war; as he feared his generals and distrusted his ministers; the triumph of his arms served only to establish the reign of the *eunuchs* over the Roman world. Those unhappy beings, the ancient production of oriental jealousy and despotism,[1] were introduced into Greece and Rome by the contagion of Asiatic luxury.[2] Their progress was rapid; and the eunuchs, who, in the time of Augustus, had been abhorred, as the monstrous retinue of an Egyptian queen,[3] were gradually admitted into the families of matrons, of senators, and of the emperors themselves.[4] Restrained by the severe edicts of Domitian and Nerva,[5] cherished by the pride

Power of the eunuchs

---

[1] Ammianus (l. xiv. c. 6) imputes the first practice of castration to the cruel ingenuity of Semiramis, who was supposed to have reigned above nineteen hundred years before Christ. The use of eunuchs is of high antiquity, both in Asia and Egypt. They are mentioned in the law of Moses, Deuteron. xxiii. 1. See Goguet, Origines des Loix, &c. part i. l. i. c. 3.

[2] Eunuchum dixti velle te;
Quia solæ utuntur his reginæ ——
　　　　　　　　　　　　Terent. Eunuch. Act i. scene 2.
This play is translated from Menander, and the original must have appeared soon after the eastern conquests of Alexander.

[3] Miles . . . spadonibus
Servire rugosis potest.
　　　　　　Horat. Carm. v. 9 [Epode 9], and Dacier ad loc.
By the word *spado* the Romans very forcibly expressed their abhorrence of this mutilated condition. The Greek appellation of eunuchs, which insensibly prevailed, had a milder sound and a more ambiguous sense.

[4] We need only mention Posides, a freedman and eunuch of Claudius, in whose favour the emperor prostituted some of the most honourable rewards of military valour. See Sueton. in Claudio, c. 28. Posides employed a great part of his wealth in building.

　　　　　Ut *spado* vincebat Capitolia nostra
　　　　　Posides.　　　　　　　　　　Juvenal. Sat. xiv. [91].
[5] Castrari mares vetuit. Sueton. in Domitian. c. 7. See Dion Cassius, l. lxvii. p. 1107 [2]; l. lxviii. p. 1119 [2].

of Diocletian, reduced to an humble station by the prudence of Constantine,[6] they multiplied in the palaces of his degenerate sons, and insensibly acquired the knowledge, and at length the direction, of the secret councils of Constantius. The aversion and contempt which mankind has so uniformly entertained for that imperfect species appears to have degraded their character, and to have rendered them almost as incapable as they were supposed to be of conceiving any generous sentiment or of performing any worthy action.[7] But the eunuchs were skilled in the arts of flattery and intrigue ; and they alternately governed the mind of Constantius by his fears, his indolence, and his vanity.[8] Whilst he viewed in a deceitful mirror the fair appearance of public prosperity, he supinely permitted them to intercept the complaints of the injured provinces, to accumulate immense treasures by the sale of justice and of honours ; to disgrace the most important dignities by the promotion of those who had purchased at their hands the powers of oppression,[9] and to gratify their resentment against the few independent spirits who arrogantly refused to solicit the protection of slaves. Of these slaves the most distinguished was the chamberlain Eusebius, who ruled the monarch and the palace with such absolute sway that Constantius, according to the sarcasm of an

---

[6] There is a passage in the Augustan History, p. 137 [xviii. 66], in which Lampridius, whilst he praises Alexander Severus and Constantine for restraining the tyranny of the eunuchs, deplores the mischiefs which they occasioned in other reigns. Huc accedit quod eunuchos nec in consiliis nec in ministeriis habuit ; qui soli principes perdunt, dum eos more gentium aut regum Persarum volunt vivere ; qui a populo etiam amicissimum semovent ; qui internuntii sunt, aliud quam respondetur referentes ; claudentes principem suum, et agentes ante omnia ne quid sciat.

[7] Xenophon (Cyropædia, l. viii. [leg. vii.] p. 540 [c. 5, 60]) has stated the specious reasons which engaged Cyrus to entrust his person to the guard of eunuchs. He had observed in animals that, although the practice of castration might tame their ungovernable fierceness, it did not diminish their strength or spirit ; and he persuaded himself that those who were separated from the rest of human kind would be more firmly attached to the person of their benefactor. But a long experience has contradicted the judgment of Cyrus. Some particular instances may occur of eunuchs distinguished by their fidelity, their valour, and their abilities ; but, if we examine the general history of Persia, India, and China, we shall find that the power of the eunuchs has uniformly marked the decline and fall of every dynasty.

[8] See Ammianus Marcellinus, l. xxi. c. 16, l. xxii. c. 4. The whole tenor of his impartial history serves to justify the invectives of Mamertinus, of Libanius, and of Julian himself, who have insulted the vices of the court of Constantius.

[9] Aurelius Victor censures the negligence of his sovereign in choosing the governors of the provinces and the generals of the army, and concludes his history with a very bold observation, as it is much more dangerous under a feeble reign to attack the ministers than the master himself. " Uti verum absolvam brevi, ut Imperatore ipso clarius ita apparitorum plerisque magis atrox nihil " [Cæs. 42].

impartial historian, possessed some credit with his haughty
favourite.[10] By his artful suggestions, the emperor was persuaded to subscribe the condemnation of the unfortunate
Gallus, and to add a new crime to the long list of unnatural
murders which pollute the honour of the house of Constantine.

When the two nephews of Constantine, Gallus and Julian, Education of
were saved from the fury of the soldiers, the former was about Julian
twelve, and the latter about six, years of age ; and, as the eldest
was thought to be of a sickly constitution, they obtained with
the less difficulty a precarious and dependent life from the
affected pity of Constantius, who was sensible that the execution
of these helpless orphans would have been esteemed by all
mankind an act of the most deliberate cruelty.[11] Different
cities of Ionia and Bithynia were assigned for the places of their
exile and education ; but, as soon as their growing years excited
the jealousy of the emperor, he judged it more prudent to secure
those unhappy youths in the strong castle of Macellum, near [c. 344 A.D.]
Cæsarea. The treatment which they experienced during a six
years' confinement was partly such as they could hope from a
careful guardian, and partly such as they might dread from a
suspicious tyrant.[12] Their prison was an ancient palace, the
residence of the kings of Cappadocia ; the situation was pleasant,
the buildings stately, the inclosure spacious. They pursued their
studies, and practised their exercises, under the tuition of the
most skilful masters ; and the numerous household, appointed to
attend, or rather to guard, the nephews of Constantine, was not
unworthy of the dignity of their birth. But they could not
disguise to themselves that they were deprived of fortune, of

[10] Apud quem (si vere dici debeat) multum Constantius potuit.   Ammian. l.
xviii. c. 4.

[11] Gregory Nazianzen (Orat. iii. p. 90) reproaches the apostate with his ingratitude towards Mark, bishop of Arethusa, who had contributed to save his life ; and
we learn, though from a less respectable authority (Tillemont, Hist. des Empereurs,
tom. iv. p. 916), that Julian was concealed in the sanctuary of a church. [Gallus
and Julian were step-brothers, being sons of Galla and Basilina respectively. The
exact date of Julian's birth has been recently a subject of discussion. Schwarz (de
vita et scr. Jul. imp. p. 16) gives Nov.-Dec., 331 ; Kellerbauer, Sept., 331 ; C.
Radinger (Philologus, 50, p. 761 ; 1891), May, 331, comparing lemma to Anth. Pal.
14, 148,—very probably as regards the month. But C. J. Neumann, Das Geburts-
jahr K. Julians (ib.), shews that if we accept May from Radinger, the year must be
332 ; for he died in his thirty-second year (Amm. 25, 3, 23) in June. If born in
May, 331, his death must have occurred in his thirty-third year.]

[12] The most authentic account of the education and adventures of Julian is contained in the epistle or manifesto which he himself addressed to the senate and
people of Athens. Libanius (Orat. Parentalis), on the side of the Pagans, and
Socrates (l. iii. c. 1), on that of the Christians, have preserved several interesting
circumstances.

freedom, and of safety; secluded from the society of all whom they could trust or esteem; and condemned to pass their melancholy hours in the company of slaves, devoted to the commands of a tyrant, who had already injured them beyond the hope of reconciliation. At length, however, the emergencies of the state compelled the emperor, or rather his eunuchs, to invest Gallus, in the twenty-fifth year of his age, with the title of Cæsar,[13] and to cement this political connexion by his marriage with the princess Constantina.[14] After a formal interview, in which the two princes mutually engaged their faith never to undertake anything to the prejudice of each other, they repaired without delay to their respective stations. Constantius continued his march towards the West, and Gallus fixed his residence at Antioch, from whence, with a delegated authority, he administered the five great dioceses of the eastern præfecture.[15] In this fortunate change, the new Cæsar was not unmindful of his brother Julian, who obtained the honours of his rank, the appearances of liberty, and the restitution of an ample patrimony.[16]

The writers the most indulgent to the memory of Gallus, and even Julian himself, though he wished to cast a veil over the frailties of his brother, are obliged to confess that the Cæsar was incapable of reigning. Transported from a prison to a throne, he possessed neither genius nor application, nor docility to compensate for the want of knowledge and experience. A temper naturally morose and violent, instead of being corrected, was soured, by solitude and adversity; the remembrance of what he had endured disposed him to retaliation rather than to sympathy; and the ungoverned sallies of his rage were often fatal to those who approached his person or were subject to his power.[17] Constantina, his wife, is described, not as a

Gallus declared Cæsar. A.D. 351, March 5 [15]

Cruelty and imprudence of Gallus

---

13 [Flavius Claudius Constantius.]

14 [Widow of Hannibalianus.]

15 For the promotion of Gallus, see Idatius [date 15th, not 5th March], Zosimus, and the two Victors. According to Philostorgius (l. iv. c. 1), Theophilus, an Arian bishop, was the witness, and, as it were, the guarantee, of this solemn engagement. He supported that character with generous firmness; but M. de Tillemont (Hist. des Empereurs, tom. iv. p. 1120) thinks it very improbable that an heretic should have possessed such virtue.

16 Julian was at first permitted to pursue his studies at Constantinople, but the reputation which he acquired soon excited the jealousy of Constantius; and the young prince was advised to withdraw himself to the less conspicuous scenes of Bithynia and Ionia.

17 See Julian ad S. P. Q. A. p. 271 [350], Jerom. in Chron., Aurelius Victor [Cæs. 42. 8], Eutropius, x. 14 [leg. 13]. I shall copy the words of Eutropius, who wrote his abridgment about fifteen years after the death of Gallus, when there was

woman, but as one of the infernal furies tormented with an insatiate thirst of human blood.[18]   Instead of employing her influence to insinuate the mild counsels of prudence and humanity, she exasperated the fierce passions of her husband ; and, as she retained the vanity, though she had renounced the gentleness, of her sex, a pearl necklace was esteemed an equivalent price for the murder of an innocent and virtuous nobleman.[19]   The cruelty of Gallus was sometimes displayed in the undissembled violence of popular or military executions ; and was sometimes disguised by the abuse of law, and the forms of judicial proceedings.   The private houses of Antioch and the places of public resort were besieged by spies and informers ; and the Cæsar himself, concealed in a plebeian habit, very frequently condescended to assume that odious character.   Every apartment of the palace was adorned with the instruments of death and torture, and a general consternation was diffused through the capital of Syria.   The Prince of the East, as if he had been conscious how much he had to fear, and how little he deserved to reign, selected for the objects of his resentment the provincials, accused of some imaginary treason, and his own courtiers, whom with more reason he suspected of incensing, by their secret correspondence, the timid and suspicious mind of Constantius.   But he forgot that he was depriving himself of his only support, the affection of the people ; whilst he furnished the malice of his enemies with the arms of truth, and afforded the emperor the fairest pretence of exacting the forfeit of his purple, and of his life.[20]

As long as the civil war suspended the fate of the Roman world, Constantius dissembled his knowledge of the weak and cruel administration to which his choice had subjected the East ; and the discovery of some assassins, secretly dispatched to

Massacre of the imperial ministers. A.D. 354

---

no longer any motive either to flatter or to depreciate his character. "Multis incivilibus gestis Gallus Cæsar . . . vir naturâ ferox [leg. ferus] et ad tyrannidem pronior, si suo jure imperare licuisset."

[18] Megæra quidem mortalis, inflammatrix sævientis assidua, humani cruoris avida, &c. Ammian. Marcellin. l. xiv. c. 1.   The sincerity of Ammianus would not suffer him to misrepresent facts or characters, but his love of *ambitious* ornaments frequently betrayed him into an unnatural vehemence of expression.

[19] His name was Clematius of Alexandria, and his only crime was a refusal to gratify the desires of his mother-in-law ; who solicited his death, because she had been disappointed of his love.   Ammian. l. xiv. c. 1.

[20] See in Ammianus (l. xiv. c. 1 [and c.] 7) a very ample detail of the cruelties of Gallus.   His brother Julian (p. 272 [351]) insinuates that a secret conspiracy had been formed against him; and Zosimus names (l. ii. p. 135 [c. 55]) the persons engaged in it ; a minister of considerable rank, and two obscure agents, who were resolved to make their fortune.

Antioch by the tyrant of Gaul, was employed to convince the
public, that the emperor and the Cæsar were united by the
same interest and pursued by the same enemies.[21]   But, when
the victory was decided in favour of Constantius, his dependent
colleague became less useful and less formidable.   Every circumstance of his conduct was severely and suspiciously examined, and it was privately resolved either to deprive Gallus
of the purple or at least to remove him from the indolent
luxury of Asia to the hardships and dangers of a German war.
The death of Theophilus, consular of the province of Syria, who
in a time of scarcity had been massacred by the people of
Antioch with the connivance, and almost at the instigation, of
Gallus, was justly resented, not only as an act of wanton
cruelty, but as a dangerous insult on the supreme majesty of
Constantius.   Two ministers of illustrious rank, Domitian, the
oriental præfect, and Montius, quæstor of the palace, were
empowered by a special commission to visit and reform the
state of the East.[22]   They were instructed to behave towards
Gallus with moderation and respect, and, by the gentlest arts
of persuasion, to engage him to comply with the invitation of
his brother and colleague.   The rashness of the præfect disappointed these prudent measures, and hastened his own ruin as
well as that of his enemy.   On his arrival at Antioch, Domitian
passed disdainfully before the gates of the palace, and, alleging
a slight pretence of indisposition, continued several days in
sullen retirement to prepare an inflammatory memorial, which
he transmitted to the Imperial court.   Yielding at length to
the pressing solicitations of Gallus, the præfect condescended
to take his seat in council ; but his first step was to signify a
concise and haughty mandate, importing that the Cæsar should
immediately repair to Italy, and threatening that he himself

---

[21] Zonaras, l. xiii. tom. ii. p. 17, 18 [c. 8].   The assassins had seduced a great
number of legionaries ; but their designs were discovered and revealed by an old
woman in whose cottage they lodged.

[22] [So Schiller (ii. p. 300) : " Constantius therefore sent the præf. præt. orientis
Domitian, and the minister of justice (quæstor palatii) Montius," &c.   But Ammian
only says that Domitian was commissioned (xiv. 7, 9) ; nothing is said of the sending
of Montius,—for the simple reason that he was not sent.   Neither Gibbon, nor
Schiller, nor Milman (who writes *ad hunc loc.*: " The commission seems to have
been granted to Domitian alone.   Montius interfered to support his authority "—
but does not explain how Montius came to be there) realized that Montius was the
quæstor palatii of the Cæsar, not of Constantius.   The Cæsars had a household
(like the Augusti) and palace officials ; thus we find Nebridius as qu. palat. of Julian
(Amm. xx. 9, 5).   These officials were probably appointed by the Augustus, as we
may infer from Julian's demand that Constantius should allow him to appoint all
officials in his own province except the prætorian præfect. Amm. xx. 8, 14.]

would punish his delay or hesitation by suspending the usual allowance of his household. The nephew and daughter of Constantine, who could ill brook the insolence of a subject, expressed their resentment by instantly delivering Domitian to the custody of a guard. The quarrel still admitted of some terms of accommodation. They were rendered impracticable by the imprudent behaviour of Montius, a statesman whose art and experience were frequently betrayed by the levity of his disposition.[23] The quæstor reproached Gallus in haughty language that a prince who was scarcely authorized to remove a municipal magistrate should presume to imprison a prætorian præfect; convoked a meeting of the civil and military officers; and required them, in the name of their sovereign, to defend the person and dignity of his representatives. By this rash declaration of war, the impatient temper of Gallus was provoked to embrace the most desperate counsels. He ordered his guards to stand to their arms, assembled the populace of Antioch, and recommended to their zeal the care of his safety and revenge. His commands were too fatally obeyed. They rudely seized the præfect and the quæstor, and, tying their legs together with ropes, they dragged them through the streets of the city, inflicted a thousand insults and a thousand wounds on these unhappy victims, and at last precipitated their mangled and lifeless bodies into the stream of the Orontes.[24]

After such a deed, whatever might have been the designs of Gallus, it was only in a field of battle that he could assert his innocence with any hope of success. But the mind of that prince was formed of an equal mixture of violence and weakness. Instead of assuming the title of Augustus, instead of employing in his defence the troops and treasures of the East, he suffered himself to be deceived by the affected tranquillity of Constantius, who, leaving him the vain pageantry of a court, imperceptibly recalled the veteran legions from the provinces of Asia. But, as it still appeared dangerous to arrest Gallus

Dangerous situation of Gallus

[23] In the present text of Ammianus, we read, *Asper* quidem sed ad *lenitatem* propensior; which forms a sentence of contradictory nonsense. With the aid of an old manuscript Valesius has rectified the first of these corruptions, and we perceive a ray of light in the substitution of the word *vafer*. If we venture to change *lenitatem* into *levitatem*, this alteration of a single letter will render the whole passage clear and consistent. [The best MS. (Vatican, ninth cent.) has *afen*, whence Kiessling has restored *Afer*, which Gardthausen accepts.]

[24] Instead of being obliged to collect scattered and imperfect hints from various sources, we now enter into the full stream of the history of Ammianus, and need only refer to the seventh and ninth chapters of his fourteenth book. Philostorgius, however (l. iii. c. 28), though partial to Gallus, should not be entirely overlooked.

in his capital, the slow and safer arts of dissimulation were practised with success. The frequent and pressing epistles of Constantius were filled with professions of confidence and friendship; exhorting the Cæsar to discharge the duties of his high station, to relieve his colleague from a part of the public cares, and to assist the West by his presence, his counsels and his arms. After so many reciprocal injuries, Gallus had reason to fear and to distrust. But he had neglected the opportunities of flight and of resistance; he was seduced by the flattering assurances of the tribune Scudilo, who, under the semblance of a rough soldier, disguised the most artful insinuation; and he depended on the credit of his wife Constantina, till the unseasonable death of that princess completed the ruin in which he had been involved by her impetuous passions.[25]

His disgrace and death.
A D 354, December

After a long delay, the reluctant Cæsar set forwards on his journey to the Imperial court. From Antioch to Hadrianople, he traversed the wide extent of his dominions with a numerous and stately train; and, as he laboured to conceal his apprehensions from the world, and perhaps from himself, he entertained the people of Constantinople with an exhibition of the games of the circus. The progress of the journey might, however, have warned him of the impending danger. In all the principal cities he was met by ministers of confidence, commissioned to seize the offices of government, to observe his motions, and to prevent the hasty sallies of his despair. The persons dispatched to secure the provinces which he left behind passed him with cold salutations or affected disdain; and the troops, whose station lay along the public road, were studiously removed on his approach, lest they might be tempted to offer their swords for the service of a civil war.[26] After Gallus had been permitted to repose himself a few days at Hadrianople he received a mandate, expressed in the most haughty and absolute style, that his splendid retinue should halt in that city, while the Cæsar himself, with only ten post-carriages, should hasten to the Imperial residence at Milan. In this rapid journey, the

[25] She had preceded her husband; but died of a fever on the road, at a little place in Bitnvnia, called Cœnum Gallicanum [Cœni Gallicani. There is a good, straightforward narrative of the episode of Gallus in Vita Artemü, Act. Sct., Oct. 20].

[26] The Thebæan legions, which were then quartered at Hadrianople, sent a deputation to Gallus, with a tender of their services. Ammian. l. xiv. c. 11 [15]. The Notitia (s. 6, 20, 38, edit. Labb.) mentions three several legions which bore the name of Thebæan. The zeal of M. de Voltaire, to destroy a despicable though celebrated legend, has tempted him on the slightest grounds to deny the existence of a Thebæan legion in the Roman armies. See Oeuvres de Voltaire, tom. xv. p. 414, quarto edition.

profound respect which was due to the brother and colleague
of Constantius was insensibly changed into rude familiarity;
and Gallus, who discovered in the countenances of the attendants that they already considered themselves as his guards,
and might soon be employed as his executioners, began to
accuse his fatal rashness, and to recollect with terror and remorse the conduct by which he had provoked his fate. The
dissimulation which had hitherto been preserved, was laid
aside at Poetovio in Pannonia. He was conducted to a palace [Pettau]
in the suburbs, where the general Barbatio, with a select band
of soldiers, who could neither be moved by pity nor corrupted
by rewards, expected the arrival of his illustrious victim. In
the close of the evening he was arrested, ignominiously stripped
of the ensigns of Cæsar, and hurried away to Pola in Istria, a
sequestered prison which had been so recently polluted with
royal blood. The horror which he felt was soon increased by
the appearance of his implacable enemy the eunuch Eusebius,
who, with the assistance of a notary and a tribune, proceeded
to interrogate him concerning the administration of the East.
The Cæsar sunk under the weight of shame and guilt, confessed
all the criminal actions, and all the treasonable designs, with
which he was charged; and, by imputing them to the advice of
his wife, exasperated the indignation of Constantius, who re-
viewed with partial prejudice the minutes of the examination.
The emperor was easily convinced that his own safety was incompatible with the life of his cousin: the sentence of death
was signed, dispatched, and executed; and the nephew of
Constantine, with his hands tied behind his back, was beheaded in prison like the vilest malefactor.[27] Those who are
inclined to palliate the cruelties of Constantius assert that he
soon relented and endeavoured to recall the bloody mandate:
but that the second messenger entrusted with the reprieve was
detained by the eunuchs, who dreaded the unforgiving temper
of Gallus, and were desirous of reuniting to *their* empire the
wealthy provinces of the East.[28]

Besides the reigning emperor, Julian alone survived, of all The danger
and escape
of Julian

[27] See the complete narrative of the journey and death of Gallus in Ammianus,
l. 14, c. 11. Julian complains that his brother was put to death without a trial;
attempts to justify, or at least to excuse, the cruel revenge which he had inflicted
on his enemies; but seems at last to acknowledge that he might justly have been
deprived of the purple.
[28] Philostorgius, l. iv. c. 1. Zonaras, l. xiii. tom. ii. p. 19 [c. 9]. But the former
was partial towards an Arian monarch, and the latter transcribed, without choice
or criticism, whatever he found in the writings of the ancients.

the numerous posterity of Constantius Chlorus. The misfortune of his royal birth involved him in the disgrace of Gallus. From [End of A.D. 354] his retirement in the happy country of Ionia, he was conveyed under a strong guard to the court of Milan ; where he languished [to June, A.D. 355] above seven months, in the continual apprehension of suffering the same ignominious death which was daily inflicted, almost before his eyes, on the friends and adherents of his persecuted family. His looks, his gestures, his silence, were scrutinized with malignant curiosity, and he was perpetually assaulted by enemies whom he had never offended, and by arts to which he was a stranger.[29] But, in the school of adversity, Julian insensibly acquired the virtues of firmness and discretion. He defended his honour, as well as his life, against the ensnaring subtleties of the eunuchs, who endeavoured to extort some declaration of his sentiments ; and, whilst he cautiously suppressed his grief and resentment, he nobly disdained to flatter the tyrant by any seeming approbation of his brother's murder. Julian most devoutly ascribes his miraculous deliverance to the protection of the gods, who had exempted his innocence from the sentence of destruction pronounced by their justice against the impious house of Constantine.[30] As the most effectual instrument of their providence, he gratefully acknowledges the steady and generous friendship of the empress Eusebia,[31] a woman of beauty and merit, who, by the ascendant which she had gained over the mind of her husband, counterbalanced, in some measure, the powerful conspiracy of the eunuchs. By the intercession of his patroness, Julian was admitted into the Imperial presence ; he pleaded his cause with a decent freedom, he was heard with favour ; and, notwithstanding the efforts of his enemies, who urged the danger of sparing an avenger of the blood of Gallus, the milder sentiment of Eusebia prevailed in the council. But the effects of a second interview were

[29] See Ammianus Marcellin. l. xv. c. 1, 3, 8.   Julian himself, in his epistle to the Athenians, draws a very lively and just picture of his own danger, and of his sentiments.   He shews, however, a tendency to exaggerate his sufferings, by insinuating, though in obscure terms, that they lasted above a year ; a period which cannot be reconciled with the truth of chronology.

[30] Julian has worked the crimes and misfortunes of the family of Constantine into an allegorical fable, which is happily conceived and agreeably related.   It forms the conclusion of the seventh Oration, from whence it has been detached and translated by the Abbé de la Blétérie, Vie de Jovien, tom. ii. p. 385-408.

[31] She was a native of Thessalonica in Macedonia, of a noble family, and the daughter as well as sister of consuls.   Her marriage with the emperor may be placed in the year 352 [or beginning of 353].   In a divided age the historians of all parties agree in her praises.   See their testimonies collected by Tillemont, Hist. des Empereurs, tom. iv. p. 750-754.

dreaded by the eunuchs; and Julian was advised to withdraw
for a while into the neighbourhood of Milan, till the emperor He is sent to
thought proper to assign the city of Athens for the place of Athens. A.D. 355,
his honourable exile.   As he had discovered from his earliest May [at Athens, July
youth a propensity, or rather passion, for the language, the to October]
manners, the learning, and the religion of the Greeks, he
obeyed with pleasure an order so agreeable to his wishes.   Far
from the tumult of arms and the treachery of courts, he spent
six months amidst the groves of the academy, in a free intercourse with the philosophers of the age, who studied to cultivate
the genius, to encourage the vanity, and to inflame the devotion, of their royal pupil.   Their labours were not unsuccessful; and Julian inviolably preserved for Athens that tender
regard which seldom fails to arise in a liberal mind from the
recollection of the place where it has discovered and exercised
its growing powers.   The gentleness and affability of manners,
which his temper suggested and his situation imposed, insensibly
engaged the affections of the strangers, as well as citizens, with
whom he conversed.   Some of his fellow-students might perhaps
examine his behaviour with an eye of prejudice and aversion;
but Julian established, in the schools of Athens, a general prepossession in favour of his virtues and talents, which was soon
diffused over the Roman world.[32]

Whilst his hours were passed in studious retirement, the Recalled to Milan
empress, resolute to achieve the generous design which she had
undertaken, was not unmindful of the care of his fortune.   The
death of the late Cæsar had left Constantius invested with the
sole command, and oppressed by the accumulated weight, of a
mighty empire.   Before the wounds of civil discord could be
healed, the provinces of Gaul were overwhelmed by a deluge of
Barbarians.   The Sarmatians no longer respected the barrier of
the Danube.   The impunity of rapine had increased the boldness and numbers of the wild Isaurians: those robbers descended
from their craggy mountains to ravage the adjacent country,
and had even presumed, though without success, to besiege the
important city of Seleucia, which was defended by a garrison of

[32] Libanius and Gregory Nazianzen have exhausted the arts as well as the powers
of their eloquence, to represent Julian as the first of heroes, or the worst of tyrants.
Gregory was his fellow-student at Athens; and the symptoms, which he so
tragically describes, of the future wickedness of the apostate amount only to some
bodily imperfections and to some peculiarities in his speech and manner.   He protests, however, that he *then* foresaw and foretold the calamities of the church and
state (Greg. Nazianzen, Orat. iv. p. 121, 122).   [See Libanius, *Epitaphios*, 526
sqq., ed. Reiske.]

three Roman legions. Above all, the Persian monarch, elated by victory, again threatened the peace of Asia, and the presence of the emperor was indispensably required both in the West and in the East. For the first time, Constantius sincerely acknowledged that his single strength was unequal to such an extent of care and of dominion.[33] Insensible to the voice of flattery, which assured him that his all-powerful virtue and celestial fortune would still continue to triumph over every obstacle, he listened with complacency to the advice of Eusebia, which gratified his indolence, without offending his suspicious pride. As she perceived that the remembrance of Gallus dwelt on the emperor's mind, she artfully turned his attention to the opposite characters of the two brothers, which from their infancy had been compared to those of Domitian and of Titus.[34] She accustomed her husband to consider Julian as a youth of a mild unambitious disposition, whose allegiance and gratitude might be secured by the gift of the purple, and who was qualified to fill, with honour, a subordinate station, without aspiring to dispute the commands, or to shade the glories, of his sovereign and benefactor. After an obstinate, though secret, struggle, the opposition of the favourite eunuchs submitted to the ascendency of the empress; and it was resolved that Julian, after celebrating his nuptials with Helena, sister of Constantius, should be appointed, with the title of Cæsar, to reign over the countries beyond the Alps.[35]

Although the order which recalled him to court was probably accompanied by some intimation of his approaching greatness, he appeals to the people of Athens to witness his tears of undissembled sorrow, when he was reluctantly torn away from his beloved retirement.[36] He trembled for his life, for his fame, and even for his virtue; and his sole confidence was derived from the persuasion that Minerva inspired all his actions, and that he was protected by an invisible guard of angels, whom for that purpose she had borrowed from the Sun and Moon.

---

[33] Succumbere tot necessitatibus tamque crebris unum se, quod nunquam fecerat, aperte demonstrans. Ammian. l. xv. c. 8 [2]. He then expresses, in their own words, the flattering assurances of the courtiers.

[34] Tantum a temperatis moribus Juliani differens fratris, quantum inter Vespasiani filios fuit Domitianum et Titum. Amm. l. xiv. c. 11 [28]. The circumstances and education of the two brothers were so nearly the same as to afford a strong example of the innate difference of characters.

[35] Ammianus, l. xv. c. 8. Zosimus, l. iii. p. 137, 138 [2].

[36] Julian. ad S. P. Q. A. p. 275, 276 [354-5]. Libanius, Orat. x. p. 268. Julian did not yield till the gods had signified their will by repeated visions and omens. His piety then forbade him to resist.

He approached with horror the palace of Milan; nor could the ingenuous youth conceal his indignation, when he found himself accosted with false and servile respect by the assassins of his family. Eusebia, rejoicing in the success of her benevolent schemes, embraced him with the tenderness of a sister; and endeavoured, by the most soothing caresses, to dispel his terrors and reconcile him to his fortune. But the ceremony of shaving his beard, and his awkward demeanour, when he first exchanged the cloak of a Greek philosopher for the military habit of a Roman prince, amused, during a few days, the levity of the imperial court.[37]

The emperors of the age of Constantine no longer deigned to consult with the senate in the choice of a colleague; but they were anxious that their nomination should be ratified by the consent of the army. On this solemn occasion, the guards, with the other troops whose stations were in the neighbourhood of Milan, appeared under arms; and Constantius ascended his lofty tribunal, holding by the hand his cousin Julian, who entered the same day into the twenty-fifth year of his age.[38] In a studied speech, conceived and delivered with dignity, the emperor represented the various dangers which threatened the prosperity of the republic, the necessity of naming a Cæsar for the administration of the West, and his own intention, if it was agreeable to their wishes, of rewarding with the honours of the purple the promising virtues of the nephew of Constantine. The approbation of the soldiers was testified by a respectful murmur: they gazed on the manly countenance of Julian, and observed with pleasure that the fire which sparkled in his eyes was tempered by a modest blush, on being thus exposed, for the first time, to the public view of mankind. As soon as the ceremony of his investiture had been performed, Constantius addressed him with the tone of authority which his superior age and station permitted him to assume; and, exhorting the new Cæsar to deserve, by heroic deeds, that sacred and immortal name, the emperor gave his colleague the strongest assurances of a friendship which should never be impaired by time, nor interrupted by their separation into the most distant climates. As soon as the speech was ended, the troops, as a

[37] Julian himself relates (p. 274 [353]), with some humour, the circumstances of his own metamorphosis, his downcast looks, and his perplexity at being thus suddenly transported into a new world, where every object appeared strange and hostile.

[38] See Ammian. Marcellin. l. xv. c. 8. Zosimus, l. iii. p. 139 [1, 2]. Aurelius Victor [Cæs. 42, 16]. Victor Junior in Epitom. [42, 12]. Eutrop. x. 14.

token of applause, clashed their shields against their knees;[39] while the officers who surrounded the tribunal expressed, with decent reserve, their sense of the merits of the representative of Constantius.

The two princes returned to the palace in the same chariot; and, during the slow procession, Julian repeated to himself a verse of his favourite Homer, which he might equally apply to his fortune and to his fears.[40] The four-and-twenty days which the Cæsar spent at Milan after his investiture, and the first months of his Gallic reign, were devoted to a splendid but severe captivity; nor could the acquisition of honour compensate for the loss of freedom.[41] His steps were watched, his correspondence was intercepted; and he was obliged, by prudence, to decline the visits of his most intimate friends. Of his former domestics, four only were permitted to attend him; two pages, his physician, and his librarian; the last of whom was employed in the care of a valuable collection of books, the gift of the empress, who studied the inclinations as well as the interest of her friend. In the room of these faithful servants, an household was formed, such indeed as became the dignity of a Cæsar; but it was filled with a crowd of slaves, destitute and perhaps incapable of any attachment for their new master, to whom, for the most part, they were either unknown or suspected. His want of experience might require the assistance of a wise council; but the minute instructions which regulated the service of his table, and the distribution of his hours, were adapted to a youth still under the discipline of his preceptors, rather than to the situation of a prince entrusted with the conduct of an important war. If he aspired to deserve the esteem of his subjects, he was checked by the fear of dis-

---

[39] Militares omnes horrendo fragore scuta genibus illidentes; quod est prosperitatis indicium plenum; nam contra cum hastis clypei feriuntur, iræ documentum est et doloris. . . . Ammianus [xv. 8, 16] adds, with a nice distinction, Eumque ut potiori reverentia servaretur, nec supra modum laudabant nec infra quam decebat.

[40] ἔλλαβε πορφύρεος θάνατος καὶ μοῖρα κραταιή. The word *purple*, which Homer had used as a vague but common epithet for death, was applied by Julian to express, very aptly, the nature and object of his own apprehensions [Amm. xv. 8, 17].

[41] He represents in the most pathetic terms (p. 277 [357]) the distress of his new situation. The provision for his table was, however, so elegant and sumptuous that the young philosopher rejected it with disdain. Quum legeret libellum assidue, quem Constantius ut privignum ad studia mittens manû suâ conscripserat, præclicenter disponens quid in convivio Cæsaris impendi deberet, phasianum et vulvam et sumen exigi vetuit et inferri. Ammian. Marcellin. l. xvi. c. 5.

pleasing his sovereign; and even the fruits of his marriage-bed were blasted by the jealous artifices of Eusebia [42] herself, who, on this occasion alone, seems to have been unmindful of the tenderness of her sex and the generosity of her character. The memory of his father and of his brothers reminded Julian of his own danger, and his apprehensions were increased by the recent and unworthy fate of Sylvanus. In the summer which preceded his own elevation, that general had been chosen to deliver Gaul from the tyranny of the Barbarians; but Sylvanus soon discovered that he had left his most dangerous enemies in the Imperial court. A dexterous informer, countenanced by several of the principal ministers, procured from him some recommendatory letters; and erazing the whole of the contents, except the signature, filled up the vacant parchment with matters of high and treasonable import. By the industry and courage of his friends, the fraud was however detected, and in a great council of the civil and military officers, held in the presence of the emperor himself, the innocence of Sylvanus was publicly acknowledged. But the discovery came too late; the report of the calumny and the hasty seizure of his estate had already provoked the indignant chief to the rebellion of which he was so unjustly accused. He assumed the purple at his head-quarters of Cologne, and his active powers appeared to menace Italy with an invasion, and Milan with a siege. In this emergency, Ursicinus, a general of equal rank, regained, by an act of treachery, the favour which he had lost by his eminent services in the East. Exasperated, as he might speciously allege, by injuries of a similar nature, he hastened with a few followers to join the standard, and to betray the confidence, of his too credulous friend. After a reign of only twenty-eight days, Sylvanus was assassinated: the soldiers who, without any criminal intention, had blindly followed the example of their leader, immediately returned to their allegiance; and the flatterers of Constantius celebrated the wisdom and felicity of

[42] If we recollect that Constantine, the father of Helena, died above eighteen years before in a mature old age, it will appear probable that the daughter, though a virgin, could not be very young at the time of her marriage. She was soon afterwards delivered of a son, who died immediately, quod obstetrix, corrupta mercede, mox natum præsecto plusquam convenerat umbilico necavit. She accompanied the emperor and empress in their journey to Rome, and the latter, quæsitum venenum bibere per fraudem illexit, ut quotiescunque concepisset, immaturum abjiceret partum. Ammian. l. xvi. c. 10 [18]. Our physicians will determine whether there exists such a poison. For my own part, I am inclined to hope that the public malignity imputed the effects of accident as the guilt of Eusebia. [The charge seems highly improbable.]

the monarch who had extinguished a civil war without the hazard of a battle.[43]

The protection of the Rhætian frontier, and the persecution of the Catholic Church, detained Constantius in Italy above eighteen months after the departure of Julian. Before the emperor returned into the East, he indulged his pride and curiosity in a visit to the ancient capital.[44] He proceeded from Milan to Rome along the Æmilian and Flaminian ways ; and, as soon as he approached within forty miles of the city, the march of a prince who had never vanquished a foreign enemy assumed the appearance of a triumphal procession. His splendid train was composed of all the ministers of luxury ; but in a time of profound peace, he was encompassed by the glittering arms of the numerous squadrons of his guards and cuirassiers. Their streaming banners of silk, embossed with gold and shaped in the form of dragons, waved round the person of the emperor. Constantius sat alone in a lofty car resplendent with gold and precious gems ; and, except when he bowed his head to pass under the gates of the cities, he affected a stately demeanour of inflexible and, as it might seem, of insensible gravity. The severe discipline of the Persian youth had been introduced by the eunuchs into the Imperial palace ; and such were the habits of patience which they had inculcated that, during a slow and sultry march, he was never seen to move his hand towards his face or to turn his eyes either to the right or to the left. He was received by the magistrates and senate of Rome ; and the emperor surveyed, with attention, the civil honours of the republic and the consular images of the noble families. The streets were lined with an innumerable multitude. Their repeated acclamations expressed their joy at beholding, after an absence of thirty-two years, the sacred person of their sovereign ; and Constantius himself expressed, with some pleasantry, his affected surprise that the human race should thus suddenly be collected on the same spot. The son of Constantine was lodged in the ancient palace of Augustus : he presided in the senate, harangued the people from the tribunal which Cicero had so often ascended, assisted with unusual courtesy at the games of the circus, and accepted the crowns of gold as well as the

[43] Ammianus (xv. 5) was perfectly well informed of the conduct and fate of Sylvanus. He himself was one of the few followers who attended Ursicinus in his dangerous enterprise.

[44] For the particulars of the visit of Constantius to Rome, see Ammianus, l. xvi c. 10. We have only to add that Themistius was appointed deputy from Constantinople, and that he composed his fourth Oration for this ceremony.

panegyrics which had been prepared for this ceremony by the deputies of the principal cities. His short visit of thirty days was employed in viewing the monuments of art and power which were scattered over the seven hills and the interjacent valleys. He admired the awful majesty of the capitol, the vast extent of the baths of Caracalla and Diocletian, the severe simplicity of the Pantheon, the massy greatness of the amphitheatre of Titus, the elegant architecture of the theatre of Pompey and the Temple of Peace, and, above all, the stately structure of the Forum and column of Trajan ; acknowledging that the voice of fame, so prone to invent and to magnify, had made an inadequate report of the metropolis of the world. The traveller, who has contemplated the ruins of ancient Rome, may conceive some imperfect idea of the sentiments which they must have inspired when they reared their heads in the splendour of unsullied beauty.

The satisfaction which Constantius had received from this *A new obelisk* journey excited him to the generous emulation of bestowing on the Romans some memorial of his own gratitude and munificence. His first idea was to imitate the equestrian and colossal statue which he had seen in the Forum of Trajan ; but, when he had maturely weighed the difficulties of the execution,[45] he chose rather to embellish the capital by the gift of an Egyptian obelisk. In a remote but polished age, which seems to have preceded the invention of alphabetical writing, a great number of these obelisks had been erected, in the cities of Thebes and Heliopolis, by the ancient sovereigns of Egypt, in a just confidence that the simplicity of their form and the hardness of their substance would resist the injuries of time and violence.[46] Several of these extraordinary columns had been transported to Rome by Augustus and his successors, as the most durable monuments of their power and victory ;[47] but there remained

[45] Hormisdas, a fugitive prince of Persia, observed to the emperor that, if he made such a horse, he must think of preparing a similar stable (the Forum of Trajan). Another saying of Hormisdas is recorded, " that one thing only had *displeased* him, to find that men died at Rome as well as elsewhere ". If we adopt his reading of the text of Ammianus (*displicuisse* instead of *placuisse*), we may consider it as a reproof of Roman vanity. The contrary sense would be that of a misanthrope. [There is no authority for *displ.*, a guess of Valesius.]

[46] When Germanicus visited the ancient monuments of Thebes, the eldest of the priests explained to him the meaning of these hieroglyphics. Tacit. Annal. ii. c. 60. But it seems probable that before the useful invention of an alphabet these natural or arbitrary signs were the common characters of the Egyptian nation. See Warburton's Divine Legation of Moses, vol. iii. p. 69-243.

[47] See Plin. Hist. Natur. l. xxxvi. c. 14, 15.

one obelisk which, from its size or sanctity, escaped for a long
time the rapacious vanity of the conquerors. It was designed
by Constantine to adorn his new city ;[48] and, after being removed by his order from the pedestal where it stood before the
Temple of the Sun at Heliopolis, was floated down the Nile to
Alexandria. The death of Constantine suspended the execution
of his purpose, and this obelisk was destined by his son to the
ancient capital of the empire. A vessel of uncommon strength
and capaciousness was provided to convey this enormous weight
of granite, at least an hundred and fifteen feet in length, from
the banks of the Nile to those of the Tiber. The obelisk of
Constantius was landed about three miles from the city, and
elevated by the efforts of art and labour, in the great Circus of
Rome.[49]

The Quadian
and Sarma-
tian war.
A.D. 357, 358,
359   The departure of Constantius from Rome was hastened by
the alarming intelligence of the distress and danger of the
Illyrian provinces. The distractions of civil war, and the irreparable loss which the Roman legions had sustained in the battle
of Mursa, exposed those countries, almost without defence, to
the light cavalry of the Barbarians ; and particularly to the
inroads of the Quadi, a fierce and powerful nation, who seem to
have exchanged the institutions of Germany for the arms and
military arts of their Sarmatian allies.[50] The garrisons of the
frontier were insufficient to check their progress ; and the
indolent monarch was at length compelled to assemble, from the

[48] Ammian. Marcellin. l. xvii. c. 4. He gives us a Greek interpretation of the
hieroglyphics, and his commentator Lindenbrogius adds a Latin inscription, which,
in twenty verses of the age of Constantius, contain a short history of the obelisk.
[The Greek interpretation of Hermapion given by Ammian cannot refer to the
obelisk transferred from Heliopolis by Constantius, as may be seen by comparing it
with Birch's translation of the hieroglyphics (see Parker's Twelve Egyptian
Obelisks). This obelisk was erected by Thothmes III., completed by Thothmes IV.
and restored by Ramses II. But the words of Ammian (qui autem notarum textus
obelisco incisus est ueteri quem uidemus in Circo) rather suggest, I think, the
obelisk of Augustus, which he had mentioned above. This obelisk, now in the
Piazza del Popolo, begun by Seti, was completed by Ramses ; and the στίχος δεύτερος
and στίχος τριτος of Hermapion (Amm. ib. 8, 19, 20) correspond sufficiently
closely to he " 2nd left column, south side," and the " left column, south side," in
Birch's translation (Parker, ib. p. 18). The whole question is passed over in Mr.
Parker's work.]

[49] See Donat. Roma Antiqua, l. iii. c. 14, l. iv. c. 12, and the learned, though
confused, Dissertation of Bargæus on Obelisks, inserted in the fourth volume of
Grævius's Roman Antiquities, p. 1897-1936. This Dissertation is dedicated to
Pope Sixtus V., who erected the obelisk of Constantius in the square before the
patriarchal church of St. John Lateran.

[50] The events of this Quadian and Sarmatian war are related by Ammianus, xvi.
10 ; xvii. 12, 13 ; xix. 11

extremities of his dominions, the flower of the Palatine troops,[51] to take the field in person, and to employ a whole campaign, with the preceding autumn and the ensuing spring, in the serious prosecution of the war. The emperor passed the Danube on a bridge of boats, cut in pieces all that encountered his march, penetrated into the heart of the country of the Quadi, and severely retaliated the calamities which they had inflicted on the Roman province. The dismayed Barbarians were soon reduced to sue for peace : they offered the restitution of his captive subjects as an atonement for the past, and the noblest hostages as a pledge of their future conduct. The generous courtesy which was shown to the first among their chieftains who implored the clemency of Constantius encouraged the more timid, or the more obstinate, to imitate their examples ; and the Imperial camp was crowded with the princes and ambassadors of the most distant tribes, who occupied the plains of the Lesser Poland, and who might have deemed themselves secure behind the lofty ridge of the Carpathian mountains. While Constantius gave laws to the Barbarians beyond the Danube, he distinguished with specious compassion the Sarmatian exiles who had been expelled from their native country by the rebellion of their slaves, and who formed a very considerable accession to the power of the Quadi. The emperor, embracing a generous but artful system of policy, released the Sarmatians from the bands of this humiliating dependence, and restored them, by a separate treaty, to the dignity of a nation united under the government of a king, the friend and ally of the republic. He declared his resolution of asserting the justice of their cause, and of securing the peace of the provinces by the extirpation, or at least the banishment, of the Limigantes, whose manners were still infected with the vices of their servile origin. The execution of this design was attended with more difficulty than glory. The territory of the Limigantes was protected against the Romans by the Danube, against the hostile Barbarians by the Theiss. The marshy lands which lay between those rivers, and were often covered by their inundations, formed an intricate wilderness, pervious only to the inhabitants, who were acquainted with its secret paths and inaccessible fortresses. On the approach of Constantius, the Limigantes tried the efficacy of prayers, of fraud, and of arms ; but he sternly rejected their supplications, defeated their rude stratagems, and repelled with skill and

---

[51] [Rather the Comitatenses. See above, p. 177.]

firmness the efforts of their irregular valour. One of their most warlike tribes, established in a small island towards the conflux of the Theiss and the Danube, consented to pass the river with the intention of surprising the emperor during the security of an amicable conference. They soon became the victims of the perfidy which they meditated. Encompassed on every side, trampled down by the cavalry, slaughtered by the swords of the legions, they disdained to ask for mercy; and with an undaunted countenance still grasped their weapons in the agonies of death. After this victory a considerable body of Romans was landed on the opposite banks of the Danube; the [Taifali] Taifalæ, a Gothic tribe engaged in the service of the empire, invaded the Limigantes on the side of the Theiss; and their former masters, the free Sarmatians, animated by hope and revenge, penetrated through the hilly country into the heart of their ancient possessions. A general conflagration revealed the huts of the Barbarians, which were seated in the depth of the wilderness; and the soldier fought with confidence on marshy ground, which it was dangerous for him to tread. In this extremity the bravest of the Limigantes were resolved to die in arms, rather than to yield: but the milder sentiment, enforced by the authority of their elders, at length prevailed; and the suppliant crowd, followed by their wives and children, repaired to the Imperial camp, to learn their fate from the mouth of the conqueror. After celebrating his own clemency, which was still inclined to pardon their repeated crimes and to spare the remnant of a guilty nation, Constantius assigned for the place of their exile a remote country, where they might enjoy a safe and honourable repose. The Limigantes obeyed with reluctance; but before they could reach, at least before they could occupy, their destined habitations, they returned to the banks of the Danube, exaggerating the hardships of their situation, and requesting, with fervent professions of fidelity, that the emperor would grant them an undisturbed settlement within the limits of the Roman provinces. Instead of consulting his own experience of their incurable perfidy, Constantius listened to his flatterers, who were ready to represent the honour and advantage of accepting a colony of soldiers, at a time when it was much easier to obtain the pecuniary contributions than the military service of the subjects of the empire. The Limigantes were permitted to pass the Danube; and the emperor gave audience to the multitude in a large plain near the modern [Acumincum Slankamen] city of Buda. They surrounded the tribunal, and seemed to hear with respect an oration full of mildness and dignity ; when one of the Barbarians, casting his shoe into the air, exclaimed with a loud voice, *Marha ! Marha !* a word of defiance, which was received as the signal of the tumult. They rushed with fury to seize the person of the emperor ; his royal throne and golden couch were pillaged by these rude hands ; but the faithful defence of his guards, who died at his feet, allowed him a moment to mount a fleet horse, and to escape from the confusion. The disgrace which had been incurred by a treacherous surprise was soon retrieved by the numbers and discipline of the Romans ; and the combat was only terminated by the extinction of the name and nation of the Limigantes. The free Sarmatians were reinstated in the possession of their ancient seats ; and, although Constantius distrusted the levity of their character, he entertained some hopes that a sense of gratitude might influence their future conduct. He had remarked the lofty stature and obsequious demeanour of Zizais, one of the noblest of their chiefs. He conferred on him the title of King ; and Zizais proved that he was not unworthy to reign by a sincere and lasting attachment to the interest of his benefactor, who, after this splendid success, received the name of *Sarmaticus* from the acclamations of his victorious army.[52]

While the Roman emperor and the Persian monarch, at the distance of three thousand miles, defended their extreme limits against the Barbarians of the Danube and of the Oxus, their intermediate frontier experienced the vicissitudes of a languid war, and a precarious truce. Two of the eastern ministers of Constantius, the prætorian præfect Musonian, whose abilities were disgraced by the want of truth and integrity, and Cassian, duke of Mesopotamia, a hardy and veteran soldier, opened a secret negotiation with the satrap Tamsapor.[53] These overtures of peace, translated into the servile and flattering language of Asia, were transmitted to the camp of the Great King ; who resolved to signify, by an ambassador, the terms which he was inclined to grant to the suppliant Romans. Narses, whom he invested with that character, was honourably received in his passage through Antioch and Constantinople : he reached Sirmium after a long journey, and, at his first audience, respectfully unfolded the silken veil which covered the haughty epistle

The Persian negotiation. A.D. 358

---

[52] Genti Sarmatarum magno decore considens apud eos regem dedit. Aurelius Victor [Cæs. 42]. In a pompous oration pronounced by Constantius himself, he expatiates on his own exploits with much vanity, and some truth.

[53] Ammian. xvi. 9.

of his sovereign. Sapor, King of Kings, and Brother of the Sun and Moon (such were the lofty titles affected by oriental vanity), expressed his satisfaction that his brother, Constantius Cæsar, had been taught wisdom by adversity. As the lawful successor of Darius Hystaspes, Sapor asserted that the river Strymon in Macedonia was the true and ancient boundary of his empire ; declaring, however, that, as an evidence of his moderation, he would content himself with the provinces of Armenia and Mesopotamia, which had been fraudulently extorted from his ancestors. He alleged that, without the restitution of these disputed countries, it was impossible to establish any treaty on a solid and permanent basis ; and he arrogantly threatened that, if his ambassador returned in vain, he was prepared to take the field in the spring, and to support the justice of his cause by the strength of his invincible arms. Narses, who was endowed with the most polite and amiable manners, endeavoured, as far as was consistent with his duty, to soften the harshness of the message.[54] Both the style and the substance were maturely weighed in the Imperial council, and he was dismissed with the following answer : " Constantius had a right to disclaim the officiousness of his ministers, who had acted without any specific orders from the throne : he was not, however, averse to an equal and honourable treaty ; but it was highly indecent, as well as absurd, to propose to the sole and victorious emperor of the Roman world the same conditions of peace which he had indignantly rejected at the time when his power was contracted within the narrow limits of the East : the chance of arms was uncertain ; and Sapor should recollect that, if the Romans had sometimes been vanquished in battle, they had almost always been successful in the event of the war ". A few days after the departure of Narses, three ambassadors were sent to the court of Sapor, who was already returned from the Scythian expedition to his ordinary residence of Ctesiphon. A count, a notary, and a sophist had been selected for this important commission ; and Constantius, who was secretly anxious for the conclusion of the peace, entertained some hopes that the dignity of the first of these ministers, the dexterity of the second, and the rhetoric of the third [55] would persuade the

---

[54] Ammianus (xvii. 5) transcribes the haughty letter. Themistius (Orat. iv. p. 57, edit. Petav.) takes notice of the silk covering. Idatius and Zonaras mention the journey of the ambassador ; and Peter the Patrician (in Excerpt. Legat. p. 28 [fr. 17, in F. H. G., iv.]) has informed us of his conciliating behaviour.

[55] Ammianus, xvii. 5, and Valesius ad loc. The sophist, or philosopher (in that age these words were almost synonymous), was Eustathius the Cappadocian,

Persian monarch to abate the rigour of his demands. But the
progress of their negotiation was opposed and defeated by the
hostile arts of Antoninus,[56] a Roman subject of Syria, who had
fled from the oppression, and was admitted into the councils of
Sapor, and even to the royal table, where, according to the
custom of the Persians, the most important business was frequently discussed.[57] The dexterous fugitive promoted his
interest by the same conduct which gratified his revenge. He
incessantly urged the ambition of his new master to embrace
the favourable opportunity when the bravest of the Palatine
troops were employed with the emperor in a distant war on the
Danube. He pressed Sapor to invade the exhausted and defenceless provinces of the East, with the numerous armies of Persia,
now fortified by the alliance and accession of the fiercest Barbarians. The ambassadors of Rome retired without success,
and a second embassy of a still more honourable rank was
detained in strict confinement, and threatened either with death
or exile.

The military nistorian,[58] who was himself dispatched to observe the army of the Persians, as they were preparing to construct a bridge of boats over the Tigris, beheld from an eminence the plain of Assyria, as far as the edge of the horizon,
covered with men, with horses, and with arms. Sapor appeared
in the front, conspicuous by the splendour of his purple. On
his left hand, the place of honour among the Orientals, Grumbates, king of the Chionites,[59] displayed the stern countenance
of an aged and renowned warrior. The monarch had reserved
a similar place on his right hand for the king of the Albanians, who
led his independent tribes from the shores of the Caspian. The
satraps and generals were distributed according to their several
ranks, and the whole army, besides the numerous train of oriental
luxury, consisted of more than one hundred thousand effective

(marginal note:) Invasion of Mesopotamia by Sapor. A.D. 359

the disciple of Jamblichus, and the friend of St. Basil. Eunapius (in vit. Ædesii,
p. 44-47) fondly attributes to this philosophic ambassador the glory of enchanting
the Barbarian king by the persuasive charms of reason and eloquence. See
Tillemont, Hist. des Empereurs, tom. iv. p. 828, 1132.

[56] Ammian. xviii. 5, 6, 8. The decent and respectful behaviour of Antoninus
towards the Roman general sets him in a very interesting light: and Ammianus
himself speaks of the traitor with some compassion and esteem.

[57] This circumstance, as it is noticed by Ammianus, serves to prove the veracity
of Herodotus (l. i. c. 133), and the permanency of the Persian manners. In every
age the Persians have been addicted to intemperance, and the wines of Shiraz
have triumphed over the law of Mahomet. Brisson de Regno Pers. l. ii. p. 462-
472, and Chardin, Voyages en Perse, tom. iii. p. 90.

[58] Ammian. l. xviii. 6, 7, 8, 10.

[59] [An uncertain people: some have sought to identify them with the Huns.]

men, inured to fatigue, and selected from the bravest nations of
Asia. The Roman deserter, who in some measure guided the
councils of Sapor, had prudently advised that, instead of wasting
the summer in tedious and difficult sieges, he should march
directly to the Euphrates, and press forwards without delay to
seize the feeble and wealthy metropolis of Syria. But the
Persians were no sooner advanced into the plains of Mesopotamia than they discovered that every precaution had been used
which could retard their progress or defeat their design. The
inhabitants, with their cattle, were secured in places of strength,
the green forage throughout the country was set on fire, the
fords of the river were fortified by sharp stakes; military engines
were planted on the opposite banks, and a seasonable swell of
the waters of the Euphrates deterred the Barbarians from
attempting the ordinary passage of the bridge of Thapsacus.
Their skilful guide, changing his plan of operations, then conducted the army by a longer circuit, but through a fertile territory, towards the head of the Euphrates, where the infant
river is reduced to a shallow and accessible stream. Sapor overlooked, with prudent disdain, the strength of Nisibis; but, as he
passed under the walls of Amida, he resolved to try whether the
majesty of his presence would not awe the garrison into immediate submission. The sacrilegious insult of a random dart, which
glanced against the royal tiara, convinced him of his error; and
the indignant monarch listened with impatience to the advice
of his ministers, who conjured him not to sacrifice the success of his
ambition to the gratification of his resentment. The following
day Grumbates advanced towards the gates with a select body
of troops, and required the instant surrender of the city as the
only atonement which could be accepted for such an act of rashness and insolence. His proposals were answered by a general
discharge, and his only son, a beautiful and valiant youth, was
pierced through the heart by a javelin, shot from one of the
balistæ. The funeral of the prince of the Chionites was celebrated according to the rites of his country; and the grief of his
aged father was alleviated by the solemn promise of Sapor that
the guilty city of Amida should serve as a funeral pile to expiate
the death, and to perpetuate the memory, of his son.

Siege of
Amida

  The ancient city of Amid or Amida,[60] which sometimes assumes

[60] For the description of Amida, see d'Herbelot, Bibliothèque Orientale, p. 108;
Histoire de Timur Bec, par Cherefeddin Ali, l. iii. c. 41; Ahmed Arabsiades, tom.
i. p. 331, c. 43; Voyages de Tavernier, tom. i. p. 301; Voyages d'Otter, tom. ii.
p. 273; and Voyages de Niebuhr, tom. ii. p. 324-328. The last of these travellers,
a learned and accurate Dane, has given a plan of Amida, which illustrates the
operations of the siege.

the provincial appellation of Diarbekir,[61] is advantageously situate in a fertile plain, watered by the natural and artificial channels of the Tigris, of which the least inconsiderable stream bends in a semicircular form round the eastern part of the city. The emperor Constantius had recently conferred on Amida the honour of his own name, and the additional fortifications of strong walls and lofty towers. It was provided with an arsenal of military engines, and the ordinary garrison had been reinforced to the amount of seven legions, when the place was invested by the arms of Sapor.[62] His first and most sanguine hopes depended on the success of a general assault. To the several nations which followed his standard their respective posts were assigned; the south to the Vertæ, the north to the Albanians, the east to the Chionites, inflamed with grief and indignation; the west to the Segestans, the bravest of his warriors, who covered their front with a formidable line of Indian elephants.[63] The Persians, on every side, supported their efforts, and animated their courage; and the monarch himself, careless of his rank and safety, displayed, in the prosecution of the siege, the ardour of a youthful soldier. After an obstinate combat the Barbarians were repulsed; they incessantly returned to the charge; they were again driven back with a dreadful slaughter, and two rebel legions of Gauls, who had been banished into the East, signalized their undisciplined courage by a nocturnal sally into the heart of the Persian camp. In one of the fiercest of these repeated assaults, Amida was betrayed by the treachery of a deserter, who indicated to the Barbarians a secret and neglected staircase, scooped out of the rock that hangs over the stream of the Tigris. Seventy chosen archers of the royal guard ascended in silence to the third story of a lofty tower which commanded the precipice; they elevated on high

[61] Diarbekir, which is styled Amid, or Kara-Amid, in the public writings of the Turks, contains above 16,000 houses, and is the residence of a pasha with three tails. The epithet of *Kara* is derived from the *blackness* of the stone which composes the strong and ancient wall of Amida.

[62] The operations of the siege of Amida are very minutely described by Ammianus (xix. 1-9), who acted an honourable part in the defence, and escaped with difficulty when the city was stormed by the Persians.

[63] Of these four nations, the Albanians are too well known to require any description. The Segestans inhabited a large and level country, which still preserves their name, to the south of Khorasan, and the west of Hindostan (see Geographia Nubiensis, p. 133, and d'Herbelot, Bibliothèque Orientale, p. 797). Notwithstanding the boasted victory of Bahram (vol. i. p. 410), the Segestans, above fourscore years afterwards, appear as an independent nation, the ally of Persia. We are ignorant of the situation of the Vertæ and Chionites, but I am inclined to place them (at least the latter) towards the confines of India and Scythia. See Ammian. xvi. 9.

the Persian banner, the signal of confidence to the assailants and of dismay to the besieged ; and, if this devoted band could have maintained their post a few minutes longer, the reduction of the place might have been purchased by the sacrifice of their lives. After Sapor had tried, without success, the efficacy of force and of stratagem, he had recourse to the slower but more certain operations of a regular siege, in the conduct of which he was instructed by the skill of the Roman deserters. The trenches were opened at a convenient distance, and the troops destined for that service advanced under the portable cover of strong hurdles, to fill up the ditch and undermine the foundations of the walls. Wooden towers were at the same time constructed, and moved forwards on wheels, till the soldiers, who were provided with every species of missile weapons, could engage almost on level ground with the troops who defended the rampart. Every mode of resistance which art could suggest, or courage could execute, was employed in the defence of Amida, and the works of Sapor were more than once destroyed by the fire of the Romans. But the resources of a besieged city may be exhausted. The Persians repaired their losses, and pushed their approaches ; a large breach was made by the battering-ram,[63a] and the strength of the garrison, wasted by the sword and by disease, yielded to the fury of the assault. The soldiers, the citizens, their wives, their children, all who had not time to escape through the opposite gate, were involved by the conquerors in a promiscuous massacre.

Of Singara, &c. A.D. 360

But the ruin of Amida was the safety of the Roman provinces. As soon as the first transports of victory had subsided, Sapor was at leisure to reflect that, to chastise a disobedient city, he had lost the flower of his troops, and the most favourable season for conquest.[64] Thirty thousand of his veterans had fallen under

[63a] [Gibbon has curiously transferred to Amida (which was taken by the crumbling of a mound) the battering-ram which decided the fate of Singara. Cp. Amm. 19, 8, 2, with 20, 6, 5.]

[64] Ammianus has marked the chronology of this year by three signs, which do not perfectly coincide with each other, or with the series of the history. 1. The corn was ripe when Sapor invaded Mesopotamia ; "Cum jam stipulâ flavente turgerent ; " a circumstance which, in the latitude of Aleppo, would naturally refer us to the month of April or May. See Harmer's Observations on Scripture, vol. i. p. 41. Shaw's Travels, p. 335, edit. 4to. 2. The progress of Sapor was checked by the overflowing of the Euphrates, which generally happens in July and August. Plin. Hist. Nat. v. 21. Viaggi di Pietro della Valle, tom. i. p. 696. 3. When Sapor had taken Amida, after a siege of seventy-three days, the autumn was far advanced. "Autumno præcipiti hædorumque improbo sidere exorto." To reconcile these apparent contradictions, we must allow for some delay in the Persian king, some inaccuracy in the historian, and some disorder in the seasons. [But see Clinton, Fasti Romani, i. p. 442; we may suppose that Sapor crossed the Tigris early in May, spent two months in Mesopotamia, began siege c. July 27; Amida taken c. Oct. 6-7.]

the walls of Amida during the continuance of a siege which lasted seventy-three days; and the disappointed monarch returned to his capital with affected triumph and secret mortification. It was more than probable that the inconstancy of his Barbarian allies was tempted to relinquish a war in which they had encountered such unexpected difficulties; and that the aged king of the Chionites, satiated with revenge, turned away with horror from a scene of action where he had been deprived of the hope of his family and nation. The strength as well as spirit of the army with which Sapor took the field in the ensuing spring was no longer equal to the unbounded views of his ambition. Instead of aspiring to the conquest of the East, he was obliged to content himself with the reduction of two fortified cities of Mesopotamia, Singara and Bezabde;[65] the one situate in the midst of a sandy desert, the other in a small peninsula, surrounded almost on every side by the deep and rapid stream of the Tigris. Five Roman legions, of the diminutive size to which they had been reduced in the age of Constantine, were made prisoners, and sent into remote captivity on the extreme confines of Persia. After dismantling the walls of Singara, the conqueror abandoned that solitary and sequestered place; but he carefully restored the fortifications of Bezabde, and fixed in that important post a garrison or colony of veterans, amply supplied with every means of defence, and animated by high sentiments of honour and fidelity. Towards the close of the campaign, the arms of Sapor incurred some disgrace by an unsuccessful enterprise against Virtha, or Tecrit, a strong, or as it was universally esteemed till the age of Tamerlane, an impregnable fortress of the independent Arabs.[66]

[Bezabde = Jeziret-ibn-Omar]

The defence of the East against the arms of Sapor required, and would have exercised, the abilities of the most consummate general: and it seemed fortunate for the state that it was the actual province of the brave Ursicinus, who alone deserved the confidence of the soldiers and people. In the hour of danger, Ursicinus[67] was removed from his station by the intrigues of

Conduct of the Romans

---

[65] The account of these sieges is given by Ammianus, xx. 6, 7.

[66] For the identity of Virtha and Tecrit, see d'Anville, Géographie Ancienne, tom. ii. p. 201. For the siege of that castle by Timur Bec, or Tamerlane, see Cherefeddin, l. iii. c. 33. The Persian biographer exaggerates the merit and difficulty of this exploit, which delivered the caravans of Bagdad from a formidable gang of robbers. [The identity of Virta is uncertain.]

[67] Ammianus (xviii. 5, 6, xix. 3, xx. 2) represents the merit and disgrace of Ursicinus with that faithful attention which a soldier owed to his general. Some partiality may be suspected, yet the whole account is consistent and probable.

the eunuchs; and the military command of the East was bestowed, by the same influence, on Sabinian, a wealthy and
subtle veteran, who had attained the infirmities, without acquiring the experience, of age. By a second order, which issued
from the same jealous and inconstant counsels, Ursicinus was
again dispatched to the frontier of Mesopotamia, and condemned
to sustain the labours of a war, the honours of which had been
transferred to his unworthy rival. Sabinian fixed his indolent
station under the walls of Edessa; and, while he amused himself
with the idle parade of military exercise, and moved to the sound
of flutes in the Pyrrhic dance, the public defence was abandoned
to the boldness and diligence of the former general of the East.
But, whenever Ursicinus recommended any vigorous plan of
operations; when he proposed, at the head of a light and active
army, to wheel round the foot of the mountains, to intercept the
convoys of the enemy, to harass the wide extent of the Persian
lines, and to relieve the distress of Amida; the timid and en-
vious commander alleged that he was restrained by his positive
orders from endangering the safety of the troops. Amida was
at length taken; its bravest defenders, who had escaped the
sword of the Barbarians, died in the Roman camp by the hand
of the executioner; and Ursicinus himself, after supporting the
disgrace of a partial inquiry, was punished for the misconduct
of Sabinian by the loss of his military rank. But Constantius
soon experienced the truth of the prediction which honest
indignation had extorted from his injured lieutenant, that, as
long as such maxims of government were suffered to prevail, the
emperor himself would find it no easy task to defend his eastern
dominions from the invasion of a foreign enemy. When he had
subdued or pacified the Barbarians of the Danube, Constantius
proceeded by slow marches into the East; and, after he had
wept over the smoking ruins of Amida, he formed, with a
powerful army, the siege of Bezabde. The walls were shaken
by the reiterated efforts of the most enormous of the battering-
rams: the town was reduced to the last extremity; but it was
still defended by the patient and intrepid valour of the garrison,
till the approach of the rainy season obliged the emperor to
[A.D. 360-1] raise the siege, and ingloriously to retreat into his winter
quarters at Antioch.[68] The pride of Constantius and the in-

---

[68] Ammian. xx. 11. Omisso vano incepto, hiematurus Antiochiæ redit in
Syriam ærumnosam, perpessus et ulcerum sed et atrocia, diuque deflenda. It is
thus that James Gronovius has restored an obscure passage; and he thinks that
this correction alone would have deserved a new edition of his author; whose

genuity of his courtiers were at a loss to discover any materials for panegyric in the events of the Persian war ; while the glory of his cousin Julian, to whose military command he had entrusted the provinces of Gaul, was proclaimed to the world in the simple and concise narrative of his exploits.

In the blind fury of civil discord, Constantius had abandoned to the Barbarians of Germany the countries of Gaul, which still acknowledged the authority of his rival. A numerous swarm of Franks and Alemanni were invited to cross the Rhine by presents and promises, by the hopes of spoil, and by a perpetual grant of all the territories which they should be able to subdue.[69] But the emperor, who for a temporary service had thus imprudently provoked the rapacious spirit of the Barbarians, soon discovered and lamented the difficulty of dismissing these formidable allies, after they had tasted the richness of the Roman soil. Regardless of the nice distinction of loyalty and rebellion, these undisciplined robbers treated as their natural enemies all the subjects of the empire, who possessed any property which they were desirous of acquiring. Forty-five flourishing cities, Tongres, Cologne, Treves, Worms, Spires, Strasburg, &c., besides a far greater number of towns and villages, were pillaged, and for the most part reduced to ashes. The Barbarians of Germany, still faithful to the maxims of their ancestors, abhorred the confinement of walls, to which they applied the odious names of prisons and sepulchres ; and, fixing their independent habitations on the banks of rivers, the Rhine, the Moselle, and the Meuse, they secured themselves against the danger of a surprise by a rude and hasty fortification of large trees, which were felled and thrown across the roads. The Alemanni were established in the modern countries of Alsace and Lorraine ; the Franks occupied the island of the Batavians, together with an extensive district of Brabant, which was then known by the appellation of *Toxandria*,[70] and may deserve to be considered as the original

(marginal note: Invasion of Gaul by the Germans)

sense may now be darkly perceived. I expected some additional light from the recent labours of the learned Ernestus (Lipsiæ, 1773). [The MSS. have the unmeaning *etulerint sed*, for which Eyssenhardt, followed by Gardthausen, reads *inulta*.]

[69] The ravages of the Germans, and the distress of Gaul, may be collected from Julian himself. Orat. ad S. P. Q. Athen. p. 277. Ammian. xv. 11 [rather 8, 1]. Libanius, Orat. x. Zosimus, l. iii. p. 140 [c. 3]. Sozomen, l. iii. c. 1.

[70] Ammianus (xvi. 8). This name seems to be derived from the Toxandri of Pliny, and very frequently occurs in the histories of the middle age. Toxandria was a country of woods and morasses which extended from the neighbourhood of Tongres to the conflux of the Vahal and the Rhine. See Valesius, Notit. Galliar. p. 558.

seat of their Gallic monarchy.[71]   From the sources to the mouth of the Rhine, the conquests of the Germans extended above forty miles to the west of that river, over a country peopled by colonies of their own name and nation ; and the scene of their devastations was three times more extensive than that of their conquests.   At a still greater distance the open towns of Gaul were deserted, and the inhabitants of the fortified cities, who trusted to their strength and vigilance, were obliged to content themselves with such supplies of corn as they could raise on the vacant land within the inclosure of their walls.   The diminished legions, destitute of pay and provisions, of arms and discipline, trembled at the approach, and even at the name, of the Barbarians.

Conduct of Julian

Under these melancholy circumstances, an unexperienced youth was appointed to save and to govern the provinces of Gaul, or rather, as he expresses it himself, to exhibit the vain image of imperial greatness.   The retired scholastic education of Julian, in which he had been more conversant with books than with arms, with the dead than with the living, left him in profound ignorance of the practical arts of war and government ; and, when he awkwardly repeated some military exercise which it was necessary for him to learn, he exclaimed with a sigh, "O Plato, Plato, what a task for a philosopher ! "   Yet even this speculative philosophy, which men of business are too apt to despise, had filled the mind of Julian with the noblest precepts and the most shining examples ; had animated him with the love of virtue, the desire of fame, and the contempt of death.   The habits of temperance recommended in the schools are still more essential in the severe discipline of a camp.   The simple wants of nature regulated the measure of his food and sleep.   Rejecting with disdain the delicacies provided for his table, he satisfied his appetite with the coarse and common fare which was allotted to the meanest soldiers. During the rigour of a Gallic winter, he never suffered a fire in his bed-chamber ; and after a short and interrupted slumber he frequently rose in the middle of the night from

71 The paradox of P. Daniel, that the Franks never obtained any permanent settlement on his side of the Rhine before the time of Clovis, is refuted with much learning and good sense by M. Biet who has proved, by a chain of evidence, their uninterrupted possession of Toxandria one hundred and thirty years before the accession of Clovis.   The Dissertation of M. Biet was crowned by the Academy of Soissons in the year 1736, and seems to have been justly preferred to the discourse of his more celebrated competitor, the Abbé le Bœuf, an antiquarian whose name was happily expressive of his talents.

a carpet spread on the floor, to dispatch any urgent business, to visit his rounds, or to steal a few moments for the prosecution of his favourite studies.[72] The precepts of eloquence which he had hitherto practised on fancied topics of declamation were more usefully applied to excite or to assuage the passions of an armed multitude: and, although Julian, from his early habits of conversation and literature, was more familiarly acquainted with the beauties of the Greek language, he had attained a competent knowledge of the Latin tongue.[73] Since Julian was not originally designed for the character of a legislator or a judge, it is probable that the civil jurisprudence of the Romans had not engaged any considerable share of his attention: but he derived from his philosophic studies an inflexible regard for justice, tempered by a disposition to clemency; the knowledge of the general principles of equity and evidence; and the faculty of patiently investigating the most intricate and tedious questions which could be proposed for his discussion. The measures of policy and the operations of war must submit to the various accidents of circumstance and character, and the unpractised student will often be perplexed in the application of the most perfect theory. But in the acquisition of this important science, Julian was assisted by the active vigour of his own genius, as well as by the wisdom and experience of Sallust, an officer of rank, who soon conceived a sincere attachment for a prince so worthy of his friendship; and whose incorruptible integrity was adorned by the talent of insinuating the harshest truths without wounding the delicacy of a royal ear.[74]

Immediately after Julian had received the purple at Milan, he was sent into Gaul, with a feeble retinue of three hundred and sixty soldiers. At Vienna, where he passed a painful and anxious winter, in the hands of those ministers to whom

His first campaign in Gaul. A.D. 356

[72] The private life of Julian in Gaul, and the severe discipline which he embraced, are displayed by Ammianus (xvi. 5), who professes to praise, and by Julian himself, who affects to ridicule (Misopogon, p. 340), a conduct which, in a prince of the house of Constantine, might justly excite the surprise of mankind.

[73] Aderat Latine quoque disserenti [leg. disserendi] sufficiens sermo. Ammianus, xvi. 5. But Julian, educated in the schools of Greece, always considered the language of the Romans as a foreign and popular dialect, which he might use on necessary occasions.

[74] We are ignorant of the actual office of this excellent minister, whom Julian afterwards created præfect of Gaul. Sallust was speedily recalled by the jealousy of the emperor; and we may still read a sensible but pedantic discourse (p. 240-252), in wh.ch Julian deplores the loss of so valuable a friend, to whom he acknowledges himself indebted for his reputation. See La Blèterie, Préface à la Vie de Jovien, p. 20.

Constantius had entrusted the direction of his conduct, the Cæsar was informed of the siege and deliverance of Autun. That large and ancient city, protected only by a ruined wall and pusillanimous garrison, was saved by the generous resolution of a few veterans, who resumed their arms for the defence of their country. In his march from Autun through the heart of the Gallic provinces, Julian embraced with ardour the earliest opportunity of signalizing his courage. At the head of a small body of archers and heavy cavalry, he preferred the shorter but the more dangerous of two roads; and sometimes eluding, and sometimes resisting, the attacks of the Barbarians, who were masters of the field, he arrived with honour and safety at the camp near Rheims, where the Roman troops had been ordered to assemble. The aspect of their young prince revived the drooping spirit of the soldiers, and they marched from Rheims in search of the enemy, with a confidence which had almost proved fatal to them. The Alemanni, familiarized to the knowledge of the country, secretly collected their scattered forces and, seizing the opportunity of a dark and rainy day, poured with unexpected fury on the rear-guard of the Romans.[75] Before the inevitable disorder could be remedied two legions were destroyed; and Julian was taught by experience that caution and vigilance are the most important lessons of the art of war. In a second and more successful action, he recovered and established his military fame: but, as the agility of the Barbarians saved them from the pursuit, his victory was neither bloody nor decisive. He advanced, however, to the banks of the Rhine, surveyed the ruins of Cologne, convinced himself of the difficulties of the war, and retreated on the approach of winter, discontented with the court, with his army, and with his own success.[76] The power of the enemy was yet unbroken; and the Cæsar had no sooner separated his troops, and fixed his own quarters at Sens, in the centre of Gaul, than he was surrounded and besieged by a numerous host of Germans. Reduced in this extremity to the resources of his own mind, he displayed a prudent intrepidity which compensated for all the deficiencies of the place and garrison; and the Barbarians, at the end of thirty days, were obliged to retire with disappointed rage.

[At Autun. 24th June, 356]

[Remi]

[Battle of Brotomagus (= Brumath)]

[Senones]

75 [Julian was on his way to *Decempagi*, now Dieuze, in Lothringen.]
76 Ammianus (xvi. 2, 3) appears much better satisfied with the success of his first campaign than Julian himself; who very fairly owns that he did nothing of consequence, and that he fled before the enemy.

The conscious pride of Julian, who was indebted only to his sword for this signal deliverance, was embittered by the reflexion that he was abandoned, betrayed, and perhaps devoted to destruction, by those who were bound to assist him by every tie of honour and fidelity. Marcellus, master-general of the cavalry in Gaul, interpreting too strictly the jealous orders of the court, beheld with supine indifference the distress of Julian, and had restrained the troops under his command from marching to the relief of Sens. If the Cæsar had dissembled in silence so dangerous an insult, his person and authority would have been exposed to the contempt of the world; and, if an action so criminal had been suffered to pass with impunity, the emperor would have confirmed the suspicions which received a very specious colour from his past conduct towards the princes of the Flavian family. Marcellus was recalled, and gently dismissed from his office.[77] In his room Severus was appointed general of the cavalry; an experienced soldier, of approved courage and fidelity, who could advise with respect and execute with zeal; and who submitted, without reluctance, to the supreme command which Julian, by the interest of his patroness Eusebia, at length obtained over the armies of Gaul.[78] A very judicious plan of operations was adopted for the approaching campaign. Julian himself, at the head of the remains of the veteran bands, and of some new levies which he had been permitted to form, boldly penetrated into the centre of the German cantonments and carefully re-established the fortifications of Saverne[79] in an advantageous post, which would either check the incursions, or intercept the retreat, of the enemy. At the same time Barbatio, general of the infantry, advanced from Milan with an army of thirty thousand men,[80] and passing the mountains prepared to throw a bridge over the Rhine, in the neighbourhood of Basil. It was reasonable to expect that the Alemanni, pressed on either side by the Roman arms, would soon be forced to evacuate the provinces of Gaul, and to hasten to the defence of their native country. But the hopes of the campaign were defeated by the

His second campaign. A.D. 357

[Tres Tabernae]

[Basilea]

[77] Ammian. xvi. 7. Libanius speaks rather more advantageously of the military talents of Marcellus, Orat. x. p. 272. And Julian insinuates that he would not have been so easily recalled, unless he had given other reasons of offence to the court, p. 278.

[78] Severus, non discors, non arrogans, sed longa militiæ frugalitate compertus; et eum recta præeuntem secuturus, ut ductorem morigerus miles. Ammian. xvi. 11. Zosimus, l. iii. p. 140 [c. 2].

[79] [In Elsass, the German form of the name, Zabern, is now more familiar. On the restoration of the forts cp. Mommsen, Hermes 16, 489.]

[80] [Rather 25,000; see Amm. ib.]

incapacity, or the envy, or the secret instructions, of Barbatio; who acted as if he had been the enemy of the Cæsar and the secret ally of the Barbarians. The negligence with which he permitted a troop of pillagers freely to pass, and to return almost before the gates of his camp, may be imputed to his want of abilities; but the treasonable act of burning a number of boats, and a superfluous stock of provisions, which would have been of the most essential service to the army of Gaul, was an evidence of his hostile and criminal intentions. The Germans despised an enemy who appeared destitute either of power or of inclination to offend them; and the ignominious retreat of Barbatio deprived Julian of the expected support, and left him to extricate himself from a hazardous situation, where he could neither remain with safety nor retire with honour.[81]

Battle of Strasburg. A D 357. August

As soon as they were delivered from the fears of invasion, the Alemanni prepared to chastise the Roman youth, who presumed to dispute the possession of that country which they claimed as their own by the right of conquest and of treaties. They employed three days and as many nights in transporting over the Rhine their military powers. The fierce Chnodomar, shaking the ponderous javelin, which he had victoriously wielded against the brother of Magnentius, led the van of the Barbarians, and moderated by his experience the martial ardour which his example inspired.[82] He was followed by six other kings, by ten princes of regal extraction, by a long train of high-spirited nobles, and by thirty-five thousand of the bravest warriors of the tribes of Germany. The confidence derived from the view of their own strength was increased by the intelligence which they received from a deserter, that the Cæsar, with a feeble army of thirteen thousand men, occupied a post about one-and-twenty miles from their camp of Strasburg. With this inadequate force, Julian resolved to seek and to encounter the

[Argentoratum]

[81] On the design and failure of the co-operation between Julian and Barbatio, see Ammianus, xvi. 11, and Libanius, Orat. x. p. 273. [The "pillagers" who passed were Læti; they surprised Lyons.]

[82] Ammianus (xvi. 12) describes with his inflated eloquence the figure and character of Chnodomar. Audax et fidens ingenti robore lacertorum, ubi ardor prœlii sperabatur immanis, equo spumante, sublimior, erectus in jaculum formidandæ vastitatis, armorumque nitore conspicuus: antea strenuus et miles, et utilis præter cæteros ductor. . . . Decentium Cæsarem superavit æquo marte congressus. [For criticism of the sources for the history of this campaign see Appendix 1. It may be noted that a very important hint for the topography of the battle has been missed by Gibbon. Libanius mentions that a part of the enemy was posted ὑπ' ὀχετῷ μετεώρῳ, a bit of the old aqueduct of Strasburg where it crosses the Musauthal. See F. Vogel, Hist. Zeitschrift, vol. 24, p. 89, 1888.]

Barbarian host; and the chance of a general action was preferred to the tedious and uncertain operation of separately engaging the dispersed parties of the Alemanni. The Romans marched in close order, and in two columns, the cavalry on the right, the infantry on the left; and the day was so far spent when they appeared in sight of the enemy, that Julian was desirous of deferring the battle till the next morning, and of allowing his troops to recruit their exhausted strength by the necessary refreshments of sleep and food. Yielding, however, with some reluctance to the clamours of the soldiers, and even to the opinion of his council, he exhorted them to justify by their valour the eager impatience, which, in case of a defeat, would be universally branded with the epithets of rashness and presumption. The trumpets sounded, the military shout was heard through the field, and the two armies rushed with equal fury to the charge. The Cæsar, who conducted in person his right wing, depended on the dexterity of his archers, and the weight of his cuirassiers. But his ranks were instantly broken by an irregular mixture of light-horse and of light-infantry, and he had the mortification of beholding the flight of six hundred of his most renowned cuirassiers.[83] The fugitives were stopped and rallied by the presence and authority of Julian, who, careless of his own safety, threw himself before them, and, urging every motive of shame and honour, led them back against the victorious enemy. The conflict between the two lines of infantry was obstinate and bloody. The Germans possessed the superiority of strength and stature, the Romans that of discipline and temper; and, as the Barbarians who served under the standard of the empire united the respective advantages of both parties, their strenuous efforts, guided by a skilful leader, at length determined the event of the day. The Romans lost four tribunes, and two hundred and forty-three soldiers, in this memorable battle of Strasburg, so glorious to the Cæsar,[84] and

---

[83] After the battle, Julian ventured to revive the rigour of ancient discipline by exposing these fugitives in female apparel to the derision of the whole camp. In the next campaign, these troops nobly retrieved their honour. Zosimus, l. iii. p. 142 [c. 3].

[84] Julian himself (ad S. P. Q. Athen. p. 279 [359, ed. Hertl.]) speaks of the battle of Strasburg with the modesty of conscious merit; ἐμαχεσάμην οὐκ ἀκλεῶς, ἴσως καὶ εἰς ὑμᾶς ἀφίκετο ἡ τοιαύτη μάχη. Zosimus compares it with the victory of Alexander over Darius; and yet we are at a loss to discover any of those strokes of military genius which fix the attention of ages on the conduct and success of a single day. [Julian wrote an account of the battle, which is not extant but is mentioned by Eunapius (fr. 9, F. H. G. iv.), and may be the basis of Ammian's account.]

so salutary to the afflicted provinces of Gaul. Six thousand of the Alemanni were slain in the field, without including those who were drowned in the Rhine or transfixed with darts whilst they attempted to swim across the river.[85] Chnodomar himself was surrounded and taken prisoner, with three of his brave companions, who had devoted themselves to follow in life or death the fate of their chieftain. Julian received him with military pomp in the council of his officers ; and, expressing a generous pity for the fallen state, dissembled his inward contempt for the abject humiliation, of his captive. Instead of exhibiting the vanquished king of the Alemanni, as a grateful spectacle to the cities of Gaul, he respectfully laid at the feet of the emperor this splendid trophy of his victory. Chnodomar experienced an honourable treatment : but the impatient Barbarian could not long survive his defeat, his confinement, and his exile.[86]

Julian subdues the Franks. A.D. 358

After Julian had repulsed the Alemanni from the provinces of the Upper Rhine, he turned his arms against the Franks, who were seated nearer to the ocean on the confines of Gaul and Germany, and who, from their numbers, and still more from their intrepid valour, had ever been esteemed the most formidable of the Barbarians.[87] Although they were strongly actuated by the allurements of rapine, they professed a disinterested love of war, which they considered as the supreme honour and felicity of human nature ; and their minds and bodies were so completely hardened by perpetual action that, according to the lively expression of an orator, the snows of winter were as pleasant to them as the flowers of spring. In the month of December, which followed the battle of Strasburg, Julian attacked a body of six hundred Franks, who had thrown themselves into two castles on the Meuse.[88] In the midst of that severe season

[85] Ammianus, xvi. 12. Libanius adds 2000 more to the number of the slain (Orat. x. p. 274). But these trifling differences disappear before the 60,000 Barbarians whom Zosimus has sacrificed to the glory of his hero (l. iii. p. 141 [c. 3]). We might attribute this extravagant number to the carelessness of transcribers, if this credulous or partial historian had not swelled the army of 35,000 Alemanni to an innumerable multitude of Barbarians, πλῆθος ἄπειρον βαρβάρων. It is our own fault if this detection does not inspire us with proper distrust on similar occasions.

[86] Ammian. xvi. 12. Libanius, Orat. x. p. 276.

[87] Libanius (Orat. iii. p. 137) draws a very lively picture of the manners of the Franks.

[88] Ammianus, xvii. 2. Libanius, Orat. x. p. 278. The Greek orator, by misapprehending a passage of Julian, has been induced to represent the Franks as consisting of a thousand men ; and, as his head was always full of the Peloponnesian war, he compares them to the Lacedæmonians, who were besieged and taken in the island of Sphacteria.

they sustained, with inflexible constancy, a siege of fifty-four days; till at length, exhausted by hunger, and satisfied that the vigilance of the enemy in breaking the ice of the river left them no hopes of escape, the Franks consented, for the first time, to dispense with the ancient law which commended them to conquer or to die.   The Cæsar immediately sent his captives to the court of Constantius, who, accepting them as a valuable present,[89] rejoiced in the opportunity of adding so many heroes to the choicest troops of his domestic guards.   The obstinate resistance of this handful of Franks apprized Julian of the difficulties of the expedition which he meditated for the ensuing spring against the whole body of the nation.   His rapid diligence surprised and astonished the active Barbarians.   Ordering his soldiers to provide themselves with biscuit for twenty days, he suddenly pitched his camp near Tongres, while the enemy still supposed him in his winter quarters of Paris, expecting the slow arrival of his convoys from Aquitain. Without allowing the Franks to unite or to deliberate, he skilfully spread his legions from Cologne to the ocean; and by the terror as well as by the success of his arms soon reduced the suppliant tribes to implore the clemency, and to obey the commands, of their conqueror.   The Chamavians submissively retired to their former habitations beyond the Rhine: but the Salians were permitted to possess their new establishment of Toxandria, as the subjects and auxiliaries of the Roman empire.[90]   The treaty was ratified by solemn oaths; and perpetual inspectors were appointed to reside among the Franks, with the authority of enforcing the strict observance of the conditions.   An incident is related, interesting enough in itself, and by no means repugnant to the character of Julian, who ingeniously contrived both the plot and the catastrophe of the tragedy.   When the Chamavians sued for peace, he required the son of their king, as the only hostage on whom he could rely.   A mournful silence, interrupted by tears and groans,

---

[89] Julian. ad S. P. Q. Athen. p. 280. Libanius, Orat. x. p. 278. According to the expression of Libanius, the emperor δῶρα ὠνόμαζε, which la Bléterie understands (Vie de Julien, p. 118) as an honest confession, and Valesius (ad Ammian. xvii. 2) as a mean evasion, of the truth.   Dom. Bouquet (Historiens de France, tom. i. p. 733), by substituting another word, ἐνόμισε, would suppress both the difficulty and the spirit of this passage.

[90] Ammian. xvii. 8.   Zosimus l. iii. p. 146-150 [c. 4-7] (his narrative is darkened by a mixture of fable); and Julian. ad S. P. Q. Athen. p. 280 [361, ed. Hertl.]. His expression, ὑπεδεξάμην μὲν μοίραν τοῦ Σαλίων ἔθνους, Χαμάβους δὲ ἐξήλασα.   This difference of treatment confirms the opinion that the Salian Franks were permitted to retain the settlements in Toxandria. [Cp. Eunapius, 12, 13, ap. Müller, F. H. G. 4. Zosimus has confused Chnodomar with Vadomar.]

declared the sad perplexity of the Barbarians; and their aged chief lamented in pathetic language that his private loss was now embittered by a sense of the public calamity. While the Chamavians lay prostrate at the foot of his throne, the royal captive, whom they believed to have been slain, unexpectedly appeared before their eyes; and, as soon as the tumult of joy was hushed into attention, the Cæsar addressed the assembly in the following terms: "Behold the son, the prince, whom you wept. You had lost him by your fault. God and the Romans have restored him to you. I shall still preserve and educate the youth, rather as a monument of my own virtue than as a pledge of your sincerity. Should you presume to violate the faith which you have sworn, the arms of the republic will avenge the perfidy, not on the innocent, but on the guilty." The Barbarians withdrew from his presence, impressed with the warmest sentiments of gratitude and admiration.[91]

Makes three expeditions beyond the Rhine. A.D. 357, 358, 359

It was not enough for Julian to have delivered the provinces of Gaul from the Barbarians of Germany. He aspired to emulate the glory of the first and most illustrious of the emperors; after whose example he composed his own commentaries of the Gallic war.[92] Cæsar has related, with conscious pride, the manner in which he *twice* passed the Rhine. Julian could boast that, before he assumed the title of Augustus, he had carried the Roman Eagles beyond that great river in *three* successful expeditions.[93] The consternation of the Germans, after the battle of Strasburg, encouraged him to the first attempt; and the reluctance of the troops soon yielded to the persuasive eloquence of a leader who shared the fatigues and dangers which he imposed on the meanest of the soldiers. The villages on either side of

[Moenus]

the Main, which were plentifully stored with corn and cattle, felt the ravages of an invading army. The principal houses, constructed with some imitation of Roman elegance, were consumed by the flames; and the Cæsar boldly advanced about ten miles, till his progress was stopped by a dark and impenetrable

---

91 This interesting story, which Zosimus has abridged, is related by Eunapius (in Excerpt. Legationum, p. 15, 16, 17) with all the amplifications of Grecian rhetoric: but the silence of Libanius, of Ammianus, and of Julian himself, renders the truth of it extremely suspicious.

92 Libanius, the friend of Julian, clearly insinuates (Orat. iv. p. 178) that his hero had composed the history of his Gallic campaigns. But Zosimus (l. iii. p. 140 [c. 2]) seems to have derived his information only from the Orations (λογοι) and the Epistles of Julian. The discourse which is addressed to the Athenians contains an accurate, though general, account of the war against the Germans.

93 See Ammian. xvii. 1. 10, xviii. 2, and Zosim. l. iii. p. 144. Julian. ad S. P. Q. Athen. p. 280.

forest, undermined by subterraneous passages, which threatened, with secret snares and ambush, every step of the assailant.   The ground was already covered with snow; and Julian, after repairing an ancient castle which had been erected by Trajan,[94] granted a truce of ten months to the submissive Barbarians.   At the expiration of the truce, Julian undertook a second expedition beyond the Rhine, to humble the pride of Surmar[95] and Hortaire, two of the kings of the Alemanni, who had been present at the battle of Strasburg.   They promised to restore all the Roman captives who yet remained alive; and, as the Cæsar had procured an exact account from the cities and villages of Gaul, of the inhabitants whom they had lost, he detected every attempt to deceive him with a degree of readiness and accuracy which almost established the belief of his supernatural knowledge.   His third expedition was still more splendid and important than the two former.   The Germans had collected their military powers, and moved along the opposite banks of the river, with a design of destroying the bridge and of preventing the passage of the Romans.   But this judicious plan of defence was disconcerted by a skilful diversion.   Three hundred light-armed and active soldiers were detached in forty small boats, to fall down the stream in silence, and to land at some distance from the posts of the enemy.   They executed their orders with so much boldness and celerity that they had almost surprised the Barbarian chiefs, who returned in the fearless confidence of intoxication from one of their nocturnal festivals.   Without repeating the uniform and disgusting tale of slaughter and devastation, it is sufficient to observe that Julian dictated his own conditions of peace to six of the haughtiest kings of the Alemanni, three of whom were permitted to view the severe discipline and martial pomp of a Roman camp.   Followed by twenty thousand captives, whom he had rescued from the chains of the Barbarians, the Cæsar repassed the Rhine, after terminating a war, the success of which has been compared to the ancient glories of the Punic and Cimbric victories.

As soon as the valour and conduct of Julian had secured an interval of peace, he applied himself to a work more congenial to his humane and philosophic temper.   The cities of Gaul, which had suffered from the inroads of the Barbarians, he diligently repaired; and seven important posts, between Mainz and the mouth of the Rhine, are particularly mentioned, as

Restores the cities of Gaul

[Moguntiacum]

---

[94] [Variously supposed to be Gustavsburg or Lupudunum (Ladenburg).]
[95] [The name is Suomar.]

having been rebuilt and fortified by the order of Julian.[96] The vanquished Germans had submitted to the just but humiliating condition of preparing and conveying the necessary materials. The active zeal of Julian urged the prosecution of the work ; and such was the spirit which he had diffused among the troops that the auxiliaries themselves, waving their exemption from any duties of fatigue, contended in the most servile labours with the diligence of the Roman soldiers. It was incumbent on the Cæsar to provide for the subsistence, as well as for the safety, of the inhabitants and of the garrisons. The desertion of the former, and the mutiny of the latter, must have been the fatal and inevitable consequences of famine. The tillage of the provinces of Gaul had been interrupted by the calamities of war ; but the scanty harvests of the continent were supplied, by his paternal care, from the plenty of the adjacent island. Six hundred large barks, framed in the forest of the Ardennes, made several voyages to the coast of Britain ; and, returning from thence laden with corn, sailed up the Rhine, and distributed their cargoes to the several towns and fortresses along the banks of the river.[97] The arms of Julian had restored a free and secure navigation, which Constantius had offered to purchase at the expense of his dignity, and of a tributary present of two thousand pounds of silver. The emperor parsimoniously refused to his soldiers the sums which he granted with a lavish and trembling hand to the Barbarians. The dexterity, as well as the firmness, of Julian was put to a severe trial, when he took the field with a discontented army, which had already served two campaigns without receiving any regular pay or any extraordinary donative.[98]

Civil adminis-
tration of
Julian

A tender regard for the peace and happiness of his subjects

[96] Ammian. xviii. 2. Libanius, Orat. x. p. 279, 280. Of these seven posts, four are at present towns of some consequence ; Bingen, Andernach, Bonn, and Neuss. The other three, Tricesimæ [has been identified with Kellen], Quadriburgium [Schenkenschanz], and Castra Herculis, or Heraclea [Erkelens], no longer subsist ; but there is room to believe that, on the ground of Quadriburgium, the Dutch have constructed the fort of Schenk, a name so offensive to the fastidious delicacy of Boileau. See d'Anville, Notice de l'ancienne Gaule, p. 183. Boileau, Epître iv. and the notes.

[97] We may credit Julian himself, Orat. ad. S. P. Q. Atheniensem p. 280 [361, ed. Hertl.], who gives a very particular account of the transaction. Zosimus adds two hundred vessels more, l. iii. p. 145 [c. 5]. If we compute the 600 corn ships of Julian at only seventy tons each, they were capable of exporting 120,000 quarters (see Arbuthnot s Weights and Measures, p. 237) ; and the country which could bear so large an exportation must already have attained an improved state of agriculture.

[98] The troops once broke out into a mutiny, immediately before the second passage of the Rhine. Ammian. xvii. 9.

was the ruling principle which directed, or seemed to direct, the administration of Julian.[99] He devoted the leisure of his winter quarters to the offices of civil government, and affected to assume with more pleasure the character of a magistrate than that of a general. Before he took the field, he devolved on the provincial governors most of the public and private causes which had been referred to his tribunal ; but, on his return, he carefully revised their proceedings, mitigated the rigour of the law, and pronounced a second judgment on the judges themselves. Superior to the last temptation of virtuous minds, an indiscreet and intemperate zeal for justice, he restrained, with calmness and dignity, the warmth of an advocate who prosecuted, for extortion, the president of the Narbonnese province. "Who will ever be found guilty," exclaimed the vehement Delphidius, "if it be enough to deny ? " "And who," replied Julian, "will ever be innocent, if it be sufficient to affirm ? " In the general administration of peace and war, the interest of the sovereign is commonly the same as that of his people ; but Constantius would have thought himself deeply injured, if the virtues of Julian had defrauded him of any part of the tribute which he extorted from an oppressed and exhausted country. The prince, who was invested with the ensigns of royalty, might sometimes presume to correct the rapacious insolence of the inferior agents, to expose their corrupt arts, and to introduce an equal and easier mode of collection. But the management of the finances was more safely entrusted to Florentius, Prætorian præfect of Gaul, an effeminate tyrant, incapable of pity or remorse ; and the haughty minister complained of the most decent and gentle opposition, while Julian himself was rather inclined to censure the weakness of his own behaviour. The Cæsar had rejected with abhorrence a mandate for the levy of an extraordinary tax ; a new superindiction, which the præfect had offered for his signature ; and the faithful picture of the public misery, by which he had been obliged to justify his refusal, offended the court of Constantius. We may enjoy the pleasure of reading the sentiments of Julian, as he expresses them with warmth and freedom in a letter to one of his most intimate friends. After stating his own conduct, he proceeds in the following terms : "Was it possible for the disciple of Plato and Aristotle to act otherwise than I have done ? Could I abandon the unhappy subjects entrusted to my care ? Was I

[99] Ammian. xvi. 5. xviii. 1.   Mamertinus in Panegyr. Vet. xi. 4.

not called upon to defend them from the repeated injuries of
these unfeeling robbers ? A tribune who deserts his post is
punished with death and deprived of the honours of burial.[100]
With what justice could I pronounce *his* sentence, if, in the
hour of danger, I myself neglected a duty far more sacred and
far more important ? God has placed me in this elevated post ;
his providence will guard and support me. Should I be condemned to suffer, I shall derive comfort from the testimony of a
pure and upright conscience. Would to heaven that I still
possessed a councillor like Sallust ! If they think proper to
send me a successor, I shall submit without reluctance ; and had
much rather improve the short opportunity of doing good than
enjoy a long and lasting impunity of evil." [101] The precarious
and dependent situation of Julian displayed his virtues and
concealed his defects. The young hero who supported, in Gaul,
the throne of Constantius was not permitted to reform the vices
of the government ; but he had courage to alleviate or to pity
the distress of the people. Unless he had been able to revive
the martial spirit of the Romans, or to introduce the arts of
industry and refinement among their savage enemies, he could
not entertain any rational hopes of securing the public tranquillity, either by the peace or conquest of Germany. Yet the
victories of Julian suspended, for a short time, the inroads of
the Barbarians, and delayed the ruin of the Western Empire.

Description
of Paris

His salutary influence restored the cities of Gaul, which had
been so long exposed to the evils of civil discord, barbarian war,
and domestic tyranny ; and the spirit of industry was revived
with the hopes of enjoyment. Agriculture, manufactures, and
commerce again flourished under the protection of the laws ;
and the *curiæ*, or civil corporations, were again filled with useful
and respectable members : the youth were no longer apprehensive of marriage ; and married persons were no longer apprehensive of posterity : the public and private festivals were
celebrated with customary pomp ; and the frequent and secure
intercourse of the provinces displayed the image of national
prosperity.[102] A mind like that of Julian must have felt the
general happiness of which he was the author ; but he viewed

---

[100] [The reading and meaning of this sentence of Julian are uncertain.]

[101] Ammian. xvii. 3. Julian. Epistol. xv. [*leg.* xvii.] edit. Spanheim [497, ed. Hertl.].
Such a conduct almost justifies the encomium of Mamertinus. Ita illi anni spatia
divisa sunt, ut aut Barbaros domitet, aut civibus jura restituat ; perpetuum professus,
aut contra hostem, aut contra vitia, certamen.

[102] Libanius, Orat. Parental. in Imp. Julian. c. 38, in Fabricius Bibliothec. Græc.
tom. vii. p. 263, 264.

with peculiar satisfaction and complacency the city of Paris, the seat of his winter residence, and the object even of his partial affection.[103] That splendid capital, which now embraces an ample territory on either side of the Seine, was originally confined to the small island in the midst of the river, from whence the inhabitants derived a supply of pure and salubrious water. The river bathed the foot of the walls ; and the town was accessible only by two wooden bridges. A forest overspread the northern side of the Seine ; but on the south, the ground, which now bears the name of the university, was insensibly covered with houses, and adorned with a palace and amphi- theatre, baths, an aqueduct, and a field of Mars for the exercise for the Roman troops. The severity of the climate was tempered by the neighbourhood of the ocean ; and with some precautions, which experience had taught, the vine and fig-tree were success- fully cultivated. But in remarkable winters, the Seine was deeply frozen ; and the huge pieces of ice that floated down the stream might be compared, by an Asiatic, to the blocks of white marble which were extracted from the quarries of Phrygia. The licentiousness and corruption of Antioch recalled to the memory of Julian the severe and simple manners of his beloved Lutetia ;[104] where the amusements of the theatre were unknown or despised. He indignantly contrasted the effeminate Syrians with the brave and honest simplicity of the Gauls, and almost forgave the intemperance which was the only stain of the Celtic character.[105] If Julian could now revisit the capital of France, he might converse with men of science and genius, capable of understanding and of instructing a disciple of the Greeks ; he might excuse the lively and graceful follies of a nation whose martial spirit has never been enervated by the indulgence of luxury ; and he must applaud the perfection of that inestimable art which softens and refines and embellishes the intercourse of social life.

[103] See Julian. in Misopogon. p. 340, 341 [438, 439, ed. Hertl.]. The primitive state of Paris is illustrated by Henry Valesius (ad Ammian. xx. 4), his brother Hadrian Valesius, or de Valois, and M. d'Anville (in their respective Notitias of Ancient Gaul), the Abbé de Longuerue, Description de la France, tom. i. p. 12, 13, and M. Bonamy (in the Mém. de l'Académie des Inscriptions, tom. xv. p. 656-691).

[104] Τὴν φίλην Λευκετιαν [Λουκετίαν]. Julian. in Misopogon. p. 340 [438, ed. Hertl.]. Leucetia, or Lutetia, was the ancient name of the city which, according to the fashion of the fourth century, assumed the territorial appellation of *Parisii*.

[105] Julian. in Misopogon. p. 359, 360 [463, 465, ed. Hertl.].

CHAPTER XX

*The Motives, Progress, and Effects of the Conversion of Constantine
    —Legal Establishment and Constitution of the Christian or
    Catholic Church*

THE public establishment of Christianity may be considered as
one of those important and domestic revolutions which excite
the most lively curiosity and afford the most valuable instruction.   The victories and the civil policy of Constantine no
longer influence the state of Europe ; but a considerable portion
of the globe still retains the impression which it received from
the conversion of that monarch ; and the ecclesiastical institutions of his reign are still connected, by an indissoluble chain,
with the opinions, the passions, and the interests of the present
generation.

Date of the   In the consideration of a subject which may be examined
conversion of   with impartiality, but cannot be viewed with indifference, a
Constantine
difficulty immediately arises of a very unexpected nature ; that
of ascertaining the real and precise date of the conversion of
A.D. 306   Constantine.   The eloquent Lactantius, in the midst of his
court, seems impatient[1] to proclaim to the world the glorious
example of the sovereign of Gaul ; who, in the first moments of
his reign, acknowledged and adored the majesty of the true
and only God.[2]   The learned Eusebius has ascribed the faith of

---

[1] The date of the Divine Institutions of Lactantius has been accurately discussed,
difficulties have been started, solutions proposed, and an expedient imagined of two
original editions : the former published during the persecution of Diocletian, the
latter under that of Licinius.   See Dufresnoy, Préfat. p. v.   Tillemont, Mém Ecclésiast. tom. vi. p. 465-470.   Lardner's Credibility, part ii. vol. vii. p. 78-86.   For
my own part, I am *almost* convinced that Lactantius dedicated his Institutions to
the sovereign of Gaul, at a time when Galerius, Maximin, and even Licinius, persecuted the Christians ; that is, between the years 306 and 311.   [The work was
probably begun about 304, and finished perhaps by 308, certainly before 311.]

[2] Lactant. Divin. Institut. i. 1, vii. 27.   The first and most important of these
passages is indeed wanting in twenty-eight manuscripts; but it is found in nineteen.
If we weigh the comparative value of those manuscripts, one of 900 years old, in
the king of France's library, may be alleged in its favour ; but the passage is
omitted in the correct manuscript of Bologna, which the P. de Montfaucon
ascribes to the sixth or seventh century (Diarium Italic. p. 409).   The taste of most
of the editors (except Isæus, see Lactant. edit. Dufresnoy, tom. i. p. 596) has felt

Constantine to the miraculous sign which was displayed in the heavens whilst he meditated and prepared the Italian expedi- A.D. 312 tion.[3]   The historian Zosimus maliciously asserts that the emperor had imbrued his hands in the blood of his eldest son, before he publicly renounced the gods of Rome and of his ancestors.[4]   The perplexity produced by these discordant A.D. 326 authorities is derived from the behaviour of Constantine himself.   According to the strictness of ecclesiastical language, the first of the *Christian* emperors was unworthy of that name, till the moment of his death; since it was only during his last illness that he received, as a catechumen, the imposition of A.D. 337 hands,[5] and was afterwards admitted, by the initiatory rites of baptism, into the number of the faithful.[6]   The Christianity of Constantine must be allowed in a much more vague and qualified sense ; and the nicest accuracy is required in tracing the slow and almost imperceptible gradations by which the monarch declared himself the protector, and at length the proselyte, of the church.   It was an arduous task to eradicate the habits and prejudices of his education, to acknowledge the divine power of Christ, and to understand that the truth of his revelation was incompatible with the worship of the gods. The obstacles which he had probably experienced in his own mind instructed him to proceed with caution in the momentous change of a national religion ; and he insensibly discovered his new opinions, as far as he could enforce them with safety and with effect.   During the whole course of his reign, the stream of Christianity flowed with a gentle, though accelerated, motion :

the genuine style of Lactantius. [On these and other minor interpolations, see Brandt's papers in the Sitzungsberichte of the Vienna Academy, 118 and 119 ; cp. Appendix 1.]

  [3] Euseb. in Vit. Constant. l. i. c. 27-32.

  [4] Zosimus, l. ii. p. 104 [c. 29].

  [5] That rite was *always* used in making a catechumen (see Bingham's Antiquities, l. x. c. 1, p. 419 ; Dom. Chardon, Hist. des Sacremens, tom. i. p. 62) and Constantine received it for the *first* time (Euseb. in Vit. Constant. l. iv. c. 61) immediately before his baptism and death. From the connexion of these two facts, Valesius (ad loc. Euseb.) has drawn the conclusion, which is reluctantly admitted by Tillemont (Hist. des Empereurs, tom. iv. p. 628), and opposed with feeble arguments by Mosheim (p. 968).

  [6] Euseb. in Vit. Constant. l. iv. c. 61, 62, 63. The legend of Constantine's baptism at Rome, thirteen years before his death, was invented in the eighth century, as a proper motive for his *donation*. Such has been the gradual progress of knowledge that a story of which Cardinal Baronius (Annal. Ecclesiast. A.D. 324, No. 43-49) declared himself the unblushing advocate is now feebly supported, even within the verge of the Vatican. See the Antiquitates Christianæ, tom. ii. p. 232 ; a work published with six approbations at Rome, in the year 1751, by Father Mamachi, a learned Dominican.

but its general direction was sometimes checked, and sometimes diverted, by the accidental circumstances of the times, and by the prudence, or possibly by the caprice, of the monarch. His ministers were permitted to signify the intentions of their master in the various language which was best adapted to their respective principles ;[7] and he artfully balanced the hopes and fears of his subjects by publishing in the same A.D. 321 year two edicts ; the first of which enjoined the solemn observance of Sunday,[8] and the second directed the regular consultation of the Aruspices.[9] While this important revolution yet remained in suspense, the Christians and the Pagans watched the conduct of their sovereign with the same anxiety, but with very opposite sentiments. The former were prompted by every motive of zeal, as well as vanity, to exaggerate the marks of his favour, and the evidences of his faith. The latter, till their just apprehensions were changed into despair and resentment, attempted to conceal from the world, and from themselves, that the gods of Rome could no longer reckon the emperor in the number of their votaries. The same passions and prejudices have engaged the partial writers of the times to connect the public profession of Christianity with the most glorious or the most ignominious æra of the reign of Constantine.

His Pagan superstition   Whatever symptoms of Christian piety might transpire in the discourses or actions of Constantine, he persevered till he was near forty years of age in the practice of the established religion ;[10] and the same conduct, which in the court of Nicomedia might be imputed to his fear, could be ascribed only to the inclination or policy of the sovereign of Gaul. His liberality restored and enriched the temples of the gods : the medals which issued from his Imperial mint are impressed with the

---

[7] The quæstor, or secretary, who composed the law of the Theodosian Code, makes his master say with indifference, "hominibus supradictæ religionis" (l. xvi. tit. ii. leg. 1). The minister of ecclesiastical affairs was allowed a more devout and respectful style, τῆς ἐνθέσμου καὶ ἁγιωτάτης καθολικῆς θρησκείας, the legal, most holy, and catholic worship. See Euseb. Hist. Eccl. l. x. c. 6.

[8] Cod. Theodos. l. ii. tit. viii. leg. 1. Cod. Justinian. l. iii. tit. xii. leg. iii. Constantine styles the Lord's day dies solis, a name which could not offend the ears of his Pagan subjects.

[9] Cod. Theod. l. xvi. tit. x. leg. 1. Godefroy, in the character of a commentator, endeavours (tom. vi. p. 257) to excuse Constantine ; but the more zealous Baronius (Annal. Eccl. A.D. 321, No. 18) censures his profane conduct with truth and asperity.

[10] Theodoret (l. i. c. 18) seems to insinuate that Helena gave her son a Christian education ; but we may be assured, from the superior authority of Eusebius (in Vit. Constant. l. iii. c. 47), that she herself was indebted to Constantine for the knowledge of Christianity.

figures and attributes of Jupiter and Apollo, of Mars and
Hercules; and his filial piety increased the council of Olympus
by the solemn apotheosis of his father Constantius.[11] But the
devotion of Constantine was more peculiarly directed to the
genius of the Sun, the Apollo of Greek and Roman mythology;
and he was pleased to be represented with the symbols of the
God of Light and Poetry. The unerring shafts of that deity,
the brightness of his eyes, his laurel wreath, immortal beauty,
and elegant accomplishments, seem to point him out as the
patron of a young hero. The altars of Apollo were crowned
with the votive offerings of Constantine; and the credulous
multitude were taught to believe that the emperor was permitted to behold with mortal eyes the visible majesty of their
tutelar deity, and that, either waking or in a vision, he was
blessed with the auspicious omens of a long and victorious reign.
The Sun was universally celebrated as the invincible guide and
protector of Constantine; and the Pagans might reasonably
expect that the insulted god would pursue with unrelenting
vengeance the impiety of his ungrateful favourite.[12]

As long as Constantine exercised a limited sovereignty over
the provinces of Gaul, his Christian subjects were protected by
the authority, and perhaps by the laws, of a prince who wisely
left to the gods the care of vindicating their own honour. If
we may credit the assertion of Constantine himself, he had been
an indignant spectator of the savage cruelties which were inflicted, by the hands of Roman soldiers, on those citizens whose
religion was their only crime.[13] In the East and in the West, he
had seen the different effects of severity and indulgence; and,
as the former was rendered still more odious by the example of
Galerius, his implacable enemy, the latter was recommended to
his imitation by the authority and advice of a dying father.
The son of Constantius immediately suspended or repealed the
edicts of persecution, and granted the free exercise of their

He protects
the Christians
of Gaul. A.D.
306-312

---

[11] See the medals of Constantine in Ducange and Banduri. As few cities had
retained the privilege of coining, almost all the medals of that age issued from the
mint under the sanction of the Imperial authority.

[12] The panegyric of Eumenius (vii. inter Panegyr. Vet.), which was pronounced
a few months before the Italian war, abounds with the most unexceptionable evidence of the Pagan superstition of Constantine, and of his particular veneration for
Apollo, or the Sun; to which Julian alludes (Orat. vii. p. 228, ἀπολείπων σε).
See Commentaire de Spanheim sur les Césars, p. 317.

[13] Constantin. Orat. ad Sanctos, c. 25. But it might easily be shewn that the
Greek translator has improved the sense of the Latin original; and the aged
emperor might recollect the persecution of Diocletian with a more lively abhorrence
than he had actually felt in the days of his youth and Paganism.

religious ceremonies to all those who had already professed themselves members of the church. They were soon encouraged to depend on the favour as well as on the justice of their sovereign, who had imbibed a secret and sincere reverence for the name of Christ and for the God of the Christians.[14]

A.D. 313.
March.
Edict of
Milan

About five months after the conquest of Italy, the emperor made a solemn and authentic declaration of his sentiments, by the celebrated edict of Milan, which restored peace to the Catholic Church. In the personal interview of the two western princes, Constantine, by the ascendant of genius and power, obtained the ready concurrence of his colleague Licinius; the union of their names and authority disarmed the fury of Maximin; and, after the death of the tyrant of the East, the edict of Milan was received as a general and fundamental law of the Roman world.[15] The wisdom of the emperors provided for the restitution of all the civil and religious rights of which the Christians had been so unjustly deprived. It was enacted that the places of worship, and public lands, which had been confiscated, should be restored to the church, without dispute, without delay, and without expense: and this severe injunction was accompanied with a gracious promise that, if any of the purchasers had paid a fair and adequate price, they should be indemnified from the Imperial treasury. The salutary regulations which guard the future tranquillity of the faithful are framed on the principles of enlarged and equal toleration; and such an equality must have been interpreted by a recent sect as an advantageous and honourable distinction. The two emperors proclaim to the world that they have granted a free and absolute power to the Christians, and to all others, of following the religion which each individual thinks proper to prefer, to which he has addicted his mind, and which he may deem the best adapted to his own use. They carefully explain every ambiguous word, remove every exception, and exact from the governors of the provinces a strict obedience to the true and simple meaning of an edict which was designed to establish and secure, without any limitation, the claims of religious liberty. They condescend to assign two weighty reasons which have induced them to allow this universal toleration: the hu-

14 See Euseb. Hist. Eccles. l. viii. 13, l. ix. 9, and in Vit. Const. l. i. c. 16, 17. Lactant. Divin. Institut. i. 1.   Cæcilius de Mort. Persecut. c. 25.

15 Cæcilius (de Mort. Persecut. c. 48) has preserved the Latin original; and Eusebius (Hist. Eccles. l. x. c. 5) has given a Greek translation of this perpetual edict, which refers to some provisional regulations.   [O. Seeck holds that there was no such thing as the Edict of Milan, Zeitsch. f. Kirchengesch., 12, p. 181; cp. Gesch. des Untergangs der antiken Welt, i., p. 457.]

mane intention of consulting the peace and happiness of their
people; and the pious hope that, by such a conduct, they shall
appease and propitiate *the Deity*, whose seat is in heaven. They
gratefully acknowledge the many signal proofs which they
have received of the divine favour; and they trust that the
same Providence will for ever continue to protect the prosperity
of the prince and people. From these vague and indefinite
expressions of piety, three suppositions may be deduced, of a
different, but not of an incompatible, nature. The mind of
Constantine might fluctuate between the Pagan and the
Christian religions. According to the loose and complying
notions of Polytheism, he might acknowledge the God of the
Christians as *one* of the *many* deities who composed the hierarchy of heaven. Or perhaps he might embrace the philosophic
and pleasing idea that, notwithstanding the variety of names,
of rites, and of opinions, all the sects and all the nations of
mankind are united in the worship of the common Father and
Creator of the universe.[16]

But the counsels of princes are more frequently influenced by
views of temporal advantage than by considerations of abstract
and speculative truth. The partial and increasing favour of
Constantine may naturally be referred to the esteem which he
entertained for the moral character of the Christians; and to
a persuasion that the propagation of the gospel would inculcate
the practice of private and public virtue. Whatever latitude
an absolute monarch may assume in his own conduct, whatever
indulgence he may claim for his own passions, it is undoubtedly
his interest that all his subjects should respect the natural and
civil obligations of society. But the operation of the wisest
laws is imperfect and precarious. They seldom inspire virtue,
they cannot always restrain vice. Their power is insufficient to
prohibit all that they condemn, nor can they always punish the
actions which they prohibit. The legislators of antiquity had
summoned to their aid the powers of education and of opinion.
But every principle which had once maintained the vigour and
purity of Rome and Sparta was long since extinguished in a
declining and despotic empire. Philosophy still exercised her

Use and beauty of the Christian morality

[16] A panegyric of Constantine, pronounced seven or eight months after the edict
of Milan (see Gothofred. Chronolog. Legum, p. 7, and Tillemont, Hist. des
Empereurs, tom. iv. p. 246), uses the following remarkable expression: "Summe
rerum sator, cujus tot nomina sunt, quot linguas gentium esse voluisti, quem enim
te ipse dici velis, scire non possumus". Panegyr. Vet. ix. 26. In explaining
Constantine's progress in the faith, Mosheim (p. 971, &c.) is ingenious, subtle,
prolix.

temperate sway over the human mind, but the cause of virtue derived very feeble support from the influence of the Pagan superstition. Under these discouraging circumstances, a prudent magistrate might observe with pleasure the progress of a religion, which diffused among the people a pure, benevolent, and universal system of ethics, adapted to every duty and every condition of life ; recommended as the will and reason of the Supreme Deity, and enforced by the sanction of eternal rewards or punishments. The experience of Greek and Roman history could not inform the world how far the system of national manners might be reformed and improved by the precepts of a divine revelation ; and Constantine might listen with some confidence to the flattering, and indeed reasonable, assurances of Lactantius. The eloquent apologist seemed firmly to expect, and almost ventured to promise, *that* the establishment of Christianity would restore the innocence and felicity of the primitive age ; *that* the worship of the true God would extinguish war and dissension among those who mutually considered themselves as the children of a common parent ; *that* every impure desire, every angry or selfish passion, would be restrained by the knowledge of the gospel ; and *that* the magistrates might sheathe the sword of justice among a people who would be universally actuated by the sentiments of truth and piety, of equity and moderation, of harmony and universal love.[17]

Theory and practice of passive obedience

The passive and unresisting obedience which bows under the yoke of authority, or even of oppression, must have appeared, in the eyes of an absolute monarch, the most conspicuous and useful of the evangelic virtues.[18] The primitive Christians derived the institution of civil government, not from the consent of the people, but from the decrees of heaven. The reigning emperor, though he had usurped the sceptre by treason and murder, immediately assumed the sacred character of vicegerent of the Deity. To the Deity alone he was accountable for the abuse of his power ; and his subjects were indissolubly bound, by their oath of fidelity, to a tyrant who had violated every law of nature and society. The humble Christians were sent into the world as sheep among wolves ; and, since they were not permitted to employ force, even in the defence of their

[17] See the elegant description of Lactantius (Divin. Institut. v. 8), who is much more perspicuous and positive than it becomes a discreet prophet.

[18] The political system of the Christians is explained by Grotius, de Jure Belli et Pacis, l. i. c. 3, 4. Grotius was a republican and an exile, but the mildness of his temper inclined him to support the established powers.

religion, they should be still more criminal if they were tempted to shed the blood of their fellow-creatures in disputing the vain privileges, or the sordid possessions, of this transitory life. Faithful to the doctrine of the apostle who in the reign of Nero had preached the duty of unconditional submission, the Christians of the three first centuries preserved their conscience pure and innocent of the guilt of secret conspiracy or open rebellion. While they experienced the rigour of persecution, they were never provoked either to meet their tyrants in the field or indignantly to withdraw themselves into some remote and sequestered corner of the globe.[19] The Protestants of France, of Germany, and of Britain, who asserted with such intrepid courage their civil and religious freedom, have been insulted by the invidious comparison between the conduct of the primitive and of the reformed Christians.[20] Perhaps, instead of censure, some applause may be due to the superior sense and spirit of our ancestors, who had convinced themselves that religion cannot abolish the unalienable rights of human nature.[21] Perhaps the patience of the primitive church may be ascribed to its weakness, as well as to its virtue. A sect of unwarlike plebeians, without leaders, without arms, without fortifications, must have encountered inevitable destruction in a rash and fruitless resistance to the master of the Roman legions. But the Christians, when they deprecated the wrath of Diocletian, or solicited the favour of Constantine, could allege, with truth and confidence, that they held the principle of passive obedience, and that, in the space of three centuries, their conduct had always been conformable to their principles. They might add that the throne of the emperors would be established on a fixed and permanent basis, if all their subjects, embracing the Christian doctrine, should learn to suffer and to obey.

In the general order of Providence, princes and tyrants are considered as the ministers of Heaven, appointed to rule or to

Divine right of Constantine

[19] Tertullian. Apolog. c. 32, 34, 35, 36. Tamen nunquam Albiniani, nec Nigriani vel Cassiani inveniri potuerunt Christiani. Ad Scapulam, c. 2. If this assertion be strictly true, it excludes the Christians of that age from all civil and military employments, which would have compelled them to take an active part in the service of their respective governors. See Moyle's Works, vol. ii. p. 349.

[20] See the artful Bossuet (Hist. des Variations des Eglises Protestantes, tom. iii. p. 210-258), and the malicious Bayle (tom. ii. p. 620). I *name* Bayle, for he was certainly the author of the Avis aux Refugiés; consult the Dictionnaire Critique de Chauffepié, tom. i. part ii. p. 145.

[21] Buchanan is the earliest, or at least the most celebrated, of the reformers, who has justified the theory of resistance. See his Dialogue de Jure Regni apud Scotos, tom. ii. p. 28, 30, edit. fol. Ruddiman.

chastise the nations of the earth. But sacred history affords
many illustrious examples of the more immediate interposition
of the Deity in the government of his chosen people. The
sceptre and the sword were committed to the hands of Moses,
of Joshua, of Gideon, of David, of the Maccabees ; the virtues
of those heroes were the motive or the effect of the divine
favour, the success of their arms was destined to achieve the
deliverance or the triumph of the church. If the judges of
Israel were occasional and temporary magistrates, the kings of
Judah derived from the royal unction of their great ancestor an
hereditary and indefeasible right, which could not be forfeited
by their own vices, nor recalled by the caprice of their subjects.
The same extraordinary providence, which was no longer confined to the Jewish people, might elect Constantine and his
family as the protectors of the Christian world ; and the devout
Lactantius announces, in a prophetic tone, the future glories
of his long and universal reign.[22]   Galerius and Maximin,
Maxentius and Licinius, were the rivals who shared with the
favourite of Heaven the provinces of the empire.   The tragic
deaths of Galerius and Maximin soon gratified the resentment,
and fulfilled the sanguine expectations, of the Christians. The
success of Constantine against Maxentius and Licinius removed
the two formidable competitors who still opposed the triumph
of the second David, and his cause might seem to claim the
peculiar interposition of Providence.   The character of the
Roman tyrant disgraced the purple and human nature ; and,
though the Christians might enjoy his precarious favour, they
were exposed, with the rest of his subjects, to the effects of his
wanton and capricious cruelty.   The conduct of Licinius soon
betrayed the reluctance with which he had consented to the
wise and humane regulations of the edict of Milan.   The
convocation of provincial synods was prohibited in his dominions ;
his Christian officers were ignominiously dismissed ; and, if he
avoided the guilt, or rather danger, of a general persecution, his
partial oppressions were rendered still more odious by the
violation of a solemn and voluntary engagement.[23]   While the

[22] Lactant. Divin. Institut. i. 1.   Eusebius, in the course of his history, his life,
and his oration, repeatedly inculcates the divine right of Constantine to the empire.

[23] Our imperfect knowledge of the persecution of Licinius is derived from Eusebius (Hist. Eccles. l. x. c. 8 ; Vit. Constantin. l. i. c. 49-56, l. ii. c. 1, 2).
Aurelius Victor mentions his cruelty in general terms. [Cp. Gorres, die Lici-
nianische Christenverfolgung.   He has shown that the persecution was not attended
with much bloodshed.   Some bishops were executed. P. 32 sqq.]

East, according to the lively expression of Eusebius, was involved in the shades of infernal darkness, the auspicious rays of celestial light warmed and illuminated the provinces of the West. The piety of Constantine was admitted as an unexceptionable proof of the justice of his arms; and his use of victory confirmed the opinion of the Christians, that their hero was inspired, and conducted by the Lord of Hosts. The conquest of Italy produced a general edict of toleration : and, as soon as the defeat of Licinius had invested Constantine with the sole dominion of the Roman world, he immediately, by circular letters, exhorted A.D. 324 all his subjects to imitate, without delay, the example of their sovereign, and to embrace the divine truth of Christianity.[24]

The assurance that the elevation of Constantine was intimately connected with the designs of Providence instilled into the minds of the Christians two opinions, which, by very different means, assisted the accomplishment of the prophecy. Their warm and active loyalty exhausted in his favour every resource of human industry ; and they confidently expected that their strenuous efforts would be seconded by some divine and miraculous aid. The enemies of Constantine have imputed to interested motives the alliance which he insensibly contracted with the Catholic church, and which apparently contributed[24a] to the success of his ambition. In the beginning of the fourth century, the Christians still bore a very inadequate proportion to the inhabitants of the empire ; but among a degenerate people, who viewed the change of masters with the indifference of slaves, the spirit and union of a religious party might assist the popular leader to whose service, from a principle of conscience, they had devoted their lives and fortunes.[25] The example of his father had instructed Constantine to esteem and to reward the merit of the Christians ; and in the distribution of public offices, he had the advantage of strengthening his government, by the choice of ministers or generals in whose fidelity he could repose a just and unreserved confidence. By the influence of these dignified missionaries, the proselytes of the new faith must have multiplied in the court and army ; the Barbarians of Germany, who filled the ranks of the legions, were

Loyalty and zeal of the Christian party

[24] Euseb. in Vit. Constant. l. ii. c. 24-42, 48-60.

[24a] [This seems a necessary correction of "contributes," which appears in the quarto ed.]

[25] In the beginning of the last century, the Papists of England were only a *thirtieth*, and the Protestants of France only a *fifteenth*, part of the respective nations, to whom their spirit and power were a constant object of apprehension. See the relations which Bentivoglio (who was then nuncio at Brussels, and afterwards cardinal) transmitted to the court of Rome (Relazione, tom. ii. p. 211. 241). Bentivoglio was curious, well-informed, but somewhat partial.

of a careless temper, which acquiesced without resistance in the religion of their commander ; and, when they passed the Alps, it may fairly be presumed that a great number of the soldiers had already consecrated their swords to the service of Christ and of Constantine.[26]   The habits of mankind, and the interest of religion, gradually abated the horror of war and bloodshed, which had so long prevailed among the Christians ; and, in the councils which were assembled under the gracious protection of Constantine, the authority of the bishops was seasonably employed to ratify the obligation of the military oath, and to inflict the penalty of excommunication on those soldiers who threw away their arms during the peace of the church.[27]   While Constantine, in his own dominions, increased the number and zeal of his faithful adherents, he could depend on the support of a powerful faction in those provinces which were still possessed or usurped by his rivals.   A secret disaffection was diffused among the Christian subjects of Maxentius and Licinius ; and the resentment which the latter did not attempt to conceal served only to engage them still more deeply in the interest of his competitor.   The regular correspondence which connected the bishops of the most distant provinces enabled them freely to communicate their wishes and their designs, and to transmit without danger any useful intelligence, or any pious contributions, which might promote the service of Constantine, who publicly declared that he had taken up arms for the deliverance of the church.[28]

Expectation and belief of a miracle

The enthusiasm which inspired the troops, and perhaps the emperor himself, had sharpened their swords, while it satisfied their conscience.   They marched to battle with the full assurance that the same God, who had formerly opened a passage to the Israelites through the waters of Jordan, and had thrown down the walls of Jericho at the sound of the trumpets

[26] This careless temper of the Germans appears almost uniformly in the history of the conversion of each of the tribes.   The legions of Constantine were recruited with Germans (Zosimus, l. ii. p. 86 [c. 15]); and the court even of his father had been filled with Christians.   See the first book of the Life of Constantine, by Eusebius.

[27] De his qui arma projiciunt in *pace*, placuit eos abstinere a communione. Concil. Arelat. Canon iii.   The best critics apply these words to the *peace of the church*.

[28] Eusebius always considers the second civil war against Licinius as a sort of religious crusade.   At the invitation of the tyrant, some Christian officers had resumed their *zones ;* or, in other words, had returned to the military service.   Their conduct was afterwards censured by the 12th canon of the Council of Nice ; if this particular application may be received, instead of the loose and general sense of the Greek interpreters, Balsamon, Zonaras, and Alexis Aristenus.   See Beveridge, Pandect. Eccles. Græc. tom. i. p. 72 tom. ii. p. 78, Annotation.

of Joshua, would display his visible majesty and power in the victory of Constantine. The evidence of ecclesiastical history is prepared to affirm that their expectations were justified by the conspicuous miracle to which the conversion of the first Christian emperor has been almost unanimously ascribed. The real or imaginary cause of so important an event deserves and demands the attention of posterity; and I shall endeavour to form a just estimate of the famous vision of Constantine, by a distinct consideration of the *standard*, the *dream*, and the *celestial sign;* by separating the historical, the natural, and the marvellous parts of this extraordinary story, which, in the composition of a specious argument, have been artfully confounded in one splendid and brittle mass.

I. An instrument of the tortures which were inflicted only on slaves and strangers became an object of horror in the eyes of a Roman citizen; and the ideas of guilt, of pain, and of ignominy were closely united with the idea of the cross.[29] The piety rather than the humanity of Constantine soon abolished in his dominions the punishment which the Saviour of mankind had condescended to suffer;[30] but the emperor had already learned to despise the prejudices of his education, and of his people, before he could erect in the midst of Rome his own statue, bearing a cross in its right hand, with an inscription which referred the victory of his arms, and the deliverance of Rome, to the virtue of that salutary sign, the true symbol of force and courage.[31] The same symbol sanctified the arms of the soldiers of Constantine; the cross glittered on their helmets, was engraved on their shields, was interwoven into their banners; and the consecrated emblems which adorned the person of the emperor himself were distinguished only by richer materials and

The "Labarum," or standard of the cross

[29] Nomen ipsum *crucis* absit non modo a corpore civium Romanorum, sed etiam a cogitatione, oculis, auribus. Cicero pro Rabirio, c. 5. The Christian writers, Justin, Minucius Felix, Tertullian, Jerom, and Maximus of Turin, have investigated with tolerable success the figure or likeness of a cross in almost every object of nature or art; in the intersection of the meridian and equator, the human face, a bird flying, a man swimming, a mast and yard, a plough, a *standard*, &c. &c. &c. See Lipsius de Cruce, l. i. c. 9.

[30] See Aurelius Victor, who considers this law as one of the examples of Constantine's piety. An edict so honourable to Christianity deserved a place in the Theodosian Code, instead of the indirect mention of it, which seems to result from the comparison of the vth and xviiith titles of the ixth book.

[31] Eusebius, in Vit. Constantin. l. i. c. 40. The statue, or at least the cross and inscription, may be ascribed with more probability to the second, or even the third, visit of Constantine to Rome. Immediately after the defeat of Maxentius, the minds of the senate and people were scarcely ripe for this public monument. [See App. 19.]

more exquisite workmanship.[32]   But the principal standard which
displayed the triumph of the cross was styled the *Labarum*,[33] an
obscure though celebrated name, which has been vainly derived
from almost all the languages of the world.   It is described [34] as
a long pike intersected by a transversal beam.   The silken veil
which hung down from the beam was curiously enwrought with
the images of the reigning monarch and his children.   The summit of the pike supported a crown of gold which inclosed the
mysterious monogram, at once expressive of the figure of the
cross and the initial letters of the name of Christ.[35]   The safety
of the labarum was entrusted to fifty guards, of approved valour
and fidelity; their station was marked by honours and emoluments; and some fortunate accidents soon introduced an
opinion that, as long as the guards of the labarum were engaged
in the execution of their office, they were secure and invulnerable amidst the darts of the enemy.   In the second civil war
Licinius felt and dreaded the power of this consecrated banner,
the sight of which, in the distress of battle, animated the
soldiers of Constantine with an invincible enthusiasm, and
scattered terror and dismay through the ranks of the adverse
legions.[36]   The Christian emperors, who respected the example

---

[32] Agnoscas regina libens mea signa necesse est;
     In quibus effigies *crucis* aut gemmata refulget
     Aut longis solido ex auro praefertur in hastis.
     Hoc signo invictus, transmissis Alpibus Ultor
     Servitium solvit miserabile Constantinus.

   *   *   *   *   *   *   *

     Christus *purpureum* gemmanti textus in auro
     Signabat *Labarum*, clypeorum insignia Christus
     Scripserat; ardebat summis *crux* addita cristis.
                    Prudentius, in Symmachum, l. ii. 464, 486.
[33] The derivation and meaning of the word *Labarum* or *Laborum*, which is
employed by Gregory Nazianzen, Ambrose, Prudentius, &c. still remain totally
unknown; in spite of the efforts of the critics, who have ineffectually tortured the
Latin, Greek, Spanish, Celtic, Teutonic, Illyric, Armenian, &c. in search of an
etymology.   See Ducange, in Gloss. Med. et infim. Latinitat. sub voce *Labarum*,
and Godefroy, ad Cod. Theodos. tom. ii. p. 143.
[34] Euseb. in Vit. Constant. l. i. c. 30, 31.   Baronius (Annal. Eccles. A.D. 312,
No. 26) has engraved a representation of the Labarum.
[35] Transversâ X literâ, summo capite circumflexo, Christum in scutis notat.
Cæcilius de M. P. c. 44.   Cuper (ad. M. P. in edit. Lactant. tom. ii. p. 500) and
Baronius (A.D. 312, No. 25) have engraved from ancient monuments several
specimens (as thus ☧ or ☧) of these monograms, which became extremely
fashionable in the Christian world.
[36] Euseb. in Vit. Constantin. l. ii. c. 7, 8, 9.   He introduces the Labarum before
the Italian expedition; but his narrative seems to indicate that it was never shewn
at the head of an army, till Constantine, above ten years afterwards, declared
himself the enemy of Licinius and the deliverer of the church.

of Constantine, displayed in all their military expeditions the standard of the cross; but, when the degenerate successors of Theodosius had ceased to appear in person at the head of their armies, the labarum was deposited as a venerable but useless relic in the palace of Constantinople.[37] Its honours are still preserved on the medals of the Flavian family. Their grateful devotion has placed the monogram of Christ in the midst of the ensigns of Rome. The solemn epithets of, safety of the republic, glory of the army, restoration of public happiness, are equally applied to the religious and military trophies; and there is still extant a medal of the emperor Constantius, where the standard of the labarum is accompanied with these memorable words, BY THIS SIGN THOU SHALT CONQUER.[38]

II. In all occasions of danger or distress, it was the practice of the primitive Christians to fortify their minds and bodies by the sign of the cross, which they used, in all their ecclesiastical rites, in all the daily occurrences of life, as an infallible preservative against every species of spiritual or temporal evil.[39] The authority of the church might alone have had sufficient weight to justify the devotion of Constantine, who, in the same prudent and gradual progress, acknowledged the truth, and assumed the symbol, of Christianity. But the testimony of a contemporary writer, who in a former treatise has avenged the cause of religion, bestows on the piety of the emperor a more awful and sublime character. He affirms, with the most perfect confidence, that, in the night which preceded the last battle against Maxentius, Constantine was admonished in a dream to inscribe the shields of his soldiers with the *celestial sign of God*, the sacred monogram of the name of Christ; that he executed the commands of heaven; and that his valour and obedience were rewarded by the decisive victory of the Milvian Bridge. Some considerations might perhaps incline a sceptical mind to suspect the judgment or the veracity of the rhetorician, whose

The dream of Constantine

---

[37] See Cod. Theod. l. vi. tit. xxv. Sozomen, l. i. c. 2. Theophan. Chronogr. p. 11. Theophanes lived towards the end of the eighth century, almost five hundred years after Constantine. The modern Greeks were not inclined to display in the field the standard of the empire and of Christianity; and, though they depended on every superstitious hope of *defence*, the promise of *victory* would have appeared too bold a fiction.

[38] The Abbé du Voisin, p. 103, &c. alleges several of these medals, and quotes a particular dissertation of a Jesuit, the Père de Grainville, on this subject.

[39] Tertullian de Corona, c. 3. Athanasius, tom. i. p. 101. The learned Jesuit Petavius (Dogmata Theolog. l. xv. c. 9, 10) has collected many similar passages on the virtues of the cross, which in the last age embarrassed our Protestant disputants.

pen, either from zeal or interest, was devoted to the cause of the prevailing faction.[40] He appears to have published his deaths of the persecutors at Nicomedia about three years after the Roman victory; but the interval of a thousand miles, and a thousand days, will allow an ample latitude for the invention of declaimers, the credulity of party, and the tacit approbation of the emperor himself; who might listen without indignation to a marvellous tale, which exalted his fame and promoted his designs.   In favour of Licinius, who still dissembled his animosity to the Christians, the same author has provided a similar vision, of a form of prayer, which was communicated by an angel, and repeated by the whole army before they engaged the legions of the tyrant Maximin.   The frequent repetition of miracles serves to provoke, where it does not subdue, the reason of mankind; [41] but, if the dream of Constantine is separately considered, it may be naturally explained either by the policy or the enthusiasm of the emperor.   Whilst his anxiety for the approaching day, which must decide the fate of the empire, was suspended by a short and interrupted slumber, the venerable form of Christ, and the well-known symbol of his religion, might forcibly offer themselves to the active fancy of a prince who reverenced the name, and had perhaps secretly implored the power, of the God of the Christians.   As readily might a consummate statesman indulge himself in the use of one of those military stratagems, one of those pious frauds, which Philip and Sertorius had employed with such art and effect.[42]

---

[40] Cæcilius, de M. P. c. 44.   It is certain that this historical declamation was composed and published while Licinius, sovereign of the East, still preserved the friendship of Constantine and of the Christians.   Every reader of taste must perceive that the style is of a very different and inferior character to that of Lactantius; and such indeed is the judgment of Le Clerc and Lardner (Bibliothèque Ancienne et Moderne, tom. iii. p. 438.   Credibility of the Gospel, &c. part ii. vol. vii. p. 94).   Three arguments from the title of the book, and from the names of Donatus and Cæcilius, are produced by the advocates for Lactantius (see the P. Lestocq, tom. ii. p. 46-60).   Each of these proofs is singly weak and defective; but their concurrence has great weight.   I have often fluctuated, and shall *tamely* follow the Colbert Ms. in calling the author (whoever he was) Cæcilius.   [See Appendix 1.]

[41] Cæcilius, de M. P. c. 46.   There seems to be some reason in the observation of M. de Voltaire (Oeuvres, t. xiv. p. 307), who ascribes to the success of Constantine the superior fame of his Labarum above the angel of Licinius.   Yet even this angel is favourably entertained by Pagi, Tillemont, Fleury, &c. who are fond of increasing their stock of miracles.

[42] Besides these well-known examples, Tollius (Preface to Boileau's translation of Longinus) has discovered a vision of Antigonus, who assured his troops that he had seen a pentagon (the symbol of safety) with these words, " In this conquer ". But Tollius has most inexcusably omitted to produce his authority; and his own character, literary as well as moral, is not free from reproach (see Chauffepié,

The præternatural origin of dreams was universally admitted by the nations of antiquity, and a considerable part of the Gallic army was already prepared to place their confidence in the salutary sign of the Christian religion. The secret vision of Constantine could be disproved only by the event; and the intrepid hero who had passed the Alps and the Apennine might view with careless despair the consequences of a defeat under the walls of Rome. The senate and people, exulting in their own deliverance from an odious tyrant, acknowledged that the victory of Constantine surpassed the powers of man, without daring to insinuate that it had been obtained by the protection of the *Gods*. The triumphal arch which was erected about three years after the event proclaims, in ambiguous language, that, by the greatness of his own mind and by an *instinct* or impulse of the Divinity, he had saved and avenged the Roman republic.[43] The pagan orator, who had seized an earlier opportunity of celebrating the virtues of the conqueror, supposes that he alone enjoyed a secret and intimate commerce with the Supreme Being, who delegated the care of mortals to his subordinate deities; and thus assigns a very plausible reason why the subjects of Constantine should not presume to embrace the new religion of their sovereign.[44]

III. The philosopher, who with calm suspicion examines the dreams and omens, the miracles and prodigies, of profane or even of ecclesiastical history, will probably conclude that, if the eyes of the spectators have sometimes been deceived by fraud, the understanding of the readers has much more frequently been insulted by fiction. Every event, or appearance, or accident, which seems to deviate from the ordinary course of nature, has been rashly ascribed to the immediate action of the Deity; and the astonished fancy of the multitude has sometimes given shape and colour, language and motion, to the fleeting but uncommon meteors of the air.[45] Nazarius and Eusebius are the

Appearance of a cross in the sky

Dictionnaire Critique, t. iv. p. 460). Without insisting on the silence of Diodorus, Plutarch. Justin, &c. it may be observed that Polyænus, who in a separate chapter (l. iv. c. 6) has collected nineteen military stratagems of Antigonus, is totally ignorant of this remarkable vision.

[43] Instinctu Divinitatis, mentis magnitudine. [Seeck thinks this an allusion to the dream.] The inscription on the triumphal arch of Constantine, which has been copied by Baronius, Gruter, &c., may still be perused by every curious traveller.

[44] Habes profecto aliquid cum illâ mente Divinâ secretum ; quæ delegatâ nostrâ Diis Minoribus curâ uni se tibi dignatur ostendere. Panegyr. Vet. ix. 2.

[45] M. Freret (Mémoires de l'Académie des Inscriptions, t. iv. p. 411-437) explains, by physical causes, many of the prodigies of antiquity ; and Fabricius, who is abused by both parties, vainly tries to introduce the celestial cross of Constantine among the solar halos. Bibliothec. Græc. tom. vi. p. 8-29.

two most celebrated orators who, in studied panegyrics, have laboured to exalt the glory of Constantine. Nine years after the Roman victory, Nazarius[46] describes an army of divine warriors, who seemed to fall from the sky: he marks their beauty, their spirit, their gigantic forms, the stream of light which beamed from their celestial armour, their patience in suffering themselves to be heard, as well as seen, by mortals; and their declaration that they were sent, that they flew, to the assistance of the great Constantine. For the truth of this prodigy, the Pagan orator appeals to the whole Gallic nation, in whose presence he was then speaking; and seems to hope that the ancient apparitions[47] would now obtain credit from this recent and public event. The Christian fable of Eusebius, which in the space of twenty-six years might arise from the original dream, is cast in a much more correct and elegant mould. In one of the marches of Constantine, he is reported to have seen with his own eyes the luminous trophy of the cross, placed above the meridian sun, and inscribed with the following words: BY THIS CONQUER. This amazing object in the sky astonished the whole army, as well as the emperor himself, who was yet undetermined in the choice of a religion; but his astonishment was converted into faith by the vision of the ensuing night. Christ appeared before his eyes; and, displaying the same celestial sign of the cross, he directed Constantine to frame a similar standard, and to march, with an assurance of victory, against Maxentius and all his enemies.[48] The learned bishop of Cæsarea appears to be sensible that the recent discovery of this marvellous anecdote would excite some surprise and distrust among the most pious of his readers. Yet instead of ascertaining the precise circumstances of time and place, which always serve to detect falsehood or establish truth;[49] instead of collecting and recording the evidence of so

[46] Nazarius inter Panegyr. Vet. x. 14, 15. It is unnecessary to name the moderns, whose undistinguishing and ravenous appetite has swallowed even the Pagan bait of Nazarius.

[47] The apparitions of Castor and Pollux, particularly to announce the Macedonian victory, are attested by historians and public monuments. See Cicero de Naturâ Deorum, ii. 2, iii. 5, 6, Florus, ii. 12. Valerius Maximus, l. i. c. 8, No. 1. Yet the most recent of these miracles is omitted, and indirectly denied, by Livy (xlv. 1).

[48] Eusebius, l. i. c. 28, 29, 30. The silence of the same Eusebius, in his Ecclesiastical History, is deeply felt by those advocates for the miracle who are not absolutely callous.

[49] The narrative of Constantine seems to indicate that he saw the cross in the sky before he passed the Alps against Maxentius. The scene has been fixed by provincial vanity at Treves, Besançon, &c. See Tillemont, Hist. des Empereurs, tom. iv. p. 573.

many living witnesses, who must have been spectators of this stupendous miracle;[50] Eusebius contents himself with alleging a very singular testimony; that of the deceased Constantine, who, many years after the event, in the freedom of conversation, had related to him this extraordinary incident of his own life, and had attested the truth of it by a solemn oath. The prudence and gratitude of the learned prelate forbade him to suspect the veracity of his victorious master; but he plainly intimates that, in a fact of such a nature, he should have refused his assent to any meaner authority. This motive of credibility could not survive the power of the Flavian family; and the celestial sign, which the Infidels might afterwards deride,[51] was disregarded by the Christians of the age which immediately followed the conversion of Constantine.[52] But the Catholic Church, both of the East and of the West, has adopted a prodigy, which favours, or seems to favour, the popular worship of the cross. The vision of Constantine maintained an honourable place in the legend of superstition, till the bold and sagacious spirit of criticism presumed to depreciate the triumph, and to arraign the truth of the first Christian emperor.[53]

The protestant and philosophic readers of the present age will incline to believe that, in the account of his own conversion Constantine attested a wilful falsehood by a solemn and deliberate perjury. They may not hesitate to pronounce that, in the choice of a religion, his mind was determined only by a sense of interest; and that (according to the expression of a

The conversion of Constantine might be sincere

---

[50] The pious Tillemont (Mém. Eccles. tom. vii. p. 1317) rejects with a sigh the useful Acts of Artemius, a veteran and a martyr, who attests as an eye-witness the vision of Constantine. [Acta Sanctorum, Oct. 20; cp. App. 15.]

[51] Gelasius Cyzic. in Act. Concil. Nicen. l. i. c. 4.

[52] The advocates for the vision are unable to produce a single testimony from the Fathers of the fourth and fifth centuries, who, in their voluminous writings, repeatedly celebrate the triumph of the church and of Constantine. As these venerable men had not any dislike to a miracle, we may suspect (and the suspicion is confirmed by the ignorance of Jerom) that they were all unacquainted with the life of Constantine by Eusebius. This tract was recovered by the diligence of those who translated or continued his Ecclesiastical History, and who have represented in various colours the vision of the cross.

[53] Godefroy was the first who, in the year 1643 (Not. ad Philostorgium, l. i. c. 6, p. 16), expressed any doubt of a miracle which had been supported with equal zeal by Cardinal Baronius and the Centuriators of Magdeburg. Since that time, many of the Protestant critics have inclined towards doubt and disbelief. The objections are urged, with great force, by M. Chauffepié (Dictionnaire Critique, tom. iv. p. 6-11), and, in the year 1774, a doctor of Sorbonne, the Abbé du Voisin, published an Apology, which deserves the praise of learning and moderation.

profane poet [54]) he used the altars of the church as a convenient
footstool to the throne of the empire. A conclusion so harsh
and so absolute is not, however, warranted by our knowledge
of human nature, of Constantine, or of Christianity. In an age
of religious fervour, the most artful statesmen are observed to
feel some part of the enthusiasm which they inspire; and the
most orthodox saints assume the dangerous privilege of defending the cause of truth by the arms of deceit and falsehood.
Personal interest is often the standard of our belief, as well
as of our practice; and the same motives of temporal advantage
which might influence the public conduct and professions of
Constantine would insensibly dispose his mind to embrace a
religion so propitious to his fame and fortunes. His vanity
was gratified by the flattering assurance that *he* had been chosen
by Heaven to reign over the earth; success had justified his
divine title to the throne, and that title was founded on the
truth of the Christian revelation. As real virtue is sometimes
excited by undeserved applause, the specious piety of Constantine, if at first it was only specious, might gradually, by
the influence of praise, of habit, and of example, be matured
into serious faith and fervent devotion. The bishops and
teachers of the new sect, whose dress and manners had not
qualified them for the residence of a court, were admitted to
the Imperial table; they accompanied the monarch in his expeditions; and the ascendant which one of them, an Egyptian
or a Spaniard,[55] acquired over his mind was imputed by the
Pagans to the effect of magic.[56] Lactantius, who has adorned

[54] Lors Constantin dit ces propres paroles :
  J'ai renversé le culte des idoles ;
  Sur les débris de leurs temples fumans
  Au Dieu du Ciel j'ai prodigué l'encens.
  Mais tous mes soins pour sa grandeur suprême
  N'eurent jamais d'autre objet que moi-même ;
  Les saints autels n'étoient à mes regards
  Qu'un marchepié du trône des Césars.
  L'ambition, la fureur, les délices
  Etoient mes Dieux, avoient mes sacrifices.
  L'or des Chrétiens, leurs intrigues, leur sang
  Ont cimenté ma fortune et mon rang.
The poem which contains these lines may be read with pleasure, but cannot be
named with decency.

[55] This favourite was probably the great Osius, bishop of Cordova, who preferred the pastoral care of the whole church to the government of a particular
diocese. His character is magnificently, though concisely, expressed by Athanasius (tom. i. p. 703). See Tillemont, Mém. Ecclés. tom. vii. p. 524-561. Osius
was accused, perhaps unjustly, of retiring from court with a very ample fortune.

[56] See Eusebius (in Vit. Constant. passim), and Zosimus, l. ii. p. 104 [c. 29].

the precepts of the gospel with the eloquence of Cicero,[57] and Eusebius, who has consecrated the learning and philosophy of the Greeks to the service of religion,[58] were both received into the friendship and familiarity of their sovereign : and those able masters of controversy could patiently watch the soft and yielding moments of persuasion, and dexterously apply the arguments which were the best adapted to his character and understanding. Whatever advantages might be derived from the acquisition of an Imperial proselyte, he was distinguished by the splendour of his purple, rather than by the superiority of wisdom or virtue, from the many thousands of his subjects who had embraced the doctrines of Christianity. Nor can it be deemed incredible that the mind of an unlettered soldier should have yielded to the weight of evidence, which, in a more enlightened age, has satisfied or subdued the reason of a Grotius, a Pascal, or a Locke. In the midst of the incessant labours of his great office, this soldier employed, or affected to employ, the hours of the night in the diligent study of the Scriptures and the composition of theological discourses ; which he afterwards pronounced in the presence of a numerous and applauding audience. In a very long discourse, which is still extant, the royal preacher expatiates on the various proofs of religion ; but he dwells with peculiar complacency on the Sybilline verses,[59] and the fourth eclogue of Virgil.[60] Forty years before the birth of Christ, the Mantuan bard, as if inspired by the celestial muse of Isaiah, had celebrated, with all the pomp of oriental metaphor, the return of the Virgin, the fall of the serpent, the approaching birth of a god-like child, the offspring of the great Jupiter, who should expiate the guilt of human kind, and govern the peaceful universe with the virtues of his father ; the rise and appearance of an heavenly race, a primitive nation throughout the world : and the gradual restoration of

The fourth eclogue of Virgil

---

[57] The Christianity of Lactantius was of a moral rather than of a mysterious cast. " Erat pæne rudis (says the orthodox Bull) disciplinæ Christianæ, et in rhetoricâ melius quam in theologiâ versatus." Defensio Fidei Nicenæ, sect. ii. c. 14.

[58] Fabricius, with his usual diligence, has collected a list of between three and four hundred authors quoted in the Evangelical Preparation of Eusebius. See Bibliothec. Græc. l. v. c. 4, tom. vi. p. 37-56.

[59] See Constantin. Orat. ad Sanctos, c. 19, 20. He chiefly depends on a mysterious acrostic, composed in the sixth age after the Deluge by the Erythræan Sybil, and translated by Cicero into Latin. The initial letters of the thirty-four Greek verses form this prophetic sentence : JESUS CHRIST, SON OF GOD, SAVIOUR OF THE WORLD.

[60] In his paraphrase of Virgil, the emperor has frequently assisted and improved the literal sense of the Latin text. See Blondel des Sybilles, l. i. c. 14, 15, 16.

the innocence and felicity of the golden age. The poet was perhaps unconscious of the secret sense and object of these sublime predictions, which have been so unworthily applied to the infant son of a consul or a triumvir : [61] but, if a more splendid, and indeed specious, interpretation of the fourth eclogue contributed to the conversion of the first Christian emperor, Virgil may deserve to be ranked among the most successful missionaries of the gospel.[62]

Devotion and privileges of Constantine The awful mysteries of the Christian faith and worship were concealed from the eyes of strangers, and even of catechumens, with an affected secrecy, which served to excite their wonder and curiosity.[63] But the severe rules of discipline which the prudence of the bishops had instituted were relaxed by the same prudence in favour of an Imperial proselyte, whom it was so important to allure, by every gentle condescension, into the pale of the church ; and Constantine was permitted, at least by a tacit dispensation, to enjoy *most* of the privileges, before he had contracted *any* of the obligations, of a Christian. Instead of retiring from the congregation when the voice of the deacon dismissed the profane multitude, he prayed with the faithful, disputed with the bishops, preached on the most sublime and intricate subjects of theology, celebrated with sacred rites the vigil of Easter, and publicly declared himself, not only a partaker, but in some measure a priest and hierophant of the Christian mysteries.[64] The pride of Constantine might assume, and his services had deserved, some extraordinary distinction : an ill-timed rigour might have blasted the unripened fruits of his conversion ; and, if the doors of the church had been strictly closed against a prince who had deserted the altars of the gods, the master of the empire would have been left destitute of any form

[61] The different claims of an elder and younger son of Pollio, of Julia, of Drusus, of Marcellus, are found to be incompatible with chronology, history, and the good sense of Virgil.

[62] See Lowth de Sacra Poesi Hebræorum Prælect. xxi. p. 289-293. In the examination of the fourth eclogue, the respectable bishop of London has displayed learning, taste, ingenuity, and a temperate enthusiasm, which exalts his fancy without degrading his judgment.

[63] The distinction between the public and the secret parts of divine service, the *missa catechumenorum*, and the *missa fidelium*, and the mysterious veil which piety or policy had cast over the latter, are very judiciously explained by Thiers, Exposition du Saint Sacrement, l. i. c. 8-12, p. 59-91 : but as, on this subject, the Papists may reasonably be suspected, a Protestant reader will depend with more confidence on the learned Bingham, Antiquities, l. x. c. 5.

[64] See Eusebius in Vit. Const. l. iv. c. 15-32, and the whole tenor of Constantine's Sermon. The faith and devotion of the emperor has furnished Baronius with a specious argument in favour of his early baptism.

of religious worship.   In his last visit to Rome, he piously disclaimed and insulted the superstition of his ancestors by refusing
to lead the military procession of the equestrian order and to
offer the public vows to the Jupiter of the Capitoline Hill.[65]
Many years before his baptism and death, Constantine had proclaimed to the world that neither his person nor his image should
ever more be seen within the walls of an idolatrous temple;
while he distributed through the provinces a variety of medals
and pictures, which represented the emperor in an humble and
suppliant posture of Christian devotion.[66]

The pride of Constantine, who refused the privileges of a
catechumen, cannot easily be explained or excused; but the
delay of his baptism may be justified by the maxims and the
practice of ecclesiastical antiquity.   The sacrament of baptism [67]
was regularly administered by the bishop himself, with his
assistant clergy, in the cathedral church of the diocese, during
the fifty days between the solemn festivals of Easter and Pentecost; and this holy term admitted a numerous band of infants
and adult persons into the bosom of the church.   The discretion
of parents often suspended the baptism of their children till they
could understand the obligations which they contracted; the
severity of ancient bishops exacted from the new converts a
noviciate of two or three years; and the catechumens themselves,
from different motives of a temporal or a spiritual nature, were
seldom impatient to assume the character of perfect and initiated
Christians.   The sacrament of baptism was supposed to contain
a full and absolute expiation of sin; and the soul was instantly
restored to its original purity, and entitled to the promise of
eternal salvation.   Among the proselytes of Christianity, there
were many who judged it imprudent to precipitate a salutary
rite, which could not be repeated; to throw away an inestimable
privilege, which could never be recovered.   By the delay of their
baptism, they could venture freely to indulge their passions in
the enjoyments of this world, while they still retained in their
own hands the means of a sure and easy absolution.[68]   The sub-

Delay of his baptism till the approach of death

[65] Zosimus, l. ii. p. 105 [29, ad fin.].

[66] Eusebius in Vit. Constant. l. iv. c. 15, 16.

[67] The theory and practice of antiquity with regard to the sacrament of baptism
have been copiously explained by Dom. Chardon, Hist. des Sacremens, tom. i. p. 3-
405; Dom. Martenne, de Ritibus Ecclesiæ Antiquis, tom. i.; and by Bingham, in
the tenth and eleventh books of his Christian Antiquities.   One circumstance may
be observed, in which the modern churches have materially departed from the
ancient custom.   The sacrament of baptism (even when it was administered to
infants) was immediately followed by confirmation and the holy communion.

[68] The fathers, who censured this criminal delay, could not deny the certain and

lime theory of the gospel had made a much fainter impression
on the heart than on the understanding of Constantine himself.
He pursued the great object of his ambition through the dark
and bloody paths of war and policy ; and, after the victory, he
abandoned himself, without moderation, to the abuse of his
fortune.   Instead of asserting his just superiority above the imperfect heroism and profane philosophy of Trajan and the Anton-
nines, the mature age of Constantine forfeited the reputation
which he had acquired in his youth.   As he gradually advanced in
the knowledge of truth, he proportionably declined in the practice
of virtue ; and the same year of his reign in which he convened
the council of Nice was polluted by the execution, or rather
murder, of his eldest son.   This date is alone sufficient to refute
the ignorant and malicious suggestions of Zosimus,[69] who affirms
that, after the death of Crispus, the remorse of his father
accepted from the ministers of Christianity the expiation which
he had vainly solicited from the Pagan Pontiffs.   At the
time of the death of Crispus, the emperor could no longer
hesitate in the choice of a religion ; he could no longer be ignorant that the church was possessed of an infallible remedy, though
he chose to defer the application of it, till the approach of death
had removed the temptation and danger of a relapse.   The
bishops, whom he summoned in his last illness to the palace of
Nicomedia, were edified by the fervour with which he requested
and received the sacrament of baptism, by the solemn protestation that the remainder of his life should be worthy of a disciple
of Christ, and by his humble refusal to wear the imperial purple
after he had been clothed in the white garment of a neophyte.
The example and reputation of Constantine seemed to countenance the delay of baptism.[70]   Future tyrants were encouraged

victorious efficacy even of a deathbed baptism.   The ingenious rhetoric of Chrysostom could find only three arguments against these prudent Christians.   1. That
we should love and pursue virtue for her own sake, and not merely for the reward.
2. That we may be surprised by death without an opportunity of baptism.   3. That,
although we shall be placed in heaven, we shall only twinkle like little stars, when
compared to the suns of righteousness who have run their appointed course with
labour, with success, and with glory.   Chrysostom in Epist. ad Hebræos Homil.
xiii apud Chardon, Hist. des Sacremens, tom. i. p. 49.   I believe that this delay
of baptism, though attended with the most pernicious consequences, was never condemned by any general or provincial council, or by any public act or declaration of
the church.   The zeal of the bishops was easily kindled on much slighter occasions.

[69] Zosimus, l. ii. p. 104 [c. 29].   For this disingenuous falsehood he has deserved and
experienced the harshest treatment from all the ecclesiastical writers, except Cardinal
Baronius (A.D. 324, No. 15-28), who had occasion to employ the Infidel on a
particular service against the Arian Eusebius.

[70] Eusebius, l. iv. c. 61, 62, 63.   The bishop of Cæsarea supposes the salvation
of Constantine with the most perfect confidence.

to believe that the innocent blood which they might shed in a long reign would instantly be washed away in the waters of regeneration ; and the abuse of religion dangerously undermined the foundations of moral virtue.

The gratitude of the church has exalted the virtues and excused the failings of a generous patron, who seated Christianity on the throne of the Roman world ; and the Greeks, who celebrate the festival of the Imperial saint, seldom mention the name of Constantine without adding the title of *equal to the Apostles.*[71] Such a comparison, if it allude to the character of those divine missionaries, must be imputed to the extravagance of impious flattery. But, if the parallel is confined to the extent and number of their evangelic victories, the success of Constantine might perhaps equal that of the Apostles themselves. By the edicts of toleration he removed the temporal disadvantages which had hitherto retarded the progress of Christianity ; and its active and numerous ministers received a free permission, a liberal encouragement, to recommend the salutary truths of revelation by every argument which could affect the reason or piety of mankind. The exact balance of the two religions continued but a moment ; and the piercing eye of ambition and avarice soon discovered that the profession of Christianity might contribute to the interest of the present, as well as of a future, life.[72] The hopes of wealth and honours, the example of an emperor, his exhortations, his irresistible smiles, diffused conviction among the venal and obsequious crowds which usually fill the apartments of a palace. The cities which signalized a forward zeal by the voluntary destruction of their temples were distinguished by municipal privileges, and rewarded with popular donatives ; and the new capital of the East gloried in the singular advantage that Constantinople was never profaned by the worship of idols.[73] As the lower ranks of society are governed by imitation, the conversion of those who possessed any eminence of birth, of power,

(marginal note: Propagation of Christianity)

(marginal note: [Ἰσαπόσ- τολος])

[71] See Tillemont, Hist. des Empereurs, tom. iv. p. 429. The Greeks, the Russians, and, in the darker ages, the Latins themselves have been desirous of placing Constantine in the catalogue of saints.

[72] See the third and fourth books of his life. He was accustomed to say that, whether Christ was preached in pretence or in truth, he should still rejoice (l. iii. c. 58).

[73] M. de Tillemont (Hist. des Empereurs, tom. iv. p. 374, 616) has defended, with strength and spirit, the virgin purity of Constantinople against some malevolent insinuations of the Pagan Zosimus.

or of riches, was soon followed by dependent multitudes.[74]   The
salvation of the common people was purchased at an easy rate,
if it be true that, in one year, twelve thousand men were
baptized at Rome, besides a proportionable number of women
and children ; and that a white garment, with twenty pieces
of gold, had been promised by the emperor to every convert.[75]
The powerful influence of Constantine was not circumscribed
by the narrow limits of his life, or of his dominions.   The
education which he bestowed on his sons and nephews secured
to the empire a race of princes whose faith was still more
lively and sincere, as they imbibed, in their earliest infancy,
the spirit, or at least the doctrine, of Christianity.   War and
commerce had spread the knowledge of the gospel beyond the
confines of the Roman provinces ; and the Barbarians, who had
disdained an humble and proscribed sect, soon learned to
esteem a religion which had been so lately embraced by the
greatest monarch and the most civilized nation of the globe.[76]
The Goths and Germans who enlisted under the standard of
Rome revered the cross which glittered at the head of the
legions, and their fierce countrymen received at the same time
the lessons of faith and of humanity.   The kings of Iberia and
Armenia worshipped the God of their protector ; and their
subjects, who have invariably preserved the name of Christians,
soon formed a sacred and perpetual connexion with their Roman
brethren.   The Christians of Persia were suspected, in time of

[74] The author of the Histoire Politique et Philosophique des deux Indes (tom. i.
p. 9) condemns a law of Constantine, which gave freedom to all the slaves who
should embrace Christianity.   The emperor did indeed publish a law which restrained the Jews from circumcising, perhaps from keeping, any Christian slaves
(see Euseb. in Vit. Constant. l. iv. c. 27 and Cod. Theod. l. xvi. tit. ix. with
Godefroy's Commentary, tom. vi. p. 247).   But this imperfect exception related
only to the Jews ; and the great body of slaves, who were the property of Christian
or Pagan masters, could not improve their temporal condition by changing their religion.   I am ignorant by what guides the Abbé Raynal was deceived ; as the total
absence of quotations is the unpardonable blemish of his entertaining history.

[75] See Acta Sti Silvestri, and Hist. Eccles. Nicephor. Callist. l. vii. c. 34, ap.
Baronium Annal. Eccles. A.D. 324. No. 67, 74.   Such evidence is contemptible
enough ; but these circumstances are in themselves so probable that the learned
Dr. Howell (History of the World, vol. iii. p. 14) has not scrupled to adopt
them.

[76] The conversion of the Barbarians under the reign of Constantine is celebrated
by the ecclesiastical historians (see Sozomen, l. ii. c. 6, and Theodoret, l. i. c. 23,
24).   But Rufinus, the Latin translator of Eusebius, deserves to be considered as
an original authority.   His information was curiously collected from one of the
companions of the Apostle of Æthiopia, and from Bacurius, an Iberian prince,
who was count of the domestics.   Father Mamachi has given an ample compilation
on the progress of Christianity, in the first and second volumes of his great but
imperfect work.   [Rufinus, at first a friend afterwards an opponent of Jerome, also
translated some works of Origen.]

war, of preferring their religion to their country; but, as long as peace subsisted between the two empires, the persecuting spirit of the Magi was effectually restrained by the interposition of Constantine.[77] The rays of the gospel illuminated the coast of India. The colonies of Jews, who had penetrated into Arabia and Æthiopia,[78] opposed the progress of Christianity; but the labour of the missionaries was in some measure facilitated by a previous knowledge of the Mosaic revelation; and Abyssinia still reveres the memory of Frumentius, who, in the time of Constantine, devoted his life to the conversion of those sequestered regions. Under the reign of his son Constantius, Theophilus,[79] who was himself of Indian extraction, was invested with the double character of ambassador and bishop. He embarked on the Red Sea with two hundred horses of the purest breed of Cappadocia, which were sent by the emperor to the prince of the Sabæans, or Homerites. Theophilus was entrusted with many other useful or curious presents, which might raise the admiration and conciliate the friendship of the Barbarians; and he successfully employed several years in a pastoral visit to the churches of the torrid zone.[80] *[c. A.D. 330 and following years]*

The irresistible power of the Roman emperors was displayed in the important and dangerous change of the national religion. *Change of the national religion* The terrors of a military force silenced the faint and unsupported murmurs of the Pagans, and there was reason to expect that the cheerful submission of the Christian clergy, as well as people, would be the result of conscience and gratitude. It was long since established, as a fundamental maxim of the Roman constitution, that every rank of citizens were alike subject to the laws, and that the care of religion was the right as well as duty of the civil magistrate. Constantine and his successors could not easily persuade themselves that they had

---

[77] See in Eusebius (in Vit. Constant. l. ib. c. 9) the pressing and pathetic epistle of Constantine in favour of his Christian brethren of Persia.

[78] See Basnage, Hist. des Juifs, tom. vii. p. 182, tom. viii. p. 333, tom. ix. p. 810. The curious diligence of this writer pursues the Jewish exiles to the extremities of the globe.

[79] Theophilus had been given in his infancy as a hostage by his countrymen of the isle of Diva, and was educated by the Romans in learning and piety. The Maldives, of which Male, or *Diva*, may be the capital, are a cluster of 1900 or 2000 minute islands in the Indian ocean. The ancients were imperfectly acquainted with the Maldives; but they are described in the two Mahometan travellers of the ninth century, published by Renaudot, Geograph. Nubiensis, p. 30, 31. D'Herbelot, Bibliothèque Orientale, p. 704. Hist. Générale des Voyages, tom. viii.

[80] Philostorgius, l. iii. c. 4, 5, 6, with Godefroy's learned observations. The historical narrative is soon lost in an inquiry concerning the seat of paradise, strange monsters, &c.

forfeited, by their conversion, any branch of the Imperial prerogatives, or that they were incapable of giving laws to a
religion which they had protected and embraced. The emperors
still continued to exercise a supreme jurisdiction over the
ecclesiastical order; and the sixteenth book of the Theodosian
A.D. 312-438 code represents, under a variety of titles, the authority which
they assumed in the government of the Catholic church.

Distinction of the spiritual and temporal powers

But the distinction of the spiritual and temporal powers,[81]
which had never been imposed on the free spirit of Greece and
Rome, was introduced and confirmed by the legal establishment
of Christianity. The office of supreme pontiff, which, from the
time of Numa to that of Augustus, had always been exercised
by one of the most eminent of the senators, was at length
united to the Imperial dignity. The first magistrate of the
state, as often as he was prompted by superstition or policy,
performed with his own hands the sacerdotal functions;[82] nor
was there any order of priests, either at Rome or in the provinces, who claimed a more sacred character among men, or
a more intimate communication with the Gods. But in the
Christian church, which entrusts the service of the altar to a
perpetual succession of consecrated ministers, the monarch,
whose spiritual rank is less honourable than that of the meanest
deacon, was seated below the rails of the sanctuary, and confounded with the rest of the faithful multitude.[83] The emperor
might be saluted as the father of his people, but he owed a
filial duty and reverence to the fathers of the church; and
the same marks of respect which Constantine had paid to the
persons of saints and confessors were soon exacted by the pride
of the episcopal order.[84] A secret conflict between the civil

[81] See the epistle of Osius, ap. Athanasium, vol. i. p. 840. The public remon-
strance which Osius was forced to address to the son contained the same principles
of ecclesiastical and civil government which he had secretly instilled into the mind
of the father.

[82] M. de la Bastie (Mémoires de l'Académie des Inscriptions, tom. xv. p. 38-
61) has evidently proved that Augustus and his successors exercised in person all
the sacred functions of pontifex maximus, or high-priest of the Roman empire.

[83] Something of a contrary practice had insensibly prevailed in the church of
Constantinople; but the rigid Ambrose commanded Theodosius to retire below
the rails, and taught him to know the difference between a king and a priest. See
Theodoret, l. v. c. 18.

[84] At the table of the emperor Maximus, Martin, bishop of Tours, received the
cup from an attendant, and gave it to the presbyter his companion, before he
allowed the emperor to drink; the empress waited on Martin at table. Sulpicius
Severus, in Vit. Sti Martin, c. 23, and Dialogue ii. 7. Yet it may be doubted,
whether these extraordinary compliments were paid to the bishop or the saint.
The honours usually granted to the former character may be seen in Bingham's
Antiquities, l. ii. c. 9, and Vales. ad Theodoret, l. iv. c. 6. See the haughty

and ecclesiastical jurisdictions embarrassed the operations of the Roman government; and a pious emperor was alarmed by the guilt and danger of touching with a profane hand the ark of the covenant. The separation of men into the two orders of the clergy and of the laity was, indeed, familiar to many nations of antiquity; and the priests of India, of Persia, of Assyria, of Judea, of Æthiopia, of Egypt, and of Gaul, derived from a celestial origin the temporal power and possessions which they had acquired. These venerable institutions had gradually assimilated themselves to the manners and government of their respective countries; [85] but the opposition or contempt of the civil power served to cement the discipline of the primitive church. The Christians had been obliged to elect their own magistrates, to raise and distribute a peculiar revenue, and to regulate the internal policy of their republic by a code of laws, which were ratified by the consent of the people and the practice of three hundred years. When Constantine embraced the faith of the Christians, he seemed to contract a perpetual alliance with a distinct and independent society; and the privileges granted or confirmed by that emperor, or by his successors, were accepted, not as the precarious favours of the court, but as the just and unalienable rights of the ecclesiastical order.

The Catholic Church was administered by the spiritual and legal jurisdiction of eighteen hundred bishops; [86] of whom one thousand were seated in the Greek, and eight hundred in the Latin, provinces of the empire. The extent and boundaries of their respective dioceses had been variously and accidentally decided by the zeal and success of the first missionaries, by the wishes of the people, and by the propagation of the gospel. Episcopal churches were closely planted along the banks of the Nile, on the sea-coast of Africa, in the proconsular Asia, and through the southern provinces of Italy. The bishops of Gaul and Spain, of Thrace and Pontus, reigned over an ample ter-

State of the bishops under the Christian emperors

---

ceremonial which Leontius, bishop of Tripoli, imposed on the empress. Tillemont, Hist. des Empereurs, tom. iv. p. 754. Patres Apostol. tom. ii. p. 179.

[85] Plutarch, in his treatise of Isis and Osiris, informs us that the kings of Egypt, who were not already priests, were initiated, after their election, into the sacerdotal order.

[86] The numbers are not ascertained by any ancient writer, or original catalogue; for the partial lists of the eastern churches are comparatively modern. The patient diligence of Charles a Sto Paolo, of Luke Holstenius, and of Bingham, has laboriously investigated all the episcopal sees of the Catholic Church, which was almost commensurate with the Roman empire. The ninth book of the Christian Antiquities is a very accurate map of ecclesiastical geography. [Cp. Append. 20.]

ritory, and delegated their rural suffragans to execute the sub-ordinate duties of the pastoral office.[87]   A Christian diocese might be spread over a province or reduced to a village ; but all the bishops possessed an equal and indelible character : they all derived the same powers and privileges from the apostles, from the people, and from the laws.   While the *civil* and *military* professions were separated by the policy of Constantine, a new and perpetual order of *ecclesiastical* ministers, always respectable, sometimes dangerous, was established in the church and state.   The important review of their station and attributes may be distributed under the following heads : I. Popular election. II. Ordination of the clergy. III. Property. IV. Civil jurisdiction. V. Spiritual censures. VI. Exercise of public oratory. VII. Privilege of legislative assemblies.

I. Election of bishops   I. The freedom of elections subsisted long after the legal establishment of Christianity ; [88] and the subjects of Rome enjoyed in the church the privilege which they had lost in the republic, of choosing the magistrates whom they were bound to obey. As soon as a bishop had closed his eyes, the metro-politan issued a commission to one of his suffragans to administer the vacant see, and prepare, within a limited time, the future election. The right of voting was vested in the inferior clergy, who were best qualified to judge of the merit of the candidates ; in the senators or nobles of the city, all those who were dis-tinguished by their rank or property ; and finally in the whole body of the people, who, on the appointed day, flocked in multitudes from the most remote parts of the diocese,[89] and sometimes silenced, by their tumultuous acclamations, the voice of reason and the laws of discipline. These acclamations might accidentally fix on the head of the most deserving competitor ; of some ancient presbyter, some holy monk, or some layman,

[87] On the subject of the rural bishops, or *Chorepiscopi*, who voted in synods, and conferred the minor orders, see Thomassin, Discipline de l'Eglise, tom. i. p. 447, &c. and Chardon, Hist. des Sacremens, tom. v. p. 395, &c. They do not appear till the fourth century ; and this equivocal character, which had excited the jealousy of the prelates, was abolished before the end of the tenth both in the East and the West.

[88] Thomassin (Discipline de l'Eglise, tom. ii. l. ii. c. i.-8, p. 673-721) has copiously treated of the election of bishops during the five first centuries, both in the East and in the West ; but he shews a very partial bias in favour of the epis-copal aristocracy. Bingham (l. iv. c. 2) is moderate ; and Chardon (Hist. des Sacremens, tom. v. p. 108-128) is very clear and concise.

[89] Incredibilis multitudo, non solum ex eo oppido (*Tours*), sed etiam ex vicinis urbibus ad suffragia ferenda convenerat, &c. Sulpicius Severus, in Vit. Martin. c. 7. The council of Laodicea (canon xiii.) prohibits mobs and tumults ; and Justinian confines the right of election to the nobility. Novell. cxxiii. 1.

conspicuous for his zeal and piety. But the episcopal chair was solicited, especially in the great and opulent cities of the empire, as a temporal rather than as a spiritual dignity. The interested views, the selfish and angry passions, the arts of perfidy and dissimulation, the secret corruption, the open and even bloody violence, which had formerly disgraced the freedom of election in the commonwealths of Greece and Rome, too often influenced the choice of the successors of the apostles. While one of the candidates boasted the honours of his family, a second allured his judges by the delicacies of a plentiful table, and a third, more guilty than his rivals, offered to share the plunder of the church among the accomplices of his sacrilegious hopes.[90] The civil as well as ecclesiastical laws attempted to exclude the populace from this solemn and important transaction. The canons of ancient discipline, by requiring several episcopal qualifications of age, station, &c., restrained in some measure the indiscriminate caprice of the electors. The authority of the provincial bishops, who were assembled in the vacant church to consecrate the choice of the people, was interposed to moderate their passions and to correct their mistakes. The bishops could refuse to ordain an unworthy candidate, and the rage of contending factions sometimes accepted their impartial mediation. The submission, or resistance, of the clergy and people, on various occasions, afforded different precedents, which were insensibly converted into positive laws and provincial customs : [91] but it was everywhere admitted, as a fundamental maxim of religious policy, that no bishop could be imposed on an orthodox church without the consent of its members. The emperors, as the guardians of the public peace, and as the first citizens of Rome and Constantinople, might effectually declare their wishes in the choice of a primate : but those absolute monarchs respected the freedom of ecclesiastical elections; and, while they distributed and resumed the honours of the state and army, they allowed eighteen hundred perpetual magistrates to receive their important offices from the free suffrages of the people.[92]   It was

[90] The epistles of Sidonius Apollinaris (iv. 25, vii. 5, 9) exhibit some of the scandals of the Gallican church ; and Gaul was less polished and less corrupt than the East.

[91] A compromise was sometimes introduced by law or by consent : either the bishops or the people chose one of the three candidates who had been named by the other party.

[92] All the examples quoted by Thomassin (Discipline de l'Eglise, tom. ii. l. ii. c. 6, p. 704-714) appear to be extraordinary acts of power, and even of oppression. The confirmation of the bishop of Alexandria is mentioned by Philostorgius as a more regular proceeding (Hist. Eccles. l. ii. 11).

agreeable to the dictates of justice, that these magistrates should not desert an honourable station from which they could not be removed; but the wisdom of councils endeavoured, without much success, to enforce the residence, and to prevent the translation, of bishops. The discipline of the West was indeed less relaxed than that of the East; but the same passions which made those regulations necessary rendered them ineffectual. The reproaches which angry prelates have so vehemently urged against each other serve only to expose their common guilt and their mutual indiscretion.

II. Ordination of the clergy

II. The bishops alone possessed the faculty of *spiritual* generation; and this extraordinary privilege might compensate, in some degree, for the painful celibacy[93] which was imposed as a virtue, as a duty, and at length as a positive obligation. The religions of antiquity, which established a separate order of priests, dedicated a holy race, a tribe or family, to the perpetual service of the Gods.[94] Such institutions were founded for possession rather than conquest. The children of the priests enjoyed, with proud and indolent security, their sacred inheritance; and the fiery spirit of enthusiasm was abated by the cares, the pleasures, and the endearments of domestic life. But the Christian sanctuary was open to every ambitious candidate who aspired to its heavenly promises or temporal possessions. The office of priests, like that of soldiers or magistrates, was strenuously exercised by those men whose temper and abilities had prompted them to embrace the ecclesiastical profession, or who had been selected by a discerning bishop as the best qualified to promote the glory and interest of the church. The bishops[95] (till the abuse was restrained by the

[93] The celibacy of the clergy during the first five or six centuries is a subject of discipline, and indeed of controversy, which has been very diligently examined. See in particular Thomassin, Discipline de l'Eglise, tom. i. l. ii. c. lx. lxi. p. 886-902, and Bingham's Antiquities, l. iv. c. 5. By each of these learned but partial critics, one half of the truth is produced, and the other is concealed.

[94] Diodorus Siculus attests and approves the hereditary succession of the priesthood among the Egyptians, the Chaldeans, and the Indians (l. i. p. 84 [c. 73], l. ii. p. 142, 153 [29, 40 and 41 ad fin.], edit. Wesseling). The magi are described by Ammianus as a very numerous family: "Per sæcula multa ad præsens unâ eâdemque prosapiâ multitudo creata, Deorum cultibus dedicata" (xxiii. 6). Ausonius celebrates the *Stirps Druidarum* (De Professorib. Burdigal. iv.); but we may infer from the remark of Cæsar (vi. 13), that, in the Celtic hierarchy, some room was left for choice and emulation.

[95] The subject of the vocation, ordination, obedience, &c. of the clergy, is laboriously discussed by Thomassin (Discipline de l'Eglise, tom. ii. p. 1-83) and Bingham (in the fourth book of his Antiquities, more especially the fourth, sixth, and seventh chapters). When the brother of St. Jerom was ordained in Cyprus, the deacons forcibly stopped his mouth, lest he should make a solemn protestation which might invalidate the holy rites.

prudence of the laws) might constrain the reluctant, and protect the distressed ; and the imposition of hands for ever bestowed some of the most valuable privileges of civil society. The whole body of the Catholic clergy, more numerous perhaps than the legions, was exempted by the emperors from all service, private or public, all municipal offices, and all personal taxes and contributions which pressed on their fellow-citizens with intolerable weight ; and the duties of their holy profession were accepted as a full discharge of their obligations to the republic.[96] Each bishop acquired an absolute and indefeasible right to the perpetual obedience of the clerk whom he ordained : the clergy of each episcopal church, with its dependent parishes, formed a regular and permanent society ; and the cathedrals of Constantinople[97] and Carthage[98] maintained their peculiar establishment of five hundred ecclesiastical ministers.   Their ranks[99] and numbers were insensibly multiplied by the superstition of the times, which introduced into the church the splendid ceremonies of a Jewish or Pagan temple ; and a long train of priests, deacons, sub-deacons, acolytes, exorcists, readers, singers, and door-keepers, contributed, in their respective stations, to swell the pomp and harmony of religious worship.   The clerical name and privilege were extended to many pious fraternities, who devoutly supported the ecclesiastical throne.[100] Six hundred *parabolani*, or adventurers, visited the sick at [παραβαλα Alexandria ; eleven hundred *copiatæ*, or gravediggers, buried νεῖς] the dead at Constantinople ; and the swarms of monks, who arose from the Nile, overspread and darkened the face of the Christian world.

[96] The charter of immunities which the clergy obtained from the Christian emperors is contained in the sixteenth book of the Theodosian code ; and is illustrated with tolerable candour by the learned Godefroy, whose mind was balanced by the opposite prejudices of a civilian and a protestant.

[97] Justinian. Novell. ciii.   Sixty presbyters or priests, one hundred deacons, forty deaconesses, ninety sub-deacons, one hundred and ten readers, twenty-five chanters, and one hundred door-keepers ; in all, five hundred and twenty-five. This moderate number was fixed by the emperor, to relieve the distress of the church, which had been involved in debt and usury by the expense of a much higher establishment.

[98] Universus clerus ecclesiæ Carthaginiensis . . . fere *quinginti* vel amplius ; inter quos quamplurimi erant lectores infantuli.   Victor Vitensis, de Persecut. Vandal. v. 9, p. 78, edit. Ruinart.   This remnant of a more prosperous state subsisted under the oppression of the Vandals.

[99] The number of *seven* orders has been fixed in the Latin church, exclusive of the episcopal character.   But the four inferior ranks, the minor orders, are now reduced to empty and useless titles.

[100] See Cod. Theodos. l. xvi. tit. 2, leg. 42, 43.   Godefroy's Commentary, and the Ecclesiastical History of Alexandria, shew the danger of these pious institutions, which often disturbed the peace of that turbulent capital.

III. The edict of Milan secured the revenue as well as the peace of the church.[101] The Christians not only recovered the lands and houses of which they had been stripped by the persecuting laws of Diocletian, but they acquired a perfect title to all the possessions which they had hitherto enjoyed by the connivance of the magistrate. As soon as Christianity became the religion of the emperor and the empire, the national clergy might claim a decent and honourable maintenance : and the payment of an annual tax might have delivered the people from the more oppressive tribute which superstition imposes on her votaries. But, as the wants and expenses of the church increased with her prosperity, the ecclesiastical order was still supported and enriched by the voluntary oblations of the faithful. Eight

years after the edict of Milan, Constantine granted to all his subjects the free and universal permission of bequeathing their fortunes to the holy Catholic church ;[102] and their devout liberality, which during their lives was checked by luxury or avarice, flowed with a profuse stream at the hour of their death. The wealthy Christians were encouraged by the example of their sovereign. An absolute monarch, who is rich without patrimony, may be charitable without merit ; and Constantine too easily believed that he should purchase the favour of Heaven, if he maintained the idle at the expense of the industrious, and distributed among the saints the wealth of the republic. The same messenger who carried over to Africa the head of Maxentius might be entrusted with an epistle to Cæcilian, bishop of Carthage. The emperor acquaints him that the treasurers of the province are directed to pay into his hands the sum of three thousand *folles,* or eighteen thousand pounds sterling, and to obey his farther requisitions for the relief of the churches of Africa, Numidia, and Mauritania.[103] The liberality of Constantine increased in a just proportion to his faith, and to his vices. He assigned in each city a regular

---

[101] The edict of Milan (de M. P. c. 48) acknowledges, by reciting, that there existed a species of landed property, ad jus corporis eorum, id est, ecclesiarum non hominum singulorum pertinentia. Such a solemn declaration of the supreme magistrate must have been received in all the tribunals as a maxim of civil law. [Cp. above, p. 292, n. 15.]

[102] Habeat unusquisque licentiam sanctissimo Catholicæ (*ecclesiæ*) venerabilique concilio, decedens bonorum quod optavit relinquere. Cod. Theodos. l. xvi. tit. ii. leg. 4. This law was published at Rome, A.D. 321, at a time when Constantine might foresee the probability of a rupture with the emperor of the East.

[103] Eusebius, Hist. Eccles. l. x. 6; in Vit. Constant. l. iv. c. 28. He repeatedly expatiates on the liberality of the Christian hero, which the bishop himself had an opportunity of knowing and even of tasting.

allowance of corn, to supply the fund of ecclesiastical charity; and the persons of both sexes who embraced the monastic life became the peculiar favourites of their sovereign. The Christian temples of Antioch, Alexandria, Jerusalem, Constantinople, &c. displayed the ostentatious piety of a prince ambitious, in a declining age, to equal the perfect labours of antiquity.[104] The form of these religious edifices was simple and oblong; though they might sometimes swell into the shape of a dome, and sometimes branch into the figure of a cross. The timbers were framed for the most part of cedars of Libanus; the roof was covered with tiles, perhaps of gilt brass; and the walls, the columns, the pavement, were incrusted with variegated marbles. The most precious ornaments of gold and silver, of silk and gems, were profusely dedicated to the service of the altar; and this specious magnificence was supported on the solid and perpetual basis of landed property. In the space of two centuries, from the reign of Constantine to that of Justinian, the eighteen hundred churches of the empire were enriched by the frequent and unalienable gifts of the prince and people. An annual income of six hundred pounds sterling may be reasonably assigned to the bishops, who were placed at an equal distance between riches and poverty,[105] but the standard of their wealth insensibly rose with the dignity and opulence of the cities which they governed. An authentic but imperfect[106] rent-roll specifies some houses, shops, gardens, and farms, which belonged to the three *Basilicæ* of Rome, St. Peter, St. Paul, and St. John Lateran, in the provinces of Italy, Africa, and the East. They produce, besides a reserved rent of oil, linen, paper, aromatics, &c. a clear annual revenue of twenty-two thousand pieces of gold, or twelve thousand pounds sterling. In the age of Constantine and Justinian, the bishops no longer possessed, perhaps they no longer deserved, the unsuspecting

---

[104] Eusebius, Hist. Eccles. l. x. c. 2, 3, 4. The bishop of Cæsarea, who studied and gratified the taste of his master, pronounced in public an elaborate description of the church of Jerusalem (in Vit. Const. l. iv. c. 46). It no longer exists, but he has inserted in the Life of Constantine (l. iii. c. 36) a short account of the architecture and ornaments. He likewise mentions the church of the holy Apostles at Constantinople (l. iv. c. 59).

[105] See Justinian. Novell. cxxiii. 3. The revenue of the patriarchs, and the most wealthy bishops, is not expressed; the highest annual valuation of a bishopric is stated at *thirty*, and the lowest at *two*, pounds of gold; the medium might be taken at *sixteen*, but these valuations are much below the real value.

[106] See Baronius (Annal. Eccles. A.D. 324, No. 58, 65, 70, 71). Every record which comes from the Vatican is justly suspected; yet these rent-rolls have an ancient and authentic colour; and it is at least evident, that, if forged, they were forged in a period when *farms*, not *kingdoms*, were the objects of papal avarice.

confidence of their clergy and people.   The ecclesiastical revenues of each diocese were divided into four parts; for the respective uses, of the bishop himself, of his inferior clergy, of the poor, and of the public worship; and the abuse of this sacred trust was strictly and repeatedly checked.[107]   The patrimony of the church was still subject to all the public impositions of the state.[108]   The clergy of Rome, Alexandria, Thessalonica, &c. might solicit and obtain some partial exemptions; but the premature attempt of the great council of Rimini, which aspired to universal freedom, was successfully resisted by the son of Constantine.[109]

[A.D. 360]

IV. Civil jurisdiction

IV.   The Latin clergy, who erected their tribunal on the ruins of the civil and common law, have modestly accepted as the gift of Constantine [110] the independent jurisdiction which was the fruit of time, of accident, and of their own industry. But the liberality of the Christian emperors had actually endowed them with some legal prerogatives, which secured and dignified the sacerdotal character.[111]   1. Under a despotic govern-

---

[107] See Thomassin, Discipline de l'Eglise, tom. iii. l. ii. c. 13, 14, 15, p. 689-706.   The legal division of the ecclesiastical revenue does not appear to have been established in the time of Ambrose and Chrysostom.   Simplicius and Gelasius, who were bishops of Rome in the latter part of the fifth century, mention it in their pastoral letters as a general law, which was already confirmed by the custom of Italy.

[108] Ambrose, the most strenuous asserter of ecclesiastical privileges, submits without a murmur to the payment of the land-tax.   "Si tributum petit Imperator, non negamus; agri ecclesiæ solvunt tributum; solvimus quæ sunt Cæsaris Cæsari, et quæ sunt Dei Deo: tributum Cæsaris est; non negatur."   Baronius labours to interpret this tribute as an act of charity rather than of duty (Annal. Eccles. A.D. 387); but the words, if not the intent ons, of Ambrose, are more candidly explained by Thomassin, Discipline de l'Eglise, tom. iii. l. i. c. 34, p. 268.

[109] In Ariminense synodo super ecclesiarum et clericorum privilegiis tractatû habito, usque eo dispositio progressa est, ut juga quæ viderentur ad ecclesiam pertinere, a publicâ functione cessarent inquietudine desistente: quod nostra videtur dudum sanctio repulsisse.   Cod. Theod. l. xvi. tit. ii. leg. 15.   Had the synod of Rimini carried this point, such practical merit might have atoned for some speculative heresies.

[110] From Eusebius (in Vit. Constant. l. iv. c. 27) and Sozomen (l. i. c. 9) we are assured that the episcopal jurisdiction was extended and confirmed by Constantine; but the forgery of a famous edict, which was never fairly inserted in the Theodosian Code (see at the end, tom. vi. p. 303), is demonstrated by Godefroy in the most satisfactory manner.   It is strange that M. de Montesquieu, who was a lawyer as well as a philosopher, should allege this edict of Constantine (Esprit des Loix, l. xxix. c. 16) without intimating any suspicion.

[111] The subject of ecclesiastical jurisdiction has been involved in a mist of passion, of prejudice, and of interest.   Two of the fairest books which have fallen into my hands are the Institutes of Canon Law, by the Abbé de Fleury, and the Civil History of Naples, by Giannone.   Their moderation was the effect of situation as well as of temper.   Fleury was a French ecclesiastic, who respected the authority of the parliaments; Giannone was an Italian lawyer, who dreaded the power of the church.   And here let me observe that, as the general pro-

ment, the bishops alone enjoyed and asserted the inestimable privilege of being tried only by their *peers ;* and even in a capital accusation, a synod of their brethren were the sole judges of their guilt or innocence.   Such a tribunal, unless it was inflamed by personal resentment or religious discord, might be favourable, or even partial, to the sacerdotal order : but Constantine was satisfied[112] that secret impunity would be less pernicious than public scandal : and the Nicene council was edified by his public declaration that, if he surprised a bishop in the act of adultery, he should cast his Imperial mantle over the episcopal sinner.   2. The domestic jurisdiction of the bishops was at once a privilege and a restraint of the ecclesiastical order, whose civil causes were decently withdrawn from the cognizance of a secular judge.   Their venial offences were not exposed to the shame of a public trial or punishment ; and the gentle correction, which the tenderness of youth may endure from its parents or instructors, was inflicted by the temperate severity of the bishops.   But, if the clergy were guilty of any crime which could not be sufficiently expiated by their degradation from an honourable and beneficial profession, the Roman magistrate drew the sword of justice without any regard to ecclesiastical immunities.   3. The arbitration of the bishops was ratified by a positive law ; and the judges were instructed to execute, without appeal or delay, the episcopal decrees, whose validity had hitherto depended on the consent of the parties.   The conversion of the magistrates themselves, and of the whole empire, might gradually remove the fears and scruples of the Christians. But they still resorted to the tribunal of the bishops, whose abilities and integrity they esteemed : and the venerable Austin enjoyed the satisfaction of complaining that his spiritual functions were perpetually interrupted by the invidious labour of deciding the claim or the possession of silver and gold, of lands and cattle.   4. The ancient privilege of sanctuary was transferred to the Christian temples, and extended, by the liberal piety of the younger Theodosius, to the precincts of consecrated ground.[113]

positions which I advance are the result of *many* particular and imperfect facts, I must either refer the reader to those modern authors who have expressly treated the subject or swell these notes to a disagreeable and disproportioned size.

[112] Tillemont has collected from Rufinus, Theodoret, &c. the sentiments and language of Constantine.   Mém. Ecclés. t. iii. p. 749, 750.

[113] See Cod. Theod. l. ix. tit. xlv. leg. 4.   In the works of Fra Paolo (tom. iv. p. 192, &c.) there is an excellent discourse on the origin, claims, abuses, and limits of sanctuaries.   He justly observes that ancient Greece might perhaps contain fifteen or twenty *asyla* or sanctuaries ; a number which at present may be found in Italy within the walls of a single city.

The fugitive, and even guilty, suppliants were permitted to implore either the justice or the mercy of the Deity and his ministers. The rash violence of despotism was suspended by the mild interposition of the church; and the lives or fortunes of the most eminent subjects might be protected by the mediation of the bishop.

V. Spiritual censures

V. The bishop was the perpetual censor of the morals of his people. The discipline of penance was digested into a system of canonical jurisprudence,[114] which accurately defined the duty of private or public confession, the rules of evidence, the degrees of guilt, and the measure of punishment. It was impossible to execute this spiritual censure, if the Christian pontiff, who punished the obscure sins of the multitude, respected the conspicuous vices and destructive crimes of the magistrate; but it was impossible to arraign the conduct of the magistrate without controlling the administration of civil government. Some considerations of religion, or loyalty, or fear, protected the sacred persons of the emperors from the zeal or resentment of the bishops; but they boldly censured and excommunicated the subordinate tyrants who were not invested with the majesty of the purple. St. Athanasius excommunicated one of the ministers of Egypt; and the interdict which he pronounced, of fire and water, was solemnly transmitted to the churches of Cappadocia.[115] Under the reign of the younger Theodosius, the polite and eloquent Synesius, one of the descendants of Hercules,[116] filled the episcopal seat of Ptolemais, near the ruins of ancient Cyrene,[117] and the philosophic bishop supported, with dignity,

114 The penitential jurisprudence was continually improved by the canons of the councils. But, as many cases were still left to the discretion of the bishops, they occasionally published, after the example of the Roman Prætor, the rules of discipline which they proposed to observe. Among the canonical epistles of the fourth century, those of Basil the Great were the most celebrated. They are inserted in the Pandects of Beveridge (tom. ii. p. 47-151), and are translated by Chardon, Hist. des Sacremens, tom. iv. p. 219-277.

115 Basil Epistol. xlvii. in Baronius (Annal. Eccles. A.D. 370, No, 91), who declares that he purposely relates it, to convince governors that they were not exempt from a sentence of excommunication. In his opinion, even a royal head is not safe from the thunders of the Vatican; and the cardinal shews himself much more consistent than the lawyers and theologians of the Gallican church.

116 The long series of his ancestors, as high as Eurysthenes, the first Doric king of Sparta, and the fifth in lineal descent from Hercules, was inscribed in the public registers of Cyrene, a Lacedæmonian colony. (Synes. Epist. lvii. p. 197, edit. Petav.) Such a poor and illustrious pedigree of seventeen hundred years, without adding the royal ancestors of Hercules, cannot be equalled in the history of mankind.

117 Synesius (de Regno, p. 2) pathetically deplores the fallen and ruined state of Cyrene, πόλις Ἑλληνίς, παλαιὸν ὄνομα καὶ σεμνὸν, καὶ ἐν ᾠδῇ μυρίᾳ τῶν πάλαι σοφῶν, νῦν πένης καὶ κατηφὴς, καὶ μέγα ἐρείπιον. Ptolemais, a new city, 82 miles to the

the character which he had assumed with reluctance.[118] He vanquished the monster of Libya, the president Andronicus, who abused the authority of a venal office, invented new modes of rapine and torture, and aggravated the guilt of oppression by that of sacrilege.[119] After a fruitless attempt to reclaim the haughty magistrate by mild and religious admonition, Synesius proceeds to inflict the last sentence of ecclesiastical justice,[120] which devotes Andronicus, with his associates and their *families*, to the abhorrence of earth and heaven. The impenitent sinners, more cruel than Phalaris or Sennacherib, more destructive than war, pestilence, or a cloud of locusts, are deprived of the name and privileges of Christians, of the participation of the sacraments, and of the hope of Paradise. The bishop exhorts the clergy, the magistrates, and the people, to renounce all society with the enemies of Christ ; to exclude them from their houses and tables ; and to refuse them the common offices of life and the decent rites of burial. The church of Ptolemais, obscure and contemptible as she may appear, addresses this declaration to all her sister churches of the world ; and the profane who reject her decrees will be involved in the guilt and punishment of Andronicus and his impious followers. These spiritual terrors were enforced by a dexterous application to the Byzantine court ; the trembling president implored the mercy of the church ; and the descendant of Hercules enjoyed the satisfaction of raising a prostrate

westward of Cyrene, assumed the metropolitan honours of the Pentapolis, or Upper Libya, which were afterwards transferred to Sozusa. See Wesseling Itinerar. p. 67, 68, 732. Cellarius Geograph. tom. ii. part. ii. p. 72, 74. Carolus a Sto Paulo Geograph. Sacra, p. 273, D'Anville Géographie ancienne, tom. iii. p. 43, 44, Mémoires de l'Acad. des Inscriptions, tom. xxxvii. p. 363-391.

[118] Synesius had previously represented his own disqualifications (Epist. cv. p. 246-250). He loved profane studies and profane sports ; he was incapable of supporting a life of celibacy ; he disbelieved the resurrection ; and he refused to preach *fables* to the people, unless he might be permitted to *philosophize* at home. Theophilus, primate of Egypt, who knew his merit, accepted this extraordinary compromise. See the Life of Synesius in Tillemont, Mém Ecclés. tom. xii. p. 499-554.

[119] See the invective of Synesius, Epist. lvii. p. 191-201. The promotion of Andronicus was illegal ; since he was a native of Berenice, in the same province. The instruments of torture are curiously specified, the πιεστήριον, or press, the ʹακτυλήθρα, the ποδοστράβη, the ῥινολαβίς, the ὠτάγρα, and the χειλοστρόφιον, that variously pressed or distended the fingers, the feet, the nose, the ears, and the lips of the victims [in Ep. lviii. p. 1399, ed. Migne].

[120] The sentence of excommunication is expressed in a rhetorical style. (Synesius, Epist. lviii. p. 201-203.) The method of involving whole families, though somewhat unjust, was improved into national interdicts.

tyrant from the ground.[121]   Such principles and such examples insensibly prepared the triumph of the Roman pontiffs, who have trampled on the necks of kings.

VI. Freedom of public preaching

VI. Every popular government has experienced the effects of rude or artificial eloquence. The coldest nature is animated, the firmest reason is moved, by the rapid communication of the prevailing impulse; and each hearer is affected by his own passions, and by those of the surrounding multitude. The ruin of civil liberty had silenced the demagogues of Athens and the tribunes of Rome; the custom of preaching, which seems to constitute a considerable part of Christian devotion, had not been introduced into the temples of antiquity; and the ears of monarchs were never invaded by the harsh sound of popular eloquence, till the pulpits of the empire were filled with sacred orators who possessed some advantages unknown to their profane predecessors.[122]   The arguments and rhetoric of the tribune were instantly opposed, with equal arms, by skilful and resolute antagonists; and the cause of truth and reason might derive an accidental support from the conflict of hostile passions. The bishop, or some distinguished presbyter, to whom he cautiously delegated the powers of preaching, harangued, without the danger of interruption or reply, a submissive multitude, whose minds had been prepared and subdued by the awful ceremonies of religion. Such was the strict subordination of the Catholic church that the same concerted sounds might issue at once from an hundred pulpits of Italy or Egypt, if they were *tuned* [123] by the master hand of the Roman or Alexandrian primate. The design of this institution was laudable, but the fruits were not always salutary. The preachers recommended the practice of the social duties; but they exalted the perfection of monastic virtue, which is painful to the individual and useless to mankind. Their charitable exhortations betrayed a secret wish that the clergy might be permitted to manage the wealth of the faithful

---

[121] See Synesius, Epist. xlvii. p. 186, 187.   Epist. lxxii. p. 218, 219.   Epist. lxxxix. p. 230, 231.

[122] See Thomassin (Discipline de l'Eglise, tom. ii. l. iii. c. 83, p. 1761-1770) and Bingham (Antiquities, vol. i. l. xiv. c. 4, p. 688-717).   Preaching was considered as the most important office of the bishop; but this function was sometimes entrusted to such presbyters as Chrysostom and Augustin.

[123] Queen Elizabeth used this expression, and practised this art, whenever she wished to prepossess the minds of her people in favour of any extraordinary measure of government.   The hostile effects of this *music* were apprehended by her successor, and severely felt by his son.   "When pulpit, drum ecclesiastic," &c. see Heylin's Life of Archbishop Laud, p. 153.

for the benefit of the poor. The most sublime representations of the attributes and laws of the Deity were sullied by an idle mixture of metaphysical subtleties, puerile rites, and fictitious miracles: and they expatiated, with the most fervent zeal, on the religious merit of hating the adversaries, and obeying the ministers, of the church. When the public peace was distracted by heresy and schism, the sacred orators sounded the trumpet of discord, and perhaps of sedition. The understandings of their congregations were perplexed by mystery, their passions were inflamed by invectives: and they rushed from the Christian temples of Antioch or Alexandria, prepared either to suffer or to inflict martyrdom. The corruption of taste and language is strongly marked in the vehement declamations of the Latin bishops; but the compositions of Gregory and Chrysostom have been compared with the most splendid models of Attic, or at least of Asiatic, eloquence.[124]

VII. The representatives of the Christian republic were regularly assembled in the spring and autumn of each year: and these synods diffused the spirit of ecclesiastical discipline and legislation through the hundred and twenty provinces of the Roman world.[125] The archbishop or metropolitan was empowered, by the laws, to summon the suffragan bishops of his province, to revise their conduct, to vindicate their rights, to declare their faith, and to examine the merit of the candidates who were elected by the clergy and people to supply the vacancies of the episcopal college. The primates of Rome, Alexandria, Antioch, Carthage, and afterwards Constantinople, who exercised a more ample jurisdiction, convened the numerous assembly of their dependent bishops. But the convocation of great and extraordinary synods was the prerogative of the emperor alone. Whenever the emergencies of the church required this decisive measure, he dispatched a peremptory summons to the bishops, or the deputies of each province, with an order for the use of post-horses, and a competent allowance for the expenses of their journey. At an early period, when Con-

VII. Privilege of legislative assemblies

A.D. 314

---

[124] Those modest orators acknowledged that, as they were destitute of the gift of miracles, they endeavoured to acquire the arts of eloquence.

[125] The council of Nice, in the fourth, fifth, sixth, and seventh canons, has made some fundamental regulations concerning synods, metropolitans, and primates. The Nicene canons have been variously tortured, abused, interpolated, or forged, according to the interest of the clergy. The *Suburbicarian* churches, assigned (by Rufinus) to the bishop of Rome, have been made the subject of vehement controversy. See Sirmond. Opera, tom. iv. p. 1-238.

stantine was the protector, rather than the proselyte, of Christianity, he referred the African controversy to the council of Arles ; in which the bishops of York, of Treves, of Milan, and of Carthage, met as friends and brethren, to debate in their native tongue on the common interest of the Latin or Western A.D. 325 church.[126]   Eleven years afterwards, a more numerous and celebrated assembly was convened at Nice in Bithynia, to extinguish, by their final sentence, the subtle disputes which had arisen in Egypt on the subject of the Trinity.   Three hundred and eighteen bishops obeyed the summons of their indulgent master ; the ecclesiastics, of every rank and sect and denomination, have been computed at two thousand and forty-eight persons ;[127] the Greeks appeared in person ; and the consent of the Latins was expressed by the legates of the Roman pontiff. The session, which lasted about two months, was frequently honoured by the presence of the emperor.   Leaving his guards at the door, he seated himself (with the permission of the council) on a low stool in the midst of the hall.   Constantine listened with patience and spoke with modesty : and, while he influenced the debates, he humbly professed that he was the minister, not the judge, of the successors of the apostles, who had been established as priests and as gods upon earth.[128]   Such profound reverence of an absolute monarch towards a feeble and unarmed assembly of his own subjects can only be compared to the respect with which the senate had been treated by the Roman princes, who adopted the policy of Augustus.   Within the space of fifty years, a philosophic spectator of the vicissitude of human affairs might have contemplated Tacitus in the senate of Rome, and Constantine in the council of Nice.   The fathers of the capitol and those of the church had alike degenerated from the virtues of their founders ; but, as the bishops were more deeply rooted in the public opinion, they sustained their dignity with more decent pride, and sometimes opposed, with a manly spirit, the wishes of their sovereign.   The progress of time and

[126] We have only thirty-three or forty-seven episcopal subscriptions : but Ado, a writer indeed of small account, reckons six hundred bishops in the council of Arles.   Tillemont, Mém. Ecc.és. tom. vi. p. 422.

[127] See Tillemont, tom vi. p. 915, and Beausobre, Hist. du Manichéisme, tom. i. p. 529.   The name of *bishop*, which is given by Eutychius to the 2048 ecclesiastics (Annal. tom. i. p. 440, vers. Pococ̄), must be extended far beyond the limits of an orthodox or even episcopal ordination.

[128] See Euseb. in Vit. Constantin. l. iii. c. 6-21.   Tillemont, Mém. Ecclésiastiques, tom. vi. p. 669-759.

superstition erased the memory of the weakness, the passion, the ignorance, which disgraced these ecclesiastical synods; and the Catholic world has unanimously submitted [129] to the *infallible* decrees of the general councils.[130]

[129] Sancimus igitur vicem legum obtinere, quæ a quatuor Sanctis Conciliis . . . expositæ sunt aut firmatæ. Prædictarum enim quatuor synodorum dogmata sicut sanctas Scripturas et regulas sicut leges observamus. Justinian. Novell. cxxxi. Beveridge (ad Pandect. proleg. p. 2) remarks that the emperors never made new laws in ecclesiastical matters; and Giannone observes, in a very different spirit, that they gave a legal sanction to the canons of councils. Istoria Civile di Napoli, tom. i. p. 136.

[130] See the article CONCILE in the Encyclopédie, tom. iii. p. 668-679, édition de Lucoues. The author, M. le docteur Bouchaud, has discussed, according to the principles of the Gallican church, the principal questions which relate to the form and constitution of general, national, and provincial councils. The editors (see Preface, p. xvi.) have reason to be proud of *this* article. Those who consult their immense compilation seldom depart so well satisfied.

CHAPTER XXI

Persecution of Heresy—The Schism of the Donatists—The Arian Controversy—Athanasius—Distracted State of the Church and Empire under Constantine and his Sons—Toleration of Paganism

THE grateful applause of the clergy has consecrated the memory of a prince who indulged their passions and promoted their interest. Constantine gave them security, wealth, honours, and revenge : and the support of the orthodox faith was considered as the most sacred and important duty of the civil magistrate. The edict of Milan, the great charter of toleration, had confirmed to each individual of the Roman world the privilege of choosing and professing his own religion. But this inestimable privilege was soon violated : with the knowledge of truth, the emperor imbibed the maxims of persecution ; and the sects which dissented from the Catholic church were afflicted and oppressed by the triumph of Christianity. Constantine easily believed that the Heretics, who presumed to dispute *his* opinions or to oppose *his* commands, were guilty of the most absurd and criminal obstinacy ; and that a seasonable application of moderate severities might save those unhappy men from the danger of an everlasting condemnation. Not a moment was lost in excluding the ministers and teachers of the separated congregations from any share of the rewards and immunities which the emperor had so liberally bestowed on the orthodox clergy. But, as the sectaries might still exist under the cloud of royal disgrace, the conquest of the East was immediately followed by an edict which announced their total destruction.[1] After a preamble filled with passion and reproach, Constantine absolutely prohibits the assemblies of the Heretics, and confiscates their public property to the use either of the revenue or of the Catholic church. The sects against whom the Imperial severity was directed appear to have been the adherents of Paul of Samosata ; the Montanists of Phrygia, who maintained

---

[1] Eusebius in Vit. Constantin. l. iii. c. 63, 64, 65, 66.

an enthusiastic succession of prophecy; the Novatians, who sternly rejected the temporal efficacy of repentance; the Marcionites and Valentinians, under whose leading banners the various Gnostics of Asia and Egypt had insensibly rallied; and perhaps the Manichæans, who had recently imported from Persia a more artful composition of Oriental and Christian theology.[2] The design of extirpating the name, or at least of restraining the progress, of these odious Heretics was prosecuted with vigour and effect. Some of the penal regulations were copied from the edicts of Diocletian; and this method of conversion was applauded by the same bishops who had felt the hand of oppression and had pleaded for the rights of humanity. Two immaterial circumstances may serve, however, to prove that the mind of Constantine was not entirely corrupted by the spirit of zeal and bigotry. Before he condemned the Manichæans and their kindred sects, he resolved to make an accurate enquiry into the nature of their religious principles. As if he distrusted the impartiality of his ecclesiastical counsellors, this delicate commission was entrusted to a civil magistrate, whose learning and moderation he justly esteemed, and of whose venal character he was probably ignorant.[3] The emperor was soon convinced that he had too hastily proscribed the orthodox faith and the exemplary morals of the Novatians, who had dissented from the church in some articles of discipline which were not perhaps

[2] After some examination of the various opinions of Tillemont, Beausobre, Lardner, &c. I am convinced that Manes did not propagate this sect, even in Persia, before the year 270. It is strange that a philosophic and foreign heresy should have penetrated so rapidly into the African provinces; yet I cannot easily reject the edict of Diocletian against the Manichæans, which may be found in Baronius. (Annal. Eccl. A.D. 287.) [The earliest mention of the Manichæans is in Eusebius, H. E. vii. 31. (For Diocletian's edict, see Cod. Gregorianus, ed. Haenel, 14, 4, where it is said that the doctrine came *in hunc mundum de Persica adversaria nobis gente.*) For the life and doctrines of Manes, we have now two important eastern sources: (*a*) His Life written by Muhammed ben Ishak, towards close of the 10th century and published with a translation by Flugel (in *Mani, seine Lehre und seine Schriften*) from which we learn that Manes wrote his works (some Persian, some Syriac) in a special "Manichæan" alphabet, derived from Persian and Syriac. (*b*) Albîrûnî's Chronology of Ancient Nations (transl. by Sachau, 1879), written early in 11th cent. at Khiva, which preserves central Asian traditions of Manes, and shows that some of his works existed there then. Of the works of Manes may be mentioned his *Gospel, The Treasure of Life, Book of Mysteries*. Baur wrote a treatise on Manichæism (*das Manich. Religionssystem*, 1831). Compare Chwolsohn, *Die Ssabier*, vol. i., and the excellent article in the Dict. of Christian Biography.]

[3] Constantius enim, cum limatius superstitionum quæreret sectas, Manichæorum et similium, &c. Ammian. xv. 15. Strategius, who from this commission obtained the surname of *Musonianus*, was a Christian of the Arian sect. He acted as one of the counts at the council of Sardica. Libanius praises his mildness and prudence. Vales. ad locum Ammian.

essential to salvation. By a particular edict, he exempted them
from the general penalties of the law ;[4] allowed them to build
a church at Constantinople, respected the miracles of their
saints, invited their bishop Acesius to the council of Nice, and
gently ridiculed the narrow tenets of his sect by a familiar jest,
which, from the mouth of a sovereign, must have been received
with applause and gratitude.[5]

African controversy.
A.D. 312
   The complaints and mutual accusations which assailed the
throne of Constantine, as soon as the death of Maxentius had
submitted Africa to his victorious arms, were ill adapted to
edify an imperfect proselyte. He learned with surprise that
the provinces of that great country, from the confines of Cyrene
to the columns of Hercules, were distracted with religious
discord.[6] The source of the division was derived from a double
[A.D. 311] election in the church of Carthage ; the second, in rank and
opulence, of the ecclesiastical thrones of the West. Cæcilian
and Majorinus were the two rival primates of Africa ; and the
death of the latter soon made room for Donatus, who, by his
superior abilities and apparent virtues, was the firmest support
of his party. The advantage which Cæcilian might claim from
the priority of his ordination was destroyed by the illegal, or at
least indecent, haste with which it had been performed, without
expecting the arrival of the bishops of Numidia. The authority
[A.D. 312] of these bishops, who, to the number of seventy, condemned
Cæcilian and consecrated Majorinus, is again weakened by the
infamy of some of their personal characters ; and by the female
intrigues, sacrilegious bargains, and tumultuous proceedings

---

[4] Cod. Theod. l. xvi. tit. v. leg. 2. As the general law is not inserted in the
Theodosian code, it is probable, that in the year 438 the sects which it had
condemned were already extinct.

[5] Sozomen, l. i. c. 22. Socrates, l. i. c. 10. These historians have been
suspected, but I think without reason, of an attachment to the Novatian doctrine.
The emperor said to the bishop, " Acesius, take a ladder, and get up to Heaven
by yourself ". Most of the Christian sects have, by turns, borrowed the ladder of
Acesius.

[6] The best materials for this part of ecclesiastical history may be found in the
edition of Optatus Milevitanus, published (Paris, 1700 [*leg.* 1702]) by M. Dupin,
who has enriched it with critical notes, geographical discussions, original records,
and an accurate abridgment of the whole controversy. M. de Tillemont has
bestowed on the Donatists the greatest part of a volume (tom. vi. part i.) : and I
am indebted to him for an ample collection of all the passages of his favourite St.
Augustin which relate to those heretics. [The particular point on which the
controversy at first turned is not made quite clear in Gibbon's text. It was
whether Felix, who ordained Cæcilian, was a *traditor* or not, that is, one of those
who in the recent persecution had handed over holy vessels and sacred writings to
the officers of the government. Constantine, inquiring into the question in 313,
decided in favour of Felix. It is to be observed that his supporters maintained not
that consecration by a traditor was allowable but that Felix was not a traditor.]

which are imputed to this Numidian council.[7] The bishops of the contending factions maintained, with equal ardour and obstinacy, that their adversaries were degraded, or at least dishonoured, by the odious crime of delivering the Holy Scriptures to the officers of Diocletian. From their mutual reproaches, as well as from the story of this dark transaction, it may justly be inferred that the late persecution had embittered the zeal, without reforming the manners, of the African Christians. That divided church was incapable of affording an impartial judicature; the controversy was solemnly tried in five successive tribunals which were appointed by the emperor; and the whole proceeding, from the first appeal to the final sentence, lasted above three years. A severe inquisition, which was taken by the Prætorian vicar and the proconsul of Africa, the report of two episcopal visitors who had been sent to Carthage, the decrees of the councils of Rome and of Arles, and the supreme judgment of Constantine himself in his sacred consistory, were all favourable to the cause of Cæcilian; and he was unanimously acknowledged by the civil and ecclesiastical powers as the true and lawful primate of Africa. [Council of Rome, A.D. 313, Oct. 2-4; of Arles, 314, Aug. 1; Constantine's Judgment, 316] The honours and estates of the church were attributed to *his* suffragan bishops, and it was not without difficulty that Constantine was satisfied with inflicting the punishment of exile on the principal leaders of the Donatist faction. As their cause was examined with attention, perhaps it was determined with justice. Perhaps their complaint was not without foundation, that the credulity of the emperor had been abused by the insidious arts of his favourite Osius. The influence of falsehood and corruption might procure the condemnation of the innocent, or aggravate the sentence of the guilty. Such an act, however, of injustice, if it concluded an importunate dispute, might be numbered among the transient evils of a despotic administration, which are neither felt nor remembered by posterity.

But this incident, so inconsiderable that it scarcely deserves a place in history, was productive of a memorable schism, which afflicted the provinces of Africa above three hundred years, and [Schism of the Donatists. A.D. 315]

---

[7] Schisma agitur illo tempore confusæ mulieris iracundia peperit; ambitus nutrivit, avaritia roboravit. Optatus, l. i. c. 19. The language of Purpurius is that of a furious madman. Dicitur te necasse filios sororis tuæ duos. Purpurius respondit, Putas me terreri a te . . . occidi; et occido eos qui contra me faciunt. Acta Concil. Cirtensis, ad calc. Optat. p. 274. When Cæcilian was invited to an assembly of bishops, Purpurius said to his brethren, or rather to his accomplices, "Let him come hither to receive our imposition of hands; and we will break his head by way of penance". Optat. l. i. c. 19.

was extinguished only with Christianity itself. The inflexible
zeal of freedom and fanaticism animated the Donatists to refuse
obedience to the usurpers whose election they disputed and
whose spiritual powers they denied. Excluded from the civil
and religious communion of mankind, they boldly excommunicated the rest of mankind, who had embraced the impious
party of Cæcilian, and of the Traditors, from whom he derived
his pretended ordination. They asserted with confidence, and
almost with exultation, that the Apostolical succession was
interrupted ; that *all* the bishops of Europe and Asia were
infected by the contagion of guilt and schism ; and that the
prerogatives of the Catholic church were confined to the chosen
portion of the African believers, who alone had preserved
inviolate the integrity of their faith and discipline. This rigid
theory was supported by the most uncharitable conduct. Whenever they acquired a proselyte, even from the distant provinces
of the East, they carefully repeated the sacred rites of baptism [8]
and ordination ; as they rejected the validity of those which he
had already received from the hands of heretics or schismatics.
Bishops, virgins, and even spotless infants were subjected to
the disgrace of a public penance, before they could be admitted
to the communion of the Donatists. If they obtained possession
of a church which had been used by their Catholic adversaries,
they purified the unhallowed building with the same jealous
care which a temple of idols might have required. They
washed the pavement, scraped the walls, burnt the altar, which
was commonly of wood, melted the consecrated plate, and cast
the Holy Eucharist to the dogs, with every circumstance of
ignominy which could provoke and perpetuate the animosity of
religious factions.[9] Notwithstanding this irreconcileable aversion, the two parties, who were mixed and separated in all the
cities of Africa, had the same language and manners, the same
zeal and learning, the same faith and worship. Proscribed by
the civil and ecclesiastical powers of the empire, the Donatists
still maintained in some provinces, particularly in Numidia, their
superior numbers ; and four hundred bishops acknowledged the
jurisdiction of their primate. But the invincible spirit of the

[8] The councils of Arles, of Nice and of Trent confirmed the wise and
moderate practice of the church of Rome. The Donatists, however, had the
advantage of maintaining the sentiment of Cyprian, and of a considerable part of
the primitive church. Vincentius Lirinensis (p. 332, ap. Tillemont, Mém. Ecclés.
tom. vi. p. 138) has explained why the Donatists are eternally burning with the
Devil, while St. Cyprian reigns in heaven with Jesus Christ. [Cp. App. 19.]

[9] See the sixth book of Optatus Milevitanus, p. 91-100.

sect sometimes preyed on his own vitals ; and the bosom of
their schismatical church was torn by intestine divisions.   A
fourth part of the Donatist bishops followed the independent
standard of the Maximianists.   The narrow and solitary path
which their first leaders had marked out continued to deviate [c. 393 A.D.]
from the great society of mankind.   Even the imperceptible
sect of the Rogatians could affirm, without a blush, that, when
Christ should descend to judge the earth, he would find his
true religion preserved only in a few nameless villages of the
Cæsarean Mauritania.[10]

The schism of the Donatists was confined to Africa : the The Trinita-
more diffusive mischief of the Trinitarian controversy successively rian contro-
penetrated into every part of the Christian world.   The former versy.
was an accidental quarrel, occasioned by the abuse of freedom ;
the latter was a high and mysterious argument, derived from
the abuse of philosophy.   From the age of Constantine to that
of Clovis and Theodoric, the temporal interests both of the
Romans and Barbarians were deeply involved in the theological
disputes of Arianism.   The historian may therefore be permitted respectfully to withdraw the veil of the sanctuary ; and
to deduce the progress of reason and faith, of error and passion,
from the school of Plato to the decline and fall of the empire.

The genius of Plato, informed by his own meditation, or by The system of
the traditional knowledge of the priests of Egypt,[11] had ventured Plato. Before
to explore the mysterious nature of the Deity.   When he had Christ 360
elevated his mind to the sublime contemplation of the first
self-existent, necessary cause of the universe, the Athenian sage
was incapable of conceiving *how* the simple unity of his essence
could admit the infinite variety of distinct and successive ideas
which compose the model of the intellectual world ; *how* a Being
purely incorporeal could execute that perfect model, and mould
with a plastic hand the rude and independent chaos.   The vain
hope of extricating himself from these difficulties, which must
ever oppress the feeble powers of the human mind, might

[10] Tillemont, Mém Ecclésiastiques, tom. vi. part. i. p. 253.   He laughs at their
partial credulity.   He revered Augustin, the great doctor of the system of predes-
ination.
[11] Plato Ægyptum peragravit ut a sacerdotibus Barbaris numeros et *caelestia*
acciperet.   Cicero de Finibus, v. 25.   The Egyptians might still preserve the
traditional creed of the Patriarchs.   Josephus has persuaded many of the Christian
fathers that Plato derived a part of his knowledge from the Jews; but this vain
opinion cannot be reconciled with the obscure state and unsocial manners of the
Jewish people, whose scriptures were not accessible to Greek curiosity till more
than one hundred years after the death of Plato.   See Marsham, Canon. Chron.
p. 144.   Le Clerc, Epistol. Critic. vii. p. 177-194.

induce Plato to consider the divine nature under the threefold
modification : of the first cause, the reason or *Logos,* and the soul
or spirit of the universe. His poetical imagination sometimes
fixed and animated these metaphysical abstractions ; the three
archical or original principles were represented in the Platonic
system of three Gods, united with each other by a mysterious
and ineffable generation ; and the Logos was particularly considered under the more accessible character of the Son of an
Eternal Father, and the Creator and Governor of the world.
Such appear to have been the secret doctrines which were
cautiously whispered in the gardens of the academy ; and which,
according to the more recent disciples of Plato, could not be
perfectly understood, till after an assiduous study of thirty
years.[12]

The arms of the Macedonians diffused over Asia and Egypt
the language and learning of Greece ; and the theological
system of Plato was taught with less reserve, and perhaps with
some improvements, in the celebrated school of Alexandria.[13]
A numerous colony of Jews had been invited, by the favour of
the Ptolemies, to settle in their new capital.[14] While the bulk
of the nation practised the legal ceremonies, and pursued the
lucrative occupations of commerce, a few Hebrews, of a more
liberal spirit, devoted their lives to religious and philosophical
contemplation.[15] They cultivated with diligence, and embraced
with ardour, the theological system of the Athenian sage. But
their national pride would have been mortified by a fair confession of their former poverty : and they boldly marked, as the
sacred inheritance of their ancestors, the gold and jewels which
they had so lately stolen from their Egyptian masters. One
hundred years before the birth of Christ, a philosophical
treatise, which manifestly betrays the style and sentiments of
the school of Plato, was produced by the Alexandrian Jews, and

The LOGOS

taught in the
school of
Alexandria
Before Christ
300

Before Christ
100

[12] The modern guides who lead me to the knowledge of the Platonic System are
Cudworth (Intellectual System, p. 568-620), Basnage (Hist. des Juifs, l. iv. c. iv.
p. 53-86), Le Clerc (Epist. Crit. vii. p. 194-209), and Brucker (Hist. Philos.
tom. i. p. 675-706). As the learning of these writers was equal, and their intention
different, an inquisitive observer may derive instruction from their disputes, and
certainty from their agreement.

[13] Brucker, Hist. Philosoph. tom. i. p. 1349-1357. The Alexandrian school is
celebrated by Strabo (l. xvii.) and Ammianus (xxii. 6). [Cp. Vacherot, Ecole
d'Alexandrie.]

[14] Joseph. Antiquitat. l. xii. c. 1. 3. Basnage, Hist. des Juifs. l. vii. c. 7.

[15] For the origin of the Jewish philosophy, see Eusebius, Præparat. Evangel.
viii. 9, 10. According to Philo, the Therapeutæ studied philosophy ; and Brucker
has proved (Hist. Philosoph. tom. ii. p. 787) that they gave the preference to that
of Plato.

unanimously received as a genuine and valuable relic of the inspired Wisdom of Solomon.[16] A similar union of the Mosaic faith and the Grecian philosophy distinguishes the works of Philo, which were composed, for the most part, under the reign of Augustus.[17] The material soul of the universe[18] might offend the piety of the Hebrews: but they applied the character of the Logos to the Jehovah of Moses and the patriarchs; and the Son of God was introduced upon earth under a visible, and even human, appearance, to perform those familiar offices which seem incompatible with the nature and attributes of the Universal Cause.[19]

The eloquence of Plato, the name of Solomon, the authority of the school of Alexandria, and the consent of the Jews and Greeks, were insufficient to establish the truth of a mysterious doctrine which might please, but could not satisfy, a rational mind. A prophet or apostle, inspired by the Deity, can alone exercise a lawful dominion over the faith of mankind; and the theology of Plato might have been for ever confounded with the philosophical visions of the Academy, the Porch, and the Lyceum, if the name and divine attributes of the *Logos* had not been confirmed by the celestial pen of the last and most sublime of the Evangelists.[20] The Christian Revelation, which was

Revealed by the Apostle St. John. A.D. 97

[16] See Calmet, Dissertations sur la Bible, tom. ii. p, 277. The book of the Wisdom of Solomon was received by many of the fathers as the work of that monarch; and, although rejected by the Protestants for want of a Hebrew original, it has obtained, with the rest of the Vulgate, the sanction of the council of Trent.

[17] The Platonism of Philo, which was famous to a proverb, is proved beyond a doubt by Le Clerc (Epist. Crit. viii. p. 211-228). Basnage (Hist. des Juifs, l. iv. c. 5) has clearly ascertained that the theological works of Philo were composed before the death, and most probably before the birth, of Christ. In such a time of darkness, the knowledge of Philo is more astonishing than his errors. Bull, Defens. Fid. Nicen. s. i. c. i. p. 12. [Philo may have been about 25 years old at birth of Christ. For chronol. of his works see Masseb.eau, Le classement des œuvres de Philon.]

[18] Mens agitat molem, et magno se corpori *miscet*.
Besides this material soul, Cudworth has discovered (p. 562) in Amelius, Porphyry, Plotinus, and, as he thinks, in Plato himself, a superior, spiritual, *hupercosmian* soul of the universe. But this double soul is exploded by Brucker, Basnage, and Le Clerc, as an idle fancy of the latter Platonists.

[19] Petav. Dogmata Theologica, tom. ii. l. viii. c. 2, p. 791. Bull, Defens. Fid. Nicen. s. i. c. 1, p. 8, 13. This notion, till it was abused by the Arians, was freely adopted in the Christian theology. Tertullian (adv. Praxeam, c. 16) has a remarkable and dangerous passage. After contrasting, with indiscreet wit, the nature of God and the actions of Jehovah, he concludes: Scilicet ut hæc de filio Dei non credenda fuisse si non scripta essent; fortasse non credenda de Patre licet scripta.

[20] The Platonists admired the beginning of the Gospel of St. John, as containing an exact transcript of their own principles. Augustin. de Civitat. Dei, x. 29. Amelius apud Cyril. advers. Julian. l. viii. p. 283. But in the third and fourth centuries, the Platonists of Alexandria might improve their Trinity by the secret study of the Christian theology.

consummated under the reign of Nerva, disclosed to the world
the amazing secret that the Logos, who was with God from the
beginning and was God, who had made all things and for whom
all things had been made, was incarnate in the person of Jesus
of Nazareth ; who had been born of a virgin, and suffered death
on the cross. Besides the general design of fixing on a perpetual basis the divine honours of Christ, the most ancient and
respectable of the ecclesiastical writers have ascribed to the
evangelic theologian a particular intention to confute two
opposite heresies, which disturbed the peace of the primitive
church.[21]   I. The faith of the Ebionites,[22] perhaps of the Nazarenes,[23] was gross and imperfect.   They revered Jesus as the
greatest of the prophets, endowed with supernatural virtue and
power.   They ascribed to his person and to his future reign all
the predictions of the Hebrew oracles which relate to the
spiritual and everlasting kingdom of the promised Messiah.[24]
Some of them might confess that he was born of a virgin : but
they obstinately rejected the preceding existence and divine
perfections of the *Logos,* or Son of God, which are so clearly
defined in the Gospel of St. John.   About fifty years afterwards,
the Ebionites, whose errors are mentioned by Justin Martyr
with less severity than they seem to deserve,[25] formed a very
inconsiderable portion of the Christian name.   II. The Gnostics,
who were distinguished by the epithet of *Docetes,* deviated into
the contrary extreme, and betrayed the human, while they
asserted the divine, nature of Christ.   Educated in the school

The Ebionites and Docetes

[21] See Beausobre, Hist. Critique du Manichéisme, tom. i. p. 377.   The Gospel
according to St. John is supposed to have been published about seventy years after
the death of Christ. [The controversy as to the date and the authorsnip is still hot.
It betrays the influence of Alexandrian theology.   The influence of Plato, which
Gibbon dwells on, is more particularly that of the Jew Philo.   His view of the
Logos as the εἰκὼν θεοῦ, image of God, &c. may be considered the origin of the
doctrine of the Word, developed by Christian theologians.]

[22] The sentiments of the Ebionites are fairly stated by Mosheim (p. 331) and Le
Clerc (Hist. Eccles. p. 535).   The Clementines published among the apostolical
Fathers, are attributed by the critics to one of these sectaries. [See above, p. 10, note 22.]

[23] Staunch polemics, like Bull (Judicium Eccles. Cathol. c. 2), insist on the
orthodoxy of the Nazarenes ; which appears less pure and certain in the eyes of
Mosheim (p. 330).

[24] The humble condition and sufferings of Jesus have always been a stumbling
block to the Jews.   "Deus . . . contrariis coloribus Messiam depinxerat ; futurus
erat Rex, Judex, Pastor," &c.   See Limborch et Orobio Amica Collat. p. 8, 19, 53-
76, 192-234.   But this objection has obliged the believing Christians to lift up their
eyes to a spiritual and everlasting kingdom.

[25] Justin. Martyr. Dialog. cum Tryphonte, p. 143, 144.   See Le Clerc, Hist.
Eccles. p. 615.   Bull and his editor Grabe (Judicium Eccles. Cathol. c. 7, and
Appendix) attempt to distort either the sentiments or the words of Justin ; but
their violent correction of the text is rejected even by the Benedictine editors.

of Plato, accustomed to the sublime idea of the *Logos*, they readily conceived that the brightest *Æon*, or *Emanation* of the Deity, might assume the outward shape and visible appearances of a mortal; [26] but they vainly pretended that the imperfections of matter are incompatible with the purity of a celestial substance. While the blood of Christ yet smoked on Mount Calvary, the Docetes invented the impious and extravagant hypothesis that, instead of issuing from the womb of the Virgin,[27] he had descended on the banks of the Jordan in the form of perfect manhood; that he had imposed on the senses of his enemies, and of his disciples; and that the ministers of Pilate had wasted their impotent rage on an airy phantom, who *seemed* to expire on the cross and, after three days, to rise from the dead.[28]

The divine sanction which the Apostle had bestowed on the fundamental principle of the theology of Plato encouraged the learned proselytes of the second and third centuries to admire and study the writings of the Athenian sage, who had thus marvellously anticipated one of the most surprising discoveries of the Christian revelation. The respectable name of Plato was used by the orthodox,[29] and abused by the heretics,[30] as the common support of truth and error: the authority of his

Mysterious nature of the Trinity

[26] The Arians reproached the orthodox party with borrowing their Trinity from the Valentinians and Marcionites. See Beausobre, Hist. du Manichéisme, l. iii. c. 5, 7.

[27] Non dignum est ex utero credere Deum, et Deum Christum . . . non dignum est ut tanta majestas per sordes et squalores mulieris transire credatur. The Gnostics asserted the impurity of matter, and of marriage; and they were scandalized by the gross interpretations of the fathers, and even of Augustin himself. See Beausobre, tom. ii. p. 523. [That Christ was not born was the view of Marcion, not that of the early Docetæ, who accepted the incarnation by Mary, but regarded her as passive, and not contributing her substance,—like a pipe through which water flows.]

[28] Apostolis adhuc in sæculo superstitibus apud Judæam Christi sanguine recente et *phantasma* corpus Domini asserebatur. Cotelerius thinks (Patres Apostol. tom. ii. p. 24) that those who will not allow the *Docetes* to have arisen in the time of the Apostles may with equal reason deny that the sun shines at noon-day. These *Docetes*, who formed the most considerable party among the Gnostics, were so called because they granted only a *seeming* body to Christ.

[29] Some proofs of the respect which the Christians entertained for the person and doctrine of Plato may be found in De la Mothe le Vayer, tom. v. p. 135, &c. edit. 1757; and Basnage, Hist. des Juifs, tom. iv. p. 29, 79, &c.

[30] Doleo bona fide, Platonem omnium hæreticorum condimentarium factum. Tertullian. de Anima, c. 23. Petavius (Dogm. Theolog. tom. iii. proleg. 2) shews that this was a general complaint. Beausobre (tom. i. l. iii. c. 9, 10) has deduced the Gnostic errors from Platonic principles; and, as in the school of Alexandria those principles were blended with the oriental philosophy (Brucker, tom. i. p. 1356), the sentiment of Beausobre may be reconciled with the opinion of Mosheim (General History of the Church, vol. i. p. 37).

skilful commentators, and the science of dialects, were employed to justify the remote consequences of his opinions, and to supply the discreet silence of the inspired writers. The same subtle and profound questions concerning the nature, the generation, the distinction, and the equality of the three divine persons of the mysterious *Triad*, or Trinity,[31] were agitated in the philosophical, and in the Christian, schools of Alexandria. An eager spirit of curiosity urged them to explore the secrets of the abyss ; and the pride of the professors and of their disciples was satisfied with the science of words. But the most sagacious of the Christian theologians, the great Athanasius himself, has candidly confessed [32] that, whenever he forced his understanding to meditate on the divinity of the *Logos,* his toilsome and unavailing efforts recoiled on themselves ; that the more he thought, the less he comprehended ; and the more he wrote, the less capable was he of expressing his thoughts. In every step of the enquiry, we are compelled to feel and acknowledge the immeasurable disproportion between the size of the object and the capacity of the human mind. We may strive to abstract the notions of time, of space, and of matter, which so closely adhere to all the perceptions of our experimental knowledge. But, as soon as we presume to reason of infinite substance, of spiritual generation ; as often as we deduce any positive conclusions from a negative idea, we are involved in darkness, perplexity, and inevitable contradiction. As these difficulties arise from the nature of the subject, they oppress, with the same insuperable weight, the philosophic and the theological disputant ; but we may observe two essential and peculiar circumstances which discriminated the doctrines of the Catholic church from the opinions of the Platonic school.

Zeal of the Christians

I. A chosen society of philosophers, men of a liberal education and curious disposition, might silently meditate, and temperately discuss, in the gardens of Athens or the library of Alexandria, the abstruse questions of metaphysical science. The lofty speculations which neither convinced the understanding, nor agitated the passions, of the Platonists themselves were carelessly overlooked by the idle, the busy, and even the studious

---

[31] If Theophilus, bishop of Antioch, (see Dupin, Bibliothèque Ecclésiastique, tom i. p. 66) was the first who employed the word *Triad, Trinity,* that abstract term which was already familiar to the schools of philosophy, must have been introduced into the theology of the Christians after the middle of the second century.

[32] Athanasius, tom. i. p. 808. His expressions have an uncommon energy ; and as he was writing to Monks, there could not be any occasion for him to *affect* rational language.

part of mankind.[33] But, after the *Logos* had been revealed as the sacred object of the faith, the hope, and the religious worship of the Christians, the mysterious system was embraced by a numerous and increasing multitude in every province of the Roman world. Those persons who, from their age, or sex, or occupations, were the least qualified to judge, who were the least exercised in the habits of abstract reasoning, aspired to contemplate the economy of the Divine Nature ; and it is the boast of Tertullian [34] that a Christian mechanic could readily answer such questions as had perplexed the wisest of the Grecian sages. Where the subject lies so far beyond our reach, the difference between the highest and the lowest of human understandings may indeed be calculated as infinitely small ; yet the degree of weakness may perhaps be measured by the degree of obstinacy and dogmatic confidence. These speculations, instead of being treated as the amusement of a vacant hour, became the most serious business of the present, and the most useful preparation for a future, life. A theology, which it was incumbent to believe, which it was impious to doubt, and which it might be dangerous, and even fatal, to mistake, became the familiar topic of private meditation and popular discourse. The cold indifference of philosophy was inflamed by the fervent spirit of devotion; and even the metaphors of common language suggested the fallacious prejudices of sense and experience. The Christians, who abhorred the gross and impure generation of the Greek mythology,[35] were tempted to argue from the familiar analogy of the filial and paternal relations. The character of *Son* seemed to imply a perpetual subordination to the voluntary author of his existence ; [36] but, as the act of generation, in the

[33] In a treatise which professed to explain the opinions of the ancient philosophers concerning the nature of the gods we might expect to discover the theological Trinity of Plato. But Cicero very honestly confessed that, though he had translated the Timæus, he could never understand that mysterious dialogue. See Hieronym. præf. ad l. xii. in Isaiam, tom. v. p. 154.

[34] Tertullian in Apolog. c. 46. See Bayle, Dictionnaire, au mot *Simonide*. His remarks on the presumption of Tertullian are profound and interesting.

[35] Lactantius, iv. 8. Yet the *Probole*, or *Prolatio*, which the most orthodox divines borrowed without scruple from the Valentinians, and illustrated by the comparisons of a fountain and stream, the sun and its rays, &c. either meant nothing or favoured a material idea of the divine generation. See Beausobre, tom. i. l. iii. c. 7, p. 548.

[36] Many of the primitive writers have frankly confessed that the Son owed his being to the *will* of the Father. See Clarke s Scripture Trinity, p. 280-287. On the other hand, Athanasius and his followers seem unwilling to grant what they are afraid to deny. The schoolmen extricate themselves from this difficulty by the distinction of a *preceding* and a *concomitant* will. Petav. Dogm. Theolog. tom. ii. l. vi. c. 8, p. 587-603.

most spiritual and abstracted sense, must be supposed to transmit the properties of a common nature,[37] they durst not presume to circumscribe the powers of the duration of the Son of an eternal and omnipotent Father. Fourscore years after the death of Christ, the Christians of Bithynia declared before the tribunal of Pliny that they invoked him as a god ; and his divine honours have been perpetuated in every age and country by the various sects who assume the name of his disciples.[38] Their tender reverence for the memory of Christ and their horror for the profane worship of any created being would have engaged them to assert the equal and absolute divinity of the *Logos*, if their rapid ascent towards the throne of heaven had not been imperceptibly checked by the apprehension of violating the unity and sole supremacy of the great Father of Christ and of the Universe. The suspense and fluctuation produced in the minds of the Christians by these opposite tendencies may be observed in the writings of the theologians who flourished after the end of the apostolic age and before the origin of the Arian controversy. Their suffrage is claimed, with equal confidence, by the orthodox and by the heretical parties ; and the most inquisitive critics have fairly allowed that, if they had the good fortune of possessing the Catholic verity, they have delivered their conceptions in loose, inaccurate, and sometimes contradictory language.[39]

Authority of the church

II. The devotion of individuals was the first circumstance which distinguished the Christians from the Platonists ; the second was the authority of the church. The disciples of philosophy asserted the rights of intellectual freedom, and their respect for the sentiments of their teachers was a liberal and voluntary tribute, which they offered to superior reason. But the Christians formed a numerous and disciplined society ; and the jurisdiction of their laws and magistrates was strictly exercised over the minds of the faithful. The loose wanderings of the imagination were gradually confined by creeds and confes-

[37] See Petav. Dogm. Theolog. tom. ii. l. ii. c. 10, p. 159.

[38] Carmenque Christo quasi Deo dicere secum invicem. Plin. Epist. x. 97. The sense of *Deus*, Θεός, *Elohim*, in the ancient languages, is critically examined by Le Clerc (Ars Critica, p. 150-156), and the propriety of worshipping a very excellent creature is ably defended by the Socinian Emlyn (Tracts, p. 29-36, 51-145).

[39] See Daillé de Usu Patrum, and Le Clerc, Bibliothèque Universelle, tom. x. p. 409. To arraign the faith of the Anti-Nicene fathers was the object, or at least has been the effect, of the stupendous work of Petavius on the Trinity (Dogm. Theolog. tom. ii.) ; nor has the deep impression been erased by the learned defence of Bishop Bull.

sions;[40] the freedom of private judgment submitted to the public wisdom of synods; the authority of a theologian was determined by his ecclesiastical rank; and the episcopal successors of the apostles inflicted the censures of the church on those who deviated from the orthodox belief. But in an age of religious controversy every act of oppression adds new force to the elastic vigour of the mind; and the zeal or obstinacy of a spiritual rebel was sometimes stimulated by secret motives of ambition or avarice. A metaphysical argument became the cause or pretence of political contests; the subtleties of the Platonic school were used as the badges of popular factions, and the distance which separated their respective tenets was enlarged or magnified by the acrimony of dispute. As long as the dark heresies of Praxeas and Sabellius laboured to confound the *Father* with the *Son*,[41] the orthodox party might be excused if they adhered more strictly and more earnestly to the *distinction*, than to the *equality*, of the divine persons. But, as soon as the heat of controversy had subsided, and the progress of the Sabellians was no longer an object of terror to the churches of Rome, of Africa, or of Egypt; the tide of theological opinion began to flow with a gentle but steady motion toward the contrary extreme; and the most orthodox doctors allowed themselves the use of the terms and definitions which had been censured in the mouth of the sectaries.[42] After the edict of toleration had restored peace and leisure to the Christians, the Trinitarian controversy was revived in the ancient seat of Platonism, the learned, the opulent,

(margin note: Factions)

---

[40] The most ancient creeds were drawn up with the greatest latitude. See Bull (Judicium Eccles. Cathol.), who tries to prevent Episcopius from deriving any advantage from this observation. [Before the Nicene Council, no creed had been drawn up as a test of orthodoxy. There were various formulæ of Christian belief (πίστεις) in various places for the use of catechumens. This has been emphasized by Mr. Gwatkin.]

[41] The heresies of Praxeas, Sabellius, &c. are accurately explained by Mosheim (p. 425, 680-714). Praxeas, who came to Rome about the end of the second century, deceived, for some time, the simplicity of the bishop, and was confuted by the pen of the angry Tertullian. [These are the *Monarchian* heresies; see below, p. 347.]

[42] Socrates acknowledges that the heresy of Arius proceeded from his strong desire to embrace an opinion the most diametrically opposite to that of Sabellius. [For the comprehension of the theological import of the Arian controversy, consult Gwatkin's *Arianism*, p. 9. "Arianism laid down a merely external, Sabellianism a merely economic, Trinity." As neither satisfied, it "became necessary to fall back on Scripture to revise the idea of a divine personality, and acknowledge not three individuals but three eternal aspects (ὑποστάσεις) of the divine, facing inward on each other as well as outward on the world". The earlier conception of God, so far as distinguished from the world, was one of abstract simplicity; the expulsion of this inadequate conception from the doctrine of the Trinity is the chief result won out of the Arian controversy.]

the tumultuous city of Alexandria ; and the flame of religious discord was rapidly communicated from the schools to the clergy, the people, the province, and the East.   The abstruse question of the eternity of the *Logos* was agitated in ecclesiastical conferences and popular sermons ;   and the heterodox opinions of Arius [43] were soon made public by his own zeal and by that of his adversaries.   His most implacable adversaries have acknowledged the learning and blameless life of that eminent presbyter, who, in a former election, had declared, and perhaps generously declined, his pretensions to the episcopal throne.[44]   His competitor Alexander assumed the office of his judge.   The important cause was argued before him ;   and, if at first he seemed to hesitate, he at length pronounced his final sentence, as an absolute rule of faith.[45]   The undaunted presbyter, who presumed to resist the authority of his angry bishop, was separated from the communion of the church.   But the pride of Arius was supported by the applause of a numerous party.   He reckoned among his immediate followers two bishops of Egypt, seven presbyters, twelve deacons, and (what may appear almost incredible) seven hundred virgins.   A large majority of the bishops of Asia appeared to support or favour his cause ;   and their measures were conducted by Eusebius of Cæsarea, the most learned of the Christian prelates, and by Eusebius of Nicomedia, who had acquired the reputation of a statesman without forfeiting that of a saint.   Synods in Palestine and Bithynia were opposed to the synods of Egypt.   The attention of the prince and people was attracted by this theological dispute ;   and the decision, at the end of six years,[46] was referred to the supreme authority of the general council of Nice.

Arius

A.D. 318-325

Three systems of the Trinity

When the mysteries of the Christian faith were danger-

[43] The figure and manners of Arius, the character and numbers of his first proselytes, are painted in very lively colours by Epiphanius (tom. i. Hæres. lxix. 3, p. 729) ; and we cannot but regret that he should soon forget the historian, to assume the task of controversy.

[44] See Philostorgius (l. i. c. 3) and Godefroy's ample Commentary.   Yet the credibility of Philostorgius is lessened in the eyes of the orthodox by his Arianism ; and in those of rational critics by his passion, his prejudice, and his ignorance.

[45] Sozomen (l. i. c. 15) represents Alexander as indifferent, and even ignorant, in the beginning of the controversy ; while Socrates (l. i. c. 5) ascribes the origin of the dispute to the vain curiosity of his theological speculations.   Dr. Jortin (Remarks on Ecclesiastical History, vol. ii. p. 178) has censured, with his usual freedom, the conduct of Alexander : πρὸς ὀρ-ὴν ἐξάπτεται . . . ὁμοίως φρονεῖν ἐκέλευσε.

[46] The flames of Arianism might burn for some time in secret ; but there is reason to believe that they burst out with violence as early as the year 319.   Tillemont, Mém. Ecclés. tom. vi. p. 774-780.

ously exposed to public debate, it might be observed that the human understanding was capable of forming three distinct, though imperfect, systems concerning the nature of the Divine Trinity ; and it was pronounced that none of these systems, in a pure and absolute sense, were exempt from heresy and error.[47] I. According to the first hypothesis, which was maintained by Arianism Arius and his disciples, the *Logos* was a dependent and spontaneous production, created from nothing by the will of the Father. The Son, by whom all things were made,[48] had been begotten before all worlds, and the longest of the astronomical periods could be compared only as a fleeting moment to the extent of his duration ; yet this duration was not infinite,[49] and there *had* been a time which preceded the ineffable generation of the *Logos*. On this only-begotten Son the Almighty Father had transfused his ample spirit, and impressed the effulgence of his glory. Visible image of invisible perfection, he saw, at an immeasurable distance beneath his feet, the thrones of the brightest archangels : yet he shone only with a reflected light, and, like the sons of the Roman emperors who were invested with the titles of Cæsar or Augustus,[50] he governed the universe in obedience to the will of his Father and Monarch. II. In Tritheism the second hypothesis, the *Logos* possessed all the inherent, incommunicable perfections which religion and philosophy appropriate to the Supreme God. Three distinct and infinite minds or substances, three co-equal and co-eternal beings, com-

---

[47] Quid credidit? Certe, *aut* tria nomina audiens tres Deos esse credidit, et idololatra effectus est ; *aut* in tribus vocabulis trinominem credens Deum, in Sabelli hæresim incurrit ; *aut* edoctus ab Arianis unum esse verum Deum, Patrem, filium et spiritum sanctum credidit creaturas. Aut extra hæc quid credere potuerit nescio. Hieronym. adv. Luciferianos. Je⁀om reserves for the last the orthodox system, which is more complicated and difficult.

[48] As the doctrine of absolute creation from nothing was gradually introduced among the Christians (Beausobre, tom. ii. p. 165-215), the dignity of the *workman* very naturally rose with that of the *work*. [A statement by Arius of his own doctrine is preserved by Theodoret, H. E. i. 5. "By will and counsel the Son existed (ὑπέστη) before time (πρὸ χρόνων καὶ πρὸ αἰώνων), full, God, only begotten, unchangeable ; and before his begetting or creation or defining or founding, he was not ; for he was not unbegotten." Another formulation of his doctrine, after his own work *Thalia*, is given by Athanasius in the Orat. contra Arianos, i. 5. Gibbon brings out the point that the Son was created though he began to be before time.]

[49] The metaphysics of Dr. Clarke (Scripture Trinity, p. 276-280) could digest an eternal generation from an infinite cause.

[50] This profane and absurd simile is employed by several of the primitive fathers, particularly by Athenagoras, in his Apology to the emperor Marcus and his son ; and it is alleged, without censure, by Bull himself, See Defens. Fid. Nicen. s. iii. c. 5, No. 4.

posed the Divine Essence;[51] and it would have implied contradiction that any of them should not have existed or that they should ever cease to exist.[52]   The advocates of a system which seemed to establish three independent Deities attempted to preserve the unity of the First Cause, so conspicuous in the design and order of the world, by the perpetual concord of their administration and the essential agreement of their will. A faint resemblance of this unity of action may be discovered in the societies of men, and even of animals.   The causes which disturb their harmony proceed only from the imperfection and inequality of their faculties: but the omnipotence which is guided by infinite wisdom and goodness cannot fail of choosing the same means for the accomplishment of the same ends.   III.

Sabellianism Three Beings, who, by the self-derived necessity of their existence, possess all the divine attributes in the most perfect degree; who are eternal in duration, infinite in space, and intimately present to each other and to the whole universe; irresistibly force themselves on the astonished mind as one and the same Being,[53] who, in the economy of grace, as well as in that of nature, may manifest himself under different forms, and be considered under different aspects.   By this hypothesis, a real substantial Trinity is refined into a trinity of names and abstract modifications, that subsist only in the mind which conceives them.   The *Logos* is no longer a person, but an attribute; and it is only in a figurative sense that the epithet of Son can be applied to the eternal reason which was with God from the beginning, and by *which*, not by *whom*, all things were made.   The incarnation of the *Logos* is reduced to a mere inspiration of the Divine Wisdom, which filled the soul, and directed all the actions, of the man Jesus.   Thus, after revolving round the theological circle, we are surprised to find that the Sabellian ends where the Ebionite had begun; and that

[51] See Cudworth's Intellectual System, p. 559, 579.   This dangerous hypothesis was countenanced by the two Gregories of Nyssa and Nazianzen [Nazianzus], by Cyril of Alexandria, John of Damascus, &c.   See Cudworth, p. 603.   Le Clerc, Bibliothèque Universelle, tom. xviii. p. 97-105.   [Observe that Tritheism as the technical name of a heresy does not appear till the sixth century, when it designates a form of Monophysitism.]

[52] Augustin seems to envy the freedom of the philosophers.   Liberis verbis loquuntur philosophi. . . . Nos autem non dicimus duo vel tria principia, duos vel tres Deos.   De Civitat. Dei, x. 23.

[53] Boetius, who was deeply versed in the philosophy of Plato and Aristotle, explains the unity of the Trinity by the *in-difference* of the three persons.   See the judicious remarks of Le Clerc, Bibliothèque Choisie, tom. xvi. p. 225, &c.

the incomprehensible mystery which excites our adoration eludes our enquiry.[54]

If the bishops of the council of Nice [55] had been permitted to follow the unbiassed dictates of their conscience, Arius and his associates could scarcely have flattered themselves with the hopes of obtaining a majority of votes, in favour of an hypothesis so directly adverse to the two most popular opinions of the Catholic world. The Arians soon perceived the danger of their situation, and prudently assumed those modest virtues which, in the fury of civil and religious dissensions, are seldom practised, or even praised, except by the weaker party. They recommended the exercise of Christian charity and moderation ; urged the incomprehensible nature of the controversy ; disclaimed the use of any terms or definitions which could not be found in the scriptures ; and offered, by very liberal concessions, to satisfy their adversaries without renouncing the integrity of their own principles. The victorious faction received all their proposals with haughty suspicion ; and anxiously sought for some irreconcileable mark of distinction, the rejection of which might involve the Arians in the guilt and consequences of heresy. A letter was publicly read, and ignominiously torn, in which their patron, Eusebius of Nicomedia, ingenuously confessed that the admission of the Homoousion, or Consubstantial, a word already familiar to the Platonists, was incompatible with the principles of their theological system. The fortunate opportunity was eagerly embraced by the bishops who governed the resolutions of the synod ; and, according to the lively ex-

---

[54] If the Sabellians were startled at this conclusion, they were driven down another precipice into the confession, that the Father was born of a virgin, that *he* had suffered on the cross ; and thus deserved the odious epithet of *Patri-passians*, with which they were branded by their adversaries [in the West]. See the invectives of Tertullian against Praxeas, and the temperate reflections of Mosheim (p. 423, 681) ; and Beausobre, tom. i. l. iii. c. 6, p. 533. [Sabellianism was a particular form of the more general heresy of Monarchianism (initiated by Praxeas towards close of second century), which, with the purpose of avoiding the danger of the Gnostic doctrines which seemed by their "emanations" to weaken the absolute unity of God's government, insisted on the *Monarchy* of the Father and fell into the other extreme of endangering Christ's divinity. See Harnack's article on Monarchianism in Herzog and Plitt's *Realencyclopädie*.—Sabellius lived c. 200 A.D. He used the phrase *persons* (πρόσωπα) of the Trinity in the literal sense of masks.]

[55] The transactions of the council of Nice are related by the ancients not only in a partial, but in a very imperfect, manner. Such a picture as Fra Paolo would have drawn can never be recovered; but such rude sketches as have been traced by the pencil of bigotry, and that of reason, may be seen in Tillemont (Mém. Ecclés. tom. vi. p. 669-759) and in Le Clerc (Bibliothèque Universelle, tom. x. p. 435-454).

pression of Ambrose,[56] they used the sword, which heresy itself had drawn from the scabbard, to cut off the head of the hated monster. The consubstantiality of the Father and the Son was established by the council of Nice, and has been unanimously received as a fundamental article of the Christian faith, by the consent of the Greek, the Latin, the Oriental, and the Protestant churches. But, if the same word had not served to stigmatize the heretics and to unite the Catholics, it would have been inadequate to the purpose of the majority by whom it was introduced into the orthodox creed. This majority was divided into two parties, distinguished by a contrary tendency to the sentiments of the Tritheists and of the Sabellians. But, as those opposite extremes seemed to overthrow the foundations either of natural or revealed religion, they mutually agreed to qualify the rigour of their principles and to disavow the just, but invidious, consequences which might be urged by their antagonists. The interest of the common cause inclined them to join their numbers and to conceal their differences; their animosity was softened by the healing councils of toleration, and their disputes were suspended by the use of the mysterious *Homoousion*, which either party was free to interpret according to their peculiar tenets. The Sabellian sense, which, about fifty years before, had obliged the council of Antioch [57] to prohibit this celebrated term, had endeared it to those theologians who entertained a secret but partial affection for a nominal Trinity. But the more fashionable saints of the Arian times, the intrepid Athanasius, the learned Gregory Nazianzen, and the other pillars of the church, who supported with ability and success the Nicene doctrine, appeared to consider the expression of *substance* as if it had been synonymous with that of *nature;* and they ventured to illustrate their meaning by affirming that three men, as they belong to the same common species, are consubstantial or homoousian to each other.[58] This pure and distinct equality was tempered, on the one hand, by the

[56] We are indebted to Ambrose (de Fide, l. iii. cap. ult.) for the knowledge of this curious anecdote. Hoc verbum posuerunt Patres, quod viderunt adversariis esse formidini; ut tanquam evaginato ab ipsis gladio, ipsum nefandæ caput hæreseos amputarent.

[57] See Bull, Defens. Fid. Nicen. sect. ii. c. i. p. 25-36. He thinks it his duty to reconcile two orthodox synods.

[58] According to Aristotle, the stars were homoousian to each other. "That *Homoousius* means of one substance in *kind*, hath been shown by Petavius, Curcellæus, Cudworth, Le Clerc, &c., and to prove it would be *actum agere*." This is the just remark of Dr. Jortin (vol. ii. p. 212), who examines the Arian controversy with learning, candour, and ingenuity.

internal connexion, and spiritual penetration, which indissolubly unites the divine persons; [59] and on the other, by the pre-eminence of the Father, which was acknowledged as far as it is compatible with the independence of the Son.[60] Within these limits the almost invisible and tremulous ball of orthodoxy was allowed securely to vibrate. On either side, beyond this consecrated ground, the heretics and the demons lurked in ambush to surprise and devour the unhappy wanderer. But, as the degrees of theological hatred depend on the spirit of the war rather than on the importance of the controversy, the heretics who degraded, were treated with more severity than those who annihilated, the person of the Son. The life of Athanasius was consumed in irreconcileable opposition to the impious *madness* of the Arians; [61] but he defended above twenty years the Sabellianism of Marcellus of Ancyra; and, when at last he was compelled to withdraw himself from his communion, he continued to mention, with an ambiguous smile, the venial errors of his respectable friend.[62]

The authority of a general council, to which the Arians themselves had been compelled to submit, inscribed on the banners of the orthodox party the mysterious characters of the word *Homoousion*, which essentially contributed, notwithstanding some obscure disputes, some nocturnal combats, to maintain and perpetuate the uniformity of faith, or at least of language. The Consubstantialists, who by their success have deserved and obtained the title of Catholics, gloried in the simplicity and steadiness of their own creed, and insulted the repeated variations of their adversaries, who were destitute of any certain rule of faith. The sincerity or the cunning of the Arian chiefs, the fears of the laws or of the people, their reverence for Christ, their hatred of Athanasius, all the causes, human and divine, that influence and disturb the counsels of a theological faction,

Arian creeds

---

[59] See Petavius (Dogm. Theolog. tom. ii. l. iv. c. 16, p. 453, &c.), Cudworth (p. 559), Bull (sect. iv. p. 285-290, edit. Grab.). The περιχώρησις or *circumincessio* is perhaps the deepest and darkest corner of the whole theological abyss.

[60] The third section of Bull's Defence of the Nicene Faith, which some of his antagonists have called nonsense, and others heresy, is consecrated to the supremacy of the Father.

[61] The ordinary appellation with which Athanasius and his followers chose to compliment the Arians was that of *Ariomanites*.

[62] Epiphanius, tom. i. Hæres. lxxii. 4, p. 837. See the adventures of Marcellus in Tillemont (Mém. Ecclés. tom. vii. p. 880-899). His work, in *one* book, of the unity of God, was answered in the *three* books, which are still extant, of Eusebius. After a long and careful examination, Petavius (tom. ii. l. i. c. 14, p. 78) has reluctantly pronounced the condemnation of Marcellus.

introduced among the sectaries a spirit of discord and inconstancy, which, in the course of a few years, erected eighteen
different models of religion,[63] and avenged the violated dignity
of the church.   The zealous Hilary,[64] who, from the peculiar
hardships of his situation, was inclined to extenuate rather than
to aggravate the errors of the Oriental clergy, declares that in
the wide extent of the ten provinces of Asia, to which he had
been banished, there could be found very few prelates who had
preserved the knowledge of the true God.[65]   The oppression
which he had felt, the disorders of which he was the spectator
and the victim, appeased, during a short interval, the angry
passions of his soul ; and in the following passage, of which I
shall transcribe a few lines, the bishop of Poitiers unwarily
deviates into the style of a Christian philosopher.   " It is a
thing," says Hilary, " equally deplorable and dangerous, that
there are as many creeds as opinions among men, as many
doctrines as inclinations, and as many sources of blasphemy as
there are faults among us ; because we make creeds arbitrarily,
and explain them as arbitrarily.   The Homoousion is rejected,
and received, and explained away by successive synods.   The
partial or total resemblance of the Father and of the Son is a
subject of dispute for these unhappy times.   Every year, nay
every moon, we make new creeds to describe invisible mysteries.
We repent of what we have done, we defend those who repent,
we anathematize those whom we defended.   We condemn
either the doctrine of others in ourselves or our own in that
of others ; and, reciprocally tearing one another to pieces, we
have been the cause of each other's ruin." [66]

It will not be expected, it would not perhaps be endured,
that I should swell this theological digression by a minute

[63] Athanasius in his epistle concerning the synods of Seleucia and Rimini (tom.
i. p. 886-905) has given an ample list of Arian creeds, which has been enlarged and
improved by the labours of the indefatigable Tillemont (Mém. Ecclés. tom. vi. p.
477).
[64] Erasmus, with admirable sense and freedom, has delineated the just character
of Hilary.   To revise his text, to compose the annals of his life, and to justify his
sentiments and conduct, is the province of the Benedictine editors.
[65] Absque episcopo Eleusio et paucis cum eo, ex majore parte Asianæ decem
provinciæ, inter quas consisto, vere Deum nesciunt.   Atque utinam penitus
nescirent ! cum procliviore enim veniâ ignorarent quam obtrectarent.   Hilar. de
Synodis, sive de Fide Orientalium, c. 63, p. 1186, edit. Benedict.   In the celebrated
parallel between atheism and superstition, the bishop of Poitiers would have been
surprised in the philosophic society of Bayle and Plutarch.
[66] Hilarius ad Constantium, l. ii. c. 4, 5, p. 1227, 1228.   This remarkable
passage deserved the attention of Mr. Locke, who has transcribed it (vol. iii. p.
470) into the model of his new common-place book.

examination of the eighteen creeds, the authors of which, for the most part, disclaimed the odious name of their parent Arius. It is amusing enough to delineate the form, and to trace the vegetation, of a singular plant; but the tedious detail of leaves without flowers, and of branches without fruit, would soon exhaust the patience, and disappoint the curiosity, of the laborious student. One question which gradually arose from the Arian controversy may however be noticed, as it served to produce and discriminate the three sects who were united only by their common aversion to the Homoousion of the Nicene synod. 1. If they were asked, whether the Son was *like* unto the Father, the question was resolutely answered in the negative by the heretics who adhered to the principles of Arius, [Anomœans] or indeed to those of philosophy; which seem to establish an infinite difference between the Creator and the most excellent of his creatures. This obvious consequence was maintained by Aetius,[67] on whom the zeal of his adversaries bestowed the surname of the Atheist. His restless and aspiring spirit urged him to try almost every profession of human life. He was successively a slave, or at least a husbandman, a travelling tinker, a goldsmith, a physician, a schoolmaster, a theologian, and at last the apostle of a new church, which was propagated by the abilities of his disciple Eunomius.[68] Armed with texts of scripture, and with captious syllogisms from the logic of Aristotle, the subtle Aetius had acquired the fame of an invincible disputant, whom it was impossible either to silence or to convince. Such talents engaged the friendship of the Arian bishops, till they were forced to renounce and even to persecute a dangerous ally, who by the accuracy of his reasoning had prejudiced their cause in the popular opinion and offended the piety of their most devoted followers. 2. The omnipotence of the Creator suggested a specious and respectful solution of the [Homœans] *likeness* of the Father and the Son; and faith might humbly receive what reason could not presume to deny, that the

---

[67] In Philostorgius (l. iii. c. 15) the character and adventures of Aetius appear singular enough, though they are carefully softened by the hand of a friend. The editor Godefroy (p. 153), who was more attached to his principles than to his author, has collected the odious circumstances which his various adversaries have preserved or invented. [Aetius was honest and downright. He and his party were disgusted by the endless shufflings of the semi-Arians.]

[68] According to the judgment of a man who respected both those sectaries, Aetius had been endowed with a stronger understanding, and Eunomius had acquired more art and learning (Philostorgius, l. viii. c. 18). The confession and apology of Eunomius (Fabricius, Biblioth. Græc. tom. viii. p. 258-305) is one of the few heretical pieces which have escaped.

Supreme God might communicate his infinite perfections, and create a being similar only to himself.[69] These Arians were powerfully supported by the weight and abilities of their leaders, who had succeeded to the management of the Eusebian interest, and who occupied the principal thrones of the East. They detested, perhaps with some affectation, the impiety of Aetius; they professed to believe, either without reserve, or according to the scriptures, that the Son was different from all *other* creatures and similar only to the Father. But they denied that he was either of the same or of a similar substance; sometimes boldly justifying their dissent, and sometimes objecting to the use of the word substance, which seems to imply an adequate, or at least a distinct, notion of the nature of the Deity. 3. The sect which asserted the doctrine of a similar substance was the most numerous, at least in the provinces of Asia; and, when the leaders of both parties were assembled in the council of Seleucia,[70] *their* opinion would have prevailed by a majority of one hundred and five to forty-three bishops. The Greek word which was chosen to express this mysterious resemblance bears so close an affinity to the orthodox symbol, that the profane of every age have derided the furious contests which the difference of a single diphthong excited between the Homoousians and the Homoiousians. As it frequently happens that the sounds and characters which approach the nearest to each other accidentally represent the most opposite ideas, the observation would be itself ridiculous, if it were possible to mark any real and sensible distinction between the doctrine of the Semi-Arians, as they were improperly styled, and that of the Catholics themselves. The bishop of Poitiers, who in his Phrygian exile very wisely aimed at a coalition of parties, endeavours to prove that, by a pious and faithful interpretation,[71] the *Homoiousion* may be reduced to a consubstantial

[69] Yet, according to the opinion of Estius and Bull (p. 297), there is one power, that of creation, which God *cannot* communicate to a creature. Estius, who so accurately defined the limits of Omnipotence, was a Dutchman by birth, and by trade a scholastic divine. Dupin, Bibliot. Eccles. tom. xvii. p. 45. [The chief leader of the Homœans was Acacius.]

[70] Sabinus (ap. Socrat. l. ii. c. 39) had copied the acts; Athanasius and Hilary have explained the divisions of this Arian synod; the other circumstances which are relative to it are carefully collected by Baronius and Tillemont.

[71] Fideli et piâ intelligentiâ . . . De Synod. c. 77, p. 1193. In his short apologetical notes (first published by the Benedictines from a Ms. of Chartres) he observes, that he used this cautious expression, qui intelligerem et impiam, p. 1206. See p. 1146. Philostorgius, who saw those objects through a different medium, is inclined to forget the difference of the important diphthong. See in particular viii. 17, and Godefroy, p. 352.

sense. Yet he confesses that the word has a dark and suspicious aspect; and, as if darkness were congenial to theological disputes, the Semi-Arians, who advanced to the doors of the church, assailed them with the most unrelenting fury.

The provinces of Egypt and Asia, which cultivated the language and manners of the Greeks, had deeply imbibed the venom of the Arian controversy. The familiar study of the Platonic system, a vain and argumentative disposition, a copious and flexible idiom, supplied the clergy and people of the East with an inexhaustible flow of words and distinctions; and, in the midst of their fierce contentions, they easily forgot the doubt which is recommended by philosophy, and the submission which is enjoined by religion. The inhabitants of the West were of a less inquisitive spirit; their passions were not so forcibly moved by invisible objects; their minds were less frequently exercised by the habits of dispute, and such was the happy ignorance of the Gallican church that Hilary himself, above thirty years after the first general council, was still a stranger to the Nicene creed.[72] The Latins had received the rays of divine knowledge through the dark and doubtful medium of a translation. The poverty and stubbornness of their native tongue was not always capable of affording just equivalents for the Greek terms, for the technical words of the Platonic philosophy,[73] which had been consecrated by the gospel or by the church to express the mysteries of the Christian faith; and a verbal defect might introduce into the Latin theology a long train of error or perplexity.[74] But, as the western provincials had the good fortune of deriving their religion from an orthodox source, they preserved with steadiness the doctrine which they had accepted with docility; and, when the Arian pestilence approached their frontiers, they were supplied with the seasonable preservative of the Homoousion, by the paternal care of the Roman pontiff. Their sentiments and their temper were displayed in the memorable synod of Rimini, which surpassed in

Faith of the Western or Latin Church

Council of Rimini. A.D. 360

[72] Testor Deum cæli atque terræ me cum neutrum audissem, semper tamen utrumque sensisse. . . . Regeneratus pridem et in episcopatu aliquantisper manens idem Nicenam nunquam nisi exsulaturus audivi. Hilar. de Synodis, c. xci. p. 205. The Benedictines are persuaded that he governed the diocese of Poitiers several years before nis exile.

[73] Seneca (Epist. lviii.) complains that even the τὸ ὄν of the Platonists (the *ens* of the boxde schoolmen) could not be expressed by a Latin noun.

[74] The preference which the fourth council of the Lateran at length gave to a *numerical* rather than a *generical* unity (see Petav. tom. ii. l. iv. c. 13, p. 424) was favoured by the Latin language; τριάς seems to excite the idea of substance, *trinitas* of qualities.

numbers the council of Nice, since it was composed of above four hundred bishops of Italy, Africa, Spain, Gaul, Britain and Illyricum. From the first debates it appeared that only fourscore prelates adhered to the party, though *they* affected to anathematize the name and memory of Arius. But this inferiority was compensated by the advantages of skill, of experience, and of discipline; and the minority was conducted by Valens and Ursacius, two bishops of Illyricum, who had spent their lives in the intrigues of courts and councils, and who had been trained under the Eusebian banner in the religious wars of the East. By their arguments and negotiations, they embarrassed, they confounded, they at last deceived, the honest simplicity of the Latin bishops; who suffered the palladium of the faith to be extorted from their hands by fraud and importunity rather than by open violence. The council of Rimini was not allowed to separate, till the members had imprudently subscribed a captious creed, in which some expressions, susceptible of an heretical sense, were inserted in the room of the Homoousion. It was on this occasion that, according to Jerom, the world was surprised to find itself Arian.[75] But the bishops of the Latin provinces had no sooner reached their respective dioceses than they discovered their mistake and repented of their weakness. The ignominious capitulation was rejected with disdain and abhorrence; and the Homoousian standard, which had been shaken but not overthrown, was more firmly replanted in all the churches of the West.[76]

Conduct of the emperors in the Arian controversy

Such was the rise and progress and such were the natural revolutions of those theological disputes which disturbed the peace of Christianity under the reigns of Constantine and of his sons. But, as those princes presumed to extend their despotism over the faith, as well as over the lives and fortunes, of their subjects; the weight of their suffrage sometimes inclined the ecclesiastical balance: and the prerogatives of the King of Heaven were settled, or changed, or modified, in the cabinet of an earthly monarch.

Indifference of Constantine. A.D. 324

The unhappy spirit of discord which pervaded the provinces of the East interrupted the triumph of Constantine; but the

[75] Ingemuit totus orbis, et Arianum se esse miratus est. Hieronym. adv. Lucifer. tom. i. p. 145.

[76] The story of the council of Rimini is very elegantly told by Sulpicius Severus (Hist. Sacra, l. ii. p. 419-430, edit. Lugd. Bat. 1647 [c. 41]), and by Jerom in his dialogue against the Luciferians. The design of the latter is to apologize for the conduct of the Latin bishops, who were deceived, and who repented. [The council of Rimini was a victory for Acacius and his Homœans.]

emperor continued for some time to view, with cool and careless indifference, the object of the dispute. As he was yet ignorant of the difficulty of appeasing the quarrels of theologians, he addressed to the contending parties, to Alexander and to Arius, a moderating epistle;[77] which may be ascribed, with far greater reason, to the untutored sense of a soldier and statesman than to the dictates of any of his episcopal counsellors. He attributes the origin of the whole controversy to a trifling and subtle question, concerning an incomprehensible point of the law, which was foolishly asked by the bishop, and imprudently resolved by the presbyter. He laments that the Christian people, who had the same God, the same religion, and the same worship, should be divided by such inconsiderable distinctions; and he seriously recommends to the clergy of Alexandria the example of the Greek philosophers; who could maintain their arguments without losing their temper, and assert their freedom without violating their friendship. The indifference and contempt of the sovereign would have been, perhaps, the most effectual method of silencing the dispute, if the popular current had been less rapid and impetuous, and if Constantine himself, in the midst of faction and fanaticism, could have preserved the calm possession of his own mind. But his ecclesiastical ministers soon contrived to seduce the impartiality of the magistrate, and to awaken the zeal of the proselyte. He was provoked by the His zeal. A.D. insults which had been offered to his statues; he was alarmed 325 by the real, as well as the imaginary, magnitude of the spreading mischief; and he extinguished the hope of peace and toleration, from the moment that he assembled three hundred bishops within the walls of the same palace. The presence of the monarch swelled the importance of the debate; his attention multiplied the arguments; and he exposed his person with a patient intrepidity, which animated the valour of the combatants. Notwithstanding the applause which has been bestowed on the eloquence and sagacity of Constantine,[78] a Roman general, whose religion might be still a subject of doubt, and whose mind had not been enlightened either by study or by inspiration, was indifferently qualified to discuss, in the Greek language, a metaphysical question, or an article of faith. But

[77] Eusebius, in Vit. Constantin. l. ii. c. 64-72. The principles of toleration and religious indifference, contained in this epistle, have given great offence to Baronius, Tillemont, &c. who suppose that the emperor had some evil counsellor, either Satan or Eusebius, at his elbow. See Jortin's Remarks, tom. ii. p. 183.

[78] Eusebius, in Vit. Constantin. l. iii. c. 13.

the credit of his favourite Osius, who appears to have presided in the council of Nice, might dispose the emperor in favour of the orthodox party ; and a well-timed insinuation that the same Eusebius of Nicomedia, who now protected the heretic, had lately assisted the tyrant,[79] might exasperate him against their adversaries. The Nicene creed was ratified by Constantine ; and his firm declaration that those who resisted the divine judgment of the synod must prepare themselves for an immediate exile annihilated the murmurs of a feeble opposition ; which from seventeen, was almost instantly reduced to two, protesting bishops. Eusebius of Cæsarea yielded a reluctant and ambiguous consent to the Homoousion ;[80] and the wavering conduct of the Nicomedian Eusebius served only to delay, about three months, his disgrace and exile.[81] The impious Arius was banished into one of the remote provinces of Illyricum ; his person and disciples were branded by law with the odious name of Porphyrians ; his writings were condemned to the flames : and a capital punishment was denounced against those in whose possession they should be found. The emperor had now imbibed the spirit of controversy, and the angry sarcastic style of his edicts was designed to inspire his subjects with the hatred which he had conceived against the enemies of Christ.[82]

He persecutes the Arian

and the orthodox party. A.D. 328-337

But, as if the conduct of the emperor had been guided by passion instead of principle, three years from the council of Nice were scarcely elapsed before he discovered some symptoms of mercy, and even of indulgence, towards the proscribed sect, which was secretly protected by his favourite sister. The

[79] Theodoret has preserved (l. i. c. 20) an epistle from Constantine to the people of Nicomedia, in which the monarch declares himself the public accuser of one of his subjects ; he styles Eusebius, ὁ τῆς τυραννικῆς ὠμότητος συμμύστης, and complains of his hostile behaviour during the civil war.

[80] See in Socrates (l. i. c. 8), or rather in Theodoret (l. i. c. 12), an original letter of Eusebius of Cæsarea, in which he attempts to justify his subscribing the Homoousion. The character of Eusebius has always been a problem ; but those who have read the second critical epistle of Le Clerc (Ars Crit. tom. iii. p. 30-69) must entertain a very unfavourable opinion of the orthodoxy and sincerity of the bishop of Cæsarea. [It is interesting to remark that Eusebius proposed that the creed (πίστις) in use at Cæsarea, which he had learnt as a catechumen, should be adopted by the council ; that the council accepted the suggestion ; but so altered the wording, especially by adding the attribute Homoousios, that a Cæsarean could not have recognized it and Eusebius hesitated to subscribe.]

[81] Athanasius, tom. i. p. 727 ; Philostorgius, l. i. c. 10, and Godefroy, Commentary, p. 41.

[82] Socrates, l. i. c. 9. In his circular letters, which were addressed to the several cities, Constantine employed against the heretics the arms of ridicule and *comic* raillery. [As to the result of the council : "the triumph was rather a surprise than a solid victory," Gwatkin (Arian Controversy, p. 39).]

exiles were recalled ; and Eusebius, who gradually resumed his influence over the mind of Constantine, was restored to the episcopal throne from which he had been ignominiously degraded. Arius himself was treated by the whole court with the respect which would have been due to an innocent and oppressed man. His faith was approved by the synod of Jerusalem ; and the emperor seemed impatient to repair his injustice, by issuing an absolute command that he should be solemnly admitted to the communion in the cathedral of Constantinople. On the same day which had been fixed for the triumph of Arius, he expired ; and the strange and horrid circumstances of his death might excite a suspicion that the orthodox saints had contributed more efficaciously than by their prayers to deliver the church from the most formidable of her enemies.[83] The three principal leaders of the Catholics, Athanasius of Alexandria, Eustathius of Antioch, and Paul of Constantinople, were deposed on various accusations, by the sentence of numerous councils ; and were afterwards banished into distant provinces by the first of the Christian emperors, who, in the last moments of his life, received the rites of baptism from the Arian bishop of Nicomedia. The ecclesiastical government of Constantine cannot be justified from the reproach of levity and weakness. But the credulous monarch, unskilled in the stratagems of theological warfare, might be deceived by the modest and specious professions of the heretics, whose sentiments he never perfectly understood ; and, while he protected Arius, and persecuted Athanasius, he still considered the council of Nice as the bulwark of the Christian faith and the peculiar glory of his own reign.[84]

The sons of Constantine must have been admitted from their childhood into the rank of catechumens, but they imitated, in the delay of their baptism, the example of their father. Like him, they presumed to pronounce their judgment on mysteries

Constantius
favours the
Arians. A.D
337-361

[83] We derive the original story from Athanasius (tom. i. p. 670), who expresses some reluctance to stigmatize the memory of the dead. He might exaggerate ; but the perpetual commerce of Alexandria and Constantinople would have rendered it dangerous to invent. Those who press the literal narrative of the death of Arius (his bowels suddenly burst out in a privy) must make their option between *poison* and *miracle*.

[84] The change in the sentiments, or at least in the conduct, of Constantine, may be traced in Eusebius (in Vit. Constant. l. iii. c. 23, l. iv. c. 41), Socrates (l. i. c. 23-39), Sozomen (l. ii. c. 16-34), Theodoret (l. i. c. 14-34), and Philostorgius (l. ii. c. 1-17). But the first of these writers was too near the scene of action and the others were too remote from it. It is singular enough that the important task of continuing the history of the church should have been left for two laymen and a heretic. [Mr. Gwatkin rejects the view that Constantine turned Arian.]

into which they had never been regularly initiated : [85] and the
fate of the Trinitarian controversy depended, in a great measure,
on the sentiments of Constantius ; who inherited the provinces
of the East, and acquired the possession of the whole empire.
The Arian presbyter or bishop, who had secreted for his use the
testament of the deceased emperor, improved the fortunate
occasion which had introduced him to the familiarity of a prince
whose public counsels were always swayed by his domestic
favourites.   The eunuchs and slaves diffused the spiritual
poison through the palace, and the dangerous infection was
communicated, by the female attendants to the guards, and by
the empress to her unsuspicious husband.[86]   The partiality
which Constantius always expressed towards the Eusebian
faction [87] was insensibly fortified by the dexterous management
of their leaders ; and his victory over the tyrant Magnentius
increased his inclination, as well as ability, to employ the arms
of power in the cause of Arianism.   While the two armies were
engaged in the plains of Mursa, and the fate of the two rivals
depended on the chance of war, the son of Constantine passed
the anxious moments in a church of the martyrs, under the
walls of the city.   His spiritual comforter, Valens, the Arian
bishop of the diocese, employed the most artful precautions to
obtain such early intelligence as might secure either his favour
or his escape.   A secret chain of swift and trusty messengers
informed him of the vicissitudes of the battle ; and, while the
courtiers stood trembling round their affrighted master, Valens
assured him that the Gallic legions gave way ; and insinuated
with some presence of mind that the glorious event had been
revealed to him by an angel.   The grateful emperor ascribed
his success to the merits and intercession of the bishop of Mursa,
whose faith had deserved the public and miraculous approbation
of Heaven.[88]   The Arians, who considered as their own the

[85] Quia etiam tum catechumenus sacramentum fidei merito videretur potuisse
nescire.   Sulp. Sever. Hist. Sacra, l. ii. p. 410 [c. 39].

[86] Socrates, l. ii. c. 2.   Sozomen, l. iii. c. 18.   Athanas. tom. i. p. 813, 834.
He observes that the eunuchs are the natural enemies of the *Son*.   Compare Dr.
Jortin's Remarks on Ecclesiastical History, vol. iv. p. 3, with a certain genealogy
in *Candide* (ch. ix.), which ends with one of the first companions of Christopher
Columbus.

[87] [It is important to note that the anti-Nicenes, headed by Eusebius and
opposed to Athanasius, did not dare to avow open Arianism till A.D. 357.   The
strength of the opposition, as Mr. Gwatkin has well brought out, rested on a
"formidable mass of conservative discontent," including Jews, pagans, &c. and
especially strong in the province of Asia.]

[88] Sulpicius Severus, in Hist. Sacra, l. ii. p. 405, 406 [c. 38].

victory of Constantius, preferred his glory to that of his father.[89] Cyril, bishop of Jerusalem, immediately composed the description of a celestial cross encircled with a splendid rainbow ; which during the festival of Pentecost, about the third hour of the day, had appeared over the Mount of Olives, to the edification of the devout pilgrims and the people of the holy city.[90] The size of the meteor was gradually magnified ; and the Arian historian has ventured to affirm that it was conspicuous to the two armies in the plains of Pannonia ; and that the tyrant, who is purposely represented as an idolater, fled before the auspicious sign of orthodox Christianity.[91]

The sentiments of a judicious stranger, who has impartially considered the progress of civil or ecclesiastical discord, are always entitled to our notice : and a short passage of Ammianus, who served in the armies, and studied the character, of Constantius, is perhaps of more value than many pages of theological invectives. "The Christian religion, which, in itself," says that moderate historian, "is plain and simple, *he* confounded by the dotage of superstition. Instead of reconciling the parties by the weight of his authority, he cherished and propagated, by verbal disputes, the differences which his vain curiosity had excited. The highways were covered with troops of bishops, galloping from every side to the assemblies, which they call synods ; and, while they laboured to reduce the whole sect to their own particular opinions, the public establishment of the posts was almost ruined by their hasty and repeated journies." [92] Our more intimate knowledge of the ecclesiastical

Arian
councils

---

[89] Cyril (apud Baron. A.D. 353, No. 26) expressly observes that in the reign of Constantine the cross had been found in the bowels of the earth ; but that it had appeared, in the reign of Constantius, in the midst of the heavens. This opposition evidently proves that Cyril was ignorant of the stupendous miracle to which the conversion of Constantine is attributed ; and this ignorance is the more surprising, since it was no more than twelve years after his death that Cyril was consecrated bishop of Jerusalem by the immediate successor of Eusebius of Cæsarea. See Tillemont, Mém. Ecclés. tom. viii. p. 715.

[90] It is not easy to determine how far the ingenuity of Cyril might be assisted by some natural appearances of a solar halo.

[91] Philostorgius, l. iii. c. 26. He is followed by the author of the Alexandrian Chronicle, by Cedrenus, and by Nicephorus (see Gothofred. Dissert. p. 188). They could not refuse a miracle, even from the hand of an enemy.

[92] So curious a passage well deserves to be transcribed. Christianam religionem absolutam et simplicem, anili superstitione confundens ; in quâ scrutandâ perplexius quam componendâ gravius excitaret discidia plurima ; quæ progressa fusius aluit concertatione verborum, ut catervis antistitum jumentis publicis ultro citroque discurrentibus, per synodos (quas appellant) dum ritum omnem ad suum trahere conantur ([so best Ms.], Valesius reads *conatur*) rei vehiculariæ concideret nervos. Ammianus, xxi. 16.

transactions of the reign of Constantius would furnish an ample
commentary on this remarkable passage; which justifies the
rational apprehensions of Athanasius that the restless activity of
the clergy, who wandered round the empire in search of the
true faith, would excite the contempt and laughter of the unbelieving world.[93]   As soon as the emperor was relieved from
the terrors of the civil war, he devoted the leisure of his winter
quarters at Arles, Milan, Sirmium, and Constantinople, to the
amusement or toils of controversy: the sword of the magistrate, and even of the tyrant, was unsheathed, to enforce the
reasons of the theologian; and, as he opposed the orthodox
faith of Nice, it is readily confessed that his incapacity and
ignorance were equal to his presumption.[94]   The eunuchs, the
women, and the bishops, who governed the vain and feeble
mind of the emperor, had inspired him with an insuperable
dislike to the Homoousion; but his timid conscience was
alarmed by the impiety of Aetius.   The guilt of that atheist was
aggravated by the suspicious favour of the unfortunate Gallus;
and even the deaths of the Imperial ministers who had been
massacred at Antioch were imputed to the suggestions of that
dangerous sophist.   The mind of Constantius, which could
neither be moderated by reason nor fixed by faith, was blindly
impelled to either side of the dark and empty abyss by his
horror of the opposite extreme: he alternately embraced and
condemned the sentiments, he successively banished and recalled
the leaders, of the Arian and Semi-Arian factions.[95]   During the
season of public business or festivity, he employed whole days,
and even nights, in selecting the words, and weighing the
syllables, which composed his fluctuating creeds.   The subject
of his meditation still pursued and occupied his slumbers; the
incoherent dreams of the emperor were received as celestial
visions; and he accepted with complacency the lofty title of
bishop of bishops, from those ecclesiastics who forgot the interest
of their order for the gratification of their passions.   The design

---

[93] Athanas. tom. i. p. 870.

[94] Socrates, l. ii. c. 35-47.   Sozomen, l. iv. c. 12-30.   Theodoret, l. ii. c. 18-32.
Philostorg. l. iv. c. 4-12; l. v. c. 1-4; l. vi. c. 1-5.

[95] Sozomen, l. iv. c. 23, Athanas. tom. i. p. 831.   Tillemont (Mém. Ecclés.
tom. vii. p. 947) has collected several instances of the haughty fanaticism ot
Constantius from the detached treatises of Lucifer of Cagliari.   The very titles of
these treatises inspire zeal and terror; "Moriendum pro Dei Filio," "De Regibus
Apostaticis," "De non conveniendo cum Hæretico," "De non parcendo in
Deum delinquentibus".   [Exiled 355-361.   His strictness led him to renounce
communion with Athanasius as tainted by Arianism.   His works are printed in
Migne, Patrol. xiii., and there is a new ed. by Hartel, 1886.]

of establishing an uniformity of doctrine, which had engaged him to convene so many synods in Gaul, Italy, Illyricum, and Asia, was repeatedly baffled by his own levity, by the divisions of the Arians, and by the resistance of the Catholics; and he resolved, as the last and decisive effort, imperiously to dictate the decrees of a general council. The destructive earthquake of Nicomedia, the difficulty of finding a convenient place, and perhaps some secret motives of policy, produced an alteration in the summons. The bishops of the East were directed to meet at Seleucia, in Isauria; while those of the West held their deliberations at Rimini, on the coast of the Hadriatic; and, instead of two or three deputies from each province, the whole episcopal body was ordered to march. The eastern council, after consuming four days in fierce and unavailing debate, separated without any definitive conclusion. The council of the West was protracted till the seventh month. Taurus, the prætorian præfect, was instructed not to dismiss the prelates till they should all be united in the same opinion; and his efforts were supported by a power of banishing fifteen of the most refractory, and a promise of the consulship if he achieved so difficult an adventure. His prayers and threats, the authority A.D. 360 of the sovereign, the sophistry of Valens and Ursacius, the distress of cold and hunger, and the tedious melancholy of a hopeless exile, at length extorted the reluctant consent of the bishops of Rimini. The deputies of the East and of the West attended the emperor in the palace of Constantinople, and he enjoyed the satisfaction of imposing on the world a profession of faith which established the *likeness*, without expressing the *consubstantiality*, of the Son of God.[96] But the triumph of Arianism had been preceded by the removal of the orthodox clergy, whom it was impossible either to intimidate or to corrupt; and the reign of Constantius was disgraced by the unjust and ineffectual persecution of the great Athanasius.

We have seldom an opportunity of observing, either in active or speculative life, what effect may be produced, or what obstacles may be surmounted, by the force of a single mind when it is inflexibly applied to the pursuit of a single object. The immortal name of Athanasius [97] will never be separated

Character and adventures of Athanasius

---

[96] Sulp. Sever. Hist. Sacra, l. ii. p. 418-430 [c. 41-44]. The Greek historians were very ignorant of the affairs of the West.

[97] We may regret that Gregory Nazianzen composed a panegyric instead of a life of Athanasius; but we should enjoy and improve the advantage of drawing our most authentic materials from the rich fund of his own epistles and apologies (tom. i. p. 670-951). I shall not imitate the example of Socrates (l. ii. c. 1), who

from the Catholic doctrine of the Trinity, to whose defence he consecrated every moment and every faculty of his being.   Educated in the family of Alexander, he had vigorously opposed the early progress of the Arian heresy : he exercised the important functions of secretary under the aged prelate ; and the fathers of the Nicene council beheld, with surprise and respect, the rising virtues of the young deacon.   In a time of public danger, the dull claims of age and of rank are sometimes superseded ; and within five months after his return from Nice,[98] the deacon

Athanasius was seated on the archiepiscopal throne of Egypt. He filled that eminent station above forty-six years, and his long administration was spent in a perpetual combat against the powers of Arianism.   Five times was Athanasius expelled from his throne ; twenty years he passed as an exile or a fugitive ; and almost every province of the Roman empire was successively witness to his merit, and his sufferings in the cause of the Homoousion, which he considered as the sole pleasure and business, as the duty, and as the glory, of his life.   Amidst the storms of persecution, the archbishop of Alexandria was patient of labour, jealous of fame, careless of safety ; and, although his mind was tainted by the contagion of fanaticism, Athanasius displayed a superiority of character and abilities, which would have qualified him, far better than the degenerate sons of Constantine, for the government of a great monarchy.   His learning was much less profound and extensive than that of Eusebius of Cæsarea, and his rude eloquence could not be compared with the polished oratory of Gregory or Basil ; but, whenever the primate of Egypt was called upon to justify his sentiments or his conduct, his unpremeditated style, either of speaking or writing, was clear, forcible, and persuasive.   He has always been revered in the orthodox school, as one of the most accurate masters of the Christian theology ; and he was supposed to possess two profane sciences, less adapted to the episcopal character, the knowledge of jurisprudence [99] and that of divination.[100]   Some fortunate conjectures of future events, which

published the first edition of his history without giving himself the trouble to consult the writings of Athanasius. Yet even Socrates, the more curious Sozomen, and the learned Theodoret, connect the life of Athanasius with the series of ecclesiastical history. The diligence of Tillemont (tom. viii.) and of the Benedictine editors has collected every fact, and examined every difficulty.

[98] [The Coptic date is 17th April, 326.]

[99] Sulpicius Severus (Hist. Sacra, l. ii. p. 396 [c. 36, ad init.]) calls him a lawyer, a jurisconsult. This character cannot now be discovered either in the life or writings of Athanasius [*uirum sanctum* is the true reading, not *iuris consultum*].

[100] Dicebatur enim fatidicarum sortium fidem, quæve augurales portenderent

impartial reasoners might ascribe to the experience and judgment of Athanasius, were attributed by his friends to heavenly inspiration, and imputed by his enemies to infernal magic.

But, as Athanasius was continually engaged with the prejudices and passions of every order of men, from the monk to the emperor, the knowledge of human nature was his first and most important science. He preserved a distinct and unbroken view of a scene which was incessantly shifting; and never failed to improve those decisive moments which are irrecoverably past before they are perceived by a common eye. The archbishop of Alexandria was capable of distinguishing how far he might boldly command, and where he must dexterously insinuate; how long he might contend with power, and when he must withdraw from persecution; and, while he directed the thunders of the church against heresy and rebellion, he could assume, in the bosom of his own party, the flexible and indulgent temper of a prudent leader. The election of Athanasius has not escaped the reproach of irregularity and precipitation;[101] but the propriety of his behaviour conciliated the affections both of the clergy and of the people. The Alexandrians were impatient to rise in arms for the defence of an eloquent and liberal pastor. In his distress he always derived support, or at least consolation, from the faithful attachment of his parochial clergy; and the hundred bishops of Egypt adhered, with unshaken zeal, to the cause of Athanasius. In the modest equipage which pride and policy would affect, he frequently performed the episcopal visitation of his provinces, from the mouth of the Nile to the confines of Æthiopia; familiarly conversing with the meanest of the populace, and humbly saluting the saints and hermits of the desert.[102] Nor was it only in ecclesiastical assemblies, among men whose education and manners were similar to his own, that Athanasius displayed the ascendancy of his genius. He appeared with easy and respect-

alites scientissime callens aliquoties prædixisse futura. Ammianus, xv. 7. A prophecy, or rather a joke, is related by Sozomen (l. iv. c. 10), which evidently proves (if the crows speak Latin) that Athanasius understood the language of the crows.

[101] The irregular ordination of Athanasius was slightly mentioned in the councils which were held against him. See Philostorg. l. ii. c. 11, and Godefroy, p. 71: but it can scarcely be supposed that the assembly of the bishops of Egypt would solemnly attest a *public* falsehood. Athanas. tom. i. p. 726.

[102] See the History of the Fathers of the Desert, published by Rosweide; and Tillemont, Mém. Ecclés. tom. vii. in the lives of Anthony, Pachomius, &c. Athanasius himself, who did not disdain to compose the life of his friend Anthony, has carefully observed how often the holy monk deplored and prophesied the mischiefs of the Arian heresy. Athanas. tom. ii. p. 492, 498, &c.

ful firmness in the courts of princes ; and in the various turns of
his prosperous and adverse fortune, he never lost the confidence
of his friends or the esteem of his enemies.

Persecution
against
Athanasius.
A.D. 330
In his youth, the primate of Egypt resisted the great Constantine, who had repeatedly signified his will that Arius should
be restored to the Catholic communion.[103] The emperor
respected, and might forgive, this inflexible resolution ; and the
faction who considered Athanasius as their most formidable
enemy were constrained to dissemble their hatred, and silently
to prepare an indirect and distant assault.   They scattered
rumours and suspicions, represented the archbishop as a proud
and oppressive tyrant, and boldly accused him of violating the
treaty which had been ratified in the Nicene council with the
schismatic followers of Meletius.[104]   Athanasius had openly
disapproved that ignominious peace, and the emperor was
disposed to believe that he had abused his ecclesiastical and
civil power, to persecute those odious sectaries ; that he had
sacrilegiously broken a chalice in one of their churches of
Mareotis : that he had whipped or imprisoned six of their
bishops ; and that Arsenius, a seventh bishop of the same party,
had been murdered, or at least mutilated, by the cruel hand
of the primate.[105]   These charges, which affected his honour
[A.D. 332] and his life, were referred by Constantine to his brother Dalmatius the censor, who resided at Antioch ; the synods of
Cæsarea and Tyre were successively convened ; and the bishops
of the East were instructed to judge the cause of Athanasius

[103] At first Constantine threatened in *speaking*, but requested in *writing*,
καὶ ἀγράφως μὲν ἠπείλει, γράφων δὲ, ἠξίου. [The first menaces were from Eusebius.
Afterwards Constantine wrote threateningly, Socrates, i. 27.] His letters gradually
assumed a menacing tone ; but, while he required that the entrance of the church
should be open to *all*, he avoided the odious name of Arius.   Athanasius, like a
skilful politician, has accurately marked these distinctions (tom. i. p. 788), which
allowed him some scope for excuse and delay.

[104] The Meletians in Egypt, like the Donatists in Africa, were produced by an
episcopal quarrel which arose from the persecution.   I have not leisure to pursue
the obscure controversy, which seems to have been misrepresented by the partiality
of Athanasius, and the ignorance of Epiphanius.   See Mosheim's General History
of the Church, vol. i. p. 201.

[105] The treatment of the six bishops is specified by Sozomen (l. ii. c. 25) ;
but Athanasius himself, so copious on the subject of Arsenius and the chalice,
leaves this grave accusation without a reply. [Gibbon omits to mention that
Athanasius was summoned to Nicomedia (331-2) to answer a first set of charges, and
was victorious (cp. Athanasius, Festal letter iv.).   The charge as to Arsenius was
made subsequently and was to be heard by Dalmatius, but Constantine,
hearing from Egypt that Arsenius was alive, stopped the proceedings, and then
Athanasius was reconciled with his opponent Arcaph, the leader of the Meletians.
Thus there is an interval between this episode and the council of Cæsarea summoned in 334 at the instigation of Eusebius.]

efore they proceeded to consecrate the new church of the
Resurrection at Jerusalem. The primate might be conscious
of his innocence ; but he was sensible that the same implacable
spirit which had dictated the accusation would direct the proceeding, and pronounce the sentence. He prudently declined
he tribunal of his enemies, despised the summons of the [A.D. 334]
synod of Cæsarea ; and, after a long and artful delay, submitted
to the peremptory commands of the emperor, who threatened
to punish his criminal disobedience if he refused to appear in
he council of Tyre.[106] Before Athanasius, at the head of fifty A.D. 335
Egyptian prelates, sailed from Alexandria, he had wisely secured
the alliance of the Meletians ; and Arsenius himself, his imaginary victim and his secret friend, was privately concealed in his
train. The synod of Tyre was conducted by Eusebius of Cæsarea
with more passion, and with less art, than his learning and experience might promise ; his numerous faction repeated the
names of homicide and tyrant ; and their clamours were encouraged by the seeming patience of Athanasius ; who expected
the decisive moment to produce Arsenius alive and unhurt in
the midst of the assembly. The nature of the other charges
did not admit of such clear and satisfactory replies ; yet the
archbishop was able to prove that, in the village where he was
accused of breaking a consecrated chalice, neither church nor
altar nor chalice could really exist. The Arians, who had
secretly determined the guilt and condemnation of their enemy,
attempted, however, to disguise their injustice by the imitation
of judicial forms : the synod appointed an episcopal commission
of six delegates to collect evidence on the spot; and this
measure, which was vigorously opposed by the Egyptian bishops,
opened new scenes of violence and perjury.[107] After the return
of the deputies from Alexandria, the majority of the council
pronounced the final sentence of degradation and exile against
the primate of Egypt. The decree, expressed in the fiercest
language of malice and revenge, was communicated to the emperor and the Catholic church ; and the bishops immediately

---

[106] Athanas. tom. i. p. 788. Socrates, l. i. c. 28. Sozomen, l. ii. c. 25. The
emperor, in his epistle of Convocation (Euseb. in Vit. Constant. l. iv. c. 42),
seems to prejudge some members of the clergy, and it was more than probable
that the synod would apply those reproaches to Athanasius.

[107] See, in particular, the second Apology of Athanasius (tom. i. p. 763-808),
and his Epistles to the Monks (p. 808-866). They are justified by original and
authentic documents ; but they would inspire more confidence if he appeared less
innocent, and his enemies less absurd. [It is clear from the authorities that the
commission was a mere farce.]

resumed a mild and devout aspect, such as became their holy pilgrimage to the sepulchre of Christ.[108]

His first
exile,
A.D. 38

But the injustice of these ecclesiastical judges had not been countenanced by the submission, or even by the presence, of Athanasius. He resolved to make a bold and dangerous experiment, whether the throne was inaccessible to the voice of truth ; and, before the final sentence could be pronounced at Tyre, the intrepid primate threw himself into a bark which was ready to hoist sail for the Imperial city. The request of a formal audience might have been opposed or eluded ; but Athanasius concealed his arrival, watched the moment of Constantine's return from an adjacent villa, and boldly encountered his angry sovereign as he passed on horseback through the principal street of Constantinople. So strange an apparition excited his surprise and indignation ; and the guards were ordered to remove the importunate suitor ; but his resentment was subdued by involuntary respect ; and the haughty spirit of the emperor was awed by the courage and eloquence of a bishop, who implored his justice and awakened his conscience.[109] Constantine listened to the complaints of Athanasius with impartial and even gracious attention ; the members of the synod of Tyre were summoned to justify their proceedings ; and the arts of the Eusebian faction would have been confounded, if they had not aggravated the guilt of the primate by the dexterous supposition of an unpardonable offence ; a criminal design to intercept and detain the corn-fleet of Alexandria, which supplied the subsistence of the new capital.[110] The emperor was satisfied that the peace of Egypt would be secured by the absence of a popular leader ; but he refused to fill the vacancy of the archiepiscopal throne ; and the sentence which, after a long hesitation, he pronounced was that of a jealous ostracism, rather than of an ignominious exile. In the remote province of Gaul, but in the hospitable court of Treves, Athana-

---

[108] Eusebius in Vit. Constantin. l. iv. c. 41-47.

[109] Athanas. tom. i. p. 804. In a church dedicated to St. Athanasius this situation would afford a better subject for a picture than most of the stories of miracles and martyrdoms.

[110] Athanas. tom. i. p. 729. Eunapius has related (in Vit. Sophist. p. 36, 37, edit. Commelin) a strange example of the cruelty and credulity of Constantine on a similar occasion. The eloquent Sopater, a Syrian philosopher, enjoyed his friendship, and provoked the resentment of Ablavius, his Prætorian præfect. The corn-fleet was detained for want of a south wind ; the people of Constantinople were discontented ; and Sopater was beheaded, on a charge that he had *bound* the winds by the power of magic. Suidas adds that Constantine wished to prove, by this execution, that he had absolutely renounced the superstition of the Gentiles.

sius passed about twenty-eight months. The death of the emperor changed the face of public affairs ; and, amidst the general indulgence of a young reign, the primate was restored to his country by an honourable edict of the younger Constantine, who expressed a deep sense of the innocence and merit of his venerable guest.[111] and restoration, A.D. 338

The death of that prince exposed Athanasius to a second persecution ; and the feeble Constantius, the sovereign of the East, soon became the secret accomplice of the Eusebians. Ninety bishops of that sect or faction assembled at Antioch, under the specious pretence of dedicating the cathedral. They composed an ambiguous creed, which is faintly tinged with the colours of Semi-Arianism, and twenty-five canons, which still regulate the discipline of the orthodox Greeks.[112] It was decided, with some appearance of equity, that a bishop, deprived by a synod, should not resume his episcopal functions, till he had been absolved by the judgment of an equal synod ; the law was immediately applied to the case of Athanasius, the council of Antioch pronounced, or rather confirmed, his degradation : a stranger, named Gregory, was seated on his throne ; and Philagrius,[113] the præfect of Egypt, was instructed to support the new primate with the civil and military powers of the province. Oppressed by the conspiracy of the Asiatic prelates Athanasius withdrew from Alexandria, and passed three [114] His second exile, A.D. 341 [Easter A.D. 340]

[111] In his return he saw Constantius twice, at Viminiacum and at Cæsarea in Cappadocia (Athanas. tom. i. p. 676). Tillemont supposes that Constantine introduced him to the meeting of the three royal brothers in Pannonia (Mémoires Ecclés. tom. viii. p. 69).

[112] See Beveridge, Pandect. tom. i. p. 429-452, and tom. ii. Annotation. p. 182. Tillemont, Mém. Ecclés. tom. vi. p. 310-324. St. Hilary of Poitiers has mentioned this synod of Antioch with too much favour and respect. He reckons ninety-seven bishops.

[113] This magistrate, so odious to Athanasius, is praised by Gregory Nazianzen, tom. i. Orat. xxi. p. 390, 391.

Sæpe premente Deo fert Deus alter opem.

For the credit of human nature, I am always pleased to discover some good qualities in those men whom party has represented as tyrants and monsters.

[114] The chronological difficulties which perplex the residence of Athanasius at Rome are strenuously agitated by Valesius (Observat. ad Calcem, tom. ii. Hist. Eccles. l. i. c. 1-5) and Tillemont (Mém. Ecclés. tom. viii. p. 674, &c.). I have followed the simple hypothesis of Valesius, who allows only one journey, after the intrusion of Gregory. [Rightly ; but the date must be Easter 340. This follows from the true date of the Council of Sardica, fixed by Hefele (Conciliengeschichte, i. p. 503-516) to A.D. 343, autumn—344, spring (Mansi had put it in 344) ; wh.ch date itself depends on the true date of the return of Athanasius to Alexandria. This had been formerly placed in 349 ; but the fragment of an anonymous biographer of Athanasius (c. 385 A.D.), published by Maffei in Osservazioni litterarie, iii. p. 60, in 1738, gave the right date, 346 (21st Oct.), and occasioned an admirable discussion of the chronology by Mansi, Concilia, 3, p. 87 sqq. This was confirmed

years as an exile and a suppliant on the holy threshold of the Vatican.[115]   By the assiduous study of the Latin language, he soon qualified himself to negotiate with the western clergy ; his decent flattery swayed and directed the haughty Julius : the Roman Pontiff was persuaded to consider his appeal as the peculiar interest of the Apostolic see ; and his innocence was unanimously declared in a council of fifty bishops of Italy.[116]   At the end of three years, the primate was summoned to the court of Milan by the emperor Constans, who, in the indulgence of unlawful pleasures, still professed a lively regard for the orthodox faith.   The cause of truth and justice was promoted by the influence of gold,[117] and the ministers of Constans advised their sovereign to require the convocation of an ecclesiastical assembly, which might act as the representatives of the Catholic church.   Ninety-four bishops of the West, seventy-six bishops of the East, encountered each other at Sardica on the verge of the two empires, but in the dominions of the protector of Athanasius.   Their debates soon degenerated into hostile altercations ; the Asiatics, apprehensive for their personal safety, retired to Philippopolis in Thrace ; and the rival synods reciprocally hurled their spiritual thunders against their enemies, whom they piously condemned as the enemies of the true God. Their decrees were published and ratified in their respective provinces ; and Athanasius, who in the West was revered as a saint, was exposed as a criminal to the abhorrence of the East.[118]

A.D. 346
[343]

by one of the Festal Letters (Ep. 19), written after the return of Athanasius, in 347 ; and agrees with the Historia Acephala, and Jerome's Chronicle (Migne, 8, 682). Hefele's correction of Mansi as to the Council takes account of the date 343, given in the Index to the Festal Letters.]

[115] I cannot forbear transcribing a judicious observation of Wetstein (Prolegomen. N. T. p. 19) : Si tamen Historiam Ecclesiasticam velimus consulere patebit jam inde a seculo quarto, cum, ortis controversiis, ecclesiæ Græciæ doctores in duas partes scinderentur, ingenio, eloquentiâ, numero, tantum non æquales, eam partem quæ vincere cupiebat Romam confugisse, majestatemque pontificis comiter coluisse, eoque pacto oppressis per pontificem et episcopos Latinos adversariis prævaluisse, atque orthodoxiam in consiliis stabilivisse.   Eam ob causam Athanasius, non sine comitatu, Romam petiit, pluresque annos ibi hæsit.

[116] [A letter of Pope Julius, reporting the decision of the Synod to the Easterns, is extant, which Mr. Gwatkin describes as " one of the ablest documents of the entire controversy ".]

[117] Philostor. l. iii. c. 12.   If any corruption was used to promote the interest of religion, an advocate of Athanasius might justify or excuse this questionable conduct by the example of Cato and Sidney ; the former of whom is *said* to have given, and the latter to have received, a bribe, in the cause of liberty.

[118] The Canon which allows appeals to the Roman pontiffs ["in honour of the memory of Peter"] has almost raised the council of Sardica to the dignity of a general council ; and its acts have been ignorantly or artfully confounded with those of the Nicene synod.   See Tillemont, tom. viii. p. 689, and Geddes's Tracts, vol. ii. p. 419-460.

The council of Sardica reveals the first symptoms of discord and schism between the Greek and Latin churches, which were separated by the accidental difference of faith and the permanent distinction of language.

During the second exile in the West, Athanasius was fre- and sto-quently admitted to the imperial presence; at Capua, Lodi, ration, A.D. 349 Milan, Verona, Padua, Aquileia, and Treves. The bishop of [346] the diocese usually assisted at these interviews; the master of the offices stood before the veil or curtain of the sacred apartment; and the uniform moderation of the primate might be attested by these respectable witnesses, to whose evidence he solemnly appeals.[119] Prudence would undoubtedly suggest the mild and respectful tone that became a subject and a bishop. In these familiar conferences with the sovereign of the West, Athanasius might lament the error of Constantius; but he boldly arraigned the guilt of his eunuchs and his Arian prelates; deplored the distress and danger of the Catholic church; and excited Constans to emulate the zeal and glory of his father. The emperor declared his resolution of employing the troops and treasures of Europe in the orthodox cause; and signified, by a concise and peremptory epistle to his brother Constantius, that, unless he consented to the immediate restoration of Athanasius, he himself, with a fleet and army, would seat the archbishop on the throne of Alexandria.[120] But this religious war, so horrible to nature, was prevented by the timely com- [345 A.D.] pliance of Constantius; and the emperor of the East condescended to solicit a reconciliation with a subject whom he had injured. Athanasius waited with decent pride, till he had received three successive epistles full of the strongest assurances of the protection, the favour, and the esteem of his sovereign; who invited him to resume his episcopal seat, and who added the humiliating precaution of engaging his principal ministers to attest the sincerity of his intentions. They were manifested in a still more public manner by the strict orders which were dispatched into Egypt to recall the adherents of Athanasius, to restore their privileges, to proclaim their innocence, and to erase from the public registers the illegal proceedings which

[119] As Athanasius dispersed secret invectives against Constantius (see the Epistle to the Monks), at the same time that he assured him of his profound respect, we might distrust the professions of the archbishop, tom. i. p. 677.
[120] Notwithstanding the discreet silence of Athanasius, and the manifest forgery of a letter inserted by Socrates, these menaces are proved by the unquestionable evidence of Lucifer of Cagliari, and even of Constantius himself. See Tillemont, tom. viii. p. 693.

had been obtained during the prevalence of the Eusebian faction. After every satisfaction and security had been given, which justice or even delicacy could require, the primate proceeded, by slow journeys, through the provinces of Thrace, Asia, and Syria; and his progress was marked by the abject homage of the oriental bishops, who excited his contempt without deceiving his penetration.[121] At Antioch he saw the emperor Constantius; sustained, with modest firmness, the embraces and protestations of his master, and eluded the proposal of allowing the Arians a single church at Alexandria, by claiming, in the other cities of the empire, a similar toleration for his own party; a reply which might have appeared just and moderate in the mouth of an independent prince. The entrance of the archbishop into his capital was a triumphal procession; absence and persecution had endeared him to the Alexandrians; his authority, which he exercised with rigour, was more firmly established; and his fame was diffused from Æthiopia to Britain, over the whole extent of the Christian world.[122]

Resentment
of Constan-
tius.
A.D. 351

But the subject who has reduced his prince to the necessity of dissembling can never expect a sincere and lasting forgiveness; and the tragic fate of Constans soon deprived Athanasius of a powerful and generous protector. The civil war between the assassin and the only surviving brother of Constans, which afflicted the empire above three years, secured an interval of repose to the Catholic church; and the two contending parties were desirous to conciliate the friendship of a bishop who, by the weight of his personal authority, might determine the fluctuating resolutions of an important province. He gave audience to the ambassadors of the tyrant, with whom he was afterwards accused of holding a secret correspondence;[123] and the emperor Constantius repeatedly assured his dearest father,

---

[121] I have always entertained some doubts concerning the retractation of Ursacius and Valens (Athanas. tom. i. p. 776). Their epistles to Julius, bishop of Rome, and to Athanasius himself, are of so different a cast from each other that they cannot both be genuine. The one speaks the language of criminals who confess their guilt and infamy; the other of enemies who solicit on equal terms an honourable reconciliation.

[122] The circumstances of his second return may be collected from Athanasius himself, tom. i. p. 769 and 822, 843; Socrates, l. ii. c. 18; Sozomen, l. iii. c. 19; Theodoret, l. ii. c. 11, 12; Philostorgius, l. iii. c. 12.

[123] Athanasius (tom. i. p. 677, 678) defends his innocence by pathetic complaints, solemn assertions, and specious arguments. He admits that letters had been forged in his name, but he requests that his own secretaries, and those of the tyrant, may be examined, whether those letters had been written by the former or received by the latter.

the most reverend Athanasius, that, notwithstanding the malicious rumours which were circulated by their common enemies, he had inherited the sentiments, as well as the throne, of his deceased brother.[124] Gratitude and humanity would have disposed the primate of Egypt to deplore the untimely fate of Constans, and to abhor the guilt of Magnentius; but, as he clearly understood that the apprehensions of Constantius were his only safeguard, the fervour of his prayers for the success of the righteous cause might perhaps be somewhat abated. The ruin of Athanasius was no longer contrived by the obscure malice of a few bigoted or angry bishops, who abused the authority of a credulous monarch. The monarch himself avowed the resolution, which he had so long suppressed, of avenging his private injuries;[125] and the first winter after his victory, which he passed at Arles, was employed against an enemy more odious to him than the vanquished tyrant of Gaul.

If the emperor had capriciously decreed the death of the most eminent and virtuous citizen of the republic, the cruel order would have been executed without hesitation, by the ministers of open violence or of specious injustice. The caution, the delay, the difficulty with which he proceeded in the condemnation and punishment of a popular bishop, discovered to the world that the privileges of the church had already revived a sense of order and freedom in the Roman government. The sentence which was pronounced in the synod of Tyre, and subscribed by a large majority of the eastern bishops, had never been expressly repealed; and, as Athanasius had been once degraded from his episcopal dignity by the judgment of his brethren, every subsequent act might be considered as irregular, and even criminal. But the memory of the firm and effectual support which the primate of Egypt had derived from the attachment of the western church engaged Constantius to suspend the execution of the sentence, till he had obtained the concurrence of the Latin bishops. Two years were consumed in ecclesiastical negotiations; and the important cause between the emperor and one of his subjects was solemnly debated, first in the synod of Arles, and afterwards in the great council of

Councils of Arles and Milan.
A.D. 353-355

---

[124] Athanas. tom. i. p. 825-844.

[125] Athanas. tom. i. p. 861. Theodoret, l. ii. c. 16. The emperor declared that he was more desirous to subdue Athanasius than he had been to vanquish Magnentius or Sylvanus.

Milan,[126] which consisted of above three hundred bishops. Their integrity was gradually undermined by the arguments of the Arians, the dexterity of the eunuchs, and the pressing solicitations of a prince, who gratified his revenge at the expense of his dignity, and exposed his own passions, whilst he influenced those of the clergy. Corruption, the most infallible symptom of constitutional liberty, was successfully practised : honours, gifts, and immunities were offered and accepted as the price of an episcopal vote ;[127] and the condemnation of the Alexandrian primate was artfully represented as the only measure which could restore the peace and union of the Catholic church. The friends of Athanasius were not, however, wanting to their leader, or to their cause. With a manly spirit, which the sanctity of their character rendered less dangerous, they maintained in public debate, and in private conference with the emperor, the eternal obligation of religion and justice. They declared that neither the hope of his favour nor the fear of his displeasure should prevail on them to join in the condemnation of an absent, an innocent, a respectable brother.[128] They affirmed, with apparent reason, that the illegal and obsolete decrees of the council of Tyre had long since been tacitly abolished by the Imperial edicts, the honourable re-establishment of the archbishop of Alexandria, and the silence or recantation of his most clamorous adversaries. They alleged that his innocence had been attested by the unanimous bishops of Egypt, and had been acknowledged, in the councils of Rome and Sardica,[129] by the impartial judgment of the Latin church.

[126] The affairs of the council of Milan are so imperfectly and erroneously related by the Greek writers that we must rejoice in the supply of some letters of Eusebius, extracted by Baronius from the archives of the church of Vercellæ, and of an old life of Dionysius of Milan, published by Bollandus. See Baronius, A.D. 355, and Tillemont, tom. vii. p. 1415.

[127] The honours, presents, feasts, which seduced so many bishops, are mentioned with indignation by those who were too pure or too proud to accept them. " We combat (says Hilary of Poitiers) against Constantius the antichrist ; who strokes the belly instead of scourging the back ;" qui non dorsa cædit, sed ventrem palpat. Hilarius contra Constant. c. 5, p. 1240.

[128] Something of this opposition is mentioned by Ammianus (xv. 7), who had a very dark and superficial knowledge of ecclesiastical history. Liberius . . . perseveranter renitebatur, nec visum hominem, nec auditum damnare nefas ultimum sæpe exclamans ; aperte scilicet recalcitrans Imperatoris arbitrio. Id enim ille Athanasio semper infestus, &c.

[129] More properly by the orthodox part of the council of Sardica. If the bishops of both parties had fairly voted, the division would have been 94 to 76. M. de Tillemont (see t. viii. p. 1147-1158) is justly surprised that so small a majority should have proceeded so vigorously against their adversaries, the principal of whom they immediately deposed.

They deplored the hard condition of Athanasius, who, after enjoying so many years his seat, his reputation, and the seeming confidence of his sovereign, was again called upon to confute the most groundless and extravagant accusations. Their language was specious; their conduct was honourable: but in this long and obstinate contest, which fixed the eyes of the whole empire on a single bishop, the ecclesiastical factions were prepared to sacrifice truth and justice to the more interesting object of defending, or removing, the intrepid champion of the Nicene faith. The Arians still thought it prudent to disguise, in ambiguous language, their real sentiments and designs: but the orthodox bishops, armed with the favour of the people and the decrees of a general council, insisted on every occasion, and particularly at Milan, that their adversaries should purge themselves from the suspicion of heresy, before they presumed to arraign the conduct of the great Athanasius.[130]

But the voice of reason (if reason was indeed on the side of Athanasius) was silenced by the clamours of a factious or venal majority; and the councils of Arles and Milan were not dissolved, till the archbishop of Alexandria had been solemnly condemned and deposed by the judgment of the Western, as well as of the Eastern, church. The bishops who had opposed, were required to subscribe, the sentence; and to unite in religious communion with the suspected leaders of the adverse party. A formulary of consent was transmitted by the messengers of state to the absent bishops: and all those who refused to submit their private opinion to the public and inspired wisdom of the councils of Arles and Milan were immediately banished by the emperor, who affected to execute the decrees of the Catholic church. Among those prelates who led the honourable band of confessors and exiles, Liberius of Rome, Osius of Cordova, Paulinus of Treves, Dionysius of Milan, Eusebius of Vercellæ, Lucifer of Cagliari, and Hilary of Poitiers, may deserve to be particularly distinguished. The eminent station of Liberius, who governed the capital of the empire; the personal merit and long experience of the venerable Osius, who was revered as the favourite of the great Constantine, and the father of the Nicene faith; placed those prelates at the head of the Latin church: and their example, either of submission or resistance, would probably be imitated by the episcopal crowd. But the repeated attempts of the emperor to seduce or to intimidate

Condemnation of Athanasius. A.D. 355

---

[130] Sulp. Severus in Hist. Sacra, l. ii. p. 412 [c. 39].

the bishops of Rome and Cordova were for some time ineffectual.
The Spaniard declared himself ready to suffer under Constantius,
as he had suffered threescore years before under his grandfather
Maximian.   The Roman, in the presence of his sovereign, asserted the innocence of Athanasius, and his own freedom.
When he was banished to Berœa in Thrace, he sent back a large
sum which had been offered for the accommodation of his
journey ; and insulted the court of Milan by the haughty remark that the emperor and his eunuchs might want that gold
to pay their soldiers and their bishops.[131]   The resolution of
Liberius and Osius was at length subdued by the hardships of
exile and confinement.   The Roman pontiff purchased his return
by some criminal compliances ; and afterwards expiated his guilt
by a seasonable repentance.   Persuasion and violence were employed to extort the reluctant signature of the decrepit bishop
of Cordova, whose strength was broken, and whose faculties were
perhaps impaired, by the weight of an hundred years ; and the
insolent triumph of the Arians provoked some of the orthodox
party to treat with inhuman severity the character, or rather the
memory, of an unfortunate old man, to whose former services
Christianity itself was so deeply indebted.[132]

Exiles   The fall of Liberius and Osius reflected a brighter lustre on
the firmness of those bishops who still adhered, with unshaken
fidelity, to the cause of Athanasius and religious truth.   The
ingenious malice of their enemies had deprived them of the
benefit of mutual comfort and advice, separated those illustrious
exiles into distant provinces, and carefully selected the most inhospitable spots of a great empire.[133]   Yet they soon experienced
that the deserts of Libya and the most barbarous tracts of Cappadocia were less inhospitable than the residence of those
cities in which an Arian bishop could satiate, without restraint,
the exquisite rancour of theological hatred.[134]   Their consolation

[131] The exile of Liberius is mentioned by Ammianus, xv. 7.   See Theodoret, l.
ii. c. 16 ; Athanas. tom. i. p. 834-837 ; Hilar. Fragment. i.

[132] The life of Osius is collected by Tillemont (tom. vii. p. 524-561), who in the
most extravagant terms first admires, and then reprobates, the bishop of Cordova.
In the midst of their lamentations on his fall, the prudence of Athanasius may be
distinguished from the blind and intemperate zeal of Hilary.

[133] The confessors of the West were successively banished to the deserts of
Arabia or Thebais, the lonely places of Mount Taurus, the wildest parts of
Phrygia, which were in the possession of the impious Montanists, &c.   When the
heretic Aetius was too favourably entertained at Mopsuestia in Cilicia, the place of
his exile was changed, by the advice of Acacius, to Amblada, a district inhabited
by savages and infested by war and pestilence.   Philostorg. l. v. c. 2.

[134] See the cruel treatment and strange obstinacy of Eusebius, in his own
letters, published by Baronius, A.D. 356, No. 92-102.

was derived from the consciousness of rectitude and independence, from the applause, the visits, the letters, and the liberal alms of their adherents,[135] and from the satisfaction which they soon enjoyed of observing the intestine divisions of the adversaries of the Nicene faith. Such was the nice and capricious taste of the emperor Constantius, and so easily was he offended by the slightest deviation from his imaginary standard of Christian truth, that he persecuted, with equal zeal, those who defended the *consubstantiality,* those who asserted the *similar substance,* and those who denied the *likeness,* of the Son of God. Three bishops, degraded and banished for those adverse opinions, might possibly meet in the same place of exile; and, according to the difference of their temper, might either pity or insult the blind enthusiasm of their antagonists, whose present sufferings would never be compensated by future happiness.

The disgrace and exile of the orthodox bishops of the West were designed as so many preparatory steps to the ruin of Athanasius himself.[136] Six and twenty months had elapsed, during which the Imperial court secretly laboured, by the most insidious arts, to remove him from Alexandria, and to withdraw the allowance which supplied his popular liberality. But, when the primate of Egypt, deserted and proscribed by the Latin church, was left destitute of any foreign support, Constantius dispatched two of his secretaries with a verbal commission to announce and execute the order of his banishment. As the justice of the sentence was publicly avowed by the whole party, the only motive which could restrain Constantius from giving his messengers the sanction of a written mandate must be imputed to his doubt of the event; and to a sense of the danger to which he might expose the second city, and the most fertile province of the empire, if the people should persist in the resolution of defending, by force of arms, the innocence of their spiritual father. Such extreme caution afforded Athanasius a specious pretence respectfully to dispute the truth of an order,

Third expulsion of Athanasius from Alexandria. A.D. 356

[135] Cæterum exules satis constat, totius orbis studiis celebratos pecuniasque eis in sumptum affatim congestas legationibus quoque eos plebis Catholicæ ex omnibus fere provinciis frequentatos. Sulp. Sever. Hist. Sacra, p. 414 [c. 39]. Athanas. tom. i. p. 836, 840.

[136] Ample materials for the history of this third persecution of Athanasius may be found in his own works. See particularly his very able Apology to Constantius (tom. i. p. 673), his first Apology for his flight (p. 701), his prolix Epistle to the Solitaries (p. 808), and the original Protest of the People of Alexandria against the violences committed by Syrianus (p. 866). Sozomen (l. iv. c. 9) has thrown into the narrative two or three luminous and important circumstances.

which he could not reconcile either with the equity, or with the former declarations, of his gracious master. The civil powers of Egypt found themselves inadequate to the task of persuading or compelling the primate to abdicate his episcopal throne; and they were obliged to conclude a treaty with the popular leaders of Alexandria, by which it was stipulated that all proceedings and hostilities should be suspended till the emperor's pleasure had been more distinctly ascertained. By this seeming moderation, the Catholics were deceived into a false and fatal security; while the legions of the Upper Egypt and of Libya advanced, by secret orders and hasty marches, to besiege, or rather to surprise, a capital habituated to sedition and inflamed by religious zeal.[137] The position of Alexandria, between the sea and the lake Mareotis, facilitated the approach and landing of the troops; who were introduced into the heart of the city, before any effectual measures could be taken either to shut the gates or to occupy the important posts of defence. At the hour of midnight, twenty-three days after the signature of the treaty, Syrianus, duke of Egypt, at the head of five thousand soldiers, armed and prepared for an assault, unexpectedly invested the church of St. Theonas, where the archbishop, with a party of his clergy and people, performed their nocturnal devotions. The doors of the sacred edifice yielded to the impetuosity of the attack, which was accompanied with every horrid circumstance of tumult and bloodshed; but, as the bodies of the slain and the fragments of military weapons remained the next day an unexceptionable evidence in the possession of the Catholics, the enterprise of Syrianus may be considered as a successful irruption, rather than as an absolute conquest. The other churches of the city were profaned by similar outrages; and, during at least four months, Alexandria was exposed to the insults of a licentious army, stimulated by the ecclesiastics of an hostile faction. Many of the faithful were killed; who may deserve the name of martyrs, if their deaths were neither provoked nor revenged; bishops and presbyters were treated with cruel ignominy; consecrated virgins were stripped naked, scourged, and violated; the houses of wealthy citizens were plundered; and, under the mask of religious zeal, lust, avarice, and private

---

[137] Athanasius had lately sent for Anthony and some of his chosen Monks. They descended from their mountain, announced to the Alexandrians the sanctity of Athanasius, and were honourably conducted by the archbishop as far as the gates of the city. Athanas. tom. ii. p. 491, 492. See likewise Rufinus, iii. 164, in Vit. Patr. p. 524.

resentment were gratified with impunity, and even with applause. The Pagans of Alexandria, who still formed a numerous and discontented party, were easily persuaded to desert a bishop whom they feared and esteemed. The hopes of some peculiar favours, and the apprehension of being involved in the general penalties of rebellion, engaged them to promise their support to the destined successor of Athanasius, the famous George of Cappadocia. The usurper, after receiving the consecration of an Arian synod, was placed on the episcopal throne by the arms of Sebastian, who had been appointed Count of Egypt for the execution of that important design. In the use, as well as in the acquisition, of power, the tyrant George disregarded the laws of religion, of justice, and of humanity ; and the same scenes of violence and scandal which had been exhibited in the capital were repeated in more than ninety episcopal cities of Egypt. Encouraged by success, Constantius ventured to approve the conduct of his ministers. By a public and passionate epistle, the emperor congratulates the deliverance of Alexandria from a popular tyrant, who deluded his blind votaries by the magic of his eloquence ; expatiates on the virtues and piety of the most reverend George, the elected bishop ; and aspires, as the patron and benefactor of the city, to surpass the fame of Alexander himself. But he solemnly declares his unalterable resolution to pursue with fire and sword the seditious adherents of the wicked Athanasius, who, by flying from justice, has confessed his guilt, and escaped the ignominious death which he had so often deserved.[138]

Athanasius had indeed escaped from the most imminent dangers ; and the adventures of that extraordinary man deserve and fix our attention. On the memorable night when the church of St. Theonas was invested by the troops of Syrianus, the archbishop, seated on his throne, expected, with calm and intrepid dignity, the approach of death. While the public devotion was interrupted by shouts of rage and cries of terror, he animated his trembling congregation to express their religious confidence, by chanting one of the psalms of David, which celebrates the triumph of the God of Israel over the haughty and impious tyrant of Egypt. The doors were at length burst open ; a cloud of arrows was discharged among the people ; the soldiers, with drawn swords, rushed forwards into the sanctuary ; and the dreadful gleam of their armour was reflected

His behaviour

---

[138] Athanas. tom. i. p. 694. The emperor, or his Arian secretaries, while they express their resentment, betray their fears and esteem of Athanasius.

by the holy luminaries which burnt round the altar.[139] Athanasius still rejected the pious importunity of the Monks and Presbyters, who were attached to his person ; and nobly refused to desert his episcopal station, till he had dismissed in safety the last of the congregation.   The darkness and tumult of the night favoured the retreat of the archbishop ; and, though he was oppressed by the waves of an agitated multitude, though he was thrown to the ground, and left without sense or motion, he still recovered his undaunted courage, and eluded the eager search of the soldiers, who were instructed by their Arian guides that the head of Athanasius would be the most acceptable present to the emperor.   From that moment the primate of Egypt disappeared from the eyes of his enemies, and remained above six years concealed in impenetrable obscurity.[140]

His retreat.
A.D. 356-362

The despotic power of his implacable enemy filled the whole extent of the Roman world ; and the exasperated monarch had endeavoured, by a very pressing epistle to the Christian princes of Æthiopia, to exclude Athanasius from the most remote and sequestered regions of the earth.   Counts, præfects, tribunes, whole armies, were successively employed to pursue a bishop and a fugitive ; the vigilance of the civil and military powers were excited by the Imperial edicts ; liberal rewards were promised to the man who should produce Athanasius, either alive or dead ; and the most severe penalties were denounced against those who should dare to protect the public enemy.[141] But the deserts of Thebais were now peopled by a race of wild yet submissive fanatics, who preferred the commands of their abbot to the laws of their sovereign.   The numerous disciples of Anthony and Pachomius received the fugitive primate as their father, admired the patience and humility with which he conformed to their strictest institutions, collected every word which dropt from his lips as the genuine effusions of inspired wisdom ; and persuaded themselves that their prayers, their fasts, and

139 These minute circumstances are curious, as they are literally transcribed from the protest which was publicly presented three days afterwards by the Catholics of Alexandria.   See Athanas. tom. i. p. 867.

140 The Jansenists have often compared Athanasius and Arnauld, and have expatiated with pleasure on the faith and zeal, the merit and exile, of those celebrated doctors.   This concealed parallel is very dexterously managed by the Abbé de la Bléterie, Vie de Jovien, tom. i. p. 130.

141 Hinc jam toto orbe profugus Athanasius, nec ullus ei tutus ad latendum super erat locus.   Tribuni, Præfecti, Comites, exercitus quoque, ad pervestigandum eum moventur edictis imperialibus : præmia delatoribus proponuntur, si quis eum vivum, si id minus, caput certe Athanasii detulisset. Rufin. l. i. c. 16.

their vigils, were less meritorious than the zeal which they expressed, and the dangers which they braved, in the defence of truth and innocence.[142] The monasteries of Egypt were seated in lonely and desolate places, on the summit of mountains, or in the islands of the Nile; and the sacred horn or trumpet of Tabenne was the well-known signal which assembled several thousand robust and determined Monks, who, for the most part, had been the peasants of the adjacent country. When their dark retreats were invaded by a military force, which it was impossible to resist, they silently stretched out their necks to the executioner, and supported their national character that tortures could never wrest from an Egyptian the confession of a secret which he was resolved not to disclose.[143] The archbishop of Alexandria, for whose safety they eagerly devoted their lives, was lost among a uniform and well-disciplined multitude; and on the nearer approach of danger, he was swiftly removed, by their officious hands, from one place of concealment to another, till he reached the formidable deserts, which the gloomy and credulous temper of superstition had peopled with demons and savage monsters. The retirement of Athanasius, which ended only with the life of Constantius, was spent, for the most part, in the society of the Monks, who faithfully served him as guards, as secretaries, and as messengers; but the importance of maintaining a more intimate connection with the Catholic party tempted him, whenever the diligence of the pursuit was abated, to emerge from the desert, to introduce himself into Alexandria, and to trust his person to the discretion of his friends and adherents. His various adventures might have furnished the subject of a very entertaining romance. He was once secreted in a dry cistern, which he had scarcely left before he was betrayed by the treachery of a female slave;[144] and he was once concealed in a still more extraordinary asylum, the house of a virgin, only twenty years of age, and who was celebrated in the whole city for her exquisite beauty. At the hour of midnight, as

[142] Gregor. Nazianzen. tom. i. Orat. xxi. p. 384, 385. See Tillemont, Mém. Ecclés. tom. vii. p. 176-410, 820-880.

[143] Et nulla tormentorum vis inveniri adhuc potuit; quæ obdurato illius tractûs latroni invito elicere potuit, ut nomen proprium dicat. Ammian. xxii. 16 and Valesius ad locum.

[144] Rufin. l. i. c. 18. Sozomen, l. iv. c. 10. This and the following story will be rendered impossible, if we suppose that Athanasius always inhabited the asylum which he accidentally or occasionally had used. [Compare the story of the virgin Eudæmonis, tortured to betray Athanasius whom she hid, in the Index to the Festal Letters.]

she related the story many years afterwards, she was surprised by the appearance of the archbishop in a loose undress, who, advancing with hasty steps, conjured her to afford him the protection which he had been directed by a celestial vision to seek under her hospitable roof. The pious maid accepted and preserved the sacred pledge which was entrusted to her prudence and courage. Without imparting the secret to any one, she instantly conducted Athanasius into her most secret chamber, and watched over his safety with the tenderness of a friend and the assiduity of a servant. As long as the danger continued, she regularly supplied him with books and provisions, washed his feet, managed his correspondence, and dexterously concealed from the eye of suspicion this familiar and solitary intercourse between a saint whose character required the most unblemished chastity and a female whose charms might excite the most dangerous emotions.[145] During the six years of persecution and exile, Athanasius repeated his visits to his fair and faithful companion ; and the formal declaration that he *saw* the councils of Rimini and Seleucia [146] forces us to believe that he was secretly present at the time and place of their convocation. The advantage of personally negotiating with his friends, and of observing and improving the divisions of his enemies, might justify, in a prudent statesman, so bold and dangerous an enterprise ; and Alexandria was connected by trade and navigation with every seaport of the Mediterranean. From the depth of his inaccessible retreat, the intrepid primate waged an incessant and offensive war against the protector of the Arians ; and his seasonable writings, which were diligently circulated and eagerly perused, contributed to unite and animate the orthodox party. In his public apologies, which he addressed to the emperor himself, he sometimes affected the praise of moderation ; whilst at the same time, in secret and vehement invectives, he exposed Constantius as a weak and wicked prince, the executioner of his family, the tyrant of the republic, and the antichrist of the church. In the height of his prosperity, the victorious monarch, who had chastised the rashness of Gallus, and suppressed the revolt of Sylvanus, who had taken the diadem from the head of

---

[145] Palladius (Hist. Lausiac. c. 136, in Vit. Patr. p. 776), the original author of this anecdote, had conversed with the damsel, who in her old age still remembered with pleasure so pious and honourable a connexion. I cannot indulge the delicacy of Baronius, Valesius, Tillemont, &c. who almost reject a story so unworthy, as they deem it, of the gravity of ecclesiastical history

[146] Athanas. tom. i. p. 869. I agree with Tillemont (t. viii. p. 1197), that his expressions imply a personal, though perhaps secret, visit to the synods.

Vetranio, and vanquished in the field the legions of Magnentius, received from an invisible hand a wound which he could neither heal nor revenge ; and the son of Constantine was the first of the Christian princes who experienced the strength of those principles which, in the cause of religion, could resist the most violent exertions of the civil power.[147]

The persecution of Athanasius and of so many respectable *Arian bishops* bishops, who suffered for the truth of their opinions, or at least for the integrity of their conscience, was a just subject of indignation and discontent to all Christians, except those who were blindly devoted to the Arian faction. The people regretted the loss of their faithful pastors, whose banishment was usually followed by the intrusion of a stranger[148] into the episcopal chair ; and loudly complained that the right of election was violated, and that they were condemned to obey a mercenary usurper, whose person was unknown, and whose principles were suspected. The Catholics might prove to the world that they were not involved in the guilt and heresy of their ecclesiastical governor, by publicly testifying their dissent, or by *Divisions* totally separating themselves from his communion. The first of these methods was invented at Antioch, and practised with such success that it was soon diffused over the Christian world. The doxology or sacred hymn, which celebrates the *glory* of the Trinity, is susceptible of very nice, but material, inflexions ; and the substance of an orthodox, or an heretical, creed may be expressed by the difference of a disjunctive, or a copulative, particle. Alternate responses, and a more regular psalmody,[149] were introduced into the public service by Flavianus and Diodorus, two devout and active laymen, who were attached to the Nicene faith. Under their conduct, a swarm of monks issued from the adjacent desert, bands of well-disciplined singers were stationed in the cathedral of Antioch, the Glory

[147] The Epistle of Athanasius to the Monks is filled with reproaches, which the public must feel to be true (vol. i. p. 834, 856) ; and, in compliment to his readers, he has introduced the comparisons of Pharaoh, Ahab, Belshazzar, &c. The boldness of Hilary was attended with less danger, if he published his invective in Gaul after the revolt of Julian ; but Lucifer sent his libels to Constantius, and almost challenged the reward of martyrdom. See Tillemont, tom. vii. p. 905.

[148] Athanasius (tom. i. p. 811) complains in general of this practice, which he afterwards exemplifies (p. 861) in the pretended election of Felix. Three eunuchs represented the Roman people, and three prelates, who followed the court, assumed the functions of the bishops of the Suburbicarian provinces.

[149] Thomassin (Discipline de l'Eglise, tom. i. l. ii. c. 72, 73, p. 966-984) has collected many curious facts concerning the origin and progress of church-singing, both in the East and West.

to the Father, AND the Son, AND the Holy Ghost,[150] was triumphantly chanted by a full chorus of voices; and the Catholics insulted, by the purity of their doctrine, the Arian prelate who had usurped the throne of the venerable Eustathius. The same zeal which inspired their songs prompted the more scrupulous members of the orthodox party to form separate assemblies, which were governed by the presbyters, till the death of their exiled bishop allowed the election and con secration of a new episcopal pastor.[151] The revolutions of the court multiplied the number of pretenders; and the same city was often disputed, under the reign of Constantius, by two, or three, or even four bishops, who exercised their spiritual jurisdiction over their respective followers, and alternately lost and regained the temporal possessions of the church. The abuse of Christianity introduced into the Roman government new causes of tyranny and sedition; the bands of civil society were torn asunder by the fury of religious factions; and the obscure citizen, who might calmly have surveyed the elevation and fall of successive emperors, imagined and experienced that his own life and fortune were connected with the interests of a popular ecclesiastic. The example of the two capitals, Rome and Constantinople, may serve to represent the state of the empire, and the temper of mankind, under the reign of the sons of Constantine.

Rome

I. The Roman pontiff, as long as he maintained his station and his principles, was guarded by the warm attachment of a great people; and could reject with scorn the prayers, the menaces, and the oblations of an heretical prince. When the eunuchs had secretly pronounced the exile of Liberius, the well-grounded apprehension of a tumult engaged them to use the [A.D. 355] utmost precautions in the execution of the sentence. The capital was invested on every side, and the præfect was commanded to seize the person of the bishop, either by stratagem or by open force. The order was obeyed; and Liberius, with

---

[150] Philostorgius, l. iii. c. 13. Godefroy has examined this subject with singular accuracy (p. 147, &c.). There were three heterodox forms: "To the Father *by* the Son, *and* in the Holy Ghost:" "To the Father *and* the Son *in* the Holy Ghost:" and "To the Father *in* the Son *and* the Holy Ghost".

[151] After the exile of Eustathius, under the reign of Constantine, the rigid party of the orthodox formed a separation, which afterwards degenerated into a schism, and lasted above fourscore years. See Tillemont, Mém. Ecclés. tom. vii. p. 35-54, 1137-1158, tom. viii. p. 537-632, 1314-1332. In many churches, the Arians and Homoousians, who had renounced each other's *communion*, continued for some time to join in prayer. Philostorgius, l. iii. c. 14.

the greatest difficulty, at the hour of midnight, was swiftly
conveyed beyond the reach of the Roman people, before their
consternation was turned into rage. As soon as they were informed of his banishment into Thrace, a general assembly was
convened, and the clergy of Rome bound themselves, by a
public and solemn oath, never to desert their bishop, never to
acknowledge the usurper Felix ; who, by the influence of the
eunuchs, had been irregularly chosen and consecrated within [A.D. 356]
the walls of a profane palace. At the end of two years, their
pious obstinacy subsisted entire and unshaken; and, when Constantius visited Rome, he was assailed by the importunate
solicitations of a people, who had preserved, as the last remnant
of their ancient freedom, the right of treating their sovereign
with familiar insolence. The wives of many of the senators and
most honourable citizens, after pressing their husbands to in-
tercede in favour of Liberius, were advised to undertake a
commission, which, in their hands, would be less dangerous and
might prove more successful. The emperor received with [May, A.D.
politeness these female deputies, whose wealth and dignity 357]
were displayed in the magnificence of their dress and ornaments : he admired their inflexible resolution of following their
beloved pastor to the most distant regions of the earth, and
consented that the two bishops, Liberius and Felix, should
govern in peace their respective congregations. But the ideas
of toleration were so repugnant to the practice, and even to
the sentiments, of those times that, when the answer of Constantius was publicly read in the Circus of Rome, so reasonable
a project of accommodation was rejected with contempt and
ridicule. The eager vehemence which animated the spectators
in the decisive moment of a horse-race was now directed
towards a different object ; and the Circus resounded with the
shout of thousands, who repeatedly exclaimed, "One God, One
Christ, One Bishop". The zeal of the Roman people in the
cause of Liberius was not confined to words alone; and the
dangerous and bloody sedition which they excited soon after
the departure of Constantius determined that prince to accept
the submission of the exiled prelate, and to restore him to the
undivided dominion of the capital. After some ineffectual resistance, his rival was expelled from the city by the permission [Aug. 2, A.D.
of the emperor, and the power of the opposite faction ; the 358]
adherents of Felix were inhumanly murdered in the streets, in
the public places, in the baths, and even in the churches ; and
the face of Rome, upon the return of a Christian bishop, re-

newed the horrid image of the massacres of Marius and the proscriptions of Sylla.[152]

Constanti-
nople

II. Notwithstanding the rapid increase of Christians under the reign of the Flavian family, Rome, Alexandria, and the other great cities of the empire, still contained a strong and powerful faction of Infidels, who envied the prosperity, and who ridiculed, even on their theatres, the theological disputes, of the church. Constantinople alone enjoyed the advantage of being born and educated in the bosom of the faith. The capital of the East had never been polluted by the worship of idols; and the whole body of the people had deeply imbibed the opinions, the virtues, and the passions, which distinguished the Christians of that age

[A.D. 336]
[A.D. 342]

from the rest of mankind. After the death of Alexander, the episcopal throne was disputed by Paul and Macedonius. By their zeal and abilities they both deserved the eminent station to which they aspired; and, if the moral character of Mace-donius was less exceptionable, his competitor had the advantage of a prior election and a more orthodox doctrine. His firm attachment to the Nicene creed, which has given Paul a place in the calendar among saints and martyrs, exposed him to the resentment of the Arians. In the space of fourteen years he was five times driven from the throne; to which he was more frequently restored by the violence of the people than by the permission of the prince; and the power of Macedonius could be secured only by the death of his rival. The unfortunate Paul was dragged in chains from the sandy deserts of Mesopotamia

[End of A.D. 350]

to the most desolate places of Mount Taurus,[153] confined in a dark and narrow dungeon, left six days without food, and at length strangled, by the order of Philip, one of the principal ministers of the emperor Constantius.[154] The first blood which stained the new capital was spilt in this ecclesiastical contest;

[152] See, on this ecclesiastical revolution of Rome, Ammianus, xv. 7; Athanas. tom. i. p. 834, 861; Sozomen, l. iv. c. 15; Theodoret, l. ii. c. 17; Sulp. Sever. Hist. Sacra, l. ii. p. 413 [c. 39]; Hieronym. Chron. Marcellin. et Faustin. Libell. p. 3, 4; Tillemont, Mém. Ecclés. tom. vi. p. 336.

[153] Cucusus was the last stage of his life and sufferings. The situation of that lonely town, on the confines of Cappadocia, Cilicia, and the Lesser Armenia, has occasioned some geographical perplexity; but we are directed to the true spot by the course of the Roman road from Cæsarea to Anazarbus. See Cellarii Geograph. tom. ii. p. 213; Wesseling ad Itinerar. p. 179, 703.

[154] Athanasius (t. i. p. 703, 813, 814) affirms, in the most positive terms, that Paul was murdered; and appeals, not only to common fame, but even to the un-suspicious testimony of Philagrius, one of the Arian persecutors. Yet he acknow-ledges that the heretics attributed to disease the death of the bishop of Constanti-nople. Athanasius is servilely copied by Socrates (l. ii. c. 26); but Sozomen, who discovers a more liberal temper, presumes (l. iv. c. 2) to insinuate a prudent doubt.

and many persons were slain on both sides, in the furious and obstinate seditions of the people. The commission of enforcing a sentence of banishment against Paul had been entrusted to Hermogenes, the master-general of the cavalry; but the execution of it was fatal to himself. The Catholics rose in the defence of their bishop; the palace of Hermogenes was consumed; the first military officer of the empire was dragged by the heels through the streets of Constantinople, and, after he expired, his lifeless corpse was exposed to their wanton insults.[155] The fate of Hermogenes instructed Philip, the Prætorian præfect, to act with more precaution on a similar occasion. In the most gentle and honourable terms, he required the attendance of Paul in the baths of Zeuxippus, which had a private communication with the palace and the sea. A vessel, which lay ready at the garden-stairs, immediately hoisted sail; and, while the people were still ignorant of the meditated sacrilege, their bishop was already embarked on his voyage to Thessalonica. They soon beheld, with surprise and indignation, the gates of the palace thrown open, and the usurper Macedonius seated by the side of the præfect on a lofty chariot, which was surrounded by troops of guards with drawn swords. The military procession advanced towards the cathedral; the Arians and the Catholics eagerly rushed to occupy that important post; and three thousand one hundred and fifty persons lost their lives in the confusion of the tumult. Macedonius, who was supported by a regular force, obtained a decisive victory; but his reign was disturbed by clamour and sedition; and the causes which appeared the least connected with the subject of dispute were sufficient to nourish and to kindle the flame of civil discord. As the chapel in which the body of the great Constantine had been deposited was in a ruinous condition, the bishops transported those venerable remains into the church of St. Acacius. This prudent and even pious measure was represented as a wicked profanation by the whole party which adhered to the Homoousian doctrine. The factions immediately flew to arms, the consecrated ground was used as their field of battle; and one of the ecclesiastical historians has observed, as a real fact, not as a figure of rhetoric, that the well before the church overflowed with a stream of blood, which filled the porticoes and the adjacent courts. The writer who should impute these tumults solely to a religious

---

[155] Ammianus (xiv. 10) refers to his own account of this tragic event. But we no longer possess that part of his history.

principle would betray a very imperfect knowledge of human nature ; yet it must be confessed that the motive which misled the sincerity of zeal, and the pretence which disguised the licentiousness of passion, suppressed the remorse which, in another cause, would have succeeded to the rage of the Christians of Constantinople.[156]

Cruelty of the Arians

The cruel and arbitrary disposition of Constantius, which did not always require the provocations of guilt and resistance, was justly exasperated by the tumults of his capital and the criminal behaviour of a faction, which opposed the authority and religion of their sovereign. The ordinary punishments of death, exile, and confiscation were inflicted with partial rigour ; and the Greeks still revere the holy memory of two clerks, a reader and a sub-deacon, who were accused of the murder of Hermogenes, and beheaded at the gates of Constantinople. By an edict of Constantius against the Catholics, which has not been judged worthy of a place in the Theodosian code, those who refused to communicate with the Arian bishops, and particularly with Macedonius, were deprived of the immunities of ecclesiastics and of the rights of Christians ; they were compelled to relinquish the possession of the churches ; and were strictly prohibited from holding their assemblies within the walls of the city. The execution of this unjust law, in the provinces of Thrace and Asia Minor, was committed to the zeal of Macedonius ; the civil and military powers were directed to obey his commands ; and the cruelties exercised by this Semi-Arian tyrant in the support of the *Homoiousion*, exceeded the commission, and disgraced the reign, of Constantius. The sacraments of the church were administered to the reluctant victims, who denied the vocation, and abhorred the principles, of Macedonius. The rites of baptism were conferred on women and children, who, for that purpose, had been torn from the arms of their friends and parents ; the mouths of the communicants were held open, by a wooden engine, while the consecrated bread was forced down their throat ; the breasts of tender virgins were either burnt with red-hot egg-shells or inhumanly compressed between sharp and heavy boards.[157] The Novatians of Constantinople

---

[156] See Socrates, . ii. c. 6, 7, .-2, 13, 15, 16, 26, 27, 38, and Sozomen, l. iii. 3, 7, 9 ; l. iv. c. 2, 21. The acts of St. Paul of Constantinople, of which Photius has made an abstract (Phot. Bibliot. p. 1419-1430), are an indifferent copy of these historians ; but a modern Greek, who could write the life of a saint without adding fables and miracles, is entitled to some commendation.

[157] Socrates, l. ii. c. 27, 38. Sozomen, l. iv. c. 21. The principal assistants of Macedonius, in the work of persecution, were the two bishops of Nicomedia and

and the adjacent country, by their firm attachment to the Homoousian standard, deserved to be confounded with the Catholics themselves. Macedonius was informed that a large district of Paphlagonia [158] was almost entirely inhabited by those sectaries. He resolved either to convert or to extirpate them; and, as he distrusted, on this occasion, the efficacy of an ecclesiastical mission, he commanded a body of four thousand legionaries to march against the rebels, and to reduce the territory of Mantinium under his spiritual dominion. The Novatian peasants, animated by despair and religious fury, boldly encountered the invaders of their country; and, though many of the Paphlagonians were slain, the Roman legions were vanquished by an irregular multitude, armed only with scythes and axes; and, except a few who escaped by an ignominious flight, four thousand soldiers were left dead on the field of battle. The successor of Constantius has expressed, in a concise but lively manner, some of the theological calamities which afflicted the empire, and more especially the East, in the reign of a prince who was the slave of his own passions and of those of his eunuchs. "Many were imprisoned, and persecuted, and driven into exile. Whole troops of those who were styled heretics were massacred, particularly at Cyzicus, and at Samosata. In Paphlagonia, Bithynia, Galatia, and in many other provinces, towns and villages were laid waste and utterly destroyed." [159]

While the flames of the Arian controversy consumed the vitals of the empire, the African provinces were infested by their peculiar enemies the savage fanatics, who, under the name of Circumcellions, formed the strength and scandal of the Donatist party. [160] The severe execution of the laws of Constantine had

The revolt and fury of the Donatist Circumcellions. A.D. 345, &c.

Cyzicus, who were esteemed for their virtues, and especially for their charity. I cannot forbear reminding the reader that the difference between the *Homoousion* and *Homoiousion* is almost invisible to the nicest theological eye.

[158] We are ignorant of the precise situation of Mantinium. In speaking of these *four* bands of legionaries, Socrates, Sozomen, and the author of the Acts of St. Paul, use the indefinite terms of ἀριθμοί, φάλαγγες, τάγματα, which Nicephorus very properly translates *thousands*. Vales. ad Socrat. l. ii. c. 38. [Mantinium was in Honorias; see Ramsay, Hist. Geogr. of Asia Minor, p. 194, where Acta Sanct. 24th Aug., Mart. S. Tatiani, and *ib.* 12th Sept., Vit. S. Autonomi, are quoted. The position of the place is still unknown.]

[159] Julian. Epistol. lii. p. 436, edit. Spanheim.

[160] See Optatus Milevitanus (particularly iii. 4), with the Donatist history, by M. Dupin, and the original pieces at the end of his edition. The numerous circumstances which Augustin has mentioned of the fury of the Circumcellions against others, and against themselves, have been laboriously collected by Tillemont, Mém Eccles. tom. vi. p. 147-165; and he has often, though without design, exposed the injuries which had provoked those fanatics.

excited a spirit of discontent and resistance ; the strenuous efforts of his son Constans to restore the unity of the church exasperated the sentiments of mutual hatred which had first occasioned the separation ; and the methods of force and corruption employed by the two imperial commissioners, Paul and Macarius, furnished the schismatics with a specious contrast between the maxims of the apostles and the conduct of their pretended successors.[161] The peasants who inhabited the villages of Numidia and Mauritania were a ferocious race, who had been imperfectly reduced under the authority of the Roman laws ; who were imperfectly converted to the Christian faith ; but who were actuated by a blind and furious enthusiasm in the cause of their Donatist teachers. They indignantly supported the exile of their bishops, the demolition of their churches, and the interruption of their secret assemblies. The violence of the officers of justice, who were usually sustained by a military guard, was sometimes repelled with equal violence ; and the blood of some popular ecclesiastics, which had been shed in the quarrel, inflamed their rude followers with an eager desire of revenging the death of these holy martyrs. By their own cruelty and rashness, the ministers of persecution sometimes provoked their fate ; and the guilt of an accidental tumult precipitated the criminals into despair and rebellion. Driven from their native villages, the Donatist peasants assembled in formidable gangs on the edge of the Gætulian desert ; and readily exchanged the habits of labour for a life of idleness and rapine, which was consecrated by the name of religion and faintly condemned by the doctors of the sect. The leaders of the Circumcellions assumed the title of captains of the saints ; their principal weapon, as they were indifferently provided with swords and spears, was a huge and weighty club, which they termed an *Israelite ;* and the well-known sound of " Praise be to God," which they used as their cry of war, diffused consternation over the unarmed provinces of Africa. At first their depredations

---

[161] It is amusing enough to observe the language of opposite parties, when they speak of the same men and things. Gratus, bishop of Carthage, begins the acclamations of an orthodox synod, "Gratias Deo omnipotenti et Christo Jesu . . . qui imperavit religiosissimo Constanti Imperatori, ut votum gereret unitatis, et mitteret ministros sancti operis *famulos Dei* Paulum et Macarium". Mon. Vet. ad Calcem Optati, p. 313.   "Ecce subito" (says the Donatist author of the Passion of Marculus), "de Constantis regis tyrannicâ domo . . . pollutum Macarianæ persecutionis murmur increpuit, et *duabus bestiis* ad Africam missis, eodem scilicet Macario et Paulo execrandum prorsus ac dirum ecclesiæ certamen indictum est ; ut populus Christianus ad unionem cum traditoribus faciendam, nudatis militum gladiis et draconum præsentibus signis, et tubarum vocibus cogeretur." Monument. p. 304.

were coloured by the plea of necessity; but they soon exceeded the measure of subsistence, indulged without control their intemperance and avarice, burnt the villages which they had pillaged, and reigned the licentious tyrants of the open country. The occupations of husbandry, and the administration of justice, were interrupted; and, as the Circumcellions pretended to restore the primitive equality of mankind and to reform the abuses of civil society, they opened a secure asylum for the slaves and debtors, who flocked in crowds to their holy standard. When they were not resisted, they usually contented themselves with plunder, but the slightest opposition provoked them to acts of violence and murder; and some Catholic priests, who had imprudently signalized their zeal, were tortured by the fanatics with the most refined and wanton barbarity. The spirit of the Circumcellions was not always exerted against their defenceless enemies; they engaged, and sometimes defeated, the troops of the province; and in the bloody action of Bagai, they attacked in the open field, but with unsuccessful valour, an advanced guard of the Imperial cavalry. The Donatists who were taken in arms received, and they soon deserved, the same treatment which might have been shewn to the wild beasts of the desert. The captives died, without a murmur, either by the sword, the axe, or the fire; and the measures of retaliation were multiplied in a rapid proportion, which aggravated the horrors of rebellion, and excluded the hope of mutual forgiveness. In the beginning of the present century, the example of the Circumcellions has been renewed in the persecution, the boldness, the crimes, and the enthusiasm of the Camisards; and, if the fanatics of Languedoc surpassed those of Numidia by their military achievements, the Africans maintained their fierce independence with more resolution and perseverance.[162]

Such disorders are the natural effects of religious tyranny; but the rage of the Donatists was inflamed by a frenzy of a very extraordinary kind; and which, if it really prevailed among them in so extravagant a degree, cannot surely be paralleled in any country or in any age. Many of these fanatics were possessed with the horror of life, and the desire of martyrdom; and they deemed it of little moment by what means, or by what hands, they perished, if their conduct was sanctified by the intention of devoting themselves to the glory of the true faith and

Their religious suicides

---

[162] The Histoire des Camisards, in 3 vols. 12mo. Villefranche, 1760, may be recommended as accurate and impartial. It requires some attention to discover the religion of the author.

the hope of eternal happiness.[163] Sometimes they rudely disturbed the festivals and profaned the temples of paganism, with the design of exciting the most zealous of the idolaters to revenge the insulted honour of their gods. They sometimes forced their way into the courts of justice, and compelled the affrighted judge to give orders for their immediate execution. They frequently stopped travellers on the public highways, and obliged them to inflict the stroke of martyrdom, by the promise of a reward, if they consented, and by the threat of instant death, if they refused to grant so very singular a favour. When they were disappointed of every other resource, they announced the day on which, in the presence of their friends and brethren, they should cast themselves headlong from some lofty rock ; and many precipices were shewn, which had acquired fame by the number of religious suicides. In the actions of these desperate enthusiasts, who were admired by one party as the martyrs of God, and abhorred by the other as the victims of Satan, an impartial philosopher may discover the influence and the last abuse of that inflexible spirit, which was originally derived from the character and principles of the Jewish nation.

General character of the Christian sects. A.D. 312-361

The simple narrative of the intestine divisions, which distracted the peace, and dishonoured the triumph, of the church, will confirm the remark of a pagan historian, and justify the complaint of a venerable bishop. The experience of Ammianus had convinced him that the enmity of the Christians towards each other surpassed the fury of savage beasts against man ;[164] and Gregory Nazianzen most pathetically laments that the kingdom of heaven was converted, by discord, into the image of chaos, of a nocturnal tempest, and of hell itself.[165] The fierce and partial writers of the times, ascribing *all* virtue to themselves, and imputing *all* guilt to their adversaries, have painted the battle of the angels and dæmons. Our calmer reason will reject such pure and perfect monsters of vice or sanctity, and will impute an equal, or at least an indiscriminate, measure of good and evil to the hostile sectaries, who assumed and bestowed the appellations of orthodox and heretics. They had been educated in the same religion, and the same civil society. Their hopes

---

[163] The Donatist suicides alleged in their justification the example of Razias, which is related in the 14th chapter of the second book of the Maccabees.

[164] Nullas infestas hominibus bestias, ut sunt sibi ferales plerique Christianorum expertus. Ammian. xxii. 5.

[165] Gregor. Nazianzen, Orat. i. p. 33. See Tillemont, tom. vi. p. 501, quarto edit.

and fears in the present, or in a future, life were balanced in the same proportion. On either side, the error might be innocent, the faith sincere, the practice meritorious or corrupt. Their passions were excited by similar objects ; and they might alternately abuse the favour of the court, or of the people. The metaphysical opinions of the Athanasians and the Arians could not influence their moral character; and they were alike actuated by the intolerant spirit which has been extracted from the pure and simple maxims of the gospel.

A modern writer, who, with a just confidence, has prefixed to his own history the honourable epithets of political and philosophical,[166] accuses the timid prudence of Montesquieu for neglecting to enumerate, among the causes of the decline of the empire, a law of Constantine, by which the exercise of the pagan worship was absolutely suppressed, and a considerable part of his subjects was left destitute of priests, of temples, and of any public religion. The zeal of the philosophic historian for the rights of mankind has induced him to acquiesce in the ambiguous testimony of those ecclesiastics, who have too lightly ascribed to their favourite hero the *merit* of a general persecution.[167] Instead of alleging this imaginary law, which would have blazed in the front of the Imperial codes, we may safely appeal to the original epistle which Constantine addressed to the followers of the ancient religion ; at a time when he no longer disguised his conversion nor dreaded the rivals of his throne. He invites and exhorts, in the most pressing terms, the subjects of the Roman empire to imitate the example of their master ; but he declares that those who still refuse to open their eyes to the celestial light may freely enjoy their temples and their fancied gods. A report that the ceremonies of paganism were suppressed is formally contradicted by the emperor himself, who wisely assigns, as the principle of his moderation, the invincible force of habit, of prejudice, and of superstition.[168]

[166] Histoire Politique et Philosophique des Etablissemens des Européens dans les deux Indes, tom. i. p. 9.

[167] According to Eusebius (in Vit. Constantin. l. ii. c. 45) the emperor prohibited, both in cities and in the country, τὰ μυσαρὰ . . . τῆς Εἰδωλολατρείας ; the abominable acts or parts of idolatry. Socrates (l. i. c. 17) and Sozomen (l. ii. c. 4, 5) have represented the conduct of Constantine with a just regard to truth and history ; which has been neglected by Theodoret (l. v. c. 21) and Orosius (vii. 28). Tum deinde (says the latter) primus Constantinus *justo* ordine et *pio* vicem vertit edicto; siquidem statuit citra ullam hominum cædem paganorum templa claudi.

[168] See Eusebius, in Vit. Constantin. l. ii. c. 56, 60. In the sermon to the assembly of saints, which the emperor pronounced when he was mature in years and piety, he declares to the idolaters (c. xi.) that they are permitted to offer sacrifices and to exercise every part of their religious worship.

Without violating the sanctity of his promise, without alarming the fears of the pagans, the artful monarch advanced, by slow and cautious steps, to undermine the irregular and decayed fabric of polytheism. The partial acts of severity which he occasionally exercised, though they were secretly prompted by a Christian zeal, were coloured by the fairest pretences of justice and the public good; and, while Constantine designed to ruin the foundations, he seemed to reform the abuses, of the ancient religion. After the example of the wisest of his predecessors, he condemned, under the most rigorous penalties, the occult and impious arts of divination; which excited the vain hopes, and sometimes the criminal attempts, of those who were discontented with their present condition. An ignominious silence was imposed on the oracles, which had been publicly convicted of fraud and falsehood; the effeminate priests of the Nile were abolished; and Constantine discharged the duties of a Roman censor, when he gave orders for the demolition of several temples of Phœnicia, in which every mode of prostitution was devoutly practised in the face of day, and to the honour of Venus.[169] The Imperial city of Constantinople was, in some measure, raised at the expense, and was adorned with the spoils, of the opulent temples of Greece and Asia; the sacred property was confiscated; the statues of gods and heroes were transported, with rude familiarity, among a people who considered them as objects, not of adoration, but of curiosity: the gold and silver were restored to circulation; and the magistrates, the bishops, and the eunuchs, improved the fortunate occasion of gratifying at once their zeal, their avarice, and their resentment. But these depredations were confined to a small part of the Roman world; and the provinces had been long since accustomed to endure the same sacrilegious rapine, from the tyranny of princes and proconsuls, who could not be suspected of any design to subvert the established religion.[170]

and his sons   The sons of Constantine trod in the footsteps of their father, with more zeal and with less discretion. The pretences of

[169] See Eusebius, in Vit. Constantin. l. iii. c. 54-58, and l. iv. c. 23, 25. These acts of authority may be compared with the suppression of the Bacchanals, and the demolition of the temple of Isis, by the magistrates of pagan Rome.

[170] Eusebius (in Vit. Constant. l. iii. c. 54) and Libanius (Orat. pro Templis, p. 9, 10, edit. Gothofred.) both mention the pious sacrilege of Constantine, which they viewed in very different lights. The latter expressly declares that " he made use of the sacred money, but made no alteration in the legal worship; the temples indeed were impoverished, but the sacred rites were performed there". Lardner's Jewish and Heathen Testimonies, vol. iv. p. 140.

rapine and oppression were insensibly multiplied ; [171] every indulgence was shewn to the illegal behaviour of the Christians ; every doubt was explained to the disadvantage of paganism ; and the demolition of the temples was celebrated as one of the auspicious events of the reign of Constans and Constantius.[172] The name of Constantius is prefixed to a concise law, which might have superseded the necessity of any future prohibitions. "It is our pleasure that in all places, and in all cities, the temples be immediately shut, and carefully guarded, that none may have the power of offending. It is likewise our pleasure that all our subjects should abstain from sacrifices. If any one should be guilty of such an act, let him feel the sword of vengeance, and, after his execution, let his property be confiscated to the public use. We denounce the same penalties against the governors of the provinces, if they neglect to punish the criminals." [173] But there is the strongest reason to believe that this formidable edict was either composed without being published, or was published without being executed. The evidence of facts, and the monuments which are still extant of brass and marble, continue to prove the public exercise of the pagan worship during the whole reign of the sons of Constantine. In the east, as well as in the west, in cities, as well as in the country, a great number of temples were respected, or at least were spared ; and the devout multitude still enjoyed the luxury of sacrifices, of festivals, and of processions, by the permission, or by the connivance, of the civil government. About four years after the supposed date of his bloody edict, Constantius visited the temples of Rome ; and the decency of his behaviour is recommended by a pagan orator as an example worthy of the

---

[171] Ammianus (xxii. 4) speaks of some court eunuchs who were spoliis templorum pasti. Libanius says (Orat. pro Templ. p. 23), that the emperor often gave away a temple, like a dog, or a horse, or a slave, or a gold cup : but the devout philosopher takes care to observe that these sacrilegious favourites very seldom prospered.

[172] See Gothofred. Cod. Theodos. tom. vi. p. 262 ; Liban. Orat. Parental. c. x. in Fabric. Bibl. Græc. tom. vii. p. 235.

[173] Placuit omnibus locis atque urbibus universis claudi protinus templa, et accessu vetitis omnibus licentiam delinquendi perditis abnegari. Volumus etiam cunctos a sacrificiis abstinere. Quod siquis aliquid forte hujusmodi perpetraverit, gladio sternatur : facultates etiam perempti fisco decernimus vindicari : et similiter adfligi rectores provinciarum si facinora vindicare neglexerint. Cod. Theodos. l. xvi. tit. x. leg. 4. Chronology has discovered some contradiction in the date of this extravagant law ; the only one, perhaps, by which the negligence of magistrates is punished by death and confiscation. M. de la Bastie (Mém. de l Académie, tom. xv. p. 98) conjectures, with a show of reason, that this was no more than the minutes of a law, the heads of an intended bill, which were found in Scriniis Memoriæ, among the papers of Constantius, and afterwards inserted, as a worthy model, in the Theodosian code.

imitation of succeeding princes. "That emperor," says Symmachus, "suffered the privileges of the vestal virgins to remain inviolate ; he bestowed the sacerdotal dignities on the nobles of Rome, granted the customary allowance to defray the expenses of the public rites and sacrifices : and, though he had embraced a different religion, he never attempted to deprive the empire of the sacred worship of antiquity."[174] The senate still presumed to consecrate, by solemn decrees, the *divine* memory of their sovereigns ; and Constantine himself was associated, after his death, to those gods whom he had renounced and insulted during his life. The title, the ensigns, the pre-rogatives of SOVEREIGN PONTIFF, which had been instituted by Numa, and assumed by Augustus, were accepted, without hesitation, by seven Christian emperors ; who were invested with a more absolute authority over the religion which they had deserted than over that which they professed.[175]

The divisions of Christianity suspended the ruin of *paganism*;[176]

[174] Symmach. Epistol. x. 54.

[175] The fourth Dissertation of M. de la Bastie, sur le Souverain Pontificat des Empereurs Romains (in Mém. de l'Acad. tom. xv. p. 75-144), is a very learned and judicious performance, which explains the state, and proves the toleration, of paganism from Constantine to Gratian. The assertion of Zosimus that Gratian was the first who refused the pontifical robe is confirmed beyond a doubt ; and the murmurs of bigotry, on that subject, are almost silenced.

[176] As I have freely anticipated the use of *pagans* and paganism, I shall now trace the singular revolutions of those celebrated words. 1. Παγή [παγά], in the Doric dialect, so familiar to the Italians, signifies a fountain ; and the rural neighbourhood which frequented the same fountain derived the common appellation of *pagus* and *pagans* (Festus sub voce, and Servius ad Virgil. Georgic. ii. 382). 2. By an easy extension of the word, *pagan* and rural became almost synonymous (Plin. Hist. Natur. xxviii. 5) ; and the meaner rustics acquired that name, which has been corrupted into *peasants* in the modern languages of Europe. 3. The amazing increase of the military order introduced the necessity of a correlative term (Hume's Essays, vol. i. p. 555) ; and all the *people* who were not enlisted in the service of the prince were branded with the contemptuous epithet of pagans (Tacit. Hist. iii. 24, 43, 77. Juvenal. Satir. xvi. [33]. Tertullian. de Pallio, c. 4). 4. The Christians were the soldiers of Christ ; their adversaries, who refused his *sacrament*, or military oath of baptism, might deserve the metaphorical name of pagans : and this popular reproach was introduced as early as the reign of Valentinian (A.D. 365) into Imperial laws (Cod. Theodos. l. xvi. tit. ii. leg. 18) and theological writings. 5. Christianity gradually filled the cities of the empire ; the old religion, in the time of Prudentius (advers. Symmachum, l. i. ad fin.) and Orosius (in Præfat. Hist.), retired and languished in obscure villages ; and the word *pagans*, with its new signification, reverted to its primitive origin. 6. Since the worship of Jupiter and his family has expired, the vacant title of pagans has been successively applied to all the idolaters and polytheists of the old and new world. 7. The Latin Christians bestowed it, without scruple, on their mortal enemies the Mahometans ; and the purest *unitarians* were branded with the unjust reproach of idolatry and paganism. See Gerard Vossius, Etymologicon Linguæ Latinæ, in his works, tom. i. p. 420. Godefroy's Commentary on the Theodosian Code, tom. vi. p. 250, and Ducange, mediæ et infimæ Latinitat. Glossar. [Latin *pagus*, canton or village, has nothing to do with πηγή.]

and the holy war against the infidels was less vigorously prosecuted by princes and bishops who were more immediately alarmed by the guilt and danger of domestic rebellion. The extirpation of *idolatry* [177] might have been justified by the established principles of intolerance : but the hostile sects, which alternately reigned in the imperial court, were mutually apprehensive of alienating, and perhaps exasperating, the minds of a powerful, though declining, faction. Every motive of authority and fashion, of interest and reason, now militated on the side of Christianity ; but two or three generations elapsed before their victorious influence was universally felt. The religion which had so long and so lately been established in the Roman empire was still revered by a numerous people, less attached indeed to speculative opinion than to ancient custom. The honours of the state and army were indifferently bestowed on all the subjects of Constantine and Constantius ; and a considerable portion of knowledge and wealth and valour was still engaged in the service of polytheism. The superstition of the senator and of the peasant, of the poet and the philosopher, was derived from very different causes, but they met with equal devotion in the temples of the gods. Their zeal was insensibly provoked by the insulting triumph of a proscribed sect ; and their hopes were revived by the well-grounded confidence that the presumptive heir of the empire, a young and valiant hero, who had delivered Gaul from the arms of the Barbarians, had secretly embraced the religion of his ancestors.

[177] In the pure language of Ionia and Athens, Εἴδωλον and Λατρεία were ancient and familiar words. The former expressed a likeness, an apparition (Homer, Odyss. xi. 601), a representation, an *image*, created either by fancy or art. The latter denoted any sort of *service* or slavery. The Jews of Egypt, who translated the Hebrew scriptures, restrained the use of these words (Exodus xx. 4, 5) to the religious worship of an image. The peculiar idiom of the Hellenists, or Grecian Jews, has been adopted by the sacred and ecclesiastical writers ; and the reproach of *idolatry* (Εἰδωλολατρεία) has stigmatized that visible and abject mode of superstition which some sects of Christianity should not hastily impute to the polytheists of Greece and Rome.

CHAPTER XXII

*Julian is declared Emperor by the Legions of Gaul—His Marc.
and Success—The Death of Constantius—Civil Administratio
of Julian*

The jealousy
of Constantius
against
Julian

WHILE the Romans languished under the ignominious tyrann
of eunuchs and bishops, the praises of Julian were repeate
with transport in every part of the empire, except in the palac
of Constantius.   The Barbarians of Germany had felt, and stil
dreaded, the arms of the young Cæsar; his soldiers were th
companions of his victory; the grateful provincials enjoyed th
blessings of his reign; but the favourites who had opposed hi
elevation were offended by his virtues; and they justly con
sidered the friend of the people as the enemy of the court.   A
long as the fame of Julian was doubtful, the buffoons of th
palace, who were skilled in the language of satire, tried th
efficacy of those arts which they had so often practised wit
success.   They easily discovered that his simplicity was no
exempt from affectation: the ridiculous epithets of an hair
savage, of an ape invested with the purple, were applied to th
dress and person of the philosophic warrior; and his modes
dispatches were stigmatized as the vain and elaborate fiction
of a loquacious Greek, a speculative soldier, who had studie
the art of war amidst the groves of the academy.[1]   The voic
of malicious folly was at length silenced by the shouts of victory
the conqueror of the Franks and Alemanni could no longer b
painted as an object of contempt; and the monarch himse
was meanly ambitious of stealing from his lieutenant th
honourable reward of his labours.   In the letters crowned wit

---

[1] Omnes qui plus poterant in palatio, adulandi professores jam docti, rec
consulta prospereque completa vertebant in deridiculum : talia sine modo strepent
insulse ; in odium venit cum victoriis suis capella, non homo; ut hirsutum Julianu
carpentes, appellantesque loquacem talpam, et purpuratam simiam, et litterione
Græcum : et his congruentia plurima atque vernacula [*legendum cum Unge*
aeque ut tintinnabula] principi resonantes, audire hæc taliaque gestienti, virtut
ejus obruere verbis impudentibus conabantur, ut segnem incessentes et timidu
et umbratilem, gestaque secus verbis comptioribus exornantem.   Ammiant
xvii. 11.

laurel, which, according to ancient custom, were addressed to the provinces, the name of Julian was omitted. "Constantius had made his dispositions in person ; *he* had signalized his valour in the foremost ranks ; *his* military conduct had secured the victory ; and the captive king of the Barbarians was presented to *him* on the field of battle," from which he was at that time distant about forty days' journey.[2] So extravagant a fable was incapable, however, of deceiving the public credulity, or even of satisfying the pride of the emperor himself. Secretly conscious that the applause and favour of the Romans accompanied the rising fortunes of Julian, his discontented mind was prepared to receive the subtle poison of those artful sycophants who coloured their mischievous designs with the fairest appearances of truth and candour.[3] Instead of depreciating the merits of Julian, they acknowledged, and even exaggerated, his popular fame, superior talents, and important services. But they darkly insinuated that the virtues of the Cæsar might instantly be converted into the most dangerous crimes, if the inconstant multitude should prefer their inclinations to their duty ; or if the general of a victorious army should be tempted from his allegiance by the hopes of revenge and independent greatness. The personal fears of Constantius were interpreted by his council as a laudable anxiety for the public safety ; whilst in private, and perhaps in his own breast, he disguised, under the less odious appellation of fear, the sentiments of hatred and envy, which he had secretly conceived for the inimitable virtues of Julian. *Fears and envy of Constantius*

The apparent tranquillity of Gaul and the imminent danger of the eastern provinces offered a specious pretence for the design which was artfully concerted by the Imperial ministers. They resolved to disarm the Cæsar ; to recall those faithful troops who guarded his person and dignity ; and to employ in a distant war against the Persian monarch the hardy veterans who had vanquished, on the banks of the Rhine, the fiercest *The legions of Gaul are ordered to march into the East. A.D. 360, April*

---

[2] Ammian. xvi. 12. The orator Themistius (iv p. 56, 57) believed whatever was contained in the Imperial letters which were addressed to the senate of Constantinople. Aurelius Victor, who published his Abridgment in the last year of Constantius, ascribes the German victories to the *wisdom* of the emperor, and the *fortune* of the Cæsar. Yet the historian, soon afterwards, was indebted to the favour or esteem of Julian for the honour of a brass statue, and the important offices of consular of the second Pannonia, and præfect of the city. Ammian. xxi. 10.

[3] Callido nocendi artificio, accusatoriam diritatem laudum titulis peragebant. . . . Hæ voces fuerunt ad inflammanda odia probris omnibus potentiores. See Mamertin. in Actione Gratiarum in Vet. Panegyr. xi. 5, 6.

nations of Germany. While Julian used the laborious hours of his winter quarters at Paris in the administration of power, which, in his hands, was the exercise of virtue, he was surprised by the hasty arrival of a tribune and a notary, with positive orders from the emperor, which *they* were directed to execute, and *he* was commanded not to oppose. Constantius signified his pleasure, that four entire legions, the Celtæ, and Petulants, the Heruli, and the Batavians,[4] should be separated from the standard of Julian, under which they had acquired their fame and discipline; that in each of the remaining bands three hundred of the bravest youths should be selected;[5] and that this numerous detachment, the strength of the Gallic army, should instantly begin their march, and exert their utmost diligence to arrive, before the opening of the campaign, on the frontiers of Persia.[6] The Cæsar foresaw, and lamented, the consequences of this fatal mandate. Most of the auxiliaries, who engaged their voluntary service, had stipulated that they should never be obliged to pass the Alps. The public faith of Rome and the personal honour of Julian had been pledged for the observance of this condition. Such an act of treachery and oppression would destroy the confidence, and excite the resentment, of the independent warriors of Germany, who considered truth as the noblest of their virtues, and freedom as the most valuable of their possessions. The legionaries, who enjoyed the title and privileges of Romans, were enlisted for the general defence of the republic; but those mercenary troops heard with cold indifference the antiquated names of the Republic and of Rome. Attached, either from birth or long habit, to the climate and manners of Gaul, they loved and admired Julian; they despised, and perhaps hated, the emperor; they dreaded the laborious march, the Persian arrows, and the burning deserts of Asia. They claimed as their own the country which they had saved; and excused their want of spirit by pleading the sacred and more immediate duty of protecting their families

---

[4] [These are *auxilia palatina* (not legions; see Appendix 12); the best troops in the army, τέτταρας ἀριθμοὺς (*numeros*) τῶν κρατίστων πεζῶν, Julian, ad S. P. Q. Ath. p. 361, ed. Hertl.]

[5] [*Ex numeris aliis* (Amm. 20, 4, 2), a general expression for "from other troops," inclusive of the legions.]

[6] The minute interval, which may be interposed, between the *hyeme adultâ* and the *primo vere* of Ammianus (xx. 1 [3], 4, [2]), instead of allowing a sufficient space for a march of three thousand miles, would render the orders of Constantius as extravagant as they were unjust. The troops of Gaul could not have reached Syria till the end of autumn. The memory of Ammianus must have been inaccurate, and his language incorrect. [As to this criticism, see App. 1.]

and friends. The apprehensions of the Gauls were derived from the knowledge of the impending and inevitable danger. As soon as the provinces were exhausted of their military strength, the Germans would violate a treaty which had been imposed on their fears; and, notwithstanding the abilities and valour of Julian, the general of a nominal army, to whom the public calamities would be imputed, must find himself, after a vain resistance, either a prisoner in the camp of the Barbarians or a criminal in the palace of Constantius. If Julian complied with the orders which he had received, he subscribed his own destruction, and that of a people who deserved his affection. But a positive refusal was an act of rebellion and a declaration of war. The inexorable jealousy of the emperor, the peremptory, and perhaps insidious, nature of his commands, left not any room for a fair apology or candid interpretation; and the dependent station of the Cæsar scarcely allowed him to pause or to deliberate. Solitude increased the perplexity of Julian; he could no longer apply to the faithful counsels of Sallust, who had been removed from his office by the judicious malice of the eunuchs: he could not even enforce his representations by the concurrence of the ministers, who would have been afraid or ashamed to approve the ruin of Gaul. The moment had been chosen, when Lupicinus,[7] the general of the cavalry, was dispatched into Britain, to repulse the inroads of the Scots and Picts; and Florentius was occupied at Vienna by the assessment of the tribute. The latter, a crafty and corrupt statesman, declining to assume a responsible part on this dangerous occasion, eluded the pressing and repeated invitations of Julian, who represented to him that in every important measure, the presence of the præfect was indispensable in the council of the prince. In the meanwhile the Cæsar was oppressed by the rude and importunate solicitations of the Imperial messengers, who presumed to suggest that, if he expected the return of his ministers, he would charge himself with the guilt of the delay, and reserve for them the merit of the execution. Unable to resist, unwilling to comply, Julian expressed, in the most serious terms, his wish, and even his intention, of resigning the purple,

---

[7] Ammianus, xx. 1. The valour of Lupicinus, and his military skill, are acknowledged by the historian, who, in his affected language, accuses the general of exalting the horns of his pride, bellowing in a tragic tone, and exciting a doubt whether he was more cruel or avaricious. The danger from the Scots and Picts was so serious that Julian himself had some thoughts of passing over into the island. [Constantius was doubtless ignorant of this danger.]

which he could not preserve with honour, but which he could not abdicate with safety.

Their discontents

After a painful conflict, Julian was compelled to acknowledge that obedience was the virtue of the most eminent subject, and that the sovereign alone was entitled to judge of the public welfare   He issued the necessary orders for carrying into execution the commands of Constantius; a part of the troops began their march for the Alps; and the detachments from the several garrisons moved towards their respective places of assembly. They advanced with difficulty through the trembling and affrighted crowds of provincials; who attempted to excite their pity by silent despair or loud lamentations; while the wives of the soldiers, holding their infants in their arms, accused the desertion of their husbands, in the mixed language of grief, of tenderness, and of indignation.   This scene of general distress afflicted the humanity of the Cæsar; he granted a sufficient number of post-waggons to transport the wives and families of the soldiers,[8] endeavoured to alleviate the hardships which he was constrained to inflict, and increased, by the most laudable arts, his own popularity and the discontent of the exiled troops. The grief of an armed multitude is soon converted into rage; their licentious murmurs, which every hour were communicated from tent to tent with more boldness and effect, prepared their minds for the most daring acts of sedition; and by the connivance of their tribunes, a seasonable libel was secretly dispersed, which painted in lively colours the disgrace of the Cæsar, the oppression of the Gallic army, and the feeble vices of the tyrant of Asia.   The servants of Constantius were astonished and alarmed by the progress of this dangerous spirit.   They pressed the Cæsar to hasten the departure of the troops: but they imprudently rejected the honest and judicious advice of Julian; who proposed that they should not march through Paris, and suggested the danger and temptation of a last interview.

They proclaim Julian emperor

As soon as the approach of the troops was announced, the Cæsar went out to meet them, and ascended his tribunal, which had been erected in a plain before the gates of the city.   After distinguishing the officers and soldiers who by their rank or merit deserved a peculiar attention, Julian addressed himself in a studied oration to the surrounding multitude: he celebrated their exploits with grateful applause: encouraged them to

---

[8] He granted them the permission of the *cursus clavularis*, or *clabularis*. These post-waggons are often mentioned in the Code, and were supposed to carry fifteen hundred pounds weight.   See Vales. ad Ammian. xx. 4.

accept, with alacrity, the honour of serving under the eyes of a powerful and liberal monarch ; and admonished them that the commands of Augustus required an instant and cheerful obedience. The soldiers, who were apprehensive of offending their general by an indecent clamour, or of belying their sentiments by false and venal acclamations, maintained an obstinate silence, and, after a short pause, were dismissed to their quarters. The principal officers were entertained by the Cæsar, who professed, in the warmest language of friendship, his desire and his inability to reward, according to their deserts, the brave companions of his victories. They retired from the feast, full of grief and perplexity ; and lamented the hardship of their fate, which tore them from their beloved general and their native country. The only expedient which could prevent their separation was boldly agitated and approved ; the popular resentment was insensibly moulded into a regular conspiracy ; their just reasons of complaint were heightened by passion, and their passions were inflamed by wine ; as, on the eve of their departure, the troops were indulged in licentious festivity. At the hour of midnight, the impetuous multitude, with swords and bowls [8a] and torches in their hands, rushed into the suburbs ; encompassed the palace ; [9] and, careless of future dangers, pronounced the fatal and irrevocable words, JULIAN AUGUSTUS ! The prince, whose anxious suspense was interrupted by their disorderly acclamations, secured the doors against their intrusion ; and, as long as it was in his power, secluded his person and dignity from the accidents of a nocturnal tumult. At the dawn of day, the soldiers, whose zeal was irritated by opposition, forcibly entered the palace, seized, with respectful violence, the object of their choice, guarded

---

[8a] [So quarto rightly (Zos. iii. 9); Smith's text and others give *bows !*]

[9] Most probably the palace of the baths (*Thermarum*), of which a solid and lofty hall still subsists in the *rue de la Harpe*. The buildings covered a considerable space of the modern quarter of the University; and the gardens, under the Merovingian kings, communicated with the abbey of St. Germain des Prez. By the injuries of time and the Normans, this ancient palace was reduced, in the twelfth century, to a maze of ruins; whose dark recesses were the scene of licentious love.

> Explicat aula sinus montemque amplectitur alis ;
> Multiplici latebrâ scelerum tersura ruborem.
> ... ... pereuntis sæpe pudoris
> Celatura nefas, Venerisque accommoda *furtis*.

(These lines are quoted from the Architrenius, l. iv. c. 8, a poetical work of John de Hauteville, or Hanville [Altavilla or Auvilla, near Rouen], a Monk of St. Alban's about the year 1190 [1184]. See Warton's Hist. of English Poetry, vol. i. dissert. ii.) Yet such *thefts* might be less pernicious to mankind than the theological disputes of the Sorbonne, which have been since agitated on the same ground. Bonamy, Mém. de l'Académie, tom. xv. p. 678-682.

Julian with drawn swords through the streets of Paris, placed him on the tribunal, and with repeated shouts saluted him as their emperor. Prudence as well as loyalty inculcated the propriety of resisting their treasonable designs and of preparing for his oppressed virtue the excuse of violence. Addressing himself by turns to the multitude and to individuals, he sometimes implored their mercy, and sometimes expressed his indignation; conjured them not to sully the fame of their immortal victories; and ventured to promise that, if they would immediately return to their allegiance, he would undertake to obtain from the emperor, not only a free and gracious pardon, but even the revocation of the orders which had excited their resentment. But the soldiers, who were conscious of their guilt, chose rather to depend on the gratitude of Julian than on the clemency of the emperor. Their zeal was insensibly turned into impatience, and their impatience into rage. The inflexible Cæsar sustained, till the third hour of the day, their prayers, their reproaches, and their menaces; nor did he yield, till he had been repeatedly assured that, if he wished to live, he must consent to reign. He was exalted on a shield in the presence, and amidst the unanimous acclamations, of the troops; a rich military collar, which was offered by chance, supplied the want of a diadem;[10] the ceremony was concluded by the promise of a moderate donative;[11] and the new emperor, overwhelmed with real or affected grief, retired into the most secret recesses of his apartment.[12]

His protestations of innocence   The grief of Julian could proceed only from his innocence; but his innocence must appear extremely doubtful[13] in the eyes of those who have learned to suspect the motives and the pro-

[10] Even in this tumultuous moment, Julian attended to the forms of superstitious ceremony, and obstinately refused the inauspicious use of a female necklace, or a horse-collar, which the impatient soldiers would have employed in the room of a diadem.

[11] An equal proportion of gold and silver, five pieces of the former, one pound of the latter; the whole amounting to about five pounds ten shillings of our money.

[12] For the whole narrative of this revolt, we may appeal to authentic and original materials; Julian himself (ad S. P. Q. Atheniensem, p. 282, 283, 284 [p. 362-366, ed. Hertl.]), Libanius (Orat. Parental, c. 44-48, in Fabricius Bibliot. Græc. t. vii. p. 269-273), Ammianus (xx. 4), and Zosimus (l. iii. p. 151, 152, 153, [c. 9]), who, in the reign of Julian, appears to follow the more respectable authority of Eunapius. With such guides we *might* neglect the abbreviators and ecclesiastical historians.

[13] Eutropius, a respectable witness, uses a doubtful expression, " consensu militum " (x. 15). Gregory Nazianzen, whose ignorance might excuse his fanaticism, directly charges the apostate with presumption, madness, and impious rebellion, αὐθάδεια, ἀπόνοια, ἀσέβεια. Orat. iii. [= iv. ed Migne] p. 67 [c. 26].

fessions of princes. His lively and active mind was susceptible of the various impressions of hope and fear, of gratitude and revenge, of duty and of ambition, of the love of fame and of the fear of reproach. But it is impossible for us to calculate the respective weight and operation of these sentiments; or to ascertain the principles of action, which might escape the observation, while they guided or rather impelled the steps, of Julian himself. The discontent of the troops was produced by the malice of his enemies; their tumult was the natural effect of interest and of passion; and, if Julian had tried to conceal a deep design under the appearances of chance, he must have employed the most consummate artifice without necessity, and probably without success. He solemnly declares, in the presence of Jupiter, of the Sun, of Mars, of Minerva, and of all the other deities, that, till the close of the evening which preceded his elevation, he was utterly ignorant of the designs of the soldiers; [14] and it may seem ungenerous to distrust the honour of a hero and the truth of a philosopher. Yet the superstitious confidence that Constantius was the enemy, and that he himself was the favourite, of the gods, might prompt him to desire, to solicit, and even to hasten the auspicious moment of his reign, which was predestined to restore the ancient religion of mankind. When Julian had received the intelligence of the conspiracy, he resigned himself to a short slumber; and afterwards related to his friends that he had seen the Genius of the empire waiting with some impatience at his door, pressing for admittance, and reproaching his want of spirit and ambition.[15] Astonished and perplexed, he addressed his prayers to the great Jupiter; who immediately signified, by a clear and manifest omen, that he should submit to the will of heaven and of the army. The conduct which disclaims the ordinary maxims of reason excites our suspicion and eludes our inquiry. Whenever the spirit of fanaticism, at once so credulous and so crafty, has insinuated itself into a noble mind, it insensibly corrodes the vital principles of virtue and veracity.

[14] Julian. ad S. P. Q. Athen. p. 284 [p. 365, ed. H.]. The *devout* Abbé de la Blèterie (Vie de Julien, p. 159) is almost inclined to respect the *devout* protestations of a Pagan.

[15] Ammian. xx. 5, with a note of Lindenbrogius on the Genius of the empire. Julian himself, in a confidential letter to his friend and physician, Oribasius (Epist. xvii. p. 384 [p. 496, ed. H.]), mentions another dream, to which, before the event, he gave credit; of a stately tree thrown to the ground, of a small plant striking a deep root into the earth. Even in his sleep, the mind of Cæsar must have been agitated by the hopes and fears of his fortune. Zosimus (l. iii. p. 155 [c. 9]) relates a subsequent dream.

To moderate the zeal of his party, to protect the persons of his enemies,[16] to defeat and to despise the secret enterprises which were formed against his life and dignity, were the cares which employed the first days of the reign of the new emperor. Although he was firmly resolved to maintain the station which he had assumed, he was still desirous of saving his country from the calamities of civil war, of declining a contest with the superior forces of Constantius, and of preserving his own character from the reproach of perfidy and ingratitude. Adorned with the ensigns of military and Imperial pomp, Julian showed himself in the field of Mars to the soldiers, who glowed with ardent enthusiasm in the cause of their pupil, their leader, and their friend. He recapitulated their victories, lamented their sufferings, applauded their resolution, animated their hopes, and checked their impetuosity; nor did he dismiss the assembly, till he had obtained a solemn promise from the troops that, if the emperor of the East would subscribe an equitable treaty, they would renounce any views of conquest, and satisfy themselves with the tranquil possession of the Gallic provinces. On this foundation he composed, in his own name, and in that of the army, a specious and moderate epistle,[17] which was delivered to Pentadius, his master of the offices, and to his chamberlain Eutherius; two ambassadors whom he appointed to receive the answer, and observe the dispositions, of Constantius. This epistle is inscribed with the modest appellation of Cæsar; but Julian solicits in a peremptory, though respectful, manner the confirmation of the title of Augustus. He acknowledges the irregularity of his own election, while he justifies, in some measure, the resentment and violence of the troops which had extorted his reluctant consent. He allows the supremacy of his brother Constantius; and engages to send him an annual present of Spanish horses, to recruit his army with a select number of Barbarian youths, and to accept from his choice a Prætorian præfect of approved discretion and fidelity. But he reserves for himself the nomination of his other civil and military officers, with the troops, the revenue, and the sovereignty of the provinces beyond the Alps. He admonishes the emperor to consult the dictates of justice; to distrust the arts of those

[16] The difficult situation of the prince of a rebellious army is finely described by Tacitus (Hist. 1, 80-85). But Otho had much more guilt, and much less abilities, than Julian.

[17] To this ostensible epistle he added, says Ammianus, private letters, objurgatorias et mordaces, which the historian had not seen, and would not have published. Perhaps they never existed.

venal flatterers who subsist only by the discord of princes; and to embrace the offer of a fair and honourable treaty, equally advantageous to the republic and to the house of Constantine. In this negociation Julian claimed no more than he already possessed. The delegated authority which he had long exercised over the provinces of Gaul, Spain, and Britain was still obeyed under a name more independent and august. The soldiers and the people rejoiced in a revolution which was not stained even with the blood of the guilty. Florentius was a fugitive; Lupicinus a prisoner. The persons who were disaffected to the new government were disarmed and secured; and the vacant offices were distributed, according to the recommendation of merit, by a prince who despised the intrigues of the palace and the clamours of the soldiers.[18]

The negociations of peace were accompanied and supported by the most vigorous preparations for war. The army, which Julian held in readiness for immediate action, was recruited and augmented by the disorders of the times. The cruel persecution of the faction of Magnentius had filled Gaul with numerous bands of outlaws and robbers. They cheerfully accepted the offer of a general pardon from a prince whom they could trust, submitted to the restraints of military discipline, and retained only their implacable hatred to the person and government of Constantius.[19] As soon as the season of the year permitted Julian to take the field, he appeared at the head of his legions; threw a bridge over the Rhine in the neighbourhood of Cleves; and prepared to chastise the perfidy of the Attuarii, a tribe of Franks, who presumed that they might ravage, with impunity, the frontiers of a divided empire. The difficulty, as well as glory, of this enterprise, consisted in a laborious march; and Julian had conquered, as soon as he could penetrate into, a country which former princes had considered as inaccessible. After he had given peace to the Barbarians, the emperor carefully visited the fortifications along the Rhine from Cleves to Basil; surveyed, with peculiar attention, the territories which he had recovered from the hands of the Alemanni, passed through

His fourth and fifth expedition beyond the Rhine. A.D. 360, 361

---

[18] See the first transactions of his reign, in Julian. ad S. P. Q. Athen. p. 285, 286 [p. 367, 368]. Ammianus, xx. 5, 8. Liban. Orat. Parent. c. 49, 50, p. 273-275.

[19] Liban. Orat. Parent. c. 50, p. 275, 276. A strange disorder, since it continued above seven years. In the factions of the Greek republics, the exiles amounted to 20,000 persons; and Isocrates assures Philip that it would be easier to raise an army from the vagabonds than from the cities. See Hume's Essays, tom. i. p. 426, 427.

[Vienne]

Besançon,[20] which had severely suffered from their fury, and fixed his head-quarters at Vienna for the ensuing winter. The barrier of Gaul was improved and strengthened with additional fortifications; and Julian entertained some hopes that the Germans, whom he had so often vanquished, might, in his absence, be restrained by the terror of his name. Vadomair [21] was the only prince of the Alemanni whom he esteemed or feared; and, while the subtle Barbarian affected to observe the faith of treaties, the progress of his arms threatened the state with an unseasonable and dangerous war. The policy of Julian condescended to surprise the prince of the Alemanni by his own arts; and Vadomair who, in the character of a friend, had incautiously accepted an invitation from the Roman governors, was seized in the midst of the entertainment, and sent away prisoner into the heart of Spain. Before the Barbarians were recovered from their amazement, the emperor appeared in arms on the banks of the Rhine, and, once more crossing the river, renewed the deep impressions of terror and respect which had been already made by four preceding expeditions.[22]

Fruitless treaty and declaration of war. A.D. 361

The ambassadors of Julian had been instructed to execute, with the utmost diligence, their important commission. But, in their passage through Italy and Illyricum, they were detained by the tedious and affected delays of the provincial governors; they were conducted by slow journeys from Constantinople to

[Summer, A.D. 360]

Cæsarea in Cappadocia; and, when at length they were admitted to the presence of Constantius, they found that he had already conceived, from the dispatches of his own officers, the most unfavourable opinion of the conduct of Julian and of the Gallic army. The letters were heard with impatience; the trembling messengers were dismissed with indignation and contempt; and the looks, the gestures, the furious language of the monarch expressed the disorder of his soul. The domestic connexion, which might have reconciled the brother and the husband of Helena, was recently dissolved by the death of that princess, whose pregnancy had been several times fruitless, and

---

[20] Julian (Epist. xxxviii. p. 414 [p. 535, ed. H.]) gives a short description of Vesontio, or Besançon; a rocky peninsula almost encircled by the river Doux [Doubs]; once a magnificent city, filled with temples, &c. now reduced to a small town, emerging however from its ruins.

[21] Vadomair entered into the Roman service, and was promoted from a Barbarian kingdom to the military rank of duke of Phœnicia. He still retained the same artful character (Ammian. xxi. 4): but, under the reign of Valens, he signalized his valour in the Armenian war (xxix. 1).

[22] Ammian. xx. 10, xxi. 3, 4. Zosimus, l. iii. p. 155 [10].

was at last fatal to herself.[23] The empress Eusebia had preserved, to the last moment of her life, the warm and even
jealous affection which she had conceived for Julian ; and her
mild influence might have moderated the resentment of a prince
who, since her death, was abandoned to his own passions and to
the arts of his eunuchs. But the terror of a foreign invasion
obliged him to suspend the punishment of a private enemy ; he
continued his march towards the confines of Persia, and thought
it sufficient to signify the conditions which might entitle Julian
and his guilty followers to the clemency of their offended
sovereign. He required that the presumptuous Cæsar should
expressly renounce the appellation and rank of Augustus, which
he had accepted from the rebels ; that he should descend to his
former station of a limited and dependent minister ; that he
should vest the powers of the state and army in the hands of
those officers who were appointed by the Imperial court ; and
that he should trust his safety to the assurances of pardon,
which were announced by Epictetus, a Gallic bishop, and one of
the Arian favourites of Constantius. Several months were ineffectually consumed in a treaty which was negotiated at the
distance of three thousand miles between Paris and Antioch ;
and, as soon as Julian perceived that his moderate and respectful behaviour served only to irritate the pride of an implacable
adversary, he boldly resolved to commit his life and fortune to
the chance of a civil war. He gave a public and military
audience to the quæstor Leonas : the haughty epistle of Constantius was read to the attentive multitude ; and Julian protested, with the most flattering deference, that he was ready to
resign the title of Augustus, if he could obtain the consent of
those whom he acknowledged as the authors of his elevation.
The faint proposal was impetuously silenced ; and the acclamations of "Julian Augustus, continue to reign, by the
authority of the army, of the people, of the republic, which you
have saved," thundered at once from every part of the field, and
terrified the pale ambassador of Constantius. A part of the

---

[23] Her remains were sent to Rome, and interred near those of her sister
Constantina, in the suburb of the *Via Nomentana*, Ammian. xxi. 1. Libanius
has composed a very weak apology to justify his hero from a very absurd charge ;
of poisoning his wife, and rewarding her physician with his mother's jewels. (See
the seventh of seventeen new orations, published at Venice 1754 [by A. Bongiovanni],
from a Ms. in St. Mark s library. p. 117-127 [Or. 36, ed. Reiske].) Elpidius, the
Prætorian præfect of the East, to whose evidence the accuser of Julian appeals, is
arraigned by Libanius as *effeminate* and ungrateful ; yet the religion of Elpidius is
praised by Jerom (tom. i. p. 243), and his humanity by Ammianus (xxi. 6) [and
Libanius praises him elsewhere, cp. Epp. 176 and 192].

letter was afterwards read, in which the emperor arraigned the ingratitude of Julian, whom he had invested with the honours of the purple; whom he had educated with so much care and tenderness; whom he had preserved in his infancy, when he was left a helpless orphan; "an orphan!" interrupted Julian, who justified his cause by indulging his passions; "does the assassin of my family reproach me that I was left an orphan? He urges me to revenge those injuries which I have long studied to forget." The assembly was dismissed; and Leonas, who, with some difficulty, had been protected from the popular fury, was sent back to his master, with an epistle, in which Julian expressed, in a strain of the most vehement eloquence, the sentiments of contempt, of hatred, and of resentment, which had been suppressed and embittered by the dissimulation of twenty years. After this message, which might be considered as a signal of irreconcileable war, Julian, who some weeks before had celebrated the Christian festival of the Epiphany,[24] made a public declaration that he committed the care of his safety to the IMMORTAL GODS; and thus publicly renounced the religion, as well as the friendship, of Constantius.[25]

Julian prepares to attack Constantius

The situation of Julian required a vigorous and immediate resolution. He had discovered from intercepted letters that his adversary, sacrificing the interest of the state to that of the monarch, had again excited the Barbarians to invade the provinces of the West. The position of two magazines, one of them collected on the banks of the lake of Constance, the other formed at the foot of the Cottian Alps, seemed to indicate the march of two armies; and the size of those magazines, each of which consisted of six hundred thousand quarters of wheat, or rather flour,[26] was a threatening evidence

[24] Feriarum die quem celebrantes mense Januario Christiani *Epiphania* dictitant, progressus in eorum ecclesiam, solemniter numine orato discessit. Ammian. xxi. 2. Zonaras observes that it was on Christmas-day, and his assertion is not inconsistent; since the churches of Egypt, Asia, and perhaps Gaul, celebrated on the same day (the sixth of January) the nativity and the baptism of their Saviour. The Romans, as ignorant as their brethren of the real date of his birth, fixed the solemn festival on the 25th of December, the *Brumalia*, or winter solstice, when the Pagans annually celebrated the birth of the Sun. See Bingham's Antiquities of the Christian Church, l. xx. c. 4, and Beausobre, Hist. Critique du Manichéisme, tom. ii. p. 690-700.

[25] The public and secret negotiations between Constantius and Julian must be extracted, with some caution, from Julian himself (Orat. ad S. P. Q. Athen. p. 286), Libanius (Orat. Parent. c. 51, p. 276), Ammianus (xx. 9), Zosimus (l. iii. p. 154 [c. 9]), and even Zonaras (tom. ii. l. xiii. p. 20, 21, 22 [c. 10]), who, on this occasion, appears to have possessed and used some valuable materials.

[26] Three hundred myriads or three millions of *medimni*, a corn-measure familiar to the Athenians, and which contained six Roman *modii*. Julian explains, like a

of the strength and numbers of the enemy, who prepared to surround him. But the Imperial legions were still in their distant quarters of Asia; the Danube was feebly guarded; and, if Julian could occupy by a sudden incursion the important provinces of Illyricum, he might expect that a people of soldiers would resort to his standard, and that the rich mines of gold and silver would contribute to the expenses of the civil war. He proposed this bold enterprise to the assembly of the soldiers; inspired them with a just confidence in their general and in themselves; and exhorted them to maintain their reputation, of being terrible to the enemy, moderate to their fellow-citizens, and obedient to their officers. His spirited discourse was received with the loudest acclamations, and the same troops which had taken up arms against Constantius, when he summoned them to leave Gaul, now declared with alacrity, that they would follow Julian to the farthest extremities of Europe or Asia. The oath of fidelity was administered; and the soldiers, clashing their shields, and pointing their drawn swords to their throats, devoted themselves, with horrid imprecations, to the service of a leader whom they celebrated as the deliverer of Gaul and the conqueror of the Germans.[27] This solemn engagement, which seemed to be dictated by affection rather than by duty, was singly opposed by Nebridius, who had been admitted to the office of Prætorian præfect. That faithful minister, alone and unassisted, asserted the rights of Constantius in the midst of an armed and angry multitude, to whose fury he had almost fallen an honourable, but useless, sacrifice. After losing one of his hands by the stroke of a sword, he embraced the knees of the prince whom he had offended. Julian covered the præfect with his Imperial mantle, and, protecting him from the zeal of his followers, dismissed him to his own house, with less respect than was perhaps due to the virtue of an enemy.[28] The high office of Nebridius was bestowed on Sallust; and the provinces of Gaul, which were now delivered from the intolerable oppression of taxes, enjoyed the mild and equitable administration of the friend of Julian, who was permitted to

soldier and a statesman, the danger of his situation, and the necessity and advantages of an offensive war (ad S. P. Q. Athen. p. 286, 287).

[27] See his oration, and the behaviour of the troops, in Ammian. xxi. 5.

[28] He sternly refused his hand to the suppliant præfect, whom he sent into Tuscany (Ammian. xxi. 5). Libanius, with savage fury, insults Nebridius, applauds the soldiers, and almost censures the humanity of Julian (Orat. Parent. c. 53, p. 278).

practise those virtues which he had instilled into the mind of his pupil.[29]

The hopes of Julian depended much less on the number of his troops than on the celerity of his motions. In the execution of a daring enterprise, he availed himself of every precaution, as far as prudence could suggest; and, where prudence could no longer accompany his steps, he trusted the event to valour and to fortune. In the neighbourhood of Basil he assembled and divided his army.[30] One body, which consisted of ten thousand men, was directed, under the command of Nevitta, general of the cavalry, to advance through the midland parts of Rhætia and Noricum. A similar division of troops, under the orders of Jovius and Jovinus, prepared to follow the oblique course of the highways, through the Alps and the northern confines of Italy. The instructions to the generals were conceived with energy and precision: to hasten their march in close and compact columns, which, according to the disposition of the ground, might readily be changed into any order of battle; to secure themselves against the surprises of the night by strong posts and vigilant guards; to prevent resistance by their unexpected arrival; to elude examination by their sudden departure; to spread the opinion of their strength and the terror of his name; and to join their sovereign under the walls of Sirmium. For himself, Julian had reserved a more difficult and extraordinary part. He selected three thousand brave and active volunteers, resolved, like their leader, to cast behind them every hope of a retreat: at the head of this faithful band, he fearlessly plunged into the recesses of the Marcian or black forest, which conceals the sources of the Danube;[31] and, for many days, the fate of Julian was unknown to the world. The secrecy of his march, his diligence and vigour, surmounted every obstacle; he forced his way over mountains and morasses, occupied the bridges or swam the rivers, pursued his direct course,[32] without reflecting whether he traversed the territory

[29] Ammian. xxi. 8. In this promotion, Julian obeyed the law which he publicly imposed on himself. Neque civilis quisquam judex nec militaris [*leg.* militiæ] rector, alio quodam præter merita suffragante, ad potiorum [*leg.* potiorem] veniat gradum (Ammian. xx. 5). Absence did not weaken his regard for Sallust, with whose name (A.D. 363) he honoured the consulship.

[30] Ammianus (xxi. 8) ascribes the same practice, and the same motive, to Alexander the Great and other skilful generals.

[31] This wood was a part of the great Hercynian forest, which, in the time of Cæsar, stretched away from the country of the Rauraci (Basil) into the boundless regions of the North. See Cluver, Germania Antiqua, l. iii. c. 47.

[32] Compare Libanius, Orat. Parent. c. 53, p. 278, 279, with Gregory Nazianzen,

of the Romans or of the Barbarians, and at length emerged, between Ratisbon and Vienna, at the place where he designed to embark his troops on the Danube. By a well-concerted stratagem, he seized a fleet of light brigantines,[33] as it lay at anchor; secured a supply of coarse provisions sufficient to satisfy the indelicate, but voracious, appetite of a Gallic army; and boldly committed himself to the stream of the Danube. The labours of his mariners, who plied their oars with incessant diligence, and the steady continuance of a favourable wind, carried his fleet above seven hundred miles in eleven days;[34] and he had already disembarked his troops at Bononia, only nineteen miles from Sirmium, before his enemies could receive any certain intelligence that he had left the banks of the Rhine. In the course of this long and rapid navigation, the mind of Julian was fixed on the object of his enterprise; and, though he accepted the deputation of some cities, which hastened to claim the merit of an early submission, he passed before the hostile stations, which were placed along the river, without indulging the temptation of signalizing an useless and ill-timed valour. The banks of the Danube were crowded on either side with spectators, who gazed on the military pomp, anticipated the importance of the event, and diffused through the adjacent country the fame of a young hero, who advanced with more than mortal speed at the head of the innumerable forces of the West. Lucilian, who, with the rank of general of the cavalry, commanded the military powers of Illyricum, was alarmed and perplexed by the doubtful reports which he could neither reject nor believe. He had taken some slow and irresolute measures for the purpose of collecting his troops; when he was surprised by Dagalaiphus, an active officer, whom Julian, as soon as he landed at Bononia, had pushed forwards with some light infantry. The captive general, uncertain of

Orat. iii. p. 68 [iv. c. 47]. Even the saint admires the speed and secrecy of this march. A modern divine might apply to the progress of Julian the lines which were originally designed for another apostate:—

——— ———So eagerly the fiend,
        O'er bog, or steep, through strait, rough, dense, or rare,
        With head, hands, wings, or feet, pursues his way
        And swims, or sinks, or wades, or creeps, or flies.

[33] In that interval the *Notitia* places two or three fleets, the Lauriacensis (at Lauriacum, or Lorch), the Arlapensis, the Maginensis; and mentions five legions, or cohorts, of Liburnarii, who should be a sort of marines. Sect. lviii. edit. Labb.

[34] Zosimus alone (l. iii. p. 156 [c. 10]) has specified this interesting circumstance. Mamertinus (in Panegyr. Vet. xi. 6, 7, 8), who accompanied Julian, as count of the sacred largesses, describes this voyage in a florid and picturesque manner, challenges Triptolemus and the Argonauts of Greece, &c,

his life or death, was hastily thrown upon a horse, and conducted to the presence of Julian ; who kindly raised him from the ground, and dispelled the terror and amazement which seemed to stupefy his faculties.   But Lucilian had no sooner recovered his spirits than he betrayed his want of discretion, by presuming to admonish his conqueror that he had rashly ventured, with a handful of men, to expose his person in the midst of his enemies.   " Reserve for your master Constantius these timid remonstrances," replied Julian, with a smile of contempt ; " when I gave you my purple to kiss, I received you not as a counsellor, but as a suppliant."   Conscious that success alone could justify his attempt, and that boldness only could command success, he instantly advanced, at the head of three thousand soldiers, to attack the strongest and most populous city of the Illyrian provinces.   As he entered the long suburb of Sirmium, he was received by the joyful acclamations of the army and people ; who, crowned with flowers, and holding lighted tapers in their hands, conducted their acknowledged sovereign to his Imperial residence.   Two days were devoted to the public joy, which was celebrated by the games of the Circus ; but, early on the morning of the third day, Julian [Kapudžik, or marched to occupy the narrow pass of Succi, in the defiles Trojanova Vrata] of Mount Hæmus ; which, almost in the mid-way between Sirmium and Constantinople, separates the provinces of Thrace and Dacia, by an abrupt descent towards the former and a simple declivity on the side of the latter.[35]   The defence of this important post was entrusted to the brave Nevitta ; who, as well as the generals of the Italian division, successfully executed the plan of the march and junction which their master had so ably conceived.[36]

He justifies
his cause
        The homage which Julian obtained, from the fears or the inclination of the people, extended far beyond the immediate effect of his arms.[37]   The præfectures of Italy and Illyricum were administered by Taurus and Florentius, who united that important office with the vain honours of the consulship ; and,

[35] The description of Ammianus, which might be supported by collateral evidence, ascertains the precise situation of the *Angustiæ Succorum*, or passes of *Succi*.   M. d'Anville, from the trifling resemblance of names, has placed them between Sardica and Naissus.   For my own justification, I am obliged to mention the *only* error which I have discovered in the maps or writings of that admirable geographer.   [The road from Constantinople crosses here the mountains which form the watershed between the Thracian plain and the basin of Sofia.   Jireček, Gesch. der Bulgaren, p. 15.]
[36] Whatever circumstances we may borrow elsewhere, Ammianus (xxi. 8, 9, 10) still supplies the series of the narrative.
[37] Ammian. xxi. 9, 10.   Libanius, Orat. Parent. c. 54, p. 279, 280.   Zosimus, l. iii. p. 156, 157 [c. 10].

as those magistrates had retired with precipitation to the court of Asia, Julian, who could not always restrain the levity of his temper, stigmatized their flight by adding, in all the Acts of the Year, the epithet of *fugitive* to the names of the two consuls. The provinces which had been deserted by their first magistrates acknowledged the authority of an emperor, who, conciliating the qualities of a soldier with those of a philosopher, was equally admired in the camps of the Danube and in the cities of Greece. From his palace, or, more properly, from his head-quarters of Sirmium and Naissus, he distributed to the principal cities of the empire a laboured apology for his own conduct; published the secret dispatches of Constantius; and solicited the judgment of mankind between two competitors, the one of whom had expelled, and the other had invited, the Barbarians.[38] Julian, whose mind was deeply wounded by the reproach of ingratitude, aspired to maintain, by argument as well as by arms, the superior merits of his cause; and to excel, not only in the arts of war, but in those of composition. His epistle to the senate and people of Athens[39] seems to have been dictated by an elegant enthusiasm; which prompted him to submit his actions and his motives to the degenerate Athenians of his own times, with the same humble deference as if he had been pleading, in the days of Aristides, before the tribunal of the Areopagus. His application to the senate of Rome, which was still permitted to bestow the titles of Imperial power, was agreeable to the forms of the expiring republic. An assembly was summoned by Tertullus, præfect of the city; the epistle of Julian was read; and, as he appeared to be master of Italy, his claims were admitted without a dissenting voice. His oblique censure of the innovations of Constantine, and his passionate invective against the vices of Constantius, were heard with less satisfaction; and the senate, as if Julian had been present, unanimously exclaimed,

[38] Julian (ad S. P. Q. Athen. p. 286 [p. 368, ed. H.]) positively asserts that he intercepted the letters of Constantius to the Barbarians: and Libanius as positively affirms that he read them on his march to the troops and the cities. Yet Ammianus (xxi. 4) expresses himself with cool and candid hesitation, si *famæ solius* admittenda est fides. He specifies, however, an intercepted letter from Vadomair to Constantius, which supposes an intimate correspondence between them : " Cæsar tuus disciplinam non habet ".

[39] Zosimus mentions his epistles to the Athenians, the Corinthians, and the Lacedæmonians. The substance was probably the same, though the address was properly varied. The epistle to the Athenians is still extant (p. 268-287), and has afforded much valuable information. It deserves the praises of the Abbé de la Bléterie (Préf. à l'Histoire de Jovien, p. 24, 25), and is one of the best manifestos to be found in any language.

"Respect, we beseech you, the author of your own fortune".[40] An artful expression, which, according to the chance of war, might be differently explained; as a manly reproof of the ingratitude of the usurper, or as a flattering confession that a single act of such benefit to the state ought to atone for all the failings of Constantius.

Hostile preparations

The intelligence of the march and rapid progress of Julian was speedily transmitted to his rival, who, by the retreat of Sapor, had obtained some respite from the Persian war.   Disguising the anguish of his soul under the semblance of contempt, Constantius professed his intention of returning into Europe, and of giving chase to Julian; for he never spoke of this military expedition in any other light than that of a hunting party.[41]   In the camp of Hierapolis, in Syria, he communicated this design to his army, slightly mentioned the guilt and rashness of the Cæsar, and ventured to assure them that, if the mutineers of Gaul presumed to meet them in the field, they would be unable to sustain the fire of their eyes and the irresistible weight of their shout of onset.   The speech of the emperor was received with military applause, and Theodotus, the president of the council of Hierapolis, requested, with tears of adulation, that *his* city might be adorned with the head of the vanquished rebel.[42]   A chosen detachment was dispatched away in post-waggons, to secure, if it were yet possible, the pass of Succi; the recruits, the horses, the arms, and the magazines which had been prepared against Sapor, were appropriated to the service of the civil war; and the domestic victories of Constantius inspired his partisans with the most sanguine assurances of success.   The notary Gaudentius had occupied in his name the provinces of Africa; the subsistence of Rome was intercepted; and the distress of Julian was increased by an unexpected event which might have been productive of fatal consequences.   Julian had received the submission of two legions and a cohort of archers, who were stationed at Sirmium; but he suspected, with reason, the fidelity of those troops, which had been dis-

---

[40] *Auctori tuo reverentiam rogamus.*   Ammian. xxi. 10.   It is amusing enough to observe the secret conflicts of the senate between flattery and fear.   See Tacit. Hist. i. 85.

[41] Tanquam venaticiam prædam caperet: hoc enim ad leniendum suorum metum subinde prædicabat.   Ammian. xxi. 7.

[42] See the speech and preparations in Ammianus, xxi. 13.   The vile Theodotus afterwards implored and obtained his pardon from the merciful conqueror, who signified his wish of diminishing his enemies, and increasing the number of his friends (xxii. 14).

tinguished by the emperor; and it was thought expedient, under the pretence of the exposed state of the Gallic frontier, to dismiss them from the most important scene of action. They advanced, with reluctance, as far as the confines of Italy; but, as they dreaded the length of the way and the savage fierceness of the Germans, they resolved, by the instigation of one of their tribunes, to halt at Aquileia, and to erect the banners of Constantius on the walls of that impregnable city. The vigilance of Julian perceived at once the extent of the mischief and the necessity of applying an immediate remedy. By his order, Jovinus led back a part of the army into Italy; and the siege of Aquileia was formed with diligence and prosecuted with vigour. But the legionaries, who seemed to have rejected the yoke of discipline, conducted the defence of the place with skill and perseverance; invited the rest of Italy to imitate the example of their courage and loyalty; and threatened the retreat of Julian, if he should be forced to yield to the superior numbers of the arms of the East.[43]

But the humanity of Julian was preserved from the cruel alternative, which he pathetically laments, of destroying or of being himself destroyed: and the seasonable death of Constantius delivered the Roman empire from the calamities of civil war. The approach of winter could not detain the monarch at Antioch; and his favourites durst not oppose his impatient desire of revenge. A slight fever, which was perhaps occasioned by the agitation of his spirits, was increased by the fatigues of the journey; and Constantius was obliged to halt at the little town of Mopsucrene, twelve miles beyond Tarsus, where he expired, after a short illness, in the forty-fifth year of his age, and the twenty-fourth of his reign.[44] His genuine character, which was

and death of Constantius. A.D. 361, November 3

[43] Ammian. xxi. 7. 11, 12. He seems to describe, with superfluous labour, the operations of the siege of Aquileia, which, on this occasion, maintained its impregnable fame. Gregory Nazianzen (Orat. iii. p. 68 [iv. c. 48]) ascribes this accidental revolt to the wisdom of Constantius, whose assured victory he announces with some appearance of truth. Constantio quem credebat procul dubio fore victorem: nemo enim omnium tunc ab hac constanti sententia discrepabat. Ammian. xxi. 7.

[44] His death and character are faithfully delineated by Ammianus (xxi. 14, 15, 16); and we are authorized to despise and detest the foolish calumny of Gregory (Orat. iii. p. 68), who accuses Julian of contriving the death of his benefactor. The private repentance of the emperor that he had spared and promoted Julian (p. 69, and Orat. xxi. p. 389) is not improbable in itself, nor incompatible with the public verbal testament which prudential considerations might dictate in the last moments of his life. [Our text of Ammianus gives 5th Oct. as date of death of Constantius, cp. Ranke. Weltgeschichte, iv. 102. Idatius and Socrates give 3rd Nov. See Büttner Wobst, *der Tod des K. Julians* (Philologus, 52, p. 561), who points out that the astronomical datum of the oracle in Amm. 21, 2, 2 agrees neither with 5th Oct. nor 3rd Nov. but is rather nearer the latter.]

composed of pride and weakness, of superstition and cruelty, has been fully displayed in the preceding narrative of civil and ecclesiastical events. The long abuse of power rendered him a considerable object in the eyes of his contemporaries; but, as personal merit can alone deserve the notice of posterity, the last of the sons of Constantine may be dismissed from the world with the remark, that he inherited the defects, without the abilities, of his father. Before Constantius expired, he is said to have named Julian for his successor; nor does it seem improbable that his anxious concern for the fate of a young and tender wife, whom he left with child, may have prevailed, in his last moments, over the harsher passions of hatred and revenge. Eusebius, and his guilty associates, made a faint attempt to prolong the reign of the eunuchs by the election of another emperor: but their intrigues were rejected with disdain by an army which now abhorred the thought of civil discord; and two officers of rank were instantly dispatched, to assure Julian that every sword in the empire would be drawn for his service. The military designs of that prince, who had formed three different attacks against Thrace, were prevented by this fortunate event. Without shedding the blood of his fellow-citizens, he escaped the dangers of a doubtful conflict and acquired the advantages of a complete victory. Impatient to visit the place of his birth and the new capital of the empire, he advanced from Naissus through the mountains of Hæmus and the cities of Thrace. When he reached Heraclea, at the distance of sixty miles, all Constantinople was poured forth to receive him; and he made his triumphal entry, amidst the dutiful acclamations of the soldiers, the people, and the senate. An innumerable multitude pressed around him with eager respect; and were perhaps disappointed when they beheld the small stature and simple garb of a hero whose unexperienced youth had vanquished the Barbarians of Germany, and who had now traversed, in a successful career, the whole continent of Europe, from the shores of the Atlantic to those of the Bosphorus.[45] A few days afterwards, when the remains of the deceased emperor were landed in the harbour, the subjects of Julian applauded the real or affected humanity of their sovereign. On foot, without his diadem, and clothed in a mourning habit, he accompanied the funeral as far as the church of the Holy Apostles, where the body was deposited: and, if

Julian enters Constantinople, December 11

---

[45] In describing the triumph of Julian, Ammianus (xxii. 1, 2) assumes the lofty tone of an orator or poet: while Libanius (Orat. Parent. c. 56. p. 281) sinks to the grave simplicity of an historian.

these marks of respect may be interpreted as a selfish tribute to the birth and dignity of his Imperial kinsman, the tears of Julian professed to the world that he had forgot the injuries, and remembered only the obligations, which he had received from Constantius.[46] As soon as the legions of Aquileia were assured of the death of the emperor, they opened the gates of the city, and, by the sacrifice of their guilty leaders, obtained an easy pardon from the prudence or lenity of Julian; who, in the thirty-second year of his age, acquired the undisputed possession of the Roman empire.[47] *and is acknowledged by the whole empire*

Philosophy had instructed Julian to compare the advantages of action and retirement; but the elevation of his birth and the accidents of his life never allowed him the freedom of choice. *His civil government, and private life* He might perhaps sincerely have preferred the groves of the academy and the society of Athens; but he was constrained, at first by the will, and afterwards by the injustice, of Constantius, to expose his person and fame to the dangers of Imperial greatness; and to make himself accountable to the world, and to posterity, for the happiness of millions.[48] Julian recollected with terror the observation of his master Plato,[49] that the government of our flocks and herds is always committed to beings of a superior species; and that the conduct of nations requires and deserves the celestial powers of the Gods or of the Genii. From this principle he justly concluded that the man who presumes to reign should aspire to the perfection of the divine nature; that he should purify his soul from her mortal and terrestrial part; that he should extinguish his appetites, enlighten his understanding, regulate his passions, and subdue the wild beast which, according to the lively metaphor of

---

[46] The funeral of Constantius is described by Ammianus (xxi. 16), Gregory Nazianzen (Orat. iv. [v. ed. Migne] p. 119 [c. 17]), Mamertinus (in Panegyr. Vet. xi. 27), Libanius (Orat. Parent. c. lvi. p. 283), and Philostorgius (l. vi. c. 6, with Godefroy's Dissertations, p. 265). These writers, and their followers, Pagans, Catholics, Arians, beheld with very different eyes both the dead and the living emperor.

[47] The day and year of the birth of Julian are not perfectly ascertained. The day is probably the sixth of November, and the year must be either 331 or 332. Tillemont, Hist. des Empereurs, tom. iv. p. 693. Ducange, Fam. Byzantin. p. 50. I have preferred the earlier date.

[48] Julian himself (p. 253-267) has expressed these philosophical ideas with much eloquence, and some affectation, in a very elaborate epistle to Themistius. The Abbé de la Bléterie (tom. ii. p. 146-193), who has given an elegant translation, is inclined to believe that it was the celebrated Themistius, whose orations are still extant.

[49] Julian. ad Themist. p. 258 [p. 334]. Petavius (note, p. 95) observes that this passage is taken from the fourth book de Legibus; but either Julian quoted from memory, or his Mss. were different from ours. Xenophon opens the Cyropædia with a similar reflection.

Aristotle,[50] seldom fails to ascend the throne of a despot.   The
throne of Julian, which the death of Constantius fixed on an
independent basis, was the seat of reason, of virtue, and perhaps
of vanity.   He despised the honours, renounced the pleasures,
and discharged with incessant diligence the duties, of his
exalted station ; and there were few among his subjects who
would have consented to relieve him from the weight of the
diadem, had they been obliged to submit their time and their
actions to the rigorous laws which their philosophic emperor
imposed on himself.   One of his most intimate friends,[51] who
had often shared the frugal simplicity of his table, has remarked
that his light and sparing diet (which was usually of the vegetable kind) left his mind and body always free and active for
the various and important business of an author, a pontiff, a
magistrate, a general, and a prince.   In one and the same day,
he gave audience to several ambassadors, and wrote, or dictated,
a great number of letters to his generals, his civil magistrates,
his private friends, and the different cities of his dominions.
He listened to the memorials which had been received, considered the subject of the petitions, and signified his intentions
more rapidly than they could be taken in shorthand by the
diligence of his secretaries.   He possessed such flexibility of
thought, and such firmness of attention, that he could employ
his hand to write, his ear to listen, and his voice to dictate ;
and pursue at once three several trains of ideas without hesitation and without error   While his ministers reposed, the prince
flew with agility from one labour to another, and, after a hasty
dinner, retired into his library, till the public business, which he
had appointed for the evening, summoned him to interrupt the
prosecution of his studies.   The supper of the emperor was still
less substantial than the former meal ; his sleep was never
clouded by the fumes of indigestion ; and, except in the short
interval of a marriage, which was the effect of policy rather
than love, the chaste Julian never shared his bed with a female
companion.[52]   He was soon awakened by the entrance of fresh

---

[50] Ὁ δὲ ἄνθρωπον κελεύων ἄρχειν, προστίθησι καὶ θηρίον.   Aristot. ap. Julian. p.
261 [338, ed. Hertl.].   The Ms. of Vossius, unsatisfied with a single beast,
affords the stronger reading of θηρία, which the experience of despotism may
warrant.   [This (Leiden) Ms. is the best ; θηρία is right.]

[51] Libanius (Orat. Parentalis, c. lxxxiv. lxxxv. p. 310, 311, 312) has given this
interesting detail of the private life of Julian.   He himself (in Misopogon. p. 350)
mentions his vegetable diet, and upbraids the gross and sensual appetite of the
people of Antioch.

[52] Lectulus . . . Vestalium toris purior, is the praise which Mamertinus (Panegyr.
Vet. xi. 13) addresses to Julian himself.   Libanius affirms, in sober peremptory

secretaries, who had slept the preceding day; and his servants were obliged to wait alternately, while their indefatigable master allowed himself scarcely any other refreshment than the change of occupations. The predecessors of Julian, his uncle, his brother, and his cousin, indulged their puerile taste for the games of the circus, under the specious pretence of complying with the inclinations of the people; and they frequently remained the greatest part of the day, as idle spectators, and as a part of the splendid spectacle, till the ordinary round of twenty-four races [53] was completely finished. On solemn festivals, Julian, who felt and professed an unfashionable dislike to these frivolous amusements, condescended to appear in the circus; and, after bestowing a careless glance on five or six of the races, he hastily withdrew, with the impatience of a philosopher, who considered every moment as lost that was not devoted to the advantage of the public or the improvement of his own mind.[54] By this avarice of time, he seemed to protract the short duration of his reign; and, if the dates were less securely ascertained, we should refuse to believe that only sixteen months elapsed between the death of Constantius and the departure of his successor for the Persian war. The actions of Julian can only be preserved by the care of the historian; but the portion of his voluminous writings which is still extant remains as a monument of the application, as well as of the genius, of the emperor. The Misopogon, the Cæsars, several of his orations, and his elaborate work against the Christian religion, were composed in the long nights of the two winters, the former of which he passed at Constantinople, and the latter at Antioch.

December, A.D. 361
March, A.D 363

---

language, that Julian never knew a woman before his marriage or after the death of his wife (Orat. Parent. c. lxxxviii. p. 313). The chastity of Julian is confirmed by the impartial testimony of Ammianus (xxv. 4), and the partial silence of the Christians. Yet Julian ironically urges the reproach of the people of Antioch that he *almost always* (ὡς ἐπίπαν, in Misopogon. p. 345 [p. 445, ed. H.]) lay alone. This suspicious expression is explained by the Abbé de la Bléterie (Hist. de Jovien, tom. ii. p. 103-109) with candour and ingenuity.

[53] See Salmasius ad Sueton. in Claud. c. xxi. A twenty-fifth race, or *missus*, was added, to complete the number of one hundred chariots, four of which, the four colours, started each heat.

Centum quadrijugos agitabo ad flumina currus.

It appears that they ran five or seven times round the *Meta* (Sueton. in Domitian. c. 4); and (from the measure of the Circus Maximus at Rome, the Hippodrome at Constantinople, &c.) it might be about a four-mile course.

[54] Julian. in Misopogon. p. 340 [p. 437, ed. H.]. Julius Cæsar had offended the Roman people by reading his dispatches during the actual race. Augustus indulged their taste, or his own, by his constant attention to the important business of the circus, for which he professed the warmest inclination. Sueton. in August. c. xlv.

Reformation
of the palace   The reformation of the Imperial court was one of the first and
most necessary acts of the government of Julian.[55] Soon after
his entrance into the palace of Constantinople, he had occasion
for the service of a barber. An officer, magnificently dressed,
immediately presented himself. " It is a barber," exclaimed
the prince, with affected surprise, " that I want, and not a
receiver-general of the finances." [56] He questioned the man
concerning the profits of his employment ; and was informed
that, besides a large salary and some valuable perquisites, he
enjoyed a daily allowance for twenty servants and as many
horses. A thousand barbers, a thousand cup-bearers, a thousand
cooks, were distributed in the several offices of luxury ; and the
number of eunuchs could be compared only with the insects of
a summer's day.[57] The monarch who resigned to his subjects
the superiority of merit and virtue was distinguished by the
oppressive magnificence of his dress, his table, his buildings,
and his train. The stately palaces erected by Constantine and
his sons were decorated with many coloured marbles and ornaments of massy gold. The most exquisite dainties were procured, to gratify their pride rather than their taste ; birds of
the most distant climates, fish from the most remote seas, fruits
out of their natural season, winter roses, and summer snows.[58]
The domestic crowd of the palace surpassed the expense of the
legions ; yet the smallest part of this costly multitude was
subservient to the use, or even to the splendour, of the
throne. The monarch was disgraced, and the people was
injured, by the creation and sale of an infinite number of obscure,
and even titular employments ; and the most worthless of
mankind might purchase the privilege of being maintained,
without the necessity of labour, from the public revenue. The
waste of an enormous household, the increase of fees and per-

---

[55] The reformation of the palace is described by Ammianus (xxii. 4), Libanius
(Orat. Parent. c. lxii. p. 288, &c.), Mamertinus (in Panegyr. Vet. xi. 11),
Socrates (l. iii. c. 1), and Zonaras (tom. ii. l. xiii. p. 24 [c. 12]).

[56] Ego non *rationalem* jussi sed tonsorem acciri. Zonaras uses the less natural
image of a *senator*. Yet an officer of the finances, who was satiated with wealth,
might desire and obtain the honours of the senate.

[57] Μαγείρους μὲν χιλίους, κουρέας δὲ οὐκ ἐλάττους, οἰνοχόους δὲ πλείους, σμήνη
τραπεζοποιῶν, εὐνούχους ὑπὲρ τὰς μυίας παρὰ τοῖς ποιμέσι ἐν ἦρι, are the original
words of Libanius, which I have faithfully quoted, lest I should be suspected of
magnifying the abuses of the royal household.

[58] The expressions of Mamertinus are lively and forcible. Quin etiam pran-
diorum et cenarum laboratas magnitudines Romanus populus sensit [leg.
pop. Rom. sentiebat] ; cum quæsitissimæ dapes non gustu sed difficultatibus
æstimarentur ; miracula avium longinqui maris pisces, alieni temporis poma,
æstivæ nives hibernæ rosæ.

quisites, which were soon claimed as a lawful debt, and the bribes which they extorted from those who feared their enmity or solicited their favour, suddenly enriched these haughty menials. They abused their fortune, without considering their past, or their future, condition; and their rapine and venality could be equalled only by the extravagance of their dissipations. Their silken robes were embroidered with gold, their tables were served with delicacy and profusion; the houses which they built for their own use would have covered the farm of an ancient consul; and the most honourable citizens were obliged to dismount from their horses, and respectfully to salute an eunuch whom they met on the public highway. The luxury of the palace excited the contempt and indignation of Julian, who usually slept on the ground, who yielded with reluctance to the indispensable calls of nature, and who placed his vanity, not in emulating, but in despising, the pomp of royalty. By the total extirpation of a mischief which was magnified even beyond its real extent, he was impatient to relieve the distress, and to appease the murmurs, of the people; who support with less uneasiness the weight of taxes, if they are convinced that the fruits of their industry are appropriated to the service of the state. But in the execution of this salutary work Julian is accused of proceeding with too much haste and inconsiderate severity. By a single edict, he reduced the palace of Constantinople to an immense desert, and dismissed with ignominy the whole train of slaves and dependents,[59] without providing any just, or at least benevolent, exceptions, for the age, the services, or the poverty, of the faithful domestics of the Imperial family. Such indeed was the temper of Julian, who seldom recollected the fundamental maxim of Aristotle that true virtue is placed at an equal distance between the opposite vices. The splendid and effeminate dress of the Asiatics, the curls and paint, the collars and bracelets, which had appeared so ridiculous in the person of Constantine, were consistently rejected by his philosophic successor. But with the fopperies, Julian affected to renounce the decencies, of dress; and seemed to value himself for his neglect of the laws of cleanliness. In a satirical performance, which was designed for the public eye, the emperor descants with pleasure, and even with pride, on the length of his nails, and the inky blackness of his hands; protests

---

[59] Yet Julian himself was accused of bestowing whole towns on the eunuchs Orat. vii. against Polyclet. p. 117-127). Libanius contents himself with a cold but positive denial of the fact, which seems indeed to belong more properly to Constantius. This charge however may allude to some unknown circumstance.

that, although the greatest part of his body was covered with hair, the use of the razor was confined to his head alone ; and celebrates, with visible complacency, the shaggy and *populous* [60] beard, which he fondly cherished after the example of the philosophers of Greece. Had Julian consulted the simple dictates of reason, the first magistrate of the Romans would have scorned the affectation of Diogenes as well as that of Darius.

Chamber of Justice

But the work of public reformation would have remained imperfect, if Julian had only corrected the abuses, without punishing the crimes, of his predecessor's reign. "We are now delivered," says he, in a familiar letter to one of his intimate friends, "we are now surprisingly delivered from the voracious jaws of the Hydra.[61] I do not mean to apply that epithet to my brother Constantius. He is no more ; may the earth lie light on his head ! But his artful and cruel favourites studied to deceive and exasperate a prince whose natural mildness cannot be praised without some efforts of adulation. It is not, however, my intention that even those men should be oppressed : they are accused, and they shall enjoy the benefit of a fair and impartial trial." To conduct this inquiry, Julian named six judges of the highest rank in the state and army ; and, as he wished to escape the reproach of condemning his personal enemies, he fixed this extraordinary tribunal at Chalcedon, on the Asiatic side of the Bosphorus ; and transferred to the commissioners an absolute power to pronounce and execute their final sentence, without delay and without appeal. The office of president was exercised by the venerable præfect of the East, a *second* Sallust,[62] whose virtues conciliated the esteem of Greek sophists and of Christian bishops. He was assisted by the elo-

---

[60] In the Misopogon (p. 338, 339 [p. 434-436]) he draws a very singular picture of himself, and the following words are strangely characteristic: αὐτὸς προστέθεικα τὸν βαθὺν τουτονὶ πώγωνα . . . ταῦτά τοι διαθεόντων ἀνέχομαι τῶν φθειρῶν ὥσπερ ἐν λοχμῇ τῶν θηρίων. The friends of the Abbé de la Blèterie adjured him, in the name of the French nation, not to translate this passage, so offensive to their delicacy (Hist. de Jovien, tom. ii. p. 94). Like him, I have contented myself with a transient allusion ; but the little animal, which Julian *names*, is a beast familiar to man, and signifies love.

[61] Julian, epist. xxiii. p. 389 [p. 503, ed. H.]. He uses the words πολυκέφαλον ὕδραν, in writing to his friend Hermogenes, who, like himself, was conversant with the Greek poets.

[62] The two Sallusts, the præfect of Gaul and the præfect of the East, must be carefully distinguished (Hist. des Empereurs, tom. iv. p. 696). I have used the surname of *Secundus*, as a convenient epithet. The second Sallust extorted the esteem of the Christians themselves ; and Gregory Nazianzen, who condemned his religion, has celebrated his virtues (Orat. iii. p. 90 [iv. c. 91]). See a curious note of the Abbé de la Blèterie, Vie de Julien, p. 363.

quent Mamertinus,[63] one of the consuls elect, whose merit is loudly celebrated by the doubtful evidence of his own applause. But the civil wisdom of two magistrates was overbalanced by the ferocious violence of four generals, Nevitta, Agilo, Jovinus, and Arbetio. Arbetio, whom the public would have seen with less surprise at the bar than on the bench, was supposed to possess the secret of the commission ; the armed and angry leaders of the Jovian and Herculian bands encompassed the tribunal ; and the judges were alternately swayed by the laws of justice, and by the clamours of faction.[64]

The chamberlain Eusebius, who had so long abused the favour of Constantius, expiated, by an ignominious death, the insolence, the corruption, and cruelty of his servile reign. The executions of Paul and Apodemius (the former of whom was burnt alive) were accepted as an inadequate atonement by the widows and orphans of so many hundred Romans, whom those legal tyrants had betrayed and murdered. But Justice herself (if we may use the pathetic expression of Ammianus)[65] appeared to weep over the fate of Ursulus, the treasurer of the empire ; and his blood accused the ingratitude of Julian, whose distress had been seasonably relieved by the intrepid liberality of that honest minister. The rage of the soldiers, whom he had provoked by his indiscretion, was the cause and the excuse of his death ; and the emperor, deeply wounded by his own reproaches and those of the public, offered some consolation to the family of Ursulus, by the restitution of his confiscated fortunes. Before the end of the year in which they had been adorned with the ensigns of the præfecture and consulship,[66] Taurus and Florentius were reduced to implore the clemency of the inexorable tribunal of Chalcedon. The former was banished to Vercellæ in Italy, and a sentence of death was pronounced against the latter. A wise prince should have rewarded the crime of Taurus : the faithful minister, when he was no longer able to oppose the

Punishment of the innocent and the guilty

---

[63] Mamertinus praises the emperor (xi. 1) for bestowing the offices of Treasurer and Præfect on a man of wisdom, firmness, integrity, &c. like himself. Yet Ammianus ranks him (xxi. 1) among the ministers of Julian, quorum merita nôrat et fidem.

[64] The proceedings of this chamber of justice are related by Ammianus (xxii. 3), and praised by Libanius (Orat. Parent. c. 74, p. 299, 300).

[65] Ursuli vero necem ipsa mihi videtur flêsse justitia. Libanius, who imputes his death to the soldiers, attempts to criminate the count of the largesses.

[66] Such respect was still entertained for the venerable names of the commonwealth that the public was surprised and scandalized to hear Taurus summoned as a criminal under the consulship of Taurus. The summons of his colleague Florentius was probably delayed till the commencement of the ensuing year.

progress of a rebel, had taken refuge in the court of his benefactor and his lawful sovereign.   But the guilt of Florentius
justified the severity of the judges ; and his escape served to
display the magnanimity of Julian ; who nobly checked the interested diligence of an informer, and refused to learn what
place concealed the wretched fugitive from his just resentment.[67]   Some months after the tribunal of Chalcedon had been
dissolved, the prætorian vicegerent of Africa, the notary Gaudentius, and Artemius,[68] duke of Egypt, were executed at Antioch.
Artemius had reigned the cruel and corrupt tyrant of a great
province ; Gaudentius had long practised the arts of calumny
against the innocent, the virtuous, and even the person of Julian
himself.   Yet the circumstances of their trial and condemnation
were so unskilfully managed, that these wicked men obtained,
in the public opinion, the glory of suffering for the obstinate
loyalty with which they had supported the cause of Constantius.
The rest of his servants were protected by a general act of
oblivion ; and they were left to enjoy with impunity the bribes
which they had accepted either to defend the oppressed or to
oppress the friendless.   This measure, which, on the soundest
principles of policy, may deserve our approbation, was executed
in a manner which seemed to degrade the majesty of the throne.
Julian was tormented by the importunities of a multitude, particularly of Egyptians, who loudly demanded the gifts which
they had imprudently or illegally bestowed ; he foresaw the
endless prosecution of vexatious suits ; and he engaged a
promise, which ought always to have been sacred, that, if they
would repair to Chalcedon, he would meet them in person, to
hear and determine their complaints.   But, as soon as they were
landed, he issued an absolute order, which prohibited the water-
men from transporting any Egyptian to Constantinople ; and
thus detained his disappointed clients on the Asiatic shore, till,
their patience and money being utterly exhausted, they were
obliged to return with indignant murmurs to their native
country.[69]

[67] Ammian. xx. 7.

[68] For the guilt and punishment of Artemius, see Julian (Epist. x. p. 379), and
Ammianus (xxii. 6, and Vales. ad loc.).   The merit of Artemius, who demolished
temples, and was put to death by an apostate, has tempted the Greek and Latin
churches to honour him as a martyr.   But, as ecclesiastical history attests that he
was not only a tyrant, but an Arian, it is not altogether easy to justify this indiscreet promotion.   Tillemont, Mém. Ecclés. tom. vii. p. 1319.

[69] See Ammian. xxii. 6, and Vales. ad locum ; and the Codex Theodosianus,
l. ii. tit. xxxix. leg. 1 ; and Godefroy's Commentary, tom. i. p. 218, ad locum.

The numerous army of spies, of agents, and informers, en-^{clemency of}
listed by Constantius to secure the repose of one man and to ^{Julian}
interrupt that of millions, was immediately disbanded by his
generous successor.   Julian was slow in his suspicions and gentle
in his punishments ; and his contempt of treason was the result
of judgment, of vanity, and of courage.   Conscious of superior
merit, he was persuaded that few among his subjects would dare
to meet him in the field, to attempt his life, or even to seat
themselves on his vacant throne.   The philosopher could excuse
the hasty sallies of discontent ; and the hero could despise the
ambitious projects which surpassed the fortune or the abilities
of the rash conspirators.   A citizen of Ancyra had prepared for
his own use a purple garment ; and this indiscreet action,
which, under the reign of Constantius, would have been considered as a capital offence,[70] was reported to Julian by the
officious importunity of a private enemy.   The monarch, after
making some inquiry into the rank and character of his rival,
dispatched the informer with a present of a pair of purple
slippers, to complete the magnificence of his Imperial habit.   A
more dangerous conspiracy was formed by ten of the domestic
guards, who had resolved to assassinate Julian in the field of
exercise near Antioch.   Their intemperance revealed their guilt ;
and they were conducted in chains to the presence of their injured sovereign, who, after a lively representation of the wickedness and folly of their enterprise, instead of a death of torture,
which they deserved and expected, pronounced a sentence of
exile against the two principal offenders.   The only instance in
which Julian seemed to depart from his accustomed clemency
was the execution of a rash youth, who, with a feeble hand, had
aspired to seize the reins of empire.   But that youth was the
son of Marcellus, the general of cavalry, who in the first campaign of the Gallic war had deserted the standard of the Cæsar
and the republic.   Without appearing to indulge his personal
resentment, Julian might easily confound the crime of the son
and of the father : but he was reconciled by the distress of Marcellus, and the liberality of the emperor endeavoured to heal
the wound which had been inflicted by the hand of justice.[71]

---

[70] The president Montesquieu (Considérations sur la Grandeur, &c. des Romains,
c. xiv., in his works, tom. iii. p. 448, 449) excuses this minute and absurd tyranny,
by supposing that actions the most indifferent in our eyes might excite, in a
Roman mind, the idea of guilt and danger.   This strange apology is supported
by a strange misapprehension of the English laws, "chez une nation . . . où il est
défendu de boire à la santé d'une certaine personne".

[71] The clemency of Julian, and the conspiracy which was formed against his

Julian was not insensible of the advantages of freedom.[72]
From his studies he had imbibed the spirit of ancient sages and
heroes; his life and fortunes had depended on the caprice of a
tyrant; and, when he ascended the throne, his pride was
sometimes mortified by the reflection that the slaves who would
not dare to censure his defects were not worthy to applaud his
virtues.[73] He sincerely abhorred the system of Oriental despotism which Diocletian, Constantine, and the patient habits
of fourscore years had established in the empire. A motive of
superstition prevented the execution of the design which Julian
had frequently meditated, of relieving his head from the weight
of a costly diadem:[74] but he absolutely refused the title of
Dominus or *Lord*,[75] a word which was grown so familiar to the
ears of the Romans that they no longer remembered its servile
and humiliating origin. The office, or rather the name, of
consul, was cherished by a prince who contemplated with
reverence the ruins of the republic; and the same behaviour
which had been assumed by the prudence of Augustus was
adopted by Julian from choice and inclination. On the calends
of January, at break of day, the new consuls, Mamertinus and
Nevitta, hastened to the palace to salute the emperor. As
soon as he was informed of their approach, he leaped from his
throne, eagerly advanced to meet them, and compelled the
blushing magistrates to receive the demonstrations of his
affected humility. From the palace they proceeded to the
senate. The emperor, on foot, marched before their litters;
and the gazing multitude admired the image of ancient times,
or secretly blamed a conduct which, in their eyes, degraded

life at Antioch, are described by Ammianus (xxii. 9, 10, and Vales. ad loc.), and
Libanius (Orat. Parent. c. 99, p. 323).

[72] According to some, says Aristotle (as he is quoted by Julian ad Themist. p.
261 [p. 338, ed. H.]), the form of absolute government, the παρβασίλεια, is contrary
to nature. [Politics, iii. 16, 2 = 1287a.] Both the prince and the philosopher
choose, however, to involve this eternal truth in artful and laboured obscurity.

[73] That sentiment is expressed almost in the words of Julian himself. Ammian.
xxii. 10.

[74] Libanius (Orat. Parent. c. 95, p. 320), who mentions the wish and design
of Julian, insinuates, in mysterious language (θεῶν οὕτω γνόντων . . . ἀλλ᾽ ἦν ἀμείνων
ὁ κωλύων), that the emperor was restrained by some particular revelation.

[75] Julian. in Misopogon. p. 343 [p. 442, ed. H.]. As he never abolished, by any
public law, the proud appellations of *Despot* or *Dominus*, they are still extant on
his medals (Ducange, Fam. Byzantin. p. 38, 39); and the private displeasure
which he affected to express only gave a different tone to the servility of the
court. The Abbé de la Blétere (Hist. de Jovien, tom. ii. p. 99-102) has curiously
traced the origin and progress of the word *Dominus* under the Imperial
government.

the majesty of the purple.[76] But the behaviour of Julian was uniformly supported. During the games of the Circus, he had, imprudently or designedly, performed the manumission of a slave in the presence of the consul. The moment he was reminded that he had trespassed on the jurisdiction of *another* magistrate, he condemned himself to pay a fine of ten pounds of gold; and embraced this public occasion of declaring to the world that he was subject, like the rest of his fellow-citizens, to the laws,[77] and even to the forms, of the republic. The spirit of his administration, and his regard for the place of his nativity, induced Julian to confer on the senate of Constantinople, the same honours, privileges, and authority, which were still enjoyed by the senate of ancient Rome.[78] A legal fiction was introduced, and gradually established, that one half of the national council had migrated into the East : and the despotic successors of Julian, accepting the title of Senators, acknowledged themselves the members of a respectable body, which was permitted to represent the majesty of the Roman name. From Constantinople, the attention of the monarch was extended to the municipal senates of the provinces. He abolished, by repeated edicts, the unjust and pernicious exemptions which had withdrawn so many idle citizens from the service of their country ; and by imposing an equal distribution of public duties he restored the strength, the splendour, or, according to the glowing expression of Libanius,[79] the soul of the expiring cities of his empire. The venerable age of Greece excited the most tender compassion in the mind of Julian ; which kindled into rapture when he recollected the gods, the heroes, and the men,   His care of the Grecian cities

---

[76] Ammian. xxii. 7. The consul Mamertinus (in Panegyr. Vet. xi. 28, 29, 30) celebrates the auspicious day, like an eloquent slave, astonished and intoxicated by the condescension of his master.

[77] Personal satire was condemned by the laws of the twelve tables :

> Si male condiderit in quem quis carmina, jus est
> Judiciumque——

Julian (in Misopogon. p. 337 [ad init.]) owns himself subject to the law ; and the Abbé de la Blèterie (Hist. de Jovien, tom. ii. p. 92) has eagerly embraced a declaration so agreeable to his own system, and indeed to the true spirit of the imperial constitution.

[78] Zosimus, l. iii. p. 158.

[79] Ἡ τῆς βουλῆς ἰσχὺς ψύχη πόλεώς ἐστιν. See Libanius (Orat. Parent. c. 71, p. 296), Ammianus (xxii. 9), and the Theodosian Code (l. xii. tit. i. leg. 50-55), with Godefroy's Commentary (tom. iv. p. 390-402). Yet the whole subject of the *Curiae*, notwithstanding very ample materials, still remains the most obscure in the legal history of the empire.

superior to heroes and to gods, who had bequeathed to the latest posterity the monuments of their genius or the example of their virtues. He relieved the distress, and restored the beauty, of the cities of Epirus and Peloponnesus.[80] Athens acknowledged him for her benefactor ; Argos, for her deliverer. The pride of Corinth, again rising from her ruins with the honours of a Roman colony, exacted a tribute from the adjacent republics, for the purpose of defraying the games of the Isthmus, which were celebrated in the amphitheatre with the hunting of bears and panthers. From this tribute the cities of Elis, of Delphi, and of Argos, which had inherited from their remote ancestors the sacred office of perpetuating the Olympic, the Pythian, and the Nemean games, claimed a just exemption. The immunity of Elis and Delphi was respected by the Corinthians ; but the poverty of Argos tempted the insolence of oppression ; and the feeble complaints of its deputies were silenced by the decree of a provincial magistrate, who seems to have consulted only the interest of the capital in which he resided. Seven years after this sentence, Julian[81] allowed the cause to be referred to a superior tribunal ; and his eloquence was interposed, most probably with success, in the defence of a city which had been the royal seat of Agamemnon[82] and had given to Macedonia a race of kings and conquerors.[83]

Julian, an orator and a judge

The laborious administration of military and civil affairs, which were multiplied in proportion to the extent of the empire, exercised the abilities of Julian ; but he frequently

[80] Quæ paulo ante arida et siti anhelantia visebantur, ea nunc perlui, mundari, madere ; Fora, Deambulacra, Gymnasia, lætis et gaudentibus populis frequentari ; dies festos, et celebrari veteres, et novos in honorem principis consecrari (Mamertin. xi. 9). He particularly restored the city of Nicopolis, and the Actiac games, which had been instituted by Augustus.

[81] Julian, Epist. xxxv. p. 407-411. This epistle, which illustrates the declining age of Greece, is omitted by the Abbé de la Bléterie ; and strangely disfigured by the Latin translator, who, by rendering ἀτέλεια, tributum, and ἰδιῶται, populus, directly contradicts the sense of the original.

[82] He reigned in Mycenæ, at the distance of fifty stadia, or six miles, from Argos : but these cities, which alternately flourished, are confounded by the Greek poets. Strabo, l. viii. p. 579, edit. Amstel. p. 1707.

[83] Marsham, Canon. Chron. p. 421. This pedigree from Temenus and Hercules may be suspicious ; yet it was allowed, after a strict inquiry by the judges of the Olympic games (Herodot. l. v. c. 22), at a time when the Macedonian kings were obscure and unpopular in Greece. When the Achæan league declared against Philip, it was thought decent that the deputies of Argos should retire (T. Liv. xxxii. 22).

assumed the two characters of Orator [84] and of Judge,[85] which are almost unknown to the modern sovereigns of Europe. The arts of persuasion, so diligently cultivated by the first Cæsars, were neglected by the military ignorance, and Asiatic pride, of their successors ; and, if they condescended to harangue the soldiers, whom they feared, they treated with silent disdain the senators, whom they despised. The assemblies of the senate, which Constantius had avoided, were considered by Julian as the place where he could exhibit, with the most propriety, the maxims of a republican and the talents of a rhetorician. He alternately practised, as in a school of declamation, the several modes of praise, of censure, of exhortation ; and his friend Libanius has remarked that the study of Homer taught him to imitate the simple, concise style of Menelaus, the copiousness of Nestor, whose words descended like the flakes of a winter's snow, or the pathetic and forcible eloquence of Ulysses. The functions of a judge, which are sometimes incompatible with those of a prince, were exercised by Julian, not only as a duty, but as an amusement : and, although he might have trusted the integrity and discernment of his Prætorian præfects, he often placed himself by their side on the seat of judgment. The acute penetration of his mind was agreeably occupied in detecting and defeating the chicanery of the advocates, who laboured to disguise the truth of facts and to pervert the sense of the laws. He sometimes forgot the gravity of his station, asked indiscreet or unseasonable questions, and betrayed, by the loudness of his voice and the agitation of his body, the earnest vehemence with which he maintained his opinion against the judges, the advocates, and their clients. But his knowledge of his own temper prompted him to encourage, and even to solicit, the reproof of his friends and ministers ; and, whenever they ventured to oppose the

[84] His eloquence is celebrated by Libanius (Orat. Parent. c. 75, 76, p. 300, 301), who distinctly mentions the orators of Homer. Socrates (l. iii. c. 1) has rashly asserted that Julian was the only prince, since Julius Cæsar, who harangued the senate. All the predecessors of Nero (Tacit. Annal. xiii. 3), and many of his successors, possessed the faculty of speaking in public ; and it might be proved, by various examples, that they frequently exercised it in the senate.

[85] Ammianus (xxii. 10) has impartially stated the merits and defects of his judicial proceedings. Libanius (Orat. Parent. c. 90, 91, p. 315, &c.) has seen only the fair side, and his picture, if it flatters the person, expresses at least the duties, of the Judge. Gregory Nazianzen (Orat. iv. p. 120), who suppresses the virtues, and exaggerates even the venial faults, of the apostate, triumphantly asks, Whether such a judge was fit to be seated between Minos and Rhadamanthus, in the Elysian fields?

irregular sallies of his passions, the spectators could observe the shame, as well as the gratitude, of their monarch. The decrees of Julian were almost always founded on the principles of justice; and he had the firmness to resist the two most dangerous temptations which assault the tribunal of a sovereign under the specious forms of compassion and equity. He decided the merits of the cause without weighing the circumstances of the parties; and the poor, whom he wished to relieve, were condemned to satisfy the just demands of a noble and wealthy adversary. He carefully distinguished the judge from the legislator;[86] and, though he meditated a necessary reformation of the Roman jurisprudence, he pronounced sentence according to the strict and literal interpretation of those laws which the magistrates were bound to execute and the subjects to obey.

His character   The generality of princes, if they were stripped of their purple and cast naked into the world, would immediately sink to the lowest rank of society, without a hope of emerging from their obscurity. But the personal merit of Julian was, in some measure, independent of his fortune. Whatever had been his choice of life, by the force of intrepid courage, lively wit, and intense application, he would have obtained, or at least he would have deserved, the highest honours of his profession; and Julian might have raised himself to the rank of minister, or general, of the state in which he was born a private citizen. If the jealous caprice of power had disappointed his expectations; if he had prudently declined the paths of greatness, the employment of the same talents in studious solitude would have placed, beyond the reach of kings, his present happiness and his immortal fame. When we inspect, with minute or perhaps malevolent attention, the portrait of Julian, something seems wanting to the grace and perfection of the whole figure. His genius was less powerful and sublime than that of Cæsar; nor did he possess the consummate prudence of Augustus. The virtues of Trajan appear more steady and natural, and the philosophy of Marcus is more simple and consistent. Yet Julian sustained adversity with firmness, and prosperity with moderation. After an interval of one hundred and twenty years from the death of Alexander Severus, the Romans beheld

---

[86] Of the laws which Julian enacted in a reign of sixteen months, fifty-four have been admitted into the Codes of Theodosius and Justinian (Gothofred. Chron. Legum, p. 64-67). The Abbé de la Bléterie (tom. ii. p. 329-336) has chosen one of these laws to give an idea of Julian's Latin style, which is forcible and elaborate, but less pure than his Greek.

an emperor who made no distinction between his duties and his pleasures; who laboured to relieve the distress, and to revive the spirit, of his subjects; and who endeavoured always to connect authority with merit, and happiness with virtue. Even faction, and religious faction, was constrained to acknowledge the superiority of his genius, in peace as well as in war; and to confess, with a sigh, that the apostate Julian was a lover of his country, and that he deserved the empire of the world.[87]

[87] . . . . . Ductor fortissimus armis;
Conditor et legum celeberrimus; ore manûque
Consultor patriæ; sed non consultor habendæ
Religionis; amans tercentûm millia Divûm.
Perfidus ille Deo, sed non et [*leg.* quamuis non] perfidus orbi.
Prudent. Apotheosis, 450, &c. [ed. Dressel, p. 102].

The consciousness of a generous sentiment seems to have raised the Christian poet above his usual mediocrity

CHAPTER XXIII

The Religion of Julian—Universal Toleration—He attempts to re-
store and reform the Pagan Worship; to rebuild the Temple of
Jerusalem—His artful Persecution of the Christians—Mutual
Zeal and Injustice

Religion of
Julian

THE character of Apostate has injured the reputation of Julian;
and the enthusiasm which clouded his virtues has exaggerated
the real and apparent magnitude of his faults.   Our partial
ignorance may represent him as a philosophic monarch, who
studied to protect, with an equal hand, the religious factions
of the empire ; and to allay the theological fever which had inflamed the minds of the people from the edicts of Diocletian to
the exile of Athanasius.   A more accurate view of the character
and conduct of Julian will remove this favourable prepossession
for a prince who did not escape the general contagion of the
times.   We enjoy the singular advantage of comparing the
pictures which have been delineated by his fondest admirers and
his implacable enemies.   The actions of Julian are faithfully related by a judicious and candid historian, the impartial spectator
of his life and death.   The unanimous evidence of his contemporaries is confirmed by the public and private declarations of
the emperor himself; and his various writings express the
uniform tenor of his religious sentiments, which policy would
have prompted him to dissemble rather than to affect.   A devout
and sincere attachment for the gods of Athens and Rome
constituted the ruling passion of Julian ; [1] the powers of an enlightened understanding were betrayed and corrupted by the
influence of superstitious prejudice ; and the phantoms which
existed only in the mind of the emperor had a real and pernicious effect on the government of the empire.   The vehement
zeal of the Christians, who despised the worship, and overturned

[1] I shall transcribe some of his own expressions from a short religious discourse
which the imperial pontiff composed to censure the bold impiety of a Cynic:
Ἀλλ' ὅμως οὕτω δή τι τοὺς θεοὺς πέφρικα, καὶ φιλῶ, καὶ σέβω, καὶ ἄζομαι, καὶ πάνθ'
ἁπλῶς τὰ τοιαῦτα πάσχω, ὅσαπερ ἄν τις καὶ οἷα πρὸς ἀγαθοὺς δεσπότας, πρὸς διδασκάλους,
πρὸς πατέρας, πρὸς κηδεμόνας.   Orat. vii. p. 212 [275, ed. Hertl.].   The variety and
copiousness of the Greek tongue seems inadequate to the fervour of his devotion.

the altars, of those fabulous deities, engaged their votary in a
state of irreconcileable hostility with a very numerous party of
his subjects; and he was sometimes tempted, by the desire of
victory or the shame of a repulse, to violate the laws of prudence, and even of justice.   The triumph of the party which he
deserted and opposed has fixed a stain of infamy on the name
of Julian; and the unsuccessful apostate has been overwhelmed
with a torrent of pious invectives, of which the signal was given
by the sonorous trumpet[2] of Gregory Nazianzen.[3]   The interesting nature of the events which were crowded into the short
reign of this active emperor deserves a just and circumstantial
narrative.   His motives, his counsels, and his actions, as far as
they are connected with the history of religion, will be the
subject of the present chapter.

The cause of his strange and fatal apostacy may be derived   His education
from the early period of his life, when he was left an orphan in   and apostacy
the hands of the murderers of his family.   The names of Christ
and of Constantius, the ideas of slavery and of religion, were
soon associated in a youthful imagination, which was susceptible
of the most lively impressions.   The care of his infancy was entrusted to Eusebius, bishop of Nicomedia,[4] who was related to
him on the side of his mother; and, till Julian reached the
twentieth year of his age, he received from his Christian preceptors the education, not of a hero, but of a saint.   The
emperor, less jealous of a heavenly than of an earthly crown,
contented himself with the imperfect character of a catechumen,
while he bestowed the advantages of baptism[5] on the nephews

---

[2] The orator, with some eloquence, much enthusiasm, and more vanity, addresses his discourse to heaven and earth, to men and angels, to the living and the
dead; and above all, to the great Constantius (εἴ τις αἴσθησις, an odd Pagan expression [cp. Isocr. *Evagoras*, 1, 2]).   He concludes with a bold assurance that he
has erected a monument not less durable, and much more portable, than the columns
of Hercules.   See Greg. Nazianzen, Orat. iii. p. 50, iv. p. 134 [iv. c. 3, v. ad fin. c. 42].

[3] See this long invective, which has been injudiciously divided into two orations
in Gregory's Works, tom. i. p. 49-134.   Paris, 1630.   It was published by Gregory
and his friend Basil (iv. p. 133 [v. c. 39]) about six months after the death of Julian,
when his remains had been carried to Tarsus (iv. p. 120 [v. c. 18]); but while Jovian
was still on the throne (iii. p. 54, iv. p. 117 [v. c. 15]).   I have derived much
assistance from a French version and remarks, printed at Lyons 1735.

[4] Nicomediæ ab Eusebio educatus Episcopo, quem genere longius contingebat
(Ammian. xxii. 9).   Julian never expresses any gratitude towards that Arian prelate;
but he celebrates his preceptor, the eunuch Mardonius, and describes his mode of
education, which inspired his pupil with a passionate admiration for the genius,
and perhaps the religion, of Homer.   Misopogon. p. 351, 352.

[5] Greg. Naz. iii. p. 70 [iv. c. 52].   He laboured to efface that holy mark in the
blood, perhaps, of a Taurobolium.   Baron. Annal. Eccles. A.D. 361, No. 3, 4.

of Constantine.[6]   They were even admitted to the inferior offices of the ecclesiastical order; and Julian publicly read the Holy Scriptures in the church of Nicomedia.   The study of religion, which they assiduously cultivated, appeared to produce the fairest fruits of faith and devotion.[7]   They prayed, they fasted, they distributed alms to the poor, gifts to the clergy, and oblations to the tombs of the martyrs; and the splendid monument of St. Mamas, at Cæsarea, was erected, or at least was undertaken, by the joint labour of Gallus and Julian.[8]   They respectfully conversed with the bishops who were eminent for superior sanctity, and solicited the benediction of the monks and hermits who had introduced into Cappadocia the voluntary hardships of the ascetic life.[9]   As the two princes advanced towards the years of manhood, they discovered, in their religious sentiments, the difference of their characters.   The dull and obstinate understanding of Gallus embraced, with implicit zeal, the doctrines of Christianity; which never influenced his conduct or moderated his passions.   The mild disposition of the younger brother was less repugnant to the precepts of the gospel; and his active curiosity might have been gratified by a theological system which explains the mysterious essence of the Deity and opens the boundless prospect of invisible and future worlds.   But the independent spirit of Julian refused to yield the passive and unresisting obedience which was required, in the name of religion, by the haughty ministers of the church. Their speculative opinions were imposed as positive laws, and guarded by the terrors of eternal punishments; but, while they prescribed the rigid formulary of the thoughts, the words, and the actions of the young prince; whilst they silenced his objections and severely checked the freedom of his enquiries,

6 Julian himself (Epist. li. p. 434 [558, ed. Hertl.]) assures the Alexandrians that he had been a Christian (he must mean a sincere one) till the twentieth year of his age.

7 See his Christian and even ecclesiastical education, in Gregory (iii. p. 58 [iv. c. 23 sqq.]), Socrates (l. iii. c. 1), and Sozomen (l. v. c. 2).   He escaped very narrowly from being a bishop, and perhaps a saint.

8 The share of the work which had been allotted to Gallus was prosecuted with vigour and success; but the earth obstinately rejected and subverted the structures which were imposed by the sacrilegious hand of Julian.   Greg. iii. p. 59, 60, 61 [c. 26 sqq.].   Such a partial earthquake, attested by many living spectators, would form one of the clearest miracles in ecclesiastical story.

9 The *philosopher* (Fragment, p. 228) ridicules the iron chains, &c. of these solitary fanatics (see Tillemont, Mém Ecclés. tom. ix. p. 661, 662), who had forgot that man is by nature a gentle and social animal, ἀνθρώπου φύσει πολιτικοῦ ζώου καὶ ἡμέρου.   The *Pagan* supposes that, because they had renounced the gods, they were possessed and tormented by evil dæmon

they secretly provoked his impatient genius to disclaim the
authority of his ecclesiastical guides.   He was educated in the
Lesser Asia, amidst the scandals of the Arian controversy.[10]
The fierce contests of the eastern bishops, the incessant alterations of their creeds, and the profane motives which appeared
to actuate their conduct, insensibly strengthened the prejudice
of Julian, that they neither understood nor believed the religion
for which they so fiercely contended.   Instead of listening to
the proofs of Christianity with that favourable attention which
adds weight to the most respectable evidence, he heard with
suspicion, and disputed with obstinacy and acuteness, the doctrines for which he already entertained an invincible aversion.
Whenever the young princes were directed to compose
declamations on the subject of the prevailing controversies,
Julian always declared himself the advocate of Paganism ; under
the specious excuse that, in the defence of the weaker cause,
his learning and ingenuity might be more advantageously
exercised and displayed.

As soon as Gallus was invested with the honours of the
purple, Julian was permitted to breathe the air of freedom, of
literature, and of Paganism.[11]   The crowd of sophists, who were
attracted by the taste and liberality of their royal pupil, had
formed a strict alliance between the learning and the religion of
Greece ; and the poems of Homer, instead of being admired
as the original productions of human genius, were seriously
ascribed to the heavenly inspiration of Apollo and the muses.
The deities of Olympus, as they are painted by the immortal
bard, imprint themselves on the minds which are the least
addicted to superstitious credulity.   Our familiar knowledge of
their names and characters, their forms and attributes, *seems* to
bestow on those airy beings a real and substantial existence ;
and the pleasing enchantment produces an imperfect and
momentary assent of the imagination to those fables which are
the most repugnant to our reason and experience.   In the age
of Julian every circumstance contributed to prolong and fortify
the illusion ; the magnificent temples of Greece and Asia ; the
works of those artists who had expressed, in painting or in

He embraces the mythology of Paganism

---

[10] See Julian apud Cyril. l. vi. p. 206, l. viii. p. 253, 262.   "You persecute,"
says he, "those heretics who do not mourn the dead man precisely in the way
which you approve."   He shews himself a tolerable theologian ; but he maintains
that the Christian Trinity is not derived from the doctrine of Paul, of Jesus, or of
Moses.

[11] Libanius, Orat. Parentalis. c. 9, 10, p. 232, &c.   Greg. Nazianzen, Orat. iii.
p. 61 [iv. c. 31].   Eunap. Vit. Sophist. in Maximo, p. 68, 69, 70, edit. Commelin.

sculpture, the divine conceptions of the poet; the pomp of festivals and sacrifices; the successful arts of divination; the popular traditions of oracles and prodigies; and the ancient practice of two thousand years. The weakness of polytheism was, in some measure, excused by the moderation of its claims; and the devotion of the Pagans was not incompatible with the most licentious scepticism.[12]   Instead of an indivisible and regular system, which occupies the whole extent of the believing mind, the mythology of the Greeks was composed of a thousand loose and flexible parts, and the servant of the gods was at liberty to define the degree and measure of his religious faith. The creed which Julian adopted for his own use was of the largest dimensions; and, by a strange contradiction, he disdained the salutary yoke of the gospel, whilst he made a voluntary offering of his reason on the altars of Jupiter and Apollo. One of the orations of Julian is consecrated to the honour of Cybele, the mother of the gods, who required from her effeminate priests the bloody sacrifice, so rashly performed by the madness of the Phrygian boy. The pious emperor condescends to relate, without a blush, and without a smile, the voyage of the goddess from the shores of Pergamus to the mouth of the Tiber, and the stupendous miracle, which convinced the senate and people of Rome that the lump of clay which their ambassadors had transported over the seas was endowed with life, and sentiment, and divine power.[13]   For the truth of this prodigy, he appeals to the public monuments of the city; and censures, with some acrimony, the sickly and affected taste of those men who impertinently derided the sacred traditions of their ancestors.[14]

The allegories   But the devout philosopher, who sincerely embraced and warmly encouraged the superstition of the people, reserved for himself the privilege of a liberal interpretation; and silently

---

[12] A modern philosopher has ingeniously compared the different operation of theism and polytheism, with regard to the doubt or conviction which they produce in the human mind. See Hume's Essays, vol. ii. p. 444 457, in 8vo edit. 1777.

[13] The Idæan mother landed in Italy about the end of the second Punic war. The miracle of Claudia, either virgin or matron, who cleared her fame by disgracing the graver modesty of the Roman ladies, is attested by a cloud of witnesses. Their evidence is collected by Drakenborch (ad Silium Italicum, xvii. 33) : but we may observe that Livy (xxix. 14) slides over the transaction with discreet ambiguity.

[14] I cannot refrain from transcribing the emphatical words of Julian: ἐμοὶ δὲ δοκεῖ ταῖς πόλεσι πιστεύειν μᾶλλον τὰ τοιαῦτα, ἢ τουτοισὶ τοῖς κομψοῖς, ὧν τὸ ψυχάριον δριμὺ μὲν, ὑγιὲς δὲ οὐδὲ ἐν βλέπει. Orat. v. p. 161 [209, ed. Hertl.].   Julian likewise declares his firm belief in the ancilia, the holy shields, which dropt from heaven on the Quirinal hill ; and pities the strange blindness of the Christians, who preferred the cross to these celestial trophies. Apud Cyril. l. vi. p. 194.

withdrew from the foot of the altars into the sanctuary of the temple. The extravagance of the Grecian mythology proclaimed with a clear and audible voice that the pious inquirer, instead of being scandalized or satisfied with the literal sense, should diligently explore the occult wisdom which had been disguised, by the prudence of antiquity, under the mask of folly and of fable.[15] The philosophers of the Platonic school,[16] Plotinus, Porphyry, and the divine Iamblichus, were admired as the most skilful masters of this allegorical science which laboured to soften and harmonize the deformed features of paganism. Julian himself, who was directed in the mysterious pursuit by Ædesius, the venerable successor of Iamblichus, aspired to the possession of a treasure which he esteemed, if we may credit his solemn asseverations, far above the empire of the world.[17] It was indeed a treasure which derived its value only from opinion ; and every artist who flattered himself that he had extracted the precious ore from the surrounding dross claimed an equal right of stamping the name and figure the most agreeable to his peculiar fancy. The fable of Atys and Cybele had been already explained by Porphyry ; but his labours served only to animate the pious industry of Julian, who invented and published his own allegory of that ancient and mystic tale. This freedom of interpretation, which might gratify the pride of the Platonists, exposed the vanity of their art. Without a tedious detail, the modern reader could not form a just idea of the strange allusions, the forced etymologies, the solemn trifling, and the impenetrable obscurity of these sages, who professed to reveal the system of the universe. As the traditions of Pagan mythology were variously related, the sacred interpreters were at liberty to select the most convenient circumstances ; and, as they translated an arbitrary cypher, they could extract from *any* fable *any* sense which was adapted to their favourite system of religion and philosophy. The lascivious form of a naked Venus was tortured into the discovery of some moral precept or some physical truth : and the castration of Atys explained

[15] See the principles of allegory in Julian (Orat. vii. p. 216, 222 [280, 288, ed. Hertl.]). His reasoning is less absurd than that of some modern theologians, who assert that an extravagant or contradictory doctrine *must* be divine ; since no man alive could have thought of inventing it.

[16] Eunapius has made these sophists the subject of a partial and fanatical history ; and the learned Brucker (Hist. Philosoph. tom. ii. p. 217-303) has employed much labour to illustrate their obscure lives and incomprehensible doctrines.

[17] Julian, Orat. vii. p. 222 [288]. He swears with the most fervent and enthusiastic devotion ; and trembles lest he should betray too much of these holy mysteries, which the profane might deride with an impious sardonic laugh,

the revolution of the sun between the tropics or the separation of the human soul from vice and error.[18]

The theological system of Julian appears to have contained the sublime and important principles of natural religion. But, as the faith which is not founded on revelation must remain destitute of any firm assurance, the disciple of Plato imprudently relapsed into the habits of vulgar superstition ; and the popular and philosophic notion of the Deity seems to have been confounded in the practice, the writings, and even in the mind of Julian.[19] The pious emperor acknowledged and adored the Eternal Cause of the universe, to whom he ascribed all the perfections of an infinite nature, invisible to the eyes, and inaccessible to the understanding, of feeble mortals. The Supreme God had created, or rather, in the Platonic language, had generated, the gradual succession of dependent spirits, of gods, of dæmons, of heroes, and of men ; and every being which derived its existence immediately from the First Cause received the inherent gift of immortality. That so precious an advantage might not be lavished upon unworthy objects, the Creator had entrusted to the skill and power of the inferior gods, the office of forming the human body, and of arranging the beautiful harmony of the animal, the vegetable, and the mineral kingdoms. To the conduct of these divine ministers he delegated the temporal government of this lower world ; but their imperfect administration is not exempt from discord or error. The earth, and its inhabitants, are divided among them, and the characters of Mars or Minerva, of Mercury or Venus, may be distinctly traced in the laws and manners of their peculiar votaries. As long as our immortal souls are confined in a mortal prison, it is our interest, as well as our duty, to solicit the favour, and to deprecate the wrath, of the powers of heaven ; whose pride is gratified by the devotion of mankind ; and whose grosser parts may be supposed to derive some nourishment from the fumes of sacrifice.[20] The inferior gods might sometimes

[18] See the fifth oration of Julian. But all the allegories which ever issued from the Platonic school are not worth the short poem of Catullus on the same extraordinary subject. The transition of Atys from the wildest enthusiasm to sober pathetic complaint, for his irretrievable loss, must inspire a man with pity, an eunuch with despair.

[19] The true religion of Julian may be deduced from the Cæsars, p. 308 [395, ed. Hertl.], with Spanheim's notes and illustrations, from the fragments in Cyril, l. ii. p. 57, 58, and especially from the theological oration in Solem Regem, p. 130-158 [168-205, Or. iv.], addressed, in the confidence of friendship, to the præfect Sallust.

[20] Julian adopts this gross conception, by ascribing it to his favourite Marcus Antoninus (Cæsares, p. 333 [428]). The Stoics and Platonists hesitated between

condescend to animate the statues, and to inhabit the temples, which were dedicated to their honour. They might occasionally visit the earth, but the heavens were the proper throne and symbol of their glory. The invariable order of the sun, moon, and stars, was hastily admitted by Julian as a proof of their *eternal* duration ; and their eternity was a sufficient evidence that they were the workmanship, not of an inferior deity, but of the Omnipotent King. In the system of the Platonists, the visible, was a type of the invisible, world. The celestial bodies, as they were informed by a divine spirit, might be considered as the objects the most worthy of religious worship. The Sun, whose genial influence pervades and sustains the universe, justly claimed the adoration of mankind, as the bright representative of the Logos, the lively, the rational, the beneficent image of the intellectual Father.[21]

In every age, the absence of genuine inspiration is supplied by the strong illusions of enthusiasm and the mimic arts of imposture. If, in the time of Julian, these arts had been practised only by the Pagan priests, for the support of an expiring cause, some indulgence might perhaps be allowed to the interest and habits of the sacerdotal character. But it may appear a subject of surprise and scandal that the philosophers themselves should have contributed to abuse the superstitious credulity of mankind,[22] and that the Grecian mysteries should have been supported by the magic or theurgy of the modern Platonists. They arrogantly pretended to control the order of nature, to explore the secrets of futurity, to command the service of the inferior dæmons, to enjoy the view and conversation of the superior gods, and, by disengaging the soul from her material bands, to re-unite that immortal particle with the Infinite and Divine Spirit.

Fanaticism of the philosophers

---

the analogy of bodies and the purity of spirits; yet the gravest philosophers inclined to the whimsical fancy of Aristophanes and Lucian that an unbelieving age might starve the immortal gods. See Observations de Spanheim, p. 284, 444, &c.

[21] Ἥλιον λέγω, τὸ ζῶν ἄγαλμα καὶ ἔμψυχον, καὶ ἔννουν, καὶ ἀγαθόεργον τοῦ νοητοῦ πατρός. Julian, epist. xli. [*leg.* li. ; p. 558, ed. Hertl.]. In another place (apud Cyril. l. ii. p. 69), he calls the Sun, God, and the throne of God. Julian believed the Platonician Trinity ; and only blames the Christians for preferring a mortal, to an immortal, *Logos*.

[22] The sophists of Eunapius perform as many miracles as the saints of the desert ; and the only circumstance in their favour is that they are of a less gloomy complexion. Instead of devils with horns and tails, Iamblichus evoked the genii of love, Eros and Anteros, from two adjacent fountains. Two beautiful boys issued from the water, fondly embraced him as their father, and retired at his command, p. 26, 27.

The devout and fearless curiosity of Julian tempted the philosophers with the hopes of an easy conquest ; which, from the situation of their young proselyte, might be productive of the most important consequences.[23]   Julian imbibed the first rudiments of the Platonic doctrines from the mouth of Ædesius, who had fixed at Pergamus his wandering and persecuted school. But, as the declining strength of that venerable sage was unequal to the ardour, the diligence, the rapid conception of his pupil, two of his most learned disciples, Chrysanthes and Eusebius, supplied, at his own desire, the place of their aged master.   These philosophers seem to have prepared and distributed their respective parts ; and they artfully contrived, by dark hints and affected disputes, to excite the impatient hopes of the *aspirant,* till they delivered him into the hands of their associate Maximus, the boldest and most skilful master of the Theurgic science.   By his hands Julian was secretly initiated at Ephesus, in the twentieth year of his age.   His residence at Athens confirmed this unnatural alliance of philosophy and superstition.   He obtained the privilege of a solemn initiation into the mysteries of Eleusis, which, amidst the general decay of the Grecian worship, still retained some vestiges of their primæval sanctity ; and such was the zeal of Julian that he afterwards invited the Eleusinian pontiff to the court of Gaul, for the sole purpose of consummating, by mystic rites and sacrifices, the great work of his sanctification.   As these ceremonies were performed in the depth of caverns, and in the silence of the night, and as the inviolable secret of the mysteries was preserved by the discretion of the initiated, I shall not presume to describe the horrid sounds and fiery apparitions, which were presented to the senses, or the imagination, of the credulous aspirant,[24] till the visions of comfort and knowledge broke upon him in a blaze of celestial light.[25]   In the caverns of Ephesus and Eleusis,[26] the mind of Julian was penetrated with sincere, deep,

[23] The dexterous management of these sophists, who played their credulous pupil into each other's hands, is fairly told by Eunapius (p. 69-76), with unsuspecting simplicity.   The Abbé de la Bléterie understands, and neatly describes, the whole comedy (Vie de Julien, p. 61-67).

[24] When Julian, in a momentary panic, made the sign of the cross, the dæmons instantly disappeared (Greg. Naz. Orat. iii. p. 71 [iv. c. 55]).   Gregory supposes that they were frightened, but the priests declared that they were indignant.   The reader, according to the measure of his faith, will determine this profound question.

[25] A dark and distant view of the terrors and joys of initiation is shewn by Dion Chrysostom, Themistius, Proclus, and Stobæus.   The learned author of the Divine Legation has exhibited their words (vol. i. p. 239, 247, 248, 280, edit. 1765), which he dexterously or forcibly applies to his own hypothesis.

[26] [Not in caverns at Eleusis, but in a great Hall, the *Telesterion.*]

OF THE ROMAN EMPIRE 441

and unalterable enthusiasm ; though he might sometimes exhibit
the vicissitudes of pious fraud and hypocrisy, which may be
observed, or at least suspected, in the characters of the most
conscientious fanatics.   From that moment he consecrated his
life to the service of the gods ; and, while the occupations of
war, of government, and of study, seemed to claim the whole
measure of his time, a stated portion of the hours of the night
was invariably reserved for the exercise of private devotion.
The temperance which adorned the severe manners of the
soldier and the philosopher was connected with some strict and
frivolous rules of religious abstinence ; and it was in honour of
Pan or Mercury, of Hecate or Isis, that Julian, on particular
days, denied himself the use of some particular food, which
might have been offensive to his tutelar deities.   By these
voluntary fasts, he prepared his senses and his understanding for
the frequent and familiar visits with which he was honoured
by the celestial powers.   Notwithstanding the modest silence
of Julian himself, we may learn from his faithful friend, the
orator Libanius, that he lived in a perpetual intercourse with
the gods and goddesses ; that they descended upon earth, to
enjoy the conversation of their favourite hero ; that they gently
interrupted his slumbers, by touching his hand or his hair ; that
they warned him of every impending danger, and conducted
him, by their infallible wisdom, in every action of his life ; and
that he had acquired such an intimate knowledge of his heavenly
guests, as readily to distinguish the voice of Jupiter from that
of Minerva, and the form of Apollo from the figure of Hercules.[27]
These sleeping or waking visions, the ordinary effects of abstinence and fanaticism, would almost degrade the emperor to the
level of an Egyptian monk.   But the useless lives of Antony
or Pachomius were consumed in these vain occupations.   Julian
could break from the dream of superstition to arm himself for
battle ; and, after vanquishing in the field the enemies of Rome,
he calmly retired into his tent, to dictate the wise and salutary
laws of an empire, or to indulge his genius in the elegant
pursuits of literature and philosophy.

The important secret of the apostacy of Julian was entrusted His religious
to the fidelity of the *initiated*, with whom he was united by the dissimulation
sacred ties of friendship and religion.[28]   The pleasing rumour

---

[27] Julian's modesty confined him to obscure and occasional hints ; but Libanius
expatiates with pleasure on the fasts and visions of the religious hero (Legat. ad
Julian. p. 157 and Orat. Parental. c. lxxxiii. p. 309, 310).

[28] Libanius, Orat. Parent. c. x. p. 233, 234.   Gallus had some reasons to

was cautiously circulated among the adherents of the ancient
worship; and his future greatness became the object of the
hopes, the prayers, and the predictions of the pagans, in every
province of the empire. From the zeal and virtues of their
royal proselyte, they fondly expected the cure of every evil and
the restoration of every blessing; and, instead of disapproving
of the ardour of their pious wishes, Julian ingenuously confessed that he was ambitious to attain a situation in which he
might be useful to his country and to his religion. But this
religion was viewed with an hostile eye by the successor of
Constantine, whose capricious passions alternately saved and
threatened the life of Julian. The arts of magic and divination were strictly prohibited under a despotic government which
condescended to fear them; and, if the pagans were reluctantly
indulged in the exercise of their superstition, the rank of Julian
would have excepted him from the general toleration. The
apostate soon became the presumptive heir of the monarchy,
and his death could alone have appeased the just apprehensions
of the Christians.[29] But the young prince, who aspired to the
glory of a hero rather than of a martyr, consulted his safety by
dissembling his religion; and the easy temper of polytheism
permitted him to join in the public worship of a sect which he
inwardly despised. Libanius has considered the hypocrisy of
his friend as a subject, not of censure, but of praise. "As the
statues of the gods," says that orator, "which have been defiled
with filth, are again placed in a magnificent temple; so the
beauty of truth was seated in the mind of Julian, after it had
been purified from the errors and follies of his education. His
sentiments were changed; but, as it would have been dangerous
to have avowed his sentiments, his conduct still continued the
same. Very different from the ass in Æsop, who disguised himself with a lion's hide, our lion was obliged to conceal himself
under the skin of an ass; and, while he embraced the dictates of
reason, to obey the laws of prudence and necessity."[30] The
dissimulation of Julian lasted above ten years, from his secret

suspect the secret apostacy of his brother; and in a letter, which may be received
as genuine, he exhorts Julian to adhere to the religion of their *ancestors;* an
argument which, as it should seem, was not yet perfectly ripe. See Julian. Op. p.
454 [613, ed. Hertl.], and Hist. de Jovien, tom. ii. p. 141.   [The letter of Gallus is
rejected by Petavius.]

[29] Gregory (iii. p. 50 [iv. c. 3]), with inhuman zeal, censures Constantius for
sparing the infant apostate (κακῶς σωθέντα). His French translator (p. 265)
cautiously observes that such expressions must not be prises à la lettre. [The
phrase implies no censure of the preserver.]

[30] Libanius, Orat. Parental. c. ix. p. 233.

initiation at Ephesus to the beginning of the civil war; when he declared himself at once the implacable enemy of Christ and of Constantius. This state of constraint might contribute to strengthen his devotion; and, as soon as he had satisfied the obligation of assisting, on solemn festivals, at the assemblies of the Christians, Julian returned, with the impatience of a lover, to burn his free and voluntary incense on the domestic chapels of Jupiter and Mercury. But, as every act of dissimulation must be painful to an ingenuous spirit, the profession of Christianity increased the aversion of Julian for a religion which oppressed the freedom of his mind and compelled him to hold a conduct repugnant to the noblest attributes of human nature, sincerity and courage.

The inclination of Julian might prefer the gods of Homer, and of the Scipios, to the new faith which his uncle had estab- He writes against lished in the Roman empire; and in which he himself had been Christianity sanctified by the sacrament of baptism. But, as a philosopher, it was incumbent on him to justify his dissent from Christianity, which was supported by the number of its converts, by the chain of prophecy, the splendour of miracles, and the weight of evidence. The elaborate work,[31] which he composed amidst the preparations of the Persian war, contained the substance of those arguments which he had long revolved in his mind. Some fragments have been transcribed and preserved by his adversary, the vehement Cyril of Alexandria;[32] and they exhibit a very singular mixture of wit and learning, of sophistry and fanaticism. The elegance of the style, and the rank of the author, recommended his writings to the public attention;[33] and in the impious list of the enemies of Christianity, the celebrated name of Porphyry was effaced by the superior merit or reputation of Julian. The minds of the faithful were either seduced, or scandalized, or alarmed; and the pagans, who

[31] Fabricius (Biblioth. Græc. l. v. c. viii. p. 88-90) and Lardner (Heathen Testimonies, vol. iv. p. 44-47) have accurately compiled all that can now be discovered of Julian's work against the Christians. [These compilations are superseded by the work of C. J. Neumann; see Appendix 1.]

[32] About seventy years after the death of Julian, he executed a task which had been feebly attempted by Philip of Side, a prolix and contemptible writer. Even the work of Cyril has not entirely satisfied the most favourable judges: and the Abbé de la Blèterie (Préface à l'Hist. de Jovien, p. 30, 32) wishes that some théologien philosophe (a strange centaur) would undertake the refutation of Julian.

[33] Libanius (Orat. Parental. c. lxxxvii. p. 313), who has been suspected of assisting his friend, prefers this divine vindication (Orat. ix. in necem Julian. p. 255, edit. Morel.) to the writings of Porphyry. His judgment may be arraigned (Socrates, l. iii. c. 23), but Libanius cannot be accused of flattery to a dead prince,

sometimes presumed to engage in the unequal dispute, derived
from the popular work of their Imperial missionary an inexhaustible supply of fallacious objections. But in the assiduous
prosecution of these theological studies, the emperor of the
Romans imbibed the illiberal prejudices and passions of a
polemic divine. He contracted an irrevocable obligation to
maintain and propagate his religious opinions; and, whilst he
secretly applauded the strength and dexterity with which he
wielded the weapons of controversy, he was tempted to distrust
the sincerity, or to despise the understandings, of his antagonists, who could obstinately resist the force of reason and
eloquence.

Universal
toleration

The Christians, who beheld with horror and indignation the
apostacy of Julian, had much more to fear from his power than
from his arguments. The pagans, who were conscious of his
fervent zeal, expected, perhaps with impatience, that the flames
of persecution should be immediately kindled against the
enemies of the gods; and that the ingenious malice of Julian
would invent some cruel refinements of death and torture,
which had been unknown to the rude and inexperienced fury
of his predecessors. But the hopes, as well as the fears, of the
religious factions were apparently disappointed by the prudent
humanity of a prince [34] who was careful of his own fame, of the
public peace, and of the rights of mankind. Instructed by
history and reflection, Julian was persuaded that, if the diseases
of the body may sometimes be cured by salutary violence,
neither steel nor fire can eradicate the erroneous opinions
of the mind. The reluctant victim may be dragged to the
foot of the altar; but the heart still abhors and disclaims
the sacrilegious act of the hand. Religious obstinacy is
hardened and exasperated by oppression; and, as soon as the
persecution subsides, those who have yielded are restored as
penitents, and whose who have resisted are honoured as saints
and martyrs. If Julian adopted the unsuccessful cruelty of
Diocletian and his colleagues, he was sensible that he should
stain his memory with the name of tyrant, and add new glories
to the Catholic church, which had derived strength and increase
from the severity of the pagan magistrates. Actuated by these

---

[34] Libanius (Orat. Parent. c. lviii. p. 283, 284) has eloquently explained the
tolerating principles and conduct of his Imperial friend. In a very remarkable
epistle to the people of Bostra, Julian himself (epist. lii) professes his moderation,
and betrays his zeal; which is acknowledged by Ammianus, and exposed by
Gregory, Orat. iii. p. 72 [iv. c. 57].

motives, and apprehensive of disturbing the repose of an un-
settled reign, Julian surprised the world by an edict which was
not unworthy of a statesman or a philosopher. He extended
to all the inhabitants of the Roman world the benefits of a free
and equal toleration; and the only hardship which he inflicted
on the Christians was to deprive them of the power of torment-
ing their fellow-subjects, whom they stigmatized with the odious
titles of idolaters and heretics. The pagans received a gracious
permission, or rather an express order, to open ALL their
temples;[35] and they were at once delivered from the oppressive laws and arbitrary vexations which they had sustained
under the reign of Constantine and of his sons. At the same
time, the bishops and clergy who had been banished by the
Arian monarch were recalled from exile and restored to their
respective churches; the Donatists, the Novatians, the Macedonians, the Eunomians, and those who, with a more prosperous
fortune, adhered to the doctrine of the council of Nice. Julian,
who understood and derided their theological disputes, invited
to the palace the leaders of the hostile sects, that he might
enjoy the agreeable spectacle of their furious encounters. The
clamour of controversy sometimes provoked the emperor to
exclaim, "Hear me! the Franks have heard me, and the
Alemanni;" but he soon discovered that he was now engaged
with more obstinate and implacable enemies; and, though he
exerted the powers of oratory to persuade them to live in concord, or at least in peace, he was perfectly satisfied, before he
dismissed them from his presence, that he had nothing to dread
from the union of the Christians. The impartial Ammianus has
ascribed this affected clemency to the desire of fomenting the
intestine divisions of the church; and the insidious design of
undermining the foundations of Christianity was inseparably
connected with the zeal which Julian professed to restore the
ancient religion of the empire.[36].

As soon as he ascended the throne, he assumed, according to   Zeal and
                                                                 devotion of
                                                                 Julian in the
                                                                 restoration of
[35] In Greece the temples of Minerva were opened by his express command,   Paganism
before the death of Constantius (Liban. Orat. Parent. c. 55, p. 280); and Julian
declares himself a pagan in his public manifesto to the Athenians. This unquestionable evidence may correct the hasty assertion of Ammianus, who seems to
suppose Constantinople to be the place where he discovered his attachment to the
gods.

[36] Ammian. xxii. 5. Sozomen, l. v. c. 5. Bestia moritur, tranquillitas redit
. . omnes episcopi, qui de propriis sedibus fuerant exterminati, per indulgentiam
novi principis ad ecclesias redeunt. Jerom. adversus Luciferianos, tom. ii. p. 143.
Optatus accuses the Donatists for owing their safety to an apostate (l. ii. c. 16,
p. 36, 37, edit. Dupin).

the custom of his predecessors, the character of supreme pontiff; not only as the most honourable title of Imperial greatness, but as a sacred and important office, the duties of which he was resolved to execute with pious diligence. As the business of the state prevented the emperor from joining every day in the public devotion of his subjects, he dedicated a domestic chapel to his tutelar deity the Sun; his gardens were filled with statues and altars of the gods; and each apartment of the palace displayed the appearance of a magnificent temple. Every morning he saluted the parent of light with a sacrifice; the blood of another victim was shed at the moment when the Sun sunk below the horizon; and the Moon, the Stars, and the Genii of the night, received their respective and seasonable honours from the indefatigable devotion of Julian. On solemn festivals, he regularly visited the temple of the god or goddess to whom the day was peculiarly consecrated, and endeavoured to excite the religion of the magistrates and people by the example of his own zeal. Instead of maintaining the lofty state of a monarch, distinguished by the splendour of his purple, and encompassed by the golden shields of his guards, Julian solicited, with respectful eagerness, the meanest offices which contributed to the worship of the gods. Amidst the sacred but licentious crowd of priests, of inferior ministers, and of female dancers, who were dedicated to the service of the temple, it was the business of the emperor to bring the wood, to blow the fire, to handle the knife, to slaughter the victim, and, thrusting his bloody hand into the bowels of the expiring animal, to draw forth the heart or liver, and to read, with the consummate skill of an haruspex, the imaginary signs of future events. The wisest of the pagans censured this extravagant superstition which affected to despise the restraints of prudence and decency. Under the reign of a prince who practised the rigid maxims of economy the expense of religious worship consumed a very large portion of the revenue; a constant supply of the scarcest and most beautiful birds was transported from distant climates, to bleed on the altars of the gods; an hundred oxen were frequently sacrificed by Julian on one and the same day; and it soon became a popular jest that, if he should return with conquest from the Persian war, the breed of horned cattle must infallibly be extinguished. Yet this expense may appear inconsiderable, when it is compared with the splendid presents which were offered, either by the hand or by order of the emperor, to all the celebrated places of devotion in the Roman world and with the sums allotted to repair and decorate the ancient temples, which had suffered the silent decay of time or the recent injuries of Christian rapine. Encouraged by the example, the exhortations, the liberality, of their pious sovereign, the cities and families resumed the practice of their neglected ceremonies. " Every part of the world," exclaims Libanius with devout transport, "displayed the triumph of religion ; and the grateful prospect of flaming altars, bleeding victims, the smoke of incense, and a solemn train of priests and prophets, without fear and without danger. The sound of prayer and of music was heard on the tops of the highest mountains ; and the same ox afforded a sacrifice for the gods and a supper for their joyous votaries." [37]

But the genius and power of Julian were unequal to the enter- *Reformation of Paganism* prise of restoring a religion which was destitute of theological principles, of moral precepts, and of ecclesiastical discipline ; which rapidly hastened to decay and dissolution, and was not susceptible of any solid or consistent reformation. The juris- diction of the supreme pontiff, more especially after that office had been united with the Imperial dignity, comprehended the whole extent of the Roman empire. Julian named for his vicars, in the several provinces, the priests and philosophers whom he esteemed the best qualified to co-operate in the execu- tion of his great design ; and his pastoral letters,[38] if we may use that name, still represent a very curious sketch of his wishes and intentions. He directs that in every city the sacerdotal order should be composed, without any distinction of birth or fortune, of those persons who were the most conspicuous for their love of the gods and of men. " If they are guilty," continues he, " of any scandalous offence, they should be censured or degraded by the superior pontiff ; but, as long as they retain their rank, they are entitled to the respect of the magistrates and people. Their humility may be shown in the plainness of

[37] The restoration of the pagan worship is described by Julian (Misopogon, p. 346 [446, ed. Hertl.]), Libanius (Orat. Parent. c. 60, p. 286, 287, and Orat. Consular. ad Julian, p. 245, 246, edit. Morel.), Ammianus (xxii. 12), and Gregory Nazianzen (Orat. iv. p. 121). These writers agree in the essential, and even minute, facts ; but the different lights in which they view the extreme devotion of Julian are expressive of the gradations of self-applause, passionate admiration, mild reproof, and partial invective.

[38] See Julian. Epistol. xlix. lxii. lxiii. and a long and curious fragment, without beginning or end, p. 288-305 [371-392]. The supreme pontiff derides the Mosaic history and the Christian discipline, prefers the Greek poets to the Hebrew prophets, and palliates, with the skill of a Jesuit, the *relative* worship of images.

their domestic garb ; their dignity, in the pomp of holy vest-
ments.   When they are summoned in their turn to officiate
before the altar, they ought not, during the appointed number
of days, to depart from the precincts of the temple ; nor should
a single day be suffered to elapse without the prayers and the
sacrifice, which they are obliged to offer for the prosperity of
the state and of individuals.   The exercise of their sacred
functions requires an immaculate purity, both of mind and
body ; and, even when they are dismissed from the temple to
the occupations of common life, it is incumbent on them to
excel in decency and virtue the rest of their fellow-citizens.
The priest of the gods should never be seen in theatres or
taverns.   His conversation should be chaste, his diet temperate,
his friends of honourable reputation ; and, if he sometimes
visits the Forum or the Palace, he should appear only as the
advocate of those who have vainly solicited either justice or
mercy.   His studies should be suited to the sanctity of his
profession.   Licentious tales, or comedies, or satires, must be
banished from his library ; which ought solely to consist of
historical and philosophical writings ; of history which is
founded in truth, and of philosophy which is connected with
religion.   The impious opinions of the Epicureans and Sceptics
deserve his abhorrence and contempt ; [39] but he should diligently
study the systems of Pythagoras, of Plato, and of the Stoics,
which unanimously teach that there *are* gods ; that the world
is governed by their providence ; that their goodness is the
source of every temporal blessing ; and that they have prepared
for the human soul a future state of reward or punishment."
The Imperial pontiff inculcates, in the most persuasive language,
the duties of benevolence and hospitality ; exhorts his inferior
clergy to recommend the universal practice of those virtues ;
promises to assist their indigence from the public treasury ; and
declares his resolution of establishing hospitals in every city,
where the poor should be received without any invidious distinction of country or of religion.   Julian beheld with envy the
wise and humane regulations of the church ; and he very frankly
confesses his intention to deprive the Christians of the applause,
as well as advantage, which they had acquired by the exclusive

[39] The exultation of Julian (p. 301) that these impious sects, and even their
writings, are extinguished may be consistent enough with the sacerdotal character :
but it is unworthy of a philosopher to wish that any opinions and arguments
the most repugnant to his own should be concealed from the knowledge of
mankind.

practice of charity and beneficence.[40] The same spirit of imitation might dispose the emperor to adopt several ecclesiastical institutions, the use and importance of which were approved by the success of his enemies. But, if these imaginary plans of reformation had been realized, the forced and imperfect copy would have been less beneficial to Paganism than honourable to Christianity.[41] The Gentiles, who peaceably followed the customs of their ancestors, were rather surprised than pleased with the introduction of foreign manners ; and, in the short period of his reign, Julian had frequent occasions to complain of the want of fervour of his own party.[42]

The enthusiasm of Julian prompted him to embrace the friends of Jupiter as his personal friends and brethren ; and, though he partially overlooked the merit of Christian constancy, he admired and rewarded the noble perseverance of those Gentiles who had preferred the favour of the gods to that of the emperor.[43] If they cultivated the literature, as well as the religion, of the Greeks, they acquired an additional claim to the friendship of Julian, who ranked the Muses in the number of his tutelar deities. In the religion which he had adopted, piety and learning were almost synonymous ;[44] and a crowd of poets, of rhetoricians, and of philosophers, hastened to the Imperial court, to occupy the vacant places of the bishops who had seduced the credulity of Constantius. His successor esteemed the ties of common initiation as far more sacred than those of

The philosophers

---

[40] Yet he insinuates that the Christians, under the pretence of charity, inveigled children from their religion and parents, conveyed them on ship-board, and devoted those victims to a life of poverty or servitude in a remote country (p. 305 [391]). Had the charge been proved, it was his duty, not to complain, but to punish. [It is very questionable whether Julian meant to insinuate this charge. He compares the conduct of the "Galilæans" in looking after the poor for the sake of proselytizing to that of kidnappers who inveigle children by giving them a cake ; the simile does not seem to be applied literally to the Christians.]

[41] Gregory Nazianzen is facetious, ingenious, and argumentative. Orat. iii. p. 101, 102, &c. [iv., c. 115 sqq.]. He ridicules the folly of such vain imitation ; and amuses himself with inquiring, what lessons, moral or theological, could be extracted from the Grecian fables.

[42] He accuses one of his pontiffs of a secret confederacy with the Christian bishops and presbyters. Epist. lxii [p. 583]. Ὁρῶν οὖν πολλὴν μὲν ὀλιγωρίαν οὖσαν ἡμῖν πρὸς τοὺς θεούς, and again, ἡμᾶς δὲ οὕτω ῥαθύμως, &c. Epist. lxiii [p. 587].

[43] He praises the fidelity of Callixene, priestess of Ceres, who had been twice as constant as Penelope, and rewards her with the priesthood of the Phrygian goddess at Pessinus. (Julian. Epist. xxi.) He applauds the firmness of Sopater of Hierapolis, who had been repeatedly pressed by Constantius and Gallus to apostatize. (Epist. xxvii. p. 401 [518].)

[44] Ὁ δὲ νομίζων ἀδελφὰ λόγους τε καὶ θεῶν ἱερά Orat. Parent. c. 77, p. 302. The same sentiment is frequently inculcated by Julian, Libanius, and the rest of their party.

consanguinity : he chose his favourites among the sages who were deeply skilled in the occult sciences of magic and divination ; and every impostor who pretended to reveal the secrets of futurity was assured of enjoying the present hour in honour and affluence.[45]   Among the philosophers, Maximus obtained the most eminent rank in the friendship of his royal disciple, who communicated, with unreserved confidence, his actions, his sentiments, and his religious designs, during the anxious suspense of the civil war.[46]   As soon as Julian had taken possession of the palace of Constantinople, he dispatched an honourable and pressing invitation to Maximus ; who then resided at Sardes in Lydia, with Chrysanthius, the associate of his art and studies. The prudent and superstitious Chrysanthius refused to undertake a journey which showed itself, according to the rules of divination, with the most threatening and malignant aspect: but his companion, whose fanaticism was of a bolder cast, persisted in his interrogations, till he had extorted from the gods a seeming consent to his own wishes and those of the emperor. The journey of Maximus through the cities of Asia displayed the triumph of philosophic vanity ; and the magistrates vied with each other in the honourable reception which they prepared for the friend of their sovereign. Julian was pronouncing an oration before the senate, when he was informed of the arrival of Maximus. The emperor immediately interrupted his discourse, advanced to meet him, and, after a tender embrace, conducted him by the hand into the midst of the assembly; where he publicly acknowledged the benefits which he had derived from the instructions of the philosopher. Maximus,[47] who soon acquired the confidence, and influenced the councils, of Julian, was insensibly corrupted by the temptations of a court. His dress became more splendid, his demeanour more lofty, and he was exposed, under a succeeding reign, to a disgraceful inquiry into the means by which the disciple of Plato had accumulated, in the short duration of his favour, a very scandalous proportion of wealth. Of the other philosophers and sophists, who were invited to the Imperial residence by the choice of Julian or by the success of Maximus,

[45] The curiosity and credulity of the emperor, who tried every mode of divination, are fairly exposed by Ammianus, xxii. 12.

[46] Julian. Epist. xxxviii. Three other epistles (xv. xvi. xxxix.) in the same style of friendship and confidence are addressed to the philosopher Maximus.

[47] Eunapius (in Maximo, p. 77, 78, 79, and in Chrysanthio, p. 147, 148) has minutely related these anecdotes, which he conceives to be the most important events of the age. Yet he fairly confesses the frailty of Maximus. His reception at Constantinople is described by Libanius (Orat. Parent. c. 86, p. 301) and Ammianus (xxii. 7).

few were able to preserve their innocence or their reputation.[48]
The liberal gifts of money, lands, and houses, were insufficient
to satiate their rapacious avarice; and the indignation of the
people was justly excited by the remembrance of their abject
poverty and disinterested professions. The penetration of
Julian could not always be deceived: but he was unwilling to
despise the characters of those men whose talents deserved his
esteem; he desired to escape the double reproach of imprudence
and inconstancy ; and he was apprehensive of degrading, in the
eyes of the profane, the honour of letters and of religion.[49]

The favour of Julian was almost equally divided between the   Conversions
Pagans, who had firmly adhered to the worship of their ancestors,
and the Christians, who prudently embraced the religion of
their sovereign. The acquisition of new proselytes[50] gratified
the ruling passions of his soul, superstition and vanity ; and he
was heard to declare with the enthusiasm of a missionary that, if
he could render each individual richer than Midas, and every
city greater than Babylon, he should not esteem himself the
benefactor of mankind, unless, at the same time, he could reclaim his subjects from their impious revolt against the immortal gods.[51] A prince, who had studied human nature, and
who possessed the treasures of the Roman empire, could adapt
his arguments, his promises, and his rewards, to every order
of Christians ; [52] and the merit of a seasonable conversion was
allowed to supply the defects of a candidate, or even to expiate
the guilt of a criminal. As the army is the most forcible engine

[48] Chrysanthius, who had refused to quit Lydia, was created high-priest of the
province. His cautious and temperate use of power secured him after the
revolution ; and he lived in peace ; while Maximus, Priscus, &c. were persecuted
by the Christian ministers. See the adventures of those fanatic sophists, collected
by Brucker, tom. ii. p. 281-293.

[49] See Libanius (Orat. Parent. c. 101, 102, p. 324, 325, 326) and Eunapius (Vit.
Sophist. in Proæresio, p. 126). Some students, whose expectations perhaps were
groundless or extravagant, retired in disgust. Greg. Naz. Orat. iv. p. 120. It
is strange that we should not be able to contradict the title of one of Tillemont's
chapters (Hist. des Empereurs, tom. iv. p. 960): "La Cour de Julien est pleine
de philosophes et de gens perdus ".

[50] Under the reign of Lewis XIV. his subjects of every rank aspired to the
glorious title of *Convertisseur*, expressive of their zeal and success in making
proselytes. The word and the idea are growing obsolete in France; may they
never be introduced into England !

[51] See the strong expressions of Libanius, which were probably those of Julian
himself. (Orat. Parent. c. 59, p. 285.)

[52] When Gregory Nazianzen (Orat. x. p. 167) is desirous to magnify the
Christian firmness of his brother Cæsarius, physician to the Imperial court, he
owns that Cæsarius disputed with a formidable adversary, πολὺν ἐν ὅπλοις, καὶ
μέγαν ἐν λόγων δεινότητι. In his invectives he scarcely allows any share of
wit or courage to the apostate.

of absolute power, Julian applied himself, with peculiar diligence, to corrupt the religion of his troops, without whose hearty concurrence every measure must be dangerous and unsuccessful; and the natural temper of soldiers made this conquest as easy as it was important. The legions of Gaul devoted themselves to the faith, as well as to the fortunes, of their victorious leader; and even before the death of Constantius, he had the satisfaction of announcing to his friends that they assisted with fervent devotion, and voracious appetite, at the sacrifices, which were repeatedly offered in his camp, of whole hecatombs of fat oxen.[53] The armies of the East, which had been trained under the standard of the cross, and of Constantius, required a more artful and expensive mode of persuasion. On the days of solemn and public festivals, the emperor received the homage, and rewarded the merits, of the troops. His throne of state was encircled with the military ensigns of Rome and the republic; the holy name of Christ was erased from the *Labarum*; and the symbols of war, of majesty, and of pagan superstition, were so dexterously blended, that the faithful subject incurred the guilt of idolatry, when he respectfully saluted the person or image of his sovereign. The soldiers passed successively in review; and each of them, before he received from the hand of Julian a liberal donative, proportioned to his rank and services, was required to cast a few grains of incense into the flame which burnt upon the altar. Some Christian confessors might resist, and others might repent; but the far greater number, allured by the prospect of gold and awed by the presence of the emperor, contracted the criminal engagement; and their future perseverance in the worship of the gods was enforced by every consideration of duty and of interest. By the frequent repetition of these arts, and at the expense of sums which would have purchased the service of half the nations of Scythia, Julian gradually acquired for his troops the imaginary protection of the gods, and for himself the firm and effectual support of the Roman legions.[54] It is indeed more than probable that the restoration and encouragement of Paganism revealed a multitude of pretended Christians, who, from

---

[53] Julian. Epist. xxxviii. Ammianus, xxii. 12 [6]. Adeo ut in dies pæne singulos milites carnis distentiore sagina victitantes incultius, potusque aviditate correpti [read, *corrupti*] humeris impositi transeuntium per plateas, ex publicis ædibus ... ad sua diversoria portarentur. The devout prince and the indignant historian describe the same scene; and in Illyricum or Antioch similar causes must have produced similar effects.

[54] Gregory (Orat. iii. p. 74, 75, 83-86 [iv., c. 65 *sqq.*, 82 *sqq.*]) and Libanius (Orat. Parent. c. lxxxi. lxxxii. p. 307, 308) περὶ ταύτην τὴν σπουδὴν, οὐκ ἀρνοῦμαι πλοῦτον ἀνηλῶσθαι μέγαν. The sophist owns and justifies the expense of these military conversions,

motives of temporal advantage, had acquiesced in the religion of the former reign; and who afterwards returned, with the same flexibility of conscience, to the faith which was professed by the successors of Julian.

While the devout monarch incessantly laboured to restore The Jews and propagate the religion of his ancestors, he embraced the extraordinary design of rebuilding the temple of Jerusalem. In a public epistle[55] to the nation or community of the Jews, dispersed through the provinces, he pities their misfortunes, condemns their oppressors, praises their constancy, declares himself their gracious protector, and expresses a pious hope that, after his return from the Persian war, he may be permitted to pay his grateful vows to the Almighty in his holy city of Jerusalem. The blind superstition and abject slavery of those unfortunate exiles must excite the contempt of a philosophic emperor; but they deserved the friendship of Julian by their implacable hatred of the Christian name. The barren synagogue abhorred and envied the fecundity of the rebellious church : the power of the Jews was not equal to their malice; but their gravest rabbis approved the private murder of an apostate;[56] and their seditious clamours had often awakened the indolence of the pagan magistrates. Under the reign of Constantine, the Jews became the subjects of their revolted children, nor was it long before they experienced the bitterness of domestic tyranny. The civil immunities which had been granted, or confirmed, by Severus were gradually repealed by the Christian princes; and a rash tumult excited by the Jews of Palestine[57] seemed to justify the lucrative modes of oppression, which were invented

[55] Julian's epistle (xxv) is addressed to the community o. the Jews. Aldus (Venet. 1499) has branded it with an εἰ γνήσιος ; but this stigma is justly removed by the subsequent editors, Petavius and Spanheim. The epistle is mentioned by Sozomen (l. v. c. 22), and the purport of it is confirmed by Gregory (Orat. iv. p. 111), and by Julian himself (Fragment. p. 295). [In a Syriac chronicle (early 6th cent.) a story is told that a number of Jews from Palestine met Julian at Tarsus, to ask leave to rebuild their Temple. As it was known that Julian objected to the Jewish monotheism, they exhibited seven idols to propitiate him, and offered incense on the altars of his heathen deities. He acceded to their request, but on their way home the Jews were murdered by Christian soldiers. See Hoffmann, Julianos der Abtrünnige, 1880 (Leiden).]

[56] The Misnah denounced death against those who abandoned the foundation. The judgment of zeal is explained by Marsham (Canon. Chron. p. 161, 162, edit. fol. London, 1672) and Basnage (Hist. des Juifs, tom. viii. p. 120). Constantine made a law to protect Christian converts from Judaism. Cod. Theod. l. xvi. tit. viii. leg. 1. Godefroy, tom. vi. p. 215.

[57] Et interea (during the civil war of Magnentius) Judæorum seditio, qui Patricium nefarie in regni speciem sustulerunt, oppressa. Aurelius Victor, in Constantio, c. xlii. See Tillemont, Hist. des Empereurs, tom. iv. p. 379 in 4to.

by the bishops and eunuchs of the court of Constantius. The Jewish patriarch, who was still permitted to exercise a precarious jurisdiction, held his residence at Tiberias;[58] and the neighbouring cities of Palestine were filled with the remains of a people who fondly adhered to the promised land. But the edict of Hadrian was renewed and enforced; and they viewed from afar the walls of the holy city, which were profaned in their eyes by the triumph of the cross and the devotion of the Christians.[59]

Jerusalem

In the midst of a rocky and barren country, the walls of Jerusalem[60] inclosed the two mountains of Sion and Acra, within an oval figure of about three English miles.[61] Towards the south, the upper town and the fortress of David were erected on the lofty ascent of Mount Sion: on the north side, the buildings of the lower town covered the spacious summit of Mount Acra; and a part of the hill, distinguished by the name of Moriah and levelled by human industry, was crowned with the stately temple of the Jewish nation. After the final destruction of the temple, by the arms of Titus and Hadrian, a ploughshare was drawn over the consecrated ground, as a sign of perpetual interdiction. Sion was deserted; and the vacant space of the lower city was filled with the public and private edifices of the Ælian colony, which spread themselves over the adjacent hill of Calvary. The holy places were polluted with monuments of idolatry; and, either from design or accident, a chapel was dedicated to Venus on the spot which had been sanctified by the death and resurrection of Christ.[62]

[The Sakhra Enclosure]

[58] The city and synagogue of Tiberias are curiously described by Reland, Palestin. tom. ii. p. 1036-1042.

[59] Basnage has fully illustrated the state of the Jews under Constantine and his successors (tom. viii. c. iv. p. 111-153). [Cp. Grätz, Ges. der Juden, iv., c. 19-21.]

[60] Reland (Palestin. l. i. p. 309, 390, l. iii. p. 838) describes, with learning and perspicuity, Jerusalem, and the face of the adjacent country. [See the article " Jerusalem " by Sir Charles Wilson, in the new ed. of Smith's Dictionary of the Bible; also the series of memoirs of the Palestine Exploration Fund; the " ordnance survey of Jerusalem," by Sir Charles Wilson, 1866. Cp. Appendix 23.]

[61] I have consulted a rare and curious treatise of M. d'Anville (sur l'ancienne Jérusalem, Paris, 1747, p. 75). The circumference of the ancient city (Euseb. Præparat. Evangel. l. ix. c. 36) was twenty-seven stadia, or 2550 *toises*. A plan taken on the spot assigns no more than 1980 for the modern town. The circuit is defined by natural land-marks which cannot be mistaken or removed. [Josephus (B. J. v. 4) gives 33 stadia; Sir C. Wilson calculates not more than 25. The dimensions of the modern town are about 1000 yards from E. to W. and the same from N. to S. A map showing the various theories as to the line of the old walls is given in the book of Mr. T. H. Lewis, The Holy Places of Jerusalem, 1888.]

[62] See two curious passages in Jerom (tom. i. p. 102, t. vi. p. 315), and the ample details of Tillemont (Hist. des Empereurs, tom. i. p. 569, tom. ii. p. 289, 294, 4to edition).

Almost three hundred years after those stupendous events, the profane chapel of Venus was demolished by the order of Constantine ; and the removal of the earth and stones revealed the holy sepulchre to the eyes of mankind. A magnificent church was erected on that mystic ground, by the first Christian emperor ; and the effects of his pious munificence were extended to every spot which had been consecrated by the footsteps of patriarchs, of prophets, and of the Son of God.[63]

The passionate desire of contemplating the original monu- Pilgrimages ments of their redemption attracted to Jerusalem a successive crowd of pilgrims, from the shores of the Atlantic ocean and the most distant countries of the East ;[64] and their piety was authorized by the example of the empress Helena, who appears to have united the credulity of age with the warm feelings of a recent conversion. Sages and heroes, who have visited the memorable scenes of ancient wisdom or glory, have confessed the inspiration of the genius of the place ;[65] and the Christian who knelt before the holy sepulchre ascribed his lively faith and his fervent devotion to the more immediate influence of the Divine spirit. The zeal, perhaps the avarice, of the clergy of Jerusalem cherished and multiplied these beneficial visits. They fixed, by unquestionable tradition, the scene of each memorable event. They exhibited the instruments which had been used in the passion of Christ ; the nails and the lance that had pierced his hands, his feet, and his side ; the crown of thorns that was planted on his head, the pillar at which he was scourged ; and, above all, they shewed the cross on which he suffered, and which was dug out of the earth in the reign of those princes who inserted the symbol of Christianity in the banners of the Roman legions.[66] Such miracles as seemed

---

[63] Eusebius, in Vit. Constantin. l. iii. c. 25-47, 51-53. The emperor likewise built churches at Bethlem, the Mount of Olives, and the oak of Mambre. The holy sepulchre is described by Sandys (Travels, p. 125-133), and curiously delineated by Le Bruyn (Voyage au Levant, p. 288-296). [For the churches of Constantine at Jerusalem, see the publication for 1891 of the Palestine Pilgrims' Text Soc., where the original sources are translated by Mr. J. H. Bernard. Cp. App. 23.]

[64] The Itinerary from Bourdeaux to Jerusalem was composed in the year 333, for the use of pilgrims ; among whom Jerom (tom. i. p. 126) mentions the Britons and the Indians. The causes of this superstitious fashion are discussed in the learned and judicious preface of Wesseling (Itin. p. 537-545). [A translation of this itinerary by Mr. A. Stewart is published by the Palestine Pilgrims' Text Soc., 1887.]

[65] Cicero (de Finibus, v. 1) has beautifully expressed the common sense of mankind.

[66] Baronius (Annal. Eccles. A.D. 326, No. 42-50) and Tillemont (Mém. Ecclés. tom. vii. p. 8-16) are the historians and champions of the miraculous *invention* of the cross, under the reign of Constantine. Their oldest witnesses are Paulinus,

necessary to account for its extraordinary preservation and seasonable discovery were gradually propagated without opposition. The custody of the *true cross,* which on Easter Sunday was solemnly exposed to the people, was entrusted to the bishop of Jerusalem; and he alone might gratify the curious devotion of the pilgrims, by the gift of small pieces, which they enchased in gold or gems, and carried away in triumph to their respective countries. But, as this gainful branch of commerce must soon have been annihilated, it was found convenient to suppose that the marvellous wood possessed a secret power of vegetation; and that its substance, though continually diminished, still remained entire and unimpaired.[67] It might perhaps have been expected that the influence of the place, and the belief of a perpetual miracle, should have produced some salutary effects on the morals as well as on the faith of the people. Yet the most respectable of the ecclesiastical writers have been obliged to confess, not only that the streets of Jerusalem were filled with the incessant tumult of business and pleasure,[68] but that every species of vice, adultery, theft, idolatry, poisoning, murder, was familiar to the inhabitants of the holy city.[69] The wealth and pre-eminence of the church of Jerusalem excited the ambition of Arian, as well as orthodox, candidates; and the virtues of Cyril, who, since his death, has been honoured with the title of Saint, were displayed in the exercise, rather than in the acquisition, of his episcopal dignity.[70]

Julian attempts to rebuild the temple

The vain and ambitious mind of Julian might aspire to restore the ancient glory of the temple of Jerusalem.[71] As the

Sulpicius Severus, Rufinus, Ambrose, and perhaps Cyril of Jerusalem. The silence of Eusebius and the Bourdeaux pilgrim, which satisfies those who think, perplexes those who believe. See Jortin's sensible remarks, vol. ii. p. 238-248. [Cp. App. 21.]

[67] This multiplication is asserted by Paulinus (epist. xxxvii. See Dupin, Biblioth. Ecclés. tom. iii. p. 149), who seems to have improved a rhetorical flourish of Cyril into a real fact. The same supernatural privilege must have been communicated to the Virgin's milk (Erasmi Opera, tom. i. p. 778. Lug. Bat. 1703, in Colloq. de Peregrinat. Religionis ergo), saints' heads, &c. and other relics, which were repeated in so many different churches.

[68] Jerom (tom. i. p. 103), who resided in the neighbouring village of Bethlem, describes the vices of Jerusalem from his personal experience.

[69] Gregor. Nyssen, apud Wesseling, p. 539. The whole epistle, which condemns either the use or the abuse of religious pilgrimage, is painful to the Catholic divines, while it is dear and familiar to our Protestant polemics.

[70] He renounced his orthodox ordination, officiated as a deacon, and was re-ordained by the hands of the Arians. But Cyril afterwards changed with the times, and prudently conformed to the Nicene faith. Tillemont (Mém. Ecclés. tom. viii.), who treats his memory with tenderness and respect, has thrown his virtues into the text, and his faults into the notes, in decent obscurity, at the end of the volume.

[71] Imperii sui memoriam magnitudine operum gestiens propagare. Ammian. xxiii. 1. The temple of Jerusalem had been famous even among the Gentiles.

Christians were firmly persuaded that a sentence of everlasting destruction had been pronounced against the whole fabric of the Mosaic law, the imperial sophist would have converted the success of his undertaking into a specious argument against the faith of the prophecy and the truth of revelation.[72] He was displeased with the spiritual worship of the synagogue; but he approved the institutions of Moses, who had not disdained to adopt many of the rites and ceremonies of Egypt.[73] The local and national deity of the Jews was sincerely adored by a polytheist who desired only to multiply the number of the gods;[74] and such was the appetite of Julian for bloody sacrifice that his emulation might be excited by the piety of Solomon, who had offered, at the feast of the dedication, twenty-two thousand oxen and one hundred and twenty thousand sheep.[75] These considerations might influence his designs; but the prospect of an immediate and important advantage would not suffer the impatient monarch to expect the remote and uncertain event of the Persian war. He resolved to erect, without delay, on the commanding eminence of Moriah, a stately temple which might eclipse the splendour of the church of the Resurrection on the adjacent hill of Calvary; to establish an order of priests, whose interested zeal would detect the arts, and resist the ambition, of their Christian rivals; and to invite a numerous colony of Jews, whose stern fanaticism would be always prepared to second, and even to anticipate, the hostile measures of the pagan government. Among the friends of the emperor (if the names of emperor and of friend are not incompatible) the first place was assigned, by Julian himself, to the

---

They had many temples in each city (at Sichem five, at Gaza eight, at Rome four hundred and twenty-four); but the wealth and religion of the Jewish nation was centered in one spot.

[72] The secret intentions of Julian are revealed by the late bishop of Gloucester, the learned and dogmatic Warburton; who, with the authority of a theologian, prescribes the motives and conduct of the Supreme Being. The discourse entitled *Julian* (2d edition, London, 1751) is strongly marked with all the peculiarities which are imputed to the Warburtonian school.

[73] I shelter myself behind Maimonides, Marsham, Spencer, Le Clerc, Warburton, &c. who have fairly derided the fears, the folly, and the falsehood of some superstitious divines. See Divine Legation, vol. iv. p. 25, &c.

[74] Julian (Fragment, p. 295) respectfully styles him μέγας θεός, and mentions him elsewhere (epist. lxiii) with still higher reverence. He doubly condemns the Christians: for believing and for renouncing the religion of the Jews. Their Deity was a *true*, but not the *only*, God. Apud Cyril. l. ix. p. 305, 306.

[75] 1 Kings, viii. 63. 2 Chronicles vii. 5. Joseph. Antiquitat. Judaic. l. viii. c. 4, p. 431, edit. Havercamp. As the blood and smoke of so many hecatombs might be inconvenient, Lightfoot, the Christian Rabbi, removes them by a miracle. Le Clerc (ad loca) is bold enough to suspect the fidelity of the numbers.

virtuous and learned Alypius.[76]   The humanity of Alypius was tempered by severe justice and manly fortitude ; and, while he exercised his abilities in the civil administration of Britain, he imitated, in his poetical compositions, the harmony and softness of the odes of Sappho.   This minister, to whom Julian communicated, without reserve, his most careless levities and his most serious counsels, received an extraordinary commission to restore, in its pristine beauty, the temple of Jerusalem ; and the diligence of Alypius required and obtained the strenuous support of the governor of Palestine.   At the call of their great deliverer, the Jews, from all the provinces of the empire, assembled on the holy mountain of their fathers ; and their insolent triumph alarmed and exasperated the Christian inhabitants of Jerusalem. The desire of rebuilding the temple has, in every age, been the ruling passion of the children of Israel.   In this propitious moment the men forgot their avarice, and the women their delicacy ; spades and pickaxes of silver were provided by the vanity of the rich, and the rubbish was transported in mantles of silk and purple.   Every purse was opened in liberal contributions, every hand claimed a share in the pious labour ; and the commands of a great monarch were executed by the enthusiasm of a whole people.[77]

The enterprise is defeated

Yet, on this occasion, the joint efforts of power and enthusiasm were unsuccessful ; and the ground of the Jewish temple, which is now covered by a Mahometan mosque,[78] still continued to exhibit the same edifying spectacle of ruin and desolation. Perhaps the absence and death of the emperor, and the new maxims of a Christian reign, might explain the interruption of an arduous work, which was attempted only in the last six months of the life of Julian.[79]   But the Christians entertained

---

[76] Julian, epist. xxix. xxx.   La Blèterie has neglected to translate the second of these epistles.

[77] See the zeal and impatience of the Jews in Gregory Nazianzen (Orat. iv. p. III [v., c. 4]) and Theodoret (l. iii. c. 20).

[78] Built by Omar, the second Khalif, who died A.D. 644.   This great mosque covers the whole consecrated ground of the Jewish temple, and constitutes almost a square of 760 *toises*, or one Roman mile in circumference.   See d'Anville, Jérusalem, p. 45.

[79] Ammianus records the consuls of the year 363, before he proceeds to mention the *thoughts* of Julian.   Templum . . . instaurare sumptibus *cogitabat* immodicis. Warburton has a secret wish to anticipate the design ; but he must have understood, from former examples, that the execution of such a work would have demanded many years.   [An examination of the evidence,—especially of Julian's own statement (ep. 25, p. 514, l. 8) that he intends to rebuild Jerusalem when he has finished the Persian War (διορθωσάμενος)—leads us to believe that the work of building was never even begun.   The whole story seems to have been (as Dr. Adler concludes in his full discussion of the subject, *Jewish Quarterly Review*, 1893, p. 615

a natural and pious expectation that, in this memorable contest, the honour of religion would be vindicated by some signal miracle. An earthquake, a whirlwind, and a fiery eruption, which overturned and scattered the new foundations of the temple, are attested, with some variations, by contemporary and respectable evidence.[80] This public event is described by Ambrose,[81] bishop of Milan, in an epistle to the emperor Theodosius, which must provoke the severe animadversion of the Jews; by the eloquent Chrysostom,[82] who might appeal to the memory of the elder part of his congregation at Antioch; and by Gregory Nazianzen,[83] who published his account of the miracle before the expiration of the same year. The last of these writers has boldly declared that this preternatural event was not disputed by the infidels; and his assertion, strange as it may seem, is confirmed by the unexceptionable testimony of Ammianus Marcellinus.[84] The philosophic soldier, who loved the virtues, without adopting the prejudices, of his master, has recorded, in his judicious and candid history of his own times, the extraordinary obstacles which interrupted the restoration of the temple of Jerusalem. "Whilst Alypius, assisted by the governor of the province, urged with vigour and diligence the execution of the work, horrible balls of fire breaking out near

perhaps by a preternatural event

---

sqq.) a deliberate fiction of Gregory Nazianzen, from whose Invective against Julian it passed into Ambrose, Chrysostom, and then (embellished with contradictions) into the ecclesiastical historians Socrates, &c. (see next notes). Ammianus, who liked a miracle, can have got the tale from the same source. Dr. Adler has disposed of the late Jewish authorities who are mustered in Wagenseil's *Tela Ignea Satanae.*]

[80] The subsequent witnesses, Socrates, Sozomen, Theodoret, Philostorgius, &c. add contradictions rather than authority. Compare the objections of Basnage (Hist. des Juifs, tom. viii. p. 157-168) with Warburton's answer (Julian, p. 174-258). The bishop has ingeniously explained the miraculous crosses which appeared on the garments of the spectators by a similar instance, and the natural effects of lightning.

[81] Ambros. tom. ii. epist. xl. p. 946, edit. Benedictin. He composed this fanatic epistle (A.D. 388) to justify a bishop, who had been condemned by the civil magistrate for burning a synagogue.

[82] Chrysostom, tom. i. p. 580, advers. Judæos et Gentes; tom. ii. p. 574, de Sancto Babylâ, edit. Montfaucon. I have followed the common and natural supposition; but the learned Benedictine, who dates the composition of these sermons in the year 383, is confident they were never pronounced from the pulpit.

[83] Greg. Nazianzen, Orat. iv. p. 110-113 [v., c. 2 *sqq.*]. Τὸ δὲ οὖν περιβόητον πᾶσι θαῦμα, καὶ οὐδὲ τοῖς ἀθέοις αὐτοῖς ἀπιστούμενον λέξων ἔρχομαι.

[84] Ammian. xxiii. 1. Cum itaque rei fortiter instaret Alypius, juvaretque provinciæ rector, metuendi globi flammarum prope fundamenta crebris assultibus erumpentes fecere locum exustis aliquoties operantibus inaccessum: hocque modo elemento destinatius repellente, cessavit inceptum. Warburton labours (p. 60-90) to extort a confession of the miracle from the mouths of Julian and Libanius, and to employ the evidence of a rabbi who lived in the fifteenth century. Such witnesses can only be received by a very favourable judge.

the foundations with frequent and reiterated attacks, rendered the place, from time to time, inaccessible to the scorched and blasted workmen; and, the victorious element continuing in this manner obstinately and resolutely bent, as it were, to drive them to a distance, the undertaking was abandoned." Such authority should satisfy a believing, and must astonish an incredulous, mind. Yet a philosopher may still require the original evidence of impartial and intelligent spectators. At this important crisis, any singular accident of nature would assume the appearance, and produce the effects, of a real prodigy. This glorious deliverance would be speedily improved and magnified by the pious art of the clergy of Jerusalem and the active credulity of the Christian world; and, at the distance of twenty years, a Roman historian, careless of theological disputes, might adorn his work with the specious and splendid miracle.[85]

Partiality of Julian

The restoration of the Jewish temple was secretly connected with the ruin of the Christian church. Julian still continued to maintain the freedom of religious worship, without distinguishing whether this universal toleration proceeded from his justice or his clemency. He affected to pity the unhappy Christians, who were mistaken in the most important object of their lives; but his pity was degraded by contempt, his contempt was embittered by hatred; and the sentiments of Julian were expressed in a style of sarcastic wit, which inflicts a deep and deadly wound whenever it issues from the mouth of a sovereign. As he was sensible that the Christians gloried in the name of their Redeemer, he countenanced, and perhaps enjoined, the use of the less honourable appellation of GALILÆANS.[86] He declared that, by the folly of the Galilæans, whom he describes as a sect of fanatics, contemptible to men, and odious to the gods, the empire had been reduced to the brink of destruction; and he insinuates in a public edict that a frantic patient might sometimes be cured by salutary violence.[87] An ungenerous

---

[85] Dr. Lardner, perhaps alone of the Christian critics, presumes to doubt the truth of this famous miracle (Jewish and Heathen Testimonies, vol. iv. p. 47-71). The silence of Jerom would lead to a suspicion that the same story, which was celebrated at a distance, might be despised on the spot. [Dr. Adler (loc. cit.) also notices the silence of Prudentius, Orosius (7, 30) and the two Cyrils.]

[86] Greg. Naz. Orat. iii. p. 81. And this law was confirmed by the invariable practice of Julian himself. Warburton has justly observed (p. 35) that the Platonists believed in the mysterious virtue of words; and Julian's dislike for the name of Christ might proceed from superstition, as well as from contempt.

[87] Fragment. Julian. p. 288 [371, ed. Hertl.]. He derides the μωρία Γαλιλαίων (epist. vii), and so far loses sight of the principles of toleration as to wish (epist. xlii) ἄκοντας ἰᾶσθαι.

distinction was admitted into the mind and counsels of Julian, that, according to the difference of their religious sentiments, one part of his subjects deserved his favour and friendship, while the other was entitled only to the common benefits that his justice could not refuse to an obedient people.[88]   According to a principle, pregnant with mischief and oppression, the emperor transferred to the pontiffs of his own religion the management of the liberal allowances from the public revenue which had been granted to the church by the piety of Constantine and his sons.   The proud system of clerical honours and immunities, which had been constructed with so much art and [A.D 362] labour, was levelled to the ground ; the hopes of testamentary donations were intercepted by the rigour of the laws ; and the priests of the Christian sect were confounded with the last and most ignominious class of the people.   Such of these regulations as appeared necessary to check the ambition and avarice of the ecclesiastics were soon afterwards imitated by the wisdom of an orthodox prince.   The peculiar distinctions which policy has bestowed, or superstition has lavished, on the sacerdotal order *must* be confined to those priests who profess the religion of the state.   But the will of the legislator was not exempt from prejudice and passion ; and it was the object of the insidious policy of Julian to deprive the Christians of all the temporal honours and advantages which rendered them respectable in the eyes of the world.[89]

A just and severe censure has been inflicted on the law which He prohibits prohibited the Christians from teaching the arts of grammar the Christians from teaching and rhetoric.[90]   The motives alleged by the emperor to justify schools [17th June, this partial and oppressive measure might command, during his A.D. 362] lifetime, the silence of slaves and the applause of flatterers. Julian abuses the ambiguous meaning of a word which might be indifferently applied to the language and the religion of the GREEKS : he contemptuously observes that the men who exalt

---

88 Οὐ γάρ μοι θέμις ἐστὶ κομιζέμεν ἢ ἐλεαίρειν.

"Ἄνδρας [*leg.* ἀνέρας] οἵ κε θεοῖσιν ἀπεχθωνντ' ἀθανάτοισιν.

These two lines, which Julian has changed and perverted in the true spirit of a bigot (Epist. xlix), are taken from the speech of Æolus, when he refuses to grant Ulysses a fresh supply of winds (Odyss. x. 73).   Libanius (Orat. Parental. c. lix. p. 286) attempts to justify this partial behaviour by an apology in which persecution peeps through the mask of candour.

89 These laws which affected the clergy may be found in the slight hints of Julian himself (Epist. lii), in the vague declamations of Gregory (Orat. iii. p. 86, 87), and in the positive assertions of Sozomen (l. v. c. 5).   [See Cod. Theod. 12, 1, 50.]

90 Inclemens . . . perenni obruendum silentio.   Ammian. xxii. 10, xxv. 5.

the merit of implicit faith are unfit to claim or to enjoy the advantages of science ; and he vainly contends that, if they refuse to adore the gods of Homer and Demosthenes, they ought to content themselves with expounding Luke and Matthew in the churches of the Galilæans.[91]   In all the cities of the Roman world, the education of the youth was entrusted to masters of grammar and rhetoric ; who were elected by the magistrates, maintained at the public expense, and distinguished by many lucrative and honourable privileges.   The edict of Julian appears to have included the physicians, and professors of all the liberal arts ; and the emperor, who reserved to himself the approbation of the candidates, was authorized by the laws to corrupt, or to punish, the religious constancy of the most learned of the Christians.[92]   As soon as the resignation of the more obstinate[93] teachers had established the unrivalled dominion of the Pagan sophists, Julian invited the rising generation to resort with freedom to the public schools, in a just confidence that their tender minds would receive the impressions of literature and idolatry.   If the greatest part of the Christian youth should be deterred by their own scruples, or by those of their parents, from accepting this dangerous mode of instruction, they must at the same time relinquish the benefits of a liberal education. Julian had reason to expect that, in the space of a few years, the church would relapse into its primæval simplicity, and that the theologians, who possessed an adequate share of the learning and eloquence of the age, would be succeeded by a generation of blind and ignorant fanatics, incapable of defending the truth of their own principles or of exposing the various follies of Polytheism.[94]

[91] The edict itself, which is still extant among the epistles of Julian (xlii.), may be compared with the loose invectives of Gregory (Orat. iii. p. 96).   Tillemont (Mém. Ecclés. t. vii. p. 1291-1294) has collected the seeming differences of ancients and moderns.   They may be easily reconciled.   The Christians were *directly* forbid to teach, they were *indirectly* forbid to learn ; since they would not frequent the schools of the Pagans.

[92] Codex Theodos. l. xiii. tit. iii. de medicis et professoribus, leg. 5 (published the 17th June, received, at Spoleto in Italy, the 29th of July, A.D. 363), with Godefroy's Illustrations, tom. v. p. 31.

[93] Orosius celebrates their disinterested resolution, Sicut a majoribus nostris compertum habemus, omnes ubique propemodum . . . . officium quam fidem deserere maluerunt, vii. 30.   Proæresius, a Christian sophist, refused to accept the partial favour of the emperor, Hieronym. in Chron. p. 185, edit. Scaliger.   Eunapius in Proæresio. p. 126.

[94] They had recourse to the expedient of composing books for their own schools.   Within a few months Apollinaris produced his Christian imitations of Homer (a sacred history in xxiv books), Pindar, Euripides, and Menander ; and Sozomen is satisfied that they equalled, or excelled, the originals.

It was undoubtedly the wish and the design of Julian to deprive the Christians of the advantages of wealth, of knowledge, and of power; but the injustice of excluding them from all offices of trust and profit seems to have been the result of his general policy rather than the immediate consequence of any positive law.[95] Superior merit might deserve, and obtain, some extraordinary exceptions; but the greater part of the Christian officers were gradually removed from their employments in the state, the army, and the provinces. The hopes of future candidates were extinguished by the declared partiality of a prince who maliciously reminded them that it was unlawful for a Christian to use the sword either of justice or war; and who studiously guarded the camp and the tribunals with the ensigns of idolatry. The powers of government were entrusted to the Pagans, who professed an ardent zeal for the religion of their ancestors; and, as the choice of the emperor was often directed by the rules of divination, the favourites whom he preferred as the most agreeable to the gods did not always obtain the approbation of mankind.[96] Under the administration of their enemies, the Christians had much to suffer, and more to apprehend. The temper of Julian was averse to cruelty; and the care of his reputation, which was exposed to the eyes of the universe, restrained the philosophic monarch from violating the laws of justice and toleration which he himself had so recently established. But the provincial ministers of his authority were placed in a less conspicuous station. In the exercise of arbitrary power, they consulted the wishes, rather than the commands, of their sovereign; and ventured to exercise a secret and vexatious tyranny against the sectaries, on whom they were not permitted to confer the honours of martyrdom. The emperor, who dissembled as long as possible his knowledge of the injustice that was exercised in his name, expressed his real sense of the conduct of his officers by gentle reproofs and substantial rewards.[97]

The most effectual instrument of oppression with which they

Disgrace and oppression of the Christians

They are condemned to restore the Pagan temples

---

[95] It was the instruction of Julian to his magistrates (Epist. vii) προτιμᾶσθαι μεν τοι τοὺς θεοσεβεῖς καὶ πάνυ φημὶ δεῖν. Sozomen (l. v. c. 18) and Socrates (l. iii. c. 13) must be reduced to the standard of Gregory (Orat. iii. p. 95), not less prone to exaggeration, but more restrained by the actual knowledge of his contemporary readers.

[96] Ψήφῳ θεῶν καὶ διδοὺς καὶ μὴ διδούς. Libanius, Orat. Parent. c. 88, p. 314.

[97] Greg. Naz. Orat. iii. p. 74, 91, 92. Socrates, l. iii. c. 14. Theodoret, l. iii. c. 6. Some drawback may however be allowed for the violence of *their* zeal, not less partial than the zeal of Julian. [On Julian's persecutions, compare Mr. Gwatkin's Arianism, p. 215 *sqq*.]

were armed was the law that obliged the Christians to make full
and ample satisfaction for the temples which they had destroyed under the preceding reign.   The zeal of the triumphant
church had not always expected the sanction of the public
authority ; and the bishops, who were secure of impunity, had
often marched, at the head of their congregations, to attack and
demolish the fortresses of the prince of darkness.   The consecrated lands, which had increased the patrimony of the sovereign or of the clergy, were clearly defined, and easily restored.
But on these lands, and on the ruins of Pagan superstition, the
Christians had frequently erected their own religious edifices :
and, as it was necessary to remove the church before the
temple could be rebuilt, the justice and piety of the emperor
were applauded by one party, while the other deplored and
execrated his sacrilegious violence.[98]   After the ground was
cleared, the restitution of those stately structures which had
been levelled with the dust and of the precious ornaments which
had been converted to Christian uses swelled into a very large
account of damages and debt.   The authors of the injury had
neither the ability nor the inclination to discharge this accumulated demand : and the impartial wisdom of a legislator would
have been displayed in balancing the adverse claims and complaints, by an equitable and temperate arbitration.   But the
whole empire, and particularly the East, was thrown into confusion by the rash edicts of Julian ; and the Pagan magistrates,
inflamed by zeal and revenge, abused the rigorous privilege of
the Roman law, which substitutes, in the place of his inadequate
property, the person of the insolvent debtor.   Under the preceding reign, Mark, bishop of Arethusa,[99] had laboured in the
conversion of his people with arms more effectual than those
of persuasion.[100]   The magistrates required the full value of a

[98] If we compare the gentle language of Libanius (Orat. Parent. c. 60, p. 286)
with the passionate exclamations of Gregory (Orat. iii. p. 86, 87), we may find it
difficult to persuade ourselves that the two orators are really describing the same
events.

[99] Restan, or Arethusa, at the equal distance of sixteen miles between Emesa
(*Hems*) and Epiphania (*Hamath*), was founded, or at least named, by Seleucus
Nicator.   Its peculiar æra dates from the year of Rome 685 according to the
medals of the city.   In the decline of the Seleucides, Emesa and Arethusa were
usurped by the Arab Sampsiceramus, whose posterity, the vassals of Rome, were
not extinguished in the reign of Vespasian.   See d'Anville's Maps and Géographie
Ancienne, tom. ii. p. 134.   Wesseling. Itineraria, p 188, and Noris. Epoch. Syro-
Macedon. p. 80, 481, 482.

[100] Sozomen, l. v. c. 10.   It is surprising that Gregory and Theodoret should
suppress a circumstance which, in their eyes, must have enhanced the religious
merit of the confessor.

temple which had been destroyed by his intolerant zeal: but, as they were satisfied of his poverty, they desired only to bend his inflexible spirit to the promise of the slightest compensation. They apprehended the aged prelate, they inhumanly scourged [A.D. 362] him, they tore his beard; and his naked body, anointed with honey, was suspended in a net between heaven and earth, and exposed to the stings of insects and the rays of a Syrian sun.[101] From this lofty station, Mark still persisted to glory in his crime and to insult the impotent rage of his persecutors. He was at length rescued from their hands, and dismissed to enjoy the honour of his divine triumph. The Arians celebrated the virtue of their pious confessor; the Catholics ambitiously claimed his alliance;[102] and the Pagans, who might be susceptible of shame or remorse, were deterred from the repetition of such unavailing cruelty.[103] Julian spared his life: but, if the bishop of Arethusa had saved the infancy of Julian,[104] posterity will condemn the ingratitude, instead of praising the clemency, of the emperor.

At the distance of five miles from Antioch, the Macedonian kings of Syria had consecrated to Apollo one of the most elegant places of devotion in the Pagan world.[105] A magnificent temple rose in honour of the god of light; and his colossal figure [106] almost filled the capacious sanctuary, which was enriched with gold and gems, and adorned by the skill of the Grecian artists. The

The temple and sacred grove of Daphne

---

[101] The sufferings and constancy of Mark, which Gregory has so tragically painted |Orat. iii. p. 88-91[iv., c. 88 *sqq.*].), are confirmed by the unexceptionable and reluctant evidence of Libanius. Μάρκος ἐκεῖνος κρεμάμενος, καὶ μαστιγούμενος, καὶ τοῦ πώγωνος αὐτῷ τιλλομένου πάντα ἐνεγκὼν ἀνδρείως νῦν ἰσόθεός ἐστι ταῖς τιμαῖς, κἂν φανῇ που περιμάχητος εὐθύς. Epist. 730, p. 350, 351, edit. Wolf. Amstel. 1738.

[102] Περιμάχητος, certatim eum sibi (Christiani) vindicant. It is thus that La Croze and Wolfius (ad loc.) have explained a Greek word whose true signification had been mistaken by former interpreters, and even by Le Clerc (Bibliothèque Ancienne et Moderne, tom. iii. p. 371). Yet Tillemont is strangely puzzled to understand (Mém. Ecclés. tom. vii. p. 1309) *how* Gregory and Theodoret could mistake a Semi-Arian bishop for a saint.

[103] See the probable advice of Sallust (Greg. Nazianzen, Orat. iii. 90, 91). Libanius intercedes for a similar offender, lest they should find many *Marks ;* yet he allows that, if Orion had secreted the consecrated wealth, he deserved to suffer the punishment of Marsyas: to be flayed alive (Epist. 730, p. 349-551).

[104] Gregory (Orat. iii. p. 90 [iv., c. 91]) is satisfied that, by saving the apostate, Mark had deserved still more than he had suffered.

[105] The grove and temple of Daphne are described by Strabo (l. xvi. p. 1089, 1090, edit. Amstel. 1707), Libanius (Nenia, p. 185, 188, Antiochic. Orat. xi. p. 380, 381), and Sozomen (l. v. c. 19). Wesseling (Itinerar. p. 581) and Casaubon (ad Hist. August. p. 64) illustrate this curious subject.

[106] Simulacrum in eo Olympiaci Jovis imitamenti æquiparans magnitudinem. Ammian. xxii. 13. The Olympic Jupiter was sixty feet high, and his bulk was consequently equal to that of a thousand men. See a curious *Mémoire* of the Abbé Gedoyn (Académie des Inscriptions, tom. ix. p. 198).

deity was represented in a bending attitude, with a golden cup in his hand, pouring out a libation on the earth ; as if he supplicated the venerable mother to give to his arms the cold and beauteous DAPHNE : for the spot was ennobled by fiction ; and the fancy of the Syrian poets had transported the amorous tale from the banks of the Peneus to those of the Orontes. The ancient rites of Greece were imitated by the royal colony of Antioch. A stream of prophecy, which rivalled the truth and reputation of the Delphic oracle, flowed from the *Castalian* fountain of Daphne.[107] In the adjacent fields a stadium was built by a special privilege,[108] which had been purchased from Elis ; the Olympic games were celebrated at the expense of the city ; and a revenue of thirty thousand pounds sterling was annually applied to the public pleasures.[109] The perpetual resort of pilgrims and spectators insensibly formed, in the neighbourhood of the temple, the stately and populous village of Daphne, which emulated the splendour, without acquiring the title, of a provincial city. The temple and the village were deeply bosomed in a thick grove of laurels and cypresses, which reached as far as a circumference of ten miles, and formed in the most sultry summers a cool and impenetrable shade. A thousand streams of the purest water, issuing from every hill, preserved the verdure of the earth and the temperature of the air ; the senses were gratified with harmonious sounds and aromatic odours ; and the peaceful grove was consecrated to health and joy, to luxury and love. The vigorous youth pursued, like Apollo, the object of his desires ; and the blushing maid was warned, by the fate of Daphne, to shun the folly of unseasonable coyness. The soldier and the philosopher wisely avoided the temptation of this sensual paradise ; [110] where pleasure, assuming the character of religion,

[107] Hadrian read the history of his future fortunes on a leaf dipped in the Castalian stream ; a trick which, according to the physician Vandale (De Oraculis, p. 281, 282), might be easily performed by chemical preparations. The emperor stopped the source of such dangerous knowledge ; which was again opened by the devout curiosity of Julian.

[108] It was purchased, A.D. 44, in the year 92 of the æra of Antioch (Noris. Epoch. Syro-Maced. p. 139-174) for the term of ninety Olympiads. But the Olympic games of Antioch were not regularly celebrated till the reign of Commodus. [Rather, Caracalla, 212 A.D. ; see Clinton, Fasti Rom.] See the curious details in the Chronicle of John Malala (tom. i. p. 293, 320, 372-381), a writer whose merit and authority are confined within the limits of his native city.

[109] Fifteen talents of gold, bequeathed by Sosibius, who died in the reign of Augustus. The theatrical merits of the Syrian cities, in the age of Constantine, are compared in the Expositio totius Mundi, p. 6 (Hudson, Geograph. Minor, tom. iii.).

[110] Avidio Cassio Syriacos legiones dedi luxuriâ diffluentes et *Daphnicis* moribus. These are the words of the emperor Marcus Antoninus in an original letter preserved by his biographer in Hist. August. p. 41 [vi. 6]. Cassius dismissed or punished every soldier who was seen at Daphne.

imperceptibly dissolved the firmness of manly virtue. But the groves of Daphne continued for many ages to enjoy the veneration of natives and strangers; the privileges of the holy ground were enlarged by the munificence of succeeding emperors; and every generation added new ornaments to the splendour of the temple.[111]

When Julian, on the day of the annual festival, hastened to adore the Apollo of Daphne, his devotion was raised to the highest pitch of eagerness and impatience. His lively imagination anticipated the grateful pomp of victims, of libations, and of incense; a long procession of youths and virgins, clothed in white robes, the symbol of their innocence; and the tumultuous concourse of an innumerable people. But the zeal of Antioch was diverted, since the reign of Christianity, into a different channel. Instead of hecatombs of fat oxen sacrificed by the tribes of a wealthy city to their tutelar deity, the emperor complains that he found only a single goose, provided at the expense of a priest, the pale and solitary inhabitant of this decayed temple.[112] The altar was deserted, the oracle had been reduced to silence, and the holy ground was profaned by the introduction of Christian and funereal rites. After Babylas [113]

---

[111] Aliquantum agrorum Daphnensibus dedit (*Pompey*), quo lucus ibi spatiosior fieret; delectatus amœnitate loci et aquarum abundantiâ. Eutropius, vi. 14. Sextus Rufus, de Provinciis, c. 16.

[112] Julian (Misopogon, p. 361, 362) discovers his own character with that *naïveté*, that unconscious simplicity, which always constitutes genuine humour.

[113] Babylas is named by Eusebius in the succession of the bishops of Antioch (Hist. Eccles. l. vi. c. 29, 39). His triumph over two emperors (the first fabulous, the second historical) is diffusely celebrated by Chrysostom (tom. ii. p. 536-579, edit. Montfaucon). Tillemont (Mém. Ecclés. t. iii. part ii. p. 287-302, 459-465) becomes almost a sceptic. [The history of the remains of Babylas is told, accurately for the most part, by Tillemont, and has been fully discussed by Bishop Lightfoot (in Apostolic Fathers, part ii. vol i. p. 41 *sqq.*), who uncovers a nest of errors in the account of Gibbon. (1) From Sozomen, v. 20, it is clear that persecutions intervened between the procession and the outbreak of the fire. Consequently Tillemont and Gibbon are wrong in stating that the fire broke out "during the night which terminated this indiscreet procession"—a false inference from Amm. xxii. 13 (Lightfoot p. 43, n. 5). (2) Gibbon seems to confound Theodorus, a young man mentioned by Rufinus, x. 36 (to whom he was known) and Socrates, 3, 19, with the presbyter and martyr Theodoret put to death by Julian's uncle, Count Julian (Soz. v. 8; Ruinart, Acta Mart. Sinc. p. 605 *sqq.*). (3) Ammian's expression *levissimus rumor* relates not to the charge against Christians, but to the story that the fire was accidentally caused by the philosopher Asclepiades. Gibbon wrongly connected *hac ex causa* with the preceding sentence: Amm. 22, 13, 3. (4) Babylas, removed by Julian's orders, was placed in his former *martyrium* within the city (Chrysostom, ii. 564-5); soon afterwards a splendid church was built in his honour, outside the city on the other side of the Orontes, and his bones were placed in it, during the bishopric of Meletius, who died 381 A.D. (Chrys. de Hier. Bab. p. 535). Gibbon apparently confounds the martyrium in Daphne with this new church, when he says "A magnificent church

(a bishop of Antioch, who died in prison in the persecution of Decius) had rested near a century in his grave, his body, by the order of the Cæsar Gallus, was transported into the midst of the grove of Daphne. A magnificent church was erected over his remains; a portion of the sacred lands was usurped for the maintenance of the clergy, and for the burial of the Christians of Antioch who were ambitious of lying at the feet of their bishop; and the priests of Apollo retired, with their affrighted and indignant votaries. As soon as another revolution seemed to restore the fortune of Paganism, the church of St. Babylas was demolished, and new buildings were added to the mouldering edifice which had been raised by the piety of Syrian kings. But the first and most serious care of Julian was to deliver his oppressed deity from the odious presence of the dead and living Christians who had so effectually suppressed the voice of fraud or enthusiasm.[114] The scene of infection was purified, according to the forms of ancient rituals; the bodies were decently removed; and the ministers of the church were permitted to convey the remains of St. Babylas to their former habitation within the walls of Antioch. The modest behaviour which might have assuaged the jealousy of an hostile government was neglected on this occasion by the zeal of the Christians. The lofty car that transported the relics of Babylas was followed, and accompanied, and received, by an innumerable multitude; who chanted, with thundering acclamations, the Psalms of David the most expressive of their contempt for idols and idolaters. The return of the saint was a triumph; and the triumph was an insult on the religion of the emperor, who exerted his pride to dissemble his resentment. During the night which terminated this indiscreet procession, the temple of Daphne was in flames; the statue of Apollo was consumed; and the walls of the edifice were left a naked and awful monument of ruin. The Christians of Antioch asserted, with religious confidence, that the powerful intercession of St. Babylas had pointed the lightnings of heaven against the devoted roof: but, as Julian was reduced to the alternative of believing either a crime or a miracle, he chose,

Removal of the dead bodies, and conflagration of the temple

[A.D. 362, 22nd Oct.]

was erected over his remains". (5) "The church of St. Babylas was subsequently demolished" is inconsistent with Chrysostom's statement (p. 565) that the martyrium in Daphne was left standing after the fire.]

[114] Ecclesiastical critics, particularly those who love relics, exult in the confession of Julian (Misopogon, p. 361) and Libanius (Nenia, p. 185), that Apollo was disturbed by the vicinity of *one* dead man. Yet Ammianus (xxii. 12) clears and purifies the whole ground, according to the rites which the Athenians formerly practised in the isle of Delos.

without hesitation, without evidence, but with some colour of probability, to impute the fire of Daphne to the revenge of the Galilæans.[115]   Their offence, had it been sufficiently proved, might have justified the retaliation which was immediately executed by the order of Julian, of shutting the doors, and confiscating the wealth, of the cathedral of Antioch.   To discover the criminals who were guilty of the tumult, of the fire, or of secreting the riches of the church, several ecclesiastics were tortured; [116] and a presbyter, of the name of Theodoret, was beheaded by the sentence of the Count of the East.   But this hasty act was blamed by the emperor; who lamented, with real or affected concern, that the imprudent zeal of his ministers would tarnish his reign with the disgrace of persecution.[117]

Julian shuts the cathedral of Antioch

The zeal of the ministers of Julian was instantly checked by the frown of their sovereign; but, when the father of his country declares himself the leader of a faction, the licence of popular fury cannot easily be restrained nor consistently punished. Julian, in a public composition, applauds the devotion and loyalty of the holy cities of Syria, whose pious inhabitants had destroyed, at the first signal, the sepulchres of the Galilæans; and faintly complains that they had revenged the injuries of the gods with less moderation than he should have recommended.[118]   This imperfect and reluctant confession may appear to confirm the ecclesiastical narratives: that in the cities of Gaza, Ascalon, Cæsarea, Heliopolis, &c. the Pagans abused, without prudence or remorse, the moment of their prosperity; that the unhappy objects of their cruelty were released from torture only by death; that, as their mangled bodies were dragged through the streets, they were pierced (such was the universal rage) by the spits of cooks and the distaffs of enraged women; and that the entrails of Christian priests and virgins, after they had been tasted by those bloody fanatics, were mixed with barley, and contemptuously thrown to the unclean animals

---

[115] Julian (in Misopogon, p. 361) rather insinuates than affirms their guilt. Ammianus (xxii. 13) treats the imputation as *levissimus rumor*, and relates the story with extraordinary candour.   [See above, p. 467, n. 113.]

[116] Quo non atroci casû repente consumpto, ad id usque imperatoris ira provexit, ut quæstiones agitare juberet solito acriores (yet Julian blames the lenity of the magistrates of Antioch), et majorem ecclesiam Antiochiæ claudi.   This interdiction was performed with some circumstances of indignity and profanation: and the seasonable death of the principal actor, Julian's uncle, is related with much superstitious complacency by the Abbé de la Blèterie.   Vie de Julien, p. 362-369.

[117] Besides the ecclesiastical historians, who are more or less to be suspected, we may allege the passion of St. Theodore, in the Acta Sincera of Ruinart, p. 591. The complaint of Julian gives it an original and authentic air.

[118] Julian, Misopogon, p. 361.

of the city.[119] Such scenes of religious madness exhibit the most contemptible and odious picture of human nature; but the massacre of Alexandria attracts still more attention, from the certainty of the fact, the rank of the victims, and the splendour of the capital of Egypt.

George of Cappadocia

George,[120] from his parents or his education surnamed the Cappadocian, was born at Epiphania in Cilicia, in a fuller's shop. From this obscure and servile origin he raised himself by the talents of a parasite: and the patrons, whom he assiduously flattered, procured for their worthless dependent a lucrative commission, or contract, to supply the army with bacon. His employment was mean; he rendered it infamous. He accumulated wealth by the basest arts of fraud and corruption; but his malversations were so notorious that George was compelled to escape from the pursuits of justice. After this disgrace, in which he appears to have saved his fortune at the expense of his honour, he embraced, with real or affected zeal, the profession of Arianism. From the love, or the ostentation, of learning, he collected a valuable library of history, rhetoric, philosophy, and theology; [121] and the choice of the prevailing faction promoted George of Cappadocia to the throne of Athanasius. The entrance of the new archbishop was that of a Barbarian conqueror; and each moment of his reign was polluted by cruelty and avarice. The Catholics of Alexandria and Egypt were abandoned to a tyrant, qualified, by nature and education, to

oppresses Alexandria and Egypt

exercise the office of persecution; but he oppressed with an impartial hand the various inhabitants of his extensive diocese. The primate of Egypt assumed the pomp and insolence of his lofty station; but he still betrayed the vices of his base and

[119] See Gregory Nazianzen, Orat. iii. p. 87 [iv. c. 86]. Sozomen (l. v. c. 9) may be considered as an original, though not impartial, witness. He was a native of Gaza, and had conversed with the confessor Zeno, who, as bishop of Maïuma, lived to the age of an hundred (l. vii. c. 28). Philostorgius (l. vii. c. 4, with Godefroy's Dissertations, p. 284) adds some tragic circumstances, of Christians who were *literally* sacrificed at the altars of the gods. &c.

[120] The life and death of George of Cappadocia are described by Ammianus (xxii. 11), Gregory Nazianzen (Orat. xxi. p. 382, 385, 389, 390 [c. 16 *sqq.*]), and Epiphanius (Hæres. lxxvi.). The invectives of the two saints might not deserve much credit, unless they were confirmed by the testimony of the cool and impartial infidel.

[121] After the massacre of George, the emperor Julian repeatedly sent orders to preserve the library for his own use, and to torture the slaves who might be suspected of secreting any books. He praises the merit of the collection, from whence he had borrowed and transcribed several manuscripts while he pursued his studies in Cappadocia. He could wish indeed that the works of the Galilæans might perish: but he requires an exact account even of those theological volumes, lest other treatises more valuable should be confounded in their loss. Julian. Epist. ix. xxxvi.

servile extraction. The merchants of Alexandria were impoverished by the unjust, and almost universal, monopoly,
which he acquired, of nitre, salt, paper, funerals, &c.; and the
spiritual father of a great people condescended to practise the
vile and pernicious arts of an informer. The Alexandrians could
never forget nor forgive the tax which he suggested on all the
houses of the city; under an obsolete claim that the royal
founder had conveyed to his successors, the Ptolemies and the
Cæsars, the perpetual property of the soil. The Pagans, who
had been flattered with the hopes of freedom and toleration,
excited his devout avarice; and the rich temples of Alexandria
were either pillaged or insulted by the haughty prelate, who
exclaimed, in a loud and threatening tone, "How long will
these sepulchres be permitted to stand?" Under the reign
of Constantius, he was expelled by the fury, or rather by the
justice, of the people; and it was not without a violent struggle
that the civil and military powers of the state could restore his
authority and gratify his revenge. The messenger who proclaimed at Alexandria the accession of Julian announced the
downfall of the archbishop. George, with two of his obsequious A.D. 361,
ministers, count Diodorus, and Dracontius, master of the mint, November 30
were ignominiously dragged in chains to the public prison. At
the end of twenty-four days, the prison was forced open by the He is mas-
rage of a superstitious multitude, impatient of the tedious forms the people
of judicial proceedings. The enemies of gods and men expired December 24
under their cruel insults; the lifeless bodies of the archbishop
and his associates were carried in triumph through the streets
on the back of a camel; and the inactivity of the Athanasian
party [122] was esteemed a shining example of evangelical patience.
The remains of these guilty wretches were thrown into the sea;
and the popular leaders of the tumult declared their resolution
to disappoint the devotion of the Christians, and to intercept
the future honours of these *martyrs*, who had been punished,
like their predecessors, by the enemies of their religion.[123]
The fears of the Pagans were just, and their precautions ineffectual. The meritorious death of the archbishop obliterated
the memory of his life. The rival of Athanasius was dear

---

[122] Philostorgius, with cautious malice, insinuates their guilt, καὶ τοῦ Ἀθανασίου
γνώμην στρατηγῆσαι τῆς πράξεως, l. vii. c. 2, Godefroy, p. 267.

[123] Cineres projecit in mare, id metuens, ut clamabat, ne, collectis supremis,
ædes illis exstruerent [*leg.* extruerentur] ut reliquis, qui deviare a religione com-
pulsi pertulere cruciabiles pœnas, ad usque gloriosam mortem intemeratâ fide
progressi, et nunc MARTYRES appellantur. Ammian. xxii. 11. Epiphanius proves
to the Arians that George was not a martyr.

and sacred to the Arians, and the seeming conversion of those sectaries introduced his worship into the bosom of the Catholic church.[124]   The odious stranger, disguising every circumstance of time and place, assumed the mask of a martyr, a saint, and a Christian hero ; [125] and the infamous George of Cappadocia has been transformed [126] into the renowned St. George of England, the patron of arms, of chivalry, and of the garter.[127]

About the same time that Julian was informed of the tumult of Alexandria, he received intelligence from Edessa that the proud and wealthy faction of the Arians had insulted the weakness of the Valentinians, and committed such disorders as ought not to be suffered with impunity in a well-regulated state. Without expecting the slow forms of justice, the exasperated prince directed his mandate to the magistrates of Edessa,[128] by which he confiscated the whole property of the church : the money was distributed among the soldiers ; the lands were added to the domain ; and this act of oppression was aggravated by the most ungenerous irony.   " I shew myself," says Julian, " the true friend of the Galilæans.   Their *admirable* law has promised the kingdom of heaven to the poor ; and they will advance with more diligence in the paths of virtue and salvation, when they are relieved by my assistance from the load of temporal possessions.   Take care," pursued the monarch, in a more serious tone, " take care how you provoke my patience and humanity.   If these disorders continue, I will revenge on

---

[124] Some Donatists (Optatus Milev. p. 60, 303, edit. Dupin ; and Tillemont, Mém. Ecclés. tom. vi. p. 713, in 4to) and Priscillianists (Tillemont, Mém Ecclés. tom. viii. p. 517, in 4to) have in like manner usurped ¦the honours of Catholic saints and martyrs.

[125] The saints of Cappadocia, Basil and the Gregories, were ignorant of their holy companion.   Pope Gelasius (A.D. 494), the first Catholic who acknowledges St. George, places him among the martyrs, " qui Deo magis quam hominibus noti sunt ".   He rejects his Acts as the composition of heretics.   Some, perhaps not the oldest, of the spurious Acts are still extant ; and, through a cloud of fiction, we may yet distinguish the combat which St. George of Cappadocia sustained, in the presence of Queen *Alexandra*, against the *magician Athanasius*.

[126] This transformation is not given as absolutely certain, but as *extremely* probable.   See the Longueruana, tom. i. p. 194. [Cp. Appendix 22.   St. George was made patron saint of England by Edward III.]

[127] A curious history of the worship of St. George, from the sixth century (when he was already revered in Palestine, in Armenia, at Rome, and at Treves in Gaul), might be extracted from Dr. Heylin (History of [that most famous saynt and souldier of Christ Jesus] St. George, 2d edition, London, 1633, in 4to, pp. 429), and the Bollandists (Act. SS. Mens. April. tom. iii. p. 100-163).   His fame and popularity in Europe, and especially in England, proceeded from the Crusades.   [Add Dr. J. Milner's Historical and Critical Inquiry into the Existence and Character of St. George, London 1792, attempting to prove that St. George of England was orthodox.]

[128] Julian. Epist. xliii.

the magistrates the crimes of the people; and you will have reason to dread, not only confiscation and exile, but fire and the sword." The tumults of Alexandria were doubtless of a more bloody and dangerous nature : but a Christian bishop had fallen by the hands of the Pagans ; and the public epistle of Julian affords a very lively proof of the partial spirit of his administration. His reproaches to the citizens of Alexandria are mingled with expressions of esteem and tenderness ; and he laments that on this occasion they should have departed from the gentle and generous manners which attested their Grecian extraction. He gravely censures the offence which they had committed against the laws of justice and humanity ; but he recapitulates, with visible complacency, the intolerable provocations which they had so long endured from the impious tyranny of George of Cappadocia. Julian admits the principle that a wise and vigorous government should chastise the insolence of the people : yet, in consideration of their founder Alexander and of Serapis their tutelar deity, he grants a free and gracious pardon to the guilty city, for which he again feels the affection of a brother.[129]

After the tumult of Alexandria had subsided, Athanasius, amidst the public acclamations, seated himself on the throne from whence his unworthy competitor had been precipitated ; and, as the zeal of the archbishop was tempered with discretion, the exercise of his authority tended not to inflame, but to reconcile, the minds of the people. His pastoral labours were not confined to the narrow limits of Egypt. The state of the Christian world was present to his active and capacious mind ; and the age, the merit, the reputation of Athanasius enabled him to assume, in a moment of danger, the office of Ecclesiastical Dictator.[130] Three years were not yet elapsed since the majority of the bishops of the West had ignorantly, or reluctantly, subscribed the Confession of Rimini. They repented, they believed, but they dreaded the unseasonable rigour of their orthodox brethren, and, if their pride was stronger than their faith, they might throw themselves into the arms of the Arians, to escape the indignity of a public penance, which must degrade them to the condition of obscure laymen. At the same time, the domestic differences concerning the union and distinction

Restoration of Athanasius. A.D. 362, February 21

---

[129] Julian. Epist. x. He allowed his friends to assuage his anger. Ammian. xxii. 11.

[130] See Athanas. ad Rufin. tom. ii. p. 40, 41 ; and Greg. Nazianzen, Orat. iii. [leg. xxi.] p. 395, 396, who justly states the temperate zeal of the primate as much more meritorious than his prayers, his fasts, his persecutions, &c.

of the divine persons were agitated with some heat among the Catholic doctors ; and the progress of this metaphysical controversy seemed to threaten a public and lasting division of the Greek and Latin churches. By the wisdom of a select synod, to which the name and presence of Athanasius gave the authority of a general council, the bishops who had unwarily deviated into error were admitted to the communion of the church, on the easy condition of subscribing the Nicene Creed ; without any formal acknowledgment of their past fault or any minute definition of their scholastic opinions.   The advice of the primate of Egypt had already prepared the clergy of Gaul and Spain, of Italy and Greece, for the reception of this salutary measure ; and, notwithstanding the opposition of some ardent spirits,[131] the fear of the common enemy promoted the peace and harmony of the Christians.[132]

He is persecuted and expelled by Julian.
A.D. 362, Oct. 23

The skill and diligence of the primate of Egypt had improved the season of tranquillity, before it was interrupted by the hostile edicts of the emperor.[133] Julian, who despised the Christians, honoured Athanasius with his sincere and peculiar hatred.   For his sake alone, he introduced an arbitrary distinction, repugnant, at least, to the spirit of his former declarations.   He maintained that the Galilæans whom he had recalled from exile were not restored, by that general indulgence, to the possession of their respective churches : and he expressed his astonishment that a criminal, who had been repeatedly condemned by the judgment of the emperors, should dare to insult the majesty of the laws, and insolently usurp the archiepiscopal throne of Alexandria,

[A.D. 262, beginning of October]

without expecting the orders of his sovereign.   As a punishment for the imaginary offence, he again banished Athanasius from the city : and he was pleased to suppose that this act of justice would be highly agreeable to his pious subjects.   The pressing

---

[131] I have not leisure to follow the blind obstinacy of Lucifer of Cagliari. See his adventures in Tillemont (Mém. Eccles. tom. vii. p. 900-916) ; and observe how the colour of the narrative insensibly changes, as the confessor becomes a schismatic.

[132] Assensus est huic sententiæ Occidens, et, per tam necessarium concilium, Satanæ faucibus mundus ereptus.   The lively and artful Dialogue of Jerom against the Luciferians (tom. ii. p. 135-155) exhibits an original picture of the ecclesiastical policy of the times.

[133] Tillemont, who supposes that George was massacred in August, crowds the actions of Athanasius into a narrow space (Mém. Eccles. tom. viii. p. 360). An original fragment, published by the Marquis Maffei, from the old Chapterlibrary of Verona (Osservazioni Litterarie, tom. iii. p. 60-92) affords many important dates, which are authenticated by the computation of Egyptian months.

solicitations of the people soon convinced him that the majority of the Alexandrians were Christians ; and that the greatest part of the Christians were firmly attached to the cause of their oppressed primate.   But the knowledge of their sentiments, instead of persuading him to recall his decree, provoked him to extend to all Egypt the term of the exile of Athanasius. The zeal of the multitude rendered Julian still more inexorable : he was alarmed by the danger of leaving at the head of a tumultuous city a daring and popular leader : and the language of his resentment discovers the opinion which he entertained of the courage and abilities of Athanasius.   The execution of the sentence was still delayed, by the caution or negligence of Ecdicius, præfect of Egypt, who was at length awakened from his lethargy by a severe reprimand.   "Though you neglect," says Julian, "to write to me on any other subject, at least it is your duty to inform me of your conduct towards Athanasius, the enemy of the gods.   My intentions have been long since communicated to you.   I swear by the great Serapis that unless, on the calends of December, Athanasius has departed from Alexandria, nay from Egypt, the officers of your government shall pay a fine of one hundred pounds of gold.   You know my temper : I am slow to condemn, but I am still slower to forgive." This epistle was enforced by a short postscript, written with the emperor's own hand.   "The contempt that is shewn for all the gods fills me with grief and indignation.   There is nothing that I should see, nothing that I should hear with more pleasure than the expulsion of Athanasius from all Egypt.   The abominable wretch !   Under my reign, the baptism of several Grecian ladies of the highest rank has been the effect of his persecutions." [134]   The death of Athanasius was not *expressly* commanded ; but the præfect of Egypt understood that it was safer for him to exceed, than to neglect, the orders of an irritated master.   The archbishop prudently retired to the monasteries of the Desert : eluded, with his usual dexterity, the snares of the enemy ; and lived to triumph over the ashes of a prince who, in words of formidable import, had declared his wish that the whole venom

[A.D. 362, 23rd Oct.]

[134] Τὸν μιαρὸν, ὃς ἐτόλμησεν Ἑλληνίδας, ἐπ᾽ ἐμοῦ, γυναῖκας τῶν ἐπισήμων βαπτίσαι διώκεσθαι.   I have preserved the ambiguous sense of the last word, the ambiguity of a tyrant who wished to find, or to create, guilt. [P. 485, ed. Hertl.   With the reading διώκεσθαι (to which Gibbon seems, by a curious blunder, to give an active meaning) we should have to render "than that Athanasius should be expelled from all Egypt, and persecuted, the abominable wretch, who dared to baptize Greek ladies".   But read with best Ms,—βαπτίσαι, διωκέσθω : "let him be persecuted".]

of the Galilæan school were contained in the single person of
Athanasius.[135]

Zeal and
imprudence
of the
Christians

I have endeavoured faithfully to represent the artful system
by which Julian proposed to obtain the effects, without incurring
the guilt, or reproach, of persecution.   But, if the deadly spirit
of fanaticism perverted the heart and understanding of a virtuous prince, it must, at the same time, be confessed, that the *real*
sufferings of the Christians were inflamed and magnified by
human passions and religious enthusiasm.   The meekness and
resignation which had distinguished the primitive disciples of
the gospel was the object of the applause rather than of the
imitation of their successors.   The Christians, who had now
possessed about forty years the civil and ecclesiastical government of the empire, had contracted the insolent vices of prosperity,[136] and the habit of believing that the saints alone were
entitled to reign over the earth.   As soon as the enmity of
Julian deprived the clergy of the privileges which had been
conferred by the favour of Constantine, they complained of the
most cruel oppression ; and the free toleration of idolaters and
heretics was a subject of grief and scandal to the orthodox
party.[137]   The acts of violence, which were no longer countenanced by the magistrates, were still committed by the zeal of
the people.   At Pessinus, the altar of Cybele was overturned
almost in the presence of the emperor ; and in the city of
Cæsarea in Cappadocia, the temple of Fortune, the sole place of
worship which had been left to the Pagans, was destroyed by the
rage of a popular tumult.   On these occasions, a prince who
felt for the honour of the gods was not disposed to interrupt the
course of justice ; and his mind was still more deeply exasperated,
when he found that the fanatics, who had deserved and suffered
the punishment of incendiaries, were rewarded with the honours of
martyrdom.[138]   The Christian subjects of Julian were assured of

[135] The three epistles of Julian which explain his intentions and conduct with
regard to Athanasius should be disposed in the following chronological order, xxvi,
x, vi. See likewise Greg. Nazianzen, xxi. p. 393 ; Sozomen, l. v. c. 15 ; Socrates,
l. iii. c. 14 ; Theodoret, l. iii. c. 9, and Tillemont, Mém. Ecclés. tom. viii. p. 361-
368, who has used some materials prepared by the Bollandists. [Cp. Schwarz,
de Vit. et Scr Julian. i. p. 20. He assigns Ep. 10 to end of Jan., Ep. 26 to end of
March, Ep. 6 to beginning of Oct., 362 A.D.   Rode regards 6 and 26 as written at
the same time.]

[136] See the fair confession of Gregory (Orat. iii. p. 61, 62).

[137] Hear the furious and absurd complaint of Optatus (de Schismat. Donatist.
l. ii. c. 16, 17).

[138] Greg. Nazianzen. Orat. iii. p. 91, iv. p. 133. He praises the rioters of
Cæsarea, τούτων δὲ τῶν μεγαλοφνῶν καὶ θερμῶν εἰς εὐσέβειαν, See Sozomen, l. v. 4,

the hostile designs of their sovereign; and, to their jealous apprehension, every circumstance of his government might afford some grounds of discontent and suspicion.   In the ordinary administration of the laws, the Christians, who formed so large a part of the people, must frequently be condemned : but their indulgent brethren, without examining the merits of the cause, presumed their innocence, allowed their claims, and imputed the severity of their judge to the partial malice of religious persecution.[139]   These present hardships, intolerable as they might appear, were represented as a slight prelude of the impending calamities.   The Christians considered Julian as a cruel and crafty tyrant who suspended the execution of his revenge, till he should return victorious from the Persian war. They expected that, as soon as he had triumphed over the foreign enemies of Rome, he would lay aside the irksome mask of dissimulation ; that the amphitheatres would stream with the blood of hermits and bishops ; and that the Christians, who still persevered in the profession of the faith, would be deprived of the common benefits of nature and society.[140]   Every calumny[141] that could wound the reputation of the Apostate was credulously embraced by the fears and hatred of his adversaries ; and their indiscreet clamours provoked the temper of a sovereign whom it was their duty to respect and their interest to flatter.   They still protested that prayers and tears were their only weapons against the impious tyrant, whose head they devoted to the justice of offended Heaven.   But they insinuated with sullen resolution, that their submission was no longer the effect of weakness ; and that, in the imperfect state of human virtue, the patience which is founded on principle may be exhausted by persecution.   It is impossible to determine how

1. Tillemont (Mém. Ecclés. tom. vii. p. 649, 650) owns that their behaviour was not dans l'ordre commun ; but he is perfectly satisfied, as the great St. Basil always celebrated the festival of these blessed martyrs.

[139] Julian determined a lawsuit against the new Christian city at Maiuma, the port of Gaza ; and his sentence, though it might be imputed to bigotry, was never reversed by his successors. Sozomen, l. v. c. 3. Reland, Palestine, tom. ii. p. 791.

[140] Gregory (Orat. iii. p. 93, 94, 95 [iv. c. 93 *sqq*.]; Orat. iv. p. 114 [v., ad init.]) pretends to speak from the information of Julian's confidants, whom Orosius (vii. 30) could not have seen.

[141] Gregory (Orat. iii. p. 91) charges the Apostate with secret sacrifices of boys and girls; and positively affirms that the dead bodies were thrown into the Orontes. See Theodoret, l. iii. c. 26, 27 ; and the equivocal candour of the Abbé de la Bléterie, Vie de Julien, p. 351, 352. Yet *contemporary* malice could not impute to Julian the troops of martyrs, more especially in the West, which Baronius so greedily swallows, and Tillemont so faintly rejects (Mém. Ecclés. tom. ii. p. 1295-1315).

far the zeal of Julian would have prevailed over his good sense
and humanity : but, if we seriously reflect on the strength and
spirit of the church, we shall be convinced that, before the emperor could have extinguished the religion of Christ, he must
have involved his country in the horrors of a civil war.[142]

---

[142] The resignation of Gregory is truly edifying (Orat. iv. p. 123, 124).   Yet,
when an officer of Julian attempted to seize the Church of Nazianzus, he would
have lost his life, if he had not yielded to the zeal of the bishop and people (Orat.
xix. p. 308 [c. 32]).   See the reflections of Chrysostom, as they are alleged by
Tillemont (Mém Ecclés. tom. vii. p. 575).

CHAPTER XXIV

Residence of Julian at Antioch—His successful Expedition against the Persians—Passage of the Tigris—The Retreat and Death of Julian—Election of Jovian—He saves the Roman Army by a disgraceful Treaty

THE philosophical fable which Julian composed under the name of the CÆSARS [1] is one of the most agreeable and instructive productions of ancient wit.[2]   During the freedom and equality of the days of the Saturnalia, Romulus prepared a feast for the deities of Olympus, who had adopted him as a worthy associate, and for the Roman princes, who had reigned over his martial people and the vanquished nations of the earth.   The immortals were placed in just order on their thrones of state, and the table of the Cæsars was spread below the Moon, in the upper region of the air.   The tyrants, who would have disgraced the society of gods and men, were thrown headlong, by the inexorable Nemesis, into the Tartarean abyss.   The rest of the Cæsars successively advanced to their seats : and, as they passed, the vices, the defects, the blemishes of their respective characters were maliciously noticed by old Silenus, a laughing moralist, who disguised the wisdom of a philosopher under the mask of a Bacchanal.[3]   As soon as the feast was ended, the voice of Mercury proclaimed the will of Jupiter, that a celestial crown should be the reward of superior merit.   Julius Cæsar, Augustus Trajan, and Marcus Antoninus were selected as the most illustrious

The Cæsars of Julian

---

[1] See this fable or satire, p. 306-336 of the Leipzig edition of Julian's works. The French version of the learned Ezekiel Spanheim (Paris, 1683) is coarse, languid, and incorrect ; and his notes, proofs, illustrations, &c. are piled on each other till they form a mass of 557 close-printed quarto pages.   The Abbé de la Bléterie (Vie de Jovien, tom. i. p. 241-393) has more happily expressed the spirit, as well as the sense, of the original, which he illustrates with some concise and curious notes.

[2] Spanheim (in his preface) has most learnedly discussed the etymology, origin, resemblance, and disagreement of the Greek *satyrs*, a dramatic piece, which was acted after the tragedy ; and the Latin *satires* (from *satura*), a *miscellaneous* composition, either in prose or verse.   But the Cæsars of Julian are of such an original cast that the critic is perplexed to which class he should ascribe them.

[3] This mixed character of Silenus is finely painted in the sixth eclogue of Virgil.

candidates; the effeminate Constantine [4] was not excluded from this honourable competition, and the great Alexander was invited to dispute the prize of glory with the Roman heroes. Each of the candidates was allowed to display the merit of his own exploits; but, in the judgment of the gods, the modest silence of Marcus pleaded more powerfully than the elaborate orations of his haughty rivals. When the judges of this awful contest proceeded to examine the heart and to scrutinize the springs of action, the superiority of the Imperial Stoic appeared still more decisive and conspicuous.[5] Alexander and Cæsar, Augustus, Trajan, and Constantine, acknowledged with a blush that fame or power or pleasure had been the important object of *their* labours: but the gods themselves beheld, with reverence and love, a virtuous mortal, who had practised on the throne the lessons of philosophy; and who, in a state of human imperfection, had aspired to imitate the moral attributes of the Deity. The value of this agreeable composition (the Cæsars of Julian) is enhanced by the rank of the author. A prince, who delineates with freedom the vices and virtues of his predecessors, subscribes, in every line, the censure or approbation of his own conduct.

He resolves to march against the Persians. A.D. 362 In the cool moments of reflection, Julian preferred the useful and benevolent virtues of Antoninus: but his ambitious spirit was inflamed by the glory of Alexander; and he solicited, with equal ardour, the esteem of the wise and the applause of the multitude. In the season of life, when the powers of the mind and body enjoy the most active vigour, the emperor, who was instructed by the experience, and animated by the success, of the German war, resolved to signalize his reign by some more splendid and memorable achievement. The ambassadors of the East, from the continent of India and the isle of Ceylon,[6]

[4] Every impartial reader must perceive and condemn the partiality of Julian against his uncle Constantine and the Christian religion. On this occasion, the interpreters are compelled, by a more sacred interest, to renounce their allegiance, and to desert the cause of their author.

[5] Julian was secretly inclined to prefer a Greek to a Roman. But, when he seriously compared a hero with a philosopher, he was sensible that mankind had much greater obligations to Socrates than to Alexander (Orat. ad Themistium, p. 264).

[6] Inde nationibus Indicis certatum cum donis optimates mittentibus . . . ab usque Divis et *Serendivis*. Ammian. xxii. 7. This island to which the names of Taprobana, Serendib, and Ceylon, have been successively applied manifests how imperfectly the seas and lands to the east of Cape Comorin were known to the Romans. 1. Under the reign of Claudius, a freedman, who farmed the customs of the Red Sea, was accidentally driven by the winds upon this strange and undiscovered coast: he conversed six months with the natives · and the king of Ceylon, who heard, for the first time, of the power and justice of Rome, was persuaded

had respectfully saluted the Roman purple.[7] The nations of the West esteemed and dreaded the personal virtues of Julian, both in peace and war. He despised the trophies of a Gothic victory[8] and was satisfied that the rapacious Barbarians of the Danube would be restrained from any future violation of the faith of treaties by the terror of his name and the additional fortifications with which he strengthened the Thracian and Illyrian frontiers. The successor of Cyrus and Artaxerxes was the only rival whom he deemed worthy of his arms; and he resolved, by the final conquest of Persia, to chastise the haughty nation which had so long resisted and insulted the majesty of Rome.[9] As soon as the Persian monarch was informed that the throne of Constantius was filled by a prince of a very different character, he condescended to make some artful, or perhaps sincere, overtures towards a negotiation of peace. But the pride of Sapor was astonished by the firmness of Julian; who sternly declared that he would never consent to hold a peaceful conference among the flames and ruins of the cities of Mesopotamia; and who added, with a smile of contempt, that it was needless to treat by ambassadors, as he himself had determined to visit speedily the court of Persia. The impatience of the emperor urged the diligence of the military preparations. The generals were named; a formidable army was destined for this important service; and Julian, marching from Constantinople through the provinces of Asia Minor, arrived at Antioch about eight months after the death of his predecessor. His ardent desire to march into the heart of Persia was checked by the indispensable duty of regulating the state of the empire; by his zeal to revive the worship of the gods; and by the advice of his wisest friends, who represented the necessity of allowing the salutary interval of winter quarters, to restore the exhausted strength of the legions

Julian proceeds from Constantinople to Antioch August [June-July]

to send an embassy to the emperor (Plin. Hist. Nat. vi. 24). 2. The geographers (and even Ptolemy) have magnified, above fifteen times, the real size of this new world, which they extended as far as the equator and the neighbourhood of China.

[7] These embassies had been sent to Constantius. Ammianus, who unwarily deviates into gross flattery, must have forgotten the length of the way, and the short duration of the reign of Julian.

[8] Gothos saepe fallaces et perfidos; hostes quaerere se meliores aiebat: illis enim sufficere mercatores Galatas per quos ubique sine conditionis discrimine venundantur [Amm. loc. cit.]. Within less than fifteen years, these Gothic slaves threatened and subdued their masters.

[9] Alexander reminds his rival Caesar, who deprecated the fame and merit of an Asiatic victory, that Crassus and Antony had felt the Persian arrows; and that the Romans, in a war of three hundred years, had not yet subdued the single province of Mesopotamia or Assyria (Caesares, p. 324 [p. 417, ed. Hertl.]).

of Gaul and the discipline and spirit of the Eastern troops. Julian was persuaded to fix, till the ensuing spring, his residence at Antioch, among a people maliciously disposed to deride the haste, and to censure the delays, of their sovereign.[10]

Licentious manners of the people of Antioch

If Julian had flattered himself that his personal connexion with the capital of the East would be productive of mutual satisfaction to the prince and people, he made a very false estimate of his own character, and of the manners of Antioch.[11] The warmth of the climate disposed the natives to the most intemperate enjoyment of tranquillity and opulence; and the lively licentiousness of the Greeks was blended with the hereditary softness of the Syrians. Fashion was the only law, pleasure the only pursuit, and the splendour of dress and furniture was the only distinction of the citizens of Antioch. The arts of luxury were honoured; the serious and manly virtues were the subject of ridicule; and the contempt for female modesty and reverent[11a] age announced the universal corruption of the capital of the East. The love of spectacles was the taste, or rather passion, of the Syrians: the most skilful artists were procured from the adjacent cities;[12] a considerable share of the revenue was devoted to the public amusements; and the magnificence of the games of the theatre and circus was considered as the happiness, and as the glory, of Antioch. The rustic manners of a prince who disdained such glory, and was insensible of such happiness, soon disgusted the delicacy of his subjects; and the effeminate Orientals could neither imitate nor admire the severe simplicity which Julian always maintained and sometimes affected. The days of festivity, consecrated by ancient custom to the honour of the gods, were the only occasions in which Julian relaxed his philosophic severity; and those festivals were the only days in which the Syrians of Antioch could reject the allurements of pleasure. The majority of the people supported the glory of the Christian

[10] The design of the Persian war is declared by Ammianus (xxii. 7, 12), Libanius (Orat. Parent. c. 79, 80, p. 305, 306), Zosimus (l. iii. p. 158 [c. 11]), and Socrates (l. iii. c. 19).

[11] The satire of Julian and the Homilies of St. Chrysostom exhibit the same picture of Antioch. The miniature which the Abbé de la Bléterie has copied from thence (Vie de Julien, p. 332) is elegant, and correct. [The date of Julian's arrival at Antioch has been contested. The first half of July seems most probable (cp. Sievers, Das Leben des Libanius, p. 247, and Gwatkin, Arianism, p. 222). Mücke (Flavius Claudius Julianus, 2, 106) puts it in September.]

[11a] [Sic quarto; should be corrected to reverend.]

[12] Laodicea furnished charioteers; Tyre and Berytus, comedians; Cæsarea, pantomimes; Heliopolis, singers; Gaza, gladiators; Ascalon, wrestlers; and Castabala, rope-dancers. See the Expositio totius Mundi, p. 6, in the third tome of Hudson's Minor Geographers.

name, which had been first invented by their ancestors; [13] they contented themselves with disobeying the moral precepts, but they were scrupulously attached to the speculative doctrines, of their religion. The church of Antioch was distracted by heresy and schism; but the Arians and the Athanasians, the followers of Meletius and those of Paulinus,[14] were actuated by the same pious hatred of their common adversary.

The strongest prejudice was entertained against the character *Their aver-* of an apostate, the enemy and successor of a prince who had *sion to Julian* engaged the affections of a very numerous sect; and the removal of St. Babylas excited an implacable opposition to the person of Julian. His subjects complained, with superstitious indignation, that famine had pursued the emperor's steps from Constantinople to Antioch; and the discontent of a hungry people was ex- *Scarcity of* asperated by the injudicious attempt to relieve their distress. *corn and public dis-* The inclemency of the season had affected the harvests of Syria; *content* and the price of bread,[15] in the markets of Antioch, had naturally risen in proportion to the scarcity of corn. But the fair and reasonable proportion was soon violated by the rapacious arts of monopoly. In this unequal contest, in which the produce of the land is claimed by one party as his exclusive property; is used by another as a lucrative object of trade; and is required by a third for the daily and necessary support of life; all the profits of the intermediate agents are accumulated on the head of the defenceless consumers. The hardships of their situation were exaggerated and increased by their own impatience and anxiety; and the apprehension of a scarcity gradually produced the appearances of a famine. When the luxurious citizens of Antioch complained of the high price of poultry and fish, Julian

---

[13] Χριστὸν δὲ ἀγαπῶντες, ἔχετε πολιοῦχον ἀντι τοῦ Διός. The people of Antioch ingeniously professed their attachment to the *Chi* (Christ), and the *Kappa* (Constantius). Julian. in Misopogon. p. 357 [460, ed. Hertl.].

[14] The schism of Antioch, which lasted eighty-five years (A.D. 330-415), was inflamed, while Julian resided in that city, by the indiscreet ordination of Paulinus. See Tillemont, Mém. Ecclés. tom. vii. p. 803, of the quarto edition (Paris, 1701, &c. [same page in earlier ed.]), which henceforward I shall quote.

[15] Julian states three different proportions of five, ten, or fifteen *modii* of wheat, for one piece of gold, according to the degrees of plenty and scarcity (in Misopogon. p. 369 [477]). From this fact, and from some collateral examples, I conclude that under the successors of Constantine the moderate price of wheat was about thirty-two shillings the English quarter, which is equal to the average price of the sixty-four first years of the present century. See Arbuthnot's Tables of Coins, Weights, and Measures, p. 88, 89; Plin. Hist. Natur. xviii. 12; Mém. de l'Académie des Inscriptions, t. xxviii. p. 718-721; Smith's Inquiry into the Nature and Causes of the Wealth of Nations, vol. i. p. 246. This last I am proud to quote, as the work of a sage and a friend.

publicly declared that a frugal city ought to be satisfied with
a regular supply of wine, oil, and bread; but he acknowledged
that it was the duty of a sovereign to provide for the subsistence
of his people. With this salutary view, the emperor ventured
on a very dangerous and doubtful step, of fixing, by legal
authority, the value of corn. He enacted that, in a time of
scarcity, it should be sold at a price which had seldom been
known in the most plentiful years; and, that his own example
might strengthen his laws, he sent into the market four hundred
and twenty-two thousand *modii*, or measures, which were drawn
by his order from the granaries of Hierapolis, of Chalcis, and
even of Egypt. The consequences might have been foreseen,
and were soon felt. The Imperial wheat was purchased by the
rich merchants; the proprietors of land, or of corn, withheld
from the city the accustomed supply; and the small quantities
that appeared in the market were secretly sold at an advanced
and illegal price. Julian still continued to applaud his own
policy, treated the complaints of the people as a vain and ungrateful murmur, and convinced Antioch that he had inherited
the obstinacy, though not the cruelty, of his brother Gallus.[16]
The remonstrances of the municipal senate served only to exasperate his inflexible mind. He was persuaded, perhaps with
truth, that the senators of Antioch who possessed lands, or were
concerned in trade, had themselves contributed to the calamities
of their country; and he imputed the disrespectful boldness
which they assumed to the sense, not of public duty, but of
private interest. The whole body, consisting of two hundred
of the most noble and wealthy citizens, were sent under a guard
from the palace to the prison; and, though they were permitted,
before the close of evening, to return to their respective houses,[17]
the emperor himself could not obtain the forgiveness which he
had so easily granted. The same grievances were still the
subject of the same complaints, which were industriously circulated by the wit and levity of the Syrian Greeks. During the
licentious days of the Saturnalia, the streets of the city resounded

[16] Nunquam a proposito declinabat, Galli similis fratris, licet incruentus,
Ammian. xxii. 14. The ignorance of the most enlightened princes may claim
some excuse: but we cannot be satisfied with Julian's own defence (in Misopogon.
p. 368, 369 [p. 475-8, ed. H.]), or the elaborate apology of Libanius (Orat. Parental.
c. xcvii. p. 321 [i. 587, ed. Reiske]).

[17] Their short and easy confinement is gently touched by Libanius, Orat.
Parental. c. xcviii. p. 322, 323. [Schiller, Gesch. der röm. Kaiserzeit, ii. p. 325, says
they were released on the following day. But Libanius, p. 322 (ap. Fabric.), says
ἀλλ' οὐδὲ νὺξ ἐπεγένετο τῷ βραχεῖ τούτῳ καὶ κούφῳ κ.τ.λ.]

with insolent songs, which derided the laws, the religion, the
personal conduct, and even the *beard*, of the emperor; and the
spirit of Antioch was manifested by the connivance of the magistrates and the applause of the multitude.[18] The disciple of
Socrates was too deeply affected by these popular insults; but
the monarch, endowed with quick sensibility, and possessed of absolute power, refused his passions the gratification of revenge. A
tyrant might have proscribed, without distinction, the lives and
fortunes of the citizens of Antioch; and the unwarlike Syrians
must have patiently submitted to the lust, the rapaciousness, and
the cruelty of the faithful legions of Gaul. A milder sentence
might have deprived the capital of the East of its honours and privileges; and the courtiers, perhaps the subjects, of Julian would
have applauded an act of justice which asserted the dignity of the
supreme magistrate of the republic.[19] But, instead of abusing,
or exerting, the authority of the state to revenge his personal
injuries, Julian contented himself with an inoffensive mode of
retaliation, which it would be in the power of few princes to
employ. He had been insulted by satires and libels; in his
turn he composed, under the title of the *Enemy of the Beard*, an
ironical confession of his own faults, and a severe satire of the
licentious and effeminate manners of Antioch. This Imperial
reply was publicly exposed before the gates of the palace; and
the MISOPOGON [20] still remains a singular monument of the resentment, the wit, the humanity, and the indiscretion, of Julian.
Though he affected to laugh, he could not forgive.[21] His contempt was expressed, and his revenge might be gratified, by the
nomination of a governor [22] worthy only of such subjects: and

Julian composes a satire against Antioch

---

[18] Libanius (ad Antiochenos de Imperatoris irâ, c. 17, 18, 19, in Fabricius
Bibliot. Græc. tom. vii. p. 221-223), like a skilful advocate, severely censures the folly
of the people, who suffered for the crime of a few obscure and drunken wretches.

[19] Libanius (ad Antiochen. c. vii. p. 213) reminds Antioch of the recent chastisement of Cæsarea: and even Julian (in Misopogon. p. 355 [p. 459, ed. H.]) insinuates
how severely Tarentum had expiated the insult to the Roman ambassadors.

[20] On the subject of the Misopogon, see Ammianus (xxii. 14), Libanius (Orat.
Parentalis, c. xcix. p. 323), Gregory Nazianzen (Orat. iv. p. 133 [v., c. 41]), and the
Chronicle of Antioch, by John Malala (tom. ii. p. 15, 16 [p. 328, ed. Bonn]). I have
essential obligations to the translation and notes of the Abbé de la Bléterie (Vie de
Jovien, tom. ii. p. 1-138).

[21] Ammianus very justly remarks, Coactus dissimulare pro tempore irâ sufflabatur internâ. The elaborate irony of Julian at length bursts forth into serious and
direct invective.

[22] Ipse autem Antiochiam egressurus, Heliopoliten quendam Alexandrum
Syriacæ jurisdictioni præfecit, turbulentum et sævum; dicebatque non illum
meruisse, sed Antiochensibus avaris et contumeliosis hujusmodi judicem convenire.
Ammian. xxiii. 2. Libanius (Epist. 722, p. 346, 347), who confesses to Julian
himself that he had shared the general discontent, pretends that Alexander was an
useful, though harsh, reformer of the manners and religion of Antioch.

the emperor, for ever renouncing the ungrateful city, proclaimed his resolution to pass the ensuing winter at Tarsus in Cilicia.[23]

Yet Antioch possessed one citizen, whose genius and virtues might atone, in the opinion of Julian, for the vice and folly of his country. The sophist Libanius was born in the capital of the East; he publicly professed the arts of rhetoric and declamation at Nice, Nicomedia, Constantinople, Athens, and, during the remainder of his life, at Antioch. His school was assiduously frequented by the Grecian youth; his disciples, who sometimes exceeded the number of eighty, celebrated their incomparable master; and the jealousy of his rivals, who persecuted him from one city to another, confirmed the favourable opinion which Libanius ostentatiously displayed of his superior merit. The preceptors of Julian had extorted a rash but solemn assurance that he would never attend the lectures of their adversary : the curiosity of the royal youth was checked and inflamed : he secretly procured the writings of this dangerous sophist, and gradually surpassed, in the perfect imitation of his style, the most laborious of his domestic pupils.[24] When Julian ascended the throne, he declared his impatience to embrace and reward the Syrian sophist, who had preserved, in a degenerate age, the Grecian purity of taste, of manners and of religion. The emperor's prepossession was increased and justified by the discreet pride of his favourite. Instead of pressing, with the foremost of the crowd, into the palace of Constantinople, Libanius calmly expected his arrival at Antioch; withdrew from court on the first symptoms of coldness and indifference; required a formal invitation for each visit; and taught his sovereign an important lesson, that he might command the obedience of a subject, but that he must deserve the attachment of a friend. The sophists of every age, despising, or affecting to despise, the accidental distinctions of birth and fortune,[25] reserve their esteem for the superior qualities of the mind, with which they themselves are so plentifully endowed. Julian might disdain the acclamations of a venal court, who adored the Imperial purple; but he was deeply flattered by the praise, the admonition, the freedom, and

[23] Julian. in Misopogon. p. 364 [p. 470, ed. H.]. Ammian. xxiii. 2, and Valesius ad loc. Libanius, in a professed oration, invites him to return to his loyal and penitent city of Antioch.

[24] Libanius, Orat. Parent. c. vii. p. 230, 231.

[25] Eunapius reports that Libanius refused the honorary rank of Prætorian præfect, as less illustrious than the title of Sophist (in Vit. Sophist. p. 135). The critics have observed a similar sentiment in one of the epistles (xviii. edit. Wolf) of Libanius himself.

the envy of an independent philosopher, who refused his favours, loved his person, celebrated his fame, and protected his memory. The voluminous writings of Libanius still exist: for the most part, they are the vain and idle compositions of an orator, who cultivated the science of words; the productions of a recluse student, whose mind, regardless of his contemporaries, was incessantly fixed on the Trojan war and the Athenian commonwealth. Yet the sophist of Antioch sometimes descended from this imaginary elevation; he entertained a various and elaborate correspondence; [26] he praised the virtues of his own times; he boldly arraigned the abuses of public and private life; and he eloquently pleaded the cause of Antioch against the just resentment of Julian and Theodosius. It is the common calamity of old age,[27] to lose whatever might have rendered it desirable; but Libanius experienced the peculiar misfortune of surviving the religion and the sciences to which he had consecrated his genius. The friend of Julian was an indignant spectator of the triumph of Christianity; and his bigotry, which darkened the prospect of the visible world, did not inspire Libanius with any lively hopes of celestial glory and happiness.[28]

The martial impatience of Julian urged him to take the field in the beginning of the spring; and he dismissed, with contempt and reproach, the senate of Antioch, who accompanied the emperor beyond the limits of their own territory, to which he was resolved never to return. After a laborious march of two days,[29] he halted on the third at Berœa, or Aleppo, where he had the mortification of finding a senate almost entirely Christian; who

March of Julian to the Euphrates. A.D. 363, March 5

[26] Near two thousand of his letters, a mode of composition in which Libanius was thought to excel, are still extant, and already published. The critics may praise their subtle and elegant brevity; yet Dr. Bentley (Dissertation upon Phalaris, p. 487) might justly, though quaintly, observe that "you feel, by the emptiness and deadness of them, that you converse with some dreaming pedant, with his elbow on his desk".

[27] His birth is assigned to the year 314. He mentions the seventy-sixth year of his age (A.D. 390), and seems to allude to some events of a still later date.

[28] Libanius has composed the vain, prolix, but curious, narrative of his own life (tom. ii. p. 1-84, edit. Morell.), of which Eunapius (p. 130-135) has left a concise and unfavourable account. Among the moderns, Tillemont (Hist. des Empereurs, tom. iv. p. 571-576), Fabricius (Bibliot. Græc. tom. vii. p. 376-414) and Lardner (Heathen Testimonies, tom. iv. p. 127-163) have illustrated the character and writings of this famous sophist. [See Appendix 1.]

[29] From Antioch to Litarbe, on the territory of Chalcis, the road, over hills and through morasses, was extremely bad; and the loose stones were cemented only with sand. Julian. epist. xxvii. It is singular enough that the Romans should have neglected the great communication between Antioch and the Euphrates. See Wesseling, Itinerar. p. 190; Bergier, Hist. des Grands Chemins, tom. ii. p. 100.

received with cold and formal demonstrations of respect the eloquent sermon of the apostle of paganism. The son of one of the most illustrious citizens of Berœa, who had embraced, either from interest or conscience, the religion of the emperor, was disinherited by his angry parent. The father and the son were invited to the Imperial table. Julian, placing himself between them, attempted, without success, to inculcate the lesson and example of toleration; supported, with affected calmness, the indiscreet zeal of the aged Christian, who seemed to forget the sentiments of nature and the duty of a subject; and at length turning towards the afflicted youth, "Since you have lost a father," said he, "for my sake, it is incumbent on me to supply [8th March] his place".[30] The emperor was received in a manner much more agreeable to his wishes at Batnæ,[31] a small town pleasantly seated in a grove of cypresses, about twenty miles from the city of Hierapolis The solemn rites of sacrifice were decently prepared by the inhabitants of Batnæ, who seemed attached to the worship of their tutelar deities, Apollo and Jupiter; but the serious piety of Julian was offended by the tumult of their applause; and he too clearly discerned that the smoke which arose from their altars was the incense of flattery rather than of devotion. The ancient and magnificent temple, which had sanctified, for so many ages, the city of Hierapolis,[32] no longer subsisted; and the consecrated wealth, which afforded a liberal maintenance to more than three hundred priests, might hasten [9th March] its downfall. Yet Julian enjoyed the satisfaction of embracing a philosopher and a friend, whose religious firmness had withstood the pressing and repeated solicitations of Constantius and Gallus, as often as those princes lodged at his house, in their passage through Hierapolis. In the hurry of military preparation, and the careless confidence of a familiar correspondence, the zeal of Julian appears to have been lively and uniform. He had now undertaken an important and difficult war; and the anxiety of the event rendered him still more attentive to

---

[30] Julian alludes to this incident (epist. xxvii), which is more distinctly related by Theodoret (l. iii. c. 22). The intolerant spirit of the father is applauded by Tillemont (Hist. des Empereurs, tom. iv. p. 534), and even by La Blétérie (Vie de Julien, p. 413).

[31] [Not to be confounded with Batnæ beyond the Euphrates, which was also a halting place of Julian. See map.]

[32] See the curious treatise de Deâ Syriâ, inserted among the works of Lucian (tom. iii. p. 451-490, edit. Reitz). The singular appellation of *Ninus vetus* (Ammian. xiv. 8) might induce a suspicion that Hierapolis had been the royal seat of the Assyrians.

observe and register the most trifling presages from which, according to the rules of divination, any knowledge of futurity could be derived.[33] He informed Libanius of his progress as far as Hierapolis, by an elegant epistle,[34] which displays the facility of his genius and his tender friendship for the sophist of Antioch.

Hierapolis, situate almost on the banks of the Euphrates,[35] had been appointed for the general rendezvous of the Roman troops, who immediately passed the great river on a bridge of boats, which was previously constructed.[36] If the inclinations of Julian had been similar to those of his predecessor, he might have wasted the active and important season of the year in the circus of Samosata, or in the churches of Edessa. But, as the warlike emperor, instead of Constantius, had chosen Alexander for his model, he advanced without delay to Carrhæ,[37] a very ancient city of Mesopotamia, at the distance of fourscore miles from Hierapolis. The temple of the Moon attracted the devotion of Julian; but the halt of a few days was principally employed in completing the immense preparations of the Persian war. The secret of the expedition had hitherto remained in his own breast; but, as Carrhæ is the point of separation of the two great roads, he could no longer conceal whether it was his design to attack the dominions of Sapor on the side of the Tigris or on that of the Euphrates. The emperor detached an army of thirty thousand men, under the command of his kinsman Procopius, and of Sebastian, who had been duke of Egypt. They were ordered to direct their march towards Nisibis, and to secure the frontier from the desultory incursions of the enemy, before they attempted the passage of the Tigris. Their subsequent operations were left to the discretion of the generals; but Julian expected that, after wasting with fire and sword the

His design of invading Persia

[13th March]

[c. 18th March]

[33] Julian (epistle xxviii [xxvii]) kept a regular account of all the fortunate omens; but he suppresses the inauspicious signs, which Ammianus (xxiii. 2) has carefully recorded.

[34] Julian, epistle xxvii. p. 399-402 [515-519].

[35] I take the earliest opportunity of acknowledging my obligations to M. d'Anville, for his recent geography of the Euphrates and Tigris (Paris, 1780, in 4to), which particularly illustrates the expedition of Julian.   [Cp. App. 24.]

[36] There are three passages within a few miles of each other: 1. Zeugma, celebrated by the ancients; 2. Bir, frequented by the moderns; and, 3. the bridge of Menbigz, or Hierapolis, at the distance of four parasangs from the city. [Membij is Hierapolis, and the city is more than twenty miles from the river.]

[37] Haran, or Carrhæ, was the ancient residence of the Sabæans and of Abraham. See the Index Geographicus of Schultens (ad calcem Vit. Saladin.), a work from which I have obtained much *Oriental* knowledge concerning the ancient and modern geography of Syria and the adjacent countries.

fertile districts of Media and Adiabene, they might arrive under the walls of Ctesiphon about the same time that he himself, advancing with equal steps along the banks of the Euphrates,

should besiege the capital of the Persian monarchy. The success of this well-concerted plan depended, in a great measure, on the powerful and ready assistance of the king of Armenia, who, without exposing the safety of his own dominions, might detach an army of four thousand horse, and twenty thousand foot, to the assistance of the Romans.[38] But the feeble Arsaces Tiranus,[39] king of Armenia, had degenerated still more shamefully than his father Chosroes from the manly virtues of the great Tiridates ; and, as the pusillanimous monarch was averse to any enterprise of danger and glory, he could disguise his timid indolence by the more decent excuses of religion and gratitude. He expressed a pious attachment to the memory of Constantius, from whose hands he had received in marriage Olympias, the daughter of the præfect Ablavius ; and the alliance of a female who had been educated as the destined wife of the emperor Constans exalted the dignity of a Barbarian king.[40] Tiranus professed the Christian religion ; he reigned over a nation of Christians ; and he was restrained, by every principle of conscience and interest, from contributing to the victory, which would consummate the ruin of the church. The alienated mind of Tiranus was exasperated by the indiscretion of Julian, who treated the king of Armenia as *his* slave, and as the enemy of the gods. The haughty and threatening style of the Imperial mandates[41] awakened the secret indignation of a prince who, in the humiliating state of dependence, was still conscious of his royal descent from the Arsacides, the lords of the East and the rivals of the Roman power.

The military dispositions of Julian were skilfully contrived to deceive the spies, and to divert the attention, of Sapor. The

[38] See Xenophon. Cyropæd. l. iii. p. 189, edit. Hutchinson [c. 1, § 33, 34]. Artavasdes might have supplied Mark Antony with 16,000 horse, armed and disciplined after the Parthian manner (Plutarch, in M. Antonio, tom. v. p. 117 [c. 50]).

[39] Moses of Chorene (Hist. Armeniac. l. iii. c. 11, p. 242) fixes his accession (A.D. 357) to the seventeenth year of Constantius.   [See Appendix 18.]

[40] Ammian. xx. 11. Athanasius (tom. i. p. 856) says, in general terms, that Constantius gave his brother's widow τοῖς βαρβάροις, an expression more suitable to a Roman than a Christian.

[41] Ammianus (xxiii. 2) uses a word much too soft for the occasion, *monuerat.* Muratori (Fabricius, Bibliothec. Græc. tom. vii. p. 86) has published an epistle from Julian to the satrap Arsaces ; fierce, vulgar, and (though it might deceive Sozomen, l. vi. c. 5), most probably spurious. La Bléterie (Hist. de Jovien, tom. ii. p. 339) translates and rejects it. [The text of this forgery will be found in Hertlein's ed. of Julian, p. 589.]

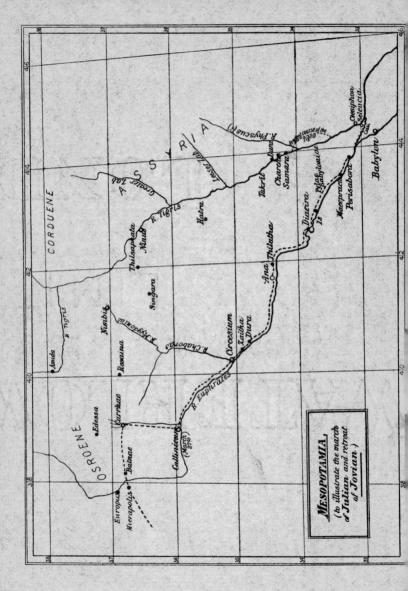

MESOPOTAMIA,
(to illustrate the march of Julian and retreat of Jovian.)

legions appeared to direct their march towards Nisibis and the Tigris. On a sudden they wheeled to the right ; traversed the level and naked plain of Carrhæ ; and reached, on the third day, the banks of the Euphrates, where the strong town [27th March] of Nicephorium, or Callinicum, had been founded by the Macedonian kings.[42] From thence the emperor pursued his march, above ninety miles, along the winding stream of the Euphrates, till, at length, about one month after his departure from [c. 2nd and Antioch, he discovered the towers of Circesium, the extreme [Karkislyä] limit of the Roman dominions. The army of Julian, the most numerous that any of the Cæsars had ever led against Persia, consisted of sixty-five thousand effective and well-disciplined soldiers. The veteran bands of cavalry and infantry, of Romans and Barbarians, had been selected from the different provinces ; and a just pre-eminence of loyalty and valour was claimed by the hardy Gauls, who guarded the throne and person of their beloved prince. A formidable body of Scythian auxiliaries had been transported from another climate, and almost from another world, to invade a distant country, of whose name and situation they were ignorant. The love of rapine and war allured to the Imperial standard several tribes of Saracens, or roving Arabs, whose service Julian had commanded, while he sternly refused the payment of the accustomed subsidies. The broad channel of the Euphrates [43] was crowded by a fleet of eleven hundred ships, destined to attend the motions, and to satisfy the wants, of the Roman army. The military strength of the fleet was composed of fifty armed galleys ; and these were accompanied by an equal number of flat-bottomed boats, which might occasionally be connected into the form of temporary bridges. The rest of the ships, partly constructed of timber and partly covered with raw hides, were laden with an almost inexhaustible supply of arms and engines, of utensils and provisions. The vigilant humanity of Julian had embarked a very large magazine of vinegar and biscuit for the use of the soldiers, but he prohibited the indulgence of wine ; and rigorously stopped a long string of

---

[42] [For a description of the locality (now Ar-Rakka) see Sachau, Reise in Syrien und Mesopotamien, p. 241 sqq.]

[43] Latissimum flumem Euphraten artabat. Ammian. xxiii. 3. Somewhat higher, at the fords of Thapsacus, the river is four stadia, or 800 yards, almost half an English mile broad (Xenophon, Anabasis, l. i. p. 41, edit. Hutchinson, with Foster's Observations, p. 29, &c. in the second volume of Spelman's translation). If the breadth of the Euphrates at Bir and Zeugma is no more than 130 yards (Voyages de Niebuhr, tom. ii. p. 335), the enormous difference must chiefly arise from the depth of the channel.

superfluous camels that attempted to follow the rear of the army. The river Chaboras falls into the Euphrates at Circesium ; [44] and, as soon as the trumpet gave the signal of march, the Romans passed the little stream which separated two mighty and hostile empires. The custom of ancient discipline required a military oration ; and Julian embraced every opportunity of displaying his eloquence. He animated the impatient and attentive legions by the example of the inflexible courage and glorious triumphs of their ancestors. He excited their resentment by a lively picture of the insolence of the Persians ; and he exhorted them to imitate his firm resolution, either to extirpate that perfidious nation or to devote his life in the cause of the republic. The eloquence of Julian was enforced by a donative of one hundred and thirty pieces of silver to every soldier ; and the bridge of the Chaboras was instantly cut away, to convince the troops that they must place their hopes of safety in the success of their arms. Yet the prudence of the emperor induced him to secure a remote frontier, perpetually exposed to the inroads of the hostile Arabs. A detachment of four thousand men was left at Circesium, which completed, to the number of ten thousand, the regular garrison of that important fortress. [45]

From the moment that the Romans entered the enemy's country, [46] the country of an active and artful enemy, the order of march was disposed in three columns. [47] The strength of the infantry, and consequently of the whole army, was placed in the centre, under the peculiar command of their master-general Victor. On the right, the brave Nevitta led a column of several legions along the banks of the Euphrates, and almost always in sight of the fleet. The left flank of the army was protected by the column of cavalry. Hormisdas and Arinthæus were ap-

[Marginal notes:]
[5th and 6th April] [Khābūr]

Julian enters the Persian territories, April 7th

His march over the desert of Mesopotamia

---

[44] Monumentum tutissimum et fabre politum, cujus mœnia Abora (the Orientals aspire Chaboras or Chabour) et Euphrates ambiunt flumina, velut spatium insulare fingentes. Ammian. xxiii. 5.

[45] The enterprise and armament of Julian are described by himself (Epist. xxvii), Ammianus Marcellinus (xxiii. 3, 4, 5), Libanius (Orat. Parent. c. 108, 109, p. 332, 333), Zosimus (l. iii. p. 160, 161, 162 [c. 12]), Sozomen (l. vi. c. 1), and John Malala (tom. ii. p. 17 [p. 328, ed. Bonn]). [Tabari's account of the war of Julian has no value (Nöldeke, p. 59 sqq.). It is derived from the Syriac Romance of Julian and Jovian, for which see Nöldeke in Ztsch. d. Morg. Ges., 28, 263 sqq., but also, in one point at least, from a second source which was also used by Malalas (p. 332, cp. Tabari, p. 61) ; see Büttner-Wobst, Philologus, 51, p. 576.]

[46] Before he enters Persia, Ammianus copiously describes (xxiii. 6, p. 396-419, edit. Gronov. in 4to) the eighteen great satrapies, or provinces (as far as the Seric, or Chinese, frontiers), which were subject to the Sassanides.

[47] Ammianus (xxiv. 1) and Zosimus (l. iii. p. 162, 163 [13]) have accurately expressed the order of march.

pointed generals of the horse; and the singular adventures of
Hormisdas [48] are not undeserving of our notice. He was a
Persian prince, of the royal race of the Sassanides, who, in the
troubles of the minority of Sapor, had escaped from prison to
the hospitable court of the great Constantine. Hormisdas at
first excited the compassion, and at length acquired the esteem,
of his new masters; his valour and fidelity raised him to the
military honours of the Roman service; and, though a Christian,
he might indulge the secret satisfaction of convincing his ungrateful country that an oppressed subject may prove the most
dangerous enemy. Such was the disposition of the three
principal columns. The front and flanks of the army were
covered by Lucillianus with a flying detachment of fifteen hundred light-armed soldiers, whose active vigilance observed the
most distant signs, and conveyed the earliest notice, of any
hostile approach. Dagalaiphus, and Secundinus duke of Os-
rhoene, conducted the troops of the rear-guard; the baggage,
securely, proceeded in the intervals of the columns; and the
ranks, from a motive either of use or ostentation, were formed in
such open order that the whole line of march extended almost
ten miles. The ordinary post of Julian was at the head of the
centre column; but, as he preferred the duties of a general to
the state of a monarch, he rapidly moved, with a small escort of
light cavalry, to the front, the rear, the flanks, wherever his
presence could animate or protect the march of the Roman
army. The country which they traversed from the Chaboras
to the cultivated lands of Assyria may be considered as a part of
the desert of Arabia, a dry and barren waste, which could never
be improved by the most powerful arts of human industry.
Julian marched over the same ground which had been trod
above seven hundred years before by the footsteps of the
younger Cyrus, and which is described by one of the companions
of his expedition, the sage and heroic Xenophon. [49] "The
country was a plain throughout, as even as the sea, and full of
wormwood; and, if any other kind of shrubs or reeds grew

---

[48] The adventures of Hormisdas are related with some mixture of fable (Zosimus, l. ii. p. 100-102 [c. 27]; Tillemont, Hist. des Empereurs, tom. iv. p. 198).
It is almost impossible that he should be the brother (frater germanus) of an *eldest*
and *posthumous* child: nor do I recollect that Ammianus ever gives him that title.
[Possibly an elder stepbrother, St. Martin suggests (on Lebeau, ii. 24).]

[49] See the first book of the Anabasis, p. 45, 46 [c. 5, § 1 *sqq.*]. This pleasing
work is original and authentic. Yet Xenophon's memory, perhaps many years
after the expedition, has sometimes betrayed him; and the distances which he
marks are often larger than either a soldier or a geographer will allow.

there, they had all an aromatic smell; out no trees could be seen. Bustards and ostriches, antelopes and wild asses,[50] appeared to be the only inhabitants of the desert; and the fatigues of the march were alleviated by the amusements of the chace." The loose sand of the desert was frequently raised by the wind into clouds of dust: and a great number of the soldiers of Julian, with their tents, were suddenly thrown to the ground by the violence of an unexpected hurricane.

His success

The sandy plains of Mesopotamia were abandoned to the antelopes and wild asses of the desert; but a variety of populous towns and villages were pleasantly situated on the banks of the Euphrates, and in the islands which are occasionally formed by

[Āna]

that river. The city of Annah, or Anatho,[51] the actual residence of an Arabian Emir, is composed of two long streets, which inclose, within a natural fortification, a small island in the midst,

[April]

and two fruitful spots on either side of the Euphrates. The warlike inhabitants of Anatho shewed a disposition to stop the march of a Roman emperor; till they were diverted from such fatal presumption by the mild exhortations of prince Hormisdas and the approaching terrors of the fleet and army. They implored, and experienced, the clemency of Julian, who transplanted the people to an advantageous settlement near Chalcis in Syria, and admitted Pusæus, the governor, to an honourable rank in his service and friendship. But the impregnable for-

[Anatelbus]

tress of Thilutha could scorn the menace of a siege; and the emperor was obliged to content himself with an insulting promise that, when he had subdued the interior provinces of Persia, Thilutha would no longer refuse to grace the triumph of the conqueror. The inhabitants of the open towns, unable to resist and unwilling to yield, fled with precipitation; and their houses, filled with spoil and provisions, were occupied by the soldiers of Julian, who massacred, without remorse, and without punishment, some defenceless women. During the march, the Surenas, or Persian general, and Malek Rodosaces, the renowned Emir of the tribe of Gassan,[52] incessantly hovered round the army:

---

[50] Mr. Spelman, the English translator of the Anabasis (vol. i. p. 51), confounds the antelope with the roe-buck, and the wild ass with the zebra.

[51] See Voyages de Tavernier, part i. l. iii. p. 316, and more especially Viaggi di Pietro della Valle, tom. i. let. xvii. p. 671, &c. He was ignorant of the old name and condition of Annah. Our blind travellers *seldom* possess any previous knowledge of the countries which they visit. Shaw and Tournefort deserve an honourable exception.

[52] Famosi nominis latro, says Ammianus; an high encomium for an Arab. The tribe of Gassan had settled on the edge of Syria, and reigned some time in Damascus, under a dynasty of thirty-one kings, or emirs, from the time of Pompey

every straggler was intercepted; every detachment was attacked; and the valiant Hormisdas escaped with some difficulty from their hands. But the Barbarians were finally repulsed; the country became every day less favourable to the operations of cavalry; and, when the Romans arrived at Mace- [April] practa, they perceived the ruins of the wall which had been constructed by the ancient kings of Assyria to secure their dominions from the incursions of the Medes. These preliminaries of the expedition of Julian appear to have employed about fifteen days; and we may compute near three hundred miles from the fortress of Circesium to the wall of Macepracta.[53]

The fertile province of Assyria,[54] which stretched beyond the Description of Assyria Tigris as far as the mountains of Media,[55] extended about four hundred miles from the ancient wall of Macepracta to the territory of Basra, where the united streams of the Euphrates and Tigris discharge themselves into the Persian Gulf.[56] The whole country might have claimed the peculiar name of Mesopotamia; as the two rivers which are never more distant than fifty, approach, between Bagdad and Babylon, within twenty-five, miles of each other. A multitude of artificial canals, dug without much labour in a soft and yielding soil, connected the rivers, and intersected the plain of Assyria. The uses of these artificial canals were various and important. They served to discharge the superfluous waters from one river into the other, at the season of their respective inundations. Subdividing

to that of the Khalif Omar. D'Herbelot, Bibliothèque Orientale, p. 360. Pocock, Specimen Hist. Arabicæ, p. 75-78. The name of Rodosaces does not appear in the list. [The identification of Ammian's *Assanitarum* with the tribe of Gassan has been questioned.]

[53] See Ammianus (xxiv. 1, 2), Libanius (Orat. Parental. c. 110, 111, p. 334), Zosimus (l. iii. p. 164-168).

[54] The description of Assyria is furnished by Herodotus (l. i. c. 192, &c.), who sometimes writes for children, and sometimes for philosophers; by Strabo (l. xvi. p. 1070-1082), and by Ammianus (l. xxiii. c. 6). The most useful of the modern travellers are Tavernier (part i. l. ii. p. 226-258), Otter (tom. ii. p. 35-69, and 189-224), and Niebuhr (tom. ii. p. 172-288). Yet I much regret that the *Irak Arabi* of Abulfeda has not been translated. [A translation by Reiske appeared in Büsching's *Magazin* for modern Hist. and Geogr. (iv. 121 *sqq.*, v. 299 *sqq.*) in Gibbon's lifetime.]

[55] Ammianus remarks that the primitive Assyria, which comprehended Ninus (Nineveh) and Arbela, had assumed the more recent and peculiar appellation of Adiabene: and he seems to fix Teredon, Vologesia, and Apollonia, as the *extreme* cities of the actual province of Assyria.

[56] The two rivers unite at Apamea, or Corna (one hundred miles from the Persian Gulf), into the broad stream of the Pasitigris, or Shat-ul-Arab. The Euphrates formerly reached the sea by a separate channel, which was obstructed and diverted by the citizens of Orchoe, about twenty miles to the south-east of modern Basra (d'Anville, in the Mémoires de l'Acad. des Inscriptions, tom. xxx. p. 170-191). [The lower courses of the Tigris and Euphrates underwent considerable changes since the middle ages; see App. 24.]

themselves into smaller and smaller branches, they refreshed the dry lands, and supplied the deficiency of rain. They facilitated the intercourse of peace and commerce ; and, as the dams could be speedily broke down, they armed the despair of the Assyrians with the means of opposing a sudden deluge to the progress of an invading army. To the soil and climate of Assyria nature had denied some of her choicest gifts, the vine, the olive, and the fig-tree ;[56a] but the food which supports the life of man, and particularly wheat and barley, were produced with inexhaustible fertility ; and the husbandman who committed his seed to the earth was frequently rewarded with an increase of two, or even of three, hundred. The face of the country was interspersed with groves of innumerable palm-trees ;[57] and the diligent natives celebrated, either in verse or prose, the three hundred and sixty uses to which the trunk, the branches, the leaves, the juice, and the fruit, were skilfully applied. Several manufactures, especially those of leather and linen, employed the industry of a numerous people, and afforded valuable materials for foreign trade ; which appears, however, to have been conducted by the hands of strangers. Babylon had been converted into a royal park ; but near the ruins of the ancient capital new cities had successively arisen, and the populousness of the country was displayed in the multitude of towns and villages, which were built of bricks, dried in the sun, and strongly cemented with bitumen, the natural and peculiar production of the Babylonian soil. While the successors of Cyrus reigned over Asia, the province of Assyria alone maintained, during a third part of the year, the luxurious plenty of the table and household of the Great King. Four considerable villages were assigned for the subsistence of his Indian dogs ; eight hundred stallions and sixteen thousand mares were constantly kept at the expense of the country, for the royal stables ; and, as the daily tribute, which was paid to the satrap, amounted to one English bushel of silver, we may compute the annual revenue of Assyria at more than twelve hundred thousand pounds sterling.[58]

[56a] [Milman has pointed out that this is not so at the present day.]

[57] The learned Kæmpfer, as a botanist, an antiquary, and a traveller, has exhausted (Amœnitat. Exoticæ, Fascicul. iv. p. 660-764) the whole subject of palm-trees.

[58] Assyria yielded to the Persian satrap an *artaba* of silver each day. The well-known proportion of weights and measures (see Bishop Hooper's elaborate Inquiry), the specific gravity of water and silver, and the value of that metal, will afford, after a short process, the annual revenue which I have stated. Yet the Great King received no more than 1000 Euboic, or Tyrian, talents (252,000*l.*) from

The fields of Assyria were devoted by Julian to the calamities of war; and the philosopher retaliated on a guiltless people the acts of rapine and cruelty which had been committed by their haughty master in the Roman provinces. The trembling Assyrians summoned the rivers to their assistance; and completed, with their own hands, the ruin of their country. The roads were rendered impracticable; a flood of waters was poured into the camp; and during several days the troops of Julian were obliged to contend with the most discouraging hardships. But every obstacle was surmounted by the perseverance of the legionaries, who were inured to toil as well as to danger, and who felt themselves animated by the spirit of their leader. The damage was gradually repaired; the [May] waters were restored to their proper channels; whole groves of palm-trees were cut down and placed along the broken parts of the road; and the army passed over the broad and deeper canals on bridges of floating rafts, which were supported by the help of bladders. Two cities of Assyria presumed to resist the arms of a Roman emperor: and they both paid the severe penalty of their rashness. At the distance of fifty miles from the royal residence of Ctesiphon, Perisabor, or Anbar,[59] held the second rank in the province; a city, large, populous, and well fortified, surrounded with a double wall, almost encompassed by a branch of the Euphrates, and defended by the valour of a numerous garrison. The exhortations of Hormisdas were repulsed with contempt; and the ears of the Persian prince were wounded by a just reproach that, unmindful of his royal birth, he conducted an army of strangers against his king and country. The Assyrians maintained their loyalty by a skilful, as well as vigorous, defence; [May] till, the lucky stroke of a battering-ram having opened a large breach by shattering one of the angles of the wall, they hastily retired into the fortifications of the interior citadel. The soldiers of Julian rushed impetuously into the town, and, after the full gratification of every military appetite, Perisabor was reduced to ashes; and the engines which assaulted the citadel were planted on the ruins of the smoking houses. The contest was continued by an incessant and mutual discharge of missile weapons; and

Assyria. The comparison of two passages in Herodotus (l. i. c. 192, l. iii. c. 89-96) reveals an important difference between the *gross*, and the *net*, revenue of Persia; the sums paid by the province, and the gold or silver deposited in the royal treasure. The monarch might annually save three millions six hundred thousand pounds, of the seventeen or eighteen millions raised upon the people.

[59] [The foundation of this place (Anbār—Ἀμβαρα, Ἀβαρα = Pêrôz—Shâpûr) is noticed in the chronicle of Tabari (Nöldeke, p. 67). Al-Anbār means "the granaries," and is to be sought in the ruins of Sifeyra (acc. to Mr. Le Strange).]

the superiority which the Romans might derive from the mechanical powers of their balistæ and catapultæ was counterbalanced by the advantage of the ground on the side of the besieged. But as soon as an *Helepolis* had been constructed, which could engage on equal terms with the loftiest ramparts, the tremendous aspect of a moving turret, that would leave no hope of resistance or of mercy, terrified the defenders of the citadel into an humble submission; and the place was surrendered only two days after Julian first appeared under the walls of Perisabor. Two thousand five hundred persons of both sexes, the feeble remnant of a flourishing people, were permitted to retire: the plentiful magazines of corn, of arms, and of splendid furniture were partly distributed among the troops, and partly reserved for the public service: the useless stores were destroyed by fire or thrown into the stream of the Euphrates; and the fate of Amida was revenged by the total ruin of Perisabor.

of Maogamalcha
[Maozar malkē]

[May]

The city, or rather fortress, of Maogamalcha, which was defended by sixteen large towers, a deep ditch, and two strong and solid walls of brick and bitumen, appears to have been constructed at the distance of eleven miles, as the safeguard of the capital of Persia. The emperor, apprehensive of leaving such an important fortress in his rear, immediately formed the siege of Maogamalcha; and the Roman army was distributed, for that purpose, into three divisions. Victor, at the head of the cavalry, and of a detachment of heavy-armed foot, was ordered to clear the country as far as the banks of the Tigris and the suburbs of Ctesiphon. The conduct of the attack was assumed by Julian himself, who seemed to place his whole dependence in the military engines which he erected against the walls; while he secretly contrived a more efficacious method of introducing his troops into the heart of the city. Under the direction of Nevitta and Dagalaiphus, the trenches were opened at a considerable distance, and gradually prolonged as far as the edge of the ditch. The ditch was speedily filled with earth; and, by the incessant labour of the troops, a mine was carried under the foundations of the walls, and sustained, at sufficient intervals, by props of timber. Three chosen cohorts, advancing in a single file, silently explored the dark and dangerous passage; till their intrepid leader whispered back the intelligence that he was ready to issue from his confinement into the streets of the hostile city. Julian checked their ardour that he might ensure their success; and immediately diverted the attention of the garrison, by the tumult and clamour of a general assault. The

Persians, who from their walls contemptuously beheld the progress of an impotent attack, celebrated, with songs of triumph, the glory of Sapor; and ventured to assure the emperor that he might ascend the starry mansion of Ormusd, before he could hope to take the impregnable city of Maogamalcha. The city was already taken. History has recorded the name of a private soldier, the first who ascended from the mine into a deserted tower. The passage was widened by his companions, who pressed forwards with impatient valour. Fifteen hundred enemies were already in the midst of the city. The astonished garrison abandoned the walls, and their only hope of safety; the gates were instantly burst open; and the revenge of the soldier, unless it were suspended by lust or avarice, was satiated by an undistinguishing massacre. The governor, who had yielded on a promise of mercy, was burnt alive, a few days afterwards, on a charge of having uttered some disrespectful words against the honour of prince Hormisdas. The fortifications were razed to the ground; and not a vestige was left that the city of Maogamalcha had ever existed. The neighbourhood of the capital of Persia was adorned with three stately palaces, laboriously enriched with every production that could gratify the luxury and pride of an Eastern monarch. The pleasant situation of the gardens along the banks of the Tigris was improved, according to the Persian taste, by the symmetry of flowers, fountains, and shady walks: and spacious parks were enclosed for the reception of the bears, lions, and wild boars, which were maintained at a considerable expense for the pleasure of the royal chase. The park-walls were broke down, the savage game was abandoned to the darts of the soldiers, and the palaces of Sapor were reduced to ashes, by the command of the Roman emperor. Julian, on this occasion, shewed himself ignorant, or careless, of the laws of civility, which the prudence and refinement of polished ages have established between hostile princes. Yet these wanton ravages need not excite in our breasts any vehement emotions of pity or resentment. A simple, naked statue, finished by the hand of a Grecian · artist, is of more genuine value, than all these rude and costly monuments of Barbaric labour: and, if we are more deeply affected by the ruin of a palace than by the conflagration of a cottage, our humanity must have formed a very erroneous estimate of the miseries of human life.[60]

[60] The operations of the Assyrian war are circumstantially related by Ammianus (xxiv. 2, 3, 4, 5), Libanius (Orat. Parent. c. 112-123, p. 335-347), Zosimus (l. iii. p.

Julian was an object of terror and hatred to the Persians : and the painters of that nation represented the invader of their country under the emblem of a furious lion, who vomited from his mouth a consuming fire.[61] To his friends and soldiers, the philosophic hero appeared in a more amiable light ; and his virtues were never more conspicuously displayed than in the last, and most active, period of his life. He practised, without effort, and almost without merit, the habitual qualities of temperance and sobriety. According to the dictates of that artificial wisdom which assumes an absolute dominion over the mind and body, he sternly refused himself the indulgence of the most natural appetites.[62] In the warm climate of Assyria, which solicited a luxurious people to the gratification of every sensual desire,[63] a youthful conqueror preserved his chastity pure and inviolate : nor was Julian ever tempted, even by a motive of curiosity, to visit his female captives of exquisite beauty,[64] who, instead of resisting his power, would have disputed with each other the honour of his embraces. With the same firmness that he resisted the allurements of love, he sustained the hardships of war. When the Romans marched through the flat and flooded country, their sovereign, on foot, at the head of his legions, shared their fatigues, and animated their diligence. In every useful labour, the hand of Julian was prompt and strenuous ; and the Imperial purple was wet and dirty, as the coarse garment of the meanest soldier. The two sieges allowed him some remarkable opportunities of signalizing his personal valour, which, in the improved state of the military art, can seldom be exerted by a prudent general. The emperor stood before the citadel of Perisabor, insensible of his extreme danger, and encouraged his troops to burst open the gates of iron, till he was almost overwhelmed under a cloud of missile weapons and

168-180), and Gregory Nazianzen (Orat. iv. p. 113, 144). The *military* criticisms of the saint are devoutly copied by Tillemont, his faithful slave.

[61] Libanius de ulciscendâ Juliani nece, c. 13, p. 162.

[62] The famous examples of Cyrus, Alexander, and Scipio were acts of justice. Julian's chastity was voluntary, and, in his opinion, meritorious.

[63] Sallust (ap. Vet. Scholiast. Juvenal, Satir. i. 104) observes that nihil corruptius moribus. The matrons and virgins of Babylon freely mingled with the men, in licentious banquets : and, as they felt the intoxication of wine and love, they gradually, and almost completely, threw aside the encumbrance of dress; ad ultimum ima corporum velamenta projiciunt. Q. Curtius, v. 1.

[64] Ex virginibus autem, quæ speciosæ sunt captæ, et in Perside, ubi fœminarum pulchritudo excellit, nec contrectare aliquam voluit nec videre. Ammian. xxiv. 4. The native race of Persians is small and ugly; but it has been improved by the perpetual mixture of Circassian blood (Herodot. l. iii. c. 97. Buffon, Hist. Naturelle, tom. iii. p. 420).

huge stones that were directed against his person. As he examined the exterior fortifications of Maogamalcha, two Persians, devoting themselves for their country, suddenly rushed upon him with drawn scimitars : the emperor dexterously received their blows on his uplifted shield ; and, with a steady and well-aimed thrust, laid one of his adversaries dead at his feet. The esteem of a prince who possesses the virtues which he approves is the noblest recompense of a deserving subject ; and the authority which Julian derived from his personal merit enabled him to revive and enforce the rigour of ancient discipline. He punished with death, or ignominy, the misbehaviour of three troops of horse, who, in a skirmish with the Surenas, had lost their honour, and one of their standards : and he distinguished with *obsidional* [65] crowns the valour of the foremost soldiers who had ascended into the city of Maogamalcha. After the siege of Perisabor, the firmness of the emperor was exercised by the insolent avarice of the army, who loudly complained that their services were rewarded by a trifling donative of one hundred pieces of silver. His just indignation was expressed in the grave and manly language of a Roman. " Riches are the object of your desires ? those riches are in the hands of the Persians; and the spoils of this fruitful country are proposed as the prize of your valour and discipline. Believe me," added Julian, " the Roman republic, which formerly possessed such immense treasures, is now reduced to want and wretchedness ; since our princes have been persuaded, by weak and interested ministers, to purchase with gold the tranquillity of the Barbarians. The revenue is exhausted ; the cities are ruined ; the provinces are dispeopled. For myself, the only inheritance that I have received from my royal ancestors is a soul incapable of fear ; and, as long as I am convinced that every real advantage is seated in the mind, I shall not blush to acknowledge an honourable poverty, which, in the days of ancient virtue, was considered as the glory of Fabricius. That glory, and that virtue, may be your own, if you will listen to the voice of Heaven, and of your leader. But, if you will rashly persist, if you are determined to renew the shameful and mischievous examples of old seditions, proceed.—As it becomes an emperor who has filled the first rank among men, I am prepared to die, standing ; and to

[65] Obsidionalibus coronis donati. Ammian. xxiv. 4. Either Julian or his historian were unskilful antiquaries. He should have given *mural* crowns. The *obsidional* were the reward of a general who had delivered a besieged city (Aulus Gellius, Noct. Attic. v. 6).

despise a precarious life, which, every hour, may depend on an accidental fever. If I have been found unworthy of the command, there are now among you (I speak it with pride and pleasure), there are many chiefs, whose merit and experience are equal to the conduct of the most important war. Such has been the temper of my reign that I can retire, without regret, and without apprehension, to the obscurity of a private station." [66] The modest resolution of Julian was answered by the unanimous applause and cheerful obedience of the Romans; who declared their confidence of victory, while they fought under the banners of their heroic prince. Their courage was kindled by his frequent and familiar asseverations (for such wishes were the oaths of Julian), "So may I reduce the Persians under the yoke!" "Thus may I restore the strength and splendour of the republic!" The love of fame was the ardent passion of his soul: but it was not before he trampled on the ruins of Maogamalcha, that he allowed himself to say, "We have now provided some materials for the sophist of Antioch".[67]

He transports his fleet from the Euphrates to the Tigris

The successful valour of Julian had triumphed over all the obstacles that opposed his march to the gates of Ctesiphon. But the reduction, or even the siege, of the capital of Persia was still at a distance: nor can the military conduct of the emperor be clearly apprehended without a knowledge of the country which was the theatre of his bold and skilful operations.[68] Twenty miles to the south of Bagdad, and on the eastern bank of the Tigris, the curiosity of travellers has observed some ruins of the palaces of Ctesiphon, which, in the time of Julian, was a great and populous city. The name and glory of the adjacent Seleucia were for ever extinguished; and the only remaining quarter of that Greek colony had resumed, with the Assyrian language and manners, the primitive appellation of Coche. Coche was situate on the western side of the Tigris; but it was naturally considered as a suburb of Ctesiphon, with which we may suppose it to have been connected by a permanent bridge of boats. The united parts contributed to

[66] I give this speech as original and genuine. Ammianus might hear, could transcribe, and was incapable of inventing, it. I have used some slight freedoms, and conclude with the most forcible sentence.

[67] Ammian. xxiv. 3. Libanius, Orat. Parent. c. 122, p. 346.

[68] M. d 'Anville (Mém. de l'Académie des Inscriptions, tom. xxviii. p. 246-259) has ascertained the true position and distance of Babylon, Seleucia, Ctesiphon, Bagdad, &c. The Roman traveller, Pietro della Valle (tom. i. lett. xvii. p. 650-780), seems to be the most intelligent spectator of that famous province. He is a gentleman and a scholar, but intolerably vain and prolix.

form the common epithet of Al Modain, THE CITIES, which the Orientals have bestowed on the winter residence of the Sassanides; and the whole circumference of the Persian capital was strongly fortified by the waters of the river, by lofty walls, and by impracticable morasses. Near the ruins of Seleucia, the camp of Julian was fixed; and secured, by a ditch and rampart, against the sallies of the numerous and enterprising garrison of Coche. In this fruitful and pleasant country, the Romans were plentifully supplied with water and forage; and several forts which might have embarrassed the motions of the army submitted, after some resistance, to the efforts of their valour. The fleet passed from the Euphrates into an artificial derivation of that river, which pours a copious and navigable stream into the Tigris, at a small distance *below* the great city. If they had followed this royal canal, which bore the name of Nahar-Malcha,[69] [Nahr-al-Mālik] the intermediate situation of Coche would have separated the fleet and army of Julian; and the rash attempt of steering against the current of the Tigris, and forcing their way through the midst of a hostile capital, must have been attended with the total destruction of the Roman navy. The prudence of the emperor foresaw the danger, and provided the remedy. As he had minutely studied the operations of Trajan in the same country, he soon recollected that his warlike predecessor had dug a new and navigable canal, which, leaving Coche on the right hand, conveyed the waters of the Nahar-Malcha into the river Tigris, at some distance *above* the cities. From the information of the peasants, Julian ascertained the vestiges of this ancient work, which were almost obliterated by design or accident. By the indefatigable labour of the soldiers, a broad and deep channel was speedily prepared for the reception of the Euphrates. A strong dyke was constructed to interrupt the ordinary current of the Nahar-Malcha: a flood of waters rushed impetuously into their new bed; and the Roman fleet, steering their triumphant course into the Tigris, derided the vain and ineffectual barriers which the Persians of Ctesiphon had erected to oppose their passage.

As it became necessary to transport the Roman army over the Tigris, another labour presented itself, of less toil, but of more danger, than the preceding expedition. The stream was broad and rapid; the ascent steep and difficult; and the intrench- [Passage of the Tigris and victory of the Romans [May]

---

[69] The royal canal (*Nahar Malcha*) might be successively restored, altered, divided, &c. (Cellarius, Geograph. Antiq. tom. ii. p. 453); and these changes may serve to explain the seeming contradictions of antiquity. In the time of Julian, it must have fallen into the Euphrates [*leg.* Tigris] *below* Ctesiphon. [Ibn Serapion describes it as falling into the Tigris three leagues below Al-Madāin. Cp. App. 24.]

ments, which had been formed on the ridge of the opposite bank, were lined with a numerous army of heavy cuirassiers, dexterous archers, and huge elephants; who (according to the extravagant hyperbole of Libanius) could trample, with the same ease, a field of corn, or a legion of Romans.[70]   In the presence of such an enemy, the construction of a bridge was impracticable; and the intrepid prince, who instantly seized the only possible expedient, concealed his design, till the moment of execution, from the knowledge of the Barbarians, of his own troops, and even of his generals themselves. Under the specious pretence of examining the state of the magazines, fourscore vessels were gradually unladen;[71] and a select detachment, apparently destined for some secret expedition, was ordered to stand to their arms on the first signal.   Julian disguised the silent anxiety of his own mind with smiles of confidence and joy; and amused the hostile nations with the spectacle of military games, which he insultingly celebrated under the walls of Coche.   The day was consecrated to pleasure; but, as soon as the hour of supper was past, the emperor summoned the generals to his tent; and acquainted them that he had fixed that night for the passage of the Tigris. They stood in silent and respectful astonishment; but, when the venerable Sallust assumed the privilege of his age and experience, the rest of the chiefs supported with freedom the weight of his prudent remonstrances.[72]   Julian contented himself with observing that conquest and safety depended on the attempt; that, instead of diminishing, the number of their enemies would be increased, by successive reinforcements; and that a longer delay would neither contract the breadth of the stream nor level the height of the bank.   The signal was instantly given, and obeyed: the most impatient of the legionaries leaped into five vessels that lay nearest to the bank; and, as they plied their oars with intrepid diligence, they were lost, after a few moments, in the darkness of the night.   A flame arose on the opposite side; and Julian, who too clearly understood that his foremost vessels, in attempting to land, had been fired by the enemy, dexterously

---

[70] Καὶ μεγέθεσιν ἐλεφάντων, οἷς ἴσον ἔργον διὰ σταχύων ἐλθεῖν, καὶ φάλαγγος [Ἐπιτάφ. c. 125].   Rien n'est beau que le vrai; a maxim which should be inscribed on the desk of every rhetorician.

[71] [We are not told that eighty vessels were unladen, but that each unladen vessel was manned with eighty soldiers—octogenis armatis, Amm. xxiv. 6, 4.]

[72] Libanius alludes to the most powerful of the generals.   I have ventured to name Sallust.   Ammianus says, of all the leaders, quod acri metû territi duces concordi precatû fieri prohibere tentarent.

converted their extreme danger into a presage of victory. "Our fellow-soldiers," he eagerly exclaimed, "are already masters of the bank ; see—they make the appointed signal : let us hasten to emulate and assist their courage." The united and rapid motion of a great fleet broke the violence of the current, and they reached the eastern shore of the Tigris with sufficient speed to extinguish the flames and rescue their adventurous companions. The difficulties of a steep and lofty ascent were increased by the weight of armour and the darkness of the night. A shower of stones, darts, and fire was incessantly discharged on the heads of the assailants ; who, after an arduous struggle, climbed the bank, and stood victorious upon the ramparts. As soon as they possessed a more equal field, Julian, who, with his light infantry, had led the attack,[73] darted through the ranks a skilful and experienced eye : his bravest soldiers, according to the precepts of Homer,[74] were distributed in the front and rear ; and all the trumpets of the imperial army sounded to battle. The Romans, after sending up a military shout, advanced in measured steps to the animating notes of martial music ; launched their formidable javelins ; and rushed forwards with drawn swords, to deprive the Barbarians, by a closer onset, of the advantage of their missile weapons. The whole engagement lasted above twelve hours ; till the gradual retreat of the Persians was changed into a disorderly flight, of which the shameful example was given by the principal leaders, and the Surenas himself. They were pursued to the gates of Ctesiphon ; and the conquerors might have entered the dismayed city,[75] if their general, Victor, who was dangerously wounded with an arrow, had not conjured them to desist from a rash attempt, which must be fatal, if it were not successful. On *their* side, the Romans acknowledged the loss of only seventy-five men ; while they affirmed that the Barbarians had left on the field of battle two thousand five hundred, or even six thousand, of their bravest soldiers. The spoil was such as might be expected from the riches and luxury of an Oriental camp ; large quantities of silver

[73] Hinc Imperator . . . (says Ammianus) ipse cum levis armaturæ auxiliis per prima postremaque discurrens, &c. Yet Zosimus, his friend, does not allow him to pass the river till two days after the battle.

[74] Secundum Homericam dispositionem. A similar disposition is ascribed to the wise Nestor, in the fourth book of the Iliad ; and Homer was never absent from the mind of Julian.

[75] Persas terrore subito miscuerunt, versisque agminibus totius gentis apertas Ctesiphontis portas victor miles intrâsset, ni major prædarum occasio fuisset, quam cura victoriæ (Sextus Rufus de Provinciis [= Festus, Breviarium], c. 28). Their avarice might dispose them to hear the advice of Victor.

and gold, splendid arms and trappings, and beds and tables of massy silver. The victorious emperor distributed, as the rewards of valour, some honourable gifts, civic and mural and naval crowns ; which he, and perhaps he alone, esteemed more precious than the wealth of Asia. A solemn sacrifice was offered to the god of war, but the appearances of the victims threatened the most inauspicious events ; and Julian soon discovered, by less ambiguous signs, that he had now reached the term of his prosperity.[76]

On the second day after the battle, the domestic guards, the Jovians and Herculians, and the remaining troops, which composed near two-thirds of the whole army, were securely wafted over the Tigris.[77] While the Persians beheld from the walls of Ctesiphon the desolation of the adjacent country, Julian cast many an anxious look towards the North, in full expectation that, as he himself had victoriously penetrated to the capital of Sapor, the march and junction of his lieutenants, Sebastian and Procopius, would be executed with the same courage and diligence. His expectations were disappointed by the treachery of the Armenian king, who permitted, and most probably directed, the desertion of his auxiliary troops from the camp of the Romans ;[78] and by the dissensions of the two generals, who were incapable of forming or executing any plan for the public service. When the emperor had relinquished the hope of this important reinforcement, he condescended to hold a council of war, and approved, after a full debate, the sentiment of those generals who dissuaded the siege of Ctesiphon as a fruitless and pernicious undertaking. It is not easy for us to conceive by what arts of fortification a city thrice besieged and taken by the predecessors of Julian could be rendered impregnable against an army of sixty thousand Romans, commanded by a brave and experienced general, and abundantly supplied with ships, provisions, batter-

---

[76] The labour of the canal, the passage of the Tigris, and the victory are described by Ammianus (xxiv. 5, 6), Libanius (Orat. Parent. c. 124-128, p. 347-353), Greg. Nazianzen (Orat. iv. p. 115), Zosimus (l. iii. p. 181-183 [c. 24 *sq.*]), and Sextus Rufus (de Provinciis, c. 28).

[77] The fleet and army were formed in three divisions, of which the first only had passed during the night (Ammian. xxiv. 6). The πᾶσα δορυφορια, whom Zosimus transports on the third day (l. iii. p. 183), might consist of the protectors, among whom the historian Ammianus, and the future emperor Jovian, actually served, some *schools* of the *domestics*, and perhaps the Jovians and Herculians, who often did duty as guards.

[78] Moses of Chorene (Hist. Armen. l. iii. c. 15, p. 246) supplies us with a national tradition, and a spurious letter. I have borrowed only the leading circumstance, which is consistent with truth, probability, and Libanius (Orat. Parent. c. 131, p. 355).

ing engines, and military stores. But we may rest assured, from the love of glory, and contempt of danger, which formed the character of Julian, that he was not discouraged by any trivial or imaginary obstacles.[79] At the very time when he declined the siege of Ctesiphon, he rejected, with obstinacy and disdain, the most flattering offers of a negotiation of peace. Sapor, who had been so long accustomed to the tardy ostentation of Constantius, was surprised by the intrepid diligence of his successor. As far as the confines of India and Scythia, the satraps of the distant provinces were ordered to assemble their troops, and to march, without delay, to the assistance of their monarch. But their preparations were dilatory, their motions slow ; and, before Sapor could lead an army into the field, he received the melancholy intelligence of the devastation of Assyria, the ruin of his palaces, and the slaughter of his bravest troops, who defended the passage of the Tigris. The pride of royalty was humbled in the dust ; he took his repasts on the ground ; and the disorder of his hair expressed the grief and anxiety of his mind. Perhaps he would not have refused to purchase, with one half of his kingdom, the safety of the remainder : and he would have gladly subscribed himself, in a treaty of peace, the faithful and dependent ally of the Roman conqueror. Under the pretence of private business, a minister of rank and confidence was secretly dispatched to embrace the knees of Hormisdas, and to request, in the language of a suppliant, that he might be introduced into the presence of the emperor. The Sassanian prince, whether he listened to the voice of pride or humanity, whether he consulted the sentiments of his birth or the duties of his situation, was equally inclined to promote a salutary measure, which would terminate the calamities of Persia, and secure the triumph of Rome. He was astonished by the inflexible firmness of a hero, who remembered, most unfortunately for himself and for his country, that Alexander had uniformly rejected the propositions of Darius. But, as Julian was sensible that the hope of a safe and honourable peace might cool the ardour of his troops, he earnestly requested that Hormisdas would privately dismiss the minister of Sapor and conceal this dangerous temptation from the knowledge of the camp.[80]

---

[79] Civitas inexpugnabilis, facinus audax et importunum, Ammianus, xxiv. 7. His fellow-soldier, Eutropius, turns aside from the difficulty, Assyriamque populatus, castra apud Ctesiphontem stativa aliquandiu habuit : remeansque victor, &c. x. 16. Zosimus is artful or ignorant, and Socrates inaccurate.

[80] Libanius, Orat. Parent. c. 130, p. 354, c. 139, p. 361 ; Socrates, l. iii. c. 21. The ecclesiastical historian imputes the refusal of peace to the advice of Maximus.

The honour, as well as interest, of Julian forbade him to consume his time under the impregnable walls of Ctesiphon; and, as often as he defied the Barbarians, who defended the city, to meet him on the open plain, they prudently replied that, if he desired to exercise his valour, he might seek the army of the Great King. He felt the insult, and he accepted the advice. Instead of confining his servile march to the banks of the Euphrates and Tigris, he resolved to imitate the adventurous spirit of Alexander, and boldly to advance into the inland provinces, till he forced his rival to contend with him, perhaps in the plains of Arbela, for the empire of Asia. The magnanimity of Julian was applauded and betrayed by the arts of a noble Persian, who, in the cause of his country, had generously submitted to act a part full of danger, of falsehood, and of shame.[81] With a train of faithful followers, he deserted to the Imperial camp; exposed, in a specious tale, the injuries which he had sustained; exaggerated the cruelty of Sapor, the discontent of the people, and the weakness of the monarchy; and confidently offered himself as the hostage and guide of the Roman march. The most rational grounds of suspicion were urged, without effect, by the wisdom and experience of Hormisdas; and the credulous Julian, receiving the traitor into his bosom, was persuaded to issue an hasty order, which, in the opinion of mankind, appeared to arraign his prudence, and to endanger his safety. He destroyed, in a single hour, the whole navy, which had been transported above five hundred miles, at so great expense of toil, of treasure, and of blood. Twelve, or, at the most, twenty-two, small vessels were saved, to accompany, on carriages, the march of the army, and to form occasional bridges for the passage of the rivers. A supply of twenty days' provisions was reserved for the use of the soldiers; and the rest of the magazines, with a fleet of eleven hundred vessels, which rode at anchor in the Tigris, were abandoned to the flames, by the absolute command of the emperor. The Christian bishops, Gregory and Augustin, insult the madness of the apostate, who executed, with his own hands, the sentence of divine justice. Their authority, of less weight, perhaps, in a military question, is confirmed by the cool judg-

Such advice was unworthy of a philosopher; but the philosopher was likewise a magician, who flattered the hopes and passions of his master.

[81] The arts of this new Zopyrus (Greg. Nazianzen, Orat. iv. p. 115, 116 [v. c. 11]) may derive some credit from the testimony of two abbreviators (Sextus Rufus and Victor), and the casual hints of Libanius (Orat. Parent. c. 134, p. 357), and Ammianus (xxiv. 7). The course of genuine history is interrupted by a most unseasonable chasm in the text of Ammianus.

ment of an experienced soldier, who was himself spectator of the conflagration, and who could not disapprove the reluctant murmurs of the troops.[82]   Yet there are not wanting some specious and perhaps solid reasons, which might justify the resolution of Julian.   The navigation of the Euphrates never ascended above Babylon, nor that of the Tigris above Opis.[83]   The distance of the last-mentioned city from the Roman camp was not very considerable ; and Julian must soon have renounced the vain and impracticable attempt of forcing upwards a great fleet against the stream of a rapid river,[84] which in several places was embarrassed by natural or artificial cataracts.[85]   The power of sails or oars was insufficient ; it became necessary to tow the ships against the current of the river ; the strength of twenty thousand soldiers was exhausted in this tedious and servile labour ; and, if the Romans continued to march along the banks of the Tigris, they could only expect to return home without achieving any enterprise worthy of the genius or fortune of their leader.   If, on the contrary, it was advisable to advance into the inland country, the destruction of the fleet and magazines was the only measure which could save that valuable prize from the hands of the numerous and active troops which might suddenly be poured from the gates of Ctesiphon.   Had the arms of Julian been victorious, we should now admire the conduct, as well as the courage, of a hero, who, by depriving his soldiers of the hopes of a retreat, left them only the alternative of death or conquest.[86]

The cumbersome train of artillery and waggons which re-   *And marches*
tards the operations of a modern army were in a great measure   *against Sapor*
unknown in the camps of the Romans.[87]   Yet, in every age,

---

[82] See Ammianus (xxiv. 7), Libanius (Orat. Parentalis, c. 132, 133, p. 356, 357), Zosimus (l. iii. p. 183), Zonaras (tom. ii. l. xiii. p. 26), Gregory (Orat. iv. p. 116 [c. 12]), Augustin (De Civitate Dei, l. iv. c. 29, l. v. c. 21).   Of these, Libanius alone attempts a faint apology for his hero ; who, according to Ammianus, pronounced his own condemnation, by a tardy and ineffectual attempt to extinguish the flames.

[83] Consult Herodotus (l. i. c. 194), Strabo (l. xvi. p. 1074), and Tavernier (p. i. l. ii. p. 152).

[84] A celeritate Tigris incipit vocari, ita appellant Medi sagittam. Plin. Hist. Natur. vi. 31.

[85] One of these dikes, which produces an artificial cascade or cataract, is described by Tavernier (part i. l. ii. p. 226), and Thévenot (part ii. l. i. p. 193).   The Persians, or Assyrians, laboured to interrupt the navigation of the river (Strabo, l. xv. p. 1075.   D'Anville, l'Euphrate et le Tigre p. 98, 99).

[86] Recollect the successful and applauded rashness of Agathocles and Cortez, who burnt their ships on the coasts of Africa and Mexico.

[87] See the judicious reflections of the author of the Essai sur la Tactique, tom. ii. p. 287-353, and the learned remarks of M. Guichardt (Nouveaux Mémoires Militaires, tom. i. p. 351-382) on the baggage and subsistence of the Roman armies.

the subsistence of sixty thousand men must have been one of
the most important cares of a prudent general; and that subsistence could only be drawn from his own or from the enemy's
country. Had it been possible for Julian to maintain a bridge
of communication on the Tigris, and to preserve the conquered
places of Assyria, a desolated province could not afford any
large or regular supplies, in a season of the year when the
lands were covered by the inundation of the Euphrates,[88] and
the unwholesome air was darkened with swarms of innumerable
insects.[89] The appearance of the hostile country was far more
inviting. The extensive region that lies between the river
Tigris and the mountains of Media was filled with villages and
towns; and the fertile soil, for the most part, was in a very
improved state of cultivation. Julian might expect that a conqueror who possessed the two forcible instruments of persuasion, steel and gold, would easily procure a plentiful subsistence from the fears or the avarice of the natives. But on
the approach of the Romans, this rich and smiling prospect was
instantly blasted. Wherever they moved, the inhabitants deserted the open villages, and took shelter in the fortified towns;
the cattle was driven away; the grass and ripe corn were consumed with fire; and, as soon as the flames had subsided which
interrupted the march of Julian, he beheld the melancholy face
of a smoking and naked desert. This desperate but effectual
method of defence can only be executed by the enthusiasm of a
people who prefer their independence to their property; or by
the rigour of an arbitrary government, which consults the public
safety without submitting to their inclinations the liberty of
choice. On the present occasion, the zeal and obedience of the
Persians seconded the commands of Sapor; and the emperor
was soon reduced to the scanty stock of provisions, which continually wasted in his hands. Before they were entirely consumed, he might still have reached the wealthy and unwarlike
cities of Ecbatana or Susa, by the effort of a well-directed
march;[90] but he was deprived of this last resource by his igno-

[88] The Tigris rises to the south, the Euphrates to the north, of the Armenian
mountains. The former overflows in March, the latter in July. These circumstances are well explained in the Geographical Dissertation of Foster, inserted in
Spelman's Expedition of Cyrus, vol. ii. p. 26.

[89] Ammianus (xxiv. 8) describes, as he had felt, the inconveniency of the flood,
the heat, and the insects. The lands of Assyria, oppressed by the Turks, and
ravaged by the Curds, or Arabs, yield an increase of ten, fifteen, and twenty-fold,
for the seed which is cast into the ground by the wretched and unskilful husbandmen. Voyages de Niebuhr, tom. ii. p. 279, 285.

[90] Isidore of Charax (Mansion. Parthic. p. 5, 6, in Hudson, Geograph. Minor.

rance of the roads, and by the perfidy of his guides. The Romans wandered several days in the country to the eastward of Bagdad : the Persian deserter, who had artfully led them into the snare, escaped from their resentment ; and his followers, as soon as they were put to the torture, confessed the secret of the conspiracy. The visionary conquests of Hyrcania and India, which had so long amused, now tormented, the mind of Julian. Conscious that his own imprudence was the cause of the public distress, he anxiously balanced the hopes of safety or success, without obtaining a satisfactory answer either from gods or men. At length, as the only practicable measure, he embraced the resolution of directing his steps towards the banks of the Tigris, with the design of saving the army by a hasty march to the confines of Corduene ; a fertile and friendly province, which acknowledged the sovereignty of Rome. The desponding troops obeyed the signal of the retreat, only seventy days after June 16 they had passed the Chaboras with the sanguine expectation of subverting the throne of Persia.[91]

As long as the Romans seemed to advance into the country, Retreat and their march was observed and insulted from a distance by distress of several bodies of Persian cavalry ; who, showing themselves army sometimes in loose, and sometimes in closer, order, faintly skirmished with the advanced guards. These detachments were, however, supported by a much greater force ; and the heads of the columns were no sooner pointed towards the Tigris than a cloud of dust arose on the plain. The Romans, who now aspired only to the permission of a safe and speedy retreat, endeavoured to persuade themselves that this formidable appearance was occasioned by a troop of wild asses, or perhaps by the approach of some friendly Arabs. They halted, pitched their tents, fortified their camp, passed the whole night in continual alarms ; and discovered, at the dawn of day, that they were surrounded by an army of Persians. This army, which might be considered only as the van of the Barbarians, was soon followed by the main body of cuirassiers, archers, and elephants, commanded by Meranes, a general of rank and reputation. He was accompanied by two of the king's sons, and many of the

tom. ii.) reckons 129 schœni from Seleucia, and Thévenot (part i. l. i. ii. p. 209-245) 128 hours of march from Bagdad, to Ecbatana, or Hamadam. These measures cannot exceed an ordinary parasang, or three Roman miles.

[91] The march of Julian from Ctesiphon is circumstantially, but not clearly, described by Ammianus (xxiv. 7, 8), Libanius (Orat. Parent. c. 134, p. 357), and Zosimus (l. iii. p. 183). The two last seem ignorant that their conqueror was retreating ; and Libanius absurdly confines him to the banks of the Tigris.

principal satraps; and fame and expectation exaggerated the strength of the remaining powers, which slowly advanced under the conduct of Sapor himself. As the Romans continued their march, their long array, which was forced to bend, or divide, according to the varieties of the ground, afforded frequent and favourable opportunities to their vigilant enemies. The Persians [22nd June] repeatedly charged with fury; they were repeatedly repulsed with firmness; and the action at Maronga, which almost deserved the name of a battle, was marked by a considerable loss of satraps and elephants, perhaps of equal value in the eyes of their monarch. These splendid advantages were not obtained without an adequate slaughter on the side of the Romans: several officers of distinction were either killed or wounded; and the emperor himself, who, on all occasions of danger, inspired and guided the valour of his troops, was obliged to expose his person and exert his abilities. The weight of offensive and defensive arms, which still constituted the strength and safety of the Romans, disabled them from making any long or effectual pursuit; and, as the horsemen of the East were trained to dart their javelins, and shoot their arrows, at full speed, and in every possible direction,[92] the cavalry of Persia was never more formidable than in the moment of a rapid and disorderly flight. But the most certain and irreparable loss of the Romans was that of time. The hardy veterans, accustomed to the cold climate of Gaul and Germany, fainted under the sultry heat of an Assyrian summer: their vigour was exhausted by the incessant repetition of march and combat; and the progress of the army was suspended by the precautions of a slow and dangerous retreat in the presence of an active enemy. Every day, every hour, as the supply diminished, the value and price of subsistence increased in the Roman camp.[93] Julian, who always contented himself with such food as a hungry soldier would have disdained, distributed for the use of his troops the provisions of the imperial household, and whatever could be spared from the sumpter-horses of the tribunes and generals. But this feeble relief served only to aggravate the sense of the public

---

[92] Chardin, the most judicious of modern travellers, describes (tom. iii. p. 57, 58, &c. edit. in 4to) the education and dexterity of the Persian horsemen. Brissonius (de Regno Persico, p. 650, 661, &c.) has collected the testimonies of antiquity.

[93] In Mark Antony's retreat, an attic chœnix sold for fifty drachmæ, or, in other words, a pound of flour for twelve or fourteen shillings: barley bread was sold for its weight in silver. It is impossible to peruse the interesting narrative of Plutarch (tom. v. p. 102-116 [c. 45]) without perceiving that Mark Antony and Julian were pursued by the same enemies and involved in the same distress.

distress; and the Romans began to entertain the most gloomy apprehensions that, before they could reach the frontiers of the empire, they should all perish, either by famine or by the sword of the Barbarians.[94]

While Julian struggled with the almost insuperable difficulties of his situation, the silent hours of the night were still devoted to study and contemplation. Whenever he closed his eyes in short and interrupted slumbers, his mind was agitated with painful anxiety; nor can it be thought surprising that the Genius of the empire should once more appear before him, covering with a funeral veil his head and his horn of abundance, and slowly retiring from the Imperial tent. The monarch started from his couch, and stepping forth, to refresh his wearied spirits with the coolness of the midnight air, he beheld a fiery meteor, which shot athwart the sky, and suddenly vanished. Julian was convinced that he had seen the menacing countenance of the god of war;[95] the council which he summoned, of Tuscan haruspices,[96] unanimously pronounced that he should abstain from action: but, on this occasion, necessity and reason were more prevalent than superstition; and the trumpets sounded at the break of day. The army marched through a hilly country; and the hills had been secretly occupied by the Persians. Julian led the van, with the skill and attention of a consummate general; he was alarmed by the intelligence that his rear was suddenly attacked. The heat of the weather had tempted him to lay aside his cuirass; but he snatched a shield from one of his attendants, and hastened, with a sufficient reinforcement, to the relief of the rear-guard. A similar danger recalled the intrepid prince to the defence of the front; and, as he galloped between the columns, the centre of the left was attacked, and almost overpowered, by a furious charge of the Persian cavalry and elephants. This huge body was soon defeated, by the well-timed evolution of the light infantry, who aimed their weapons, with dexterity and effect, against the

(margin note: Julian mortally wounded)

[94] Ammian. xxiv. 8, xxv. 1. Zosimus, l. iii. p. 184, 185, 186. Libanius, Orat. Parent. c. 134, 135, p. 357, 358, 359. The sophist of Antioch appears ignorant that the troops were hungry.

[95] Ammian. xxv. 2. Julian had sworn in a passion, nunquam se Marti sacra facturum (xxiv. 6). Such whimsical quarrels were not uncommon between the gods and their insolent votaries; and even the prudent Augustus, after his fleet had been twice shipwrecked, excluded Neptune from the honours of public processions. See Hume's Philosophical Reflections. Essays, vol. ii. p. 418.

[96] They still retained the monopoly of the vain, but lucrative, science which had been invented in Etruria; and professed to derive their knowledge of signs and omens from the ancient books of Tarquitius, a Tuscan sage.

backs of the horsemen and the legs of the elephants. The Barbarians fled ; and Julian, who was foremost in every danger, animated the pursuit with his voice and gestures. His trembling guards, scattered and oppressed by the disorderly throng of friends and enemies, reminded their fearless sovereign that he was without armour ; and conjured him to decline the fall of the impending ruin. As they exclaimed,[97] a cloud of darts and arrows was discharged from the flying squadrons ; and a javelin, after razing the skin of his arm, transpierced the ribs, and fixed in the inferior part of the liver. Julian attempted to draw the deadly weapon from his side ; but his fingers were cut by the sharpness of the steel, and he fell senseless from his horse. His guards flew to his relief; and the wounded emperor was gently raised from the ground, and conveyed out of the tumult of the battle into an adjacent tent. The report of the melancholy event passed from rank to rank ; but the grief of the Romans inspired them with invincible valour and the desire of revenge. The bloody and obstinate conflict was maintained by the two armies, till they were separated by the total darkness of the night. The Persians derived some honour from the advantage which they obtained against the left wing, where Anatolius, master of the offices, was slain, and the præfect Sallust very narrowly escaped. But the event of the day was adverse to the Barbarians. They abandoned the field, their two generals, Meranes and Nohordates,[98] fifty nobles or satraps, and a multitude of their bravest soldiers : and the success of the Romans, if Julian had survived, might have been improved into a decisive and useful victory.

[leg. Noho-dares]

[97] Clamabant hinc .nde *candidati* (see the note of Valesius) quos disjecerat terror, ut fugientium molem tanquam ruinam male compositi culminis declinaret. Ammian. xxv. 3. [It was unknown who threw the javelin, according to Ammian (25, 3, 23, *incertum unde*) and Magnus of Carrhæ (abridged in Malalas, p. 328-330 ; see App. 1), who were present. Eutropius says *hostili manu ;* on the other hand the tale was soon invented that the dart was from the hand of a Christian in Julian's army. The question is discussed by Büttner-Wobst in Philologus, 51, p. 561 *sqq.* (1892). Libanius (ii. 31, Reiske) adopted a rumour that the man whose dart dealt death to the Emperor was Ταιηνός τις, which was not understood until O. Crusius recently (Philologus, *ib.* p. 735 *sqq.*) pointed to a notice in Stephanus (p. 598) that the Taêni were an Arabic tribe to the south of the Saracens. Libanius' statement would thus prove not that a Taene killed Julian, but that there were Taenes in his army. Nöldeke (Philol. 52, p. 736) has confirmed Crusius, and showed that the name Taene first occurs in a Syriac book (c. 210 A.D.) and is rendered in the Praepar. Evangel. of Eusebius, vi. 10, 14 (Hein.), by Ταινοίς.]

[98] Sapor himself declared to the Romans that it was his practice to comfort the families of his deceased satraps by sending them, as a present, the heads of the guards and officers who had not fallen by their master's side. Libaniu, de nece Julian. ulcis. c. xiii. p. 163.

The first words that Julian uttered, after his recovery from the fainting fit into which he had been thrown by loss of blood, were expressive of his martial spirit. He called for his horse and arms, and was impatient to rush into the battle. His remaining strength was exhausted by the painful effort; and the surgeons who examined his wound discovered the symptoms of approaching death. He employed the awful moments with the firm temper of a hero and a sage; the philosophers who had accompanied him in this fatal expedition compared the tent of Julian with the prison of Socrates; and the spectators, whom duty, or friendship, or curiosity, had assembled around his couch, listened with respectful grief to the funeral oration of their dying emperor.[99] "Friends and fellow-soldiers, the seasonable period of my departure is now arrived, and I discharge, with the cheerfulness of a ready debtor, the demands of nature. I have learned from philosophy, how much the soul is more excellent than the body; and that the separation of the nobler substance should be the subject of joy, rather than of affliction. I have learned from religion, that an early death has often been the reward of piety;[100] and I accept, as a favour of the gods, the mortal stroke that secures me from the danger of disgracing a character, which has hitherto been supported by virtue and fortitude. I die without remorse, as I have lived without guilt. I am pleased to reflect on the innocence of my private life; and I can affirm, with confidence, that the supreme authority, that emanation of the Divine Power, has been preserved in my hands pure and immaculate. Detesting the corrupt and destructive maxims of despotism, I have considered the happiness of the people as the end of government. Submitting my actions to the laws of prudence, of justice, and of moderation, I have trusted the event to the care of Providence. Peace was the object of my counsels, as long as peace was consistent with the public welfare; but, when the imperious voice of my country summoned me to arms, I exposed my person to the dangers of war, with the clear fore-knowledge (which I had acquired from the art of divination)

---

[99] The character and situation of Julian might countenance the suspicion that he had previously composed the elaborate oration which Ammianus heard and has transcribed. The version of the Abbé de la Blétérie is faithful and elegant. I have followed him in expressing the Platonic idea of emanations, which is darkly insinuated in the original.

[100] Herodotus (l. i. c. 31) has displayed that doctrine in an agreeable tale. Yet the Jupiter (in the 16th book of the Iliad) who laments with tears of blood the death of Sarpedon his son had a very imperfect notion of happiness or glory beyond the grave.

that I was destined to fall by the sword. I now offer my tribute of gratitude to the Eternal Being, who has not suffered me to perish by the cruelty of a tyrant, by the secret dagger of conspiracy, or by the slow tortures of lingering disease. He has given me, in the midst of an honourable career, a splendid and glorious departure from this world; and I hold it equally absurd, equally base, to solicit, or to decline, the stroke of fate.——Thus much I have attempted to say; but my strength fails me, and I feel the approach of death.—I shall cautiously refrain from any word that may tend to influence your suffrages in the election of an emperor. My choice might be imprudent, or injudicious; and, if it should not be ratified by the consent of the army, it might be fatal to the person whom I should recommend. I shall only, as a good citizen, express my hopes that the Romans may be blessed with the government of a virtuous sovereign." After this discourse, which Julian pronounced in a firm and gentle tone of voice, he distributed, by a military testament,[101] the remains of his private fortune; and, making some inquiry why Anatolius was not present, he understood, from the answer of Sallust, that Anatolius was killed; and bewailed, with amiable inconsistency, the loss of his friend. At the same time he reproved the immoderate grief of the spectators; and conjured them not to disgrace, by unmanly tears, the fate of a prince who in a few moments would be united with heaven, and with the stars.[102] The spectators were silent; and Julian entered into a metaphysical argument with the philosophers Priscus and Maximus, on the nature of the soul. The efforts which he made, of mind as well as body, most probably hastened his death. His wound began to bleed with fresh violence; his respiration was embarrassed by the swelling of the veins: he called for a draught of cold water, and, as soon as he had drunk it, expired without pain, about the hour of midnight. Such was the end of that extraordinary man, in the thirty-second year of his age, after a reign of one year and about eight months from the death of Constantius. In his last moments he displayed, perhaps with some ostentation, the love of

---

[101] The soldiers who made their verbal, or nuncupatory, testaments upon actual service (in procinctu) were exempted from the formalities of the Roman law. See Heineccius (Antiquit. Jur. Roman. tom. i. p. 504), and Montesquieu (Esprit des Loix, l. xxvii.).

[102] This union of the human soul with the divine ætherial substance of the universe is the ancient doctrine of Pythagoras and Plato; but it seems to exclude any personal or conscious immortality. See Warburton's learned and rational observations, Divine Legation, vol. ii. p. 199-216.

virtue and of fame which had been the ruling passions of his life.[103]

The triumph of Christianity, and the calamities of the empire, may, in some measure, be ascribed to Julian himself, who had neglected to secure the future execution of his designs by the timely and judicious nomination of an associate and successor. But the royal race of Constantius Chlorus was reduced to his own person; and, if he entertained any serious thoughts of investing with the purple the most worthy among the Romans, he was diverted from his resolution by the difficulty of the choice, the jealousy of power, the fear of ingratitude, and the natural presumption of health, of youth, and of prosperity. His unexpected death left the empire without a master and without an heir, in a state of perplexity and danger, which, in the space of fourscore years, had never been experienced, since the election of Diocletian. In a government which had almost forgotten the distinction of pure and noble blood, the superiority of birth was of little moment; the claims of official rank were accidental and precarious; and the candidates who might aspire to ascend the vacant throne could be supported only by the consciousness of personal merit, or by the hopes of popular favour. But the situation of a famished army, encompassed on all sides by an host of Barbarians, shortened the moments of grief and deliberation. In this scene of terror and distress, the body of the deceased prince, according to his own directions, was decently embalmed; and, at the dawn of day, the generals convened a military senate, at which the commanders of the legions and the officers, both of cavalry and infantry, were invited to assist. Three or four hours of the night had not passed away without some secret cabals; and, when the election of an emperor was proposed, the spirit of faction began to agitate the assembly. Victor and Arinthæus collected the remains of the court of Constantius; the friends of Julian attached themselves to the Gallic chiefs, Dagalaiphus and Nevitta; and the most fatal consequences might be apprehended from the discord of two factions, so opposite in their character and interest, in their maxims of government, and perhaps in their religious principles. The superior virtues of Sallust could alone reconcile their divisions and unite their suffrages; and

Election of the emperor Jovian. A.D. 363, 27th June

---

[103] The whole relation of the death of Julian is given by Ammianus (xxv. 3), an intelligent spectator. Libanius, who turns with horror from the scene, has supplied some circumstances (Orat. Parental. c. 136-140 p. 359-362). The calumnies of Gregory, and the legends of more recent saints, may now be *silently* despised.

the venerable præfect would immediately have been declared the successor of Julian, if he himself, with sincere and modest firmness, had not alleged his age and infirmities, so unequal to the weight of the diadem. The generals, who were surprised and perplexed by his refusal, shewed some disposition to adopt the salutary advice of an inferior officer,[104] that they should act as they would have acted in the absence of the emperor; that they should exert their abilities to extricate the army from the present distress; and, if they were fortunate enough to reach the confines of Mesopotamia, they should proceed with united and deliberate counsels in the election of a lawful sovereign. While they debated, a few voices saluted Jovian, who was no more than *first* [105] of the domestics, with the names of Emperor and Augustus. The tumultuary acclamation was instantly repeated by the guards who surrounded the tent, and passed, in a few minutes, to the extremities of the line. The new prince, astonished with his own fortune, was hastily invested with the Imperial ornaments and received an oath of fidelity from the generals whose favour and protection he so lately solicited. The strongest recommendation of Jovian was the merit of his father, Count Varronian, who enjoyed, in honourable retirement, the fruit of his long services. In the obscure freedom of a private station, the son indulged his taste for wine and women; yet he supported, with credit, the character of a Christian [106] and a soldier. Without being conspicuous for any of the ambitious qualifications which excite the admiration and envy of mankind, the comely person of Jovian, his cheerful temper, and familiar wit, had gained the affection of his fellow-soldiers; and the generals of both parties acquiesced in a popular election, which had not been conducted by the arts of their enemies. The pride of this unexpected elevation was moderated by the just apprehension that the same day might terminate the life and reign of the new emperor. The pressing voice of necessity

[104] Honoratior aliquis miles; perhaps Ammianus himself. The modest and judicious historian describes the scene of the election, at which he was undoubtedly present (xxv. 5).

[105] The *primus*, or *primicerius*, enjoyed the dignity of a senator; and, though only a tribune, he ranked with the military dukes. Cod. Theodosian. l. vi. tit. xxiv. These privileges are perhaps more recent than the time of Jovian.

[106] The ecclesiastical historians, Socrates (l. iii. c. 22), Sozomen (l. vi. c. 3), and Theodoret (l. iv. c. 1), ascribe to Jovian the merit of a confessor under the preceding reign; and piously suppose that he refused the purple, till the whole army unanimously exclaimed that they were Christians. Ammianus, calmly pursuing his narrative, overthrows the legend by a single sentence. Hostiis pro Joviano extisque inspectis pronuntiatum est, &c. xxv. 6.

was obeyed without delay; and the first orders issued by Jovian, a few hours after his predecessor had expired, were to prosecute a march which could alone extricate the Romans from their actual distress.[107]

The esteem of an enemy is most sincerely expressed by his fears; and the degree of fear may be accurately measured by the joy with which he celebrates his deliverance. The welcome news of the death of Julian, which a deserter revealed to the camp of Sapor, inspired the desponding monarch with a sudden confidence of victory. He immediately detached the royal cavalry, perhaps the ten thousand *Immortals*,[108] to second and support the pursuit; and discharged the whole weight of his united forces on the rear-guard of the Romans. The rear-guard was thrown into disorder; the renowned legions, which derived their titles from Diocletian and his warlike colleague, were broke and trampled down by the elephants; and three tribunes lost their lives in attempting to stop the flight of their soldiers. The battle was at length restored by the persevering valour of the Romans; the Persians were repulsed with a great slaughter of men and elephants; and the army, after marching and fighting a long summer's day, arrived, in the evening, at Samara on the banks of the Tigris, about one hundred miles above Ctesiphon.[109] On the ensuing day, the Barbarians, instead of harassing the march, attacked the camp, of Jovian which had been seated in a deep and sequestered valley. From the hills, the archers of Persia insulted and annoyed the wearied legionaries; and a body of cavalry, which had penetrated with desperate courage through the Prætorian gate, was cut in pieces, after a doubtful conflict, near the Imperial tent. In the succeeding night, the camp of Carche was protected by the lofty dykes of the river; and the Roman army, though incessantly exposed to the vexatious pursuit of the Saracens,

(margin note: Danger and difficulty of the retreat 27th June to 1st July)

(margin note: [Samarrā])

---

[107] Ammianus (xxv. 10) has drawn from the life an impartial portrait of Jovian: to which the younger Victor has added some remarkable strokes. The Abbé de la Bléterie (Histoire de Jovien, tom. i. p. 1-238) has composed an elaborate history of his short reign; a work remarkably distinguished by elegance of style, critical disquisition, and religious prejudice.

[108] Regius equitatus. It appears from Procopius that the Immortals, so famous under Cyrus and his successors, were revived, if we may use that improper word, by the Sassanides. Brisson de Regno Persico, p. 268, &c.

[109] The obscure villages of the inland country are irrecoverably lost; nor can we name the field of battle where Julian fell: but M. d'Anville has demonstrated the precise situation of Sumere, Carche, and Dura, along the banks of the Tigris (Géographie Ancienne, tom. ii. p. 248. L'Euphrate et le Tigre, p. 95, 97). In the ninth century, Sumere, or Samara, became, with a slight change of name, the royal residence of the Khalifs of the house of Abbas. [Among the palaces at Samarrā was that of Al-Hārūni, built by Caliph Al-Wāthik.]

[Dūr]

pitched their tents near the city of Dura,[110] four days after the death of Julian. The Tigris was still on their left; their hopes and provisions were almost consumed; and the impatient soldiers, who had fondly persuaded themselves that the frontiers of the empire were not far distant, requested their new sovereign that they might be permitted to hazard the passage of the river. With the assistance of his wisest officers, Jovian endeavoured to check their rashness; by representing that, if they possessed sufficient skill and vigour to stem the torrent of a deep and rapid stream, they would only deliver themselves naked and defenceless to the Barbarians, who had occupied the opposite banks. Yielding at length to their clamorous importunities, he consented, with reluctance, that five hundred Gauls and Germans, accustomed from their infancy to the waters of the Rhine and Danube, should attempt the bold adventure, which might serve either as an encouragement, or as a warning, for the rest of the army. In the silence of the night, they swam the Tigris, surprised an unguarded post of the enemy, and displayed at the dawn of day the signal of their resolution and fortune. The success of this trial disposed the emperor to listen to the promises of his architects, who proposed to construct a floating bridge of the inflated skins of sheep, oxen, and goats, covered with a floor of earth and fascines.[111] Two important days were spent in the ineffectual labour; and the Romans, who already endured the miseries of famine, cast a look of despair on the Tigris, and upon the Barbarians; whose numbers and obstinacy increased with the distress of the Imperial army.[112]

Negotiation and treaty of peace. July

In this hopeless situation, the fainting spirits of the Romans were revived by the sound of peace. The transient presumption of Sapor had vanished: he observed, with serious concern, that, in the repetition of doubtful combats, he had lost his most faithful and intrepid nobles, his bravest troops, and the greatest part of his train of elephants: and the experienced

---

[110] Dura was a fortified place in the wars of Antiochus against the rebels of Media and Persia (Polybius, l. v. c. 48, 52, p. 548, 552, edit. Casaubon, in 8vo).

[111] A similar expedient was proposed to the leaders of the ten thousand, and wisely rejected. Xenophon, Anabasis, l. iii. p. 255, 256, 257. It appears from our modern travellers that rafts floating on bladders performed the trade and navigation of the Tigris. [On the course of the Tigris here cp. App. 24.]

[112] The first military acts of the reign of Jovian are related by Ammianus (xxv. 6), Libanius (Orat. Parent. c. 146, p. 364), and Zosimus (l. iii. p. 189, 190, 191, [c. 30]). Though we may distrust the fairness of Libanius, the ocular testimony of Eutropius (uno a Persis atque altero prœlio victus, x. 17) must incline us to suspect that Ammianus has been too jealous of the honour of the Roman arms.

monarch feared to provoke the resistance of despair, the vicissitudes of fortune, and the unexhausted powers of the Roman
empire; which might soon advance to relieve, or to revenge,
the successor of Julian. The Surenas himself, accompanied
by another satrap, appeared in the camp of Jovian; [113] and
declared that the clemency of his sovereign was not averse to
signify the conditions on which he would consent to spare and
to dismiss the Cæsar with the relics of his captive army. The
hopes of safety subdued the firmness of the Romans; the emperor
was compelled, by the advice of his council and the cries of the
soldiers, to embrace the offer of peace; and the præfect Sallust
was immediately sent, with the general Arinthæus, to understand the pleasure of the Great King. The crafty Persian
delayed, under various pretences, the conclusion of the agreement; started difficulties, required explanations, suggested ex-
pedients, receded from his concessions, increased his demands,
and wasted four days in the arts of negotiation, till he had consumed the stock of provisions which yet remained in the camp
of the Romans. Had Jovian been capable of executing a bold
and prudent measure, he would have continued his march with
unremitting diligence; the progress of the treaty would have
suspended the attacks of the Barbarians; and, before the expiration of the fourth day, he might have safely reached the
fruitful province of Corduene, at the distance only of one hundred
miles. [114] The irresolute emperor, instead of breaking through
the toils of the enemy, expected his fate with patient resignation; and accepted the humiliating conditions of peace, which
it was no longer in his power to refuse. The five provinces beyond
the Tigris, which had been ceded by the grandfather of Sapor,
were restored to the Persian monarchy. He acquired, by a
single article, the impregnable city of Nisibis; which had
sustained, in three successive sieges, the effort of his arms.
Singara, and the castle of the Moors, one of the strongest
places of Mesopotamia, were likewise dismembered from the
empire. It was considered as an indulgence, that the inhabitants
of those fortresses were permitted to retire with their effects;

[113] Sextus Rufus (de Provinciis, c. 29) embraces a poor subterfuge of national
vanity. Tanta reverentia nominis Romani fuit, ut a Persis *primus* de pace sermo
haberetur.

[114] It is presumptuous to controvert the opinion of Ammianus, a soldier and a
spectator. Yet it is difficult to understand *how* the mountains of Corduene could
extend over the plain of Assyria, as low as the conflux of the Tigris and the great
Zab; or *how* an army of sixty thousand men could march one hundred miles in
four days.

THE DECLINE AND FALL

but the conqueror rigorously insisted that the Romans should
for ever abandon the king and kingdom of Armenia. A peace,
or rather a long truce, of thirty years was stipulated between
the hostile nations; the faith of the treaty was ratified by
solemn oaths, and religious ceremonies; and hostages of
distinguished rank were reciprocally delivered to secure the
performance of the conditions.[115]

The weakness and disgrace of Jovian

The sophist of Antioch, who saw with indignation the sceptre
of his hero in the feeble hand of a Christian successor, professes
to admire the moderation of Sapor, in contenting himself with
so small a portion of the Roman empire. If he had stretched
as far as the Euphrates the claims of his ambition, he might
have been secure, says Libanius, of not meeting with a refusal.
If he had fixed, as the boundary of Persia, the Orontes, the
Cydnus, the Sangarius, or even the Thracian Bosphorus, flatterers
would not have been wanting in the court of Jovian to convince
the timid monarch that his remaining provinces would still
afford the most ample gratifications of power and luxury.[116]
Without adopting in its full force this malicious insinuation,
we must acknowledge that the conclusion of so ignominious
a treaty was facilitated by the private ambition of Jovian. The
obscure domestic, exalted to the throne by fortune rather than
by merit, was impatient to escape from the hands of the
Persians; that he might prevent the designs of Procopius, who
commanded the army of Mesopotamia, and establish his
doubtful reign over the legions and provinces, which were still
ignorant of the hasty and tumultuous choice of the camp beyond
the Tigris.[117] In the neighbourhood of the same river, at no
very considerable distance from the fatal station of Dura,[118]

[115] The treaty of Dura is recorded with grief or indignation by Ammianus (xxv.
7), Libanius (Orat. Parent. c. 142, p. 364), Zosimus (l. iii. p. 190, 191, [c. 31]),
Gregory Nazianzen (Orat. iv. p. 117, 118 [v., c. 15], who imputes the distress to
Julian, the deliverance to Jovian), and Eutropius (x. 17). The last-mentioned
writer, who was present in a military station, styles this peace necessariam
quidem sed ignobilem.

[116] Libanius, Orat. Parent. c. 143, p. 364, 365.

[117] Conditionibus . . . dispendiosis Romanæ reipublicæ impositis . . . quibus
cupidior regni quam gloriæ Jovianus imperio rudis adquievit. Sextus Rufus de
Provinciis, c. 29. La Bléterie has expressed, in a long direct oration, these
specious considerations of public and private interest. Hist. de Jovien, tom. i. p.
39, &c.

[118] The generals were murdered on the banks of the Zabatus (Anabasis, l. ii. p.
156, l. iii. p. 226), or great Zab, a river of Assyria, 400 feet broad, which falls into
the Tigris [at Al-Haditha] fourteen hours below Mosul. The error of the Greeks
bestowed on the great and lesser Zab the names of the *Wolf* (Lycus), and the *Goat*
(Capros). They created these animals to attend the *Tiger* of the East. [Another
tributary of the Tigris, the Arzan Sū, is called Nahr-adh-Dhīb or Wolf-river.]

the ten thousand Greeks, without generals, or guides, or provisions, were abandoned, above twelve hundred miles from their native country, to the resentment of a victorious monarch. The difference of *their* conduct and success depended much more on their character than on their situation. Instead of tamely resigning themselves to the secret deliberations and private views of a single person, the united councils of the Greeks were inspired by the generous enthusiasm of a popular assembly; where the mind of each citizen is filled with the love of glory, the pride of freedom, and the contempt of death. Conscious of their superiority over the Barbarians in arms and discipline, they disdained to yield, they refused to capitulate; every obstacle was surmounted by their patience, courage, and military skill; and the memorable retreat of the ten thousand exposed and insulted the weakness of the Persian monarchy.[119]

As the price of his disgraceful concessions, the emperor might He continues perhaps have stipulated that the camp of the hungry Romans his retreat to should be plentifully supplied;[120] and that they should be Nisibis permitted to pass the Tigris on the bridge which was constructed by the hands of the Persians. But, if Jovian presumed to solicit those equitable terms, they were sternly refused by the haughty tyrant of the East; whose clemency had pardoned the invaders of his country. The Saracens sometimes intercepted the stragglers of the march; but the generals and troops of Sapor respected the cessation of arms; and Jovian was suffered to explore the most convenient place for the passage of the river. The small vessels, which had been saved from the conflagration of the fleet, performed the most essential service. They first conveyed the emperor and his favourites; and afterwards transported, in many successive voyages, a great part of the army. But, as every man was anxious for his personal safety, and apprehensive of being left on the hostile shore, the soldiers, who were too impatient to wait the slow returns of the boats, boldly ventured themselves on light hurdles, or inflated skins; and, drawing after them their horses, attempted, with various success, to swim across the river. Many of these daring adventurers were swallowed by the waves; many others, who were carried

---

[119] The *Cyropædia* is vague and languid: the *Anabasis* circumstantial and animated. Such is the eternal difference between fiction and truth.

[120] According to Rufinus, an immediate supply of provisions was stipulated by the treaty; and Theodoret affirms that the obligation was faithfully discharged by the Persians. Such a fact is probable, but undoubtedly false. See Tillemont, Hist. des Empereurs, tom. iv. p. 702.

along by the violence of the stream, fell an easy prey to the avarice, or cruelty, of the wild Arabs : and the loss which the army sustained in the passage of the Tigris was not inferior to the carnage of a day of battle. As soon as the Romans had landed on the western bank, they were delivered from the hostile pursuit of the Barbarians ; but, in a laborious march of two hundred miles over the plains of Mesopotamia, they endured the last extremities of thirst and hunger. They were obliged to traverse a sandy desert, which, in the extent of seventy miles, did not afford a single blade of sweet grass, nor a single spring of fresh water ; and the rest of the inhospitable waste was untrod by the footsteps either of friends or enemies. Whenever a small measure of flour could be discovered in the camp, twenty pounds weight were greedily purchased with ten pieces of gold : [121] the beasts of burden were slaughtered and devoured ; and the desert was strewed with the arms and baggage of the Roman soldiers, whose tattered garments and meagre countenances displayed their past sufferings and actual misery. A small convoy of provisions advanced to meet the army as far as the castle of Ur ; and the supply was the more grateful, since it declared the fidelity of Sebastian and Procopius. At Thilsaphata,[122] the emperor most graciously received the generals of Mesopotamia, and the remains of a once flourishing army at length reposed themselves under the walls of Nisibis. The messengers of Jovian had already proclaimed, in the language of flattery, his election, his treaty, and his return ; and the new prince had taken the most effectual measures to secure the allegiance of the armies and provinces of Europe ; by placing the military command in the hands of those officers who, from motives of interest or inclination, would firmly support the cause of their benefactor.[123]

[121] We may recollect some lines of Lucan (Pharsal. iv. 95), who describes a similar distress of Cæsar's army in Spain :

> Sæva fames aderat————
> Miles eget : toto censû non prodigus emit
> Exiguam Cererem.   Proh lucri pallida tabes !
> Non deest prolato jejunus venditor auro.

See Guichardt (Nouveaux Mémoires Militaires, tom. i. p. 379-382). His Analysis of the two Campaigns in Spain and Africa is the noblest monument that has ever been raised to the fame of Cæsar.

[122] M. d'Anville (see his Maps, and l'Euphrate et le Tigre, p. 92, 93) traces their march, and assigns the true position of Hatra [Al-Hadr], Ur, and Thilsaphata, which Ammianus has mentioned.   He does not complain of the Samiel, the deadly hot wind, which Thévenot (Voyages, part ii. li. p. 192) so much dreaded.

[123] The retreat of Jovian is described by Ammianus (xxv. 9), Libanius (Orat. Parent. c. 143, p. 365), and Zosimus (l. iii. p. 194 [c. 33]).

The friends of Julian had confidently announced the success of his expedition. They entertained a fond persuasion that the temples of the gods would be enriched with the spoils of the East; that Persia would be reduced to the humble state of a tributary province, governed by the laws and magistrates of Rome; that the Barbarians would adopt the dress, and manners, and language, of their conquerors; and that the youth of Ecbatana and Susa would study the art of rhetoric under Grecian masters.[124] The progress of the arms of Julian interrupted his communication with the empire; and, from the moment that he passed the Tigris, his affectionate subjects were ignorant of the fate and fortunes of their prince. Their contemplation of fancied triumphs was disturbed by the melancholy rumour of his death; and they persisted to doubt, after they could no longer deny, the truth of that fatal event.[125] The messengers of Jovian promulgated the specious tale of a prudent and necessary peace: the voice of fame, louder and more sincere, revealed the disgrace of the emperor and the conditions of the ignominious treaty. The minds of the people were filled with astonishment and grief, with indignation and terror, when they were informed that the unworthy successor of Julian relinquished the five provinces which had been acquired by the victory of Galerius; and that he shamefully surrendered to the Barbarians the important city of Nisibis, the firmest bulwark of the provinces of the East.[126] The deep and dangerous question, how far the public faith should be observed, when it becomes incompatible with the public safety, was freely agitated in popular conversation; and some hopes were entertained that the emperor would redeem his pusillanimous behaviour by a splendid act of patriotic perfidy. The inflexible spirit of the Roman senate had always disclaimed the unequal conditions which were extorted from the distress of her captive armies; and, if it were necessary to satisfy the national honour by delivering the guilty general into the hands of the Barbarians, the greatest part of the subjects of Jovian

Universal clamour against the treaty of peace

---

[124] Libanius, Orat. Parent. c. 145, p. 366. Such were the natural hopes and wishes of a rhetorician.

[125] The people of Carrhæ, a city devoted to Paganism, buried the inauspicious messenger under a pile of stones. Zosimus, l. iii. p. 196 [c. 34]. Libanius, when he received the fatal intelligence, cast his eye on his sword; but he recollected that Plato had condemned suicide, and that he must live to compose the panegyric of Julian (Libanius de Vitâ suâ, tom. ii. p. 45, 46).

[126] Ammianus and Eutropius may be admitted as fair and credible witnesses of the public language and opinions. The people of Antioch reviled an ignominious peace, which exposed them to the Persians on a naked and defenceless frontier. (Excerpt. Valesiana, p. 845, ex Johanne Antiocheno.)

would have cheerfully acquiesced in the precedent of ancient times.[127]

But the emperor, whatever might be the limits of his constitutional authority, was the absolute master of the laws and arms of the state; and the same motives which had forced him to subscribe, now pressed him to execute, the treaty of peace. He was impatient to secure an empire at the expense of a few provinces; and the respectable names of religion and honour concealed the personal fears and the ambition of Jovian. Notwithstanding the dutiful solicitations of the inhabitants, decency, as well as prudence, forbade the emperor to lodge in the palace of Nisibis; but, the next morning after his arrival, Bineses, the ambassador of Persia, entered the place, displayed from the citadel the standard of the Great King, and proclaimed, in his name, the cruel alternative of exile or servitude. The principal citizens of Nisibis, who, till that fatal moment, had confided in the protection of their sovereign, threw themselves at his feet. They conjured him not to abandon, or, at least, not to deliver, a faithful colony to the rage of a barbarian tyrant, exasperated by the three successive defeats which he had experienced under the walls of Nisibis. They still possessed arms and courage to repel the invaders of their country; they requested only the permission of using them in their own defence; and, as soon as they had asserted their independence, they should implore the favour of being again admitted into the rank of his subjects. Their arguments, their eloquence, their tears, were ineffectual. Jovian alleged, with some confusion, the sanctity of oaths; and, as the reluctance with which he accepted the present of a crown of gold convinced the citizens of their hopeless condition, the advocate Sylvanus was provoked to exclaim, "O Emperor! may you thus be crowned by all the cities of your dominions!" Jovian, who, in a few weeks, had assumed the habits of a prince,[128] was displeased with freedom, and offended with truth: and, as he reasonably supposed that the discontent of the people might incline them to submit to the

---

[127] The Abbé de la Bléterie (Hist. de Jovien, tom. i. p. 212-227), though a severe casuist, has pronounced that Jovian was not bound to execute his promise; since he *could not* dismember the empire, nor alienate, without their consent, the allegiance of his people. I have never found much delight or instruction in such political metaphysics.

[128] At Nisibis he performed a *royal* act. A brave officer, his name-sake, who had been thought worthy of the purple, was dragged from supper, thrown into a well, and stoned to death, without any form of trial or evidence of guilt. Ammian. xxv. 8.

Persian government, he published an edict, under pain of death, that they should leave the city within the term of three days. Ammianus has delineated in lively colours the scene of universal despair, which he seems to have viewed with an eye of compassion.[129]   The martial youth deserted, with indignant grief, the walls which they had so gloriously defended : the disconsolate mourner dropt a last tear over the tomb of a son or husband, which must soon be profaned by the rude hand of a Barbarian master ; and the aged citizen kissed the threshold, and clung to the doors, of the house where he had passed the cheerful and careless hours of infancy.   The highways were crowded with a trembling multitude : the distinctions of rank, and sex, and age, were lost in the general calamity.   Every one strove to bear away some fragment from the wreck of his fortunes ; and, as they could not command the immediate service of an adequate number of horses or waggons, they were obliged to leave behind them the greatest part of their valuable effects. The savage insensibility of Jovian appears to have aggravated the hardships of these unhappy fugitives.   They were seated, however, in a new-built quarter of Amida ; and that rising city, with the reinforcement of a very considerable colony, soon recovered its former splendour, and became the capital of Mesopotamia.[130]   Similar orders were dispatched by the emperor for the evacuation of Singara and the castle of the Moors ; and for the restitution of the five provinces beyond the Tigris.   Sapor enjoyed the glory and the fruits of his victory ; and this ignominious peace has justly been considered as a memorable æra in th   decline and fall of the Roman empire.   The predecessors of Jovian had sometimes relinquished the dominion of distant and unprofitable provinces ; but, since the foundation of the city, the genius of Rome, the god Terminus, who guarded the boundaries of the republic, had never retired before the sword of a victorious enemy.[131]

After Jovian had performed those engagements which the voice of his people might have tempted him to violate, he hastened away from the scene of his disgrace, and proceeded with his whole court to enjoy the luxury of Antioch.[132]   With- Reflections on
the death

---

[129] See xxv. 9, and Zosimus, l. iii. p. 194, 195 [c. 33].

[130] Chron. Paschal. p. 300 [vol. i. p. 554, ed. Bonn].   The ecclesiastical Notitiæ may be consulted.

[131] Zosimus, l. iii. p. 192, 193 [c. 32].   Sextus Rufus de Provinciis, c. 29. Augustin. de Civitat. Dei, l. iv. c. 29.   This general position must be applied and interpreted with some caution.

[132] Ammianus, xxv. 9.   Zosimus, l. iii. p. 196 [c. 34].   He might be edax, et

out consulting the dictates of religious zeal, he was prompted, by humanity and gratitude, to bestow the last honours on the remains of his deceased sovereign;[133] and Procopius, who sincerely bewailed the loss of his kinsman, was removed from the command of the army, under the decent pretence of conducting the funeral. The corpse of Julian was transported from Nisibis to Tarsus, in a slow march of fifteen days; and, as it passed through the cities of the East, was saluted by the hostile factions, with mournful lamentations and clamorous insults. The Pagans already placed their beloved hero in the rank of those gods whose worship he had restored; while the invectives of the Christians pursued the soul of the apostate to hell, and his body to the grave.[134] One party lamented the approaching ruin of their altars; the other celebrated the marvellous deliverance of the church. The Christians applauded, in lofty and ambiguous strains, the stroke of divine vengeance, which had been so long suspended over the guilty head of Julian. They acknowledged[134a] that the death of the tyrant, at the instant he expired beyond the Tigris, was *revealed* to the saints of Egypt, Syria and Cappadocia;[135] and, instead of suffering him to fall by the Persian darts, their indiscretion ascribed the heroic deed to the obscure hand of some mortal or immortal champion of the faith.[136] Such imprudent declarations were eagerly adopted by the malice, or credulity, of their adversaries;[137] who darkly insinuated, or confidently

vino Venerique indulgens. But I agree with La Bléterie (tom. i. p. 148-154) in rejecting the foolish report of a Bacchanalian riot (ap. Suidam) celebrated at Antioch, by the emperor, his *wife*, and a troop of concubines.

[133] The Abbé de la Bléterie (tom. i. p. 156, 209) handsomely exposes the brutal bigotry of Baronius, who would have thrown Julian to the dogs, ne cespititiâ quidem sepulturâ dignus.

[134] Compare the sophist and the saint (Libanius, Monod. tom. ii. p. 251 and Orat. Parent. c. 145, p. 367, c. 156, p. 377, with Gregory Nazianzen, Orat. iv. p. 125-132 [v., c. 36-38]). The Christian orator faintly mutters some exhortations to modesty and forgiveness: but he is well satisfied that the real sufferings of Julian will far exceed the fabulous torments of Ixion or Tantalus.

[134a] [A necessary correction of *acknowledge*, which appears in the quarto ed.]

[135] Tillemont (Hist. des Empereurs, tom. iv. p. 549) has collected these visions. Some saint or angel was observed to be absent in the night on a secret expedition, &c.

[136] Sozomen (l. vi. 2) applauds the Greek doctrine of *tyrannicide;* but the whole passage, which a Jesuit might have translated, is prudently suppressed by the president Cousin.

[137] Immediately after the death of Julian, an uncertain rumour was scattered, telo cecidisse Romano. It was carried, by some deserters, to the Persian camp; and the Romans were reproached as the assassins of the emperor by Sapor and his subjects (Ammian. xxv. 6. Libanius de ulciscendâ Juliani nece, c. xiii. p. 162, 163). It was urged, as a decisive proof, that no Persian had appeared to claim the promised reward (Liban. Orat. Parent. c. 141, p. 363). But the flying horseman, who darted the fatal javelin, might be ignorant of its effect; or he might be slain in the same action. Ammianus neither feels nor inspires a suspicion.

asserted, that the governors of the church had instigated and directed the fanaticism of a domestic assassin.[138] Above sixteen years after the death of Julian, the charge was solemnly and vehemently urged, in a public oration, addressed by Libanius to the emperor Theodosius. His suspicions are unsupported by fact or argument; and we can only esteem the generous zeal of the sophist of Antioch for the cold and neglected ashes of his friend.[139]

It was an ancient custom in the funerals, as well as in the triumphs, of the Romans, that the voice of praise should be corrected by that of satire and ridicule; and that, in the midst of the splendid pageants, which displayed the glory of the living or of the dead, their imperfections should not be concealed from the eyes of the world.[140] This custom was practised in the funeral of Julian. The comedians, who resented his contempt and aversion for the theatre, exhibited, with the applause of a Christian audience, the lively and exaggerated representation of the faults and follies of the deceased emperor. His various character and singular manners afforded an ample scope for pleasantry and ridicule.[141] In the exercise of his uncommon talents, he often descended below the majesty of his rank. Alexander was transformed into Diogenes; the philosopher was degraded into a priest. The purity of his virtue was sullied by excessive vanity: his superstition disturbed the peace, and endangered the safety, of a mighty empire; and his irregular sallies were the less entitled to indulgence, as they appear to be the laborious efforts of art, or even of affectation. The remains of Julian were interred at Tarsus in Cilicia; but his stately tomb which arose in that city, on the banks of the cold and limpid Cydnus,[142] was displeasing to the faithful friends, who loved and

[margin note:] and funeral of Julian

[138] Ὅστις ἐντολὴν πληρῶν τῷ σφῶν αὐτῶν ἄρχοντι. This dark and ambiguous expression may point to Athanasius, the first, without a rival, of the Christian clergy (Libanius de ulcis. Jul. nece, c. 5, p. 149. La Bléterie, Hist. de Jovien, t. i. p. 179).

[139] The Orator (Fabricius, Bibliot. Græc. tom. vii. p. 145-179) scatters suspicions, demands an inquiry, and insinuates that proofs might still be obtained. He ascribes the success of the Huns to the criminal neglect of revenging Julian's death.

[140] At the funeral of Vespasian, the comedian who personated that frugal emperor anxiously inquired, how much it cost?—Fourscore thousand pounds (centies).—Give me the tenth part of the sum, and throw my body into the Tiber. Sueton. in Vespasian. c. 19, with the notes of Casaubon and Gronovius.

[141] Gregory (Orat. iv. p. 119, 120 [v., c. 16]) compares this supposed ignominy and ridicule to the funeral honours of Constantius, whose body was chaunted over mount Taurus by a choir of angels.

[142] Quintus Curtius, i. iii. c. 4. The luxuriancy of his descriptions has been often censured. Yet it was almost the duty of the historian to describe a river, whose waters had nearly proved fatal to Alexander.

revered the memory of that extraordinary man. The philosopher expressed a very reasonable wish that the disciple of Plato might have reposed amidst the groves of the academy: [143] while the soldiers exclaimed in bolder accents that the ashes of Julian should have been mingled with those of Cæsar, in the field of Mars, and among the ancient monuments of Roman virtue.[144] The history of princes does not very frequently renew the example of a similar competition.

[143] Libanius, Orat. Parent. c. 156, p. 377. Yet he acknowledges with gratitude the liberality of the two royal brothers in decorating the tomb of Julian (de ulcis. Jul. nece, c. 7, p. 152).

[144] Cujus suprema et cineres, si qui tunc juste consuleret, non Cydnus videre deberet, quamvis gratissimus amnis et liquidus: sed ad perpetuandam gloriam recte factorum praeterlambere Tiberis, intersecans urbem aeternam divorumque veterum monumenta praestringens. Ammian. xxv. 10.

APPENDIX

1. AUTHORITIES

[By an inadvertency it was not mentioned in vol. i. p. 443, that C. de Boor has shown it to be highly probable (Byzantinische Zeitschrift, i. p. 13 *sqq.*) that the Anonymous Continuer of Dion is identical with Peter the Patrician (who lived in the sixth century under Justinian).—It should also be added to the notice of Rufus Festus, on p. 448, that this writer should be simply called Festus (as C. Wagener observes in his Jahresbericht on Eutropius, in Philologus, 42, p. 521), as the addition "Rufus" appears only in inferior Mss. It is highly unsafe to speak, as some writers do, of "Rufius Festus," on the strength of a guess of Mommsen (Hermes, 16, p. 605) that the author of the Breviarium is identical with the Rufius Festus Avienus of C. I. L., 6, 103.—I am also bound to state that E. Rohde (Byz. Ztsch., 5, p. 1 *sqq.*) and C. Neumann (in the same number of the same journal) agree in ascribing to the tenth cent. the *Philopatris*, which, with Crampe, I assigned to the seventh in vol. i. p. 340; and they urge weighty arguments against Crampe's view.]

The DE MORTIBUS PERSECUTORUM, which was briefly noticed in vol i., Appendix 1, calls for some further observations here. It always seemed clear that it was ascribed to Lactantius before the end of the fourth century, and possible that L. Cæcilius (the name of the author in the unique Ms. found at Moissac, and now in the Bibl. Nationale) might be a mistake for L. Cælius, the name of Firmianus Lactantius; accordingly, fortified by the judgments of Teuffel and Ebert, I am inclined (with Schiller, Burckhardt, and others) to accept the identification, and suppose that the difference (justly noticed by Gibbon, ch. xx. n. 40) may be explained by difference of subject. Yet a study of the exhaustive investigation of Brandt might go far to convince one that Lactantius was not the author of the Mortes, and that Gibbon's hesitation was thoroughly justified. The arguments of Ebert, the chief champion of the Lactantian authorship (Ueber den Verfasser des Buches de M. P., Ber. der sächs. Ges. der Wissensch., phil.-hist. Cl. 1870), have been assailed with force by Brandt, the greatest living authority on Lactantius, in his essay Ueber die Entstehungsverhältnisse der Prosaschr. des Lact. und des Buches de M. P. (Sitzungsber. der Wiener Akad., vol. cxxv., Abh. vi. 1892).

(1) There is a serious chronological argument, which in itself (if the facts were correct) would be almost conclusive (first urged by P. Meyer in Quæst. Lactant. particula prima, 1878). The author of the Mortes was an eye-witness of the persecutions at Nicomedia, where he wrote after the middle of 313 A.D. (cp. xii. 2; xiii. 1; xxxv. 4; xlviii. 1; and xlviii. 13; xlix.; lii. 4). But the Divine Institutions, which was finished before 310 (Brandt has shown, p. 12 *sqq.*, that it was almost certainly completed in 307-8), though begun at Nicomedia, was finished at Trier, whither Lactantius must have gone before 310. Therefore, the writer who describes as an eye-witness the persecutions after 310 cannot have been Lactantius.

(2) There are peculiarities in style in the Mortes which cannot be explained by the nature of the subject; *e.g.*, "more or less strong vulgarisms, Græcisms,

&c., where Lactantius writes correctly" (p. 58, *e.g.*, *misereri* with dat., *idolum*, &c.).

(3) Advocates of the Lactantian authorship appeal to numerous passages which are verbally identical with, or echoes of, passages of Lactantius. But Brandt urges that these must be the work of an inferior imitator, and are in fact a strong argument against the Lactantian authorship. Especially instructive is a comparison of Mort. xxxviii. 1 (which Ebert is forced to regard as an interpolation) with Div. Inst. vi. 23, § 10-12.

(4) Brandt also insists that the author of the Mortes (whose want of *bona fides* is glaringly exhibited in his exaggerated descriptions of Maximin's lust, *e.g.*, or the cruelty of Galerius; xxxviii. 4; xxi. 5) stands on a lower ethical level than the Lactantius whom we know from his undoubted writings.

(5) The weak argument which rests on the fact that the Mortes is dedicated to "Donatus confessor," and that Lactantius inscribed his De Ira Dei to Donatus, is turned by Brandt into an argument on the other side. While the mere identity of a most common name proves nothing, what we know of the two Donati forbids the identification. The Donatus of the Mort. was imprisoned in 305 (cf. 16; 35), and underwent the stress of the persecution; but the only thing that Lactantius has to say to his Donatus is to warn him against trusting the authority of philosophers. There is not a hint in the De Ira Dei that the person addressed was undergoing imprisonment, which, whether the De Ira Dei was prior to 311 (as Brandt has tried to show) or subsequent (as Ebert held), is an argument against the identification of the two Donati.

On the other hand the Mortes was ascribed to Lactantius in the course of the fourth century, for Jerome had a copy in 393 A.D., on which doubtless the name of Lactantius was inscribed; De Vir. Ill. c. 80, *habemus* (I possess) *eius—de persecutione librum unum*. And Brandt has corroborated this view of Jerome's statement by showing that the person who (c. 370 or not many years later) interpolated the Divine Institutions with the addresses to the Emperors (see Brandt, die Kaiseranreden, Sitzungsber. der W. Ak. 119, 1889), made use of the Mortes, supposing it to be Lactantian. This false ascription of the treatise, the work perhaps of a pupil of Lactantius, to Lactantius himself is accounted for by Brandt by the hypothesis that it was published anonymously, and the public, anxious to discover the authorship, were led by the Lactantianisms and the Nicomedian origin to fix on the well-known writer of the Divine Institutions. *L. Cæcilii* would be, on this hypothesis, probably a mistake for L. Cælii (*i.e.* Lactantii), and not the name of the true author.

As for the date (discussed by Görres in Philologus, xxxvi. p. 597 *sqq.*, 1877), Brandt narrows it down to a short period between the end of 314 A.D. and the middle of 315 (p. 111). The Epitome of the Divine Institutions (its Lactantian authorship has been vindicated, p. 2-10) was used in the Mortes, and was written between the middle of 313 A.D. and the conclusion of the Mortes. Seeck (who accepts from Idatius 316 as date of Diocletian's death) makes the limits 317 and 321.

On Brandt's arguments I would observe that all except (1) have little cogency. (4) is especially weak; we have a much more glaring example of such inconsistency in the case of Procopius the historian. In regard to (1), Seeck urges (Gesch. des Unterg. der ant. Welt, p. 428) Jerome's statement that L. taught Crispus as Cæsar, *i.e.* after 317 A.D.; Constantine would not before his conversion (312, at earliest) have chosen a Christian preceptor for his son; in 308 Crispus was not more than two years old. There seems indeed to be no reason for supposing that L. went to Trier much before 317; therefore he could be in Nicomedia in 313; and the chief argument against the Lactantian authorship of the Mortes breaks down. It may be added that no argument, except one favourable to the identification, can be based on the difference between the names in the Mss.—Cælius and Cæcilius,— in view of the fact that *L. Cæcilius Firmianus* is found in a Numidian inscription (C. I. L. 8, 7241); and Lactantius belonged to the African Diocese (Seeck, *ib.* 426).

On the life of Lactantius see Brandt, Ueber das Leben des L., Sitzungsber. der

W. Akad., cxx., 1890; and on the interpolations in the Divine Inst. (see above chap. xx. n. 2) his two papers, Die dualistischen Zusätze, *ib.* cxviii., 1889, and Die Kaiseranreden, *ib.* cxix., 1889.

To understand the historical work of EUSEBIUS of Cæsarea, we must glance at the "Chronographies" of Sextus Julius Africanus, who flourished in the early part of the third century and wrote his chronographical work between 212 and 221 A.D. All that is known about him and his work will be found in the invaluable study of H. Gelzer, Sextus Julius Africanus und die byzantinische Chronographie (1880). He is the founder of Byzantine chronography. His system is determined by the Jewish idea of a world-epoch of 6000 years; and he divides this into two parts at the death of Phalek. He is concerned to prove that the Incarnation took place in the year 5500 (=2 B.C.); after which there are 500 years of waiting till the end of the world and the beginning of the millennium or the World-Sabbath. The date of Moses was fixed at 1020 years before the first olympiad by Justus of Tiberias, and this view, to which the apologist Justin gave currency, is maintained by Africanus, who puts Moses in 3707-8 and the first olympiad=first year of Ahaz in 4727-8. A contemporary of Africanus, Hippolytus of Rome, also wrote a chronicle of the world, which Gelzer (ii. 23) designates as a very feeble performance, in erudition far inferior to that of Africanus.

The chronicle of Eusebius, translated into Latin by Jerome, threw that of Africanus into the background. Gelzer (ii. 42 *sqq.*) gives him the credit which he deserves for his excellent critical discussion of the number of years between the Exodus and the building of Solomon's temple. Here we have a contradiction between St. Paul and the Book of Judges on one hand, and the Books of Kings on the other. Eusebius does not hesitate to criticize the inspired numbers with masterly ability, just as if they occurred in profane documents, and rejects the statement of the apostle Paul. "In later patristic literature we find nothing similar. The Greek Church was perfectly speechless at the boldness which treated the chronological sketch of the apostle like that of a profane author' (Gelzer, ii. 47).

Again the historical instinct of Eusebius is shown in the choice of his era. While Africanus began with Adam, this instinct taught Eusebius that all Hebrew events before Abraham were "prehistoric," and so he dated events by the years of Abraham, whom he places in 2017 B.C., whereas the date of Africanus was 2300. But this was little compared with his boldness in rejecting the received date of Moses, whom he placed in 1512 B.C. instead of 1795 B.C.

In the Ecclesiastical History, the Panegyric on Constantine, and the Life of Constantine (a *Denkschrift* rather than a regular biography; Ranke), the guiding idea of Eusebius is the establishment of a Christian empire, for which Constantine was the chosen instrument. See Ranke's short suggestive essay in Weltgeschichte, ii. 2, 249 *sqq.;* one of his points is that we must not press some deviations in the Life, written after Constantine's death, from the earlier works. But we must agree with the remark of O. Seeck: "Nichts hat dem Andenken des grossen Kaisers mehr geschadet als das Lügenbuch des Eusebios". Seeck declines to make any use of the documents contained in it. P. Meyer, de Vita Const. Eusebiana, 1883; V. Schultze, Quellen-untersuchungen zur Vita Const. des Eus., in Zeitsch. für Kirchengesch., xiv. p. 503 *sqq.*, 1894; Amedeo Crivellucci, Della fede storica di Eusebio nella vita di Constantino, 1888 (Livorno); Görres, Z. f. wiss. Theol., xx. 215 *sqq.;* xxi. 35 *sqq.;* xxxiii. 124 *sqq.*

Two historical fragments, one covering A.D. 293-337, the other A.D. 474-526, first printed by H. Valois at the end of his edition of Ammian (from a Ms. belonging to J. Sirmond, which afterwards passed into the Phillipps collection, and was translated in 1887 from Cheltenham to Berlin), are generally described under the name ANONYMUS VALESII. This title is misleading, by its suggestion that the two fragments belong to the same work, whereas they have nothing to do with each other; but it is still convenient to refer to them under the old title. Though they have nothing to do with Ammianus, Gardthausen, following the example of Valois, printed them at the end of his edition. The authoritative edition is now Mommsen's in the Chronica Minora (M. G. H.); the first which concerns us here, being printed under the title Origo Constantini imperatoris in vol. i. p. 7-11 (1891).

The unknown author of this fragment wrote in the fourth century, and Mommsen designates him as "optimi et Ammiano neque aetate neque auctoritate inferioris" and adds that he probably wrote "ante tempora absolute Christiana". Several passages (e.g., 20, 33, 34), which are redolent of the Christian clerical style, are shown to be interpolations derived from Orosius (Mommsen, pref. p. 6 ; cp. W. Ohnesorge, Der Anonymus Valesii de Constantino, p. 88 sqq., 1885, who has some good remarks on the author's geographical knowledge, and the probability that he wrote in Italy).

[The ANONYMI MONODIA (first published by Morelli in 1691) was supposed to be (in accordance with its title in the Palatine Ms.) a funeral oration on Constantine, the eldest son of Constantine the Great ; and on this supposition Gibbon made important use of it (p. 212, n. 26 ; cp. p. 232, n. 71). But it is only necessary to read it carefully to see that the inscription is false, and that it cannot refer to the younger Constantine. This was proved by Wesseling, who made it probable that the subject of the oration was Theodore Palæologus. As the argument of Gibbon as to Fausta's survival was recently repeated by such a capable scholar as Victor Schultze, with an appeal to the Monodia (Brieger's Zeitschr. f. Kirchengeschichte, viii. p. 541, apparently he had not read the document), it may be worth while to state briefly the chief decisive points. (I cite from the most recent edition: Anon. Græci oratio funebris, by C. E. Frotscher, 1856.) (1) The very first words are quite impossible in an orator of the fourth century : Ἄνδρες Ῥωμαῖοι, μᾶλλον δὲ τῶν Ῥωμαίων ποτὲ λείψανα δυστυχῆ. (2) The subject of the laudation died of a plague (p. 14) ; Constantine according to our authorities was killed by violence. (3) ἐπὶ τούτοις ἐκ Πελοποννήσου πρὸς ἡμᾶς πάλιν ἀνήγου (p. 16) does not apply to Constantine, nor yet (4) the statement (p. 26) that he sent ambassadors to Iberia (whether Spanish or Caucasian) to get him a wife.]

It is much to be regretted that the history of Constantine the Great, in two books, written by a young Athenian named PRAXAGORAS at the age of twenty-two, is only known to us by a brief quotation in Photius, cod. 62, p. 20, ed. Bekk. (=F. H. G. iv. p. 2). Photius does not give his date. Müller says he wrote at end of Constantine's reign, or under Constantius, ut uidetur, but does not give reasons. In accepting this date as probably right I am guided by the following consideration. Praxagoras (Photius tells us) was a pagan (Ἕλλην τὴν θρησκείαν), and yet he praised Constantine very highly, setting him above all his predecessors who held the Imperial dignity. It is extremely improbable that a pagan living in the second half of the fourth century—a contemporary of Julian and Eunapius—or in the fifth, would have adopted this attitude. Hostility to Constantine's memory is a note of Julian and all the pagans who came after him. It seems to me, therefore, that the first half of the fourth century is the only epoch which suits our data respecting Praxagoras.

JULIAN has been treated so fully in the text that only bibliographical points need be noted here. My references throughout are to the critical text of Hertlein (Gibbon used that of Spanheim, 1696), which includes the extant works, except (1) the treatise contra Christianos, which has been ingeniously reconstituted from the citations of Cyril and edited by C. J. Neumann, 1880 ; and (2) six letters which A. Papadopoulos-Kerameus discovered in a Ms. at the μονὴ τῆς Θεοτόκου in the island of Chalce near Constantinople. These are published in the Rheinisches Museum, 42 (1887), p. 15 sqq., in the Maurogordateios Bibliotheke and elsewhere [number 1, to his uncle Julian, 2, to the priestess Theodora (cp. Hertl. Ep. 5), 3, to Theodorus, high priest, 4, to Priscus, 5, to Maximin, 6, probably to a priestess]. Three of these [1, 2, 3] are considered of doubtful authenticity by Schwarz in his valuable Julianstudien, Philol. li. p. 623 sqq. (1892), where he tries to discriminate in the extant correspondence of Julian, what is genuine, spurious, and doubtful. He condemns letters 8, 18, 19, 24, 25, 34, 40, 41, 53, 54, 60, 61, 66, 67, 72, 73, 75. Doubts are attached to 28, 32, 57, 68. Letter 27 is mainly genuine, but is tainted by an interpolation, § 9-21.

(Schwarz also disproves Cumont's conjecture that a number of the letters are the work of Julian the Sophist, p. 626 *sqq.*) Julian wrote a special work in his Alamannic campaign, not extant now, which was used by Ammianus and Libanius (see below under Ammianus). The Cohortatio ad Græcos, which had been falsely ascribed to Justin, has been shown by J. Asmus to be a contemporary polemical tract against Julian (acc. to J. Dräseke, Apollinarios von Laodicea, 1891, p. 85 *sqq.*, identical with the treatise of Apollinaris on Truth, mentioned by Sozomen, v. 18). It was used by Gregory Naz., in his Invectives. See Zeitsch. für wissensch. Theologie, xxxviii. 115 *sqq.*, 1895. The *Therapeutic* of Theodoret seems to have been directed against Julian's "Rhetor-edict" and his work against the Galilæans ; see J. Asmus, Byz. Zeitsch. 3, p. 116 *sqq.* [Modern works : J. F. Mücke, Flavius Cl. Julianus, 1866-8. Rendall, The Emperor Julian, 1878. Naville, Julien l'Apostat et sa philosophie du polythéisme, 1877. Miss Gardner, Julian the Philosopher, 1895. Sievers (in his Studien), Julians Perserkrieg. Rode, Geschichte der Reaction Kaiser J. gegen die christliche Kirche, 1877. Schwarz, de vita et scriptis Juliani imperatoris, 1888. F. Cumont, Sur l'authenticité de quelques lettres de Julian, 1889. Wiegand, Die Alamannenschlacht von Strassburg (in Heft 3 of Beitr. zur Landes und Volkeskunde von Elsass-Lothr., 1887). Koch, Leyden Dissertation on Julian's Gallic campaigns, 1890. Reinhardt, Der Tod des Kaisers Julian, 1891, and Der Perserkrieg des K. J., 1892. Klimek, Zur Würdigung der Handschriften und zur Textkritik Julians, 1888. See also G. Boissier's La fin du paganisme ; Petit de Julleville's L'Ecole d'Athènes au iv͏ᵉ siècle après Jésus Christ. Others have been mentioned in the notes.]

Of the life and works of LIBANIUS (314—c. 395 A.D.) a full account will be found in the standard monograph of Sievers, Das Leben des Libanius (1868), which is full of valuable research for the general history of the time. Reiske's edition of the Orations and Declamations appeared too late (1784-1797, 4 volumes) for Gibbon to use. A new edition both of Speeches and Letters (ed. Wolf, 1738) is much needed. 1607 letters are preserved, of which Sievers gives a full dated index (p. 297 *sqq.*). Four hundred letters professing to be Latin translations from originals of Libanius have been proved by R. Förster to be forgeries (F. Zambeccari und die Briefe des Libanius, 1876 ; cp. Sievers, *ib.* Beil. T.T.). The dates of the Speeches of Libanius, which concern us in the present volume, are, according to Sievers (p. 203), as follows :—

(1) Βασιλικός (lx.)=c. 348 A.D. (349 A.D., Tillemont).
(2) Μονῳδία ἐπὶ Νικομηδείᾳ (lxii.)=c. 358 A.D. (after 24th August).
(3) Ἀντιοχικός (xi.)=360 A.D.
(4) Προσφωνητικὸς Ἰουλιανῷ (xiii.)=July 362 A.D.
(5) ὑπὲρ Ἀριστοφάνους (xiv.)=362 A.D. (intercession for a friend who had been exiled).
(6) Μονῳδία ἐπὶ τῷ ἐν Δάφνῃ νεῷ (lxi.)=362 A.D. (after 23rd October).
(7) εἰς Ἰουλιανὸν ὕπατον (xii.)=1st January 363 A.D.
(8) πρεσβευτικὸς πρὸς Ἰουλιανόν (xv.) } =after March 363 A.D.
(9) πρὸς Ἀντ. περὶ τῆς βασ. ὀργῆς (xvi.) }
(10) Μονῳδία ἐπὶ Ἰουλιανῷ (xvii.)=end July 363 A.D.
(11) Ἐπιτάφιος ἐπὶ Ἰουλιανῷ (xviii.)=368 or 369 A.D.
(12) ὑπὲρ τῆς Ἰουλιανοῦ τιμωρίας (xxiii.)=after 378 A.D.

Of the orations of THEMISTIUS (a younger contemporary and friend of Libanius) those which concern this volume are the Panegyrics of Constantius : i. A.D. 347 ; ii. A.D. 355; iii. (Πρεσβευτικός) and iv., delivered in the senate at Constantinople A.D. 357. The subject of i. is φιλανθρωπία, which Christ (Gr. Litteratur, p. 672) designates as the Schlagwort of Themistius,—a pagan whose tolerance stands out in contrast with the temper of men like Libanius and Eunapius. (Ed. Dindorf, 1832 ; E. Baret, de Them. sophista et apud imperatores oratore, Paris, 1853.)

The Latin panegyric of NAZARIUS on Constantine (see above, p. 304) and the speech of thanksgiving of CLAUDIUS MAMERTINUS to Julian are printed in Baehrens' xii. Panegyr. Lat., as x. and xi.

AMMIANUS MARCELLINUS, born c. 330, belonged to a good Antiochene family (Amm. xix. 8, 6), and was thus a *Grœcus* (xxxi. 16), though he wrote his history in Latin, which had become a second mother-tongue. His good birth and connexions gained him admission to the corps of the *domestici* (see below, App. 13). His military service probably lasted somewhat more than ten years. We find him at Nisibis in 353 under Ursicinus (xiv. 9, 1). Next year he is in the west; we catch him on the way to Milan (*ib.* 11, 5); and he goes with other *protectores*, *domestici* and *tribuni* (*scholarum ?*) on a mission to Köln (xv. 5, 2, and xviii. 8, 11). But in 357 he returns to the east, to the scene of the Persian war (xvi. 10, 21), and Gibbon notices his escape from Amida. He went through Julian's campaign and probably retired from military service soon after the conclusion of the war by Jovian's treaty (cp. Büdinger, Ammianus Marcellinus und die Eigenart seines Geschichtswerkes, 1895).

His Res Gestæ in thirty-one books was intended as a continuation of Tacitus, and began with Nerva (xxxi. 16). "The first thirteen books, a superficial epitome of 257 years, are now lost; the last eighteen, which contain no more than twenty-five years, still preserve the copious and authentic history of his own times" (Gibbon, ch. xxvi. n. 113). Book xiv. begins with the acts of the Cæsar Gallus in 353 A.D., and book xxxi. ends with the battle of Hadrianople in 378 A.D. The work seems to have been finished early in the last decade of the century, and he won by it a considerable reputation at Rome (cp. Libanius, Epp. ed. Wolf, Ep. to Amm. Marc. pp. 132 *sqq.*). Characteristic are his imitations of Tacitus and Sallust, and his contempt for the scandal-mongering popular history of Marius Maximus. The impartiality of Ammianus is appreciated by Gibbon, and generally recognized. For the Persian wars his account is not only that of a contemporary but of an eye-witness. As to his sources for Julian's German wars, see below. He was a pagan, but was not unjust to Christianity, of which he speaks with respect, and, though an admirer of Julian, shows by a very strong expression his disapprobation of that Emperor's measure which prohibited Christians from teaching (xxii. 10, 7). For his view of Christianity cp. xxi. 16, 18 (quoted by Gibbon) and xxii. 11, 5 (nihil nisi iustum suadet et lene). His remarkable phrase about the founder of Christianity was unknown until A. von Gutschmid brilliantly restored a corrupt passage, xxii. 16, 22 :—

Ex his fontibus [sc. Egyptian sources] per sublimia gradiens sermonum amplitudine Iouis æmulus non uisa Aegypto militauit sapientia gloriosa.

The name of the wise man, thus described, has disappeared from the Mss., and Valesius proposed to substitute *Platon* for *non*. But Gutschmid saw that the reference is to Jesus, and that the abbreviated name *ihs* had fallen out accidentally after *his*. Thus *ex his Iesus fontibus* now appears in Gardthausen's text. (*Non u. Aegypto* is not verbally true, according to the account of Matthew, but it is in any case true in spirit.) Ammianus was doubtless thinking of the doctrine of the Logos in the fourth Gospel.

In connexion with this passage I would hazard a conjecture. I think that when Ammianus went out of his way to connect Jesus with Egypt, he had in mind a letter of Julian to the Alexandrians (Ep. li.), where the Emperor reproaches them for the prevalence of the Galilean superstition in their cities. The general theme of the letter is : What is Alexandria to Jesus or Jesus to Alexandria ? The Ptolemies, he says (p. 557, l. 7, ed. Hertl.), οὔτι τοῖς Ἰησοῦ λογοις ηὔξησαν αὐτὴν οὐδὲ τῇ τῶν ἐχθίστων Γαλιλαίων διδασκαλίᾳ τὴν οἰκονομίαν αὐτῇ ταυτην ὑφ᾽ ἧς νῦν ἐστιν εὐδαίμων ἐξειργάσαντο. Again (p. 558, l. 7), ὃν δὲ οὔτε ὑμεῖς οὔτε οἱ πατέρες ὑμῶν ἑοράκασιν Ἰησοῦν οἴεσθε χρῆναι θεὸν λόγον ὑπάρχειν. I suggest that Ammian's words are a criticism on Julian's argument, and that *non uisa Aegypto* was suggested by the sentence last quoted.

The attitude of Ammianus to internal ecclesiastical history has been well brought out by Büdinger (*op. cit.* p. 15 *sqq.*). He declines to enter into the details of Christian controversies; his idea is that the Christians fight among themselves like wild beasts.—His ideas of morality are high and strict; he believes in progress and the enlightenment of his own age, cp. xviii. 7, 7. He has a high ideal of the imperial authority. He shows towards the Germans a certain bitterness which is never apparent in his treatment of the oriental nations. That he was in a certain measure superstitious, notwithstanding his enlightenment, has been brought out by Büdinger. A proneness to exaggerate signs and portents may partly account for the extraordinary mistake in xx. 3, 1, where it is stated that in the east of the Empire there was an eclipse of the sun visible from dawn to noon, in 360 A.D. (the month is not given),—a total eclipse, for the stars were visible. In that year there was a total eclipse, but only visible in Australia; and there was also an eclipse in the afternoon of 28th August, (1) visible in Asia but further east than the east boundary of the Empire, and (2) partial, so that *intermicabant iugiter stellæ* could not apply to it. (Query: Did Ammianus, by a lapse of memory, set down under a wrong year the total eclipse of 4th June, 364?)

One sharp criticism of Gibbon on Ammianus (see p. 398, n. 6) is due, as Mr. Hodgkin has pointed out to me, to a misunderstanding. Ammianus means in the passage in question that the troops were not to reach Persia, but to muster in Italy, at the beginning of spring.

A reference must be made to the friendship of Ammian with his fellow-citizen and fellow-pagan Libanius. Their correspondence seems to have begun (not very cordially perhaps) about 359; Libanius, ep. 141, ed. Wolf; and a very interesting letter (cited above) is extant (date 390-1) in which the rhetor admonishes Ammianus to go on with his historical work. In ep. 232 he refers to ὁ κολὸς Ἀμμιανός. In other letters addressed to Ammianus or Marcellinus there is nothing to identify the writer's correspondent.

For contemporary history Ammianus made use of the writings of Julian, the history of Eutropius and other sources. Much has been written on the subject of his *fontes*: Gardthausen, Die geographischen Quellen Ammians, 1873 (and Coniectanea Ammianea, 1869); Hertz, Aulus Gellius und Ammianus Marcellinus (Hermes 8, 1874); Sudhaus, de ratione quæ intercedat inter Zosimi et Ammiani de bello a Jul. imp. cum Pers. gesto relationes, 1870; Hugo Michael, de A. M. studiis Ciceronianis, 1874, die verlorenen Bücher des Ammianus M., 1880. In Hermes 25, 1889, E. von Borries, Die Quellen zu den Feldzügen Julians des Abtrünnigen gegen die Germanen (p. 173 *sqq.*), elaborately and ingeniously discusses the question of the relations between the sources for Julian's German campaigns (*viz.*, Ammian, Libanius' Epitaphios, and Zosimus). His results are:—

(1) Libanius used all Julian's writings including a lost work on the battle of Strassburg. Borries thinks the Ἐπιτάφιος was composed as early as end of 363.

(2) (Zosimus drew from) Eunapius (who) used a memoir of the physician Oribasius, and various writings (including lost letters) of Julian, but not the work on the campaign against the Alamanni.

(3) A lost source, x., used all the writings of Julian and the Memoir of Oribasius.

(4) Ammianus used two sources (as is shown by a number of contradictions and repetitions, and the fact that he sometimes agrees with Libanius, sometimes with Eunapius (Zosimus)). These sources were Julian's monograph on the Alamannic campaign, and x.

Borries shows that there were no "Commentaries" of Julian such as Hecker assumes in "Zur Geschichte des Kaisers Julian," 1876 (cp. Die Alamannenschlacht bei Strassburg, in Jahrbb. für class. Philol., 1879, p. 59-80).

Gardthausen's edition of Ammianus (1874) is the best.

On Ammian's geographical knowledge see Mommsen, Hermes 16, 1881.

EUNAPIUS of Sardis was born about 347, and survived 414 A.D. For the facts which are known about his life see Müller, Frag. Hist. Græc. iv. p. 7-8. He wrote (1) a continuation of the Chronicle of Dexippus, which ended in 270 A.D. and brought it down to the death of Theodosius I., in 395 A.D. Then (2) he composed (c. 405 A.D.) his Lives of [23] Philosophers and Sophists, a work which is preserved (ed. Boissonade, in Didot series, 1849), and is valuable as a history of the fourth century renascence of sophistic. (3) About ten years later, he took up his history again and continued it to 404 A.D.,—probably intending to make the death of Arcadius (408) his terminus. Of the history we have only fragments (edited by Müller, F. H. G. iv.) ; but we have further knowledge of it through the fact that it was the main source of Zosimus. It was characterized by all the weaknesses of contemporary rhetoric. For the history of events from Diocletian forward Eunapius' narrative and the Epitome of Victor seem to have been drawn from a common source, but I agree with Mendelssohn in deciding, in opposition to Opitz and Jeep, that this source was not Ammianus. For the campaigns of Julian, Eunapius used the Memoirs of Oribasius. Like Libanius, he was a firm adherent of the old religion, and an enthusiastic admirer of Julian.

For Magnus of Carrhæ and Eutychianus who wrote accounts of the Persian campaign of Julian, see Müller, F. H. G. iv. 4-6, and Mendelssohn's Preface to Zosimus, p. xxxix. sqq.

Zosimus, count and ex-advocatus fisci, wrote his history, as L. Mendelssohn (who has recently published an excellent critical edition, 1887) showed, between the years 450 and 501 A.D. He is not to be identified with either of his two contemporary namesakes, the grammarian of Ascalon or the sophist of Gaza. That he lived part of his life at Constantinople has been inferred from his accurate description of the city, ii. c. 35 sqq. Like Eunapius he was devoted to paganism, and hostile to the Christian Emperors.

Introducing his work by expressing his belief in a guiding providence in history, and appealing to the work of Polybius in which the wonderful career of Rome was unfolded, Zosimus proceeds to give a rapid sketch of Imperial history up to the death of Claudius (i. 1-46), and then begins, with the accession of Aurelian, a fuller narrative, coming down to the siege of Rome by Alaric in 410. The author clearly intended to continue his work to a later date ; if the sixth book, of which there are only thirteen chapters, had reached the average length of the first five, it would probably have ended with the death of Honorius. Between books i. and ii. there is a great gap, corresponding to the reigns of Carus, Carinus and Diocletian. We may conjecture that book ii. began with the accession of Diocletian.

The important question of the sources of Zosimus has been acutely investigated by Mendelssohn (see Preface and Notes to his edition). His results are briefly : (1) For chaps 1-46, Zosimus used a lost source, in which the account of the Gothic invasions was drawn from the Scythica of Dexippus, but the Chronica of that writer was not consulted. The hypothesis of an indirect use of the same source will explain the remarkable agreements between Zonaras and Zosimus ; and the identification of the source is bound up with the perplexed question of the *fontes* of Zonaras. (2) For the main body of the work Zosimus has chiefly relied on Eunapius, as can be shown from the Eunapian fragments. Besides oracles, and one or two passages of small importance, which he has taken from other sources, Mendelssohn makes it probable that the digression on the secular games at beginning of book ii. was derived from Phlegon's treatise on Roman Feasts ; and explains the agreements between Zosimus and Ammianus in the account of Julian's Persian expedition by a common use of Magnus of Carrhæ (cp. Zosimus' own words, iii. 2, 4, where he promises to tell of Julian μάλιστα ὅσα τοῖς ἄλλοις παραλελεῖφθαι δοκεῖ—doubtless an allusion to Eunapius). (3) For the last years, 407-410 A.D., he uses Olympiodorus, whom he mentions. It is important here to consult Sozomen, who used the same source.

There is an elaborate and admirable "characteristic" of Zosimus as an historian in the Analekten to the fourth part of Ranke's Weltgeschichte (Abth. 2, p. 264 sqq.).

The Consular Fasti of Idatius or, correctly, Hydatius, the Spaniard, consist of three parts : (1) from the first consuls to the foundation of Constantinople, 330 A.D., (2) from A.D. 330 to 395, (3) from A.D. 395 to 468. Parts i. and ii. are an epitome of a chronicle which has been more fully preserved in a Greek form in the CHRONICON PASCHALE. (Mommsen has printed the two versions side by side in Chron. Minora, i. p. 208 *sqq.*). The second part was written at Constantinople "quae etiam in chronicis urbanis hereditatem quodammodo Romae veteris sibi vindicavit". We must suppose that a copy reached Spain towards the end of the fourth century, and was continued by Idatius concurrently with his continuation of the Chronicle of Jerome, along with which it has come down (see Mommsen, l. c. p. 201. Also C. Frick, in Byz. Zeitschrift, vol. i.). In the second part, Idatius seems to have added some notices from the CHRONICLE of Jerome (composed c. 380 A.D.).

Of the four Greek ecclesiastical historians who wrote in the first half of the fifth century, the earliest, PHILOSTORGIUS (born before 365(?); flor. c. 380-412 A.D.), is the most interesting, as an Arian. Unluckily his "Ecclesiastical History" (which beginning with Constantine ended in 425 A.D.) is only known by the epitome of it made by Photius in the ninth century; it can be proved that at the beginning of the fourteenth century Nicephorus Xanthopulos had only this epitome and not the complete work before him. (For the problem as to how far the epitome differs from the original, the study of J. R. Asmus, in Byz. Zeitsch. v. 30 *sqq.*, 1895, is suggestive.) The sources of Philostorgius, Socrates and Sozomen have been elaborately studied by L. Jeep in Quæstiones Fridericianæ, 1881, and Quellenuntersuchungen zu den griechischen Kirchenhistorikern, 1884. He concludes that Philostorgius made use of Eunapius, and, for the late years of his work, Olympiodorus (see below, vol. iii. Appendix 1).

Some fragments of another Arian historian (name unknown) are preserved (as Mr. Gwatkin showed in his Studies of Arianism) in the Chronicon Paschale. P. Batiffol has tried to show that this writer was a source of Philostorgius and Theodoret (Röm. Quartalschrift, 9, p. 57 *sqq.*, 1895).

SOCRATES (orthodox; native of Constantinople) brought down his History to 439 A.D. (cp. vii. 48), in which year (or 440) he can be shown to have completed his work. His sources (referred to by himself) are: Eusebius; Rufinus (cp ii. 1); Athanasius; three Collections of Letters, of (*a*) Arius, (*b*) Constantine against Arius, (*c*) Alexander of Alexandria (cp. i. 6); Sabinus (Bishop of Thracian Heraclea, and adherent of the heresy of Macedonius), who compiled a Collection of the Acts of the Synods, beginning with Nicæa (συναγωγὴ τῶν συνοδικῶν), doubtless filling in the historical connexion, and adding comments from his own point of view. Besides these, Socrates certainly made use of the Constantinopolitan Chronicle (see above); and Jeep has tried to show that he used Philostorgius and Olympiodorus. For the relations of Socrates and Rufinus see Gwatkin, Studies of Arianism, p. 93 *sqq.*

SOZOMEN, a contemporary of Socrates and likewise orthodox (probably native of Palestine), proposed to trace the history of the Church from A.D. 324 to 439 (where Socrates ended; see Soz.'s dedication); but the work as we have it ends in 425, the last books apparently having been lost (cp. Jeep, Quellenuntersuch. p. 140). He used Socrates, but also went to the sources of Socrates; in the last book he abandons Socrates for Olympiodorus. Cp. Sarrazin, de Theodoro Lectore (in Gelzer u. Götz, Diss. Jenenses).

THEODORET (orthodox) wrote his work (which comes down to 429 A.D.) between 441 and 449 A.D. It has very little value, adding almost nothing to Socrates and Sozomen. The sources have been fully investigated by A. Güldenpenning, Die Kirchengeschichte des Theodoret von Kyrrhos, 1889. Besides Athanasius, Arius, Eustathius of Antioch, he used (according to Güldenpenning) Socrates and Sozomen, and perhaps Philostorgius; also Ephraem Syrus and the Gregories of Nazianzus and Nyssa. The most elaborate work on Theodoret is in Russian, by N. Glubokovski, 1890.

Besides these, two other Ecclesiastical Histories in Greek were composed about the same time, which are now lost and never attained the same popularity, those of (1) Philip Sidetes; cp. Socr. vii. 26-7; and Harnack, Texte u. Untersuch. I., i. 179 sqq.; and (2) Hesychius of Jerusalem, cp. Fabricius, Bib. Gr. vii. 548 sqq. All six began their histories about the same place,—where Eusebius ended. Cp. Harnack's Sokrates u. Sozomenos, in Encycl. of Herzog u. Plitt; he calls attention to the differences between western and eastern Ecclesiastical historians in motive, aim and scope.

MODERN WORKS (compare vol. i. Appendix 1). Burckhardt, Die Zeit Constantins des Grossen, 1880 (edition 2). Ranke, Weltgeschichte, iv. O. Seeck, Geschichte des Unterangs der antiken Welt, vol. i. 1895 (which, I regret, appeared too late to be used in the preparation of vol. i. of this edition. Especially noteworthy is the brilliant chapter on early German society). For early Christian art, F. X. Kraus, Geschichte der christlichen Kunst, vol. i. part i. 1895, where full bibliographical references will be found, and V. Schultze, Archäologie der altchristlichen Kunst, 1895 (cp. below, Appendix 7). On ecclesiastical matters the reader may profitably consult (besides good ecclesiastical histories, which are numerous, e.g., Neander, Schröckh, Hefele, Milman) articles in the Dictionary of Christian Biography, and in the theological encyclopædia of Herzog and Plitt.

2. ORIGIN OF GNOSTICISM—(P. 11)

Hilgenfeld has developed his view as to the rise of Gnosticism in his highly important work on early heresies, Die Ketzergeschichte des Urchristenthums. His position is that Gnosticism was founded (as Irenæus said) by the Samaritan, Simon the Magian, at the beginning of the Apostolic epoch, and thus arose strictly' outside Christianity, but yet within its atmosphere. Then it became in a way Christian, and deeply affected Christianity, both by breaking down Jewish Christianity, and by calling forth a combined opposition which led to the formation of a united Catholic Church. Hilgenfeld repeats and defends his theory in his Zeitsch. für wissenschaftliche Theologie, vol. xxxiii. 1890, p. 1 sqq., against the different view put forward in Harnack's Lehrbuch der Dogmengeschichte, vol. i., 1st edition, p. 178 sqq. Harnack holds that Gnosticism arose from pre-Christian syncretistic religious theories (a "Religionsmischung") which existed in Syria and, especially Samaria, and aimed at a universal religion. The Gnostics he describes as "the theologians of the first century" (p. 163); they took up Christianity at once as a universal religion and opposed it sharply to Judaism and other religions. In Gnosticism, he says (following Overbeck), is represented "die acute Verweltlichung" (Hellenisation) of Christianity,—a result which was only obtained by a gradual process in Catholic Christianity.

Harnack points out well (p. 172) that Gnosticism was accompanied by a number of other sects, only partially related, which on one hand shade off into Hellenism, on the other to ordinary Christianity; e.g. Carpocratians and Encratites respectively. He deals at length with the peculiar position of Marcion, p. 197 sqq. [Cp. articles on Gnosticism and Marcion, in Dict. of Christian Biography.]

Harnack has since made a valuable contribution to the study of Gnosticism by his work "Ueber das gnostische Buch Pistis Sophia" (1891). He shows that this treatise (for which see above, p. 14, n. 33), of which he gives an elaborate exegesis, was earlier than A.D. 302, and fixes it to the second half of the third century (p. 94 sqq.). He shows that it was written in Egypt, but does not represent Valentinian doctrines (as had been supposed) but rather Ophite, if we use this elastic word to connote a whole group of Syrian gnostic heresies (Ophites, Nicolaites, Sethites, Kainites, &c.). He goes on to develop an attractive theory that the Pistis Sophia is identical with a treatise mentioned by Epiphanius (De Hær. xxvi.) under the title of the Small Questions of Mary, as a work that issued from this Gnostic group, and he even tries to establish that it represents in particular the views of the Sethites.

A long and important study on Gnostic works preserved in Coptic (the Books of Jeû : Coptic text and German translation) by C. Schmidt, in Gebhardt u. Harnack, Texte u. Unters., viii. 1 and 2, deserves special mention.

3. WORLD-ERAS—(P. 24)

The system of Africanus (see above, note 1) which established 5500 years between the creation of the world and the incarnation (σάρκωσις : not the nativity, ἐνανθρώπησις) of Christ was adopted by many subsequent chroniclers : *e.g.* by Hippolytus, by Sulpicius Severus, by Eutychius. It was also accepted by Eusebius, but in his chronicle (see above, n. 1) he reckoned events from Abraham, 2017 A.D. On this system A.M. 5500 was concurrent with our 2 B.C.

The other most important eras were :—

(1) The "Byzantine" or "Roman" era (adopted in the Chronicon Paschale)= A.M. 5507 (incarnation, 21st March). As this year was identified with 1 B.C. we must, in order to reduce a date A.M. to a date A.D., subtract 5508. Thus A.M. 5958 (−5508)=A.D. 450.

(2) The "Antiochene" era (used by John Malalas)=A.M. 5967 ; but concurrent with 3-2 B.C. The rule for reducing to a date A.D. is : subtract 5970. Thus A.M. 6370 (−5970)=A.D. 400-1. Cp. Gelzer, Sex. Julius Africanus, ii. 132.

(3) The "Ecclesiastical" era of Annianus (adopted by George Syncellus and Theophanes) was A.M. 5501. (The year 5500 ended on 24th March, 5501 began 25th March, day of the immaculate conception. The same day of the month (1st Nisan) was the day of the Creation and the Crucifixion.) This year was concurrent with 9 A.D. Therefore to reduce A.M. in Theophanes to A.D. we must subtract (5501−9=) 5492. Thus A.M. 6000 (−5492)=A.D. 508.

Annianus (finished his work 412) owed much to his elder contemporary Panodorus (c. 395-408)—as has been shown by Unger, cp. Gelzer. *op. cit.* ii. 191—and both were the main foundations of the chronicle of Syncellus. Panodorus invented a different era which found little favour. He placed Christ's birth in A.M. 5493. Unger has shown that he miscalculated the length of the Ptolemaic dynasty by a year ; his era should be 5494. The eras of Annianus and Panodorus are sometimes known as the Alexandrine.

4. EARLY CHURCH INSTITUTIONS—(P. 41)

There is a considerable German literature on early Christian institutions, from Baur's Der Ursprung des Episkopats, 1838, to the present day (of recent works, E. Löning's Die Gemeindeverfassung des Urchristenthums, 1889, deserves special mention). Important contributions have been made to the subject in England by Bishop Lightfoot and by Dr. Hatch ; the latter in The Organization of the Early Christian Churches (translated into German and edited by Harnack), 1880, doing good service by pointing out resemblances with the organization of religious communities in the contemporary pagan world. The large literature relating to the Ignatian Letters is also directly concerned with the origin of episcopacy. The subject has been treated from a wider point of view by M. Réville in his Les origines de l'épiscopat, vol. i., 1894, a work which throws light on many points. A very brief summary of his results (though they are by no means incontestable) in regard to the episcopate will be appropriate.

He throws aside the πρῶτον ψεῦδος of many of his predecessors, "le funeste préjugé de l'unité du christianisme primitif," the idea that in the early church the institutions found in one community existed in all the others. Thus for Paul's time the evidence of the Pauline epistles proves that there were episcopi at Philippi, but does not give the slightest reason to assume such in Galatia. The episcopal functions were originally administrative and financial [and liturgical] ; and were distinct from the presbyteral functions, though often exercised by presbyters ; the deacons were assistants of the episcopi. Thus the current view that bishop and presbyter were originally synonymous terms is, according to Réville, erroneous ; it is only true in so far as the duties of instruction came to devolve on the bishops as well as the presbyters. (1) In the earliest documents we find a plurality of bishops (and this is still the case at Corinth, when the Epistle of Clement was written) ; (2) in the last years of the first century a single bishop is becoming the rule in the churches of Asia Minor (cp. Pastoral Epistles) ; (3) the third stage is the monarchical bishop, the ideal which Ignatius extolled in his Letters (which are certainly genuine) as the true remedy for the disorders and divisions of the Eastern Churches, but which (the monarchical, as distinguished from the "uninominal") was not yet (in the second decade of the second century), as his letters prove, a reality. For the organization of the Christian community in Palestine, consult the articles of Hilgenfeld in his Zeitschrift, vol. 33, 1890, p. 98 *sqq.*, and 223 *sqq.*

It may still be maintained that neither M. Réville nor any one else has satisfactorily explained how *bishop* and *presbyter* came to be used interchangeably at any time, as in Acts xx. 28, and the 1st chap. of Titus.

5. NUMBER OF CHRISTIANS IN THE EMPIRE UNDER DIOCLETIAN AND CONSTANTINE—(P. 61, 65)

Gibbon considers the number of Christians at Rome to have been not more than one-twentieth of the population about the middle of the third century, and he adopts the same proportion for the whole Empire. (This conclusion agrees with that of Friedländer, Sittengeschichte, iii. 531.) On the other hand, much higher proportions have been computed by more recent writers ; Stäudlin, one-half; Matter, one-fifth ; La Bastie, one-twelfth ; while Chastel gives one-fifteenth for the West, and one-tenth for the East. See Burckhardt, Die Zeit Constantin's des Grossen, edition 2, p. 137. H. Richter (whose judgment in such a matter deserves particular consideration) reckons the Christians at one-ninth of the total population 'Weströmisches Reich, 85, 86). But we have not sufficient data to fix such accurate ratios ; we may say that from Decius to Constantine the proportion probably varied from about one-twentieth to one-ninth. Burckhardt, putting aside the question of numbers, finds the main strength of the Christians in their belief in immortality (p. 140).

6. THE RESCRIPT OF ANTONINUS CONCERNING THE CHRISTIANS —(P. 94)

The authenticity of this edict has not yet been finally determined. It has come down to us in three forms : (1) in Eusebius, H. E. iv. 13, (2) in Rufinus, H. E. iv. 13, which is merely a free rendering of the Greek text in Eusebius, and does not rest on a Latin original, (3) in a fourteenth century Ms. of Justin. Harnack, who has thoroughly discussed the whole question (in his Texte u. Untersuch. xiii. 4), has shown satisfactorily that the version in Justin is not in-dependent, but is taken from Eusebius with certain " tendenziös " changes. The most striking difference between the Justin version and the Eusebian (Rufinus) is in the title ; in the former the edict is attributed to Titus, in the latter to Marcus. But the context in Eusebius shows that he regarded the edict as issuing from Titus ; and so it would seem, as Harnack suggests, that he found the incorrect title in his source and did not venture to omit or alter it, while he assumed it to be wrong. But in any case, the title is a clumsy forgery, for Marcus is described as Ἀρμένιος (he did not possess the true title Ἀρμενιακός so early as 161), and the name of Lucius Verus his colleague does not appear. In regard to the authenticity of the rescript as Eusebius gives it, Harnack points out that he had a Greek, not a Latin (as in other cases, iv. 9 ; vii. 13 ; viii. 17), copy before him, and that this cannot have been the original. The com-parison between the behaviour of Christians and pagans to the advantage of the former is clearly a Christian interpolation. Harnack attempts to restore the original Greek form of the rescript, in whose authenticity he believes (though he owns that certainty cannot be attained). The rescript was an answer to a petition of the κοινόν of Asia, and Harnack thinks that the copy used by Eusebius was preserved (and interpolated) in Christian circles.

The difference between the rescripts of Hadrian and Antoninus was that the former protected the Christians against calumnious accusation ; the latter against the accusation of atheism in general.

7. EXILE OF MARCELLUS AND EUSEBIUS, BISHOPS OF ROME— (P. 131)

Most interesting traces of the early Bishops of Rome have been found in the Catacombs. We owe them to the activity of Bishop Damasus in subterranean Rome. The subject can be studied in English, in the "Roma Sotterranea" of Messrs. Northcote and Brownlow (2 vols.), an excellent compilation from the researches of the Cavaliere di Rossi, the greatest authority of this century on Christian Rome.

Marcellus and Marcellinus *were* "different persons". Marcellinus is mentioned in the inscription of the Deacon Severus found in the Catacomb of St. Callixtus (*op. cit.* i. 350). Both Marcellus and Marcellinus were buried not in this cemetery but in that of St. Priscilla (*ib.* 304).

Eusebius, the successor of Marcellus, was like him severe to the "Lapsed," and like him banished. This is shown by the following inscription, found in the Catacomb of St. Callixtus,—the fellow of that relating to Marcellus quoted in Gibbon's note (p. 131).

> Heraclius vetuit lapsos peccata dolere ;
> Eusebius miseros docuit sua crimina flere.
> scinditur in partes populus gliscente furore ;
> seditio caedes bellum discordia lites ;
> extemplo pariter pulsi feritate tyranni,
> integra cum rector servaret foedera pacis,
> pertulit exilium domino sub iudice laetus,
> litore Trinacrio mundum vitamque reliquit.

The author of these epitaphs had a limited vocabulary. But they throw light on the divisions in the Roman Church at the time, and on the interference of Maxentius, in the interests of order,—which won for him in later times the name of a persecutor.

8. PERSECUTIONS OF THE CHRISTIANS IN THE FIRST AND SECOND CENTURIES, A.D.—(C. XVI.)

A considerable literature has sprung up in recent years regarding the attitude of the Roman government to Christianity from Nero to Marcus Aurelius (Th. Keim, Rom und das Christenthum, ed. Ziegler, 1881 ; K. J. Neumann, der römische Staat und die allgemeine Kirche, vol. i. 1890 ; Th. Mommsen, der Religionsfrevel nach römischem Recht, in Sybel's Hist. Zeitschrift, 1890 ; Professor Ramsay's The Church in the Roman Empire, 1893 ; may be mentioned). A thorough and instructive discussion of the whole question will be found in Mr. E. G. Hardy's Christianity and the Roman Government, 1894. A summary of some of his results will illustrate the sixteenth chapter of Gibbon.

From a review of the practical policy of the Roman state towards foreign cults Mr. Hardy concludes that they were tolerated in so far as they did not (1) injure the national religion, (2) encourage gross immoralties, (3) seem likely to lead to political disaffection (p. 35-6). Various considerations led to the toleration of Judaism, and Mr. Hardy points out that its toleration would by no means logically lead to that of Christianity, a religion "claiming to overstep all limits of nationality" (p. 37). The contact between the state and the Christians at Rome in 64 A.D., on the occasion of the conflagration, was accidental. The charge of incendiarism broke down at the trials, but it was converted into a charge of *odium generis humani* (a brief summary of the antisocialism and other characteristics of Christianity). It was for this that they were punished; and Suetonius does not bring their punishment into connexion with the fire, which was the occasion, not the ground, of their condemnation (Ner. 16: adflicti suppliciis Christiani genus hominum superstitionis nouæ ac maleficæ). Mr. Hardy seems to have quite made out his point that in the Neronian persecution the Christians were condemned as Christians, not on any special charge.

This charge *odium generis humani*, for the use of which the Neronian episode set a precedent, did not come under *maiestas* or the formula of any regular *quæstio*. According to Mommsen, whose view in this respect Mr. Hardy accepts, it was a matter for police regulation, to be dealt with by virtue of the *coercitio* vested in magistrates. In Rome, such cases would come under the jurisdiction of the prefect of the city (Tac. Ann. vi. 11); and the provincial governor was empowered to deal with them by his instructions to maintain the peace and tranquillity of his province, "which he will find no difficulty in effecting, if he be careful *ut malis hominibus provincia careat eosque conquirat*" (*e.g.*, *sacrilegi*, *latrones*, &c.). Mr. Ramsay holds that a new principle was introduced into the State policy towards Christians between 65 and 95 A.D., namely that whereas under Nero they were attacked by charges of special and definite crimes (incendiarism), under the Flavians Christianity itself became a punishable offence. But if Mr. Hardy is right as to the Neronian persecution, this change in attitude would disappear. "As soon as the Christians were once convicted of an *odium generis humani*, they were potentially outlaws and brigands and could be treated by the police administration as such, whether in Rome or the provinces" (p. 82). That the distinction between Judaism and Christianity had been clearly recognized in the East as early as 70 A.D., is proved by the speech of Titus in Sulpicius Severus, ii. 30 (taken from a lost book of Tacitus, as we may with some confidence assume); one of the advantages of the destruction of Jerusalem will be, that prince is reported to say, the extirpation of the Jewish and the Christian religion. We need not infer, as Mr. Hardy points out, that Titus had special designs against the Christians: "the persecution of the Christians was a standing one like that of brigands" (Mommsen).

"With Roman citizens," however, "of standing and importance a more definite charge was necessary, and this we find from Dio Cassius was primarily ἀθεότης, *i.e.*, not so much *sacrilegium* as a refusal to worship the national gods of the state" (p. 88). This was applied in the case of Flavius Clemens, cousin of Domitian, who was executed, and his wife Domitilla, who was banished, 95 A.D. The reign of Domitian introduced no new principle, but a very convenient test— *e.g.*, the observance of the imperial cult—for discovering whether a person suspected of the crime of Christianity (a crime, that is, in the eyes of the police administration, not of the law) was justly suspected.

Nor does the Bithynian persecution introduce (according to Mr. Hardy) any new principle. The letter of Trajan to Pliny is described (p. 117) as "the decision of a practical statesman who declined on the one hand to be led into severe repressive measures against a body which was only remotely and theoretically dangerous to the state, while he, on the other, refused to give up on humanitarian grounds the claim of the state to absolute obedience on the part of all its subjects". It is in no sense an edict of proscription or of toleration, but it is "an index of the imperial policy" (p. 122).[1] As to Hadrian's rescript to Minucius Fundanus (whose genuineness is by no means above suspicion), Mr. Hardy considers (143) that it "was intended, as indeed it naturally would be, for the special circumstances of Asia: it does not in any way, as I interpret it, rescind the decision of Trajan that the *nomen* was a crime, but to avoid any miscarriage of justice . . . it lays down more stringent conditions for the proof of punishable crime". Under M. Antoninus and his successor things remained theoretically the same. In the reign of the former there were some persecutions, —Ptolemæus and Lucius were executed at Rome (Justin Apol. ii. 2) and (ac-

---

[1] It is to be observed that the condemnation of Christians in Bithynia had nothing to do with the general laws or special regulations against collegia.

cording to M. Waddington's date) Polycarp at Smyrna. The remarkable point in the persecutions of Aurelius is that they take place in the western as well as the eastern provinces, and not so much their extent or the number of victims (p. 147). In general tenor these conclusions agree with the view of Mommsen and Ramsay that there were no *laws* against the Christians. I cannot see that this has been made out, for the second century at least, though it may be true of the Flavian period. It does not appear that the explicit statement of Sulpicius Severus in ii. 29, *post etiam datis legibus religio vetabatur* (referring to the whole period after Nero) is definitely disproved. Some of Mr. W. T. Arnold's criticisms (Eng. Hist. Review, 1895, p. 546 *sqq.*) are very much to the point.

Gibbon's general view of the slight extent of the early persecutions, resting as it does on the strong testimony of Origen (c. Cels. 3, 8), is commonly admitted. Compare Hardy, p. 131: "There seems good reason to suppose that this state of things—a general indulgence and toleration on the part of the emperors, occasionally interrupted by violent manifestations of popular feeling, which provincial governors had either not the will or not the strength to resist—continued throughout the second century: that the Christians were still punished for the name, but that the initiative in the way of searching them out was not taken by the governors, while accusers had to come forward in their own name; and finally, that the number of victims was on the whole a comparatively small one". It must at the same time be remembered that it was the policy of the Apologists (on whose evidence our knowledge is largely based) "to accentuate and in a measure to exaggerate the indulgent attitude of the government, especially in the period preceding their own, or at any rate to omit anything unfavourable to their own cause" (p. 132).

Two important documents give a notion of the proceedings adopted in the trials of Christians in the second century: (1) the Acts of Martyrs of Scili in Numidia, in 181 A.D. (ed. Usener, 1881, and Robinson in Texts and Studies, vol. i.), and (2) the Acts of Apollonius, tried at Rome in the first years of Commodus (Armenian version of a lost Greek original, discovered by Mr. Conybeare, who has given a translation in his Acts and Monuments of Early Christianity). The credit of these documents as trustworthy rests chiefly on the circumstance that miracles are conspicuously absent. Mr. Hardy gives an account of them in an Appendix. Cp. Mommsen, Der Process des Christen Apollonios, in the Sitzungsberichte of the Berlin Academy, xxvii. 1894.

B. Aubé has written several books dealing with the subject of the persecutions of the Christians : Les persecutions de l'église jusqu' á la fin des Antonins ; Les Chrétiens dans l'empire romain ; L'église et l'état dans le 2me moitié du 3me siècle.

On Nero's persecution also see C. F. Arnold, Die neronische Christenverfolgung, and an article by Hilgenfeld in his Zeitschrift, vol. xxxiii. p. 216 *sqq.*

On church and state from Decius to Diocletian : Görres, Jahrb. für protest. Theologie, xvi. 1890, p. 454 *sqq.*

On Diocletian's persecution : Mason's The Persecution of D., 1876 ; Hunziker, Zur Reg. u. Christenverfolgung des K. Diokletian und s. Nachfolger, in Büdinger's Untersuch. zur römischen Kaisergeschichte ; papers of F. Görres in Hilgenfeld's Zeitsch. f. wiss. Theol., xxxiii. p. 314 *sqq.* (cp. 469 *sqq.*). I. Belser, Zur Diokl. Christenverfolgung, 1891. Cp. also Schwarze, Unters. über die aüssere Er.twicklung der afrik. Kirche, 1892.

On church and state in fourth century : A. de Broglie, L'église et l'empire romain au quatrième siècle. Some other works have been mentioned in the footnotes.

An important memoir has been published as a supplement to the Acta Sincera of Ruinart by E. Le Blant : Les actes des martyrs, in Mém. of the National Institute of France (Acad. d. Belles lettres, t. xxx., 1883, p. 57-347). Le Blant is too anxious to rescue apocryphal lives, and overdoes his criticism of technical terms of Roman procedure. But he has done good work here (as well as in his essay, Sur les bases juridiques des poursuites dirigées contre les martyrs, in Comptes rendus of Académie des Inscriptions, N.S., ii. 1866), and any one studying martyrological Acta will do ill to neglect this memoir.

9. AUGUSTEUM AND FORUM OF CONSTANTINE—(P. 152, 153)[1]

The chief thoroughfare in the new city of Constantine led from the Golden Gate (in the wall of Constantine, not to be confused with the later Golden Gate in the wall of Theodosius II.) eastward (passing through the Forum Bovis, the Forum Amastrianorum, and the Forum Tauri) to the Golden Milestone in the Augusteum. Before it reached the Augusteum it passed through the Forum of Constantine in which stood the Pillar of Constantine (and the Churches of S. Constantine and S. Mary of the Forum). In the Augusteum (which we might translate Place Impériale) it came to an end, in front of the Senate house (Σενάτον) and west wall of the Palace. The Augusteum was bounded on the north by St. Sophia; on the east, by Senate house and palace buildings; on the south, by the Palace (the great entrance gate, known as the Chalkê, was here) and the north side of the Hippodrome, beside which were the Baths of Zeuxippus. There was no public way between the east side of the Hippodrome and the Palace. According to Labarte, the Augusteum was enclosed by a wall, with gates, on the west side, running from south-west of St. Sophia to the point between Palace and Hippodrome; so that the entrance to the Hippodrome and the Zeuxippus would have been outside the Augusteum. The street connecting the Augusteum with the Forum of Constantine was called Middle St.,—Μέση. The Chalkoprateia, and the Church of the Theotokos (Mother of God) in Chalkoprateia, were not in the Augusteum where Labarte places them, but west of St. Sophia, to the right of the Mese (as Mordtmann has shown, Esquisse Top. § 6, p. 4, and also Bieliaiev, cp. Byz. Zeitsch. ii. p. 138; but probably close to the Mese, cp. Krasnoseljcev, in the Annual Hist.-Phil. Publication of the Odessa University, iv. (Byz. section, 2) p. 309 sqq.). A plan of the Augusteum and adjoining buildings will appear in vol. 4, to illustrate the Nika riots under Justinian.

The chief guides to the topography of Constantinople used by Gibbon were Ducange's folio, Constantinopolis Christiana, and the little 32mo of Petrus Gyllius, de Constantinopoleos topographia, libri iv., 1632; both still of great value. The prolix work in 2 vols. of Skarlatos D. Byzantios (ἡ Κωνσταντινούπολις, Athens, 1851) is unscientific and must be used with great caution. The reconstruction of the Imperial Palace, involving a theory of the topography of the Augusteum and adjacent buildings, was undertaken by Jules Labarte (Le Palais impérial de Constantinople et ses abords, 1861), whose scholarly book marked a new departure and is of permanent value. The diligent Greek antiquarian A. G. Paspatês succeeded in establishing several valuable identifications in his Βυζαντιναὶ Μελέται (Constantinople, 1877), but his τὰ Βυζαντινὰ ἀνάκτορα (1885; in English: The Great Palace of Constantinople, translated by Mr. Metcalfe, 1893) is a retrogression compared with Labarte (see above, vol. i. Introd, p. lxii.). The problems of the Palace have been critically and thoroughly dealt with by D. Th. Bieliaiev in his Obzor glavnych chastei bolshago dvortsa Vizantiiskich tsarei (Part 1 of Byzantina), 1891, where it is shown that we must retain the main line of Labarte's reconstruction, but that in most of the details we must be content for the present to confess our ignorance.

In 1892 Dr. Mordtmann's Esquisse topographique de Constantinople appeared. It is not well arranged, but it is an important contribution to the subject; and his map has been an indispensable guide in the preparation of the plan in this volume. He clearly recognizes the true position of the Hebdomon on the Propontis; and I may observe that I had already pointed out (in 1889) that the received view which placed it near Blachernae must be wrong (Later Roman Empire, vol. ii. p. 556). The most recent work on Constantinople is: Constantinople, 2 vols., by E. A. Grosvenor, Professor of History at Robert College, Constantinople.

It is impossible to notice all the smaller contributions to the subject, but I must specially refer to some valuable articles of the late G. S. Destunis in the Zhurnal Min. Narodnago Prosviescheniia in 1882 1883.

---

[1] A new work on the topography of Constantinople, by A. van Millingen (Byzantine Constantinople, the walls of the city and adjoining historical sites, 1899) has reached me in time to be mentioned here. It supersedes all previous works on the walls and gates.

10. THE NEW MONARCHY—(C. XVII.)

All the main points in the new absolute monarchy, founded by Diocletian and organized by Constantine, have been brought out in the brilliant description of Gibbon (ch. xvii.): the new organization of the provinces; the hierarchical administration; the separation of civil from military functions; the abolition of the distinction between Italy and the Provinces; the loss of her unique position by Rome, which is closely connected with the clearly pronounced tendency of the Empire to part into an eastern and a western half. Anticipations of some of these results we have seen in the history of the third century. The formal oligarchy of Emperor and Senate, in which the Senate had been gradually becoming more and more a silent partner, formally ceases; the distinction between senatorial and imperial provinces vanishes, there are no senatorial provinces; and the *aerarium*, which had many years before lost its importance, is no longer a state treasury but merely a municipal chest. Externally the change from the Principate to undisguised monarchy is indicated by the assumption of oriental state by the emperor (here Aurelian had pointed the way). The thorough-going reformation of the military system, which was not fully understood till Mommsen's recent investigation, demands a note to itself; and the new division of provinces another. To distinguish between the work of Diocletian and that of Constantine is in many cases impossible, and Gibbon did not attempt it; it will be seen however in the two following appendices that some distinctions can be established. To Diocletian was due the separation of the civil and military authority (Lactant., de Mort. P., 7; Euseb., de Mart. Pal., 13). The dioceses and prefectures are an instructive, and I think we may say, typical instance of the relation between the work of the two great emperors. We know beyond question that the dioceses were instituted by Diocletian (Lact., *ib.*), but it has been disputed whether the prefectures were due to him or (so Zosimus) to Constantine. The latter view seems the more probable; but the quadruple division of the Empire between Diocletian, Maximian and the two Cæsars (implying four prefects; there is distinct evidence that the Cæsar Constantius had a prefect) was the suggestion and anticipation of the three (sometimes four; after 395 A.D. four) prefectures. Constantine abandoned the artificial, adoptive system of Diocletian for a dynastic principle, but he retained the geographical side of that system and stereotyped it in the prefectures.

A few words may be said here on (*a*) the new ceremonial, (*b*) the imperial titles, and (*c*) the consistorium.

(*a*) For the adoration see Godefroy on Cod. Theod., vol. ii. p. 83. Those who approached the Emperor bent the knee, and drew the edge of his purple robe to their lips. The Emperor wore a robe of silk, embroidered with gold, and adorned with gems (introduced by Aurelian); or the purple cloak of the military commander (first worn in *Rome* by Septimius Severus, and since then an imperial *insigne*). He also wore the diadem (perhaps first worn by Aurelian, see Victor, Epit. 35, 5; but the novelty is also ascribed to Diocletian, and to Constantine). Constantine introduced the gold band round the head, which was called *nimbus* (cp. Eckhel, Doct. Num., 8, 79). The emperor is officially called *deus*, and the cult of the imperial majesty, which at an early time had made its way in the camp, is further developed; and, when a new Emperor is proclaimed, his bust crowned with laurel is carried round in procession in the provinces. See Schiller, ii. p. 33, 34.

(*b*) The style of imperial titles which was usual in the latter part of the Principate was maintained until the time of Gratian. It was Imperator Cæsar pius (felix or) invictus Augustus pontifex Maximus—icus [Sarmaticus, &c.] maximus trib. pot. [ii. &c.] consul [ii. &c.] imperator [ii. &c.] pater patriae proconsul. [The order of imperator and consul is variable. The only change made was the substitution of maximus victor ac triumphator for invictus. Gratian dropped the title pontifex maximus, and the other titles were at the same time abandoned in favour of a shorter formula,

Dominus noster $\left\{\begin{array}{l} \text{pius felix semper Augustus} \\ \text{invictissimus princeps, \&c.} \end{array}\right.$

The chief reminiscence of the republican constitution of the principate, so carefully contrived by Augustus, was the practice of numbering the years of a reign by the formula *trib. pot.*, which appears as late as Theodosius ii. (on coins, Eckhel, 8, 182). Dominus, which (like deus) Aurelian had only used in the dative case, is from Constantine forward the ordinary official title of the Emperor (equivalent of "His Majesty"). Schiller, ii. 31-33.

(c) The consilium, which had been organized by Hadrian, is superseded in the new monarchy by a council called *consistorium* (the name first occurs in an inscription of 353 A.D., C. I. L. 6, 1739), which assembled at fixed times in the Emperor's presence. The chief of the Hadrianic consilium was the prætorian prefect; but, as that officer has been diverted to new administrative functions and as the provincial administration and palace offices are kept carefully apart, his position in the council is inherited by the quæstor sacri pal. who presides over the consistorium. It is however unlikely that the quæstor had this position at first under Diocletian and Constantine; for he does not belong to the class of illustres till after Valentinian I. It has been conjectured (by Mommsen) that the president of the council was at first entitled *præpositus* and afterwards developed into the quæstor, and that he had a deputy, the *vicarius a sacris consiliis*, who developed into the *magister officiorum* (Schiller, ii. 66). The members of the council (entitled at first *a consiliis sacris*, afterwards *comites consistoriani*) were divided into two classes with a difference of stipend: *ducenarii* (200,000 sesterces), *sexagenarii* (60,000 sesterces), and mainly consisted of jurists. The functions of the council were properly confined to judicature, but they also assisted the Emperor in legislation. The two finance ministers belonged to the council, and in later times prætorian prefects and masters of soldiers were sometimes invited by the Emperor, but did not belong to the consistory ex officio. See on the subject E. Cuq, Le conseil des empereurs d'Auguste à Dioclétian.

11. DIOCESES AND PROVINCES—(P. 169 *sqq.*)

Diocletian made considerable modifications in the provincial divisions of the Empire, and distributed all the provinces under twelve large Dioceses. Three changes in his diocesan arrangement were made in the course of the fourth century, and by 400 A.D. we find thirteen Dioceses. (a) Egypt, which was at first part of the Diocese of the East, was promoted to be a separate Diocese towards the end of the fourth century. (b) Diœcesis Moesiarum was broken up into Diœcesis Daciae and Diœcesis Macedoniae. (c) On the other hand, Diœcesis Galliarum and Diœcesis Viennensis were combined to form a single Diocese of Gaul. In the case of this change we find an interesting example of the survival of nomenclatures which had ceased to be appropriate. The south of Gaul was at first divided into five provinces (Novempopuli, Aquitanica, Narbonensis, Viennensis, Alpes Maritimiae). But when these became seven by the subdivision of Aquitanica and Narbonensis the Diocese (Viennensis) still continued to be known as Quinque Provinciae as well as by the amended title Septem Provinciae. But this was not all. When Northern Gaul, the original Diœcesis Galliarum, was added to the sphere of the governor of the Diœcesis Viennensis, the whole united Diocese was known not only as the Diocese of the Gauls but as the Septem Provinciae; while the old name Quinque Provinciae was appropriated to the seven southern provinces, which, though they were no longer a separate Diocese, preserved a fragment of their former integrity by having financial officers (*rationales*) to themselves.

(1) A record of the new organization as it existed in 297 A.D. has been preserved in the List of Verona (Laterculus Veronensis), published with a valuable commentary by Mommsen in the Abhandl. of the Berlin Acad., 1862, p. 489 *sqq.*, and reprinted by Seeck in his edition of the Notitia Dignitatum.[1] (2) Our next list is

[1] First published by S. Maffei in 1742.

(incomplete) in the Breviarium of Festus (above, vol. i. App. 1), dating from 369 A.D. just before the foundation of the new Britannic province Valentia. (3) This defective list is supplemented by another, dating from much the same time, of the *eastern* provinces of the Empire (dioceses of Illyricum, Thrace, Pontus, Asia, East, Egypt), which is preserved in the Laterculus of Polemius Silvius, drawn up in 449 A.D. The list of Polemius with a complete critical apparatus is edited by Mommsen in Chron. Minora, i. p. 511-551 (also printed in Seeck's Notit. Dign.). Mommsen has shown that Polemius is up to date in regard to the western provinces, but that for the eastern he practically reproduces a list dating from about the middle of the fourth century, with one or two blunders, and only adding the new provinces of Arcadia and Honorias, which bearing the names of the sons of Theodosius were more likely than other new pro-vinces to be known of in the west. (4) A list of the Gallic provinces in Ammianus (writing between 383 and 390 A.D.), xv. 11, 7 *sqq.*, who clearly used an official *laterculus.* Mommsen, Chron. Min. i. p. 552 *sqq.* Ammianus also enumerates the provinces of Egypt, xxii. 16, 1. (5) Notitia Galliarum, between 390 and 413 A.D., edited by Mommsen, *ib.*, 552-612; printed in Seeck, *op. cit.* ; the provinces are the same as in the Not. Dign. (6) Notitia Dignitatum : first years of the fifth century. Panciroli's commentary, used by Gibbon, has been completely superseded by that of Böcking (2 vols., 1839-53), which is abso-lutely indispensable to the student ; but Böcking's text has been superseded by that of O. Seeck, 1876. For a good account of work and history of the Codex, with its curious pictures, see Hodgkin, Italy and her Invaders, i. 594 *sqq.* For date cp. above, p. 158, n. 73. From the fact that the twentieth legion does not appear in the Not., it has been argued that the date is A.D. 402—at the moment when this legion was recalled from Britain and had not yet been enrolled among the Italian forces (Hodgkin, *ib.* p. 717). (7) The Laterculus of Polemius Silvius ; for the *western* provinces, A.D. 449, see above. I have arranged the data of these successive documents in parallel columns.

(Literature : L. Czwalina, Ueber das Verzeichniss der röm. Prov. v. Jahr. 297, 1881 ; L. Jullian, De la réforme provinciale attribuée à Diocl., Revue Hist., 19, 331 *sqq.* ; Schiller, Röm. Gesch. ii. 45-50 ; W. Ohnesorge, Die römische Pro-vinzliste von 297, Teil. i., 1889. Cp. also Marquardt, Staatsverwaltung, vol. i.)

	List of Verona.	List in "Polemius."	Ammianus.	Notitia Dignitatum.
Diocese of the East (L. Ver.) = Diocese of Egypt (L. Polem.).	Libya superior	Libya Pentapolis	Pentapolis	Libya superior
	Libya inferior	Libya Sicca	Libya	Libya inferior
	Thebais	Thebais	Thebais	Thebais
	Ægyptus Jovia [1]	Ægyptus	Ægyptus	Ægyptus
	Ægyptus Herculea [1]	Augustamnis [2] [3]	Augustamnica	Augustamnica
				Arcadia [4]

	List of Verona.	List in "Polemius."	Notitia Dignitatum.
Diocese of the East continued (L. Ver.) = Diocese of the East (L. Pol., Not.).	Arabia	Syria Palestina	Palestina Salutaris [6]
	Arabia Augusta Libanensis	Syria Phœnice	Arabia
	Palestina	Syria Cœle	Palestina
	Phœnice	Euphratesia	Phœnice
	Syria Cœle	Cilicia	Syria
	Augusta Euphratensis	Isauria	Euphratensis
	Cilicia	Cyprus	Cilicia
	Isauria	Mesopotamia	Isauria
	Cyprus	Osroene	Cyprus
	Mesopotamia	Sophanene [5]	Mesopotamia
	Osroena		Osroena
			—
			Palestina secunda
			Phœnice Libani
			Syria Salutaris
			Cilicia secunda

[1] These names were clearly given in honour of Diocletian and Maximian.

[2] This name first occurs in an edict of 342 A.D. C. Theod. xii. 1, 34.

[3] Arcadia is added by Polemius; it cannot have stood in the old laterculus which he used, which was prior to 384 A.D.

[4] Arcadia (and Honorias) formed after 384; Mommsen thinks perhaps as late as 393, when Arcadius became Augustus.

[5] Not a regular province; governed by a satrap.

[6] See Nöldeke, Hermes, x. 163 sqq., Ohnesorge (Die röm. Provinzliste, v. 297, p. 33 sqq.) has shown that the northern province (chief city, Bostra) was Arabia (the addition "Aug. Lib." was dropped early in the fourth century), and the southern (Diocletian's Arabia) was renamed Palestina Salutaris before 325 A.D. (p. 43).

	List of Verona.	List in "Polemius".	Notitia.
Diocese of Pontus.	Bithynia	Bithynia	Bithynia
	Cappadocia	Cappadocia	Cappadocia prima
	Galatia	Galatia [9]	Galatia
	Paphlagonia [7]	Paphlagonia	Paphlagonia
	Diospontus	Pontus Amasia	Helenopontus
	Pontus Polemoniacus	Pontus Polemoniacus	Pontus Polemoniacus
	Armenia Minor [8]	Armenia Minor	Armenia prima
	———	Armenia Maior.	———
	———	Honorias	Honorias
	———	———	Cappadocia secunda [10]
		———	Galatia Salutaris [10]
		———	Armenia secunda [10]
Diocese of Asia	Pamphylia [11]	Pamphylia	Pamphylia
	Phrygia prima	Phrygia prima	Phrygia Pacatiana
	Phrygia secunda	Phrygia Salutaris	Phrygia Salutaris
	Asia	Asia	Asia
	Lydia	Lydia	Lydia
	Caria	Caria	Caria
	Insulae	Cyclades	Insulae
	Pisidia	Pisidia	Pisidia
	Hellespontus	Hellespontus	Hellespontus
	———	Lycia	Lycia
		Lycaonia [12]	Lycaonia

[7] There is a later false adscript *nunc in duas divisa*.

[8] Another note (from the hand of the same interpolator) *et nunc maior addita* records the conquest of Diocletian.

[9] Polemius places it in the Diocese of Asia, probably by an oversight.

[10] Cappadocia II. is mentioned in an edict of 386, Cod. Theod. xiii. 11, 2 (wrong reference in Mommsen, Chron. Min. i. p. 533). Armenia I. was the northern, Armenia II. the southern, half of Little Armenia. Galatia Salutaris also existed already in 386, Cod. Theod., *ib.*

[11] *I.e.*, Lycia et Pamphylia. We find Lycia and Pamphylia as one province in 313 A.D., C. Th. xiii. 10, 2, but separate in the subscriptions (not always reliable) in the Acts of the Council of Nice, 325 A.D.

[12] Lycaonia became a separate province in 373. See Tillemont, v. 99.

	List of Verona.	Festus.	List in "Polemius".	Notitia.
Diocese of Thrace.	Europa Rhodope Thracia Haemimus mons Scythia Moesia inferior	Europa Rhodope Thracia Haemimontus Scythia Moesia inferior	Europa Rhodope Thracia [prima] Haemimontus[13] Scythia[13] Moesia inferior	Europa Rhodope Thracia Haemimontus Scythia Moesia secunda
Diocese of the Moesias (L. Ver.) = Diocese of Dacia (Not.).	Dacia Moesia superior Margensis Dardania Praevalitana —	Dacia Moesia Dacia[14] Praevalis —	Dacia Moesia superior Dardania Praevalis —	Dacia ripensis Moesia prima Dardania Praevalitana Dacia mediterranea[14]
Diocese of the Moesias continued (L. Ver.) = Diocese of Macedonia (Not.).	Macedonia Thessalia [Achaia][15] Epirus nova Epirus vetus Creta	Macedonia Thessalia Achaia Epirus Epirus Creta	Macedonia Thessalia Achaia Epirus nova Epirus vetus Creta	Macedonia Thessalia Achaia Epirus nova Epirus vetus Creta Macedonia Salutaris
Diocese of the Pannonias (L. Ver.) = Diocese of Illyricum (Not.).	Pannonia inferior Savensis Dalmatia Valeria Pannonia superior Noricus ripariensis Noricus mediterranea	Pannonia Savia Dalmatia Valeria Pannonia Noricum Noricum	Pannonia secunda Savia Dalmatia Valeria Pannonia prima Noricus ripensis Noricus mediterranea	Pannonia secunda Savia Dalmatia — Pannonia prima Noricum ripense Noricum mediterraneum

13 Polemius has put the right names Haemimontus and Scythia under the wrong diocese, Illyricum; in this place he substitutes Thracia Secunda and Scythia inferior. The list used by Polemius seems to have included the dioceses of Dacia, Macedonia and Illyricum under the head Illyricum.

14 Dacia medit. and Dardania were at this time names of the same province. Between the composition of the List of Polemius and 386 A.D. (see C. Theod. i, 32, 5) the province was divided into Dardania and Dacia med.

15 A mysterious priantina usurps the place of Achaia. Mommsen conjectured that it is a dittogram of privalitana which follows, and that Achaia has dropped out.

	List of Verona.	Festus.	Ammianus.	Notitia.	Polemius Silvius.
Diocese of the Britains	Prima Secunda Maxima Caesariensis [16] Flavia Caesariensis [16]	Britannia prima Britannia secunda Maxima Caesariensis Flavia		Britannia prima Britannia secunda Maxima Caesariensis Flavia Caesariensis Valentia [17]	Britannia prima Britannia secunda Maxima Flavia Valentiniana
Diocese of the Gauls (L. Ver. = Diocese of the Gauls (Not., Pol.).)	Belgica prima Belgica secunda Germania prima Germania secunda Sequania Lugdunensis prima Lugdunensis secunda Alpes Graiae et Poeninae — —	Belgica Belgica Germania Germania Maxima Sequanorum Lugdunensis Lugdunensis Alpes Graiae —	Belgica prima Belgica secunda Germania prima Germania secunda Sequani Lugdunensis prima Lugdunensis secunda Alpes Graiae et Poeninae — —	Belgica prima Belgica secunda Germania prima Germania secunda Maxima Sequanorum Lugdunensis prima Lugdunensis secunda Alpes Peninae et Graie Lugdunensis tertia [18] Lugdunensis Senonia [18]	Belgica prima Belgica secunda Germania prima Germania secunda Maxima Sequanorum Lugdunensis prima Lugdunensis secunda Alpes Graie Lugdunensis tertia Senonia
Diocese of Vienna (L. Ver.) = Aquitania (Fest., Amm.) = Provincie septem (Notit. Gall.) = Diocese of the Gauls (Not., Pol.).	Viennensis Narbonensis prima Narbonensis secunda Novem populi Aquitanica prima Aquitanica secunda Alpes maritime	Provincia Viennensis Narbonensis — [19] Novempopulana Aquitania Aquitania Alpes maritime	Viennensis Narbonensis — [19] Novem populi Aquitanica [19] —	Viennensis Narbonensis prima Narbonensis secunda Novem populi Aquitania prima Aquitania secunda Alpes maritime	Viennensis Narbonensis prima Narbonensis secunda Novempopulana Aquitania prima Aquitania secunda Alpes maritime

16 These names seem to be connected with the Caesar Flavius Constantius (Chlorus) who won back Britain in 296 A.D.

17 Formed 369 A.D. In Polemius Silvius an interpolator added Orcades, suggested, as Mommsen observes, by Eutropius, 7, 13.

18 Appear in the notit. Galliarum.

19 The mention of a single Narbonensis by both Festus and Ammianus, and of a single Aquitanica by Ammianus, must be regarded as merely errors.

Diocese of Italy.	List of Verona.	Notitia Dignitatum.	Polemius Silvius.
	Venetia Histria	Venetia	Venetia cum Histria
	Flaminia	Flaminia et Picenum annonarium	Flaminia
	Picenum	Picenum suburbicarium	Picenum
	Tuscia Umbria	Tuscia Umbria	Tuscia Umbria
	Apulia Calabria	Apulia Calabria	Apulia Calabria
	Lucania	Lucania Brittii	Brittia Lucania
	Corsica	Corsica	Corsica
	Alpes Cottiæ	Alpes Cottiæ	Alpes Cottiæ [22]
	Raetia ——— [20]	Raetia prima	Raetia prima
	———	Raetia secunda	Raetia secunda
	———	Campania	Campania
	———	Aemilia	Aemilia [23]
	———	Liguria	Liguria
	———	Samnium	Samnium
		Sicilia	Sicilia
		Sardinia	Sardinia
		Valeria [21]	———

[20] There is an accidental omission in the Ms., for the Italian provinces are introduced by the words *Dioecensis Italiciana habet provincias numero* xvi.; but we cannot tell how many provinces are omitted. For in the case of the other dioceses the copyist has sometimes counted rightly, sometimes wrongly. If his enumeration is correct here, seven provinces are lost; if he has counted each name as a province, only three. Probably his reckoning was based partly on the right, and partly on the wrong principle. As Valeria must have been formed by Diocletian, we can supply with certainty: Campania, Samnium (or Campania et Samnium), Sicilia, Sardinia, Valeria, and Aemilia et Liguria (which formed a single province in 385 A.D., C Th. ii. 4, 4). If we could assume that Raetia was already subdivided, the number xvi. would be correct.

[21] The Italian Valeria had a habit of vanishing and reappearing, being sometimes separate from, sometimes united with, Picenum. Thus: (1) instituted by Diocletian; (2) it disappears in 364 A.D., C. Theod. ix. 30, 1; (3) reappears in 399, C. Th. ix. 30, 5; (4) disappears in 400 C. I. L., 6, 1706; (5) reappears in the Notitia; (6) disappears in 413, C. Theod. xii. 28, 7, and is not mentioned in Polemius (interpolated in some Mss.), see Mommsen, Chron. Min. i. p. 532. Ohnesorge, holding that Flaminia and Picenum formed one province in 297 and were not divided till 364, places the separation of Valeria from Picenum suburb. after that date, op. cit., p. 8 and to.

[22] An interpolator of sixth or seventh century added Alpes Appennine. I wonder at the appearance of this province in Sieglin's atlas, in the map of the Empire under Diocletian. Liguria came down to the sea coast.

[23] The same interpolator added Nursia and Valeria.

	List of Verona.	Festus.	Notitia Dignitatum.	Polemius Silvius.
Diocese of the Spains.	Baetica	Baetica	Baetica	Baetica
	Lusitania	Lusitania	Lusitania	Lusitania
	Karthaginiensis	Karthaginiensis	Carthaginiensis	Carthaginiensis
	Gallaecia	Gallaecia	Gallaecia	Gallaecia
	Tarraconensis	Tarraconensis	Tarraconensis	Tarraconensis
	Mauritania Tingitana	Mauritania Tingitana	Tingitana	Tingitana
			Baleares	insulae Baleares
Diocese of Africa.	proconsularis Zeugitana	proconsularis	Africa	proconsularis
	Byzacena	Byzacium	Byzacium	Byzacium
	Numidia Cirtensis	Numidia	Numidia	Numidia
	Numidia miliciana [24]			
		Tripolis	Tripolitana	Tripolis
	Mauritania Caesariensis	Mauritania Caesariensis	Mauritania Caesariensis	Mauritania Caesariensis
	Mauritania [Sitifensis] [25]	Mauritania Sitifensis	Mauritania Sitifensis	Mauritania Sitifensis

[24] It is a question whether Numidia Miliciana is a name, or corruption, for Tripolitana, or is a distinct province which afterwards became obsolete (Tripolitana being accidentally omitted). The latter view is adopted in Sieglin's new Historical Atlas, and in the map of the Empire in this volume.

[25] In Ms. Mauritania Tabia insidiana.

12. THE ORGANIZATION OF THE ARMY UNDER THE NEW SYSTEM—(P. 176 *sqq.*)

Mommsen has brought light and order into the subject of the new military organization which was introduced in the epoch of Diocletian and Constantine, by his article entitled Das römische Militärwesen seit Diocletian, which appeared in Hermes in 1889 (vol. xxiv. p. 195 *sqq.*). The following brief account is based on this important study.

Under Diocletian the regular army seems to have fallen into two main divisions : the troops who followed the emperor as he moved throughout his dominion, and the troops stationed on the frontier. The latter were called *limitanei*, the former were possibly distinguished as *in sacro comitatu* (cp. C. I. L. 3, 6194). But early in Constantine's reign the troops *in sacro comitatu* were broken up into two classes, the *comitatenses* and the *Palatini* (before 310, for the *comitatenses* existed then, cp. C. I. L. 5565 ; *palatini* occurs first in a law of 365 A.D., Cod. Theod. vii. 4, 22). Thus there were three great divisions of the army : 1, (*a*) palatini, (*b*) comitatenses, and 2, limitanei. Thus Gibbon's use of *palatines* to include the *comitatenses* is erroneous.

The other most important changes introduced by Constantine were : the increase of the comitatenses (who were under the command of the magister militum) at the expense of the limitanei, who had been increased by Diocletian ; and the separation of the cavalry from the infantry.

1. *Limitanei* (commanded by *duces*). The statement that Diocletian strengthened the frontier troops (Zos. ii. 34) is borne out by the fact that if we compare the list of the legions in the time of Marcus (C. I. L. 6, 3492) with the Notitia Dignitatum, we find in the former twenty-three legions, in the latter the same twenty-three and seventeen new legions (leaving out of account Britain, Germany, Africa, for which we have not materials for comparison). And if we remember that Constantine drafted away regiments (the pseudo-comitatenses) to increase his comitatenses, we may conclude that Diocletian doubled the numbers of the frontier armies.

The limitanei consisted of both infantry and cavalry. (1) The infantry consisted of *legiones*, *auxilia* and *cohortes*. (*a*) The legions are of two kinds. The old legions of the Principate retain their old strength of 6000 men ; while the new legions correspond to the old legionary detachments, and are probably 1000 strong. But the larger legions are usually broken into detachments which are distributed in different places, and the præfectus legionis consequently disappears. (*b*) The *auxilia* are of barbarian formation, and as such are thought more highly of than the rest of the frontier infantry ; they are found only in the Illyric provinces. The size of the *auxilium* is probably 500. (*c*) The *cohortes*, 500 strong as under the Principate, are found everywhere except in the duchies on the Lower Danube. (2) The (*a*) *cunei equitum* probably differ from (*b*) *equites*, by being of barbarian formation and of higher rank. The (*c*) *ala* is generally 600 (not as before 500) strong.

Constantine's new organization reduced the limitanei to second class troops, as compared with the Imperial troops of both kinds.

2. Imperial Troops. (*a*) Comitatenses (under Masters of Soldiers) consist of infantry and cavalry : (*a*) The legion is of the smaller size, about 1000 strong ; (β) the *vexillatio* of horse is about 500 strong. Connected with the comitatenses but of lower rank are the *pseudo-comitatenses*, drawn from the frontiers (eighteen legions in the west, twenty in the east). (*b*) Palatini (under Masters of Soldiers *in præsenti*) consist of infantry and cavalry : (*a*) the legion of 1000 ; (β) the *vexillatio* of 500.

In connexion with the Palatini, the *auxilia palatina* demand notice. These are troops of light infantry, higher in rank than the legion of the *comitatenses*, lower than the *palatine* legion. They chiefly consist of Gauls and include Germans from beyond the Rhine (but virtually no orientals). Mommsen makes it probable that their formation was mainly the work of Maximian (p. 233). They were perhaps the most important troops in the army.

The *scholae*, which seem to have been instituted by Constantine, must also be mentioned here (cp. Cod. Theod. 14, 17, 9). They were probably so called from having a hall in the palace to await orders. At first they were composed of Germans (but in fifth century under Leo I., of Armenians; under Zeno, of Isaurians; afterwards of the best men who could be got, Procop., Hist. Arc. c. 24). There were at first five divisions of 500 men; then seven; finally under Justinian eleven. The division was commanded by a tribune, who was a person of much importance (*e.g.*, Valentinian I.). They ultimately lost their military character, and the excubitores (first introduced by Leo I.) took their place.

Gibbon considers the question of the size of the army under the New Monarchy. On one side, we have the fact that under Severus at the beginning of the third century there were thirty-three legions, which, reckoned, along with their adjuncts, at the usual strength, give as the total strength of the army about 300,000. On the other side we have the statement of Agathias quoted by Gibbon, which puts the nominal strength of the army in the middle of the 6th century at 645,000. Taking into account the great increase of the troops under Diocletian, the record that the army was further strengthened by Valentinian (cp. Amm. Marc., 30, 7, 6, Zos. 4, 12), and a statement of Themistius (Or. 18, p. 270) as to the strength of the frontier forces under Theodosius the Great, we might guess that at the beginning of the fifth century, when the Notitia was drawn up, the army numbered five, if not six, hundred thousand. These *a priori* considerations correspond satisfactorily with the rough calculation which Mommsen has ventured to make from the data of the Notitia. His figures deserve to be noted, though he cautions us that we must not build on them.

Limitanei	.	. Foot, 249,500; Horse, 110,500	.	. Total 360,000
Comitatenses	}	Foot, 148,000; Horse, 46,500	.	. Total 194,500
Palatini (with aux.)				
				Total 554,500

A word must be said about the *gentes*, who, outside the Roman provinces and formally independent, but within the Roman sphere of influence and virtually dependent on the Empire, helped to protect the frontiers and sometimes supplied auxiliary troops to the Roman army. (Thus in Amm. xxiii. 2, 1 we read of *legationes gentium plurimarum auxilia pollicentium;* Julian refuses such *adventicia adiumenta.*) The most important of these *gentes* are the Saracens on the borders of Syria, and the Goths on the right bank of the Danube. They are *fœderati;* and their relation to the Empire depends on a *fœdus* which determines the services they are bound to perform. Under the Principate the theory was that such *fœderati* were tributaries, but in return for their military services the tribute was either remitted or diminished. But under the new system, they are considered rather in the light of a frontier force and, like the regular riparienses, are paid for their work. Consequently the amount of the *annonæ fœderaticæ* is the chief question to be arranged in a *fœdus*. The Lazi of Colchis were an exception to this rule ; though federates they received no annonæ (Procop., B. P. 2, 15). The inclusion of the federates in the Empire is illustrated by the treaty with Persia in 532 A.D., in which the Saracens are included as a matter of course, without special mention (Procop., B. P. 1, 17 ; 2, 1). See Mommsen, *op. cit.* p. 215 *sqq.*

13. PROTECTORES AND DOMESTICI—(P. 187)

The origin and organization of the imperial guards, named Protectores and Domestici, who so often meet us is our historical authorities from the time of Constantine forward, have been elucidated, so far as the scanty material allows, by Mommsen in a paper entitled Protectores Augusti, in the Ephemeris Epigraphica, v. p. 121 *sqq.*

In the second half of the third century there existed protectores of two kinds : protectores Augusti, and protectores of the prætorian prefect. The

latter (whose existence is proved by epigraphic evidence, cp. C. I. L. vi. 3238)
naturally ceased when, under Constantine's new *régime*, the prætorian prefect
ceased to have military functions.

The earliest instance of a protector Augusti whose date we can control is
that of Taurus, who was consul in 261 A.D., and held the office of prætorian
prefect. An inscription (whose date must fall between 261 and 267 A.D.,
Orelli, 3100) mentions that he had been a protector Augusti. Mommsen calculates that he must have held that post before 253 A.D., and infers that protectors
were instituted about the middle of the century, by Decius or possibly Philip.
The full title of the protector was *protector divini lateris Augusti nostri*,
preserved in one inscription found at Ocriculæ (Orelli, 1869); for this form cp.
Cod. Theod. vi. 24, 9. The abbreviation *protector Augusti* is the regular formula
up to Diocletian ; after Diocletian it is simply *protector*.

The protectors were soldiers who had shown special competence in their
service, and were rewarded by a post in which they received higher pay (they
were called *ducenarii* from the amount of their salary) and had the expectation of being advanced to higher military commands. Gallienus hindered
Senators from serving as officers in the army, and from that time the service of
the protectors became a sort of military training school (Mommsen, l. c. p. 137)
to supply commanders (*ad regendos milites*, Ammianus). From Aurelian's
time (*ib.* 131) the protectors seem to have been organized as a bodyguard of
the Emperor, with a captain of their own. (The earliest mention of the service
in legislation is in a law of 325 A.D., Cod. Th. vii. 20, 4.)

Constantine completely abolished the prætorian and the military functions
of the praef. pract. With this change we must connect his reorganization of
the protectores (*ib.* 135). The nature of this reorganization was determined
by his abrogation of the measure of Gallienus which excluded senators from
military command. A body of guards was instituted, called Domestici or
Houseguards, which was designed to admit nobles and sons of senators to a
career in the army. Thus there were now two corps of palace guards, that of
the Protectors who were enrolled for distinguished service, and were consequently veterans, and that of the Domestics who were admitted *nobilitate et
gratia*, through birth and interest. But the two were closely connected and
jointly commanded by captains called Counts of the Domestics ; and the two
names came to be interchangeable and used indifferently of one or the other.

It cannot indeed be strictly demonstrated that Constantine organized the
Domestics, who are first mentioned in a law of 346 A.D. (Cod. Th. xii. 1, 38) ;
but this hypothesis is far more likely than any other. At the same time the
pay of the guards was probably increased—a necessary result of the new
monetary system of Constantine.[1] The epithet ducenarii was given up, and
became attached to the schola of *agentes in rebus*. The rank of a guardsman
was *perfectissimus*, but the first ten in standing (decem primi) were *clarissimi*.

By a law of Valentinian (Cod. Th. vi. 24, 2) veterans were enrolled in the
guards gratis, while all others had to pay. The ultimate result was that
veterans ceased to be enrolled altogether, and the post of domesticus or protector
was regularly purchased. The traffic in these offices in Justinian's time is
noticed by Procopius, Hist. Arc. c. 24.

14. THE TRAGEDY OF FAUSTA AND CRISPUS—(P. 208 *sqq.*)

The attempt of Gibbon to show that Fausta was not put to death by Constantine was unsuccessful ; for the text on which he chiefly relied has nothing to do
with Constantine the Great, but refers to an Emperor of the fifteenth century (see
above, App. 1, p. 534) ; and from the subsidiary passage in Julian (p. 211, n. 25) no
inference can be drawn. On the other hand, as Seeck has pointed out, the sign

---

[1] We may guess that under Diocletian they were still ducenarii, and so profited by his
raising the weight of the aureus from 1-70th to 1-60th. Constantine would not have reduced
their pay ; so that they would no longer be ducenarii.

of the Constantinople mint appears on coins of Constantine I. and II., Constantius, Constans, Helena, Theodore, Delmatius and Hannibalianus, in short all the members of the Imperial family who survived the foundation of the Capital (11th May, 330); but in the Fausta series as in the Crispus series the sign never appears, and in the Trier mint the latest coins of both belong to the same emission. Eusebius, the writer of the Anonymous Valesian fragment, and Aurelius Victor are silent as to the death of Fausta; but this proves nothing, on the principle, as Seeck observes, "im Hause des Gehenkten redet man nicht vom Stricke".

The evidence as to the circumstances of the tragedy is investigated in a suggestive manner by Seeck, "Die Verwandtenmorde Constantins des Grossen," in Ztsch. f. wiss. Theol. 33, 1890, p. 63 *sqq*. He distinguishes four independent testimonies. (1) Eutropius (on whom Jerome and Orosius depend) states simply that Constantine put to death his son and wife. (2) Sidonius Apollinaris mentions (Ep. v. 8) that Crispus was poisoned, Fausta suffocated by a hot bath. These kinds of death were suitable to avoid the appearance of violence. (3) Philostorgius (ii. 4) assigns causes. He says that Crispus, calumniated by Fausta, was put to death, and that she was afterwards found guilty of adultery with a cursor and killed in a hot bath. (4) A common source, on which the Epitome of Victor, the account of Zosimus, and that of John the Monk in the Vita S. Artemii (Acta Sanct. 8th October) depend, stated that Fausta charged Crispus with having offered her violence; Crispus was therefore executed; then Helena persuaded Constantine that Fausta was the guilty one, and induced him to kill her by an overheated bath. Then Constantine repents; the heathen priests declared that his deeds could not be expiated; Christianity offered forgiveness and he became a Christian. Seeck points out that this unknown source agrees with Philostorgius in three points: the manner of Fausta's death; her guilt in causing the death of Crispus; her connexion with a story of adultery. In the details (which Gibbon, p. 210-11, combines) they differ.

Seeck argues for the view that the drama of Fausta and Crispus was a renewal of that of Phædra and Hippolytus. It is certainly by no means impossible that this is the solution; the evidence for it is not absolutely convincing (especially as the Vita Artemii is of extremely doubtful value; cp. Görres, Z. f. wiss. Theol., 30, 1887, 243 *sqq*.). Seeck conjectures that Constantine's law of 22nd April (C. Th. ix. 7, 2) which confines the liberty to bring accusations of adultery to the husband's and the wife's nearest relatives, and in their case converts the liberty into a duty, &c., was partly occasioned by the Emperor's own experience.

But I cannot regard as successful Seeck's attempt to show that the younger Licinius (1) was not the son of Constantia, but the bastard of a slave-woman whom Constantia was compelled to adopt, and (2) was not killed in 326, but was alive in 336; by means of the rescripts Cod. Theod. iv. 6, 2 and 3. Cp. the criticisms of Görres in the same vol. of Z. f. wiss. Theol. p. 324-7.

15. DIVISIONS OF THE EMPIRE, A.D. 293 to 378—(P. 214, 224)

The chief interest of the divisions of the Empire in A.D. 335 and 337-8 lies in their connexion with the general subject of the lines of geographical division drawn by Imperial partitions in the century between Diocletian and Arcadius. The divisions in the first half of this period (A.D. 285-338) present various difficulties, from the circumstance that the statements of our best authorities are not sufficiently precise, and those of secondary authorities are often divergent. Here I would lay stress upon a principle which has not been sufficiently considered. Later writers were accustomed to certain stereotyped lines of division which had been fixed by the partitions of A.D. (364 and) 395; and they were determined by these in interpreting the geographical phrases of earlier writers. It is therefore especially important in this case to consider the testimonies of the earlier writers apart from later exegesis. It is also clear that names like Illyricum (which came to be distinguished into the diocese [Western] and the prefecture [Eastern]), Thrace (which might mean either the diocese or the province, or might bear, as in Anon. Val., its old sense, covering the four provinces south of Mount Haemus),

Gaul (which might include Spain and Britain), were very likely to mislead into false and various explanations.

I. Division of A.D. 293. (1) *a*, Maximian: Italy, Africa, Spain; *b*, Constantius: Gaul and Britain. (2) *c*, Diocletian: Dioceses of Pontus and the East, including Egypt; *d*, Galerius: Dioceses of Pannonia, Dacia, Macedonia, Thrace and Asia.

As to (1), a passage in the De Mort., our earliest authority, is quite decisive; in c. 8, Africa vel (=et) Hispania, are assigned to Maximian. Against this, we cannot entertain Julian's ascription of Spain to Constantius (Or. ii. p. 65); an error which would easily arise from the inclusion (under Constantine) of Spain in the Prefecture of Gaul. Under Diocletian the division of the west is drawn across the map, by Alps and Pyrenees, not downward. (Victor, Cæs., 39, 30, does not mention Spain; his Galliae might = Gaul + Britain, or = Gaul + Britain + Spain. Praxagoras mentions neither Africa nor Spain.) As to (2), our authorities are Praxagoras and Victor, and the truth has been obscured by following the statements of later writers. Praxagoras assigns to Galerius τῆς τε Ἑλλάδος καὶ τῆς κάτω Ἀσίας καὶ Θρᾴκης; to Diocletian τῆς τε Βιθυνίας καὶ τῆς Λιβύης καὶ τῆς Αἰγύπτου. Now in this enumeration a rough principle may be observed. *He enumerates countries which mark the lines of division.* Less well informed as to the west, he does not commit himself about Spain. Beginning at the north, he gives Britain to Constantius (κ. Βρετανίας ἐβασίλ.), and Italy to Maximian; implying that Maximian's realm began, where Constantius's ended. Thus Gaul is implicitly assigned to Constantius; Africa to Maximian. From the extreme south, Diocletian's part reaches to Bithynia, which implies the Dioceses of Pontus and the East; while Thrace and Asia (ἡ κάτω Ἀσία, to designate the diocese, not the province) mark the line of partition on the side of Galerius, whose realm in the other direction stretches, it is implied, to Italy. (Hellas is mentioned, doubtless, because the writer was an Athenian.) There is no good reason for rejecting this evidence; the same assignment of Asia is repeated (on the same authority) at the later division of 315. It is at least not contradicted by the not precise statement of Aur. Victor (*ib.*): Illyrica ora adusque Ponti fretum Galerio; cetera Valerius retentavit. Later writers, accustomed to the later division of the Prefectures of Illyricum and the East, could hardly realize this cross division; the utmost their imaginations could compass would be to connect Thrace with Illyricum instead of Asia Minor. That the statesmen of Diocletian's age did not regard the Propontis as a necessary geographical boundary, and that a part of Asia could be as easily attached to Europe as a part of Europe could be attached to Asia, is proved by the next division on incontestably good evidence.

II. A.D. 305. (1) *a*, Severus: Maximian's portion with Diocese of Pannonia; *b*, Constantius: as before, with Spain (?). (2) *c*, Maximin: Egypt, the East; Pontus (?) except Bithynia; *d*, Galerius: as before, with Bithynia, but without Pannonia.

Anon. Val. iii. 5. Maximino datum est orientis imperium: Galerius sibi Illyricum Thracias et Bithyniam tenuit. (*Thraciæ:* the point of the plural is probably to include Moesia ii. and Scythia; as, in 18, the singular excludes them. See below.) Victor, with his usual vagueness (40, 1), gives Italy to Severus; quæ Iouius obtinuerat to Maximin. Anon. Val. 4, 9. Severo Pannoniæ et Italiæ urbes et Africæ contigerunt.

III. A.D. 306 (on death of Constantius). (1) *a*, Constantine: Britain and Gaul; *b*, Severus (Maxentius): as before, with Spain. (2) *c*, *d*, As before.

It is clear that, since (according to Anon. Val.) the Cæsar Severus had Diocese of Pannonia, he could not have also had Spain; for his realm would have been quite out of proportion to that of the Augustus Constantius. We may therefore assume that on Maximian's resignation Constantius took over Spain, but that after his death it was claimed by Severus, as Augustus, and actually held for a time by Maxentius.

IV. A.D. 314. Constantine now has all the dominions that from 293 to 305 were held by Constantius, Maximian and Galerius, with the exception of Thrace. Licinius has Diocletian's part, along with Thrace. The important point in this arrangement is the beginning of an administrative connexion between Thrace and the East ; they would now be governed by the same Prætorian Prefect.

Praxagoras (F. H. G. iv. p. 3) : Ἑλλάδος τε καὶ Μακεδονίας καὶ τῆς κατω (*ita leg. pro* κατα) Ἀσίας were acquired by Constantine. Anon. Val. 18; Licinius : orientem, Asiam, Thraciam, Moesiam, minorem Scythiam.

V. A.D. 335. [The arrangement of this year was not a division of the Empire, but partly a confirmation of the assignment of administrative spheres, already made to his sons, and partly a new assignment of administrations to his nephews. Constantine did not directly sacrifice the unity of the Empire, which was still realized in his own sovereignty, though he adopted a policy which might at any moment endanger it. " Von einer Erbtheilung ist dabei nicht die Rede, sondern nur von einem Antheil an der Verwaltung " (Ranke, Weltgeschichte, iv. 2, 270).]

(1) Constantine had Gaul, Britain and Spain (= the later " Prefecture of Gaul ") ; (2) Constantius, Asia and Egypt ; (3) Constans, Italy, Africa, and Illyricum (including Thrace). For Delmatius the *ripa Gothica* was cut off from the portion of Constans ; Hannibalian had (at the expense of Constantius) a " kingdom " composed of principalities in the regions of Pontus and Armenia.

The question is, what were the limits of the province of Delmatius ? Is ripa Gothica [I have not seen noticed a parallel expression in De Mortibus, 17, where Galerius reaches Nicomedia, *per circuitum ripæ strigæ*, where the emendation *Istricæ* is doubtless right] to be interpreted as Eastern Illyricum (=dioceses of Dacia, Macedonia, and Thrace)? So Schiller (ii. 235), Ranke, Burckhardt and others. But the Epitome of Victor (41, 20) includes in the share of Constans " Dalmatia, Thrace, Macedonia and Achaia". Ranke supposes that *Dalmatiam* here is a scribe's mistake for *Dalmatius*, and that we should interpret the *ripa Gothica* of the Anonymous by the words thus amended. If we adopted this view, it would be better to read: Dalmaci⟨us Daci⟩am Thraciam Macedoniam Achaiamque.

But a view that necessitates tampering with a text which in itself gives perfect sense cannot be accepted as satisfactory. There is a further objection here. The text of the Epitome agrees remarkably with the statement of Zonaras, xiii. 5, which assigns to Constans Italy, Africa, Sicily and the islands, Illyricum, Macedonia, " Achaia, with the Peloponnesus". The Epitome was not a direct source of Zonaras ; but the agreement is explained by the fact they both (the author of the Epitome directly, Zonaras indirectly) drew from a common source (probably Ammianus : cp. L. Jeep, Quellenunt. zu den gr. Kirchenhistorikern, p. 67). Thus the assumption of a textual error in the Epitome means the assumption of an error in the text of an earlier authority ; and therefore becomes decidedly hazardous and unconvincing. Add to this that the interpretation of *ripa Gothica* to include or to imply Macedonia and Greece is extremely forced. The natural meaning of the expression is : the provinces of Dacia, Moesia I. and II. and Scythia,[1] and perhaps Pannonia and Noricum. The actual testimonies of the two best authorities, that are explicit, concur in showing that the main division of A.D 335 was tripartite—between the Emperor's three sons—and that only subsidiary (though highly responsible) posts in frontier regions were given to the two nephews. This view is also more in accordance with Zosimus, ii. 39, who distinctly marks a triple division.[2] Nor is it contradicted by Eusebius, Panegyr. ch. iii., which only proves that Delmatius (unlike Hannibalian) was a Cæsar, and thus co-ordinate in dignity with his cousins.

VI. A.D. 337-8. (1) Constantius : as before, along with the kingdom of Hannibalian, and the four provinces of D. Thrace, south of Haemus ;[3] (2) Constans : as

---

[1] Chron. Pasch., p. 532, ed. B. gives Mesopotamia to Delmatius (Godefroy accepted the statement). I conjecture that Μεσοποταμίαν may have arisen from Μυσιαν παραποταμιαν =Moesiam ripensem.

[2] He pretends to mark it as it existed at the death of Constantine (before the destruction of Delmatius); though he seems really to give the subsequent division.

[3] The dates in the early edicts of the C. Th. are not certain enough to permit us to draw an inference from xi. 1, 4 (professedly issued by Constantius at Thessalonica in November 337).

before, along with *ripa Gothica*, including Moesia II. and Scythia ; **and without** (?) Raetia or part of Africa ; (3) Constantine : as before, along with some part of Africa or of the Diocese of Italy (?).

We have not data for determining the details of this partition. The problem was to divide the provinces held by the two nephews into three parts. To secure geographical continuity Constans would naturally take the *ripa Gothica*, and hand over some part of his western dominions to Constantine ; he likewise resigned Thrace south of Haemus (not Moesia and Scythia, I infer from Zos. ii. 39, who gives to Constans and Constantine τὰ περὶ τὸν Εὔξεινον πουτον) to Constantius. The war which broke out between Constans and Constantine was probably connected with the question of the territorial compensation to be received by the latter ; seeing that Zos. ii. 41, ascribes it to a dispute about Africa and Italy.

Gibbon (with Tillemont) has accepted from the Chron. Alex. of Eutychius a curious notice (under Ol. 279) that Constantine the younger reigned for a year at Constantinople. The only possible support I can see for this statement must be derived from the passage of Zosimus. He groups together the lands of Constantine and Constans, as if they ruled jointly over an undivided realm, in which he includes "the regions of the Euxine". A defender of Eutychius might urge that for some months at least Constans did not assert his independence, that his elder brother may have governed for him, and that the transference of Thrace to Constantius may have been subsequent. But without further evidence it is better to leave the Eutychian notice aside ; and I may call attention to Ranke's remark that there is a *tendency* in the account of Zosimus, who desiring to justify Magnentius is hostile to Constans and anxious to throw on him the blame for the war with Constantine.

The division of 338 A.D. is given as follows in the Life of St. Artemius (Acta Sanct., Oct. 20)—a document which merits more criticism than it has received :—

(1) Constantine : αἱ ἄνω Γαλλίαι καὶ τὰ ἐπέκεινα Ἄλπεων (an expression often used to include Spain), αἵ τε Βρεττανικαὶ νῆσοι (Britain and the Orcades, etc. ? cp. Eutropius 7, 13, and the interpolation in the Laterculus of Polemius Silvius, see above, App. 11), καὶ ἕως τοῦ ἑσπερίου ὠκεανοῦ. (2) Constans : αἱ κάτω Γαλλίαι ἤγουν αἱ Ἰταλίαι (Italy with its adjuncts, Sicily, Africa, etc.), καὶ αὐτὴ ἡ Ῥώμη. (3) Constantius : τὸ τῆς ἀνατολῆς μέρος, Βυζάντιον, τὰ ἀπὸ τοῦ Ἰλυρικοῦ (implying that Illyricum went to Constans) μέχρι τῆς Προποντίδος ὁπόσα ὑπήκοα τοῖς Ῥωμαίοις τὴν τε Συρίαν καὶ Παλαιστίνην καὶ Μεσοποταμίαν καὶ Αἴγυπτον καὶ τὰς νήσους ἁπάσας.

The Vita Artemii (the Greek text was first published by A. Mai in Spicilegium Romanum, vol. iv.) was composed by "John the Monk," and professes to be compiled from the Ecclesiastical History of Philostorgius and some other writers. Eusebius, Socrates and Theodoret are also referred to. There is evidence that Philostorgius was largely used, and consequently the Life of Artemius becomes an important mine of material for the restoration of the history of that Arian writer. The story of Gallus is, I presume, derived from him, and I conjecture that the statement of the partition of the Empire among the sons of Constantine comes from the same source. If so, both passages ultimately depend on Eunapius, who was doubtless the source of Philostorgius.

From the same source is certainly derived the statement of the partition in Constantine Porphyrogennetos, de Them., ii. 9 (ed. Bonn, p. 57). The portion of Constantine is described in exactly the same words as in the Vita Artemii (τὰς ἄνω Γαλλίας καὶ τὰ ἐπέκεινα Ἀλπέων ἕως τοῦ ἑσπερίου Ὠκεανοῦ, except that instead of "the British Isles" the imperial geographer says "as far as the city of Canterbury itself" (Κάντάβριν). The expression αἱ κάτω Γαλλίαι is also used, but, in expanding the concise expressions of his source, Constantine falls into error and assigns Illyricum and Greece to Constantius.

VII. A.D. 364. (1) Valentinian i.: Prefectures of Gaul, and of Italy and Illyricum ; (2) Valens: Prefecture of the East, including D. of Thrace.

VIII. A.D. 378. (1) Gratian and Valentinian ii. : Prefectures of Gaul and of Italy, including Western Illyricum : (2) Theodosius : Prefecture of the East, along with Dioceses of Dacia and Macedonia (Soz. vii. 4).

This partition, which drew a new line of division between East and West, probably established definitely the system of four prefectures which Zosimus attributed to the express enactment of Constantine. Up to this time three pr. prefects seem to have been the rule, four an exception. But now, instead of adding Eastern Illyricum to the large Prefecture of the East, Theodosius instituted a new Prefecture.

16. THE SARMATIANS—(P. 216)

It is often asserted that "Sarmatian" was a generic name for Slavonic peoples. It is certain that a great many Slavonic tribes must have been often described under the name, but it is extremely doubtful whether any of the chief Sarmatian peoples—the Bastarnae, the Roxolani (? Rox-alani) or Jazyges—were Slavonic. I believe that Šafařik, in taking up a negative position on this question, was right (Slawische Alterthümer, ed. Wuttke, i. 333 *sqq.*). But I cannot think that he has quite made out the Slavonic race of the Carpi (*ib.* 213-4), though this is accepted by Jireček (Gesch. der Bulgaren, p. 77) ; he has a more plausible case, perhaps, for the Kostoboks. On the other hand it is extremely likely, though it cannot be absolutely proved, that in the great settlements of non-German peoples, made in the third and fourth centuries in the Illyrian peninsula by the Roman Emperors, some Slavonic tribes were included. This is an idea which was developed by Drinov in his rare book on the Slavic colonization of the Balkan lands, and has been accepted by Jireček. There is much probability in the view that Slavonic settlers were among the 300,000 Sarmatae, to whom Constantine assigned abodes in 334 A.D. It is an hypothesis such as, in some form, is needed to account for the appearance of Slavonic names before the beginning of the sixth century in the Illyrian provinces.

Šafařik tried to show that the Alani, Roxolani, Bastarnae, Jazyges, &c., were of Iranian race, allied to the Persians and Medes,—like the Scythians of Herodotus.

17. BATTLE OF SINGARA—(P. 227)

I have shown in the Byzantinische Zeitschrift (vol. 5) that we should accept Julian's notice as to the date of this battle (and place it in A.D. 344), instead of following Jerome's date (adopted by Idatius), A.D. 348. One might be tempted to guess that there were two battles at Singara, and that the *nocturna pugna* was placed in the wrong year by an inadvertence of Jerome ; this might be considered in connexion with Förster's reconstruction of the corrupt passage of Festus, Brev. ch. 27 : Verum pugnis Sisaruena, Singarena, et iterum Singarena praesente Constantio ac Siegarena, &c. The νυκτομαχία is described below as : nocturna Elliensi prope Singaram pugna. *Elliensi* is mysterious.

The events of the Persian wars of Constantius and Julian are briefly narrated by General F. R. Chesney in his Expedition for the Survey of the Rivers Euphrates and Tigris, vol. 2, p. 430 *sqq.* (quarto ed.).

18. SOURCES AND CHRONOLOGY OF ARMENIAN HISTORY UNDER TRDAT AND HIS SUCCESSORS—(C. XIX.)

Some works bearing on Armenia have been mentioned in connexion with general oriental history in vol. i. Appendix 13. In addition to these must now be mentioned (besides St. Martin's Mémoires sur l'Arménie and the notes to his edition of Lebeau's Bas-Empire): Ter Mikelian, Die armenische Kirche in ihren Beziehungen zur byzantinischen (saec. 4-13), 1892 ; Chalatianz, Zenob of Glak (in modern Armenian ; known to me through Stackelberg's summary in Byz. Zeitschrift, 4, 368-70), 1893 ; and above all Gelzer's highly important essay, Die Anfange der armenischen Kirche (in the Ber. der kön. sächs. Gesellschaft der Wiss.), 1895.

1. Sources. (*a*) Faustus. For Armenian history in the fourth century after death of Trdat (Tiridates), A.D. 317, our only trustworthy source is Faustus, who

wrote his History of Armenia in Greek (before the Armenian alphabet was introduced; the Greek original is quoted by Procopius, Pers. i. 5), probably in first years of King Vram Sapuh, who reigned from 395 to 416 (Gelzer, p. 116). The work is marked by enthusiasm for the clergy, and a certain prejudice against the policy of those who were loyal to the kings, also by chronological errors. "Faustus is completely a national Armenian; therein lies his strength and his weakness" (*ib.* 117). He consulted official documents in the royal archives (*ib.*) and made use of old songs. It is announced that H. Gelzer and L. Babajan will issue a translation of Faustus, and Gelzer's name is a guarantee that it will be trustworthy. (*b*) Agathangelos, who lived about half a century later, contains a work which is our only good source for the reign of Trdat. His work (preserved both in Armenian and in a Greek translation, which mutually check each other) has been dissected by A. von Gutschmid (Kleine Schriften, 3, 395, *sqq.*). It contains an earlier Life of St. Gregory (perhaps originally composed in Syriac, Gelzer, p. 114) and an Apocalypse of Gregory written between 452 and 456 by a priest of Valaršapat. The latter is valuable as throwing indirect light on the church history of the fifth century, but worthless for the history of Trdat. (*c*) The conclusion of Carrière (mentioned in vol. i. App. 13) that the date of Moses of Chorene is very late (beginning of eighth century) is accepted by Chalatianz and Gelzer, and seems to be established. (*d*) The worthlessness of the History of Taron by Zenob of Glak has been shown by the investigation of Chalatianz (*op. cit.*). Hitherto supposed to have been written in Syriac in the fourth century and translated into Armenian in the seventh, it is now shown to be an apocryphal work of an impostor of the eighth or ninth century. There is a French translation by Langlois, F. H. G. vol. v.

2. Chronology. The student who consults the translation of Langlois (Agathangelos and Faustus; *op. cit.*) must be warned that the chronological indications in the notes are set down at random and contradict one another. And, if he has read the note in Smith's edition of the Decline and Fall, vol. ii. p. 369, which is taken from St. Martin's edition of Lebeau, and compares it with the chronological list of kings in the same scholar's Mémoires, he will find that the two accounts diverge. (In the Mémoires, p. 412-3, the dates are: death of Trdat, 314; interregnum; accession of Chosroes II., 316; Tiran II., 325; Arsaces, 341; Pap, 370. According to the old view, which appears, though not consistently, in Langlois' collection, and seems to be assumed in Ter Mikelian's *op. cit.*, Trdat reigned from 286 to 342.) The following reconstruction seems most probable:—

Death of Chosrov I., accession of Trdat,			-	-	-	-	261	A.D.
Accession of Chosrov II.,	-	-	-	-	-	-	317	,,
,, Tiran,	-	-	-	-	-	-	326	,,
,, Aršak,	-	-	-	-	-	-	337	,,
,, Pap,	-	-	-	-	-	-	367	,,
							to 374	,,

There are not sufficient data for determining the dates of the Catholici; the statements of Moses will not bear criticism, see Gelzer, p. 121 *sqq.* The only certainties we have are that Aristakēs, son and successor of Gregory, attended the Council of Nicæa, 325; and that Nersēs was poisoned by King Pap before 374.

3. Trdat and Constantine (Gelzer, 165 *sqq.*). Officially the Armenian kings adopted the style "Arsaces" (just as the Severian Emperors adopted Antoninus), and he appears in Cod. Theod. xi. i. 1 (Constantine and Licinius A.D. 315) as *Arsacis regis Armeniæ*. In the previous year, he and Gregory visited Constantine in Illyricum ("the land of the Dalmatians" in the Armenian Agathangelos) in "the royal city of the Romans," probably Serdica. There the alliance mentioned by Faustus (iii. 21; Langlois, p. 232) was concluded, which endured till 363. The authenticity of the account of Agathangelos (doubted by Gutschmid) has been successfully vindicated by Gelzer.

On Trdat's death the Romans intervened to put Chosrov on the throne, and Tiran likewise owed his elevation to Constantine. In 337 he was betrayed to the Persians by his chamberlain, seized by the governor of Atropatene, and blinded. The armed intervention of Constantine and Constantius led to the elevation of

Aršak, the son of Tiran, who declined to resume the sovereignty. Aršak first married Olympias, a Greek lady connected with the Constantinian house ; and afterwards a daughter of the Persian king. His policy was to hold the balance between Rome and Persia throughout the wars of Constantius and Julian.

4. In Eusebius, H. E. vi. 46, 2, we find this notice : καὶ τοῖς κατὰ Ἀρμενίαν ὡσαύτως περὶ μετανοίας ἐπιστέλλει ὧν ἐπεσκόπευε Μερουζάνης. Gelzer (p. 171 sqq.) points out that this bishopric of Meruzanes cannot have been in the Roman provinces called Armenia, and therefore was in Great Armenia ; and he seeks to show that it may have been in the south-eastern corner, the district of Vaspurakan. The words in Eusebius are from a letter of Dionysios of Alexandria (248-265), and the inference seems to be that Christianity was introduced into an outlying district of Armenia in the fifties of the third century.[1] But the formal conversion of Armenia began about 280 under the auspices of King Trdat, through the labours of Gregory the Illuminator. The destruction of the temples of the gods, in spite of strong opposition from the priests, was one of the first parts of the change, and preceded Gregory's journey to Cæsarea (between 285 and 290 according to Gelzer) to be consecrated by Leontius. The Armenian Church was dependent on the see of Cæsarea, and under Greek influence for nearly a century. After the death of the Patriarch Nersês, it was severed and made autocephalous by King Pap (circa A.D. 373-4. Cp. Ter Mikelian, p. 31). During the fourth century the seat of the Catholicus and the spiritual centre of Armenia, was Aštišat in the southern district of Taron, as has been well brought out by Gelzer. It was afterwards removed to Valaršapat, when no longer dependent on Cæsarea, and then the priests of Valaršapat invented stories to prove the antiquity of their seat and the original independence of the Armenian Church. In the fourth century, the chief feature of the domestic history of Armenia is the struggle between the monarch and the Catholicus, between the spirit of nationality and the subjection to foreign influences. It culminated in the reign of Pap, who solved the question by poison.

In regard to the conversion of Armenia, its progress was partly determined by the feudal condition of the country (Gelzer, 132). The nobles were easily won over by the personal influence of the king ; the priests were naturally the most obstinate opponents. The new faith seems to have been slow in taking root among the people, and it is noteworthy that women, even in high rank, clung tenaciously to the old religion (like the wife of Chosrov, Faustus, iii. 3, and the mother of Pap, ib. 44).

I have read with interest the remarkable study of N. Marr, O nachalnoi istorii Armenii Anonima, in Viz. Vremennik, i. 263 sqq. (1894). He discusses the character of the brief History of Armenia, which is prefixed to Sebeos' History of the Emperor Heraclius (Russ. tr. by Patkanian, 1862) ; and its relation to Moses of Chorene. This document (which appears in the collection of Langlois under the title Pseudo-Agathange) he regards as the earliest extant Armenian history of early Armenia ; it was worked up by a later (also anonymous) writer, of whose composition a large extract has been preserved in Moses of Chorene, bk. i. c. 8 (in Langlois, under the title, Mar Apas Catina). Moses also used the original work. Marr points out a number of resemblances between Faustus and the first Anonymous, and hazards the conjecture (295 sqq.) that this history of Armenia may be part of the first two books of Faustus, whose work, as we have it, begins with book iii.

19. CONSTANTINE AND CHRISTIANITY—(C. XX.)

The attitude of Constantine to the Christian religion has been the theme of many discussions, and historians are still far from having reached a general

[1] My friend Mr. F. C. Conybeare is inclined to believe that Gregory the Illuminator used an Armenian version of New Testament Scriptures made from a pre-Peshito Syriac text, long before the time of Mesrop. This version may have been due to the Church in Vaspurakan. Apparently the non-existence of Mesrop's alphabet did not prevent literary composition in Armenian.

agreement. Burckhardt, in his attractive monograph, developed the view that Constantine was " ganz wesentlich unreligiös," constitutionally indifferent to religion, because he was a " genialer Mensch," dominated by ambition ; and that in his later years he exhibited personal inclinations rather towards paganism than towards Christianity. H. Richter has some remarkable pages on Constantine's *system of parity* between the two religions ; and Brieger, in an excellent article in his *Zeitschrift f. Kirchengesch.* (iv., 1881, p. 163 *sqq.*), agrees with Gibbon that Constantine's Christianity was due entirely to political considerations. Many of the data admit of different interpretations. Those who ascribe to him a policy of parity, or the idea of a state religion which might combine elements common to enlightened paganism and Christianity (so Schiller), appeal to the fact that the *sacerdotales* and *flamines* in Africa were granted privileges ; but it is replied that they had ceased to carry on the ritual and simply, as a matter of equity, had the old rights secured to them, while they no longer performed the old duties. If the " cult " of Tyche at Constantinople is alleged, it is urged that she had no temple-service. The temples of Constantinople are explained away ; and the "aedes Flaviae nostrae gentis " of the remarkable inscription of Hispellum (date between 326 and 337 ; Orelli, 5580) is asserted not to have been intended for the worship of the Emperors, but simply as a fine hall for public spectacles.[1] (See V. Schultze, in Brieger's *Zeitschrift*, vii. 352 *sqq.*) The indulgence to paganism was simply the toleration of a statesman who could not discreetly go too fast in the accomplishment of such a great reformation. And certainly on the hypothesis that Constantine had before his eyes, as the thing to be achieved, the ultimate establishment of Christianity as the exclusive state religion, his attitude to paganism would be, in general, the attitude we should expect from a really great statesman. Ranke's remark hits the point (Weltgesch. iii. 1, 532) : " Er konnte unmöglich zugeben dass an die Stelle der Unordnungen der Verfolgung die vielleicht noch grösseren einer gewaltsamen Reaction träten ".

It seems to me that Seeck, in holding that Constantine had really broken with the old religion and was frankly a Christian, is nearer the mark than Gibbon or Schiller. From the evidence which we have, I believe that Constantine adopted the Christian religion and intended that Christianity should be the State religion. As to a great many details, there may be uncertainty in regard to the facts themselves or their interpretation, but I would invite attention to the following general considerations.

(1) The theory that the motives of Constantine's Christian policy were purely political, and that he was religiously indifferent, seems perilously like an anachronism,—ascribing to him modern ideas. There is no reason to suppose that he was above the superstitiousness of his age. (2) The theory that he was a Deist, that he desired to put Paganism and Christianity on an equality, emphasizing some common features, and that circumstances led him to incline the balance towards Christianity in his later years, is not the view *naturally* suggested by the (*a*) Christian education he gave his children, and (*b*) the hostility of the pagan Emperor Julian to his memory. (3) The fact that he countenanced Paganism and did not completely abolish the customs of the old State religion proves nothing ; the remark of Ranke quoted above is a sufficient answer. In fact, those who have dealt with the question have sometimes failed to distinguish between two different things. It is one thing to say that Constantine's motives for establishing Christianity were purely secular. It is quite another to say that he was guided by secular considerations in the methods which he adopted to establish Christianity. The second thesis is true—Constantine would have been a bad statesman if he had not been so guided ;—but its truth is quite consistent with the falsity of the first.

Schiller (iii. 301 *sqq.*) has conveniently summarized the chief facts, and his results may be arranged as follows :—

(1) COINS. In Constantine's western mints coins appeared with *Mars*, with

---

[1] Compare the words : ne aedis nostro nomini dedicata cuiusquam contagiosae superstitionis fraudibus polluatur, insisted on by Seeck, Untergang der antiken Welt, p. 439.

genius pop. Rom., and with *Sol*, but certainly not in the two first cases, perhaps not in the last case, after 315 A.D. Further, Constantinian coins with *Juppiter* were not struck in the west, but in the mints of Licinius. Thus we may say that between 315 and 323 pagan emblems were disappearing from Constantine's coinage, and indifferent legends took their place, such as *Beata tranquillitas*.

We also find coins with ☧, as a sign of the mint; and at the end of Constantine's reign a series of copper coins was issued in which two soldiers were represented on the reverse holding the labarum, that is a flag with the monogram ☧.

We see then two stages in Constantine's policy. At first he removes from his coins symbols which might offend his Christian soldiers and subjects whom he wished to propitiate (this is Schiller's interpretation); and finally he allows to appear on his money symbols which did not indeed commit him to Christianity, but was susceptible of a Christian meaning.

(2) Laws. After the great Edict of Milan, 312-3 A.D. (which, according to Seeck, was never issued), the following measures were taken by Constantine to put Christianity on a level with the old religion. (1) 313 A.D., the Catholic clergy were freed from all state burdens. (2) 313 (or 315), the Church was freed from *annona* and *tributum*. (3) 316 (321), Manumissions in the Church were made valid. (4) 319, (1) was extended to the whole empire. (5) 320, exception to the laws against celibacy made in favour of the clergy, allowing them to inherit. (6) 321, wills in favour of the Catholic Church permitted. (7) 323, forcing of Christians to take part in pagan celebrations forbidden. On the other hand, a law of 321 (Cod. Theod. xvi. 10, 1) forbids private consultation of haruspices, but allows it in public. [Cp. further Seuffert, Constantins Gesetze und das Christenthum, 1891.]

(3) EUSEBIUS describes in his Ecclesiastical History (bk. x. 1 *sqq.*) a number of acts of Constantine after his victory over Maxentius, which attest not only toleration but decided favour towards the Christians. He entertains Christian priests, heaps presents on the Church, takes an interest in ecclesiastical questions. There is no reason to doubt these statements; but Schiller urges us to remember (1) that Eusebius does not mention what favour Constantine bestowed on the pagans, and (2) that, when the final struggle with Licinius came and that Emperor resorted to persecution, policy clearly dictated to Constantine the expediency of specially favouring Christianity. In general, according to Schiller, from 313 to 323 Constantine not only maintained impartial toleration, but bestowed positive benefits on both the old and the new religion. The account of Eusebius is a misrepresentation through omission of the other side.

One or two points may be added. Eusebius states that after the victory over Maxentius Constantine erected a statue of himself with a cross in his right hand at Rome. This statement occurs in Hist. E. ix. c. 10, 11; Paneg. ix. 18; Vit. C. i. 40. Is this to be accepted as a fact? A statement in H. E. is more trustworthy than any statement in the Vit. C.; and Brieger thought that in this case the passage in H. E. is an interpolation from that in the Vit. C. (Ztsch. f. Kirchengesch, 1880, p. 45). But Schultze (*ib.* vii. 1885, 343 *sqq.*) has shown that Eusebius mentioned the statue in question, in his speech at Tyre in 314 A.D., from H. E. x. 4, 16. This adds considerable weight to the evidence.

In regard to the monogram ☧, Rapp in his paper, Das Labarum und der Sonnenkultus (Jahrb. des Vereins von Altertumsfreunden im Rheinlande, 1866, p. 116 *sqq.*), showed that it appears on Greco-Bactrian coins of 2nd and 1st centuries B.C. It appears still earlier on Tarentine coins of the first half of the 3rd century. It is not clear that Constantine used it as an ambiguous symbol; nor yet is there a well-attested instance of its use as a Christian symbol before A.D. 323 (cp. Brieger in his Ztschr. iv. 1881, p. 201).

Several examples of the Labarum as described by Eusebius are preserved; I may refer especially to one on a Roman sarcophagus in the Lateran Museum.

For "Christian emblems on the coins of Constantine the Great, his family and his successors" see Madden in the Numismatic Chronicle, 1877-8.

For the Tyche, to whom Constantine dedicated his new city, the most recent and instructive study is the brief paper of Strzygovski, in Analecta Græciensia (Graz, 1893).

As to the connexion of Constantine with the Donatist controversy, attention may be drawn to the article of O. Seeck in Brieger's Zeitsch. f. Kirchengeschichte, x. 505-568 (Quellen und Urkunden über die Anfange des Donatismus). He fixes the date of the Council of Arles to A.D. 316 (cp. Euseb., V. C. i. 44-45). The general result of his discussion is to discredit the authority of Optatus, whom he regards as a liar, drawing from a lying source. The only value of the work of Optatus is to be found, he concludes, in the parts which rest on the protocols of the Synods of Cirta and Rome, and the lost parts of the Acta of the process of Felix (viz., I., 13, 14, 23, 24, 27, and perhaps the story of the choice of Cæcilian, 16-18).

For Constantine in mediæval legend see the Incerti Auctoris de C. Magno eiusque matre Helena, edited by Heydenreich (1879); Extracts from a popular Chronicle (Greek) given by A. Kirpitschnikow, Byz. Ztsch. i. p. 308 sqq. (1892); Heydenreich, C. der Grosse in den Sagen des Mittelalters, Deutsche Ztsch. f. Geschichts-wissenschaft, 9, 1 sqq. (1893), and Griechische Berichte über die Jugend C. des G., in Gr. Stud. H. Lipsius zum Geburtstag dargebracht, p. 88 sqq. (1894). For his father Constantius in mediæval legend see Li contes dou roi Constant l'Emperor, ed. in the Bibl. Elzevir, by MM. Moland and d'Hericault, 1856. An English translation by Mr. Wm. Morris has appeared 1896.

20. ECCLESIASTICAL GEOGRAPHY—(P. 315)

The ecclesiastical divisions of the empire, referred to incidentally by Gibbon, are not closely enough connected with the subject to require an editorial note. But, as they sometimes throw light on the political boundaries, and as they have been recently much investigated, some bibliographical indications of literature on the eastern bishoprics may be useful.

Parthey : Notitiæ Græcæ Episcopatuum (along with Hierocles).
H. Gelzer : Die Zeitbestimmung der griech. Not. Episc., Jahrb. f. protest. Theologie, xii. 556 sqq. ; Zeitsch. f. wiss. Theologie, xxxv. 419 sqq. ; Byz. Ztsch., i. 245 (on eastern Patriarchates) ; ii. 22.   Also edition of Basil's Notitia (early in ninth century) in "Georgius Cyprius" (edition Teubner, 1890).
W. Ramsay : Articles in the Journal of Hellenic Studies, 1884, 1887 ; Historical Geography of Asia Minor, 1890, passim.
De Boor : Ztsch. f. Kirchengeschichte, xii. 303 sqq., 519 sqq. (1890) ; xiv. 573 sqq. (1893).
Duchesne : Byz. Ztsch., i. 531 sqq. (eccl. geogr. of Illyricum).

21. LEGEND OF THE FINDING OF THE TRUE CROSS—(P. 456)

The legend of the discovery of the Cross by Judas for St. Helena has come down in Syriac, Greek and Latin versions.   See E. Nestle, Byz. Zeitschrift, iv. p. 319-345, who makes it probable that the original Helena legend was in Syriac, and prints the oldest Greek version extant from a Sinai Ms. of the eighth century copied by Mr. Rendel Harris.   (The Greek from later Mss. (1) in J. Gretser's huge treatise, De Cruce Christi (1600), ii. 530 sqq., and Holder, Inventio verae crucis, 1889 ; (2) in Gretser, op. cit., ii. 543 sqq. ; (3) Wotke, Wiener Studien, 1891, p. 300 sqq. ; the Latin (1) in the Sanctuarium (a rather rare book ; c. 1479) of Mombritius, and in Acta Sanct., May 4, I., 445 sqq. ; (2) in Holder, op. cit. ; (3) in Mombritius, op. cit. ; the Syriac (1) from seventh century Ms., in Nestle's De sancta Cruce, 1889 ; (2) ib. ; (3) in Bedjan's Acta Martyrum et Sanctorum, 1890, p. 326 sqq.)

22. ST. GEORGE—(P. 472)

The article on St. George by Zöckler in Herzog and Plitt's Encyclopædia has been superseded by the discussion of F. Görres in the Zeitsch. f. wiss. Theologie, xvi. 1890, p. 454 *sqq.* "Ritter St. Georg in Geschichte, Legende, u. Kunst." [There is no question that the Acta (in Act. Sanct. 23rd April) are apocryphal and legendary. They are remarkable for the horrible descriptions of scenes of martyrdom, which might serve as a text to elucidate the pictures on the walls of the curious round Church of San Stefano on the Esquiline.] Görres arrives at practically the same conclusion as Tillemont (Mém. eccl., v. 185-9, 658-60). All the details of St. George's martyrdom are uncertain ; but St. George existed and suffered as a martyr in the East in some pre-Constantinian persecution. Tillemont established the reality of St. George by the existence of his cult (he was a μεγαλόμαρτυς) in the sixth century ; Görres proves that it already existed in the fifth century. (1) The round Church of St. George at Thessalonica is not younger than the fifth century and possibly belongs to the fourth; (2) Venantius (Carm. ii. 12, p. 41, ed. M. H. G.) mentions a Gallic basilica to St. George, founded by Sidonius Apollinaris; (3) the decree of Pope Gelasius *de libris non recipiendis*, at end of fifth century, condemns the Acta of St. George as apocryphal, but confesses his historical existence.

The connexion of his name with a dragon-slaying legend does not relegate him to the region of myth. For over against the fabulous Christian dragon-slayer, Theodore of the Bithynian Heraclea, we can set Agapetus of Synnada and Arsacius, who though celebrated as dragon-slayers were historical persons.

Gibbon's theory which identifies St. George with George of Cappadocia has nothing to be said for it ; but Görres points out that it is not open to any objection on the ground that George of Cappadocia was an Arian. For there are examples of Arians admitted into the Martyrologium : he cites Agapetus of Synnada and Auxentius, afterwards bishop of Mopsuestia. (It is to be noted that one recension of the Acta S. Georgii was edited by Arians.)

23. THE CHURCHES OF CONSTANTINE AT JERUSALEM—(P. 455)

In regard to Constantine's Churches at Jerusalem it may be said, without entering upon the question as to the true positions of Golgotha and the Holy Sepulchre, that it is certain that these Churches—(1) the round Church of the Anastasis which contained the Sepulchre, and the (2) adjacent Basilica, dedicated to the Cross—stood on the site of the present Church of the Holy Sepulchre. Injured by the Persians (614 A.D.) they were restored some years later, and a plan of the buildings drawn up, towards the end of the seventh century, by the pilgrim Arculfus is extant, and is of great importance for the topography. Some traces of the old buildings still remain. "The relative position of the Churches is the same ; the circular Church of the Anastasis has preserved its form ; the south wall of the Basilica can be traced from 'Calvary' eastward, and one of the large cisterns constructed by Constantine has been discovered" (Sir C. Wilson, in Smith's Dict. of the Bible, new ed., 1893, p. 1654). Mr. Fergusson's theory which identified the Church of the Resurrection with the mosque known as Kubbet-es-Sakhrah, the Dome of the Rock (within the so-called "Haram area"), is now quite exploded.

The Dome of the Rock has its own question, but has nothing to do with Constantine. Is it of Saracenic origin dating from the end of the seventh century—built perhaps by a Greek architect? or was it originally a Christian Church, and converted into a mosque? It has been identified by Professor Sepp with a Church of St. Sophia built by Justinian. Sir C. Wilson thinks that it stands on the site of St. Sophia, which was destroyed by the Persians ; "that it was rebuilt with the old material by Abdul-Melik who covered it with a dome, and that it was again repaired and redecorated by El Mamûn" (*ib.*, p. 1657).

The adjacent mosque el-Aksa occupies the site of the mosque of Omar. It was built by Abd al Malik, "out of the ruins of Justinian's Church of St. Mary" (Wilson, *ib.*), which is fully described by Procopius; but there is a difference of opinion whether the Church was on the same site as the mosque or (so Fergusson and others) in the south-eastern corner of the "Haram area," where there are vaults apparently of the Justinianean age.

For further details see Sir C. Wilson's article Jerusalem, cited above; Mr. T. H. Lewis' essay on the Church of Constantine at Jerusalem in the Palestine Pilgrims' Text Society, 1891; Sepp, Die Felsenkuppell eine Justinianische Sophien-kirche; various papers in the Palestine Exploration Fund publications.

24. THE TIGRIS AND EUPHRATES—(P. 495)

The recent publication of a geographical description of Mesopotamia and Baghdād by an Arabic writer, Ibn Serapion, of whom nothing is known except that he wrote in the early years of the tenth century, by Mr. Guy Le Strange (with translation and commentary, in the *Journal of the Royal Asiatic Soc.*, 1895, January and April; cp. addenda in July, and 1896, October), is of considerable importance.

It shows that since the tenth century great alterations have taken place in the course of the Tigris and Euphrates, and shows what these alterations were; it gives a clear account of the canal system which drew the overflow of the Euphrates into the Tigris; and it supplies most important data for the reconstruction of the topography of Baghdād.

Before the Caliphate, the River Tigris followed its present course, from Kūt-al-Amarah (about 100 miles below Baghdād) flowing in a south-easterly direction to its junction with the Euphrates. But during the middle ages—in the tenth century for example—it flowed almost due south "running down the channel now known as the Sha*tt*-al-Hay, and passing through the city of Wāsi*t*" (Le Strange, *ib.*, Jan., p. 3). The changes in the Euphrates are thus summed up by Mr. Le Strange (p. 4): A little above Al-Kūfa "the stream bifurcated. The branch to the right—considered then as the main stream of the Euphrates, but now known as the Hindiyya Canal—ran down past Al-Kūfa, and a short distance below the city became lost in the western part of the great Swamp," which also swallowed up the waters of the Tigris. "The stream to the left or eastward called the Sūrā Canal—which, in its upper reach, follows the line of the modern Euphrates—ran a short course and then split up into numerous canals whose waters for the most part flowed out into the Tigris above Wāsi*t*." The great Swamp in which the streams of both Tigris and Euphrates lost themselves was drained by the Tidal Estuary which reached the sea at Abbadān, "a town which, on account of the recession of the Persian Gulf, now lies nearly twenty miles distant from the present shore-line".

It should be carefully remembered in reading the account of the events after Julian's death that the Tigris has also altered its course to the north of Ctesiphon since the tenth century. From a point below Samarrā to a point above Baghdād, it followed a shorter and more westerly channel than at the present day.

As to the canal Nahr-al-Malik (see above, p. 503), Mr. Le Strange says (*ib.*, Jan., p. 75), that "roughly speaking it followed the line of the modern Radhwāniyya Canal".

It may be added that the geographical work of Abu-l-Fidā, mentioned by Gibbon, p. 495, n. 54, is not very valuable, being neither good nor early. The authoritative Arabic text is that of Reinaud, 1840, and there is a French translation by S. Guyard, 1883. On early geographical works in Arabic, see Le Strange's Palestine under the Moslems (Pal. Explor. Fund).

THE ABERDEEN UNIVERSITY PRESS LIMITED

ADDENDA

P. 304, l. 17, the luminous trophy of the cross, placed above the meridian sun.
   [I cannot forbear to mention here the ingenious and plausible suggestion
   communicated to me by Professor Flinders Petrie that what Constantine saw
   was the phenomenon of mock-suns (not uncommon in northern, but rare in
   southern, latitudes). The real sun, with three mock-suns, might have appeared to his eyes as a cross.]

ADDENDA

P. 404, l. 17, the luminous canopy of the cross, placed above the meridian, still. I cannot forbear to mention how the ingenious and plausible suggestion communicated to me by Professor Rhodes Fairrie that what Constantine saw was the phenomenon of mock-suns (not uncommon in northern, but rare in southern, latitudes). The real sun, with three mock-suns, might have appeared to his eyes as a cross.